DELHI
Biography of a City

DELHI
Biography of a City

Ram Avtar Sharma
Madhukar Tewari

AAKAR

Delhi: Biography of a City
Ram Avtar Sharma and Madhukar Tewari

First Published, 2012

ISBN 978-93-5002-104-0

Published by
AAKAR BOOKS
28 E Pocket IV, Mayur Vihar Phase I, Delhi 110 091
Phone : 011 2279 5505 Telefax : 011 2279 5641
aakarbooks@gmail.com; www.aakarbooks.com

Printed at
Mudrak, 30 A, Patpar Ganj, Delhi 110 091

Dedicated to Those
Who Love the
City of Delhi

Contents

Preface

It is very fascinating to study an ancient city and its people. It is more interesting to know the past of a city like Delhi. So far plenty of literature has been written on this subject, but strange to say that still more to be written. The field is so vast and the sources are hidden, so varied and extensive that it is not possible to write about Delhi in one volume conclusively. The people residing here, whose forefathers had come at different times from different races, religions and places, had paid little attention to the history, conquest, socioreligious and political life of the city.

Despite various handicaps, it has been our constant aim and desire to treat this study without bias and prejudice; yet, at many stages, it became very difficult to know what testimony was the most reliable and what conclusion would be most just and fair. If still some facts are left or the real picture is not presented, it is not due to lack of desire.

We have sought and got encouragement and assistance from various persons and institutions, the names of all are difficult to mention here. However, some of them, whom we must acknowledge for their invaluable contribution are: Dr Sarfaraz Ahmad, Persian Scholar, Dr Kaushal Gupta, Asst. Professor, Deshbandhu College, University of Delhi, Dr J.K. Kohli, former teacher, Hindu College, University of Delhi, Dr Ram Singh Rawat, former teacher, Hindu College, Dr Khalid Ashraf, Associate Professor, Kirori Mal College, University of Delhi, Mr A.A. Abbasi, Mr Ajit Santram, Section Officer, University of Delhi, Mr Chandra Shekhar Shandilya, Section Officer, University of Delhi, Mr Nand Lal, Professional Assistant, Delhi University Library Systems and Mr Amit Gautam, Library Attendant, DULS. We are also indebted to the Central Library of the University of Delhi, Library of IIPA, Teen Murti Museum and Library and National Museum, New Delhi. We are also indebted and grateful to all those writers, publishers and owners of various websites whose works we have consulted and referred in this book.

We own the responsibility of all the shortcomings and errors which have inadvertently crept in the book. We are also indebted to Mr. K.K. Saxena, the Publisher of the book who had taken personal interest to bring out this beautiful book in a short time.

R.A. Sharma
M. Tewari

Introduction

Delhi is an ancient and historical city. It remained the capital of many empires since its inception and, except for some interludes, it has never lost its significance since the Mahabharat period. We find the references of this city in the epics as well as other philosophical literature of that time and subsequent ages irrespective of the then prevailing political and religious thought. Over the years, Delhi has generated among the people in general and scholars in particular, a widespread interest. In the past, many great kings, soldiers, scholars, poets, musicians, historians, sufis and saints have either made it their abode or just crossed over out of curiosity. This city has remained an asylum for several sagacious and wise men through the ages. However, on the other hand, it has also faced the wrath of the invaders, pillage of looters and sack by tyrants. It has witnessed many ups and downs under different rulers who ruled this magnificent city. With the passage of time, many races brought along their culture and way of life to this city and contributed enormously to the vast stock of its perennial culture. The city has been beautiful and its environs too have contributed immensely to its attractive charm. The river Yamuna and the ridge have played a central role in the overall development of the city. Here, many kings built their capital and forts with great care and named it accordingly, but subsequent rulers again abandoned it and built their own new city (capital) with added precision. The ruins of the previous cities are scattered all over this region and can still be seen in some form or the other. Of course, some materials of the old capitals have been used to build the new ones; yet, the continuity and novelty of this city have attracted writers and historians to investigate afresh. Despite vigorous and scholarly research in the past about this glorious city, still many areas and aspects remain unexplored waiting for further investigation.

The earliest written reference of a settlement at Indraprasth (Delhi) is found in the *Mahabharat*[1], which was built by Pandavs on the western bank of the river Yamuna. Padam Puran refers a forest called Khandav Van (Forest) located on the banks of Yamuna. This forest was burnt and Indraprasth or Khandavaprasth was built there. In the fire, the animals ran away for their safety—some of them were burnt completely, some partly, resisting death. Even the birds, while trying to fly, got burnt.

The *Mahabharat* (Bhishmaparv) also gives a description of Janapads and Indraprasth was one of them. The reference of Indraprasth is also given in Sabhaparv[2] when Arjun, Bhim and Shri Krishn journeyed from Indraprasth to Magadh. Adiparv also records the existence of two Kuru Janapads, namely, Uttar Kuru and Dakshin Kuru. There were three parts of this Janapad, namely, Kuru Jangal, Kuru and Kurukshetr. Kuru Jangal was a forest region and Indraprasth (Delhi) was a part of it.

The *Mahabharat* also gives lists and descriptions of various rivers and some of them are considered sacred. The river Yamuna is one of them. This river emerges from Yamunotri and meets the holy river Ganga at Prayag.[3]

The city of Indraprasth was guarded by a moat, rampart, gateways and watch-tower.[4] The name of the city was given Indraprasth by King Indr himself. The city was encircled by beautiful gardens.[5] Even Firishta, author of *Tarikh-i-Firishta*, stated that Delhi derived its name from Raja Dhilu of early times. Delhi was founded in 736 A.D. by the Tomars. A geographer of Alexander, in his map of India in first and second centuries B.C. describes 'Daidala' near Indraprasth. The Pehowa inscription of the Pratihar king, Mahendrapal I, mentions that a Tomar king ruled over the Hariyana country and Dhillika was its capital. Delhi, as name of this city, has been used for the first time during the first and second centuries A.D. by Ptolemy.

Even in the *Jataks* (Suruchi Jatak), Indraprasth is considered one of the important cities along with Mithila. The *Bhagwat Puran* describes that Yudhishthir reigned from this city and was succeeded by thirty generations of the descendants of his brother, Arjuna.

The original settlement of Delhi stood on the banks of the Yamuna (between Kotla of Firoz Shah and the tomb of Humayun). Here, a village named Indraprasth was in existence till recently; the village was uprooted by the British along with other villages for the construction of New Delhi. The river Yamuna has now shifted its stream towards the east. In early Buddhist literature, this settlement is mentioned as Indapatt, Indapath, Indapathan and Indaratth. This settlement is mentioned 29 times in the whole of *Pali Tipitika* out of which 26 references are from the *Jataks*, two from the *Cariyapitaka* and one from the *Buddhavams*.[6]

In the *Jataks*, the references of Indapatt/Indapattan or Indapatha, as a town in the Kuru country, figures and a straight road ran from there to Varanasi. It was one of the chief cities of Jambudvip. It was a paragon of beauty, its excellence being comparable to the legendry Naga city Bhogwat. Later, Naga rulers would also rule Indraprasth.

In order to avoid strife, Dhritarastr and Bhishm asked the Pandav to go to the Khandav tract and to build their capital. The Khandav tract was a forested area. It had to be cleared with the help of Agni (the Fire God).[7]

At this place, the Pandavs built a new fortified city, which was named *Indraprasth*.[8] After the *Mahabharat* war, the Pandavs moved to Hastinapur and Indraprasth was handed over to the Yadavs, the descendants of Pandavs. Later, the Pandavs shifted their capital from Hastinapur to Kausambi, because Hastinapur was washed away by the floods of the river Ganga. The Yadavs also later abandoned Indraprasth for Mathura; but it remained a city of importance.

The importance of this city declined during Gupt period. The Tomar rulers built their city at Suraj Kund, which was well protected by hills. Stone for construction and water for life was easily available. Mehrauli had also the same features.

The Delhi territory is situated between 28° 30′N-29°N latitude and 70° 45′E-77° 30′E longitude. The present area of this territory was carved out of the erstwhile state of Punjab in 1912 to which 65 villages of Meerut district (United Provinces) were added in 1915 by the British.

Some of the sites of Delhi were built on the whims of the builders and the location later had the disadvantage of poor water supply. The cities built on the western bank of the Yamuna river were also badly sited and the floods caused their abandonment and decay; but locations on the elevated land to the north proved safer and advantageous.

Delhi was very strategically positioned in the context of South Asia. It was almost in the middle of the whole of India before partition, when Afghanistan, too, was a part of the Delhi empire. Even today, it enjoys a gateway position in between the Himalayan land and Thar peninsula areas. Delhi has, 'The march land position between the North-West, ever accessible to new waves of invasion and cultural intrusion and the shock absorbing Gangetic plains … Few sites enjoy such advantages, perhaps none save Rome and Istanbul have had such long sustained significance.'[9]

Over the ages, the Yamuna, which is an ancient river, played a great role in the commercial, social and religious life of the city. It also protected the city from the eastern side. It made the land around it fertile. The climate of this area is tropical savanna type with a dry season from October to May and wet monsoon type from June to September.

The ridge has also played a great role in protecting the city from invasions and providing stones for building the various cities. It was also a good hunting ground and is now a lung of the city.

In 1451, Bahlol Lodi shifted the capital to Agra, but in 1639, Shah Jahan again shifted it back to Delhi. The British shifted their capital in 1858 to Calcutta but again shifted to Delhi in December 1911.

In fact, the nodal position of Delhi was always a matter of consideration, inherent to any situation, and this made it the potential focus of routes from contrasting zones of physical environment. The historical geography, climate, land, river and ridge suited rulers politically and militarily to keep it as their capital.

In 1955 and 1969–73, excavations were made in the Old Fort (Purana Quila) and some painted grey wares were found. The evidence of continuous habitation of the site from Mauryan (c. 300 B.C.) to the early Mughal period (16th century) was encountered. However, there are some positive indicators of the antiquity of settlements in or around Delhi. Some stone tools found at Suraj Kund also indicate earliest habitation in this region. The mounds along the eastern and western banks of the Yamuna lying between Mandoli (Nand Nagari) and Sambhaoli villages has yielded pot-shreds with some Harappan cultural affiliations, which is said to be nearly four thousand years old. Other sites with similar affiliations are Gharonda Nimka, Mem ka Khera, Timarpur, Khera Kalan, Bhor Garh, and Narela.

Asok's Minor Rock Edicts at East of Kailash are the earliest recorded evidence of the historic Delhi, and so is the Bijhli Rock inscription (district Udaipur, Rajasthan) issued by Chahaman Someshvara in v.s. 1226 (1169–70 A.D.). It is the earliest epigraphic evidence referring to 'Dhillika' which is identified with modern Delhi. An inscription of 1316–17 A.D. recording the excavation of a step well at Ladnu (in Jodhpur, Rajasthan) describes 'Dilli' as a city in the Haritan (Haryana) territory that was once ruled by the Tomars and the Chahmans. It also refers to the long sequence of Turkish rulers from Shahab-ud-Din Ghori to Ala-ud-Din Khilji (verses 6-13). The inscription refers to the current rulers of the city as Sakas.[10]

In the course of time, the name of this city has also changed in pronunciation from 'Dhilli' to 'Dilli' and from 'Dehli' to 'Delhi'. During the reign of Sultan Mohammad Tughluq (1325–57 A.D.), an inscription in 1327 A.D. was installed at Nadayana, now Naraina village, which also describes the beauty of the city of 'Dhilli' and the river. One inscription is also found in Palam village *baoli,* referring to 'Delhi' as lying in Hariyank.

The earliest monumental remains in Delhi are a pre-tenth century temple around the complex of Sultan Garhi, Suraj Kund, with its Sun Temple, the ruins of a dam; some pavilions and fortifications are associated with the Suraj Pal and Anang Pal. Lal Kot was the creation of Anang Pal, who brought the Iron pillar, which now stands in the courtyard of the Quwwat-ul-Islam mosque, Mehrauli.

The Chahmanas succeeded the Tomars. The king Prithviraj III (Rai

Pithora) reinforced the ramparts of Lal Kot and gave it a new name of 'Qila Rai Pithora'. Some historians believe that first floor of the Qutub Minar was built during the time of Prithviraj III.

The temple of Jogmaya (Yogmaya) is also mentioned in the Palam Baoli inscription (thirteenth century) as well as some Jain Pattavalis. Yognipura is also an alternative name of Delhi.

From an obscure *pargana* with a fort, it became a prominent city under the Muslim rulers. Its mosques, shrines, palaces and majestic forts, now in neglect, display the flow of many civilizations and manifest developing architectural styles.

The various cities of Delhi known as Mehrauli, Siri, Tughlaqabad, Jahanpanah, Firozabad, were built in the styles of architecture developed during the Turkish and Pathan dynasties. Purana Qila is the mixed characteristic of the Pathan and the Mughal art. Shahjahanabad exhibits the Mughal styles. Except Shahjahanabad, the earlier cities are now extinct and only their ruins remain as mute testimony of their past. After Shahjahanabad, the British built the capital city of New Delhi in a planned way and in its execution, many villages were uprooted.

The beauty of Delhi, its construction, the people, the rulers and its importance has been described variously from time to time; the famous inscription in Sanskrit dated 13 August 1276, found in a step well at Palam is one such evidence. Ibn Battuta, the great Moorish traveler who visited Delhi and stayed in the city from 1334 to 1342 A.D. during the reign of Muhammad Tughluq, also described this city similarly. Francois Bernier visited Delhi from 1659 to 1660 A.D. and also narrated the same in his accounts. The invasions of Timur, Nadir Shah, Ahmad Shah and others have also been narrated by various people. The rebellion of 1857 A.D. is also narrated by some British and poets like Ghalib.

The river Yamuna has remained the centre of various activities and the life line of Delhi from the inception of the city. It has been described by various people; now it is losing its face and charm.

Delhi has been sacked and left nacked and desolate many times. However, it emerged again and became the Empress of Indian cities.

It is not generally known that one of the Governors-General, the much maligned Warren Hastings, was firmly convinced that the permanency of the British dominion in India could never be ensured while Calcutta remained the capital city. From 1912 to 1930 A.D., the British temporarily made their capital at Civil Lines and cantonment area (now University of Delhi), the British termed it as Delhi. In 1931 A.D., New Delhi was inaugurated. This city has mostly been the capital of various rulers alien to the soil and this factor appears to have had a profound effect upon the pattern of the city as it then existed.

After the death of Harsh, for three hundred years no personality striking enough was seen through the mist which settled down like a pall over India. The death of Harsh loosened the bounds which restrained the disruptive forces always ready to operate in India, and allowed them to produce their normal result: a medley of petty states with ever varying boundaries, and engaged in unceasing internecine wars. It was not a new thing in the history of India. Hindustan always needed some strong, centralizing, magnetic forces to hold its varying atoms together. The period from 700 to 1001 A.D. is the period of chaos but India had grown inordinately rich.

The campaigns of the crescent started from 1001 to 1200 A.D. The Rajputs resisted from 1176 to 1206 A.D. but envy and strife among them led to the defeat of the Rajputs one by one. In 1206 A.D., the Empire of Delhi was founded by a slave. The Tartar dynasties ruled Delhi from 1288 to 1398 A.D. The empire expanded and new forts were built but some Darveshs (Sufis) were not having good relations with the rulers and cursed them. The capital was once shifted to Deogiri, which was rechristened as Daulatabad, or the 'Abode of Wealth'. Again the capital was shifted to Delhi with heavy loss of life and property. Many Mongol invasions were repulsed. The dreaded, often times delayed invasions of the Mongols under Timur had come to Delhi at last in 1388 to 1389 A.D. He left anarchy, famine, pestilence behind him. For two months Delhi was a city of dead and for thirty-six years India owned no government either in name or in reality. Dazed, depopulated, despairing, Delhi dreamt evil dreams.

From 1389 to 1514 A.D. India remained free from a master hand. The whole continent had split up into petty principalities governed by Muslim rulers. Gujarat, Malwa, Kanauj, Oudh, Karra, Jaunpur, Lahore, Dipalpur, Multan, Bayana, Kalpi, Mahoba, were a few places of the countless kings who rose up and warred with one another.

The South (Deccan) also had split up into five separate states: Bijapur, Golconda, Berar, Ahmadnagar and Hyderabad. Meanwhile, at Delhi, the thirty-six years of kinglessness passed into seventy three, during which the government was in the hands of three comparatively strong men, Bahlol Lodi, Sikandar Lodi and Ibrahim Lodi. The first was a warrior, the second a bigot and the third one a tyrant.

Sikandar Lodi had subordinated policy to religion. He destroyed every image and temple which he could see, or of which he could hear, and promptly put to death a Brahman who preached that 'all religions, if sincerely practiced, were equally acceptable to God'.

Tolerance was not a virtue in those days. It was during the reign of Ibrahim

Lodi that Babar, the first of great Mughals, entered India in 1514 A.D. In the first battle of Panipat (1526 A.D.) he defeated Ibrahim Lodi and established Mughal rule which lasted till 1858 A.D. with some strong and weak kings. Nadir Shah, Ahmad Shah Abdali, Marathas, Sikhs, Jats, Rohillas and others invaded Delhi during this period.

After the death of Aurangzeb in 1707 A.D., the Marathas rose to power to the extent that they became the protectors of Mughal rule. In 1803 A.D., the British became the rulers and transformed the whole system to their advantage. In 1857–8 A.D. the general grievance started from Calcutta (the then capital of the British) and carried throughout every native regiment in India, of the greased cartridges. Some native rulers of North India were not happy with the 'Policy of Lapse' of the British. The native soldiers at Meerut started the Mutiny followed by Delhi, Kanpur, Jhansi and Lucknow. The British crushed it with superior power and with the help of the native rulers.

Calcutta remained the capital of India from 1858 A.D. to December 1911 A.D. In December 1911 A.D., again the capital was shifted to Delhi. The British wanted to rule India for eternity, that is why they built a planned capital (New Delhi), but circumstances and events so happened that in August 1947 A.D. they had to leave India but left it divided.

Many dynasties, tribes and races ruled over Delhi from Jambudvip (Bharat, India) and outside it. Foreign invaders like the Greeks, the Bectrians, the Parthians, the Sakas, the Kushans, the Turks, the Mughals and last of all the British, tended to recapture the emotions of their predecessors and often built on the debris of the previous capitals.

> And thus it was that, on the Plateau chosen by the ancients, many subsequent rulers... The stone from the fallen forts and the spreading thorn bush and built strong holds for their fiery souls, which their retinue, living all around them in tents, simply accepted as the natural order imposed by the hero-king. And heroism in this area became the necessary condition of survival, because generation after generation, invasion followed infiltration by the land-hungry tribes from North, who had heard rumours of the fertile plains watered by the river Yamuna and the Ganga.[11]

Indian society was continuously adopting and absorbing many a social, artistic and religious traditions from these foreigners, who had come and settled in India. Since Delhi was the capital and trading centre of India, these people and tribes came to Delhi and in turn contributed their shares in the growth of social, political, religious and cultural life of India in general and Delhi in particular. The sources of information on such aspects can be found from the contemporary literature: Hindu, Buddhist and Jain. The *Brahmans*, the *Aryanks*, the *Upnishads*, the *Dharm* and the *Grih-Sutrs*, the *Nirukt* of Yaksh and the *Astadhyayi* of Panini, the *Mahabhashy* of Patinjali, the *Mahabharat*, the

Ramayan, the *Dharmasashtr* of Manu and *Arthasastr* of Kautilya. The *Purans*, like the *Markendey, Kurm, Vayu, Matsy, Vishnu*; *Khil* and *Harivams* are full of interesting episodes. The two most interesting treatise on dramatics and music, namely, Bharat's Natyasastr (second-third century B.C.), Matangamuni called *Brhaddesi* (sixth century A.D.) are of great value because they have recorded the cultural contribution of the foreign tribes. Among the Buddhist works, *Mahavagg*, the *Brahmajalasutt*, the *Jatakmala* as well as the *Mahavastu, Avadanasatak* and *Divyadan* are the chief sources of knowledge regarding the names of the foreign tribes, their location and other particulars.

The Jain canonical works, such as the Nayadhammakahao refers to the foreigners. The western contacts brought something new to the cuisine of ancient India, and changed the taste of the people. The change in taste points to the mutual give and take and adaptability of the period. The western ideas also crept into the coiffure art of the Ancient Indians; the jewellery and dress, festivities and many other areas.

Our social system based on four *varnas* was strengthened on the Persians social order. Large scale shifting of population from one place to another was due to the foreign invasions. The Indian pardah system and the custom of 'Sati' can be said to be the outcome of the presence of foreigners in our midst.

The Sanskrit language particularly the poetry owes much to the Sakas and the Kushans. The art of writing developed due to foreign initiative and the rise and fall of some ancient universities, in some cases, was brought about by the movements of invaders.

REFERENCES

1. Adiparv, 211, 10
2. Sabhaparv, 20, 26-27
3. Adiparv, Ch. 60, 2 (Gorakhpur)
4. Adiparv, 206; 31-32
5. Adiparv, 41-42
6. Buddhavams (Jayawickram's, PTS Ed.), XXVIII, 11
7. Mahabharata 1(19), 214-215, English tr. by J. A. B, Van Buitenen, Chicago, 1973
8. ibid. p. 199
9. O. H. K., *Spate-India and Pakistan*, Metheun, London, 1954
10. Epigraphia Indica, XII, 1913-14, No. 5, pp. 17-27
11. Mulk Raj Anand, Marg, September 1967, p. 5

1

Yamuna and the Ridge

'Environment' is a very commonly heard word, which has become a great concern for today's world. The imbalance of nature has made men more frightened and more worried about the future than the present. Environmentalists and various scientists have come to this conclusion that, if with the same speed men continue to affect nature—the water, the earth, the air, the sky and emanation of gases and cutting of forests and trees—it is sure that between 1990 and 2020, everyday, 50 species of animals and other living organisms shall vanish from the earth and this will have many negative effects on our environment.

The plants and trees grew first on the earth. Nearly 42.5 crore years back, on the surface of the earth, some simple plants came up and, nearly 40 crore years ago, big plants and trees started growing on this earth. After the development of the plants and trees, other creations came on this earth. Man came into existence only 10 lacs years ago; hence, men are the youngest progeny of nature and trees are our ancestors. They are the basis of life and that is why they have been venerated; till date we worship the sun and trees. In many parts of India, people believe that to get rid of some trouble, one has to marry a tree. The trees not only give us fresh air, they also give us food and rain. In ancient times, people acknowledged that it was impossible for men to exist without trees. That is why our ancestors assigned to them a religious sanctity and respected the forests.

In the seal and sealings found in the excavations of Harappa and Mohenjodaro, some trees and plants are depicted; they have been identified as the date palm, the pipal and the acacia. It is a significant evidence that, in the prehistoric period, our ancestors were respecting and restoring the trees and plants. In Vedic way of life, *Vanprasth*, (forest stage) is one of the very important stages of life in which men have to live in forests in their waning years.

Our forefathers were conscious that plants have life and are useful for the existence of all sentient beings. *Satapath Brahman*[1] distinguishes between living and non-living trees. *Vanaspati* is the commonly used term in scriptures for all trees and plants. There are many '*shloks*' to venerate trees. Even after the Vedic period, in the *Mahabharat*, the term used for a plant is *udbhuja*.[2] The *Mahabharat* records that the planting of trees gives merit in this world and the world hereafter. A man is honoured by his children after his death. Thus, the trees establish this reputation and are remembered by posterity. Those, who have no progeny, consider the trees as their own children.[3] The *Mahabharat* also gives an idea of the various trees and plants of that period.[4] During the Buddhist era, forests and trees were highly respected. Mahatma Buddha was born under a sal tree and for the first time when he opened his eyes he saw trees and forest. He got his enlightenment under the tree and later his nirwana under the tree.

A Drawing depicting Yamuna and Ganga, from Udaigiri caves, 4th century A.D.

Indraprasth was established by the Pandavs in the forest of Khandav Van. There were gardens around the city.[5] The city was located on the bank of Yamuna. Indraprasth is a site near the Purana Qila (the Old Fort); now there is no forest around it. From 1430 B.C. onwards, we have knowingly or unknowingly destroyed it.

The earliest reference of human settlement at 'Delhi' (the region) is found in the *Mahabharat*. It was a primeval forest and a frightful place, full of thorns and prickles, having crumbling ruins of a deserted city which was a shelter for birds and beasts and was infested with thieves and wicked men. The original inhabitants of this place were the Nags and Takshaks, who were expelled by Arjun with the help of Lord Krishn.[6] The Nags, like most of the other native tribes, had the serpent as their totem and protective diety. Shri Krishn, the hero of Yadavs, apart from being an incarnation of Vishnu, was also the son of Vasudev and great grandson of Aryak, who was a Nag chief. It is believed that Baldev, the elder brother of Krishn, is said to be the incarnation of Seshnag. It is also said that, at his death, his soul came out of his mouth in the form of a large cobra.

The role of Nags or Ahi (Serpent) is mentioned in the *Rig Ved*. In the *Atharv Ved*, there are hymns describing *ilige* and *viligi*, who were Assyrian

Shiv Temple, Neeli Chhatri, the spot is claimed to be as ancient as Pandavs.

Kings. The tradition of *nag* worship was prevalent in Babylonia, Assyria, Palestine and Iran. According to the *Rig Ved,* the language of these people was not Sanskrit but was Souraseni. The most valuable Nag images recovered from Mathura district are preserved in the Mathura Museum.[7] Nags were great warriers and they recaptured Hastinapur and Indraprasth after the war of the *Mahabharat*. They also later pushed back the Kushans and Scythians from North India. From 950 B.C., coinciding with the beginning of Vedic culture, one can see the revival of Nag culture.

Yamuna

The Kurus not only decimated the Nags but also established matrimonial relations. According to the *Mahabharat*, one of the wives of Arjun was Ulupi, who was a Nag maiden. The mother of Kunti was also a daughter of a Nag king. Subhadra, a Nag Princess, was married to Arjun.

List of Rulers of Indraprasth and Delhi Beginning from Raja Yudhishthir[8]

S. No.	Ruler	Father's name	Approx. Yr. of Acc. (B.C.)	Capital	Period of rule (Yrs.)	Event
1.	Raja Yudhishthir	Raja Pandav	1450	Hastinapur	36	After the death of Krishn Avtar, Raja Yudhishthir buried himself in the snow in Himanchal.
2.	Raja Parikshit	Abhimanyu s/o Raja Arjun s/o Raja Pandav	1414	Hastinapur	32	
3.	Raja Janmejay	Raja Parikshit	1382	Hastinapur	34	
4.	Raja Shatamikalias RajaAshwamedh	Raja Janmejay	1348	Hastinapur	33	
5.	Raja Sahnranik alias Raja Udhman	Raja Ashwamedh	1315	Hastinapur	32	
6.	Ashwamedhj alias Raja Muhaji	Raja Udhman	1283	Hastinapur	36	
7.	Asin Krishan	Raja Muhaji	1247	Hastinapur	35	
8.	Nimi alias Raja Drishtadyumn	Asim Krishan	1212	First Hastinapur. After that on the bank of the river Koshki and after that Indraprasth	35	
9.	Raja Chakr alias Ugrasain	Raja Drishtadyumn	1177	Indraprasth	36	
10.	Raja Chitr Rath alias Sursain	Raja Ugrasain	1141	Indraprasth	36	
11.	Raja Kirath	Raja Sursain	1105	Indraprasth	32	
12.	Parishat Man alias Rasmi	Raja Kirath	1073	Indraprasth	31	
13.	Sursain alias Raja Barchhal	Raja Rasmi	1042	Indraprasth	27	

14.	Raja Saunth alias Sukhpal	Raja Barchhal	1015	Indraprasth	28	
15.	Raja Narchakshu alias Narhardev	Raja Sukhpal	987	Indraprasth	23	
16.	Sakhi Nal alias Suraj Rath	Raja Narhardev	964	Indraprasth	18	
17.	Parillu alias Raja Bhupat	Suraj Rath	946	Indraprasth	26	
18.	Raja Sauni	Raja Bhupat	920	Indraprasth	25	This Raja founded Sonipat city. Also known as Dhava who built the Iron Pillar.
19.	Raja Medhavi	Raja Sauni	895	Indraprasth	23	
20.	Raja Nrip Anji alias Shravan Chatr	Raja Medhavi	872	Indraprasth	25	
21.	Raja Daurabh alias Bhikam	Raja Shravan Chatr	847	Indraprasth	19	
22.	Raja Timi alias Bidarth	Raja Bhikam	828	Indraprasth	21	
23.	Brihadrath alias Raja Daswan	Raja Bidarath	807	Indraprasth	20	
24.	Raja Sivdas alias Adni Pal	Raja Daswan	787	Indraprasth	20	
25.	Shatanik alias Abhidhar	Raja Adni Pal	767	Indraprasth	23	
26.	Raja Druman alias Dand Pan	Raja Abhidhar	744	Indraprasth	18	
27.	Raja Bahitar alias Durbal Rai	Dand Pan	726	Indraprasth	19	
28.	Raja Danda Pani alias Dushta Pal	Raja Durlabh Rai	707	Indraprasth	16	This king founded the city of Panipat.
29.	Raja Nimmi alias Raja Khem Pal	Raja Dushta Pal	691	Indraprasth	26	

30.	Raja Kishimak alias Khiman	Raja Khem Pal	665	Indraprasth	22	The above mentioned kings ruled for 807 years then Wazir Basrava killed this king and ascended the throne himself.
31.	Raja Basrava	x	643	Indraprasth	8	
32.	Raja Suraj Sain	Raja Basrava	636	Indraprasth	19	
33.	Raja Bir Sah	Raja Suraj Sain	617	Indraprasth	24	
34.	Raja Anek Sah alias Rab Sain	Raja Bir Sah	593	Indraprasth	22	
35.	Raja Harjeet alias Pitr Sal	Raja Anek Sah	571	Indraprasth	16	
36.	Raja Durabh	Raja Harjeet	555	Indraprasth	20	
37.	Raja Siddhi Pal	Raja Durabh	535	Indraprasth	13	
38.	Raja Barsat	Raja Siddhi Pal	522	Indraprasth	19	
39.	Raja Sanji	Raja Barsat	503	Indraprasth	16	
40.	Raja Amar Jodh	Raja Sanji	487	Indraprasth	13	
41.	Raja Amin Pal	Raja Amar Jodh	474	Indraprasth	12	
42.	Raja Sirohi	Raja Amin Pal	462	Indraprasth	22	
43.	Raja Padarth	Raja Sirohi	440	Indraprasth	12	
44.	Raja Budh Mal	Raja Padarth	428	Indraprasth	15	This dynasty ruled for 230 years; after that, Bir Bah Wazir killed the king and himself ascended the throne.
45.	Raja Bir Bah	x	413	Indraprasth	17	
46.	Raja Murar Singh	Raja Bir Bah	396	Indraprasth	14	
47.	Raja Shatr Kan	Raja Murar Singh	382	Indraprasth	11	
48.	Raja Mahi Pat alias Dhan Pat	Raja Shatr Kan	371	Indraprasth	12	
49.	Raja Mahabal	Raja Mahi Pat	359	Indraprasth	19	
50.	Raja Sarup Dat	Raja Mahabal	340	Indraprasth	14	Perhaps during the time of this king, a city was founded in Indraprasth in the name of Raja Dehlav of Kanauj.

51.	Raja Mitr Sain	Raja Sarup Dat	326	Dehli	12	
52.	Raja Sukh Dan	Raja Mitr Sain	314	Dehli	8	
53.	Raja Jait Mal	Raja Sukh Dan	306	Dehli	14	
54.	Raja Pal Singh	Raja Jait Mal	292	Dehli	19	
55.	Raja Kulmati	Raja Pal Singh	273	Dehli	19	
56.	Raja Shatru Mardan	Raja Kulmati	254	Dehli	6	
57.	Raja Jeevan Jat	Raja Shatru Mardan	248	Dehli	13	
58.	Raja Parichhit	Raja Jeevan Jat	235	Dehli	8	
59.	Raja Bir Sain	Raja Parichhit	227	Dehli	17	
60.	Raja Udpat	Raja Bir Sain	210	Dehli	13	This dynasty ruled for 216 years. After that Wazir Dharni Dhar killed the king and assumed the throne himself.
61.	Raja Dharni Dhar	x	197	Dehli	19	
62.	Raja Sain Dhaj	Raja Dharni Dhar	178	Dehli	25	
63.	Raja Mahi Katak	Raja Sain Dhaj	153	Dehli	19	
64.	Raja Maha Jodh	Raja Mahi Katak	134	Dehli	22	
65.	Raja Bir Nabh	Raja Maha Jodh	112	Dehli	13	
66.	Raja Jeevan Raj	Raja Bir Nath?	99	Dehli	21	
67.	Raja Udhi Sain	Raja Jeevan Raj	78	Dehli	17	
68.	Raja Anand Jag	Raja Udhi Sain	61	Dehli	25	
69.	Raja Raj Pal	Raja Anand Jag	36	Dehli	12	This dynasty ruled for 173 years. Subsequently Raja Bhagwant, ruler of Kumayun, captured Dilli.
70.	Raja Bhagwant Gohi	x	24	Dehli	13	Killed in battle with Bikramjit.
71.	Raja Bikramjit ruler of Ujjain	Raja Gandharp Sain	11 V.S. 42	Ujjain	93	When this king was killed in the battle of Salbahan, Samundar Pal Jogi assumed the throne of Dilli.
72.	Raja Samundar Pal Jogi	x	V.S. 135 78 A.D.	Dehli	24	
73.	Raja Chandra Pal	Raja Samundar Pal	V.S. 159 / 102 A.D.	Dehli	27	
74.	Raja Nai Pal	Raja Chandra Pal	V.S. 186 / 129 A.D.	Dehli	21	

No.	Ruler	Predecessor	Date	Capital	Years	Remarks
75.	Raja Din Pal	Raja Nai Pal	V.S. 207 / 150 A.D.	Dehli	14	
76.	Raja Sukh Pal	Raja Din Pal	V.S. 221 / 164 A.D.	Dehli	19	
77.	Raja Gobind Pal	Raja Sukh Pal	V.S. 240 / 183 A.D.	Dehli	18	
78.	Raja Mukh Pal	Raja Gobind Pal	V.S. 258 / 201 A.D.	Dehli	22	
79.	Raja Harchand Pal	Raja Mukh Pal	V.S. 280 / 223 A.D.	Dehli	13	
80.	Raja Mahi Pal	Raja Harchand Pal	V.S. 293 / 236 A.D.	Dehli	15	
81.	Raja Har Pal	Raja Mahi Pal	V.S. 308 / 251 A.D.	Dehli	14	
82.	Raja Madan Pal	Raja Har Pal	V.S. 322 / 265 A.D.	Dehli	18	
83.	Raja Karam Pal	Raja Madan Pal	V.S. 340 / 283 A.D.	Dehli	15	
84.	Raja Bikram Pal or Khaim Pal	Raja Karam Pal	V.S. 355 / 298 A.D.	Dehli	12	This dynasty ruled for 222 years. Then Raja Maluk Chand of Bahiraj won in the battle.
85.	Raja Maluk Chand	x	V.S. 367 / 310 A.D.	Dehli	2	
86.	Raja Bikram Chand	Raja Maluk Chand	V.S. 369 / 312 A.D.	Dehli	13	
87.	Raja Kan Chand	Raja Bikram Chand	V.S. 382 / 325 A.D.	Dehli	1	
88.	Raja Ram Chandar	Raja Kan Chand	V.S. 383 / 326 A.D.	Dehli	11	
89.	Raja Dheer Chand	Raja Ram Chandar	V.S. 394 / 337 A.D.	Dehli	15	
90.	Raja Kalyan Chand	Raja Dheer Chand	V.S. 409 / 352 A.D.	Dehli	16	
91.	Raja Bhim Chand	Raja Kalyan Chand	V.S. 425 / 368 A.D.	Dehli	12	
92.	Raja Har Chand	Raja Bhim Chand	V.S. 437 / 380 A.D.	Dehli	1	
93.	Raja Gobind Chand	Raja Har Chand	V.S. 438 / 381 A.D.	Dehli	13	
94.	Rani Paim Devi	Raja Gobind Chand	V.S. 451 / 394 A.D.	Dehli	1	This dynasty ruled for 85 years. When the queen died, the people set Faqir Har Prem on the throne.
95.	Raja Har Prem	x	V.S. 452 / 395 A.D.	Dehli	8	
96.	Raja Gobind Prem	Raja Har Prem	V.S. 460 / 403 A.D.	Dehli	20	
97.	Raja Gopal Prem	Raja Gobind Prem	V.S. 480 / 423 A.D.	Dehli	16	
98.	Raja Maha Patr	Raja Gopal Prem	V.S. 496 / 439 A.D.	Dehli	7	This dynasty ruled for 51 years. Finally, the king left the kingdom and became a Faqir. Hearing this news, the ruler of Bangale, Raja Dahi Sain, captured Dilli.
99.	Raja Dahi Sain	x	V.S. 503 / 446 A.D.	Dehli	18	
100.	Raja Bilawal Sain	Raja Dahi Sain	V.S. 521 / 464 A.D.	Dehli	12	

101.	Raja Kunwar Sain	Raja Bilawal Sain	v.s. 533 / 476 A.D.	Dehli	15	
102.	Raja Madhav Sain	Raja Kunwar Sain	v.s. 548 / 491 A.D.	Dehli	15	
103.	Raja Sur Sain	Raja Madhav Sain	v.s. 563 / 506 A.D.	Dehli	6	
104.	Raja Bhim Sain	Raja Sur Sain	v.s. 569 / 521 A.D.	Dehli	5	
105.	Raja Kan Sain	Raja Bhim Sain	v.s. 574 / 517 A.D.	Dehli	5	
106.	Raja Har Sain	Raja Kan Sain	v.s. 579 / 522 A.D.	Dehli	9	
107.	Raja Khana Sain	Raja Har Sain	v.s. 588 / 531 A.D.	Dehli	2	
108.	Raja Narain Sain	Raja Khana Sain	v.s. 590 / 533 A.D.	Dehli	27	
109.	Raja Damodar Sain	Raja Narain Sain	v.s. 617 / 560 A.D.	Dehli	11	Twelve people ruled for 125 years. At last, the Arkan kingdom conspired with Raja Deb Singh of Kohistan and called him to Dilli.
110.	Raja Deb Singh Kohi	x	v.s. 628 / 571 A.D.	Dehli	17	
111.	Raja Ran Singh	Raja Deb Singh	v.s. 645 / 588 A.D.	Dehli	14	
112.	Raja Raj Singh	Raja Ran Singh	v.s. 659 / 602 A.D.	Dehli	9	
113.	Raja Sher Singh	Raja Raj Singh	v.s. 668 / 611 A.D.	Dehli	45	
114.	Raja Har Singh	Raja Sher Singh	v.s. 713 / 656 A.D. 37 A.H.	Dehli	13	
115.	Raja Jeevan Singh	Raja Har Singh	v.s. 726 / 669 A.D. 50 A.H.	Dehli	7	Six people ruled for 105 years. Then Anang Pal Tanwar conquered Dilli.
116.	Raja Anang Pal Tanwar	Raja Ugra Sain	v.s. 733 / 676 A.D. 57 A.H.	Dehli	18	
117.	Raja Basdev	Raja Anang Pal	v.s. 751 / 694 A.D. 75 A.H.	Dehli	19 years 1 month 18 yaum (days)	
118.	Raja Kanak Pal	Raja Basdev	v.s. 770 / 713 A.D. 95 A.H.	Dehli	22 years 3 months 28 days	
119.	Raja Pirthi Pal	Raja Kanak Pal	v.s. 792 735 A.D. 117 A.H.	Dehli	19 years 6 months 19 days	
120.	Raja Jai Dev	Raja Pirthi Pal	v.s. 811 / 754 A.D. 137 A.H.	Dehli	21 years 7 months 28 days	

121.	Raja Har Pal	Raja Jai Dev	V.S. 832 / 775 A.D. 159 A.H.	Dehli	14 years 4 months 9 days	
122.	Raja Uday Raj	Raja Har Pal	V.S. 846 / 789 A.D. 173 A.H.	Dehli	26 years 7 months 11 days	
123.	Raja Bachh Raj	Raja Udai Raj	V.S. 872 / 816 A.D. 201 A.H.	Dehli	22years 2 months 13 days	
124.	Raja Anag Pal	Raja Bachh Raj	V.S. 894 / 837 A.D. 222 A.H.	Dehli	22 years 3 months 16 days	
125.	Raja Rakh Pal	Raja Anag Pal	V.S. 916 / 859 A.D. 245 A.H.	Dehli	21 years 6 months 5 days	
126.	Raja Nek Pal	Raja Rakh Pal	V.S. 938 / 881 A.D. 268 A.H.	Dehli	2 years 14 days	
127.	Raja Gopal	Raja Nek Pal	V.S. 940 / 883 A.D. 270 A.H.	Dehli	18 years 3 months 15 days	
128.	Raja Salkhan	Raja Gopal	V.S. 958 / 901 A.D. 288 A.H.	Dehli	25 years 2 months 10 days	
129.	Raja Jai Pal	Raja Salkhan	V.S. 983 / 926 A.D. 314 A.H.	Dehli	16 years 4 months 13 days	
130.	Raja Kanwar Pal	Raja Jai Pal	V.S. 1000 / 943 A.D. 332 A.H.	Dehli	29 years 9 months 11 days	
131.	Raja Anek Pal	Raja Kanwar Pal	V.S. 1029 / 972 A.D. 362 A.H.	Dehli	29 years 6 months 18 days	
132.	Raja Bijay Pal	Raja Anek Pal	V.S. 1059 / 1002 A.D. 393 A.H.	Dehli	24 years 1 month 4 days	
133.	Raja Mahi Pal	Raja Bijay Pal	V.S. 1083 / 1026 A.D. 417 A.H.	Dehli	25 years 2 months 13 days	
134.	Raja Agar Pal	Raja Mahi Pal	V.S. 1108 / 1051 A.D. 443 A.H.	Dehli	21 years 2 months 15 days	
135.	Raja Pirthi Raj	Raja Agar Pal	V.S. 1129 / 1072 A.D. 465 A.H.	Dehli	22 years 3 months 16 days	Twenty rulers of this dynasty ruled for 419 years 8 months and 28 days. Then Bildev Chauhan conquered Dilli.

136.	Raja Bildev Chauhan	Raja Anil Dev	v.s. 1152 / 1095 A.D. 495 A.H.	Dehli	6 years 1 month 4 days	
137.	Raja Amar Kanu	Raja Bildev Chauhan	v.s. 1158 / 1101 A.D. 499 A.H.	Dehli	5 years 2 months 5 days	
138.	Raja Khar Pal	Raja Amar Kanku	v.s. 1163 / 1106 A.D. 500 A.H.	Dehli	20 years 1 month 5 days	
139.	Raja Sumer	Raja Khar Pal	v.s. 1183 / 1126 A.D. 520 A.H.	Dehli	7 years 4 months 2 days	
140.	Raja Jahara	Raja Sumer	v.s. 1190 / 1133 A.D. 528 A.H.	Dehli	4 years 4 months 8 days	
141.	Raja Nag Dev	Raja Jahara	v.s. 1195 / 1138 A.D. 533 A.H.	Dehli	3 years 1 month 5 days	
142.	Raja Pirthi Raj alias Rai Pithora	Raja Nag Dev	v.s. 1198 / 1141 A.D. 536 A.H.	Dehli (Dehli+Ajmer)	49 years 5 months 9 days	Seven kings of this dynasty ruled for 95 years and seven months. Then Rai Pithora was killed in a battle with Maz-ud-din Mohammad Sam alias Sultan Shahab-ud-din Ghori and the kingdom passed on to Muslim dynasties. Although Ghayas-ud-din Mohammad bin Sam, King of Ghori, was the brother of Sultan Shahab-ud-Din, the conquest of Hindustan was Sultan Shahab-ud-din's own achievement. So, from the day of the conquest, Sultan Shahab-ud-din is reconed as King of Dilli.*

* The above list, given by Bashir-ud-Din Ahmad, is a comprehensive list of the rulers of Indraprasth and Delhi after the battle of the *Mahabharat,* mentioning the year of accession and the period of rule of the respective kings. Certainly it has come down to us from the oral as well as written native traditions which have been compiled by the author with all due care. Now the trace of these rulers cannot be ascertained in the absence of sufficient archaeological or historical evidence. Moreover, at S. No. 18 and 28, it states that the cities of Sonipat and Panipat were founded by Raja Sauni in 920 B.C. and Raja Danda Pani in 707 B.C. respectively. Whereas according to native traditions, Sonipat and Panipat were among those five villages which were demanded by the Pandavs from the Kauravs. It means that these villages were in existence even before the battle of the *Mahabharat.* Irrespective of such inaccuracies, this list of rulers is a testimony to the fact that Delhi was continuously ruled by native rulers and remaind an important and capital city even before the advent of the Muslim kings.

Indraprasth, as per the Surchi Jataka, was an important city of that period. According to the *Bhagavat Puran*, Yudhishthir reigned for a long period and was succeeded by thirty generations of descendents of his brother Arjun. Indraprasth of the *Mahabharat* period is identified as the area of the present Purana Qila, on the banks of the Yamuna. Yamuna has been flowing at this point for the past 10,000 years with little deviation.

According to the *Mahabharat* (Adiparv), young Bhim who had been administered poison in his food by his cousin, Duryodhan, and was thrown into the river Ganga, went into the deep waters and entered '*Pataal*', where he was bitten by Nags and thus cured of the effects of the poison. The description contained in a few *Purans* and the *Mahabharat* indicates that, among the nine divisions of India, one was that of the Nags and it was in the western part of the country. Virupaks, the Nag demi-God was its guardian. The Bhogavati, to some writers, was the city of the Nags. It was ruled by Vasuki, Takshak and Airavat. Bhogavati is also identified with river Sarasvati near Kurukshetr.[9]

After the *Mahabharat*, the Nags dominated northwestern India. Parikshit, the grandson of Arjun, was killed by Takshak. Janamejay performed a *yagya* and many Nags were killed. However, Astak interceded and the slaughter of the Nags stopped. Ahichhatr (serpent umbrella) was the capital of the Nags. Later, Buddh is said to have preached there and converted its Nag kings.[10]

The Pandavs also belonged to the Nag Dynasty. Yayati, the father of Puru was the son of the Nag, Nahusa, and the maternal grandfather of Astak.[11] Magadh country also belonged to Nag rulers. Brahadrath, Jarasandh and Sisunag belonged to the Nag dynasty. Many Nag rulers and people converted to Buddhism such as Mucillind and Nagaraj. The Nags were also occupants of the East, as is referred in Ramayan.[12] Nag dynasties ruled from Vidisa, Kantipura, Mathura, Padmavati, Taxila, Ayodhya and a number of other places.[13]

After the *Mahabharat*, Mathura became more important than Indraprasth. Among the rulers of Aryavart, who were extirpated by Samudra Gupt (as per his Allahabad pillar inscription), Ganapati Nag and Nagasen whose two coins were found at Padmavati, Vidisa and Mathura relating to King Ganapati Nag.

Chandragupt also married Kuber Nag, the daughter of a Nag Prince. Skand Gupt, in 446 B.C., appointed Sarv Nag as Governor of Antarvedi, a district between the Ganga and the Yamuna. The other famous kings of Padmavati are Maharaja Bhim Nag, Maharaja Skand Nag, Maharaja Brihaspati Nag, Maharaja Dev Nag, Maharaja Vibhu Nag and Maharaja Vyaghraj Nag.

After the Kushan rule, some Nag kings ruled Mathura (the coins of these rulers are kept in the Mathura Museum). Purusadatt, Uttamadatt, Ramdatt, Kamadatt, Raja Seradatt, Raja Bhavadatt and Raja Balabhuti issued coins. They ruled Mathura from the first century B.C. to the second century A.D. Virasen seems to have been a very powerful ruler of Mathura; he, too, was a

Nag ruler. Nag rulers can be found in all ages throughout the country. They were also associated with Buddh and Jain Tirthankars.[14]

In the middle of the Pleistocene times, Delhi and its surroundings were becoming warm and, with the rising in the temperature of atmosphere, ice was melting. It was a favourable time for *homo erectus* for hunting and, for this purpose, he made tools out of the quartzite boulders lying in the Aravallis and the Ridge was its integral part.[15]

The *RigVed* describes the great Saraswati River which, flowing from the 'mountain to the sea', was very ancient. Some centuries before 3000 B.C., the Yamuna (a tributary of the Ganga) and the Sutlej (a tributary of the Indus), flowed into the river Saraswati. This made the river mighty. However, diminishing rainfall and a complex geological phenomenon (plate tectonic) led to the uplifting of sections of the North Indian plane, leading to the loss of the Yamuna from the Dishadvati to the Ganga. Some time before 3000 B.C., due to tectonic shifts followed by earthquakes, the Yamuna changed its course and began to flow into the Ganga. This *sangam* was somewhere in the neighbourhood of Delhi; now it has shifted to Allahabad.[16]

During this period Delhi had plenty of vegetation and water. Man roamed freely in the ridges of Aravalli and hunted. Stone Age tools are found around Anangpur and other parts of the Aravallis. Archeologists and historians, with the help of satellite data, identified six different courses of the Yamuna. Various Stone Age tools have also been located. With this, it becomes clear that man was attracted to this area from the very beginning, in the evolutionary sequence of mankind. Man settled down on the banks of the Yamuna and around it. He shifted his activities with the shifting of the course of Yamuna.

Water is also essential for the growth and development of plants, trees, human beings, animals and all kinds of living creatures. Markandeya Puran[17] states that 'All the rivers are sacred, all flow towards the sea. All rivers are like mothers to the world, all purge away sins'. Many civilizations and cities have grown on the banks of rivers. The Yamuna is considered as one of such rivers which represent India.[18]

The Yamuna (Kalindi) has been mentioned frequently in ancient literature. In the *Rig-Ved* it is mentioned many times: (X 75; V, 52, 17, VII. 18.19; X, 75.5), *Atharvaved* (IX, 9, 10), *Aitareya Brahman* (VIII, 14.4, 23), *Satapath Brahman* (XIII. 5, 4, 11). *Pancavims Brahman* (X,4,11,XXV, 10, 24,13,4), Sankhyayan Srautasutr (XII, 29, 25, 33), Katyayan Srautasutr (XXIV 6,10,39), *Asvalayan Srautasutr* (XII, 6, 28), Patanjali's *Mahabhashya* (1.1.9., p. 436, 1.4.2. p. 670), *Yoginitantr* (2–5, 139–40) and *Kalikapuran* (Ch.15, 8). It is considered as a goddess in the ancient texts. The *Bhagwat Puran* (III.4.36, IV 8.43, IX. 4.30, X 58.22), *Mahavastu* (III.201), *Banahbatt-Kadambri* (p. 6), Purans consider it Yami, the sister of Yam, the god of the dead. In the *Ramayan* (Ayodhya Kand, 54.2.6.8; 55.4.8.12.3, 19, 21, 23, 31, 33).

In the *Mahabharat*, the Yamuna is considered a sacred river. Sage Lomas asked Yudhishthir to take a bath in the Yamuna to wash his sins. Many Asvamedhs were performed by Bhart on the banks of the river Yamuna. Chinese travelers called it Yen-mok-na. In sculptures, it is shown as dark goddess standing on a tortoise.

The people in the villages of Delhi and its surroundings still believe that, by bathing in the Yamuna, their sins will be washed away. Till date the rural people especially women come on the banks of river Yamuna on Amavasya day and take bath in this river. Of course the water of the river is very dirty and stinking, but the belief is very strong.

After completion of the period of exile, the Pandavs requested Duryodhan to give five villages, *Vrikaprasth*–Baghpat; *Indraprasth*—Indrapat (now Delhi); *Tilaprasth*—Tilpat; *Paniprasth*—Panipat and *Sonanaprasth*—Sonipat. All the abovementioned villages were situated on the banks of the Yamuna. The meandering of the Yamuna due to tectonic forces has a great bearing on the settlement in the Yamuna—Doab region. Over a period of time, Yamuna has moved towards the eastern course.[19] However for the past 10,000 years, the Yamuna is flowing on this site.

The Yamuna is the first western tributary of Ganga. It rises from Bandarpunch, a peak situated between the Yamuna and the Ganga in the Himalayas (Yamunotri shrine). Through the Shiwalik ranges and Garhwal, it enters into plains of North India and runs parallel to the Ganga. From plains to Prayag (Allahabad), it receives two tributaries at Dehradun (Tons), between Agra and Allahabad it receives Chambal, Sind, Betwa, Ken and Paisuni. Many cities and holy places are situated on its banks that is, Delhi and Agra, Mathura, Vrindaban, Gokul, Prayag, Kosala and Madura are situated on the bank of this historic river.

The Ridge

The highest point of 1722 metres in the Aravalli Hills is at Mount Abu and the lowest is at 2.5 mt. above the river Yamuna in the north and till 90 m in the south of Delhi. The Ridge in Delhi can be divided into four zones. Outside the city limits, lies the southern ridge which is private land and nearly 6200 hectare area. The South-Central ridge having 626 hectare in area (in Mehrauli) between Rajinder Nagar and Sardar Patel Marg, Central or New Delhi Ridge comprising 864 hectare of the area, and between Delhi University and Civil Lines (North or Old Delhi Ridge) having 87 hectare of the area.[20] The British not only preserved the ridge as a forest but they also took some parts of it for constructing some structures for Delhi of 1912 and New Delhi. According to the officers of the Forest Department of Delhi Government, the Ridge had been certified as reserved forests under the Indian Forest Act of 1878. But since then no government has implemented this Act and government after government started building colonies like Karol Bagh, Rajinder Nagar and Dhaula Kuan. This action rapidly started in the 1920s and 1930s. The prime agencies and people also took advantage of this situation and, according to TCPO, 1982 Reports, '40% of the Ridge had already been destroyed'.

Since time immemorial, the Ridge is very important in the life and history of Delhi. It is an extension of the Aravalli Hills, which are older than the Himalayas. It starts from the Khybar Pass (Delhi) from the western bank of the Yamuna and begins to rise and cross Delhi towards the south and reaches Gujarat through some parts of Rajasthan. It is the lung of the city, which has been preserved to some extent from encroachments due to the directions of courts and vigilance of some N.G.O's. Still, most of Delhi is situated on this ridge: Timarpur, Delhi University, Hindu Rao Hospital, Old Subzi Mandi, Bara Hindu Rao, Chandni Chowk, Jama Masjid, Daryaganj, some parts of New Delhi such as Parliament and Rastrapati Bhawan, Birla Mandir, Rajinder Nagar, Karol Bagh, Dhola Kuan and some villages around it. The Aravalli Hills provided stones for building various capital cities by many rulers from time to time.

Asok's Edicts engraved on this pillar brought by Feroz Shah Tughlaq from Topra near Ambala and placed at the top of his fort.

Asok's Pillar, near Hindu Rao Hospital

The Ridge was earlier a hunting place for kings. Firoz Shah Tughluq had built *shikar gaah* (hunting places) or *aram gaah* (resting places) at various places on the Ridge, such as, one at Jeetgarh, near University of Delhi and others at Talkatora Garden, at Kushak in Teen Murti House and at Malchha Marg on the hill. He also brought two Asok's Pillars from outside Delhi and placed one at the Ridge near Hindu Rao Hospital and the other at his fort. These pillars were created somewhere in 250 B.C. and established at the present places about 1360 A.D. The historicity of Delhi can be traced from the fact that, even during

Asok's Edict, East of Kailash near ISKCON Temple.

and before Asok's period, it was on the trunk route; Asok had created his edicts on such routes. One such rock edict of Asok can still be seen in East of Kailash (a colony in South Delhi), near ISKCON Temple.

Some constructions have come up on the Ridge over the period. On the bank of Yamuna, now Metcalfe House is situated, Timur killed more than 90 thousands captives before entering into Delhi. Metcalfe, who was the resident of Delhi, uprooted the villagers and placed them at Chandrawal (now near Kamla Nagar) to build his house. In 1857, these people looted Metcalfe House to take revenge. Some people were hanged and killed in this house in 1858 after the rebellion.

At Timarpur crossing, there is one Mosque which is said to have been built in time of Timur. Another building, which is called Hindu Rao Hospital, was built as a residence on the Ridge by Edward Colebrooke, the Resident of Delhi, and later on William Fraser purchased it from him. However, on 12 March 1835, Fraser was murdered while returning from the walled city to this house. The cousin of Mirza Ghalib, who was the Nawab of Firozpur Jhirka in Mewat, was hanged for this act. Hindu Rao, who was the brother of Baiza Bai, the famous Rani of Gwalior, occupied this house for a long period from 1835 onwards. She came along with his brother to Delhi and lived with him after the death of his young son.

On the eastern side of Flag Staff Tower, which was built by the British, some of the British soldiers, women and children stayed there during the mutiny. Just down it is the old viceregal lodge. Now it is called the Vice Chancellor's Office of the University of Delhi. In one of the rooms, which is now the Registrar's Office, Lord Mountbatten proposed to marry Lady Edwina.

The British planted lots of trees, especially *kikar* (Acacia) trees. They also planted 3000 neem and *babool* trees during 1878-9. In 1878 the Ridge was declared as a Reserve Forest, so that no tree could be felled down without permission. After the shifting of the capital from Calcutta to Delhi in 1912, forestation of the Ridge started. William Robertson Mustoe was given the charge of planting trees in the capital and on the Ridge. The Delhi Town Planning Committee supervised this work. In 1932–3 more trees were planted on the ridge.

Historically, the ridge has played a significant role in the affairs of Delhi; it was a hunting place for the earlier rulers. It provided stones for the next city. It protected the city from invaders. In 1857 it gave shelter to many British people. Now it is working as a central air-conditioning plant. It provides oxygen to increasingly polluted city. It acts as a sound insulator, blocks the dust, it gives a taste of nature where one can walk, or enjoy a picnic. Till few years back lots to hyenas, dear and jackals were seen on this ridge now they are not there. Some of the trees which vanished from Delhi region were seen on the ridge, now they are also not seen on the ridge.

The major activities which have caused this destruction of the Ridge are:

(a) construction of buildings, roads and establishment of human settlements by government and private parties;
(b) conversion of forests into parklands; and
(c) miscellaneous activities like garbage dumping, lopping for fuel and fodder and grazing by livestock.

To save the Ridge from further destruction we can take the following measures:

(i) to make aware the people of the importance of the Ridge and sensitise the people of Delhi about it;
(ii) the teach the importance of the Ridge/forest to children, who would live longer on this earth than the old people;
(iii) to bring the security for the Ridge under the control of only one agency. No further construction to be allowed and old constructions on the ridge to be reviewed; and
(iv) to make strict and upgrade the security for the Ridge. Now a wall is being erected around the remaining ridge at New Delhi. It is to be seen how effective it will be for preserving the lungs of the city.

REFERENCES

1. Satapath Brahman (9, 2, 2, 3).
2. Mahabharat (6, 17, 13, 0 R-1).
3. Anusasan Parv, Chapter 96, of Mahabharat.
4. Vanaparv, 158, 42-48, Aranyakaparv, 155, 40-6.
5. Adiparva 40, (Mahabharat).
6. Mahabharata, Ch. 228.
7. Catalogue, p. 60 No. e-13.
8. Bashir-ud-Din Ahmad, *Wakeat Dar ul Hukumat-i-Dehli, (Urdu),* (3 vols.), Urdu Akadami, Dehli, 1990, vol. 2, pp. 1-8.
9. Mahabharata – Udyogaparva, C IX, 19.
10. Beal-Buddhist Records of the Western World I, p. 200.
11. Mahabharata, Adiparva IXXXVii, 42-43; Udyoga Xvii, 17, 23.
12. Ramayana, Kiskindha, and XI, pp. 51-3.
13. JRAS, 1905, p. 233.
14. T.V. Mahalingam, 'The Nagas in Indian History and Culture', Journal of Indian History, vol. XLIII, Pt. I, 1965.
15. A.K. Sharma, *Pre-Historic Delhi and its Neighbourhood,* 1983, p. 2.
16. N.S. Rajaram, *Saraswati: Rivers and Civilization in Early Harappans and Indus-Saraswati Civilization,* Eds. D.P. Sharma and Madhuri Sharma, vol. II, Kaveri Books, 2006, p. 472.
17. Markandeya Purana, LVII, 30.
18. Vedic Index, Majjhima Nihaya, p. 39.
19. A.K. Grover and P.L. Bakliwal, 'River Migration and Floods – A study of a Section of Yamuna River through Remote Sensing', Man and Environment, vol.9, 1985, pp. 151-3.
20. Kalpavriksh, The Delhi Ridge Forest, Decline and Conservation, 1991.

2

Delhi During the Hindu Rulers

Delhi is an ancient city and for the last thousands of years it has been the capital of this country. Many empires have been built and destroyed here. Many kings and important personalities are buried here. In the ancient period, knowledge was transferred from one generation to the other through oral tradition; that is why very little was recorded or symbolized. Nevertheless, there are still some remnants of the ancient period through which one can understand and glance into the past history of Delhi.

There have been sixteen cities in Delhi, sometimes one upon another and sometimes one besides the other. Right from the city of Indraprasth to the modern city of New Delhi, evidence of the settlements of various cities can be traced. These cities have seen many ups and downs, have seen prosperity and magnificence and also have suffered the wrath and onslaught of foreign invaders. It carries many historic monuments, most of which are in ruins. During the different periods of history, many rulers of different dynasties ruled over this city.

The following dynasties ruled this city from 1500–345 B.C. to 1151–92 A.D.

1.	The Kurus	1500–345 B.C.	(1)	**Indraprasth**–Legendary city of the Pandavs
2.	The Nands	345–20 B.C.		
3.	The Mauryas	323–185 B.C.		
4.	The Indo Greeks	185–100 B.C.		
5.	The Saks and the Kushans	50 B.C.–320 A.D.		
6.	The Gupts	320–500 A.D.		
7.	The Huns	500–600 A.D.		
8.	The House of Pushya Bhuti	606–47 A.D.		
9.	The Gurjar-Pratihars	836–1018 A.D.		
10.	The Tomars	1051 A.D.	(2)	**Lal Kot**—Anangpal I was the founder of the Tanwar Dynasty. He was succeeded by the following rulers:
11.	The Chauhans or Chahamans	1151–92 A.D.	(3)	**Rai Pithora**

Visarv, the Minister of the last king of the descendents of Arjun (brother of Yudhishthir who founded Indraprasth), usurped the power and his dynasty ruled this city for 500 years.

They were taken over by the Goutam Dynasty. They, in turn, were removed by the Maurya Dynasty, with their capital at Patliputr (Patna) and the city was taken to some miles more towards the south of the present site of Mehrauli. During this period, the city was so important that Asok (273–36 B.C.), the Mauryan king, had engraved his edicts in Brahmi script and Prakrit language. (In this edict Asok had stated that people should strive to be more near to God). The location of this rock edict is in East of Kailash (a colony in South Delhi), near ISKCON Temple and, at that time, it was overlooking the river Yamuna and was lying on the trunk route connecting the main cities of India. Ptolemy called it Daidalar. One Raja Dilu established a new city and it is after him that the city is called 'Dilli'. There are various stories relating to this aspect. The Saks defeated Raja Dilu and captured the city.

Rise of Tomars at Delhi

The traditions and stories tell us that Delhi was deserted for 792 years and the Mathura became prominant during this period. The Tomar Rajputs had established themselves in the Aravalli Hills south of Delhi, which is now called Suraj Kund. There is still a village called Anangpur. King Surajpal built a reservoir in tenth century A.D. There was a sun temple on the west side of this

Suraj Kund, Anang Pal II built his capital near this place and also built a Sun Temple which is now in ruins.

reservoir. Till date, some fresh water is oozing from certain rocks near this reservoir and local people believe it to be pious. There is also a vast lake in this area and some remnants of fortification can be traced. 'Prithvi Raj Raso', the epic poetry written by Chandra Bardai, the court poet of Rai Pithora, also mentions that Delhi was built by Anangpal Tomar. The city was called Lal Kot, which is the first known regular defence-work of Delhi and first city of Delhi. It is also believed that Anangpal had also brought the iron pillar from Mathura to Delhi and installed it at Vishnu Temple.

The following descendants of Raja Anangpal ruled over Delhi:

S. No.	*Name*	*Year*	*Month*	*Day*	*Gharhi*
1.	Raja Anangpal	19	5	3	9
2.	Raja Gangey	21	3	3	9
3.	Raja Prithak	19	6	19	11
4.	Raja Sahadev	20	7	20	15
5.	Raja Rudradatt	15	3	9	3
6.	Raja Indradatt	14	4	9	9
7.	Raja Narapal	26	7	11	9
8.	Raja Bachharaj	21	2	13	11
9.	Raja Birapal	21	6	5	11
10.	Raja Gopal	20	4	4	9
11.	Raja Tolande	19	3	15	9
12.	Raja Goprend	25	10	10	16
13.	Raja Richhapal	16	4	3	1
14.	Raja Kunwarapal	28	3	11	9
15.	Raja Anangpal	19	6	19	10
16.	Raja Tejpal	24	1	6	11
17.	Raja Mahupal	15	3	17	11
18.	Raja Mukdant	12	9	16	0
19.	Raja Paliraj	22	3	6	17

The last king, Paliraj, was defeated by Bishaldev Chauhan and he ascended the throne of Delhi in V.S. 1117 on the second day of the full moon of the month of Chaitra. His dynasty ruled for seven generations extending over a period of more than 161 years. The following were the rulers of this dynasty:

S.No.	*Name*	*Year*	*Month*	*Day*	*Gharhi*
1.	Raja Bhilandev	18	1	4	9
2.	Raja Gangey	25	2	3	11
3.	Raja Paharhi	19	1	5	1
4.	Raja Jasmu	17	4	2	9
5.	Raja Biharhde	14	4	8	0
6.	Raja Jagadev	13	1	5	1

(*Note*: One Gharhi is equivalent to 24 minutes, 60 Gharhis is equal to one day)[1]

Defeat of Tomars and Rise of Chauhans at Delhi

In the early twelfth century, Ajay Raj established the Chauhan Dynasty at Sambhar, he also built the city of Ajmer. His son, Arno Raj, built Anasagar (a reservoir). In 1153 A.D., Vigar Raj IV or Vishal Dev became ruler of Sakabri. He ruled from 1157 A.D. to 1164 A.D. He was very powerful and extended his kingdom in all directions. He defeated the Chalukyas, rulers of Chittor, and captured the territory of Bhadanak (present Hissar, Bhiwani and Gurgaon) Mewar and Malwa. He defeated Amir Khusrau Shah at Jaipur and defeated the Turk invaders. He also defeated the Tomar ruler of Delhi and captured Hansi from the rulers of Gazni. He not only extended his empire but also erected some forts. He was found of poets and learned persons. He himself had written *Harkeli* a drama. He also erected a Sanskrit Institute at Ajmer, which Qutubuddin Aibak destroyed and with its material built 'Dhai-Din Ka Jhonpra'.

Vigra Raj's son, Aparjangeh, ruled for a few years and was killed by Prithvi Raj II, the son of Jaidev, who ruled from 1164 A.D. to 1169 A.D. Prithvi Raj II had no son and heir.

Someshvar, the son of Arno Raj, ruled from 1169 to 1177 A.D. His son, Prithvi Raj III, who is known as Prithvi Raj Chauhan, ruled from 1178 to 1192 A.D. After the death of his father, he was also known as Rai Pithora. From 1178 to 1180 A.D., he was guided by his mother, Karpuri Devi, and when he became adult, he started ruling himself. During his rule, he subdued the rebellion of Nagarjuna, Bhadanas, defeated Chandels, Parmardi and Jai Chand at Mahoba. This battle is so famous that it is sung in the form of a ballad 'Alha' by the rural people. He defeated the rulers of Gujarat. In the first battle of Terain he defeated Mahammad Ghori in 1191 A.D. but in the second battle of Tarain (1192 A.D.) he was defeated by Ghori.

There are various reasons for this defeat. Ghori, like Mahmud Ghazani wanted to loot India. He also wanted to establish Muslim rule in India, there was old rivalry between Rajput and Muslim rulers. Both (Ghori and Mahmud Ghaznvi) were ardent followers of Islam and wanted to establish Muslim rule in India. So it was necessary to defeat Prithvi Raj Chauhan. Secondly, Ghori wanted to get back his lost territory (Multan, Bhatinda and Hansi) from the Rajputs. Thirdly, Prithivi Raj had made his enemies all over the North India and Jai Chand was very prominent among them. In the first battle of Tarain Ghori, was not conclusively defeated but in the second battle the Rajputs because of lack of vigilance, trusted the words of Ghori who deceitfully attacked the Rajputs and they were caught unaware. In the second battle of Tarain many good warriors were killed. Prithvi Raj was killed along with Raja Samar Singh, the ruler of Chittor and Govind Raj, the Subedar of Delhi.

The results of this defeat were not ordinary; they had many far reaching effects. Muslim rule was established from now onwards till the advent of the

British. Islam was declared the state religion and many temples were destroyed and looted. Budhists also suffered immensely due to this war and subsequent defeat. They moved to other countries. With the capture of Delhi and Ajmer, slowly and steadily the whole of India came under the rule of Muslims. From now onwards, the down fall of the Hindu rulers began and the reason can be summed up in three phrases, namely. (a) internal dissensions, (b) generosity towards enemies, and (c) want of ambitions. From 1193 to 1206 A.D. Qutub-ud-Din Aibak remained the slave of Mohammad Ghori and after the death of Ghori in 1206 A.D., Aibak declared himself as the ruler of India.

REFERENCE

1. Puranchand Nahar, 'Indian Culture', Vol. II, July 1935, pp. 164-6

3

Delhi During the Muslim Rule

The Muslim rule in north-west India concided with the clear establishment of the conception of Caliphate. Mahmud of Ghazani submitted to the spiritual authority of Abbasid Khilafat. However his first slave, Sultan Qutub-ud-Din, did not live long and could not be invested by a Khalifa; yet he continued to expand the Islamic kingdom in India.

The Islamic Concept of State—the Sunni Caliphate and the Shia Imamate

There is no dichotomy in Islam between the temporal and the spiritual. The structure of Islam is essentially religious-political and in this system the state is only an effort to realize the spiritual in a human organization. The state is a politically organized community has existed in human history from very early times. The ancient Greeks called it 'polis', the Romans 'civitas', as also 'status rei, publicai; the Latin term 'status' became 'stato' in Italian, 'etat' in French and 'state' in English. Whatever the nomenclature, the concept of power was, however, always associated with a state in medieval thought. The Hindus actually called it 'dand' (rod, secpture) and, even in the seventeenth century, Hobbes conceived of it as to leviathan—a monster having several hands and wielding several Swords. It is only in the nineteenth and twentieth centuries that the concept started changing, Western political scientists began to take a deep look and theories of social contract, sovereignty of the people and government as a trust and as an organization for the welfare of the people began to emerge.

However, centuries earlier in the deserts of Arabia's Prophet Mohammad, who was the political as well as religious head of Islam, under the divine guidance, anticipated all the above wisdom and set up a state on firm foundations of solidarity through accord, equality through law and freedom, through belief in the principle of Tawhid.

The first Islamic state was set up by Prophet Mohammad himself in the city of Yathrib, later named Madinat al-Nabi which ultimately became shortened to Madina. It is the ideal model of Islam because it is Muslim belief that whatever the Prophet did, had to be perfect as he was not only a living embodiment of the Quran but also acted under divine guidance through revelations.

This first Islamic state came into existence after the Hijra from Mecca but, before that, the prophet had entered into a pact with the leaders of Banu Aws and Banu Khazraj, the two leading tribes of Medina, who had embraced Islam and had invited the Prophet to shift to Medina as the persecution of the Muslims by the Meccans had reached unbearable limits and the life of the Prophet himself was in grave danger. This pact was made at a place called Aqaha and was in the Nature of a bilateral treaty under which the Madinates on their part accepted the prophet as their religious as well as political leader and undertook to protect him from all his enemies and in particular the Quraysh, and the Prophet, on his part, bound himself in these words never to forsake them or return to Mecca. 'May in life and death I am with you and you are with me. I will fight whom you fight and I will make peace with whom you make peace'[1].

At this time in Medina, the Banu Aws and Banu Khazraj were divided into 12 clans and the Jews into ten clans and each clan was fully autonomous and they were actually weary of their traditions of unending tribal wars. The first task, therefore, was to teach the new converts the fundamental principles of the new faith; to this he first constructed a mosque, where they could collect all his followers and impart them the practical lessons of fraternity, equality, liberty and justice and thus weld them into a disciplined community with a common ideology.

After he imparted to them the injunction of the Quran (the Holy Book was codified after the demise of prophet) that 'the believers are but a single brotherhood, so make peace and reconciliation between your (contending) brothers and fear God that ye may receive mercy' (XLIX: 10). He succeeded in obliterating the distinction between the Quraysh, Aws and Khazraj and poised them into brothers in Islam. The Quraysh were still bent upon destroying the Muslims. To meet this external threat, he forged friendship with the Jews, who were in large number in Medina and made treaties of mutual security and defense and guaranting them equal civil rights, freedom of religion and mutual protection against external aggression in return for their recognition of the Prophet as the paramount executive, military and judicial authority. The Jews of Medina willingly accepted this and they became, as a body, the allies of the Muslims and thus the city state of Medina came into being as a political entity.

The duties of contracting parties along with the rights were made in writing. The basic concept of this charter was that all would accept the Prophet as the paramount authority in all matters administrative, judicial and military and obey his lawful orders. He was to be the commander of the combined army, the executive head of the state and the final court of appeal but ruler in any sense of the term as sovereignty over the universe vested in Almighty Allah alone and all without any exception were subject to his laws. The Jews and Muslims were to enjoy complete freedom of religion and was to be governed by its own laws, customs and traditions.

The practice of blood-revenge and counter-revenge was totally banned and no interference on the basis of kingship was permitted in the administration of justice. The Jews also expressly undertook that they would not in any event grant protection to the Quraysh or their allies.

The Main characteristics of this state formed at Madina are as follows:

(i) That it was an institution established through a democratic process, namely the free will and accord of the people desiring to form the same and to accept the Prophet as the paramount Authority (pledge of 'Aqaba and Agreement with the Jews')
(ii) That it was a constitutional organization functioning under a written charter (of Medina)
(iii) That it was a federal structure comprising two communities the Muslims and the Non-Muslims, and not two territories.
(iv) That it was an ideological state based on the concepts and fundamentals.

Sovereignty: The concept of human sovereignty is completely absent in the political philosophy of Islam. 'It is only for Allah to command' (Quran, XII: 40) and "to Allah belongeth the dominion of the Heavens and the Earth" (II: 110) proclaims the Quran. This is repeated again in V: 20, with greater emphasis thus: 'To Allah alone belongs the Dominion of the Heaven and the Earth and all that lies between'. Even the prophets were mere Deputies authorized to enforce his commands (see XXXVIII: 26), where Allah says 'oh David! We did indeed make a "Khalifa" on Earth—So judge thou between men in truth (and justice)'. The same word has been used in respect of Adam in II: 27 where Allah announces to the Angels that he is going to set up a 'Khalifa' on Earth. This introduces the concept of 'Niyabat Ilahi' and from this flow four important consequences:

(a) That all are equal before law;
(b) That the Exercise of power is a trust;
(c) That power has to be exercised in accordance with the commandments of Allah and in his name;
(d) That every one vested with power is accountable for his action.

Liberty: The principle of Tawhid is the fundamental principle of Islam and the Kalima Tawhid is the greatest charter of Individual liberty. When a Muslim declares 'La ilah illa Allah (There is no God but one God)' he excludes all other authority but that of God because this demands 'Loyalty to God and not to thrones'. 'But liberty did not mean license or anarchy for no one could encroach upon the rights of others or refuse to obey those in authority or revolt if those in authority are acting within the limits of the divine law' Allah ordains in IV: 62. 'Oh ye who believe! Obey Allah and obey the Messenger and those charged with Authority among you. If ye differ in anything among yourselves, refer it to Allah and his Messenger'.

Justice: Everyone is equal before the law and enjoys equal opportunities. The most important consequence of this is that appointments are made on the basis of merit alone and not on the ground of kinship, wealth or status. Office seekers were disqualified. (see ref. of Quran (II: 134), V: 9).

Fraternity: 'The believers are but a single Brotherhood' (XLIV: 10) declares Allah and describes them as 'Friends and protectors of one another' (VIII: 72) with a warning that unless they protect each other there will be 'tumult and oppression' on Earth (VIII: 74). The Prophet is reported to have explained this concept thus 'The Umma (the community) is a single fold in which each is a shepherd unto the other'. The Prophet in his last sermon declared: 'O people listen and obey, even though a mangled Abyssinian slave is appointed your Amir provided he executes the Book of Allah among you'.

In the Islamic state, the non-believers formed a separate category but not necessarily an inferior category. They were granted protection of property, life and house, freedom of religion, liberty of conscience and non-interference with their culture and traditions or their religious laws. They were exempt from military service and the Poor Tax payable by a Muslim but they paid 'jizya' for the protection afforded to them.

Democracy: The affairs of the state were not only required to be regulated in accordance with the laws of the Quran but also to be administered through mutual consultation. Even the Prophet was advised by Allah: 'Consult them (the believers) in matters of administration and when thou art resolved, then put thy trust in Allah'(III: 159). This verse and verse 38 of Sura XLII lay down the basic principle which should guide Muslims in the transaction of their national affairs.

Accountability: Authority or power to rule according to Islam is a trust (*amanat*) of the people and not the birth –right of anyone verse 58 of Sura IV says: 'verily Allah commands you to give over the trusts to those entitled to them and that when you judge between men, you judge with justice' (also Sura XXII: 41).

The state government was really a social service designed for evolving a polity based on social justice under which there was no difference between even the head of the state and the ordinary citizen. They were both equally subject to the same laws, were burdened with the same obligations and shared the same simple and frugal life. The concept of state sovereignty is non-existent as sovereignty in Islam rests in God.

The thesis propounded by the Prophet himself that 'the whole of this Earth is a mosque'. The state in Islam is only an effort to realize the spiritual in a human organization. It is not an end in itself but only means to an end.[2]

According to a Hadith narrated by both Bukhari and Muslim, the Prophet is reported to have said: '.. the affairs of state of the Banu Israil used to be in the hands of their prophets and when one prophet died another succeeded him but since after me there is no other Prophet so in the near future there will be Khalifas after me and many of them'. When asked if he would like to give instructions about them he said: 'take the oath of allegiance at the hands of him who is chosen as the first (Most fit by the Jumhur)'. The method indicated by the Prophet was thus the democratic method of selection and that was the method adopted in the selection of the first Khalifa—Abu Bakr. The Ansar wanted to elect a Khalifa from among themselves but Umar reminded the people that Abu Bakr was the senior most and the most venerated among the companions of the prophet and had been given the honor by the Prophet himself of leading the congregational prayer during the last illness and then took the oath of allegiance at the hands of Abu Bakr.

Abu Bakr proposed the name of Umar which was unanimously accepted by all the people.

Umar was stabbed by a Persian slave and it was felt that he might not survive. He was approached by the prominent companions to nominate his successor. He refused to do so but set up a council of six most important companions and asked them to select one from among themselves within three days of his death. This was done and the people accepted Uthman unanimously. By this time, the state had spread beyond Arabia so the oath of allegiance was also taken in every province of the state in the presence of the local governors.

Uthman was murdered in his own house by a select group and Ali bin Abi Talib was selected by the people of Medina including the rebels but the principle of unanimity was unfortunately lacking. There were differences even among the prominent companions. The provinces of Sham (Syria) and Kufa (Iraq) did not accept his Khilafa. This led to war with Mu'awiya and opened the floodgates of division. Attempts at reconciliation were thwarted by the assassination of Ali at Kufa.

So long as the Prophet was alive, he managed the conflict and no one questioned him, but after his death a severe religious and political struggle within the Islamic community developed into a bitter internecine conflict, ultimately splitting the Umma into two antagonistic sects: 'The people of the Sunni' and the Shia. Their mutual hostility gathered significant momentum during the Caliphate of Uthman, intensified during Umayyad period, and reached its climax in the Abbasid era.

The Prophet had left no clear instructions regarding the successorship. Before the question could be resolved, the old centrifugal forces which the prophet had suppressed but not extirpated began to reassert themselves, never to be completely subdued again. The divisive tribalistic tendencies ever afterward sought to gain the upper hand, in direct opposition to the Islamic ideas of unity and universality.

The orthodox majority, the Sunnis, defended the succession of the four Rashiduem. A small minority, however, defended the claims of Ali B. Abi Talib, Mohammad's son-in-law and cousin, insisting that the succession be based on blood kinship, and further that it be confined to the Hashimite branch of the Quraysh, termed the *ahl al-bayt* or 'people of the (Prophet) house'.

Ali's forces were defeated by those of Mu'awiya, who founded a new dynasty, the Umayyad in Damascus. The martyrdom of Al-Hussain, Ali's younger son, at the hands of the Umayyad, Yazid b Mu'awiya, was probably the most significant event in the early religions development of Shiaism, for it invested the movement, at first almost entirely political, with a spiritual, even a passionate, quality. Shiaism was becoming more than just the principal political opposition to the Umayyad 'Kings'. It was the symbol and rallying point of all discontented Muslims, especially the non-Arab ones, who suffered exploitation and humiliation at the hands of the arrogant and clannish Umayyad Arabs. The Shia emphasis on suffering and passion principally based on the martyrdom of Al-Hussain and the trials of later Immams strengthened its appeal to the oppressed. The severe persecutions undergone by the successive Shia Immams and adherents of the movement in general encouraged its further growth. The Shia actively participated in the overthrow of the Umayyads and establishment of the 'Abbasid Dynasty', but was betrayed by the new rulers after they had served their purpose.[3]

To a large discontented minority of Umayyad and later, Abbasid subjects, Shiaism thus became the embodiment of social, religions, political and economic protest which has been termed '... a rejection of the Yoke of Mohammad in all but form and Name'.[4]

For a short period in the Abbasid era, the Shiaites were fairly well treated, in the reign of al-Ma'mun, who designated Imam, Ali al-Rida as his successor. This was perhaps to win over the support of Persian and Iraqi subjects, who had Shia proclivities. Ali al-Rida died soon after his designation and, the Shia charge that he was poisoned by al-Ma'mun. The attempted reconciliation between the Sunnis and Shias was abandoned, due to increasing political pressure upon the Caliph by the Sunni majority in Baghdad and in the rest of the Empire. From then on, the Shia and their Imams were constantly persecuted.

The Shiaite 'Pretender to the throne' was not an established ruler; he was not given the title of Caliph but called instead an 'Imam.' The following list gives the names of the first six Shiaite Imams and the two rivals, who claimed to be the seventh Imam.

(1) Ali, the husband of the Prophet's daughter, Fatimah (assassinated in 661 A.D.)
(2) Hassan, the elder son of Ali, who lived in retirement and died in 669 A.D.
(3) Husain, the second son of Ali, who was killed at Karbala in 680 A.D.
(4) Ali Zayn al-Abidin, the son of Husain, who lived in retirement and died about 712 A.D.
(5) Mohammad al-Baqir, who lived at Madina and died 731 A.D.
(6) Jafar al-Saddiq, who lived at Madina and died 765 A.D.
(7) Two sons of Jafar al-Saddiq claimed to be the seventh Imam.

Ismail	*Musa al-Kazim.*
Whose descendants formed the Shiaite Party of Al-Ismailiyyah or the seveners, To which the Fatimids belonged	Whose descendants formed the Shiaite Party of the twelvers, which today is strong in Iran, Southern Iraq and other places.

Some of the Ismailis regard Ali as the Asas, so that for them Hasan was the first Imam, Ismail the sixth and his son Mohammad the seventh Imam. This, however, is a minority view. The other view which may not be correct. However, the sixth Imam appointed his son, Ismail, to be his successor, but as Ismail lived an intemperate life, the father renounced him in favour of his younger brother, Musa al-Kazim although one group of Shiaites accepted Musa-al-Kazim as the seventh Imam. The boy, Mohammad, fled to the region of Al-Rayy in Persia, due to the fear of the Caliph Harum-al-Rashid.

Sheikhs belong to two groups that have become famous in Muslim history, which are designated as the Ithna Ashariyah (followers of twelve Imams) and the Sali'iyah (followers of seven Imams).

The term 'Shia' connotes 'Party' and is used to designate all those Muslims who support the claims of Ali, the fourth Caliph, as the first and rightful successor to the Prophet.

The twelvers hold that there have been in all twelve successors of Mohammad, and that the twelfth one who mysteriously disappeared, did not die but is still living. He is concealed under divine care, and is called the Hidden Imam. They also expect him to return to earth in the character of the Mahdi, whose coming is prophesied as a sign of the last days. Another group of Shias come into existence after the death of the sixth Imam, Jafar as-siddiq. They recognize his son, Ismail, as the seventh Imam, with whose death they regard the Immamate closed.

The number of Shias cannot be definitely given, but it is estimated that they are nearly 10 to 15 per cent of the Muslim population in India, and most of them are in South India. In the North, they are in large numbers in Rampur and Lucknow.

The Muslim conquerors of India as well as the rulers who ruled Delhi and Agra were all Sunnis. But at times Shia influence from Persia was very strong. Many Shias found their way in to India, and established communities throughout the land. The armies of the Kings and Emperors of the North, up to the time of the Mughals, were largely recruited from foreign countries. These composed of Mongols, Persians, Turks, Georgians, Circassions, Calmucs and other tartars were mostly Shias.[5]

Towards the close of the fifteenth and the beginning of the sixteenth centuries, the Shia kingdoms of the Deccan in India and the Shia Safawid dynasty of Persia were founded. The rulers of Deccan and the early Safawid rulers took personal interests in their affairs. Babur did not take much interest in Shia-Sunni controversy. He also had little time with him. Shah Tahmasp took advantage of the forced visit of the Emperor Humayun to his dominions to make a daring effort to compel his royal guest to embrace the Shia religion. This happened in the year 1544 A.D. when Humayun fled to Persia after he was driven out from his throne at Delhi by Sher Shah Suri and became a refugee there. After much reluctance, Humayun is said to have adopted the Shia mode of reciting the public Prayers, and to have further indicated his change of faith by making a pilgrimage to the tomb of Sheikh Safi at Ardabil, in Northwestern Persia.[6]

On Humayun's return to India, it was of course, impossible to carry out the wishes of Tahmasp, and for all intents and, purposes he died a well regarded Sunni. Further, Shia influence was to be found also at the Mughal court in the presence of Bairam Khan and other Persians.[7] He was one of the favorite noblemen of the Persian Shah-Tahmasp, who became one of Humayun's officers. To him, also, was entrusted the case of the youthful Akbar, who made him his first Minister. On Humayun's return from Persia, the orthodox Ulema of the court looked first to their own safety, and that they kept at a discreet distance until after the fall of Bairam Khan (his murder). No doubt much of the influence that shaped Akbar's religious experience is to be found in his early contact with this ardent Shia, who was his first minister and guardian.

However, whatever his religious convictions or those of this associates, he would not allow the Shia religion to become supreme. Akbar set about winning the confidence and cooperation of every element of the population he possibly could. Jahangir loved drinking eating the meat of an animal which is prohibited in Islam. He used to drink even during the days of Ramazan (fasting). Shahjahan was having two policies, on one hand he was near to Aurangzeb and on the other he was near to Dara Shikoh, but both Jahangir and Shah Jahan did not become the disciples of Sheikh Ahmad. Basic of Sheikh Ahmad Sirhindi's thought and to that of all traditionalists Sunni Muslim, is the idea that the present is to be controlled by the laws of Islam; and the laws of Islam are not to be altered by changing circumstances. The Shias of course, did not concur, but their minority-position in the country, once their position at the court was challenged, and rendered them a group apart.

Some rulers, such as, Ala-ud-Din Khilji, Mohammad Bin-Tughluq, Jalal-ud-Din Lodi, Sikandar Lodi and later Aurangzeb, followed the policy of repression of Hindus and to some extent Shias. However, as missionaries many Sufis had to maintain a close contact with non-Muslims, if they were to be successful in their conversion; but Sheikh Ahmad however belonged to a different school. His teaching certainly played a prominent role in bringing out into the open an ideological conflict among the Muslims of India. His strict traditionalism met the heterodoxy of Indian Muslim ways head on. In the last years of Shah Jahan's rule, this struggle centered round the figures of his sons, Dara Shikoh, the liberal Sufi, and Aurangzeb, the follower of Sheikh Ahmad.

During the Delhi Sultanate period, some kind of assimilative development in Islam may have taken place due to Mongol's invasions.[8]

But the Sultans of Delhi especially welcomed the Sunni scholars; the course of tradition in India was greatly strengthened because these scholars were thoroughly conversant with the defeat of the Mutazila, the silencing of the philosophers, and the channalyzing of mysticism. Once settled in India, they became the guardians of Islamic purity and at the same time advisers to sultans and teachers in the Muslim schools and very frequently the chroniclers of medieval India as well.

Islam in India has never functioned as an organic unity. It has never developed a thorough going organization, which through its recognized representatives and hierarchy could exercise a far-reaching and effective control over the whole community. However, some earnest efforts have been made during the last century to achieve such organizations, with promising results. During the period of Muslim domination, the unity of the faithful was brought about, to a certain extent, by the ruler, who was regarded as the chief custodian of Islamic law as well as the defender of religion.

Indian Islam and the Caliphate

Caliph Umar and Caliph Uthman had eyes fixed on India as a field for the extension of Islam. But during the reign of Umayyad Caliph Wahid, Mohammad Bin Quasim invaded Sind (711 A.D.). Hajjaj, the Governor of Basrah, wrote to Mohammad Bin Qasim that throughout the cities and towns captured, 'The Khutbah should be read and the coin struck in the name of this Government[9] and throughout the period in which the Arab Governors held sway over Sind, the Khutba continued to be read in the name of the Khalifa. Even in the distribution of the booty taken by the early Arab invaders, the Khalifa was remembered in the portion of one-fifth that was reserved for him, as directed by the Quran.[10]

Mahmud of Ghazani, as ruler of his Indian possession, recognized the supreme authority of 'the successor of the Prophet of God'. Iltutmish was the first independent ruler of India (1210 A.D. to 1235 A.D.), who received a formal investiture of a diploma and title from Abbasid Caliph of Baghdad in 1229 A.D. Iltutmish had the document from the Caliph read before a great assembly at Delhi, and from that date put the name of the Caliph on his coins, and had his name read in the Khutbah. This was followed by his successors. 'The name of the last Abbasid Khalifah of Baghdad, Mustasim (1242–58 A.D.) first appears on the coins of Ala-ud-Din Masud-Shah (1241–6 A.D.); and though Mustasim was put to death by the Mongols in 1258 A.D., his name continued to appear on the coins of successive kings of Delhi, for example, Mahmud Shah Nasir al-Din (1246–65 A.D.); Ghiyas al-Din Balban (1265–87 A.D.); and Muizz-al-Din Kaiqubad (1287–90 A.D.), the last monarch of the so-called 'slave' Dynasty; and the first of these continued to have the name of Mustasim mentioned in the Khutbah.

A new dynasty arose, that of the Khilji; the same need for legitimization was apparently still felt, and the coins of Jall-al-Din Firuz Shah II (1290–5 A.D.) continued to bear the name of Mustasim, though this Caliph had been trampled to death by the Mongols more than thirty years before.

What was an unfortunate Muslim Monarch to do who felt that his title was insecure? He knew that it was only his sword that had set him on the throne, that his own dynasty might at any time he displaced, as he had himself displaced the dynasty that had preceded him, while his legal advisers and religious guides told him that the only legitimate source of authority was the Khalifah, the Imam, and he realized that all his devout Muslim subjects shared their opinion. So he went on putting the names of the dead Mustasim on his coins, because he could find no other, and the Muslim theory of the state had not succeeded in adjusting itself to the fact that there was no Khalifah or Imam in existence. His successor, Ala-al-Din Mohammad Shah I (1295–1315 A.D.) got out of the difficulty by ceasing to insert Mustasims name and by describing himself merely as Yamin al-Khilafat Nasir Amir al-Muminin, 'the right hand of the Caliphate, the helper of the commander of the faithful'; and this was sufficient for the satisfaction of tender consciences; though in reality he was giving no help to any Caliph, any more than either of his predecessors had done, who had seen the unhappy Mustasim trampled to death without moving a finger, though they had gone on making use of his name for their own selfish political purposes."[11] Some of the Indian Monarch such as Sultan Ala-ud-Din Khilji assumed the dignity of the Caliphate (1296–1316 A.D.).

Amir Khusrau, styled him, 'the Caliph of the Age,' and the 'Shadow of the Merciful on the heads of mankind'. His son, Qutb-ud-Din Muharak Shah (1316–20 A.D.) had inscribed on some of this coins the most exalted Imam, the Khalifah of the lord of the worlds, the pole-star of the earth and of the faith Abu-al-Muzaffar, Khalifah of God.[12]

Whenever a new king came to the throne of Delhi it was the custom to have Khutbah read in his name. But when Mohammad Shah Tughluq came to the throne in 1324 A.D., he got his name substituted by the name of Khalifah of Egypt, the rightful successor of the 'Abbasid dynasty' on the coins, and in 1343 A.D. his ambassador to Egypt, Haji Said Sarsari returned to the Sultan, bringing honors and a rob from the Khalifah. The reason for this was that he had come to the conclusion.

> That no King or Prince could exercise regal power without confirmation by the Khalifah of the race of Abbas and that every king who had or should hereafter reign without such confirmation had been or would be over powered ... From that date permission was given that out of respect the Khalifah's name should be repeated in the prayers for Sabbaths and holy days ... and it was also ordered that in mentioning the names of the kings in the Khutbah, they should be declared to have reigned under the authority and confirmation of the 'Abbasi Khalifah.' And the name of the Khalifah was ordered to be inscribed on lofty buildings, and no other name besides.[13]

In 1351 A.D., Firoz Shah III came to the throne and he also got permission to rule from the Khalifah. However, the fact is that if the ruler was strong and able, great was the power and glory of Islam; but if he was weak and incapable, Islam suffered in proportion. Khizr Khan (1414–21 A.D.) had the Khutbah read in the name of Shah Rukh son of Timur; who made great efforts to get himself recognized as Caliph.

The Caliphate and the Mughal Emperors

The glory, wealth and power of the Mughal Emperor's court brought about a decidedly independent attitude in respect to the over lordship of the Ottoman Caliph. After the manner of their ancestors in Transoxiana, they commonly assumed the title of Khalifah, from the reign of Akbar onwards; they called their capital Dar al-Khilafat (the abode of the Caliphate) Akbar's famous gold coin bore the inscription 'the great Sultan, the exalted Khalifah.' It certainly never formed any part of the policy of the Mughals to acknowledge the over lordship of the Ottoman Sultan nor did the current theory of the Caliphate suggested submission to some central Muslim authority. Aibak and Sultan Sulaiman (the Ottoman) were in correspondence and they were bound together with the chains of union and love.

Suleiman is addressed as 'he who has attained the exalted rank of the Caliphate', the familiar verse (Quran, XXXV, 37) is Quoted; and prayers are offered that his Caliphate may abide for ever. At the same time, the Ottoman Sultan is reminded that there is now installed on 'the seat of the Sultanate and the throne of the Khilafat of the realms of Hind and Sind' a monarch whose magnificence is equal to that of Solomon. The same claim was repeated in the reign of Shah Jahan. The title Khalifah had been adopted officially by the Imperial House. There are numerous examples, when Khalifah is used for Kings of Delhi, down to the reign of Shah Alam II (1759–1806 A.D.), whose authority for a considerable part of his life was not even effective within the walls of his own palace. Still some learned persons remained faithful to the earlier doctrine that the Caliphate could belong only to the Quraysh.[14]

Indian Muslims Relations to the Caliphate Since 1800 A.D.

The relations of Indian Muslims to the Caliphate has been very intense and provocative and full of turmoil and agitations. As there was no Muslim Sunni ruler in India who could provide temporal and religions leadership to Sunni Muslims, so they were taking special interests in the affairs of the Ottoman Caliphate and for the past many years they were mentioning the name of the Ottoman Caliph in the Khutbah. He was looked as the only hope for the defender of the faith and reviving the glory of Islam. He was the symbol of unity and strength of Islam.

During the years 1877–1908 A.D. the relation of Indian Sunnis to the Ottoman Caliphate began to assume something of form and substance. The Sultan, Abdul-al-Hamid II was developing his doctrine of Pan-Islamism, and under the leadership of such agents as Jamal-ud-Din Afghani, who made his headquarters at Hyderabad and Calcutta during his enforced stay in India (1879–81 A.D.), an extensive propaganda was developed.[15]

When the Damascus-Medina railway project was being promoted by the Caliph, Indian subscriptions were sent forward from Lahore.

During the First World War, The Caliph declared a jihad, a holy war against the allies, but Indian Muslims turned a deaf ear to the Caliph's proclamation of a 'holy war'.

The Indian Sunni Muslim desired to be loyal to the Government of India, and at the same time felt their loyalty to the Caliph, as the symbol of Islamic power and prestige. This second loyalty soon gave birth to the 'Khilafat Agitation'. Funds were collected and committees were formed to go to London and Pairs to secure the best position for Khilafat. Some Muslim leaders in India preached the doctrine of Hijrat, and declared that India was no longer a suitable place where Muslims could live and exercise the functions of their religion. Hence no less than eighteen thousand people sold their property and fled away to Afghanistan and central Asia, all because of their devotion to the Caliph.[16]

In Malabar, in 1921 A.D., Mappilles started a 'Khilafat Kingdom' and forcibly converted thousands of Hindus to Islam.[17]

Even the Hindus and Mahatma Gandhi supported Khilafat movement, but up to March 1924 when Kamal Pasha pricked the Khilafat bubble, he shattered the hope of Indian Muslims by summarily deposing the Caliph, 'Abdul-Majid,' and by banishing him and his family from the Turkish Nation to Europe.

In 1926 A.D. a conference, 'league of Muslim Nations' was held in Cairo to Elect a new Khalifa and Indian delegates in this conference supported this idea. Sunni-Shia relations have always been more or less strained.

Even in the time of Akbar, Sheikh Mubarak, father of Abul Fazal and his brother Fayzi, turned Shia as a result he was greatly persecuted and was obliged to fly with his family from Agra. Prince Suja, the son of Shah-Jahan, was a Shia, and so was regarded with aversion by the orthodox. At the same time his brother, Aurangzeb, who became a model for Muslim orthodoxy, is said to have detested the Shias almost as much as he did the Hindus.[18]

Shah Alam (1759–1806 A.D.) gave an order that the word Wasi (heir) should be used among the attributes of the Khalifah Ali in the Khutbah (Friday sermon). It was met with violent opposition. In Lahore (from where this order was given), 'the crowd killed the Khatib (preacher) of the chief Mosque'. Finally, the Emperor ordered that they should return to the form used in the reign of Aurangzeb.[19]

In April 1837, Magistrate Lindsay altered the traditional proclamation about Tazias in Delhi in favor of the Shias. The Sunnis, twice as numerous as the Shias, petitioned against this order to Thomas Metcalfe; who had it repealed.[20]

The Managing Committee of Anglo-Arabic School was sharply divided among its Sunni and Shia members but it did not affect its academic order and standard. Commissioner Hamilton issued a general order against precessions in 1878 A.D., as Delhi was a commercial city and was already too much infested with processions and religions processions which were peculiarly dangerous here. It started, due to Jain and Hindu processions. So, even the

Shia Jama Masjid, Kashmiri Gate

Shias were prohibited to take out Moharrum-procession. But later it was cleared by the Secretary of State.[21]

During the British period in Delhi, separate Shia societies/associations were formed in Delhi as they felt that their interests were not looked after by the Sunni Muslims. Even in 1877 A.D., they asked for a separate electorate in Delhi like other minorities.

With the spread of education and various employments the diversity in Islam is gaining grounds for more progressive, more reasonable and tolerant towards each other than before in the History.

The Arab Conquest of Sind

Arabia remained in the backwaters of world movements and had played no direct part in the affairs of humanity. It had woken up from its slumbers at the clarion call of the Prophet Mohammad, who was born in 570 A.D. at Mecca and belonged to the eminent tribe of Quresh. From his early life he acquired a great reputation for his noble character and generous disposition. He was the friend of the poor and the needy. He won his name of al-Amin, 'the trusted one'. Inwardly he was unhappy because his people indulged in robbery, drinking, gambling, infanticide, idolatry and they were ignorant and had many vices. The Quresh, the tribe, he belonged to, was driving much of their income from the annual pilgrimage to the Kaaba which contained 360 idols. At the age of 40 years he was ordained an apostle by God to preach indivisible unity to mankind. He was persecuted for his preaching and compelled to migrate to Medina where he was received well. When at last the truce of Hudaibiyah was violated by the Quresh he marched to Mecca, which he occupied without much resistance. He extended the General Amnesty to all his adversaries. Mecca accepted Islam and the Kaaba was cleared of all idols. In the year 632 A.D. he departed from this world. He had changed the current of human thought.

The Quran, which was revealed to the Prophet at different periods of his life and on different occasions, embodies the teaching of Islam, which means literally 'the religions of submission to the will of God'. The entire structure of the teaching of Islam is based on the fundamental conception of the unity of God. The teachings of the prophet worked a mighty change in the lives of the Arabs. They discarded their feuds, old vices and dedicated themselves to the service of the one true God.

Byzantine and Sasanian were at the borders of Arabia. They did not relish the success and unity of Arabs and time to time made inroads by the armies into Arab territory. This compelled Hadrat Abu Bakr, who had succeeded by the Prophet Mohammad as the head of the commonwealth, to cross swords with these mighty empires under Hardrat Umar, Syria, Egypt and Persia were completely conquered; and the Muslims were found battering against the frontiers of Sind under Umayyad Caliph, al-Walid (705–15 A.D.) his General Musa-Bin Nusair subjugated the whole of North Africa, his lieutenant Tariq captured Spain, Qutaibah penetrated into central Asia, Mohammad Bin Qasim conquered Sind.

In this battle against Raja Dahir, the Arabs used for the first time, *mujaniqes* or catapults which were used for bombing fortresses with large stones and metal balls. The largest of them was called *arus* (bride) and was worked by 500 men. With this equipment, Mohammad Bin Qasim marched against Daibul, through Makran.

The temple of the city was also made a target of this machine. Stones were thrown on the temple; this demoralized the people. He then marched on to Nirem; a deputation of Buddhist priests met him and produced a letter of pardon and protection from Hajjaj; a mosque was constructed there. Sehwan was also captured; Sisam was captured and crushed the opposition of the Jats.

Raja Dahir again fought a battle but his elephant got an arrow in the eye and went wild against its own army. The king fought on foot but was killed. The Muslims now besieged the fortress and captured it. After this victory at Rawer, Qasim proceeded to Brahmanabad which was near Hyderabad and Shahabad; he also conquered the town of Aror and Multan. He captured the son and wife of Dahir and converted them to Islam. His army plundered the entire town he conquered and sent the loot to Caliph. The Hajjaj died in the meantime and his brother Suleiman succeeded him; he was imprisoned and tormented to death.

The Arab not only used 'Arus' but big ships were also used. The Indian side was not using the sea or entering into it because of superstition. Subsequently Arab armies penetrated as far as Malwa and Gujarat. It had a far reaching effect on the history; this provided a big opportunity to Arabs for commercial, cultural and religious progress.

From Sind, Islam and its administration spread to other parts of the sub-continent.

The Yamini Dynasty of Ghazni

By the tenth century A.D., Central Asia, Afghanistan and eastern part of Persia were under the control of Samani dynasty, Bukhara was their capital. Ghazni was founded by one of their slaves in 963 A.D. His son and two slaves succeeded him. In the year 977 A.D., Subuktgin, another slave, set on the throne. Jaipal the Raja of Waihind, which was situated on the bank of the river Indus, a few miles above Attak, was not happy with the expansion of the power of the Muslims. A battle was fought between Subuktgin and Jaipal, Jaipal suffered a defeat and asked for peace for ten lakh of rupees, fifty elephants and part of his territory up to Lamghan (Jalalabad), but he annulled on his agreement while reaching his capital; Subuktgin attacked the territory of Lamghan and captured a number of forts. In the second battle Subuktgin again won, now he captured the territory up to Peshawar and spread Islam there. He died in 997 A.D. He left four sons behind him: Mahmud, Ismail, Narr and Yusuf.

Mahmud was more able among all; he was also married to a daughter of the Farighun dynasty and related to Samlains. But Ghazni was not given to him; he wanted it and attacked his brother Ismail, and captured Ghazni. The Samanids acknowledge his suzerainty over the lands of Balk, Herat, Tirmiz and Bust but not over Khurasan. Later by force he captured it and the Caliph accepted it. Meanwhile, Ilak Khan occupied Bukhara, with this Samanid dynasty came to an end.

Mahmud attacked Multan in 1006 A.D. In 1008 A.D., he defeated Ilak Khan. In 1012 A.D., he captured Ghuzistan and in 1017 A.D., Khwarazan. In

1025 A.D., he attacked Transoxiana, annexed the territory of Sistan and Ghur, Persia as far as Ray; his son Masud captured Hamadan and Isfahan.

Saljuq requested the Sultan to allow them to settle in Khurasan as they were unsafe in Bukhara. Sultan allowed him to do so but not to keep arms. However, soon, there was rebellion which was quelled, but after the death of the Sultan, they became a permanent menace to the house of Ghazni. In December 1008 A.D., he again defeated Anandpal, the son of Jaipal and captured the fort of Nagarkot in which he got untold riches. Shortly thereafter, Anandpal died. He was succeeded by his son, Trilochanpal; Mahmud attacked him at Nandana and captured the fort. In October 1014 A.D., he captured Thanesar; with this, the whole Punjab was brought under in his realm.

On 27 September 1018, he crossed Yamuna captured a number of towns and reached Bulandshahar (Baran) whose Hindu ruler, along with 10,000 of his followers, embraced Islam. He next proceeded to Mathura; there he received no resistance. He then captured the city of Kanauj in December 1018 A.D. Towards the end of 1019 A.D., he reached Ghazni with a huge loot. In 1021 A.D., he invaded India with the intention to capture the fort of Kalinjar, considered to be impregnable. He captured Gwalior and Kalinjar, but the Raja of Kalinjar praised the Sultan and agreed to pay annual tribute. The Sultan, with the large booty, returned to Ghazni in 1023 A.D. The Hindus believed that Somnath was not happy with the other Gods and that is why their temples and cities were defeated and looted. The Sultan heard it. He decided to destroy Somnath temple; for that, he marched from Ghazni in October 1025 A.D. After crossing Rajputana and defeating the rulers of Anhilwara, he reached Somnath on 6 January 1026 A.D. The Governor of the city fled; the people fought with the army of the Sultan for two days; ultimately, Muslims occupied the fort and the temple. The temple of Somnath was destroyed completely. The Shiva Lingam was broken. The treasurers obtained from this temple were estimated to be worth two crores of dinars. The Sultan stayed at Somnath for fifteen days. He reached Ghazni on 3 April 1026. The destruction of Somnath temple was an outstanding military feat in the annals of Islam. The Caliph of Baghdad and others praised the Sultan for this achievement. (The Somnath Temple was again built but not at its original site. It is near to the original site.)

In 1027 A.D., he invaded Sind and severely punished the Jats. Due to constant hardships, the Sultan developed phthisis. He was confined to bed ultimately and, on 30 April 1030 at 5.00 p.m., he died. He was buried in Bagh-i-Firuzi.

He was the patron of scholars in his court: Firdausi, Unsuri, Farruki, Asjadi and Abu Rihan-al-Biruni, the author of Kitab-al-Hind were there. He also established an academy at Ghazni; in its library there were rare books. Whenever a new city was captured, he would send to Ghazni rare books that were found there.

He had the zeal to spread Islam; for this, he fought many battles; he had 72 wounds on his body. He was gifted by nature with a remarkable military skill. He remained busy in fighting for thirty-three years.

He established his authority from Iraq to the Ganga and from Khwarazm to Kathiawar. He built a Minar (tower) of 144 ft high at Ghazni, which is also of the same type as the Qutub Minar. His son Masud blinded his elder brother Mahmud and imprisoned him and ruled from 1030 to 1042 A.D. Masud fought with Niyaltigin and in his expedition he captured the part of Hansi and Sonipat. The Saljuq menace had increased beyond measure. In 1042 A.D., when he was going to Lahore, his large treasure was looted and thrown in a well which was filled by stones.

The Saljuqs became so strong that Isfahan, Ray, Tabaristan and Khurasan were lost by the house of Ghazni. Ala-ud-Din ordered to burn the city of Ghazni, its library, Mosques, palaces and graves. His nephew, Muiz-ud-Din Mohammad, established Islamic rule in Hindustan, he attached Lahore in 1186, where the family of Sultan Mahmud was staying. The last person of Sultan's family was imprisoned in the fort of Ghur by Muiz-ud-Din Mohammad.

Sultan Mahmud, of course, did not invad Delhi but he had weakened its surroundings and opened the way for others in the future. He had militarily, economically and morally weakened the Hindu rulers so much that they could not repulse the coming of Islamic rulers later on.

In 1174 A.D., Ghiyas-ud-Din attacked Ghazni and captured it after defeating the Ghuzz and placed the administration in the hands of his younger brother, Mohammad-Bin-Sam and returned to his capital at Firoz Koli. Sultan Ghiyas-ud-Din died at Herat in 1202 A.D. In the meantime, Sultan Muiz-ud-Din attacked Multan and Uchh. In 1178 A.D., he conquered Anhilwara (Gujarat). At Abu, he suffered a defeat from the Raja of Gujarat. He came back to Ghur. He conquered Peshawar and the surrounding country. In 1189 A.D., he marched against Lahore and took Malik Shah's son as hostage and a rare elephant as a present. Earlier in 1186 A.D., he had captured Khusrau Malik, imprisoned him and took Lahore.

The following Muslim rulers belonging to various dynasties ruled over Delhi from 1193 to 1857 A.D.:

---

1. Shamsabanis-Muizuddin
   Mohammad bin Sam 1193–1206 A.D.
2. House of Qutub-ud-Din (Muizziya Kings) Delhi Sultanate: Aibak founded the first of a succession of dynasties collectively known as the Delhi Sultanate composed of Afghans and Turkish military lords (1206–1526 A.D.)

Ruler	Period	City
(a) Qutub-ud-Din Aibak	1206–10 A.D.	
(b) Aram Shah	1210 A.D.	
3. House of Iltutmish (Shamsia Kings)	1211–66 A.D.	
(a) Shams-ud-Din Iltutmish	1211–36 A.D.	
(b) Rukn-ud-Din Firoz	1236 A.D.	
(c) Raziya	1236–40 A.D.	
(d) Muiz-ud-Din Bahram	1240–2 A.D.	
(e) Ala-ud-Din Masud	1242–6 A.D.	
(f) Nasir-ud-Din Mahmud	1246–66 A.D.	
4. House of Balban	1266–90 A.D.	
(a) Ghiyas-ud-Din Balban	1266–87 A.D.	
(b) Muiz-ud-Din Kaiqubad	1287–90 A.D.	(4) **Kilokhari**– Kaikubad founded the city in 1287A.D.
5. The Khiljis	1290–1320 A.D.	
(a) Jalal-ud-Din Firuz	1290–6 A.D.	
(b) Rukn-ud-Din Ibrahim	1296 A.D.	
(c) Ala-ud-Din Mohammad	1296–1316 A.D.	(5) **Siri**–The city was founded by Ala-ud-Din Khilji in 1304 A.D.
(d) Shihab-ud-Din Umar	1316 A.D.	
(e) Qutub-ud-Din Mubarak	1316–20 A.D.	
(f) Nasir-ud-Din Khusru	1320 A.D.	
16. House of Tughluq	1320–1414 A.D.	
(a) Ghiyas-ud-Din (I) Tughluq	1320–5 A.D.	(6) **Tughlaqabad**–The city was founded by Ghazi Malik in 1320 A.D. who is also known as Ghiyas-ud-Din Tughluq
(b) Mohammad bin Tughluq	1325–51 A.D.	(7) **Jahanpanah**–'The refuge of the world'. It was built in 1327 A.D.
(c) Firuz bin Rajab	1351–88 A.D.	(8) **Firozabad**–It was built in 1354 A.D. by Firoz Shah Tughluq at the site of village Gawin on the bank of Yamuna seven miles North-East of Jahanpanah.
(d) Ghiyas-ud-Din (II)	1388–9 A.D.	
(e) Abu Bakr	1389–90 A.D.	
(f) Mohammad II	1390–4 A.D.	
(g) Sikandar	1394 A.D.	
(h) Mahmud	1394–6 A.D.	
(i) Nusrat Shah	1396–9 A.D.	
(j) Mahmud (restored)	1399–1413 A.D.	
(k) Daulat Khan Lodi (usurper)	1413–14 A.D.	
7. The Sayyids	1414–51 A.D.	
(a) Khizr Khan	1414–21 A.D.	(9) **Khizrabad**–Khizr Khan captured Dilli (Delhi) in 1414 A.D. and founded this city on the bank of Yamuna one mile South East of Kilokhari
(b) Muiz-ud-Din Mubarak	1421–34 A.D.	(10) **Mubarakabad**–After the death of Khizr Khan his son Muiz-ud-Din

Ruler	Period	City
		Mubarak became ruler of Dilli and constructed the new city of Mubarakabad on the bank of Yamuna in 1433 A.D. but he was Assassinated before the completion of the city. The remains of these two cities are not traceable now.
(c) Mohammad	1434–44 A.D.	
(d) Ala-ud-Din Alam Shah	1444–51 A.D.	
8. The Lodis	1451–1526 A.D.	The Lodis shifted their capital to Agra which was also used by Babar.
(a) Bahlul	1451–89 A.D.	
(b) Sikandar	1489–1517 A.D.	
(c) Ibrahim	1517–26 A.D.	
9. **Mughal Delhi**	1526–38 A.D.; 1555–1857 A.D.	
(a) Zahir-ud-Din Babur	1526–30 A.D.	
(b) Nasir-ud-Din Humayun	1530–8 A.D.	(11) **Dinpanah**–On the ancient site of Indraprasth, Humayun constructed his new capital in 1533 A.D.
10. The Surs	1538–55 A.D.	
(a) Sher Shah	1538–45 A.D.	(12) **Sher Garh**–Sher Shah who defeated Humayun and became ruler of Dilli expanded Dinpanah and named it Sher Garh.
(b) Islam Shah	1545–54 A.D.	
(c) Mohammad Adilshah	1554–5 A.D.	
(d) Ibrahim Shah	1555 A.D.	
(e) Sikandar Shah	1555 A.D.	
11. The Mughals (restored)		
(a) Humayun	1555–6 A.D.	
(b) Jalal-ud-Din Akbar	1556–1605 A.D.	
(c) Nur-ud-Din Jahangir	1605–27 A.D.	
(d) Dawar Bakhsh	1627–8 A.D.	
(e) Shihab-ud-Din Shah Jahan	1628–57 A.D.	(13) **Shahjahanabad**–Shah Jahan had built many buildings and in 1640 A.D. he decided to shift his capital from Agra to Dilli and built a new city in 1648 A.D. on the bank of Yamuna which is located one mile to the North of Firozabad.
(f) Murad Baksh	1657 A.D.	
(g) Shah Shuja	1657 A.D.	
(h) Muhi-ud-Din Aurangzeb Alamgir	1658–1707 A.D.	
(i) Azam Shah	1707 A.D.	
(j) Kam Bakhsh	1707 A.D.	

(k) Qutub-ud-Din Shah Alam I Bahadur	1707–12 A.D.	
(l) Azimush Shan	1712 A.D.	
(m) Muiz-ud-Din Jahandar Shah	1712–13 A.D.	
(n) Muhi-ud-Din Farrukhsiyar	1713–19 A.D.	
(o) Rafi-ud-Darajat	1719 A.D.	
(p) Shah Jahan II Rafi-ud-Daulah	1719 A.D.	
(q) Nasir-ud-Din Mohammad Shah	1719–48 A.D.	
(r) Mujahid-ud-Din Ahmad Shah Bahadur	1748–54 A.D.	
(s) Aziz-ud-Din Alamgir II	1754–9 A.D.	
(t) Shah Jahan III	1759 A.D.	
(u) Jalal-ud-Din Shah Alam II	1759–1806 A.D.	(In 1803 the British captured Delhi and the system of Residency began)
(v) Muin-ud-Din Mohammad Akbar II	1806–37 A.D.	
(w) Siraj-ud-Din Bahadur Shah II	1837–57 A.D.	

Muiz-ud-Din Mohammad Bin Sam (1193–1206 A.D.)

Ghori is a small town between Ghazna and Mirat in North-West of Afghanistan. In Ghazna, Turk rulers ruled for 150 years but they were overtaken by the rulers of Ghur. In the same way, the rulers of Ghur also destroyed the Ghazni dynasty from Punjab in 1187 A.D. The rulers of Ghur were called from then onwards as Pathan rulers of Delhi. Mohammad Ghori (Shihab-ud-Din) was the younger brother of Ghiyas-ud-Din Ghori and Chief of Army and Governor of Ghazna. After due management of Ghazna in 1175–6 A.D., he prepared himself for the invasion of India. He attacked India repeatedly. He also wanted to rule India apart from taking its wealth out. First he attacked Multan and after conspiring with the Queen of Sind, he captured Unch. In 1178–9 A.D., he attacked Gujarat but was defeated by the ruler of Anhilwara (Pattan). Once upon a time Pattan was the kingdom of Chalukyas. During this period, there were four Hindu kingdoms in North India such as Delhi, Ajmer, Kanwar and Gujarat. He wanted to destroy all of them.

At this time, the Tanwar ruler of Delhi did not have a son, so he adopted Prithvi Raj Chauhan, who was the son of the king's daughter; but Jai Chand, the ruler of Kanauj, was also the son of the elder daughter of the king. He was not happy with this move. After the demise of the Tanwar ruler of Delhi, Prithvi Raj became the ruler of Delhi and Ajmer and he made his younger brother Khandey Rao the Governor of Delhi. In 1191 A.D., Mohammad Ghori invaded Bhatinda and captured the fort of Sarhind. Prithvi Raj attacked Ghori at Taravri which was situated on the bank of river Sarswati; in this move, Jai Chand was not with Prithvi Raj. About 150 Rajput rulers stood with Prithvi Raj. In this battle Khandey Rao lost his front tooth and Ghori got a severe wound on his right hand and he was taken away from the battlefield. Shihab-ud-Din Ghori was defeated. Ghori's soldiers that remained alive ran towards Sind. Ghori reached Ghazna then he punished all those who fled from the battlefield. After physical recovery Ghori started building a fresh Army and started preparation for the second invasion. On the other side, the Rai Pithora (Prithvi Raj Chauhan) was celebrating this victory and became assured that now no one could attack his kingdom. The rivalry of Jai Chand and Prithvi Raj further widened from then onwards. Jai Chand organized Swyambar (a marriage ceremony) for his daughter, Samyukta and invited Prithvi Raj Chauhan for Darbani (to guard). This was a great insult for a ruler like Prithvi Raj Chauhan. He determined to take revenge. He sent an old lady to Kanoj, who was also acquainted with the mother of Samyukta; this lady persuaded Samyukta to marry Prithvi Raj Chauhan. Now he marched from Delhi with 100 swift horsemen to Kanoj. He left the horses in the jungle outside Kanoj and, dressed as fakir and mendicant reached the marriage party. Jai Chand had installed a statue of Prithvi Raj at the gate of the marriage venue. Samyukta garlanded this statute which infuriated Jai Chand and Samyukta was confined to the house. Prithvi Raj somehow took her from there and after a bloody battle, reached Delhi. The soldiers of Jai Chand persued him till the walls of the fort of Rai Pithora. Prithvi Raj married Samyukta thereafter. Jai Chand was so infuriated and insulted that he invited Ghori to attack Delhi; Ghori was already waiting for this golden opportunity.

Ghori marched towards Delhi at Tarai in 1193 A.D. where he faced the large army of Rajput. He played a trick saying that he did not wanted to fight but want to make a treaty in which he wanted only Sarhind, Punjab and Multan, but he sought some time to seek the assent of his brother. Hearing this all the Rajput soldiers let down their guard and, in the early morning, Ghori attacked them. When the battle was almost over, Prithvi Raj came out of his tent, but knowing the reality he fled towards Sirsa, where he was arrested and killed; the second version is that he was made a prisoner and taken to Ghazna and was killed later. Samyukta committed *Johar*. This defeat was the beginning of the end of Rajput rule in India.

In 1193 A.D., Ghori attacked Jai Chand. Near Yamuna Chandawar (Etava); Jai Chand got a shot in the eye and died; no one came to his support from Ajmer and Delhi. Banaras was looted; more than 1000 temples were destroyed and from Banaras alone 4000 camels laden with gold and silver taken to

Afghanistan. In 1194 A.D., he entered through Ranjit Darwaza to Delhi, which was later on named as Ghazni Darwaza, he took the reign of Delhi from the son of Khandey Rao. He marched to Ajmer, there also he looted enormously and killed many people and destroyed temples, a Sanskrit Pathshala (school) and built a *Dhai Din Ka Jhonpra* with the stones of that temple. He appointed Qutub-ud-Din Aibak as his viceroy and left to Ghazni. By 1203 A.D. Qutub-ud-Din Aibak controlled, Gujarat, Gwalior, Kalinjar, Mahoba, Chandel, Awadh, Bihar and Bengal. After the death of his brother Ghiyas-ud-Din, Shihab-ud-Din Ghori again marched towards Punjab in 1205 A.D. to suppress the rebellion of Khokars. He killed many people and after crushing the rebellion he marched towards Afghanistan in the way he camped at the bank of river Nilaob (Sind), there some Khokars whose relatives were killed by Ghori, killed him in March 1206 in the night. He ruled 32 years and few months.

Slave Dynasty (1206-1290 A.D.)

Qutub-ud-Din Aibak 1206–10 A.D.)

After the death of Mohammad Ghori, the Viceroy Qutub-ud-Din Aibak became the King of India in 1206 A.D. and he was the first Muslim King of India. He married into the families of high status with this he raised and consolidated his position. He married the daughter of Taj-ud-Din Yalduj, married his sister to Nasr-ud-Din-Qawacha who was the Governor of Sind, and married his daughter to Altmash, the Governor of Bihar. One of his nobles, Mohammed Bakhtiar, raided Bihar in 1197 A.D. with 200 horsemen, destroyed Buddhist establishments and killed all the priests to the extent that Buddhism could not rise again in Bihar. In 1199 A.D., Bengal was captured. In 1204–5 A.D., Mohammad Bakhtiar attacked Darjeeling. Large volumes of booty were looted in this campaign. Some believe that Qutub Minar was built by Qutub-ud-Din Aibak from 1193–8 A.D. and was completed by Sams-ud-Din, his son-in-law. The other view is that he renovated an existing minar, but the prevailing opinion is that this Minar was built by Aibak even though there are some Sanskrit slokas on its surface and its gate is on North side which is not the Islamic practice. He shifted his capital from Delhi to Lahore. One day, while playing Chaugan in Lahore, he fell down from the horse and died in 1210 A.D.

He was very generous. Minhaj said about the Sultan 'Gifts were bestowed by hundreds of thousands, and his slaughters likewise were by hundreds of thousands'. During his boyhood, Qutub-ud-Din was captured by slave traders in Turkistan and brought to Nishapur where the chief Qazi bought him and he was brought up along with the son of Qazi. He also received the training of horsemanship and shooting with the bow and arrow and soon was praised for his qualities. He was again sold and came to Ghazni. There he was purchased by Sultan-i-Ghazi, Muiz-ud-Din Mohammad, son of Sam.

He was famous for his generosity and rose steadily in rank and achieved the office of the Amir-i-Akhur (Lord of Stables). He also distinguished himself in various battles leading the armies and captured numerous Indian forts.

Shihab-ud-Din, the mentor of Qutub-ud-Din Aibak was assassinated on his way to Ghazni; he had no male heirs to succeed him. His daughter had died before him. His easygoing nephew, Nasir-ud-Din, confined to his ancestral land and declared all the slave generals of his uncle as free rulers. Aibak remained king for four and twenty years and for six months as viceroy. He was buried in Lahore and his grave became a place of worship but later on, the British converted it into a library and a place of Christian Worship.

Aram Shah and Iltutmish (1211 A.D.)

It is not very clear whether Aram Shah was the son of Qutub-ud-Din or the son of his brother but after the Sultan's death in Lahore Aram Shah was declared as King. However, every one was not pleased with it. Some Amir and the Governor of Delhi got together and sent an invitation to Iltutmish, who was the son-in-law of Qutub-ud-Din Aibak. He hastened to come to Delhi and occupied it. He defeated Aram Shah in a small battle and became ruler of Delhi.

Iltutmish was a Turk; his father, Ilam Khan was the leader of a tribe, and had large family. One day the cousin of Iltutmish sold him to Bukhara. He was brought up in kindness. Once he was given some money to purchase grapes, but he lost that amount and started weeping; seeing this, one Darvesh took him and purchased grapes for him and asked him to respect the Darvesh in future. This Iltutmish did in his whole life.

He was very handsome. He was sold again twice; at last he was brought to Ghazni along with another slave to be sold, but could not be sold as the offer was not liked by his master. The Sultan ordered that these slaves should not be sold in Ghazni. Meanwhile, Qutub-ud-Din Aibak came to Ghazni and requested the Sultan to purchase Iltutmish to which Sultan replied that these slaves could be purchased outside Ghazni as he had already made an order. So they were brought to Delhi and Iltutmish was purchased by Aibak and always kept by his side. With his abilities and sincerity he was raised electively in the ranks. After seeing his ability in crushing the Khokhar, Sultan Muiz-ud-Din Mohammad Ghori told Qutub-ud-Din Aibak to 'treat Iltutmish well, for he will distinguish himself'. He was set free from slavery.

In 1210 or 1211 A.D. Iltutmish became ruler of Delhi. By 1215–6 A.D. in the historic battlefield of Tarain he defeated Yalduz and Iltutmish became the ruler of Hindustan. His diplomacy kept Chingiz Khan away from Delhi. He consolidated his throne with the help of Turk Chiefs. He always respected the Sufis. He received the emissionary of the Caliph. On 29 April 1236, he died having ruled for 26 years.

Raziya Sultan (1236–40 A.D.)

During the life-time of Iltutmish; his son and heir Nasir-ud-Din Mohammad Shah died, his other son Rukn-ud-Din was a pleasure loving person and was not liked by the Chiefs. He blinded the younger son of Iltutmish, conspiring with his mother. After six months Raziya, whom Iltutmish had always liked and ordered her to be the ruler after his death, took the reins of the state in her hands in 1236–40 A.D. with the help of chiefs.

She was the first Muslim woman ruler in India. She was trained like a prince. She was acquainted with all the matters of the state. She was also very beautiful. She could read and write and handled the affairs of the state for six years in the absence of her father during his campaign outside Delhi. She used to wear men's clothing and remained without veil (*Purdah*). She also coined the male name on her coins as Sultan-ul-Azam Raziat-Dunia va Deen. She usually led the Army to war. She was very good in other matters of the state but she was not liked by the chiefs as she liked a Negro slave, Jamal-ud-Din-Yaqut, Mir Akhur. She married this Abyssinian. On account this the Wazir, Nizam-ul-Mulk and Malik Akhtiar-ud-Din, the Governor of Bhatinda revolted against her. A battle ensued and Yaqut died in it. Raziya was arrested but the Governor of Bhatinda released her and married her. But the chiefs at Delhi did not like it and they declared her brother Muiz-ud-Din Behram Shah a king. Another battle was fought in which both Raziya and Governor of Bhatinda died. Another story is that she fled from the battlefield and took some rest in a field under a tree and slept there; a farmer killed her and took all her ornaments. Whatever is the truth, she died in 1240 A.D. and a grave is erected

One of the graves is said to be of Sultan Raziya Begum who died in 1240 A.D., Bulbuli Khana in the walled city.

in Bulbuli Khana in old Delhi. Now there are two graves; one is said to be of Raziya and another is of her sister Sazia. The Archaeological Department in the 1990s declared these graves to be of a Sufi Saint. Ibn Batuta, in his description of the death of Raziya, claimed that she was buried on the banks of the Yamuna. She ruled for a period of 3 years, 6 months and 6 days.

The state religion was the Sunni creed of Islam, and other Islamic sects like Kiramitah and the Mulahidah were considered heretical and were abhorrent to the Sunnis. These Non-Sunnis rebelled against her; even the Sunni Chiefs were not happy with her as she was suspected to be close to a Negro and she wore the dress of a man without purdah. Even though the Caliph had lost his earlier position, his name continued on the coins and Khutba was read in his name. The temporal authority rested with the sovereign while the spiritual resided in the Shaikh-ul-Islam. The Muslim concept of Kingship derived basically from the Iranian Muslim tradition. The King must follow the teachings of the Prophet, enforce the Sharia, suppress rebellions, punish heretics, subordinate the unbelievers and protect the weak against the strong. He is responsible for order, for stability and for the safety and prosperity of his subjects. Some of the Chiefs were of the opinion that Raziya, being woman, is not capable to do so; they raised this point of view even at the time of Iltutmish; but Iltutmish was of the opinion that Raziya was far superior in all respects to her brothers.

Muiz-ud-Din Bahram Shah (1240–2 A.D.)

Iltutmish had created a group of Chihlgni nobles, who became very powerful over the period. After the death of Raziya Begum, they supported Bahram Shah in the calculation that he would rule as per their direction, but it did not happen and, in 1242 A.D., they rebelled and killed Bahram Shah.

Ala-ud-Din Masud Shah (1242–6 A.D.)

He was the son of Rukn-ud-Din Firoz; he was also put on the throne of Delhi by the Chihlgani nobles called the 'Forty'; but soon in 1246 A.D., another son of Iltutmish, Nasir-ud-Din Mahmud was put on the throne.

Nasir-ud-Din Mahmud (1246–66 A.D.)

He lived a simple life and did not take money from the state treasury. For his personal use he used to earn his livelihood by sewing caps and copying the Quran. He entrusted the affairs of state to Balban.

Balban made an intensive campaign against the turbulent Jats in the North and Khokhars; they used to help the Mongols. He also made expedition in the Doab and Bundelkhand. He was made 'Naib-ul-Mulk'. The 'Forty' Nobles grew jealous of him and due to their pressure he was removed in March 1253 and he then retired to his jagir in Hansi. He was replaced by 'Imad-ud-Din

Rihan' who alienated the nobles by his arrogance. In 1255 A.D., Balban was reinstated. When in 1257 A.D. Mongols took Multan, Balban marched towards them, they withdrew from there. The Mongol ruler, Halaku Khan, the grandson of Chingiz Khan sent an envoy to Delhi at the close of Nasir-ud-din's rule. He was well received in Delhi and he was highly overwhelmed. In 1266 A.D., Nasir-ud-din died.

Ghiyas-ud-Din Balban (1266–87 A.D.)

Ghiyas-ud-Din Balban was captured in his childhood and sold as slave in Baghdad. Khwaja Jamal-ud-din Basri purchased him and brought him up like his own child. In 1232 A.D., he was taken to Delhi where Iltutmish purchased him. As Nasir-ud-Din had no male child so he nominated him in 1266 A.D. as his heir.

When he acquired the throne of Delhi, the Nobles of the court were not in discipline, Jats were in rebellion, soldiers were not performing their duties properly, the roads were full of robbers, Mewatis were; in and around Delhi, there was rebellion in Bengal and the Mongols were plundering Sind and Multan. He managed all these and kept a strong discipline in the court. He punished all those who raised rebellion against the state; for this, he made no distinction for his own relatives. He loved the company of high born and learned persons; because of Mongol disturbances outside India, learned people were taking shelter in India, especially in Delhi. He was a great monarch who combined in himself the quality of discipline and generosity. He patronized the 'Ulema and Mashaikh'. He was an orthodox Muslim, strict in the observance of his religious duties.

In 1286 A.D., the Mongols reappeared under Timur Khan and plundered Lahore. They were defeated but Prince Mohammad, who was very dear to Balban and was nominated as heir, was killed in this raid. Balban, due to his old age, could not bear this grief and died in February 1286 A.D.

Kaiqubad (1287–9 A.D.)

Balban had now left only one son, Burga Khan, who was easygoing and lazy. Balban appointed him as his heir, but after the death of Balban he refused to take the responsibility of the Empire and went to his province (Bengal). The Nobles appointed his son Kaiqubad who was brought up under a strict discipline. But soon he too indulged in pleasure. He was warned by his father but to no effect. He shifted his capital from Mehrauli to Kilokhari, now near Nizam-ud-Din (Humayun's Tomb). Because of heavy drinking he got paralysis and had no hope for recovery. The Nobles therefore, placed Kaimurth, his 3 years old son on the throne. The Khilji Nobles were alarmed at this. They captured the capital and placed Malik Firoz as King.

The Khiljis (1290–1320 A.D.)

Jalal-ud-Din Firoz Khilji (1290–6 A.D.)

In the tenth century the Khiljis settled down between Sistan and West Punjab and were deeply affected by their long stay in Afghanistan. So the later Turks who migrated from Turkistan in the thirteenth century considered these people as Afghans. Due to this the Turks were opposed to the accession of Jalal-ud-Din Firoz Khilji as the Sultan. But with his soft nature and humility he won his enemies and also crushed the rebellion of Malik Chhajju, the nephew of Balban, who was later sent to Multan. He even let off robbers and thives after pleading with them to reform their ways. In 1292 A.D., under 'Abdullah' a grandson of Halaku, the Mongols attacked, but were defeated; one of the descendents of Chingiz Khan did not return and he embraced Islam along with his followers. The Sultan married one of his daughters to him and new converts settled in the Suburb of Delhi called 'Mughalpura' (near Roshnara Road). There are two Mughalpuras in Delhi: one is now near Roshnara Road and the other are two villages near Rohini, one is called Mongolpur Kalan and other is called Mongolpur Khurd. The inhabitants of these villages in 1739 A.D. when Nadir Shah came to Delhi attacked one of his rear parties. Nadir Shah ordered to burn this village; later the Jats settled in this land.

Mongol Invasion

After the disintegration of the Abbasid Empire, middle Eastern history also changed. The Buwayhids come to power in Iraq and Western Iran from 945 to 1055 A.D., the Samanies in Eastern Iran and Transoxania (999 A.D.) and Ghaznavids in Afghanistan and Khurasan (1040 A.D.). the decline of the Abbasid Empire also gave way to Turkish nomadic people to infiltrate into the Middle East and inner Asia. In the ninth century, Qarakhanids invaded and controlled Transoxania, in the eleventh century the Saljuqs seized Iran and Anatolia, Ghuzz and Nayman and in the thirteenth century the Mongols conquered most of the region. Soon they started exerting their pressure upon Northern India. It was more during the period of Khilji Dynasty. 1290 to 1320 A.D. The reign of Sultan Ala-ud-Din (1296–1316 A.D.) endorsed a series of Mongol invasions from the Chaghtai Khanate in Central Asia; they reached twice the outskirts of Delhi. After 1307 A.D., the Mongol raids to Delhi receded. In 1351 A.D. in the reign of Mohammad Tughluq, the Chaghtai Khan Tarmashirin led an incursion and advanced till Yamuna but returned after looting and killing the people of Delhi, they actually did not enter the main capital, but looted the streets of Delhi. Before it in 1303 A.D. a vast number of Mongols some 100,000 to 150,000, invaded India under the command of grandson of Hulaku and penetrated as for as Sunam. Firoz-ud-Din Tughluq, met the Mongol advance guard and defeated it, but afraid to face the main force of invading Mongols, made peace with them. He married one of his daughters to Ulghu, a descendent of Genghis Khan, who accepted Islam with 4000, followers. They were settled in the Suburb of Delhi, called Mongol Pura, near old Subzi Mandi, and were known as new Muslims. In 1305, Ala-al-Din faced a formidable invasion of some 50,000 Mongols under 'Ali Beg' a descendent of Genghis Khan and Tartaq, who were joined by Targhi, a leader of the last campaign. They were defeated at Amroha in 31 December 1305, Ali Beg and Tartaq were captured, many were killed and their heads were built into the Towers of the Fort of Siri.

In 1306 A.D., the Mongols again invaded India to take revenge on the death of 'Ali Beg' and 'Tartaq' but Malik Naib Kafur defeated these forces on the banks of Ravi and Nagaur; he captured many Mongols, along with their women and children who were sent to Delhi. Some fled and escaped. Those who were sent to Delhi were trampled under the feet of elephants and their heads were placed at the Badaun Gate of the fort. Their women and children were sold as slaves.

In 1306 A.D., during the reign of Ala-al-Din, Kabak invaded India. Duwa Khan, the Khan of Transoxiana again made some attempts but with his death in 1306 A.D., Mongol invasion stopped for some time. Those Mongols, who were settled in the environs of Delhi (Mongol Pura) and accepted Islam, were discontented, because of heavy taxes and had no important positions in the state and were also not given jagirs. They rebelled in Gujarat, so they all were dismissed from Ala-al-Din's Service. They hatched a plan to kill Ala-al-Din, which was exposed. So Ala-al-Din ordered all of them to be killed, some 20 to 30 thousands by them, some innocent, were also killed.

In the year 1351 A.D., during the reign of Mohammad Tughluq, the Chaghtai Khan, Tarmashirin led an incursion from Mawara' al-Nahr in which the Mongol forces once again advanced to Yamuna but retired without actually entering the capital. Hindustan was almost free from major attacks from Mongols for merely 60 years until the sack of Delhi by Timur in 1398 A.D.

There are two views of many historians regarding the Tarmashirin. Earlier he was a Buddhist converted to Islam (a Sunni) by faith; he was overthrown by Ilkham, who was Shia by faith.[22] Some say that he was driven out by the forces of the king and had suffered a loss but some say that he was bribed and an agreement was entered into. Tarmashirin looted Gujarat and on the way going back to his capital he looted Lahore, Samana, Indri and some territories bordering Badaun. The fact to be noted is that Tarmashirin attacked when the citizens of Delhi had already left for Daulatabad, but the king, Mohammad remained in the city for two years; he gathered an army and faced this attack of Mongols. In fact, Sultan Mohammad humiliated himself before the Mongols and purchased peace by giving the invaders a huge quantity of wealth. The Mongols imprisoned many people. They received almost the price of the kingdom. After the death of Tarmashirin, his son, with his sister and her husband, had sought asylum with Mohammad Tughluq. So many Mongols also came to India especially in Delhi and settled there.

Timur Lang (1336–1405 A.D.)

Timur Lang, son of Traghai and Nagina Begum was born in Kush which is famous with the name of Saher-i-Subj (green city) at that time it was a part of Persia, in 736 Hijri. The 25th of Saban (1336 A.D.), he became king in 771 Hijri at Balkh (at that time a part of Persia). He attacked India on 12th of Muharram 801 Hijri (in August 1398) at the time of King Nusrat Shah. He was a Mongol by decent and great grandson of Chingiz Khan, who formed a confederation of Inner Asian peoples and conquered the whole of the East Asia, the Middle East and the East-European steppes. Within a few years, the Mongols ruled Central Europe and the pacific. The whole Empire was divided among the sons of Changis who considered it their joint property. But the decendents of Changis fought among themselves for their control later on. Out of this dispute, many independent states came into existence such as Mongolia, China, the Golden Horde on the northern steppes, the Chaghtai Khanate in Transoxiana and Eastern Turkistan and the Ilkhan regime in Iran and Anatolia. After defeating other Chieftains, Timur grouped loyal followers and became a military adventurer. In 1370 A.D., he made Samarkand his capital and became a successor of the Chaghtai branch of Mongol rulers in Transoxiana. He was also supported by local Muslims and Sufis. From 1379 to 1402 A.D. he conquered Iran, northern India, Anatolia and northern Syria. He made there conquests in the name of Sharia, on the pretext that his enemies were traitors of Islam.

In all the subjugated states during the Timurid period the leading positions were held by the Naqshbandis. Even before the invasion of Timur, Mongols were invading India and after looting it went back but the invasion of Timur in 1398 was different from the earlier ones. He knew the political turmoil in India, its rulers, people and wealth of course. He was lame but he was well built and at the age of 60 years with a large army of Turks, Tatars and Iranians, he invaded India. He started butchering people to the extent that it became an example till date no one could kill so many people in one invasion. Heading 90,000 horsemen through Afghanistan he entered into Punjab and step by step he was moving forward with plunder, killing and destroying cities after city and people, he reached Panipat without any hindrance, from there he crossed Yamuna near Baghpat to the eastern side and captured the Fort of Loni. He camped opposite the Firoz Shah Kotla. Again he crossed the river and camped, (there is now Metcalfe House); there he killed one lakh infidels (Hindus), even those people who had never killed a sheep. From here, he camped near Firozabad, digging a ditch and placing in front of it lines of buffaloes, tied together to break a charge. After two days he reached near the place where now stands the tomb of Safdarjung. Nusrat Shah, the King of Delhi, moved out of the fort with twelve thousand cavalry, forty thousand infantry and a line of elephants. The troops of Timur were dismayed at this sight but they were veteran soldiers and soon they repulsed the fleeing enemy. Nusrat Shah fled to Gujarat. The next day, again thousands of people were slaughtered and the fort was plundered and Timur feasted by the side of Hauz Khas. Dead bodies were piled together and there was no place to move easily in the city. He stayed for few months in Delhi and during this period he inspected the masque in the Kotla of Firoz Shah and was delighted. There he was presented with two white parrots, supposed to be seventy-four years old of age which had been transferred from one to another king from the time of Tughluq Shah.

Timur did not need any excuse to invade India. There were valid reasons such as weakness of the Delhi Sultanate, the fabulous wealth of India and also the news of Muslims worshipping idols in India. But the real object was plunder. He wanted to take the wealth of India to his country. Although he proclaimed himself the 'Emperor' of Delhi, he did not have any serious desire to rule it. He moved to his home country via Meerut and repeated the ferocious performance of massacre and loot in the name of Islam. On the way, he raided all the cities along the river Ganga, reached Kashmir and Kangra and at last he crossed the river Indus, taking with him fabulous wealth, innumerable slaves including women. He left behind him a scene of horror, dead bodies sided up in the streets and houses, anarchy and famine. He destroyed whatever government existed in Delhi and for the next fifteen years there was no regular government in Delhi. There prevailed a general chaos, disorder and anarchy everywhere. Nusrat Shah came to Delhi after five months and took possession of the spoiled city, but shortly afterwards he was drawn out by one noble, Iqbal Khan Mahmud summoned to Delhi and he remained king till his death in 1412 A.D. The name of Timur even today sends a frightful feeling in the minds of the people.

Timur died in 1405 A.D. He had ordered that Albroki, the one from the tribe of Prophet Mohammad be entered into the grave along with him so that he may plead for him and also pray for him. The same was done at the demise of Timur. Albroki was tied with the body of Timur and entered in the grave of Timur at Samarkand. Today the grave, which has a Mausoleum over it, is considered as a place of pilgrimage and a pious place.

Masjids (Mosques) of Delhi

With the collapse of the Abbasid Empire in the mid-tenth century, the history of Islamic Societies in the subcontinent began to be created. In 711–3 A.D. Arab invasion of Sind started and they could establish their rule. However, in Afghanistan the Muslim rule started only after post Abbasid military regime. The Ghaznavids captured Lahore in 1030 A.D. and plundered North India. They were replaced by the local chiefs under the leadership of the Ghurid Dynasty, who began the systematic conquest of India. From 1175 to 1192 A.D., they occupied Unch, Multan, Peshawar, Lahore and Delhi. In 1206 A.D., Ghori was killed by the Turks in Afghanistan and Qutub-ud-Din Aibak, one of the Gauried-General, the conqueror of Delhi, became independent and founded first dynasties of Muslims, collectively known as the Delhi Sultanate (1206–1526 A.D.). When the Muslims were pouring through the gates of India, Delhi and Kanoj were still at feud. The other Rajput Kings, Suryavanshi and Chandravanshi, were not in good terms, and the invaders took great advantage of this situation.

> The fanatical marauders overwhelmed by luxurious cities of Lahore, Delhi and Kanoj, shouting for God and the Prophet, but caring for nothing save women and plunder. Their war cry spread terror far and wide. The Rajput Nobles and their retainers rode forth to take the field, or manned the walls and fortresses. The Multitude flocked to the temples, whilst the Brahmans performed their sacrifices and incantations, and implored the God for success. Some were huddled together in the inner chambers. Others hid themselves in secluded gardens, or flocked to the roofs of palaces to gain tidings of the fight. It was a war of Iron and rapine against Gold and beauty. They ransacked every chamber and every shrine in their thirst for jewels and treasure. They filled the street and houses with blood; they hacked and hewed at temples and idols and Brahmanical deities; they derided the relics of holy man; they profaned the altars of the Gods; they carried off young men and maidens, and even the priests and dancing girls of the temples, to sell as slaves in the bazars of Kabul and Ghazni.[23]

Islam is a very simple religion. It is not loaded with much of rituals. Its main principle is—that the God is Great and one only. Through the *namaz*—five times a day, a Muslim should pray to God (at Sunrise, at noon, at afternoon, after sunset and at night). Allah is one and the Prophet is his messenger; one should keep fast, give alms and should perform the Haj (visit the Kaaba at Mecca). These principles should be followed by all Muslims. He should surrender before Allah and consider Allah all powerful. To keep this faith, intact the masjid (mosque) plays a great role. It is a very pious place. Namaz may be performed individually but namaz performed in a masjid in a congregation has greater importance.

'Masjid is a place of Allah (Khuda). It is for Khuda. Therefore, no other name is uttered there except Khuda'[24] In the masjid everyone, rich or poor, young and old, black or brown, every one is same and there is no difference. Brotherhood and equality emanates from masjid. Namaz is not only a ritual but it is the whole philosophy of Islam. That is why Hazrat Sahib masjid at Madina has become a religions place and a model of masjid for all Muslims. Prophet Mohammad used to perform all social, political and religious activities from this masjid; so the masjid is not only a religious place but it is also a place of social gathering. The Imam has an important place in the masjid. In the second call for namaz all Muslims should come to the masjid for namaz and make a line to perform the namaz in a disciplined manner. The Madina masjid is a model for masjid; variations if it is a must according to the place and circumstances.

In Islam, masjid also caters to the needs of education (Madarsa), Sarai's Assembly, et cetera. As per Islam, Allah is present every where and all places are equal to Allah, therefore Allah can be remembered at any place, but it should not be a disturbed and disputed place. The namaz can be performed even without a masjid. This fact can be seen at many places even now in Delhi (some people perform the Friday namaz on roads). The only necessary condition of namaz is that those who perform the namaz should keep their face in the direction of Mecca.

Quwwat-ul-Islam Mosque

The meaning of the name of this mosque is 'the might of Islam'. This mosque was built after destroying 27 Hindu and Jain Temples. This is amply clear from the inscription over the eastern gate of the Mosque. Some Hindu structures inside the Mosque are still standing there, which is the proof of this fact. Even the pillars and other columns indicate the bells and figures of Hindu Gods. On the north side of the Gate on the stairs there are slabs, which has the carving of Hindu Gods. After destroying these 27 Hindu Temples, Qutub-ud-Din Aibak, used the materials of these temples to build this Mosque. Dehliwal was the name of the coin during this period. This was the currency of Rai Pithora. The material used from 27 temples, as estimated, was at a cost of 54,000,000 Dehliwals. Later also it was widened. He got made Quranic verses in Naskh and Kufi Scripts. In his conquest of Malwa and Ujjain in 1233, he devastated the temple of Mahakal and brought the images or divinities and the statue of Raja Vikramaditya to Delhi and piled them at the gate of this Mosque.

In its courtyard, the famous Iron Pillar is situated. The sculpted columns that support the roof of the prayer hall and colonnades are the most obvious relics. The roof itself is Rajput in style; particularly the domes over the entrance bays, which may originally have come from temple Mandaps. The lack of mortar in indigenous building techniques must have made such re-use of materials easy.

Dada Bari, Jain Temple, Mehrauli.

The Iron Pillar

This Pillar is situated in the compound of Quwwat-ul-Islam Mosque. This pillar is over 7 meter high; its diameter is 40 centimeter at the base and 30 centimeter at the top. At the top of this column is an inverted lotus capital, which was once crowned by a Vaishnavite emblem such as Garuda, Vishnu's vehicle.

There are many stories relating to this Pillar, coming from earlier period down to us. But the fact is that this pillar was cast before the Tomars and Turks

Iron Pillar, Mehrauli.

ruled. The fact is that in the fourth century A.D., Indian workmanship involved purifying iron and casting it. This could be done in the nineteenth century in the west. This pillar is exceptionally pure wrought iron. It does not rust. In fact, early iron making processes produced a high phosphorus content that allowed the iron to react with oxygen and hydrogen to produce a protective film of miswrite that has been slowly growing ever since its manufacturing. An inscription is given on it, the translation of it depicts that some king named Chandra erected it on 'the Vishnupada Hill'. So this pillar was taken to this place from somewhere else, even the Turks who destroyed other structures did not do anything with this iron pillar.

The Qutub Minar

The Minar is very beautiful. Its height is 72.5 m, with a diameter at the base of 14 meters and at the top it is only 3 meters. It is built in red stone; only white marble is used in the fourth storey. The construction has been done by very skilled persons. It has five stories. The first storey has conical and circular projections alternatively; the second has circular; the third only conical projections and fourth and fifth stories are all round. When Qutub-ud-Din Aibak went to Ghazna, he was directed by Sultan Muiz-ud-Din, to build something representative in the (converted) building and after coming back from Ghazni to Delhi in 1195 A.D., he built the mosque of Quwwat-ul-Islam. The Minar is said to be constructed by Iltutmish, the next ruler after Aibak. Its first level of 29 meters was built by Aibak (1192–1210 A.D.) his successor Iltutmish (1210–35 A.D.) built other stories, altered by subsequent damage and repair. The tower was damaged by lighting during the time of Firoz Shah,

Qutub Minar, Mehrauli.

Babur going in a procession to visit Maqbara of Khawja Hazrat Qutb-ud-Din near Qutub Minar. (From Journal of the United Provinces Historical Society, vol. 10, 1937.)

who partially demolished the top layer and made two out of it. In 1503 A.D., Fateh Khan, under Sultan Sikandar Lodi, repaired it. Major repairs were undertaken by Lord Lake. Originally it was 100 yards in height and seven stories, containing 378 stairs; after an Earthquake, two stories have been removed. It has now tilted a little. Some historians had raised some doubts about its originality such as its entrance on the north side, while all Muslim Madhanas open on the east; it is not built on the plinth while Muslim structures are built on the plinth. The first storey has carving of bells and chains as in the original temple; the name of Muiz-ud-Din and Aibak is carried in the same way as is done in the converted temple; the stones above the inscribed panel seem to have been fixed in situ later. The first story is definitely a Hindu structure. The storey goes that a Sun worshiper, who considered Yamuna the daughter of Sun, used to see it before taking his meal. This is a historical fact that one stream of Yamuna was flowing near the Qutub area during this period.

After the conquest of Delhi, Qutub-ud-Din Aibak, the General of Mohammad Ghori built a Mosque over the site of the temple of Rai Pithora, with its stones, and slabs unmindful that it carried with them the carvings of Hindu gods and motifs. The practice of demolishing Hindu temples and other religious structures was further followed by successive Islamic rulers. The followers of Islam settled in India in large numbers and Delhi was no exception: either they were original Muslims or they were converted from Hindus, but they remained in the beginning aloof from the normal current of the social and religious life of the country. Before the advent of Islam, many diverse cultures met in India but with the passage of time, they were all fused together

Alai Minar, Mehrauli.

Yogmaya Mandir, Mehrauli.

into a common cultural pattern. The Muslims, however, did not merge themselves into this pattern, and for the first time in Indian history, two distinct cultures stood face to face and India was divided into two units, each with its marked individuality of its own. The problem remained and continued to be faced by India in its chequered history in the next six hundred years and even the partition of India in 1947 A.D. could not solve it.

With the rapid and successive raids of the Mongols at Lahore, Delhi became more important for the rulers, while it grew into a trading, cultural and religious centre as well.

Right from the beginning it became the cherished object of the Sultans. The chroniclers mention it with reverential prefixes such as Shahr (Barani); Hadrat(Afif); Dar-al-Mulk (Sams Siraj); Dar-al-Khulafa(Amir Khusrau) In 1399 A.D., it had at least five forts, Kilokhari, Siri, Tughlaqabad, Firozabad and Rai Pithora that of Prithvi Raj. The town was surrounded by a city wall with numerous gates leading out in all directions. Magnificent monuments, splendid edifices in various shades of royal residence, mosques, madarsas, hospitals, sarais, reservoirs, khanqahs, chabutras, along with the modest dwellings of stone or brick, roofed with wood and either shining or unpaved floors, sprang up all over the Town. The extent of the Town was 40 miles and the suburbs remaining up to another 12 miles were set apart for orchards and gardens. In view of the large size of the town, beasts of draught and vehicles were available as a matter of course.[25]

Auliya Mosque: In this mosque Hazrat Khawja Moinuddin Chishti, Hazrat Qutubuddin Bakhtiyar Kaki and Baba Fariduddin Shakar Ganj, the renowned Sufis collectively performed the Namaz. Hazrat Qutubuddin used to receive the cakes (small chapatis) at this mosque that is why he was called Kaki. This mosque is situated on Hauz Shamsi covering one hundred acres of land. In earlier times it was full of clean water which was used by the inhabitants of Mehrauli for drinking. Later on one stream of water was taken to Tughulaqabad for the use of the fort. The Hauz was considered very pious that is why its mud is used on the grave of Bakhtiyar Kaki, Mehrauli.

Not only the Sultans, but the nobles, the members of the royal family got built mosques and tombs in some one's memory or on the death of some high-ups. It is not possible to give here the details of each and every Tomb and Mosque, as it is not the purpose of this book and some of them are not even traceable. However, some old and important mosques and tombs which have played some role in the life of Delhi are given below:

Kalan Masjid

It is a sturdy little mosque, black and solid, built in 1386 A.D. in Bulbuli Khana near Turkman Gate. It is a plain structure built like a fortress. It is approached by some steep stairs and to reach the front portion of this mosque, one has to climb 30 stairs. It is built on 8.5 feet high base. This mosque belongs to a period when men's minds were filled with bloodshed and repine. Therefore, the assembly of men needed a strong and safe place from sudden attack. The men in those days must have worshipped with their arms by their side and the sentinels posted to shout alarm. At that time, some channel of Yamuna was also flowing near this Mosque.

Khirki Mosque

Like Kalan masjid this is also erected by Janashah Khanejahan, the Prime Minister of Firoz-Shah Tughluq. This Mosque lies in village Khirki, with the southeastern walls of Jahanpanah. It is a double storey Mosque. In some ways, it is similar to Kalan masjid (the gateways and prayer niche, flanked by sloping towers) but other features of this Mosque are different from Kalan masjid. Hazrat Nizam-ud-Din Aulia used to come to this masjid to perform his namaz on every Jumma (Friday).

The interior having been divided into four equal quarters, each one having an open court in its centre. Out of 25 divisions of the terrace, four in the middle are open through courts, 12 have flat roofs and nine have cupola roofs, nine in one set, there being 81 cupolas in nine sets on the superstructure. It follows the style of the Mosque of Rum (Turkey).

Begumpuri Mosque

The Mosque is situated in village Begumpur near Malviya Nagar. It is said to be built in 1387 A.D. and it is entirely built of rubble and mortar. It seems to be a Pathan structure resembling with Khirki Mosque and Atala masjid at Jaunpur. Earlier, villagers encroached upon it; the British evacuated them and got it cleared. It is on a raised platform; one has to climb 15 stairs to reach the main Mosque.

Masjid Kalu Sarai

This Mosque is situated near, Begumpuri Mosque and it is also built of rubble and Mortar. This was built in 1387 A.D. Its northern and southern *dalans* have been destroyed.

Jamat Khana Masjid (Nizam-ud-Din)

This mosque is situated in the compound of the Dargah of Hazrat Nizam-ud-Din Aulia. This structure was originally built for the Mazaar of Aulia Sahib, who refused it. Later on, two sides were added to it; that is why its structure is not in tradition of building Mosque. This is the construction from Ala-ud-Din Khilji's period (1296–1316 A.D.). It is said that Khwaja, the son of Ala-ud-Din Khilji, who was the disciple of the saint got it constructed for the grave of the saint, but it was denied by the saint himself. There is one more mosque in the Nizam-ud-Din area which is also very old. It is situated on the eastern side of Nizam-ud-Din, now it is encroached and encircled from all-sides.

The Moth-ki-Masjid

This mosque is situated in the vicinity of Kotla-Mubarakpur. It was built during the reign of Sultan Sikandar Lodi in 1488–95 A.D. This is indicated from the red stone slab inside the well which was dig along with this mosque. The gateway of this mosque is carved by Quranic verses in white marble. It is believed that this mosque is built out of the proceeds of the grain of *moth* (a pulse), which was cultivated at this place; that is why it is called Moth-ki-Masjid.

Masjid Maulana Jamali

This mosque was built in 1528 A.D. by Sheikh Fadullah, who was also known as Jalal Khan, in the area of Qutub Minar, Mehrauli. It was originally a populated area; now it is in ruins. It is also a double story masjid and so famous for its corridors on the first floor that it becomes difficult to trace a person if one has gone out of sight. Its Chilla Khana is very airy and cool.

Masjid Qila-i-Kuhna (old fort)

This is a very strong and beautiful Mosque built by Sher Shah in 1541 A.D. It is built of red stone along with white marble. Quranic verses have been carved in Naskh and Kufic styles. The walls of the mosque are very thick and its height is extra ordinary. In *Akbarnamah* it has been referred as Jami masjid. It was also used during Humayun's time. After hearing the call of the Maulvi, Humayun wanted to come to this mosque for prayer but he fell down in the *sher mandal* (the library of Humayun) and died.

Masjid of Khairpur

It was built during the period of Sher-Shah in 1543 A.D. It is a fine and rare specimen of Pathan architecture. Quranic verses have been carved on the façade.

Masjid Isa Khan

It is situated in Arab-ki-Sarai, Nizam-ud-Din; Isa Khan was the famous noble of Islam Shah. It is another beautiful structure.

Masjid Dargah Hadrat Qutub Sahib

This mosque is close to the Tomb of Qutub Sahib. It is composed of three sections. The first one which is two arched is *kachcha*, of mud only; it was built by Qutub Sahib himself. The other section was added to it in 1551 A.D., by Salim Shah Sur, the third one was added by Farrukh Siyar in 1717 A.D.

Jama Masjid

The large surface was obtained after cutting the *pahari* (hill) of Bhojla, on which the foundation of present mosque of Jama masjid was laid by Shah Jahan in 1650 A.D. It is believed that Shah Jahan had designed the masjid. It is built in red granite, including its steps, but the domes and cupolas of the Minarets are of white Marble, and there are some cornices and moldings of

Jama Masjid.

Masjid Shah Jahani, Pataudi House, Daryaganj.

the same facing the building. It has three gates on the east, north and the south. In the centre, there is a pond for ablution. It took six years to compelete it and cost ten lacs of rupees.

During 1858 A.D., till the restoration, it was under the control of the British army, who not only stayed inside it but also used it as a stable and used to drink and eat inside this mosque. Later, the peace committee got it restored to the Muslims. In 1844 A.D., W.H. Sleeman visited this Mosque, the two Hindu gentlemen were not allowed by the keepers to enter into this mosque on the plea that no worshippers of idols could be admitted to the mosque by the order of the Master. One minar (northern) had been struck by lightening and had fallen down. The British Government had restored the minar in 1817 A.D., during the time of King Muin-ud-Din Mohammad Akbar Shah.

A Mukabbar (raised platform) was built in 1829 A.D. by Prince Salim, the son of Akbar Shah; some relics of the Prophet are preserved in a room in northern side. On the southern side there are 33 stairs descending below to the road. On the northern gate, there are 39 stairs, on the eastern gate side there are 35 steps and on both corners of the eastern side, two tanks of large dimensions were built. Now they have been filled in and houses have been built there. A hospital (Dar-ul-Shifa) was there on the northwestern side. On the southern side there was a Madarsa. In front of the eastern gate, there is a

Dargah and grave of Sarmad Shah, a renowned Sufi saint, who was beheaded near this mosque.

This masjid remained closed till 1862 A.D. for worship; it was opened for prayer when a Jama Masjid Committee was formed. This mosque played a great role in the religious, social, cultural and political life of Delhi.

Masjid Fatehpuri

This mosque was built by Nawab Fatehpuri Begum, the wife of Shah Jahan in 1650 A.D. It is 45 yards x 22 yards in size, a double storey built around it in red sandstone. Now a Madarsa is there. It was sold to Lala Chhuna Mal by the British in 1857 A.D. After this, many discussions were held in Fatehpuri masjid by the Hanafi and al-Hadis Muslims with the Missionaries till 1877 A.D. The masjid remained the property of Lala Chhunna Mal, who purchased it in for Rs. 39,650. It was the link between the city and the suburbs; it was patronized by the Punjabi Muslims. This masjid remained the centre of political as well as cultural and religious activities for a long period and differed in attitude from the Committee of Jama Masjid.

Fatehpuri Masjid

Masjid Akbarabadi

It was situated in Faiz Bazar inside the walled city of Shahjahanabad. Now it is Subhash Park opposite the Red Fort of Delhi. It was built at a cost of one and a half lac rupees by Akbarabadi Begum in 1650 A.D., one of the queens of Shah Jahan, named Nawab Afsar-un-Nisa Begum. It measured 63 x 17 yards.

Akbarabadi Mosque demolished by the British after the Mutiny, now there is Subhash Park.

Red stone and marble were used in its construction. The courtyard measures 154 yards x 104 yards. Some *hujras* (rooms) were also there and a madarsa was there in which Maulvi Rahamatullah used to come to teach the students. He was very much against Christianity and used to propagate against it. The masjid was so great that it was considered second to Jama Masjid. Near it there was a Kashmiri Katara (lane) that is why it was also called Kashmiri Katara ki Masjid. In the hujras the Kashmiris used to prepare shawls. During winter season the Kashmiri people used to come here, because of which the masjid was getting some rent from them which was used for its maintenance. In the later part, it was not properly maintained but it had very good *katabas* (quranic verses). When it was demolished by the British after the 'mutiny', the katabas were given to Ilahi Baksh (a relative of Bahadur Shah Zafar). When Sir Sayed Ahmad Khan asked Ilahi Baksh to give these katabas for the masjid he was making at Aligarh, Ilahi Baksh evaded it. After his death Mirza Sulaiman Jah (son of Ilahi Baksh) gave these katabas to Sir Syed Ahmad Khan, who made many parts of it and placed them at the Aligarh Muslim University masjid. They can be seen now at this masjid.

Near Akbarabadi masjid there was a *taksal* (mint) which worked till 1818 A.D. The British stopped its operations and demolished it along with other structures in the same area after the 'mutiny' in 1857.

Masjid Sirhindi

This was built in 1650 A.D. by Sirhindi Begum, another queen of Shah Jahan. It was also built in red stone. This is situated outside the Lahori-Darwaza. Its outer walls had fallen down and only the sanctuary of the mosque stands on the moat. She also laid out a garden near Subzi-Mandi. The tomb of Sirhindi Begum is also situated in the garden.

The Moti Masjid (Red Fort)

It was built by Aurangzeb in Red Fort of Delhi in 1659 A.D. It is entirely built of white marble with extremely chaste architectural style. A sum of rupees one lakh and six thousand was spent on its construction. Aurangzeb used to spend most of his time at this masjid. He used to sew the caps at this masjid and out of its proceeds he had to maintain himself.

Masjid Aurangabadi

It was built by Nawab Aurangabadi Begum, one the Queen of Aurangzeb in 1703. It is entirely built in red sand stone. This mosque is situated in the Punjabi Katra inside Shahjahanabad. There is a spacious court and a tank which was fed by canal water. Now traders live in this area and called it Punjabi Katra; the nearby houses have appropriated the land of this masjid.

Zinat-ul-Masjid

Its meaning is the ornament of mosques. It was built by Zinat-un-Nisa Begum, daughter of Aurangzeb in 1710 A.D. The mosque was built of red stone; the three domes were of white marble bearing black stone lining. A small tomb is also erected inside this area where she was buried in 1710 A.D. There were lands allotted for the support and repairs of this place amounting to rupees one lac per annum, but this has been confiscated during 1857 A.D.

Mosque of Roshan-ud-Daulah

This mosque was built by Nawab Roshan-ud-Daulah Zafar Khan in the memory of his Pir in 1721 A.D. This noble was enjoying his life with all types of activities but in his later life he became religious. This masjid is made of brick and mortar. It is a beautiful construction. It is also called Sunehri Masjid because its pinnacles and Kalash are gold polished. It was earlier next to Kotwali, now the area of Kotwali has been merged with Sis Ganj Sahib Gurudwara, so this masjid is now next to this Gurudwara. It is from here the Nadir Shah in 1739 A.D. ordered the massacre of the people of Delhi.

In 1745 A.D., Nawab Roshan-ud-Daulah Zafar Khan also got built another mosque in the Phool-ki-Mandi, at Faiz Bazar, near Qadiwara in Shahjahanabad. Qadi Faidullah Khan Sahib had it adequately repaired later.

Mosque of Sharf-ud-Daulah

This mosque is situated in Dariba. This was built by Nawab Sharf-ud-Daulah Bahadur in 1722 A.D. It is built of brick and lime-mortar; its three domes are of marble. This marble is yellow like brass.

Masjid of Mausoleum of Nawab Safdar Jang

He was the nephew of the first Nawab of Oudh and Wazir of Ahmed Shah; he was also responsible for the final ruin of the Mughal Emperors. In 1753 A.D., he called the Jats and his rivals called the Marathas to Delhi and this tomb and this masjid became the centre of many activities. In 1398 A.D., Timur crushed the armies of Muhmad Khan near this place. In this mausoleum and in the mausoleum of Ghazi-ud-Din Khan at Ajmeri Gate, two ruling houses, Oudh and Hyderabad, did so many activities and later became independent rulers.

Shah Mardan Mosque

This was built by Udham Bai, a Queen of Mohammad Shah. She belonged to the Shia sect. A mosque and a tomb were built in 1748 A.D.; the Assembly Hall by Ishrat Khan in 1808 A.D.; and a Naqqar Khana by Sadiq Ali Khan in 1821 A.D. *Taziyas* are placed here during Muharram. It is also called the Karbala.

Fakhr-ul-Masjid

This is situated in Kashmiri Gate, near old Hindu College. It was built by Fakhr-un-Nisa Begum, wife of Nawab Shujaat Khan, in 1728 A.D. in the memory of her husband who died in Afghanistan. He was the Qiledar (Keeper of the Fort) of Agra during the period of Aurangzeb; the royal treasure was kept in Agra fort. This man was very loyal to Aurangzeb. This mosque is magnificently designed and attractive.

Masjid Fatima Farrukh Jahan, Kashmiri Gate.

Chubi Masjid (The Wooden Mosque)

This Mosque was built by king Ahmad Shah in the Red Fort. Its pillars and arches are made of wood. It has been restored by the gevernment in 1850 A.D.

There are many more Mosques. These are given below:

1. Masjid –Sultan Ghazi (Sultan Nasrudin Mahmud) at Mehrauli died in 1229 A.D.
2. Masjid Firoz Shahi, at Green Park, Built by Firoz Shah Tughluq in 1352 A.D.
3. Jama Masjid at Kilokhari, Kaikubad built it (1287–90 A.D.).
4. Purani masjid, at Panchsheel Enclave, Sultan Mohammad Tughluq in 1327 A.D.
5. Chhoti Masjid, Lodi Garden, Lodi Period.
6. Aulia Masjid; Kalkaji (Tughluq Period).
7. Masjid Bagh-i-Alam at Deer Park, Hauz Khas, now in bad condition.
8. Do-Burji Masjid; Sheikh Sarai (Firoz Shah Tughluq 1387 A.D.).
9. Kanati Masjid, Munirka; built by Munir Khan, the noble of Firoz Shah Tughluq.
10. Masjid Salim Garh; built by Salim Shah Sur.
11. Masjid Zabta Gunj, near India Gate, Rohila Chieftain Zabita Khan built it in 1785 A.D.
12. New Delhi Jama Masjid, Near Parliament House.
13. Masjid Siddipura near Model Basti.
14. Masjid Hazrat Baki Billah Qutub Road built in 1891–2 A.D. in the period of Mahmud Shah.
15. Masjid, Purani Idgah at Qutub Road, built by Shah-Jahan.
16. Masjid Gulmohar Park.
17. Masjid Nawab Rukun-ud-Daulah, (Lal Masjid) in Chawri Bazar was built by Akbar Shah II who died in 1837 A.D.
18. Masjid Mehran Nagar, near Palam Airport.
19. Masjid Sunehri Bagh; near Udyog Bhawan.
20. Masjid at Curzon Road.
21. Masjid Patel Chowk.
22. Masjid Eastern Court.
23. Shahi Masjid Bhogal. Masjid Khwaja Pir, Friends Colony.
24. Masjid Bangali Market (Masjid Bachehu Shah).
25. Masjid at Kharag Singh Marg, Connaught Place.
26. Aulia Masjid, near Cinema Odeon.
27. Masjid opposite Marina Hotel.
28. Masjid Panj Piran near Cremation ground at Lodi Road.
29. Masjid Qazi Wali, Paharganj opposite New Delhi Railway Station.

30. Masjid Bhul-Bhulayan, Akbar built it in 1561 A.D. (Mehrauli).
31. Masjid Adhchini.
32. Masjid Abul Khair, Chitli Qabr, Old Delhi.

All the mosques mentioned above not only served a religious purpose but have also played a role in sociocultural and political life of Delhi at different times.

The ancient indigenous, Hindu buildings in Delhi could not survive, either due to lack of patronage or because early Muslim rulers were not tolerant of other faiths. Hindu temples were destroyed and their materials were used to make other structures. New temples and other religious places were not allowed to be constructed. Except some dilapidated structures at Suraj Kund at Lal Kot, Asok edicts at East of Kailash (a colony in South Delhi), near ISKCON Temple, temple relics of the Qutub Mosque and the Iron Pillar at Mehrauli, it becomes very difficult to trace old religious structures of the Hindu period in Delhi still in good condition.

Jizya was one such and very powerful way to spread Islam. Jizya was a 'tax' imposed on the non-Muslims. It was imposed on those (i) who did not believe in God, the last day, and the distinction between the tabooed (haram) and the non-tabooed (halal) drawn by God and his apostle, (ii) those of the scripturaries who did not accept Islam.

1. It is a Jihad provision, not a fiscal one, as sought usually to be made out;
2. In the matter of liability for jizya, scripturaries and other non-Muslims share the same fate;
3. It presupposes Islam's 'eminent domain' over the other communities.
4. It was meant to be an alternative to killing, forcible conversion, enslavement and ransom. Thereby, it transpires to be a kind of compensation fine, an indulgence tax;
5. It was a badge of humiliation for being a non-Muslim, of utter servility to Islamdom, of abject surrender to the will of God; liability to pay jizya is abject surrender to the will of Islamdom the amount of jizya does not matter.
6. It did not in value any obligation on the part of Islamdom towards the jizya paying individuals or communities, save of course the negative one of non-exterminations;
7. The long term policy behind it appears to be to compel or motivate the non-Muslims slowly to embrace Islam. It was thus a camouflaged engine of repression to that end;
8. A secondary motive behind it appears to be love of power and greed of pelf. Thus in effect it was also an engine of exploitation; and

9. Finally, jizya seems to be based on the principle that the life and property of the communities conquered by the Muslims in Jihad was at the disposal of the latter, who could enslave or kill them at will.[26] But they were let live in the hope of their conversion in course of time on the one hand and as sources of revenue by way of jizya, Karz (Land-Tax) et cetera on the other, as an alternative to death and conversion. In Fiqh literature, highly humiliating procedures were adopted for realizing jizya. Qazi Mughisu'd-Din, told Ala-ud-Din Khilji that 'if the jizya-collector asks a Hindu for silver, the latter should offer gold in all humility. If the collector wants to spit into the mouth, the latter should open his mouth without demur, so as to enable the former to spit into it.'[27]

The early rulers of Muslim religion were very cruel to their enemies on the one hand and on the other they were very enthusiastic to create their own structures so that they are remembered later on. Ala-ud-Din had 7000 construction workers in his service. They not only built their own forts, but also Tombs, apart from mosques. Some important Tombs are as follows:

1. Iltutmish Tomb (1235 A.D.)
2. Tomb of Imam Zamin (1539 A.D.)
3. Sultan Ghari's Tomb (1231 A.D.)
4. Ghyis-ud-Din's Tomb (1320–4 A.D.).
5. Lal Gumbad
6. Grave of Sheikh Hasan Tahir (1503 A.D.)
7. Bahlul Lodi Tomb (1489 A.D.)
8. Soami Nagar Tomb (15th Century)
9. Firoz Shah Tomb (1354 A.D.)
10. Tughluq Tombs (late 14th Century) Hauz Khas
11. Tomb and Mosque of Shah Alam (14th Century) near Timarpur, Wazirabad
12. Fateh Khan's Tomb, Qadam Sharif (1376 A.D.)
13. Bhuli Bhatiyari Ka Mahal (late 14th Century)
14. Malchha – on the Ridge
15. Mubarak Shah Tomb
16. Bare and Chhote Khan ka Gumbad
17. Bagh-i-Alam ka Gumbad

Sultans, 'Ulemas and Sufis'

Twenty eight sultans of three different dynasties succeeded to the throne of Delhi from 1206 to 1413 A.D. They belonged to the same race, but different not only in their intellectual faculties, personal tastes and outlooks, but also in their theories and ideals of the state. Some were highly learned in religious methods and other sciences while others were little educated or illiterate. Some of them tried to enforce the Sharia; the others did not care for it. Some even thought it to be impractical. Some wished to establish a new religion. Even if they were differing in personal beliefs and individual ideas, but all of them were obliged by some political factors to uphold Islam as it was the religion of their fighting force and a stimulant against their enemy.

They had to deal with the religious leaders, the Ulema and the Sufis. Though most of the Ulema's were also Sufis.

In the past, there had been great Empires, but on the eve of Muslim invasion India was divided into numerous local states. The Muslim conquests brought a new level of political integration; it brought a new elite and distinct form of Muslim civilization. The cultural policy, took time to develop. The Delhi Sultanate was aggressively Muslim, exclusive and hostile to the political participation of non-Muslims. The Delhi Sultans stressed the allegiance to the Caliph and support for the judicial establishment of the Ulema. Some rulers like Ala-al-Din sought Sufi rather than Ulema support for sultans, since the Sufis shared a hierarchical concept of political society. Just as the Sufi saints stood at the apex of the universal spiritual order, the sultans stood at the head of society. The Muslim concept of Kingship derived substantially from the Iranian Muslim tradition. He must follow the teaching of the Prophet, enforce the Sharia suppress rebellions, punish heretics, subordinate and unbelievers, and protect the weak against the strong.

The early Delhi Sultanate did not try to incorporate the local Hindu lords. The first gesture of the Muslim conquest was to destroy major Hindu temples and replace them with the great mosques, whose size, design, and inscription was symbols of Muslim domination. Quwwat-ul-Islam and the Qutub Minar at Delhi are some such structures.

Only in the fourteenth century, the Tughluq Dynasty began to absorb the Hindu motifs in to Muslim architecture. With the Islamic conquest, Muslim scholars, scribes, Sufis, poets and intellectuals flocked to India, seeking this patronage of the new regimes, organizing madarsas and khanqahs and opening the way for the conversion of Indian people to Islam. Till the fourteenth century, only 20 to 25 per cent people were converted to Islam and Islam remained confined to the Indus valley, North-West India and Bengal. In the fourteenth century, it spread to Assam and Deccan. The aristocracy remained of Muslim and only lower classes Hindu converted to Islam. Conversions also happened due to the growth of the cities. Cities broke down caste and geographical barriers to social interaction. People who had given up their social and political status and who were ambitious to make careers under a new regime, such as itinerant merchants, workers and peddlers, fugitive peasants and vagabonds, found in Islam a unifying ideology.

Sufi khanqahs may similarly have served as centers for converting rural Indians to Islam. In some cases Islam correlated with important changes in regional societies. In the North-West provinces, where the Jats, a hunter-gatherer and pastoral population, came into contact with a state based agricultural society and a literate form of civilization, Islam became the religion of the people who were becoming peasants; same thing happened in Bengal.

Ulemas also played a great role in promotion of Islam. There were two types of Ulemas one was those who were performing various administrative functions of the Government and others did not like to join state service, but were engaged themselves in teaching and furtherance of learning. However, the Ulema of both categories enjoyed the royal support and respect and received *Iqta*'s (financial support). All the madarsas were run by the financial help of the Sultan; the madarsas were preparing the students for qadiship and other administrative posts, most of the *Danishmands* and Ulemas went to government services and constituted an important post of the bureaucracy. They served as *Wazirs* (revenue officers) *Qadis* (judges) Shaykhu-l-Islam, Mustafwi-i-mumaliks (Auditor General), *Mushrifs* (Accountants) *Safirs* (emissaries), *Katibs*, imams, Muftis, Poets et cetera. They participated in politics and belonged to respective political groups. The case of Qadi Minhaj-us-Siraj is one such example who deserted Malik Qubacha and joined Iltutmish; afterwords he supported Bahram Shah against Maliks and Amirs.

Some of the Qadis had matrimonial relations with the ruling house. The Chief Qadi was the highest judicial authority below the Sultan and exercised both civil and criminal jurisdiction. He might be appointed for life or on hereditary basis.

Historical facts indicate that in the early period of Islam the education of the Ulemas was very low, Sultans were sometimes in a difficult position. On the one hand, he was exhorted to be the Ulema to adopt the religious injunctions and champion their cause, on the other, he was pressed by some political factions and Amirs and Maliks to disregard the religious principles and take care of their political interest.

When Ala-ud-Din Khilji became king, he came to the conclusion that policy and government are one thing and the rules and decrees of the Sharia another. Royal Commands belong to the king and Sharia decrees to the 'Ulema.' The Sultan was not bound by the Sharia.

An important conversation which took place between Sultan Ala-ud-Din Khilji and Qadi Mughith-ud-din makes it clear what policy the Sultans were adopting and how Ulemas' considering the administrative affairs. The Qadi was a very learned person and the Sultan loved and trusted him over other

Ulemas. Before this conversation started, the Qadi sought the security of his life.

The Sultan asked four questions:

The first question was about the position and treatment of the Hindus. The Qadi said that as per the opinion of Abu Hanifa, tribute (jizya) should be levied on Hindus.

The second question was about the theft, bribery, and embezzlement committed by government servants. The Qadi said that as per the Sharia the Sultan could punish as he deemed fit, but the Sharia punishment by cutting the hands was not applicable to those who stole from the public treasury.

The third question was about the booty which was acquired by the Sultan from Deogiri. The Qadi declared that this was acquired through the strength of the army of Muslims so it should be kept in the treasury.

The fourth question was about the limit of the claim of the Sultan on the public treasury. The answer was that the Sultan should take his salary as per the Sharia as is fixed for the troopers, that is 134 *takas*. He can take more if his requirement were not met with it, but the Sultan should not take more than this amount and should not give huge amount of money and gold to his wives as it would cause perdition hereafter.

Next day, the Sultan gave lots of money to the Qadi, who accepted it. The Sultan remarked that he had no intention of implementing the Sharia as he did not know what was lawful and unlawful according to Sharia, but followed what he thought to be for the good of the state; moreover, people had changed since the time of the Prophet. In spite of Ala-ud-Din out rightly rejecting the Sharia, the Ulemas and Sufis too, regarded him as a supporter of the Sharia.

After the short reign of Ghiyas-ud-Din Tughluq (1320–5 A.D.), his son, Mohammad bin Tughluq (1325–52 A.D.), succeeded to the throne. He was in complete contrast to his predecessors. He knew the Quran and the Hedaya by heart. He was a disciple of Sheikh Ala-ud-Din, the grandson of Baba Farid Ganj Shakar. He was a follower of the Sharia in state affairs also. He was the first Sultan who tried to propagate Islam through the state machinery. He rendered justice according to Sharia and did not discriminate. He was a patron of learning too. There were one thousand madarsas in Delhi and thousands of *takas* were assigned by the Sultan for teaching. He would dine with hundreds of *fuqarah* and had conversations with them on various problems. His regime had most of the characteristics to which Ulema either aspired or had been demanding from the inception of the Sultanate.

But even because of his pro- Ulema and Sufi attitude and pro-Sharia actions, he was the first Sultan who was denounced by the Ulemas as Kafir, Nimrod and Pharaoh. They accused him of revolt against Islam and condemned him to death for 'the Sharia approved of his execution'. The Ulemas, the Qadis, the khatibs, the faqihs, the mashaikhs and sufis urged a general revolt against him and aroused some chiefs of the army and governors to defy him.

The real cause of the Ulemas' bitterness was that the Sultan did not show the same hypocritical reverence for them as was shown by earlier Sultans and he transferred them to outside Delhi to preach Islam, which they felt was very inconvenient. The other aspect of the treatment was the Sultan's strictures and impartiality in administration of justice. He did not spare his own brother-in-law (Amir Saif-ud-Din Ghada). But the Ulema of those days considered themselves superior to others.

Jalal-ud-Din Khilji had to adopt some insinuative means to kill a conspirator Sufi, Sheikh Sidi Maula, when the Ulema tried to save him. Sultan Bahram (1240–62 A.D.) and Malik Qubacha did the same mistake of punishing some Ulemas and faced their opposition.

After the death of Mohammad-binTughluq, Ulemas and Sufis selected Firoz as the new Sultan and they obtained the upper hand and all political trouble ceased. The new Sultan, Firoz Shah Tughluq granted the religious leaders huge aids and stipends to gain their sympathies.

From the very beginning, Firoz Shah became a passive instrument in the hands of Ulemas and Sufis and continued to play the same role throughout his whole reign. The affairs of the state were carried on practically by the Wazir and policies were dictated by the Ulemas. He abolished twenty taxes as desired by the Ulemas and imposed jizya on Hindus including Brahmins. No post of influence was given to any Hindu. All the heretics, heterodox Muslims and some Hindu preachers were persecuted and condemned to death.[28] In fact, rigour and strictness was one sided. As a result, the entire machinery of the government deteriorated. The rebels established their autonomous states and the era of the provincial dynasties started.

In fact, in the first hundred years of the Sultanate, the Ulema played the part of second fiddle. They were with the state chariot but were not allowed to determine the political developments. The second phase was of Mohammad-bin Tughluq. The Ulemas were in better position; but the Sultan wanted them to work for Islam; this they resented for 25 years and ultimately succeeded in it.

At the time of Firoz Shah, the Ulmas and Sufis got victory and they ruled the state. They carried out their reactionary plans with full freedom and applied the Sharia in any way they liked.

At home they were rigorous and cruel with their weak subjects who held contrary views or faith, but were timid and weak in face of the armed rebels and enemies and did not dare to wage war. This policy and relationship between the Ulemas and the King continued during the reigns of later Sultans and the Mughal Emperors.

In the history of Islam, Imam Abdul Hamid Al-Ghazali of Iran is considered as one of the greatest scholars, authors and foremost thinkers. During the Middle Ages, his authority as interpreter of the Quranic verses in the light of his spiritual investigation of the underlying 'hidden wisdom' of Quran was almost unsurpassed and unchallenged. His unique contribution to Islamic thought and behavior was the reconciling adjustment of this 'intuition insight into the Quranic dicta with the Vedantic, Greek, Neo-Platonic and Buddhist metaphysical speculation and philosophies touching on mysticism. His most famous work, *Ihya-ul-uloom-ud-Din* (The Revival of the Spiritual Sciences) is a treasury of Sufi principles, practices and characteristics which are followed by all the Great Sufi dervishes of the world.

Sufi dervishes were the special class of Muslim ascetics or mystics who, by virtue of their amazing spiritual powers and overwhelming piety and devotion, were directly selected by God to guide mankind on the right path of truth and right course. They have rendered invaluable service not only in building up but also in polishing and preserving the moral, spiritual, social, cultural and even political behavior and character of the people. Chishtia *silsila* of Sufism is one such silsila of Sufis in India and Khwaja Muin-ud-Din Hassan Chishti Sanjari is the founder of this silsila. He was born in 1141 A.D. in Sijistan (Persia) and was the descendant of a noble family coming down in the direct lineage of the Holy Prophet Mohammad. He was directly and divinely inspired from Mecca and Madina to go to Ajmer (Hindustan) to preach the gospel of universal truth and brotherhood through Sufism. At the age of 52, he came to India and settled down at Ajmer and for 44 years he conducted his mission. In 1236 A.D. he died. His noble teachings are as follows:

> Love all and hate none. Mere talk of peace will avail you naught. Mere talk of God and religion will not take you far. Bring out all the latent powers of your being and reveal the full magnificence of your immortal self. Be surcharged with peace and joy, and scatter them wherever you are and wherever you go. Be a blazing flame of truth, be a beauteous blossom of love and be a smoothing palm of peace, with your spiritual light, dispel the darkness of ignorance, dissolve the clouds of discord and war and spread goodwill, peace and harmony among the people. Never seek any help, charity or favour from anybody except God. Never go to the courts of kings but never refuse to bless and help the needy and the poor, the widow and the orphan, if they come to your door. This is your mission of peace to serve the people of Hindustan. Carryout dutifully so that I assure Pir, may not be ashamed of any shortcoming on your part before the Almighty God and our holy predecessors in the 'Silsila' on the day of Qayamat.

Hazrat Qutub-ud-Din Kaki

Under the cover of conquest, the invasions and pressure of Mongols, Muslim scholars, scribes, Sufis, poets and intellectuals flocked to India, seeking their patronage of the new regions organizing madarsas, khanqahs and opening the way for the conversion of Indian people to Islam. The Mongols not only destroyed centres of learning but they made the life of peace loving people miserable. Hindustan was safe and vast place for them. Bakhtiyar Kaki became the disciple of Muin-ud-Din Chishti at Baghdad. He was from Fergana (Turkistan). At the age of twnty he lost his father, who was called Khwaja Sahib (Kamal-ud-din Ahmad Musa). He came to India (Ajmer) along with Muin-ud-Din Chishti and later settled in Delhi (Mehrauli). He was one of such dervishes who came to India along with the early invaders. In 1188, he performed the namaz of victory at Delhi. The relations of Mohammad Ghori were not good with him. In his early period, he stayed at Kilokhari and later settled at Mehrauli. He had good relations with Iltutmish. During this period, he converted many Hindus to Islam. He married in Delhi and had two sons. Sayyid Ahmad and Sayyid Mahmud, who were also buried near his grave. One story is very popular regarding Khwaja. One day, when Khwaja Qutub-ud-Din and Sultan Iltutmish were having a stroll in the fort of Delhi, a beautiful woman suddenly appeared on the scene, wailing and crying. She told the king that she was carrying the child of Khwaja Qutub-ud-Din in her womb and the king should arrange for her *nikah* (marriage) with the Khwaja. By this accusation of the woman, all were taken aback and upset. The Khwaja himself

Dargah Hazrat Bakhtiyar Kaki, Mehrauli.

Hawa Mahal or Zafar Mahal, Mehrauli.

was aghast at her statement. He turned his face towards Ajmer and invoked the help of his Pir-o-Murshid. In the next moment, the Pir came personally to this spot; he enquired from Kaki Sahib about the whole thing. He enquired from the child directly who was in the womb of the lady. The child declared that the woman was instigated and there was no truth in this accusation. To this everybody present there realized the truth. This was a nefarious plot to bring disgrace upon that holy saint. The plot failed. Even the holy persons have not been spared by the wicked in the human history.

He died in 1235 A.D. at the age of 67. King Iltutmish took personal interest in his burial. His disciple, Sheikh Farid Ganj Shakar, brought the mud from the Hauz Shamshi and put it on the grave of this Pir; till date, the grave is washed with that mud. The later Mughals built a *mahal* (Hawa Mahal) near these graves and used to stay near by; they also desired that after death they too be buried around the grave of this saint. In the compound there is one masjid, and one graveyard of Nawabs of Jhajjar; one grave of Nawab Ali Khan, one of his wives; his son, Faiz Mohammad. Abul Rehman Khan, the last Nawab of Jhajjar is also buried here; he was hanged by the British in 1857 A.D. One grave of an important eunuch of Aurangzeb, Sara Mohammad Khan is also there. This person was the custodian of the Fort of Gwalior and Agra. Four more graves are of Mirza Ilahi Bakhsh's family. Maulana Fakhr-ud-Din, Nawabs of Banda, Badr-ud-Din Ghaznavi, Imam-ud-Din Ibadat, Jabte Khan and his wife, whose son was Ghulam Qadir, a notorious fellow, Akbar Shah Sani (1837 A.D.), Shah Alam Sani (1806 A.D.) Mirza Farrukh, the son of last king of Delhi, who was killed in 1857 A.D., Maulana Fakhr-ud-Din and many more are buried there. Even a place for the burial of the last king of Delhi, Bahadur Shah Zafar was earmarked, who died in Rangoon and was buried there.

There are many strange incidents narrated by Hazrat Khwaja Qutub-ud-Din. In one such incident he narrated the story of a Fakir and that Fakir is said to be Hazrat Khwaja: that unless and until a Fakir gives up people's company, gives away all he receives, sits in seclusion, eats little, sleeps little, speaks little, he cannot attain 'nearness to God'. (Fawaid-us-Slikin part I) He lived a very simple life and never accepted any *nazrana* (gift) from the ruling Chiefs. Whatever was there in his Khanqah was distributed to the people, when nothing was left to give, simple water was served to them. He loved 'sama' and died in the state of ecstasy. He said that he learned the Holy Quran by heart by the grace of Allah, who directed him to repeat 'Surah Yusuf'. (A chapter of the Holy Quran) He used to say that

> A Sufi must always remain deeply absorbed in the love of God so much so that if, in his state of 'Sukr' both the heaven and earth enter into his chest, he should not feel their presence. If a Sufi in the path of his love and devotion to God complains against the hardships and privations, he cannot claim himself to be true lover and friend of God; he is only a hypocrite and liar. True divine friendship means that whatever, good or bad, he gets from the 'friend' (God) he must take it as a great boon and blessing from him because even by any tortuous tests, his 'friend' at least remembered him. Therefore, Hazrat Rabia Basri, the women saint, used to feel sorry and unhappy on the day when no new calamity or hardship befell her. She thought that her friend (God) had forgotten her. On the other hand, when

> she had a new calamity or trouble, she felt extremely happy because she took it as a token of her 'friend's kind remembrance of her. Hazrat Khwaja Muin-ud-Din Chishti also says that 'a Sufi who cannot bear the hardships and privations in love of his "friend" ' (God) has no right to claim his friendship, because a friend's torture comes only to a friend. The day these hardships are stopped, he should consider that he is being deprived of his friend's attention, blessings and boon. In Sufism, the names of blessings, favours or boons are tortures, hardships and privations.

The stage a Sufi must never disclose it because by doing so, he would be deprived of all other stages already attained by him. Hazrat Khwaja Qutub-ud-Din advocated strongly the strict adherence to the laws of Sharia for a Sufi.[29]

He had 27 *khalifas* (disciples) who carried on his teachings in Sufism in different parts of India, apart from Delhi and its adjoining provinces. In the contemporary period, his Dargah is also famous for *Phool Walon ki Sair,* where every year a fair is organized in the month of July. When Jahangir Shah was exterminated to Allahabad, his mother was very much upset and went to many places in Mehrauli—the Dargah of Bakhtiyar Kaki and the temple of Yogmaya. She vowed that if her son was allowed to come to Delhi she would place a *pankha* to the Dargah and Yogmaya Temple. It so happened that within six months the Prince was allowed to come to Delhi by the British. From then onwards, with a small interruption; it continued till date. It was a very important occasion some 100 years back; people of Delhi used to participate in large numbers, even today, with the passage of time this interest is diminishing but still the symbol of unity between Hindus and Muslims is demonstrated.

Hazrat Khwaja Farid-ud-Din Masud Ganj Shakar

He was the disciple of Khwaja Qutub-ud-Din Bakhtiyar Kaki. He was one of the most brilliant stars of the Chistia order of Sufi Darvish in India and is held in high esteem for his awfully difficult *mujahedas* or mortifications which enabled him to reach the pinnacle of glory in the realm of Sufism. He enjoyed 21 titles of which 'Ganj Shakar' became most popular. There are four different stories relating to this title. One is when he was getting training in spiritualism under his Pir, he was asked to go on fast for seven days at a stretch and was given a place over Ghazni Gate, at Mehrauli. After this fast, when he was going to his Pir's Khanqah, his foot accidentally slipped and he fell down in the mud and some mud entered his mouth; it became sugar. He narrated this incident to his Pir. His Pir said that if it had happened thus, then God would make him a very sweet personality and he would become sweet tongued for the benefit of the people. After this, he was called 'Ganj Shakar'. He lost his father at the age of 7 and his mother arranged for his education in Multan in a mosque where he met his Pir, who advised him to undertake a tour and study more. He went to Ghazni, Baghdad, Sawastan, Badakshan, Jerusalem, Mecca and Madina for 18 years and met very renowned Sufi saints.

The year of 1235 A.D. proved to be the most auspicious year for both the temporal as well as spiritual affairs of Hindustan. On 23 March 1235, Hazrat Khwaja Muin-ud-Din Chishti of Ajmer died. On 7 May 1235. King of Delhi the Sultan Sams-ud-Din Iltutmish, died. On 7 December 1235, Khwaja Qutub-ud-Din Bakhtiyar Kaki of Delhi died. Delhi was not peaceful for Sufis; there was struggle for the throne. By 1290 A.D., the Khiljis liquidated the Slave Dynasty forever and took possession of the throne of Delhi. In this atmosphere, Khwaja Kaki decided to leave Delhi. The people of Hansi wanted him there. He went to Ajmer to seek guidance from the Khwaja and remained in *chilla* for 40 days and ultimately got the clue. He decided to settle at Pakpatan (Ajodhan). Many plots for his murder were attempted. The Qazi of Ajodhan opposed him and tried many times to kill him.

Hazrat Khwaja Farid-ud-Din performed many *karamaat* or miracles in his life. The holy saints are gifted with divine powers. They can bring back an arrow even after it is released from the bow. Bernard Shaw said 'A miracle is an event which creates "faith", does not deceive. Therefore, it is not a fraud but a miracle.'

As per Islamic principles and faith, miracles do, and must, happen on the authority of the Sufi saint. No Sufi uses miracles for the sake of self-aggrandizement. He is obliged to display them unavoidably to fight the 'devil in man' only to meet extraordinary emergencies, like other great Sufi, Hazrat Baba Farid-ud-Din followed this rule scrupulously and avoided miracles so far as possible.

The most important step in the life of a Sufi is to control his *nafs* (appetitive Soul). He can never achieve perfection in Sufism without complete subjugation of his nafs and hence he has no desire or attraction for a married life. It is the Sharia which is also an indispensable obligation of his creed and career, as important as the control of nafs that obliges a Sufi to marry although many great Sufis adhered to celibacy. Hazrat Khwaja Nizam-ud-Din Aulia of Delhi and his successor Hazrat Khwaja Naseer-ud-Din Chirag Dilli did not marry and remained in celibacy all their life. Ghaus-ul-Azam Hazrat Abdul Qadar Jilani of Baghdad—one of the greatest Sufi married at the Age of 51 years. Hazrat Khwaja Muin-ud-Din Chishti married at the age of 52 years and Hazrat Baba Farid-ud-Din had to marry at the age of 52 years. He had 3 wives. Having fulfilled his divine mission as a true servant of God and a true friend of the suffering humanity with a brilliant saintly career, extending over a period of 75 years, as one of India's greatest Sufi saints, Hazrat Baba Farid-ud-Din also quit the stage of this world and merged his identity into the unity of his 'friend'

(God) in 1262 A.D. at the ripe age of 92 years. There is a difference of opinion among the notable chronicles of his life. But the majority of them agree to the above mentioned date. He breathed his last in prayer. He was buried only when his successor, Hazrat Nizam-ud-Din Aulia reached Ajodhan; today, there is magnificent Mausoleum over his grave. During his lifetime, kings of Slave Dynasty, that is, Qutub-ud-Din Aibak, Aaraam Shah, Iltutmish, Rukn-ud-Din, Firoz Shah I, Sultana Raziya Begum, Muiz-ud-Din Bahram Shah, Sultan Nasir-ud-Din Mahmud and Sultan Balban ruled over Delhi and some of them were the followers of the saint. Some rulers also tortured some of the Sufi saints.

Hazrat Syedi Maula

Hazrat Baba Farid Sakar Gunj once advised Syedi Maula to avoid the company of the high and wealthy persons. To avoid the atmosphere of Delhi, he chose Ajodhan for his Khanqah. He never accepted any gift from wealthy people and kings. He lived very simple life throughout his life and preached the same for other. Syedi Maula, was a Darvesh, travelled through all the Muslim countries and met many saints. He also came to Ajodhan and enjoyed the company of Hazrat Farid. After sometime, the Darvesh desired to go to Delhi and set up a Khanqah of his own. The Baba said that as far as possible he should stay away and avoid the company of kings and their courtiers because such company is dangerous for Darveshes and often proves the cause of their destruction. Hazrat Syedi Maula come to Delhi during the period of Sultan Ghiyas-ud-Din Balban and set up a magnificent Khanqah. In a short period due to the very good hospitality of Syedi Maula, thousands of people began to come to him. His hospitality even surpassed the king's hospitality, people were puzzled to see Syedi Maula's huge expenses in charity. The public of Delhi believed that the Darvesh knows the science of *Keemia* as he had no other source of income, nor did he accept any offer, *nazrana*, nor had he any *jagir*. He lived simply, with no women, no servants. He prayed most of the time. He strictly followed all the Islamic principles. He did not attend the weekly Friday prayers. After the downfall of Slave Dynasty and the rise of the Khiljis, the expense of his kitchen doubled. Many government officials and even Akbar-Khan-e-Khana, the heir apparent become his devotee. The Khanqah of Syedi Maula actually became the rendezvous of the king's courtiers, *Umrah*, and high officials. The historians of this period recorded that 500 *mans* of meat, 200 mans of misri (refined sugar) 1000 mans of floor and 200 mans of sugar were consumed every day. The Ex-high officials of the regime were staying in the Khanqah even during the night. The Qazi, Jalal-ud-Din Kasani, was the Chief Justice of Delhi in the reign of Jalal-ud-Din Khilji. He was a very intriguing person. A plot was enacted to kill the King. This was detected and

Syedi Maula along with the Qazi and a few more were called by the King for enquiry; others were let off but Syedi Maula was kept there for further questioning. The king asked one Sheikh Abu Bakar Tus to advise him in this matter. To this, one of the followers of Tus, named Behri, attacked Syedi Maula with a razor and cut his throat. And the younger son of the king, Arkil Khan, who had a grudge against his elder brother and was a devotee of Syedi Maula, signalled a person to tramp the saint under an elephant, which he did, so Syedi was crushed to death.

Maulana Ziya-ud-Din Barni in his *Tarikh-i- Firoz Shahi* had narrated this event as he was present there. That year, a devastating famine also engulfed the kingdom. Thousands of innocent people perished due to starvation, while hundreds of them committed suicide by jumping into the river Yamuna. Many intrigues and mutinies were faced by the king. He repented later on. He was also mercilessly murdered.

In fact, the Sultan Jalal-ud-Din Khilji, who was known for his respect for the Darvesh did not behave properly. Even Syedi Maula did not heed to the advice of Farid Ganj Shakar, not to keep company with wealthy people, the king, and not to receive any gifts from them. The same advice he gave to Sheikh Badr-ud-Din Ghaznavi, whose disciple was arrested in a case of embezzlement.

Hazrat Khwaja Nizam-ud-Din Aulia

After the demise of Hazrat Baba Farid-ud-Din Ganj Shakar, Hazrat Khwaja Nizam-ud-Din Aulia succeeded him as his successor. He played a great role in the cultural, spiritual and ethical life of Delhi. In addition to his spiritual attainment and perfection, he was a most distinguished scholar and administrative genius. He also founded a Khanqah at Ghyaspur, Delhi. His disciples were spread all over India.

His father, Syed Ahmed Bukhara, was a very pious person as was his mother, Bibi Zulikha. His grandfather came to Hindustan from Bukhara and first settled at Lahore and then at Badayun, where Aulia Sahib was born on 19 October 1238 A.D. However, some writers give the year as 1243 A.D. After the death of his father when he was just five years old, he came to Delhi during the period of Sultan Balban along with his mother and sister. He studied under the guidance of Maulana Kamal-ud-Din Zahid. In Delhi, he lived near the house of Hazrat Khwaja Najib-ud-Din (the brother of Hazrat Baba Farid). Hazrat Aulia wanted to become a Qazi but was not advised by Khwaja Najib-ud-Din, so he went to Ajodhan and remained under the guidance of Baba Farid. (He visited Ajodhan ten times, three times during his Pir-o-Murshid's life time and seven times later).

He witnessed the following rulers, but remained detached with all Sultans:

Balban	-	1266–87 A.D.
Kaikubad	-	1287–90 A.D.
Jalal-ud-Din Khilji	-	1290–6 A.D.
Ala-ud-Din Khilji	-	1296–1316 A.D.
Mubarak Khilji	-	1316–20 A.D.
Khusru Khan	-	1320 A.D.
Ghiyas-ud-Din Tughluq	-	1320–5 A.D.
Mohammad Bin Tughluq	-	1325–51 A.D.

The abovementioned rulers ruled Delhi, but none could change Nijam-ud-Din Aulia's decision to live in solitude. Khizr Khan was his disciple, but Aulia never took interest in his political life. Mubarak Khilji said bad words against the Aulia but he never bothered.

During the period of the Aulia, many new cities were established by various kings. The Mongols did not attack during Iltutmish's time; his descendants also followed the same policy and Delhi flourished. Balban built fifteen different clusters of people such as from Samarkand, Kashger, Gore and Khata et cetera. Aulia praised the religious policy of Balban. During the period of Ala-ud-Din Khilji, the Mongols attacked Delhi. People used to come to the Khanqah of the Aulia during the attack of the Mongols. In this period, goods were very cheap, trade was flourishing and food was very good and cheap. Ala-ud-Din Khilji never entered the Dargah of the Aulia but he never interfered in the affairs

Dargah of Mai Sahiba, Mother of Hazrat Nizamuddin Auliya, Village Adhchini.

of the Aulia either. Mubarak Khilji and Ghiyas-ud-Din Tughluq could not understand this behavior and they tried to interfere in the affairs of the Aulia's Khanqah and accordingly suffered. By this time three *silsilas* of Sufis: *Chishtiya*, *Suhrawardi* and *Firdausi* were established in India. In his early days at Delhi, Aulia lived in extreme poverty: for days together he had no food, there was problem of house and security of his mother and sister. His mother was a very pious lady. She lived in poverty but always remembered God. She had predicted that one day her son would be very fortunate person. The Aulia also loved her very much. When he was troubled by Mubarak Khilji, he went to the grave of his mother and got solace and prayed there. The prayers were answered in a positive way. Her grave is in Adhchini village near Mehrauli. In Delhi, he was guided by Sheikh Najib-ud-Din Mutvakil, who remained very poor but never allowed the Aulia to take the job of Qazi. In Ajodhan also, Aulia remained poor and many times without food, despite the fact that the dargah was receiving lots of things; but all were distributed among the poor people.

In 1265 A.D., Nizam-ud-Din moved to Ghyaspur (now it is called Nizam-ud-Din basti). It was away from the din of the capital; it was a small village. He spent the rest of his life in the Khanqah constructed by one of his disciples, Maulana Ziya-ud-Din. This was visited by men from all walks of life irrespective of caste and creed, rich and poor, even some princes were also devout followers

Chillah Khana, Hazrat Nizamuddin, near Humayun's Tomb.

of the Aulia. He was a man of vast erudition and singular piety; he used to spend his days in fasting, prayers and teaching. His way of life and magnetic personality drew around him a host of disciples whom he guided in their quest for spiritual salvation. No one went back disappointed from his door. He wished to become a man of perfect virtue and to teach others without weariness. His whole career was one continuous struggle against sin, against poverty and against the self. He is reputed to have insisted upon his disciples complete severance form all worldly ties. He was not even ready to permit them to earn their livelihood. To him, it appeared that the feeling of security about one's means of livelihood would simply depend not upon God but upon somebody else.

Visitors to the Khanqah used to bring gifts to the Aulia; he would receive their private gifts only to give them away to others. The popularity of the saint did receive the attention of contemporary Sultans of Delhi. He lived through the reign of eight rulers of Delhi, but he never cared for their favour or frown. Except Qutub-ud-Din Mubarak Shah (1316–20 A.D.) and Ghiyas-ud-Din Tughluq (1320–5 A.D.), who disturbed the peace of the Aulia, no other Sultan could dare to challenge the Aulia, rather, they were influenced by him and were respectful to him. The Aulia never begged any favour from these Sultans; rather, he refused many a time some favour offered to him. He always remembered the words of his Pir, Sheikh Farid-ud-Din Ganj-i-Shakar, 'Do not make friends with kings and nobles. Consider their visit to your home as fatal (for your spirit). Every Darvesh who makes friends with kings and nobles will end badly.'[30]

He was prepared to leave Delhi, if the Sultans disturb him in his peace. This he demonstrated many times. The above mentioned two Sultans became enemies of the Aulia, either due to his popularity among the people or because they suspected some plot against themselves, which was wrongly advised by some persons. We do not find on record any such substance in this matter. The hostile Sultans could not make out a case against the Aulia, accusing him of having dabbled in politics. He occupies a prominent place among the spiritual benefactors of mankind. Quite in keeping with the style of Sufi saints, his sterling qualities could never be tempted by any material gain. He used to say that the main object of man's creation is the love of the Supreme Being. In his view, the love of God implied the love of humanity without which the former would be incomplete. He spared no pains to inculcate this ethical ideal in the mind of his followers. His concept of life is reflected in his own utterance.

> A Muslim must abstain from doing harm of any kind to anybody; he must also abstain from every sin and should protect his eyes, tongue and hands from an undesirable act; he should direct his eyes and tongue towards the truth and keep glorifying Allah steering clear of every doubt that might develop in his mind ...

> the heart is a mirror which is in itself clear; but sins cover it with dust which can only be removed by repeating the names of Allah and his Prophet Mohammad[31]

Barni[32] gives us a good account of the impact of Nizam-ud-Din Aulia's noble presence on the character of the people and the moral of the society.

> All people, believing in him, tried to emulate him in devotion and virtue. Men and women, young and old, low and mean servants and slaves and even small boys had began to offer their prayers regularly. Rich and benevolent persons had constructed in several pleasant spots between the city and Ghyaspur terraces with thatched roofs and had wells dug there. The terraces were supplied with large jars full of water, clay jugs and mats, and keepers and reciters were posted there so that people coming from or going to the monastery of the Sheikh may not feel inconvenient in making their ablutions at prayer times. In each of these terraces one saw crowds of people offering prayers. Perpetration or talk of crime had declined among the people, and they talked mostly of religions things ... There was no quarter in the city where after twenty days or a month there was no gathering of the pious listening to Sufi music and weeping in ecstasy. Sultan Ala-ud-Din himself, with all his family, had great faith in the Sheikh and the hearts of all classes of people were inclined towards virtue and piety. Never did the name of wine and women, crime and sin, gambling or other like practices, profane the lips of people during the latter portion of Ala-ud-Din's reign. Most of the students, noble and great men who attended upon the Sheikh were seen to be busy in the study of books on Sufism or the Islamic Law.

When Ghiyas-ud-Din Tughluq was admired against the Aulia, the Sultan ordered the saint to quit Delhi before he entered it. The Sultan was coming from Lakhnauti to Delhi with a large loot and a reception was organized at the village Afghanpur near Tughlaqabad, in the outskirts of Delhi. The Sheikh said without getting perturbed, '*Hanuz Dilli Door Ast*' (Delhi is yet far off). The same thing happened. The Sultan died before entering his capital. During this period the Aulia was also becoming physically sick and weak, but he continued his religions duties as usual. He lived the life of a celibate, but he brought up the sons of his sister like his own sons. He liked Amir Khusrau, the great poet. A day before his death, he ordered his personal attendant, Iqbal, to distribute all that was in his *langar khana* and asked the people to take everything so that he may not have to give an account of the same before God. Just before his death on the morning of 18 Rabi-us-Sani 725 A.H., he distributed from his private *bughcha* presents to his various Khalifas and ordered them to go out to all directions of India to preach the gospel of truth and love. Handing over the traditional sacred relics to Hazrat Khwaja Nasir-ud-Din Chirag of Delhi, he said 'you must stay in Delhi and suffer the persecution of the people'. After this, he offered the morning prayers and sank. The whole city plunged into mourning. His body was taken to the present site of his Dargah from his Chilla-Khana which is near Humayun's Tomb.

Hazrat Sheikh Abul Fatah Rukn-ud-Din, grandson of Hazrat Khwaja Baha-ud-Din Zakaria Suhrawardi of Multan, had the honor of conducting his funeral service.

Sultan Mohammad bin Tughluq built a Tomb on his grave. The Aulia has already built a *bawri* (a pond), near his grave. Amir Khusrau, Jahan Ara Begum daughter of Shah Jahan, and many big personalities are buried in this dargah. Till date, people of all religions, from all over India and abroad come to this dargah for the blessings of the Aulia.

Timur, Babur, Humayun, Akbar, Jahangir, Shah Jahan, Aurangzeb and the later Mughal kings paid respects to this dargah and donated land and money to this dargah.

Hazrat Khwaja Nasir-ud-Din Mahmud, 'Chirag' of Delhi (725-757 A.H.)

He was appointed the spiritual successor by Hazrat Khwaja Nizam-ud-Din Aulia with the order that 'you shall have to stay in Delhi and suffer the persecution of the people'; he followed this order most dutifully. In the selection of the spiritual successor, it has always been the Divine will that must prevail. The successor had to serve a very hard apprenticeship for 20 years under his Pir-o-Murshid.

Hazrat Nizam-ud-Din Aulia too had to uphold the 'divine will'; he had to express, that '*Nizam Chahe Amir Ko Khuda Chahe Nasir Ko*' that is, Nizam-ud-Din wants Amir Khusru whereas God wants Nasir-ud-Din.

Historians differ about the lineage of Nasir-ud-Din which of course was a noble one; some claim his lineage from Hazrat Imam Husain while others say that he descended from the family of Hazrat Umar-ibn-Khatab, the second Khalifa. His forefathers came from Khurasan and his father was born in Lahore, later his family shifted to Faizabad (Awadh, India). He lost his father at the age of nine years. His mother arranged for his education. He became a scholar of Islamic subjects at an early age. At the age of 25 years, he renounced the world, remained in the jungles of Awadh, observed fasting and accompanied Darveshes.

According to Siyar-ul-Aulia and Mirat-ul-Asrat, Hazrat Nasir-ud-Din came to Delhi at the age of 43 years and joined the circle of Hazrat Nizam-ud-Din Aulia's *murids* (disciples). He served his Pir with great devotion. After his initiation, Hazrat Nasir-ud-Din devoted all his time to his spiritual training or *mujahedas* denying oneself food and water for days together. He went to stay with his mother in Awadh, but after some time he wanted to go to some lonely place and sought the permission for it from his Pir, which was denied, on the ground that 'you must stay among the people of God and suffer their intrusion with patience and toleration'. He had visited Delhi time and again but after the death of his mother he stayed at Delhi permanently.

After his succession, he shifted to 'Chirag Dilli' where his *mazaar* (tomb) stands up to this day. During his good times, although he himself used to fast daily, he ordered delicious food to be prepared and served to his guests and *mureeds*. He used to serve them personally and used to give his sermons at this time so that at the time of meal, one should think that gracious God is watching. One should eat for the sake of God and must think that whatever energy one gets from food, it would be spent in the devotion of God.

After hearing the praise of Hazrat Nasir-ud-Din, Hazrat Jalal-ud-Din Bukhari came all the way from Mecca to Delhi to meet Hazrat Nasir-ud-Din and after meeting him he was satisfied regarding all the comments he had heard. He always gave sermons on punctuality of namaz and moral and religions character. For 300 years Chishtiya mission humble fakirs, poor, famished, ragged but spiritually rich and brave Khalifas, fought the battles of truth most gracefully, defeating at every step the forces of materialism and evil, rescuing millions of people from the tyranny of oppression and putting them on the path of righteousness, peace and salvation. Sultan Mohammad Tughluq's ambitious schemes and thirst for power interfered with the pious work of Darveshes. He had to pay a severe penalty, like some of his shortsighted predecessors, who had also persecuted Hazrat Khwaja Nizam-ud-Din Aulia.

Sultan Mohammad Tughluq and his son did not enjoy good relations with Nasir-ud-Din Chirag and other mashaikhs of Delhi. When he wanted to quell the invasion of Mongols, he sought the help and advice of the Sufis. He was not liked by them. He also wanted to shift the capital from Delhi to Deogiri which no one approved of. He also wanted that Sufis should serve him like his servants. This was also not liked by the Sufis.

He executed hundreds of innocent Muslims, Ulemas, Sufis, Sayyids and mendicants. Barni writes, 'of all the Muslim rulers of India, Sultan Mohammad Tughluq was a mixture of opposites'. Moreland called him 'a man of inconsistencies'. Hazrat Nasir-ud-Din Chirag Delhi tolerated all the insults, because his Pir had ordered him to do so and remained in Delhi; but during his lifetime and just after him, the Chishtiya silsila which was going on well for the past 300 years collapsed. The main reasons for it were; (a) central organization of his silsila got weak and some *mureeds* were not following the principles of guidance given by earlier Sufis and (b) after the death of Hazrat Nasir-ud-Din (who was stabbed by a Fakir from Jallandhar in 1356 A.D. at the age of 85 years), many younger generation Darveshes of this silsila went to the provinces and they became free and did not follow the principles and warning of Baba Farid. With the burial of Hazrat Nasir-ud-Din, all the relics of this silsila were also buried as the saint did not nominate his successor. During his lifetime in 1350 A.D., a Mausoleum was erected, the wall was erected by Mohammad Shah in 1729 A.D. and the main door of his Dargah was erected by Firoz Shah in 1378 A.D. Now a full city (Chirag Dilli) is developed around this Dargah which is near Kalkaji, Delhi.

Bibi Fatima Sam

She was a renowned woman Sufi of the period of Farid-ud-Din Ganj Shakar and Khwaja Nizam-ud-Din Aulia. She remembered so many couplets on Sufism. She always remained in meditation and did not eat for days together. Sheikh Najib-ud-Din Mutvakil who was the brother of Baba Farid used to address each other as sister and brother. Sheik Nasir-ud-Din Chirag-i-Delhi met an Abdal (a religious person above Sufi, there are only forty Abdals at a time) at the grave of Bibi Fatima Sam, this itself is a proof that she was very pious women of her time. Her grave is in Kaka Nagar, near the Delhi High Court.

There are ten stages in succession to achieve spiritual excellence. The first stage is *Mokunam.* Their number is 4000, they do not recognize each other where they are stationed. The second stage is *Akhiar*. Their number is 300 and they are very near to God, and 40 Aulia are called *Kayum,* 40 Aulia are *Abdal,* 7 Aulia are called *Abrai,* 4 Aulia are called '*Avtad*' 2 Aulia are called *Imam* these two Imams are stationed on the left and right side of *Qutub*. In this group of Aulias, one is called *Qutub* and the other *Gaus*. They recognize one another and they seek help of one another. The last category of Aulia is called *Muferidan,* their place is between the Khalifa and the Prophet.[33]

The fall of Baghdad (1258 A.D.), a great seat of Sufis, at the hands of Hulagu and the establishment of a vast Mongol Empire, forced a number of Muslim refugees to seek asylum in Northern India. The Muslim population, with the conversion of many Hindus, multiplied manifold over the period of a few centuries. During a long span of about five hundred years (from the eleventh to the sixteenth centuries) the soldiers and administrators exerted themselves in order to consolidate the political power of the government while the Muslim men of religion engaged themselves in fulfilling the socioreligious needs of their community as well as in strengthening the influence of their creed outside it. In the first decade of the eleventh century, one such religious man was Sheikh Ismail of Bukhara who settled in Lahore, *Sheikh Ali bin Uthman Hujwari* (died in 1072 A.D.). This feature was already growing in the province of Lahore and on the other due to the death of Khwaja Nasir-ud-Din Chirag-i-Delhi and the foolish policies of Sultan Mohammad-bin-Tughluq against the peaceful Sufi Darveshes, many of the younger mystics entered into government service and many of the older saints established themselves and their khanqahs in various provincial towns of India which did not owe allegiance to any central authority. Some of the prominent Sufis who established their khanqahs elsewhere are as follows: Hazrat Siraj-ud-Din (1357 A.D., Bengal), Ala-ud-Din (Bengal, 1388 A.D.), Syed Shamsuddin Tahir (Ranthambhor), Hasan Tahir (Jaunpur 1503 A.D.), Hazrat Qutub-ud-Din Munawwar (Hansi), Shah Kalimullah Jahanabadi at Delhi, Maulana Khwaja at Kalpi, Qazi Abdul Muqtadir of Delhi, Hazrat Shah Barq Allah Gujarati, Hazrat Wajihuddin Yusuf (1328 A.D.) at Chanderi, and many more.

In Lahore and near by towns, some more Sufis established their khanqahs, such as, Sheikh Daud (died 1575 A.D.) of Jheni. Sheikh Hamid Qadri of Uch. Miyan Mir, Mulla Abd al-Hakim Siyalkoti, Abd al Qadri Jilani, Pir Hassen Teli (died at Lahore in 1603 A.D.), Shah Dawlah, Mir Mohammad Husayu (established his Khanqah at Delhi), Shah Badr-al-Din Shah Shams al Din Darya, Shah Husayau Lahori (1539–99 A.D.), Sultan Bahu (1631–91 A.D.), and Bulhay Shah (1680–1758 A.D.).

The Lodi rulers shifted their capital to Agra and due to this, the influence of Sufis at Delhi also waned. After the victory at Panipat in 1526 A.D., Babur visited the Tomb of Sheikh Nizam-ud-Din Aulia; before him in 1398 A.D., Timur also visited this Tomb. Humayun did try to built a new city of Jahanpanah but Sher Shah Suri ousted him for a considerable period in 1555 A.D., he again captured Delhi but died in January 1556 A.D. Of course, Humayun is buried near the Chilla Khana of Hazrat Nizam-ud-Din Aulia; Akbar did visit the dargah of the Aulia but he made his quarters first at Fatehpur Sikri and thereafter at Agra. Jahangir, in 1606 A.D., visited Aulia's tomb, but he mostly remained at Lahore or Agra; he did visit Delhi occasionally and stayed at Salimgah.

Shah Jahan decided to shift his capital from Agra to Delhi and he built a planned city of Shahjahanabad (Delhi) during 1639–49 A.D. Many Sufis, poets, fakirs and kalandars started coming to this city. During his earlier visits to Delhi he used to go to Humayun's tomb and the Dargah of Sheikh Nizam-ud-Din Aulia.

The shrine of Sheikh Nizam-ud-Din Aulia has been and still is one of the most visited places of Delhi. Thousands of Hindu, Muslim and others come daily to receive blessings. The importance of the tombs of Sufis is a well known aspect of Indo-Muslim piety. It was believed that a measure of the spiritual charisma and power of the saint persisted in his tomb to which those who require his intercession would resort. Almost all Mughal kings and nobles would have liked to be buried near the Tomb of Sufi saints and some succeeded in it.

Mas'ud Bakk

He was one of the most striking figures in early Indian Sufism. Bakk is said to be the name of a town in the vicinity of Bukhara. According to most accounts, he was born in the region of Bukhara in Transoxania. He belonged to a princely house; later, he migrated to India and is said to have been a close relative of the Sultan, Firoz Shah.

During the chaotic last year of Firoz Shah's reign (1387 A.D.), Mas'ud Bakk was put to death. At that time, there was no central authority in Delhi, only warring factions and a complete breakdown of the order. It was this shambles of imperial Delhi that Timur sacked the following year.

Soon after his arrival in India, Mas'ud was attracted to the Chishtiya order; it was most popular Sufi order in India since its inception from twelfth century. Affiliation with the Chishtis would have been rather unusual for someone having connections with the court since the Chishtis were notable for their refusal to accept royal patronage and interference. Mas'ud Bakk's writings were very popular among later generations of Indian Sufis, some of whom went to the extent of making talismans out of his writings, and his death anniversary was regularly observed along with those of other major saints. Mas'ud Bakk was the disciple of Sheikh Rukn-al-Din ibn Sheikh Shahab al-Din Imam. He was in the extremity of intoxication. He spoke intoxicated words; no one in the Chishti order had ever revealed the secret of reality so blatantly or acted so intoxicated as he. His tears were so hot that if they fell on one's hand, it would be burnt. He wrote many works on the science of Sufism and unification.[34]

The volume of his writings is also impressive and attests to his scholarship. He was in the first generation of Chishtis to engage in extensive literary production. He had also written responses to most of the odes and poems of Amir Khusrau. The detailed narrative of the causes and circumstances of his execution was given after 1815 A.D. Mohammad Gul Ahmadpuri added the earlier hagiography relating to the execution of Mas'ud Bakk which is as follows.

One day, the revered Mas'ud Bakk was carrying a pair of sandals for his master. A religious scholar met him on the road and asked, 'Whose shoes have you lifted up, that is to say on your head? He replied, 'I have lifted up the shoe of God most high'. The externalist religious scholars reached a unanimous decision; beneath the Firozabad fort on the river bank, they martyred that revered man. Having torn his blessed limbs to pieces, they cast him to the river. After the occurrence of this event, although the believers cast nets into the river's water, they found no trace of him. After much doubt, they found him, all limbs united and re-formed into a body, in the private room of the revered Nizam-ud-Din Aulia (died in 1325 A.D.). His Chilla Khana (a place of meditation) is still there on the east side of Humayun's tomb. It was on the bank of the Yamuna at that time. Raising him (Mas'ud Bakk) up from that place, they buried him in the tomb of his master, near the grave of Qutb al Islam Bakhtiyar Awshi in Lado Sarai. When this news reached the revered master (Mas'ud's master, Rukn al-Din) he asked the judge for what reason they had martyred him. The judge said, 'He affirmed that God most high has a foot'. The revered master said, 'Attribution (to God) for the lowest of things is the secret of correct relationship. Had you asked him weather the shoe of God most high was for the personal use of God most high?'

He (Rukn-ud-Din) continued saying, 'To God belong all things in heaven and on Earth. (Quran, 2.284), so the shoe undoubtedly belongs to God most high!' He said that the judge was unable to reply, so then the revered master was stirred and said, "You black face!" At once he became black, and he was ruined.'[35]

The case of Mas'ud Bakk, a Sufi mystic put to death in the late fouteenth century by Firoz Shah Tughluq, is a striking example of the growth of a martyrology in India. It is in the tradition of al-Husain ibn Mansur-al Hallaj (died 922 A.H.) the early Sufi martyr of Baghdad.

Martyrdom is the final resort of the weak against the powerful. It is an act of truth performed without regard for one's life.

Sharaf al-Din Maneri, a fourteenth century Sufi saint of Bihar, cursed the city of Delhi because of Firoz Shah's impious persecution of the saints, and the devastating invasion of Timur in 1398 A.D. was the divine punishment for the execution of these martyrs.[36]

Akbar not only made his first capital at Fatehpur Sikri near the khanqah of Salim Chishti, but he also made *jiarat* (pilgrimage) to Ajmer Sharif and to Aulia's Dargah. In 1652–3 A.D., Shah Jahan's Governor of Delhi, Khalilullah Khan, undertook the major reconstruction of the Khanqah of Nizam-ud-Din Aulia. In the fourteenth century as per one Arab account,

> ... there are one thousand Madarsa in Delhi, all belonging to the Hanafis excepting one for the Shafis. There are nearly seventy hospitals (Bimaristan) called Dar al-Shifa. Delhi and its suburbs are studded with two thousand khanqahs and sarais (inns), colossal buildings, large bazars and numerous baths. The water is supplied from wells which are not deeper than 14 feet with Persian wheel. People drink rain water which is collected in big reservoirs the diameter of each being the distance of an arrow shot or more.[37]

In eighteenth century Delhi, write Chandra Bhan Brahman and Sujan Rai Bhandari[38], there were mosques in every lane, street, bazar, courtyard, madarsa and khanqah which benefited the people to prepare themselves for this worldly and other worldly life. Shahjahanabad became an important centre for the educational and spiritual activities. There were twenty-two Sufis during the reign of Mohammad Shah.[39] Among the famous khanqahs of the period were that of Shah Kalimullah, Shah Fakhr-ud-Din Dehlvi, Mirza Mazhar Jan i-Janan, Mir Dard, Sa'dullah Gulshan and Mirza Abdul Qadir Bedil. People from far and near thronged to those khanqahs to quench their spiritual thirst. Besides these Sufis, other spiritual persons were also there who guided the people spiritually, such as, Shah Bhik, Shah Abdul Rasul, Shah Sarif, Shah Basit, Shah Abdul Manan, Shah Faqirullah Ambalavi, Shah Sondhi Ambalavi, Shah Bayazid, Shah Fuzail, Shah Ghulam Mohammad Jhatlavi, Shah Abdus Samad, Shah Kamal, Shah Budh, Shah Mubarak, Shah Ramz, Shah Abdullah, Shah Karimullah, Shah Nasir, Shah Abdul Latif, Shah Husain Waiz, Sayyid Mohammad Khan, Saeed Khan and Shah Kazim. Peace, prosperity, literary activities and spiritual endeavors shattered with a heavy blow of the attack on Delhi in 1739 A.D. by Nadir Shah. The Mughal Empire disintegrated. Its total collapse took place after 120 years in 1857 A.D.

After Nadir Shah, Ahmad Shah Abdali invaded India about nine times, forced the people of Delhi for exodus to other safer places. Most of the Sufis except Khwaja Mir Dard, constrained to say goodbye to Delhi. In 1857 A.D., Delhi was deserted again.

In 1753 A.D., Surajmal plundered Delhi, Ghulam Qadir, a Rohilla Chief plundered Delhi, thereafter Marathas started plundering it; at the end the British also did the same thing. The dependents of the Sufi Saints are serving as managers of their shrines and the organizers of the orders that flourished around them. The Pirzadas, the hereditary descendants and Managers of the Saint's Tombs, supervised the festivities commemorating the birth and death anniversaries of the saints, maintained public kitchens, led community prayers, and offered amulets along with spiritual and social advice. There are conflicting concepts about the social meaning of Islamic religious beliefs. The Sharia minded Muslim society, defines Muslim not by inherited lineage, position in the state, occupation, but by individual belief in Islam which transcended all other social ties and made men equals and brothers in religion. Islam is in their view a universal community. By contrast, popular Sufism took Islam to be an integral aspect of lineage, occupational and neighborhood ties. Sharia minded Muslims, stood for state enforcement of Islamic law and state mandated subordination of Hindus to Muslim rule by discriminatory taxes and restrictions; Aurangzeb's rule was like that, which not only antagonized Hindus but also the Sufis. During his rule, Sufis left Delhi and lived in other provinces of South India.

In the beginning of the Islamic period, the caliphate was the symbol of Islam; it grew towards the heritage of Iran, combined with Mongol, Timurid and Chaghtai concepts with Indian and Hindu motifs which introduced new qualities into Islamic culture. At the popular level Islamic beliefs and practice mixed with Hindu and Buddhist forms of beliefs and worship, it is in fact not a departure from Muslim norms but a process which has come over a long period and other Muslim societies also witnessing it.

Jamali Dehlvi

He was a famous Sufi poet of Delhi. He was so simple that he had only one 'lungi' and one hide, which he sometimes also pulled on his body. He was the disciple of Sheikh Baha-ud-Din Kambu; he also met Maulana Jalal-ud-Din Rumi and Abdul Rehman Jani. He extended a great influence on the people of Delhi.

Sheikh Muski Dehlvi

He used to live in Delhi. He was active during the period of Akbar and Jahangir. He wrote *Rubais*. In his poetry, the relationship with God is the main subject.

Ali Ahmad Nishtani Dehlvi

He was a poet of Jahangir's period. In one Mehfil (assembly), when one singer was singing the poetry of Hazrat Nizam-ud-Din Aulia, 'Every religion has right path in its place of worship said Amir Khusrau and I went to the right path due to Aulia'— King Jahangir asked the Ali Ahmad Nistani Dehlvi to explain it; he did so and died at the end of this explanation.

Sadullah Gulshan Dehlvi

He was the disciple of Sheikh Abdul Abod Sarhindi. He used one cloth for 12 years and lived alone. He went to Ahmedabad to see the Sun set. He said, 'go beyond the body and develop the soul, which give you light, go beyond soul like me so that you get the God'.

Sarmad Kasi

He was a famous fakir during the period of Aurangzeb. He remained nude. One Qazi complained to king that the fakir remained nude and did not read the full kalma. He was ordered to read the full kalma, to which he said that he had reached till 'La illah' only, and rest he did not know. This was considered against the tenets of Islam and his head was severed from his body and three times he said 'ill-ullah'. His grave is now at the east side of Jama Masjid Delhi. He was a Jew in his early life and adopted Islam later on. He was close to Dara Shikoh and was liked by him; he always remained naked, except when he appeared in the presence of the Prince, when he contented himself with a piece of cloth at his waist. One reason of his punishment was that he was liked by Dara Shikoh and Aurangzeb considered him a kafir. He praised the tenets of Mohammad, Jewish religion and Hindustani. There were Jesuit Fathers in his company like, Father Estanilas Malpica, a Neapolitan; Father Pedro Juzartee, a Portuguese and Father Henriques Buzeo, a Flamand (1653–1708 A.D.). He was much loved by Dara that every time he went to the court he received fifty rupees and two shawls.

Maulana Abdul Qadri 'Bedil'

He was a poet of Delhi during the eighteenth century. He had written a book, 'Mohit-i-Azam', and 'Chahar-un-Sur' and a book on poetry, 'Diwan-i-Bedil'. He was a Sufi poet and written extensively on Sufism.

The fifteenth century in the history of North India is a period of great cultural significance, but the Delhi Sultanate disintegrated towards the close of the fourteenth century. This gave rise to centrifugal tendencies; however its cultural and political system remained. Independent kingdoms and principalities come into existence. The cultural life and the activities of the Sufi's developed in Delhi, shifted to different cities on the eve of Timur's invasion in 1398 A.D.

The Sufis were considered indispensable for various reasons. Generally people had faith in their spiritual powers, regarded them as favorites of God and sought their blessings for success in their worldly careers as well as salvation in the hereafter. No doubt, genuine spirituality was the concern of a few only in medieval times as it is today; many Sufis sincerely endeavoured to wean away people from the lures of the worldly and provided them with solace in distress. Besides the Ulemas and the Nobles, the Sufis also played an important role in the process of urbanization and dissemination of learning in the new kingdoms. In Kalpi, Shah Madar got in touch with Hindu yogis and apparently discussed with them the yog philosophy. It is worth recalling, that the association of the Sufis with the yogis was not at all considered objectionable during the fifteenth century.

Some of the leading Chishti Saints even adopted certain yogic traditions. For instance, Sheikh Abd-al-Haqq Radaulwi and Abd-al-Quddus Gangohi regularly did the exercises of controlling breath, burying themselves alive or absorbed in devotion suspended upside down by a rope tied to the heels.[40]

In fact, the Sufis acted as a bridge between the Muslims and the Hindus and thus brought the two communities closer to each other.

Qalandars

Apart from the Sufis there was a class of Muslim ascetics called Qalandars, who were allied with the Chishti and Suhrawardi orders. These religious persons were wandering Darveshes, living in seclusion, emancipation and poverty. They were not an organized group nor had established spiritual centers like the Sufis. They were not bothered about social life and material needs and always confined themselves to their religious observances or were in a state of *Sukr* (mystic intoxication). They also did not follow fully the injunctions of Sharia.

Some of them demonstrated their spiritual power through magical and occult practices.

Muslim Women of Note

During the Mughal period, some women (related to the royal family) were faithful by nature and some by necessity. It also depended on their character and style. Each ruler had more than one wife (women) in their life. In all activities of the Mughal rulers, the woman was a part of it. They were present in the court, behind the *jali* (the intricate lattice screen). They were doing independent business; they were dealing with the domestic and foreign dignitaries; and they travelled with kings. They remained in the harem, unless they were driven out after the death of the king with whom they were related. These women included the mothers, foster-mothers, aunts, older women, wives, mistresses, concubines, daughters, grand-daughters, nieces, women slaves, eunuchs and other guests. The noblemen, their wives and daughters from all parts of the Empire used to gather in Delhi during weddings or some important functions or festivals.

Some of the women by character and accomplishment affected the functioning of the court or influenced the decisions of the ruler. They also affected the social life of the city. In the Mogul hierarchy, the Queen Mother was always the first lady, but Nur Jahan and Mumtaz Mahal were the exceptions. Sir Jadunath Sarkar[41] very aptly described their position in the following words:

> Natural bashfulness would keep on Empress from ordering the general establishment of the harem, regulating marriages and other ceremonies in the family, or presiding over female society of the capital. But the death of her husband would at once raise her to the dignity of a widow and the influence of a Queen mother, and remove from her even the possibility of any younger and fairer rival supplanting her in her husband's favour and hurling her from her seat of honor and influence. Social decorum prevented an Emperor from placing his wife above the mother, his elder sister, or his paternal aunt. Thus, it was that dowagers and old maids ruled the ladies' world in the Delhi palace.

Mahim Begum

She was the chief and favourite wife of Babur and mother of Humayun. She held a very high place in the harem of Babur, Humayun and Akbar. She was related to a Sufi of Iran, Sheikh Alum Nassar Ahmed Jan. Timur and Humayun had visited the Dargah of this Sufi Saint. Hamida Bano Begum, the mother of Akbar, was also related to this Sufi Saint. Babur had nine wives and he married Mahim Begum in 1506 A.D. at Heart. She was addressed as 'Aaka' the Chief Queen. She remained with Babur in all his battles. She gave birth to five children that is, Bar-Bul-Miza, Maher-Jahan Begum, Ashani, Daulat-Begum,

Farrukh Mirza and Humayun Mirza. She was well educated for her time and she established Khair-ul-Manazil, a madarsa; now it is no longer in existence, but it was once situated near the Old Fort. She also built a mosque beside this madarsa.

Gulbadan Begum, born from another wife of Babur was brought up by Mahim Begum along with Humayun. She remained with Mahim Begum till the age of ten years.

Gulbadan Begum

She was the step-sister of Humayun. She was born in Kabul in 1523 A.D. from Babur and Dildar Begum. She was a noted calligrapher, a distinguished writer, having written *Humayun Nama*. She was taught and brought up by Mahim Begum on whose death Gulbadan Begum was highly grieved. Gulbadan married her second cousin, Khizr-Khwaja Khan. She went to Mecca for a long pilgrimage (1576–82 A.D.) and at the age of 80 years she died in 1603 A.D. Her real brother was Mirza Hindal. She took a lot of interest in the marriage of the poor girls. She used to arrange the provisions for the hajis and fakirs and provided with stipends. She was a good poetess as well. Among the Princesses of the Timurid period, Gulbadan was considered the first highly educated lady. Akbar himself went with her dead body till her grave. From Humayunama it is evident that kings used to consult some women of the harem. She was also liked by Maryam Makani (Hamida Bano) the wife of Humayun. She was a very religious lady. Akbar was not so religious, so she was worried about it and advised Akbar about the same, but he did not heed her. She was buried at Agra by Akbar himself.

Maryam Makani (Hamida Banu)

She was the wife of Humayun and mother of Akbar. She was a very powerful personality at the Mughal court. In fact, Humayun became king again because of Hamida Banu. Her strong character is the proof of it; she initially refused to marry Humayun. She was for the encouragement of family ties but was against the presence of foreign religions. Although she had Russian slaves in her service, after her return from Mecca, she was not in favour of the Portuguese Jesuits and other Christians at the court. When the Portuguese captured the Mughal ships, she advised Akbar to arrest all the Portuguese; to this, Akbar did not act. Upon her death in 1604, Akbar was greatly affected and deeply mourned her death. She was buried in Humayun's Tomb at Delhi.

Mahim Anga

She was the wet-nurse (mother) of Akbar and loved Akbar immensely. She cooperated with Akbar in getting rid of Bairam Khan. When Adam Khan, the son of Mahim Anga turned hostile to Akbar, she supported Akbar. Until the age of 19 years she had great influence over Akbar. Thereafter, Akbar became independent and her influence on him quickly waned. She suffered a great shock after the death of her son who was thrown to the ground from the wall of the fort. She died 40 days after his death. She was an expert in arranging banquets and marital negotiations. In Delhi, she established a madarsa. She died in 1562 A.D. and is buried in Delhi.

Maryam Zamani (Jodha Bai)

She was the daughter of a Hindu noble (Raja Bihari Mal) and wife of Akbar and mother of Salim (Jahangir). It is believed that Salim was born due to the blessings of one Darvesh (Sufi) named Sheikh Salim who lived in Sikri. Akbar also shifted his capital to Sikri and built a Dargah having a high doorway in that Dargah and named his son, Salim. This Jodha Bai was later called Maryam Zamani. She was not less in anyway to any wife of Akbar. She used to do international trade. Her famous ship was named 'Rohini'. She was the first woman to engage in international trade; she had trouble with the Portuguese. She died in 1623 A.D. and was buried at Sikandar Lodi's Tomb at Agra.

Haji Begum

She was another beautiful wife of Humayun. Humayun pointed out his place of burial and, after his death, she built a mausoleum, which is now called Humayun's Tomb. Humayun died in 1556 A.D. and since then this tomb was planned but was completed in 16 years costing 15 lacs of rupees; there is no parallel to this building, even the Taj Mahal is modeled after it. Many members of royal family have been buried in this Tomb. Haji Begum is also buried in this Tomb. She also built Arab-ki-Sarai. From Mecca she brought 300 Arabs who lived there, so it is called Arab-ki-Sarai. Now it is in very bad condition and some offices of the Delhi Government are there.

Salim Sultan Begum

She was the granddaughter of Babur and daughter of Gulrukh Begum. She was first married to Bairam Khan;, when both were going on Haj, one Afghan killed Bairam Khan. After the death of Bairam Khan, she married Akbar and became his favourite wife. She used to go with the king on war and expeditions. She was sent by Akbar to Salim (Jahangir) for conciliation. She was the most highly educated lady at the court; she used to write poetry under the pen name of 'Makhfi'. Akbar used to consult her on political and administrative matters. She died in 1613 A.D. Upon her death, Jahangir states: 'She was adorned with all good qualities. In women this degree of skill and capacity is seldom found'[41]

Shah Begum (Rajkumari Man Bai)

She was the daughter of Raja Bhagwan Das and sister of Raja Man Singh of Amber. She was the first wife of Jahangir and also the mother of Khusrau. She died after Khusrau revolted against Jahangir in 1606 A.D. This behaviour of Khusrau humiliated her and one version is that she took poison and died and another version is that she became mad when humiliated by Nur Jahan. Jahangir wrote that 'In consequence of her death, from attachment I had for her, I passed some days without any kind of pleasure in life or existence'.[42]

Jagat Gosain (Jodha Bai)

She was the daughter of a Hindu nobleman, a Mansabdar of Jahangir called Mota Raja. She was also the mother of Khurram (Shah Jahan). There was tremendous jealousy between her and Nur Jahan. She died in 1619 A.D. She is also known by the name of Bilkis Makani. In one incident when a lion attacked Jahangir, Nur Jahan was frightened but Jagat Gosain killed this lion with her gun.

Nur Jahan (Mihr-un-Nisa)

When Itimad-ud-Daula Ghiyas Beg and his wife Asmat Begum were coming to Akbar's court at Agra, from Tehran, Mihr-un-Nisa was born en route at Qandhar. She was brought up in a family of importance. When young, she was married to Sher Afghan (Ali Quli Beg) who later became the Governor of Bengal. In a Skirmish in 1607 A.D., Sher Afghan was killed and Mihr-un-Nisa and her daughter, Ladli, were brought to Jahangir's court at Agra. In 1611 A.D., at the Nouroz or New Year's festival, Jahangir made her his last and eighteenth wife. She was named as Nur Mahal and also called Nur Jahan. Soon after this marriage, the power equation changed in the court. The father and brother of Nur Jahan were elevated to higher positions, and along with Sir Thomas Robert, the first English Ambassador to the Mughal court, she began to operate and virtually decided upon sovereign matters. The king was a tool in her hands; he was happy with a bottle of wine and pieces of meat. She was wise enough to conduct the affairs of the state. She used to receive gifts from foreigners. She also conducted international trade. She took great interest in the war of succession as Jahangir's health waned. She drove out other women of the harem who were jealous of her. She contributed to the advancement of Indian culture.

Mumtaz Mahal (Arjumand Banu Begum)

She was the wife of Shah Jahan, daughter of Asif Khan, and niece of Nur Jahan. She was most loved by Shahjahan and he was inspired by her to build the famous Taj Mahal. Khurram (Shah Jahan) married her in 1612 A.D. She was very loyal and devoted to him and went with him on almost all the expeditions. She delivered many children and at the time of her fourteenth delivery on 17 June 1631, she died at Burhanpur. For a week, Shah Jahan shut himself in a room and remained there without food and other entertainment. He grieved so much that in a week's time his beard grew white. In her memory, he built the Taj-Mahal, spent 50 lacs of rupees of that time and collected grain for the workers from all over India, which caused great famine in the country. Her body was put in the grave inside the Taj Mahal after its completion.

Begum Sahib (Jahan Ara Begum)

She was the eldest daughter of Shahjahan. As Mumtaz Mahal (wife) and Jagat Gosain (Mother) of Shahjahan had already died and Nur Jahan who was related to Shah Jahan had retired to Lahore, Jahan Ara ruled the harem for twenty-seven years under the title of Begum Sahib after the death of her mother the eldest Princess. She also shared the eight years of disgrace and captivity of Shahjahan in the Agra fort. During the rule of Shahjahan, Jahan Ara enjoyed the unsupervised liberty of her own place outside the confines of the Delhi Red Fort.

In virtue, she was the contrast of her younger sister, Roshan Ara. Of all the ladies in the Mughal court, she was alone and different with unassailable dignity. She was her mother's image, one who loved and forgave everybody. Of course she was openly with Dara Shikoh, tried to resolve the issue of succession, tried to persuade Aurangzeb who did not heed to her. In spite of it, she always requested Shahjahan in captivity to forgive Aurangzeb. But not long before his death on 22 January 1666, Shahjahan yielded to her gentleness. Jahan Ara got a signed pardon from Shahjahan for all the sins committed by Aurangzeb. It was really a spiritual trimph. Even two decades earlier to the death of her father she interceded for Aurangzeb's pardon, when he mysteriously fell from favour and found himself dismissed from his first viceroyalty of the Deccan. Prince Muazzam represented the king at the funeral of Shah Jahan. Jahan Ara oversaw the burial of Shah Jahan. Aurangzeb was grieved with the death of Shahjahan but reached Agra a month later. She received Aurangzeb with all atiquates and emotions. It was a union between the two after eight years.

During the year of imprisonment at Agra, she had accomplished more than what Aurangzeb could guess. She nursed Shahjahan, tutored her nieces (daughters of Dara). She completed the biography of the Muslim saints of Kashmir. She was full of compassion and no sign of bitterness was seen in her behaviour.

Aurangzeb was also moved by the affectionate protestation of her sister. He forgave her past conduct and gave her 1,00,000 gold pieces and an annual pension of Rs.17,00,000. For rest of her life she was given the title of Badshah Begum. In October 1666, she came to Delhi and took up residence in the grand mansion of the dead Persian noble, Ali Mardan Khan. She again became the favourite confidant of the King. She was the only person who could criticize the King.

She disapproved the re-imposition of jizya on Hindus, disapproved his Picayune dictates. She also visited Aurangzeb and begged him not to move for devastation of the South. But Aurangzeb did not heed to her request and advice. She predicted his end. She arranged a lavish ceremony in her house to mark the marriage of Dara's daughter, Jani, to Aurangzeb's third son Azam.

'Hindu Delhi' responded as Jahan Ara feared. Mobs gathered under the Jharokha of the Red Fort with prayers and wails, but Aurangzeb refused to acknowledge their presence. On the following Friday, thousands of Hindu supplicants thronged the entire route from the Red Fort to the great Mosque: money changers, fabric sellers, shopkeepers from the Urdu bazar, merchants and artisans, everyone abandoned work for a massive demonstration, knowing that the Emperor and his equipage of grandees must pass on their way to public prayer. Orders went out to force passage through the crowd, which stubbornly refused to disperse. Aurangzeb and his nobles fumed for an hour, after which another order went out: bring on the imperial elephants, and trample a path to the mosque. In a Macedonian phalanx of elephants and horses, many Hindus were crushed to death. The crowds continued to protest for some days more but it was hopeless; afterwards, they would submit and pay jizya. Puritanism had trumphed—at the price of alienating the Hindus at last, that bore the weight of the Mughal Empire on its shoulders'.[43]

When Aurangzeb decided to march to Deccan, Jahan Ara desired to remain in Agra and warned the king not to undertake such a difficult task. She also predicted that they would not meet again. The prophecy came true. During the march towards the Deccan, the news came to Aurangzeb that she had died on 6 September 1681 at the age of sixty seven. At the time of her death, she divided her property and jewels among her nieces and gave the finest gems and greater share of the money to Jani Begum. She was very wise, saintly and of good fame. She was buried at the Dargah of Hazrat Nizam-ud-Din Aulia. Near her grave on a plate it is written in Persian that:

'Except greenery nothing can cover my grave, and only this grass covers the grave of poor'.

She had also built a garden, part of which is now the Town Hall; this park was later called Queen's Garden during British rule. In this part, she had built a Sarai, which was called Sarai of the Princess Jahan Ara Begum. Bernier considered it as one of the finest buildings of Delhi and compared it with the 'Palais Royal' of Paris.

Roshan Ara Begum

She was younger to Jahan Ara Begum and close to Aurangzeb. She schemed and allied openly for Aurangzeb in the war of succession and during the kingship of Aurangzeb she occupied a special position in his court. On Aurangzeb's coronation in June 1659, she received half a million rupees more than the daughters of the king. For several years she enjoyed complete ascendancy over the royal harem. It was to the extent that in May 1662, for five days, Aurangzeb became ill; it was a rumor in the harem that the Emperor was going to die; in the public rumors were rampant that the king was already dead, because Aurangzeb, who used to have his Darbar twice a day and used to give *darshan* to the public from the *jharokha* (balcony), was not visible. Roshan Ara Begum was so influential at this time that without her permission no one could meet the king. She wanted that Sultan Azam who was just 9 years of age should takeover; to this she took away the royal seal and wrote to many Rajas and generals on behalf of Sultan Azam. In fact, she wanted to rule herself as the Prince was only 9 years old. This was protested by Nawab Bai, because her son Muazzam was older than Azam and she said the king was still alive. She wanted to go to the king to inform him about the acts of Roshan Ara. But she was pulled by Roshan Ara by heirs and abused and not allowed to meet the king. Some generals even wanted to free Shah Jahan from captivity at Agra.

Meanwhile, the king improved; he called a Darbar after five days and also went to Jama masjid on Friday. When Aurangzeb came to know of all this developments, he became suspicious and Roshan Ara Begum lost much of his love and he was angery at her behaviour. By June, the Emperor made full recovery; he went to Kashmir with his entire bag and baggage along with army; Roshan Ara also accompanied him. She was indiscrete. Bernier and Manucci treated her sex starved virago, hell bent for power. She wanted all liberty outside the fort like her elder sister, to which Aurangzeb declined politely. He knew that she was resorting to indiscretion within the Zenana itself. One such incident was also reported to Aurangzeb by Badr-un-Nisa, the daughter of Aurangzeb. From 1666 until 1670 A.D., she had not taken any interest in the intermarriages of Dara's and Murad's siblings whom the elder sister (Jahan Ara) reared up. Her only interest left was in sex. Aurangzeb was angery at her conduct, and in April 1670, she was poisoned, which shortened her life. She was only fifty-six at that time. She is buried in Roshan Ara Garden in Delhi near Roshan Ara Road.

Zeb-un-Nisa

She was the eldest daughter of Aurangzeb and her mother was Dilras-Begum, who was the daughter of Shahnawaz Khan Safavi. Zeb-un-Nisa was trained in the serious study of religious doctrine and in the matter of faith under the supervision of Hafza-Marriam (she was the mother of a noble, Inayatullah Khan) when Zeb-un-Nisa became *hafiz*, Aurangzeb gave her 30,000 *ashrafis* as a prize. She was a great scholar of Arabic and Persian. She was also guided by Mulla Said Asraf Mazindrani (a Persian by descent). She was the sister of Mohammad Akbar who revolted against Aurangzeb when he was sent to quell the rebellion of Rajputs in Jodhpur. Zeb-un-Nisa sided with Mohammad Akbar; their correspondence was confiscated and she was imprisoned in Salim Garh and all her property was confiscated. Some historians (Ma'asir-i-Alamgiri) describe that she participated in the condolences of the death of Rohilla Khan. It is said that she had written *Diwan-i-Makhfi* which is not found, but *Zaibut Munshiyat* is available (letters collections of Zeb-un-Nisa). She was mostly encircled by highly academic persons. She had also built a library. She also built a garden in Kashmir which was visited by Alamgir when he came to Kashmir. It is also a known fact that she had a love affair with Aqil Khan, a noble, who was ultimately boiled in a hot-water pot, in which he hid himself. She was also a good poetess. She died in 1702 A.D. at Delhi as state prisoner. At this time Aurangzeb was in South India. The couplet on her grave is similar to that of Jahan Ara.

Zinat-un-Nisa

She was another daughter of Aurangzeb. She used to take care of political prisoners on behalf of her father. Even big lords and nobles could not dare to argue with her. She was also born from Dilras Bano Begum. When Shah Alam, Bahadur Shah became the king after killing Azam Shah, the Begum was at Gwalior; she could not present herself, so Shah Alam, after becoming the king, came to her and doubled her allowances and facilities. She was a religious lady and highly respected. When Farrukh Siyar became the king, he was maneuvered by a lady. On 18 May 1721 at Delhi she died and her grave is in Daryaganj Mosque, Zinat-ul-Masjid. She was 80 years old at that time. She spent all the money to build this masjid, which she was given by Aurangzeb.

Lal Kunwar

She was the daughter of Khaqsayat Khan, a musician of note in Northern India in the last decade of the seventeeth century. She was also related to Tansen, a noted singer of Akbar's court, fifth generation from the paternal side. She was not an ordinary dancing girl. She was also related to Rupmati, a noted wife of Bazbahadur in the fourth generation from her mother's side. She was beautiful and charming but had no morals. In 1703 A.D., Jahandar Shah, the King, fell prey to a thumri sung by her at Multan. After two days, she was entered into the Royal Harem and gradually Jahandar Shah (earlier Muiz-ud-Din) was helpless and became prisoner of her voice and delicate steps. He began to suspect everyone except Lal Kunwar. Infatuation for a woman was undaring. He listened to music when Punjab was pillaged by Banda Bahadur.

After the annihilation of all his potential enemies, Jahandar Shah left the banks of Ravi for Agra on 1 May 1712 along with Lal Kunwar and it took him one month to reach the capital. They did every thing that an Emperor and his mistress should not have done. On 2 June, they reached Delhi fort and next day one noble was hanged, because the previous night he had made some unwise remarks. There was talk in the capital that Farrukh Siyar was poised to attack the capital, which was ignored on the advice of Lal Kunwar. Delhi was lit for 4 months; this caused a crisis of oil in the city, and even other commodities became very costly. To meet this crisis, Lal Kunwar devised a method to distribute the money to the people of the city. To do so she had to go to a different part of the city on a *rath* and throw money, a hundred thousand rupees a day, which caused a heavy burden on the exchequer. It gave pleasure to Lal Kunwar when others were struggling. One day, a fully loaded boat was drowned in the middle of the Yamuna River; Lal Kunwar was watching this from the roof of the Lal Qila. Only nine men could swim to the bank and the others drowned. She had no sorrow. One night, the Emperor was left in the rath by the guards after having gone to his apartment along with Lal Kunwar. The Emperor was drunk heavily and remained in sleep throughout the night in the rath. The driver of the rath was hanged next day. She was an arrogant, haughty woman who talked to one man, looked at another, and thought of someone else. She tried her best to become a mother; for this she visited the holy places but all in vain.

Jani Begum

She was the daughter of Dara Shikoh; after his death, she was brought up by Begum Jahan Ara and later married in Delhi to Mohammad Azam, the son of Aurangzeb. She was not only beautiful but also a brave woman. She participated in many wars in the Deccan along with her husband, especially war at Bijapur.

Akbarabadi Begum

She was one of the wives of Shah Jahan. She built a mosque of red stones near the Red Fort, which was demolished by the British after the Mutiny. The British cleared the front of the Red Fort till Jama masjid and placed guns at Red Fort. The mosque was at the place where now exists Subhash Park.

Qudsia Begum

Arham Bai or Qudsia Begum was the wife of Mohammad Shah. She was a very clever woman and impressed the King by her counsel. But the way of life of Mohammad Shah was alike her nature. She enjoyed wine and other entertainment. Mohammad Shah was indulged so much in the wine and women that he neglected his administration and a condition of revolt existed in the empire. The Marathas looted Delhi. In this condition, Nadir Shah attacked Delhi (1739 A.D.). He took 80 crores worth of goods and cash along with many men, women, material and Takht-i-Tauos and killed thousands of persons. This all happened because of the lifestyle of Mohammad Shah. Qudsia Begum was also an Urdu poetess and used to write under the pen name of 'Ranai'. She built a garden and a *hauz* during the reign of Ahmad Shah. This garden was encircled by a beautiful wall which is now missing. Even a small river which was full of water earlier, is now filled with earth.

Zeenat Mahal

She was the wife of the last Mughal King of Delhi, Bahadur Shah Zafar and the daughter of Ahmad Quli Khan, a Nawab, who was related to Ahmad Shah Durrani. She influenced the king in such a way and extent that in administration she exerted great influence. The King had ordered that any document which did not bear the stamp of Queen Zeenat Mahal would not be treated as valid. In the Lal Kuan area of the walled city, she had a house; the British gave it to the Raja of Patiala after 1857 A.D. She also accompanied the King during his exile and died in Rangoon.

Juliana: A Catholic Portuguese Lady at the Mughal Court

One Agastinao Dias da Costa, a native of Portugal, and his wife were taken prisoners when Shah Jahan sacked Hugli in 1631 A.D.; their daughter whose name was Dona Juliana Diaz da Costa rose to such an importance and eminence at the court of Bahadur Shah I, the grandson of Shah Jahan, that he bestowed on her the title of Khanum (the Lady or the Princess). Aurangzeb also received her very well and was charmed by her presence of mind; he confided in her the education of Bahadur Shah, his eldest son and later Mohammad Shah. Dona Juliana was the patroness of Desideri, an Italian Jesuit, who wrote very highly about her, with full of admiration. He describes her admiringly as 'an ornament of our holy faith in the Empire'. He not only credits her with 'rare intelligence, eloquence, amiability and sagacity' but also with 'supernatural, miraculous powers'. Desideri says that Juliana, by her prayers to St. John Baptist, enabled Bahadur Shah's daughter-in-law to 'miraculously' conceive a son.[44]

Bahadur Shah, having fallen into the disgrace of the Emperor (Aurangzeb), his father, was confined to the jail, deprived of even the most necessary things; but Juliana helped him to procure some of them at the risk of her life. Juliana helped Bahadur Shah usefully with her advice. Bahadur Shah made use of her advice in many cases. He said, 'If this woman were a man, I would have made her my Wazir'. Juliana made many Portuguese to come to Delhi from Goa, placed those whom she found meritful advantageously in the service of the Emperor and sent back the rest to Goa.[45]

She was at Lahore at the time of the death of Bahadur Shah; she was arranging to introduce a Dutch Ambassador (Katellar, a Dutch scholar, merchant and diplomat who had been on a mission to Lahore in 1711–13 and to Isphan in 1717–18) to the Emperor. She received Rupees 25,000 per month, a large number of male and female servants, the house of Dara Shikoh, and the dignity of crowning the Emperor, a position which became hereditary in her family.

She cured Farrukh Siyar, the Emperor, from a furuncle (boil) which no doctor could do. Mohammad Shah's mother wished to make a vow so that her son could come to the throne. She consulted Juliana who advised her to make vow to St. John Baptist to whom the Mohammedans honour under the name of 'Leia Paighamber'. Juliana, true to the principle orders of the Christian Church, herself made a vow too. When Mohammad Shah came to the throne, he wished to be crowned by Juliana.

Juliana died in 1732 A.D. at the ripe age of 75 years, and she was laid to rest in the Church of Agra. Juliana had a sister who was married to Dom Velho da Castro; she made her to come to Delhi with her husband.

Isabella Velho, her niece, widow of Dom Joseph Mendes succeeded Juliana in her post. There were five other (grand-nieces who were descendants of Isabella), who succeeded her successively till the reign of Ahmad Shah. Under the rule of Ahmad Shah, Safdarjung, a key man of the government, sold the palace of Dara Shikoh for the price of nothing. Ghazikhan, Safdar Jung and the Jats took control of the dominions of Velho and Mendes. When Ahmad Shah Abdali plundered Delhi many times, he deprived these two families of all the rest of their fortune. They came out of Delhi and a branch of the Velhos took shelter at Faizabad, the residence of Shuja-ud-Daulah, Nawab of Oudh, and son of Safdarjung. This Prince welcomed them and granted them a pension.

Colonel Gentil, the Chief of the infantry of Shuja-ud-Daulah, married one of the young ladies of the Velho family at Faizabad in 1774 A.D. She was the great grandniece of Juliana and she died in 1778 A.D. Madame Velho, her mother, died at Versailles in 1806 A.D.

Colonel Gentil went to France in 1778 A.D. and died in 1789 A.D. in difficult conditions.

Begum Samru

She was the wife of a German, Walter Reinhardt. Originally a carpenter from Strasbourg, Reinhardt came to India at the time when the great colonial powers of Europe, France and England were fighting for control of India.

After several adventures, in the year 1761 A.D., he put himself at the head of a group of soldiers who served under different native rulers. He was hated by the British, as he obstructed their march as they advanced towards the Ganges.

In the year 1773 A.D., General Samru was given the Principality of Sardhana by the Mughal Emperor of Delhi as a reward for his meritorious services. Reinhardt was a Catholic. He died in Agra in 1778 A.D. and was buried there in the Catholic cemetery. His wife (Begum Samru, later Begum Johanna), a Muslim whom he had married in 1776 A.D., erected a memorial to this German warrior, a beautiful mausoleum which exists to this day at Sardhana.

On 7 May 1781, she was baptized in Agra with the name of Johanna Nobilis by the Carmelite Priest, Gregorio. She had a big house at Chandni Chowk and a church.

Poets of Note

With the Arab conquests of India in the eigth and ninth centuries, Sind and Mansura, Daybal and Multan became the seats of Islamic learning. Under the Ghaznavid Sultans, Lahore became the seat of Islamic culture and learning. In a short period Muslim rule was established in many parts of India and Delhi became the seat of culture and learning. Many learned persons came to Delhi from various parts of the world. The Arabic literature produced in India was very meager and confined to religious topics. Later, Persian culture dominated the Arab culture.

Mahmud of Ghazani introduced Arabic and Persian languages and literature in India. Many poets and scholars such as Albiruni accompanied him. Later, many Persian poets, writers, scholars and theologians from Transoxiana, Bukhara, Khurasan and other countries took refuge in Indian courts and towns (mostly in Delhi) to escape the massacre and misfortune at the hands of the Mongols. They not only brought with them their cherished possession of books, but also set up educational institutions, which led to the growth of Persian and later Urdu in India in general and Delhi in particular.

The Muslim impact and rule in India in general and Delhi in particular generated three literary growths: a) a Muslim literature of conquest, b) Hindu literature of resistance and of psychological rejection, and c) comparative studies of other religions to widen the horizon of their knowledge.

The first 'two literary growths were planted in two different cultures, in two different languages, Persian and Hindi; in two mutually exclusive religious, cultural and historical attitudes each confronting the other in aggressive hostility. Each of these two literary growths developed in mutual ignorance of the other.'[46]

(*a*) *The Muslim Literature of Conquest* grew out of the Qasidas (panegyrics) written on the occasion of Indian campaigns by the Ghaznawid poets of Ghazna and Lahore, and later by the poets of the Sultanate like

Nasiri and Sangriza in Delhi. Amir Khusrau's Miftah al-Futuh, celebrates four victories of Jalal-ud-Din Khilji (1290–6), two of them against Hindu Rajas, one against the Mongols and one against a rebel—a Muslim governor.

Amir Khusrau's *Khazain al-Futuh* is in praise and glorification of the Turks against the Hindu. His *Ashiqa* was courtly (Bazmiya) in theme, relating the romantic story of the love of Ala al-Din Khilji's son Khizr Khan, for the Hindu Princess of Gujarat, Dewal Rani, setting the pattern for a recognized type of Indian Muslim love story in which the hero is invariably a Muslim and the heroine a Hindu, asserting the conqueror's right not only to love but to be loved. But the glorification of India is there as a consequence of the Muslim supremacy.

'Happy Hindustan, the splendour of religion, where the (Muslim only) law finds perfect honour and security ... The strong men of Hind have been trodden under foot and are ready to pay tribute. Islam is triumphant and idolatory is subdued.'[47]

In Amir Khusrau's *Nuh Sipihr*, the thematic emphasis is again on the Turk's destiny as conqueror who is decreed to hold the Hindu in subjugation, though the commander of the Turkish army in this case was a convert from Hinduism.[48]

Amir Khusrau's *Tughluq Nama*, describes the re-establishment of Muslim power in India. Isami's *Futuh al-Salatin*, glorifies the role of Mahmud of Ghazani who made the Muslim conquest of India possible.[49] It emphasizes throughout the superiority of the Turks over the Hindus.[50]

The motif was of a war waged to protect or avenge the honour of Muslim women; be it the case of Hijaz ibn Yusuf's expedition against Sind or the expeditions of Sultan Bahadur of Gujarat (1526–37) against a Hindu chieftain, or be it the expedition of Sher Shah Suri against Puran Mal, the Raja of Raisain.

Kamal al-Din 'Abd al-Razzak, the Ambassador of Shah Rukh to the Hindu courts of the Deccan, regarded the Hindus, at first sight, as a curious tribe 'neither men nor demons', nightmarish in appearance, almost naked, incomprehensibly matriarchal and, of course, idolators.[51]

Babur said on Hindustan and its people:

> Hindustan is a country that has few pleasures to recommend it. The people are not handsome. They have no idea of the charms of friendly society, of friendly mixing together, or of a familiar intercourse. They have no genius, no comprehension of mind, no politeness of manners, no kindness or fellow-feeling, no ingenuity or mechinical invention

> in planning or executing their handicraft 'works', no skill or knowledge in design or architecture; They have no horses, no good flesh, no grapes or muskmelons, no good fruits, no ice or cold water, no good food or bread in their bazars, no baths or colleges, no candles, no torches, not a candlestick.[52]

(*b*) *Hindu Intellectual Resistance* to the Muslim power did not come mainly from Brahmins. In earlier periods, the Hindus believed that Aryavart was so wide, that even if the 'Mlechchh' overran it, they could never abide there for long. The faith in this thesis dwindled as the Muslim power came to be more and more firmly entrenched in the subcontinent. The *chaturvarn* was one such cause of it. The Hindu reformers passed over the question of Muslim domination in silence as the fruit of 'Karma' without making suggestions for its overthrow.[53]

The bardic tradition of Rajputana echoed the Hindu resistance. Chandra Bardai, Prithvi Raj Raso and Alha Khand of Bundelkhand are the examples. Another literature of the Prithvi Raj cycle is *Prithvi Raj Vijaya*, composed by Jayanaka (between 1178 and 1200 A.D.). The poem accuses Muslims of confiscating charity lands and oppressing Brahmins. The Turushka (Turkish) women are condemned for bathing in the sacred lake while in their unclean period.[54]

Unhistorical poets are given in Hammir Raso and Hamir Kavya by Sarang Dhar, a bard of mid-fourteenth century.[55] Naya Chandra Suri's *Hammir Mahakavy* depicts, Hindu chivalric theme and anti-Muslim content. Another Naya Chanda Suri's work of literature is *Viranarayan*. It describes the defeat of Jalal al-Din Khilji.

The story is true that the Mongols supported Hammir against Ala-ud-Din Khilji; other Hindu chiefs supported Khilji. Khilji suspected Mongols and killed them and their houses were burnt at Mongol Pura in Delhi. This event took place after the siege of Ranthambhor.

The nineth century Khuman Raso was recast in the sixteenth century devoting a large section to Ala al-Din's sack of Chittor.[56]

Malik Mohammad Jaisi's *Padmavat* (1540 A.D.) is remarkable case of anti-Muslim literature. The first part of *Padmavat* deals with the love story of Ratan Sen for Padmini (Padmavati). The second part deals with an allegorical clue, like Gora and Badal entering the imperial fort of Delhi by a counter-ruse and rescue Ratan Sen. Even before the composition of *Padmavat* by a Muslim, other literature was written by Hindus, such as Vidyapati Thakur's *Purush Parikhsha*, which tells of the Hindu Rajas coming to the aid of Mohammad bin Tughuluq against a fellow Hindu Raja and Malik Kafoor.[57]

The idealization of Hindu women or of Muslims, passed on from Rajput literature to popular songs in other areas such as Bihar.[58]

Shivaji's idealization of Kavi Bhushan in *Granthavali*, burst into boiling fury in Maharashtra after Aurangzeb's reversal of Akbar's tolerant policies.

(c) Comparative study of other religions was undertaken to widen the horizon of their knowledge. Some Muslim and Hindu writers produced the literature to know the theological and cultural achievements of the followers of Hinduism such as: under the Abbasids (749–1258 A.D.) a large number of books on religion, medicine, astrology, astronomy, arithmetic, parables, politics, games and amusements and ethics were translated from Sanskrit into Arabic. Also, independent eminent scholars in Arabic have given useful accounts of the various branches of Hindu learning, such as Jahiz (d. 864 A.D.) refers to supreme insight of Hindus into medicine; Ya'qubi (d. 897 A.D.) acknowledges the calculations of astronomy of India as 'the most perfect'. The Arabs learnt the numbers from 1 to 9 from India. The Arab astrologers relied on the Siddhant method in the third to fifth centuries. Abu Ma'shar, the famous astronomer of the ninth century A.D., came to India and learnt Indian astronomy at Banaras. He stayed there for nine years. One can also find the description of Hindu gods, deities, modes of worship and ceremony in the writings of Ya'qub bin Ishaque Kindi, Mutahhar, Qadi Sa'ad, Ibn-i-Fiquh Hamadani, 'Abdul al-Qahir Baghdadi and Buzurg bin Shahryar of the ninth and tenth centuries A.D. These researchers culminated in Al-Biruni's Kitab-ul-Hind.

Of course the Muslims had a feeling of superiority but they did not like to display any sense of aloofness or detatchment from the beliefs and achievements of non-Islamic people. In the beginning there was, of course, a barrier between the sense of superiority of the victors and the ill feelings of the vanquished, but with the adoption of India as their homeland, and their closer contacts in daily life, religious and racial bias and prejudice subsided gradually.

Amir Khusrau might have written in favour of the Muslim rulers, may be to get money, but in the later part of the thirteenth century A.D., he gave a clarion call to shake off the mutual repugnance, and make appreciative study of everything Indian. In his *Mathnavi Nuh Sipihr* compiled in 1318 A.D., he says that in India lies concealed wisdom and learned ideas beyond compute. He also admired the knowledge of learning and languages, logic, dogmatic, theology, astrology, physics, mathematics, astronomy, divination of the past and future are known to the Indians.[59]

Amir Khusrau introduced a new tone in the Indian Music by interlinking some of its melodies with those of Iranian rhyms.

Firoz Shah Tughluq took notice of books at the temple of Nagarkot in 1361 A.D. He invited Hindu scholars and ordered some of the books to be translated. The celebrated poet of his time, 'Izzu'd-Din Khalid Khani, wrote *Dalait-i-Firuz Shahi* deriving ideas from the philosophy, astrology and divination of the Hindu books. Other books translated into Persian were: Sarawati on astronomy and Haramkhela also called *Uddisa-Tantra* or *Uddisa Shastra*; a work on astronomy, *Brihat Samhita,* of the renowned astronomer Varahamihir was made by Shams Siraj Afif. During the period of Sikandar Lodi, *Argar Mahabedak*, a work on the science of medicine, was translated into Persian by Bhuwa bin Khawass Khan in 1512–13 A.D., entitled *Tibb-i-Sikandari.* It is also known as *Ma'danu'sh-Shifa-i-Sikandar Shahi.*

The Mughal period ushered in a new era for the extensive study in Indology. Babur's Memoirs, Abu'l Fazl's *Ain-i-Akbari*, Jahangir's *Jahangir Nama* give valuable botanical and zoological statistics. *Hitopadesh* was translated by Taj-ud-Din Mufti al-Maliki' as *Mufarrihu'l-Qutub* and he dedicated it to Emperor Humayun.

Under the patronage of Akbar, the epic *Mahabharata* was translated as *Razm Namah* by Naqib Khan, Abdul Qadir Badayuni, Mulla Shiri, Sultan Haji Thanisari and Shaikh Faidi. Abdul Qadir Badayuni translated Ramayan in 1589 A.D.; *Atharvaved* was translated by Haji Ibrahim Sirhindi into Persian; *Lilavati,* a book of mathematics by Faidi; *Rajak* (astronomy) by Mukammil Khan Gujarati; *Haribans* by Mulla Shiri; *Rajtarangini* by Mulla Shah Muhammad Shahabadi; *Panchtantr* by Abul Fadal as *Iyar-i-Danish*; Faidi described the story of Nal and Damyanti; Faidi also compiled a treatise on Vedant philosophy based on *Yogvasishth*, *Bhagvat Puran*, et cetera, and called it *Shariqu'l-Ma'rifat.* In 1574–5 A.D. Mulla Abdul Qadir Badayuni translated into Persian the famous Sanskrit work Singhasan Battisi, exploits of Raja Bikramajit of Malwa; translation known as *Nama-i-Khirad-Afza*; Mulla Badayuni also translated collection of stories as *Bahrul-Asmar*; Abul Fazl, *Ain-i-Akbari*, which describes various subjects.

During Jahangir's period, Shaikh Sa'dullah Masih versified Ramayan titled as *Rama-u-Sita*; Sufi Sharif made an abstract of *Yogvasisht* in *Atvar dar Hal-i-Asrar.*

During Shah Jahan's period, Shir Khan Ludi compiled Mir'atul Khayal; in the eigth year of Shah Jahan's reign, Ataullah Rashidi, the eldest son of Ahmad Mimar, the architect of Taj Mahal and Delhi's Red Fort, translated Bhaskarachary's *Beej Ganit,* a book on algebra, into Persian.

Prince Dara Shikoh translated *Bhagwat Gita* into Persian; Mukalama-i-Dara Shikoh-wa-Baba Lal, *Yogvasishth*, *Upnishads* titled as *Sirr-i-Akbar* (1657 A.D.); Majmaul-Bahrain, depicts the religious notions of Hindus and Muslims.

He also got compiled Hindi *doha*s as *Doha Sar*. In Alamgir's reign, Mirza Khan wrote 'Tuhfa-ul-Hind'; Hidayatullah bin Mohammad Muhsin al Quraishi, compiled *Farhang-i-Aurang Shahi* and dedicated it to Alamgir. It contains the description of animals, plants and minerals of India. On astronomy, *Tanjim* and *Burhanul-Kifayal* by an unknown author; *Anwaru'n-Nujum* by Qabul Mohammad Ansari; *Huku'r-Riyadi* by Mohammad Zaman Yazdi; *Nizamu'n-Nujum* by Abu Sa'id al-Husaini are important. Jaunpur king Husain Shaqi also contributed to Indian music.

Though Islam had imposed prohibition on music, still Indian music remained popular not only with rulers but the public at large. *Risala-i-Shattariyah* by Nizam-ud-Din Hasan describes the Hindu method of meditation also, *Rayahinu'l-Basatin* discusses the *nirvan*; *Miratul-Asrar* by Maulana Abdur Rahman Chisti compiled in 1631 A.D. gives the dialogue of Mahadev and Parvati.

Talif-i-Sharif compiled by Hakim Mohammad Sharif Khan (on medicine) *Risala-i-Farasnamah* by Mohammad Ali Hazin (on Indian veterinary science).

The Hindu scholars also took upon themselves the task of acquainting their Muslim countrymen with their treasures of knowledge by bringing out abundant literature in Persian through their own efforts, such as Girdhar Das, a Kayasth of Delhi translated Ramayan into Persian in 1626 A.D.; Makhan Lal Jahan-i-Zafar; Anandghan Gosain translated *Pothi Kashi Khand*; Anand Kunwar, *Dharam Gyan Sagar*; Amar Nath, Veds into Persian (Khayalat-i-Shaida); Ram Prasad, *Amar Charitra* (Makhzanu'l-Irfan in 1812 A.D.); Harsukh Lal Sahgal (Zubdatul-Qawanin, 1797 A.D.); Medini Mal, Lilavati (Bada'iul-Funun, 1664 A.D.); Ganga Bishan Kul's Majmu'a; Rai Mannu Lal died in 1832, leaving a considerable number of works on different branches of learning, such as, *Gulistan-i-Iran, Bustan-i-Hairat, Mufradat-i-Tibb*. His son, Kundan Lal, compiled *Zich-i-Ashki* (Astronomy), *Aksir-i-Sa'adat* and *Qastas* in philosophy; in astronomy,

Raja Jai Singh Kachhwaha of Amber (Zich-i-Mohammad Shahi). Through these works, both Hindus and Muslims came to know of the learning and literature of each other.

The people of North India and Iran originally belonged to the same race and culturally there are many similarities found in these two people. This fact can be traced from *Rig Ved* and *Avesta.* Even after the advent of Islam there remained a close relation between Hindu (India) and Muslim (Iran). In the past one thousand years some of the noted poets of Iran settled down in India. Persian remained the court language in India till the advent of British. From the sixth century onwards there are many Persian works available in prose and poetry.

Amir Khusrau Dehlvi

From the earlier period of Muslim rule in Delhi Amir Khusrau was considered as Sheikh Sa'adi (a poet of Iran) of Delhi. He was the contemporary of five rulers of Delhi that is, from Kaikubad to Sultan Mohammad-bin-Tughluq. He was the son of Amir Saifuddin-Dehlvi, who was a Turk, settled in Delhi.

Amir Khusrau's grandfather, Lachin, came to India from Khota (Turkistan). Khusrau was born in 651 Hijri in Delhi. His father got a good position at the court of Iltutmish. Khusrau was brought up by his maternal uncle after the demise of his father. He lived his life among the royals but at the same time he was very close to spiritual saints, especially Hazrat Nizam-ud-Din Aulia. He was so close to the Aulia that, before his demise, he said that when God will ask me, what I have brought then I will say to God that I have brought Amir Khusrau. Amir Khusrau died six months after the death of the Aulia. He even said if it is permissible in the Shariat to bury other person along with the dead then he would have willed that Amir Khusrau be buried in his grave, so that they remain together. But at the behest of an eunuch, Amir Khusrau was buried on the platform where Aulia used to sit with his disciples. The noted books of Amir are as follows:

(i) *Tohfatus Sigar* (small gift)
(ii) *Wastul Hayat* (Mid-life)
(iii) *Gurrat-ul Kamal* (Complete life)
(iv) *Buklia-i-Naklia* (Poetry relating to old age)
(v) *Nihayat-ul-Kamal* (Poetry relating to last time)

In all there were at least 18 books relating to poetry and prose. He was an expert on *qasida, ghazal* and *masnavi.* The content of his writing reflected his spirituality. He was a soldier as well as a good poet and writer. He also narrated poetry in Hindi and was considered to be the first Hindi poet. He was also an expert in music. He was also called Tuti-e-Hind. His writings had great impact not only on kings but on the people at large for a long period.

Amir Hassan Sajzi

He was a friend of Amir Khusrau and a disciple of Hazrat Nizam-ud-Din Aulia. Ziya-ud-Din Barni was a contemporary of these poets. Hassan Sajzi was the famous poet of the period of Ala-ud-Din Khilji. In poetry, he addressed himself as the Nightingale of the Garden. His real name was Nizam-ud-Din Aulia-Sajzi. His pen name was Hassan. He was born in the city of Badayun. Hazrat Nizam-ud-Din Aulia was also born in Badayun. He was educated and lived in Delhi alone and in the last days of his life he went to Devgir and died there. He had a good command over Arabic and Persian languages. He had written poetry in praise of Prophet Mohammad in Arabic as well as in Persian. His tilt was towards spirituality.

Balban was the patron of good poets and learned persons such as: Sheikh Qutub-ud-Din, Sayyid Muntakhab-ud-Din, Sayyid Jalal-ud-Din, Sayyid Aziz, and Sayyid Maim-ud-Din. These scholars came to India from Iran, after the attack of Chingiz Khan.

Maulana Burhan-ud-din Malkh, Maulana Burhan-ud-Din Bokhari Baiaj, Maulana Nazm-ud-Din Danishki (he was the disciple of Maulana Fakr-ud-Din Raji a historian of repute) and Qazi Rafi-ud-Din were the teachers of Amir Hassan Sajzi. He became famous for his ghazals (*Ghazaliat-i-Hassan*). He died in 738 Hijri. His famous books are *Isknam Makhul Mani*, *Anisul Arwah*, *Fawaid-ul-Fawad* and *Diwan-e-Hassan*.

Qadi Abd-al-Muqtadir

He was the descendant of Shuraih bin al-Harith bin al-Hahm al-Kindi (d. A.H. 78/A.D. 697) of Yemini origin, the renowned Tabi'i (follower of the Prophet's companions) and an authority on Hadith (apostolic tradition), who served as Qadi (judge) at Kufah in the times of Caliph Ali bin Abi Talib, and Amir Mu'aneijah.[60]

Sulaiman, the Qadi's grandfather, came to India during the time of Qutb al-Din Khilji, who appointed him as Qadi of northern India; he settled at Thaneswar. Qadi Abd al-Muqtadir was born at Thaneswar. He was brought up and educated in Delhi. He was given the best education in Arabic and religious sciences. He was greatly inspired and influenced by his teachers and spiritual guides, Shaikh Shams al-Din Muhammad bin Yahya al-Awadhi and Shaikh Nasir al-Din Mahmud. He was initiated into the esoteric Chishtiyyah order.

He remained busy learning, teaching and guiding students until he died on 26th of Muharram in 791 A.H./1398 A.D. at the age of 88 years in Delhi, where he was buried near the Shamsi Hauz.

Qadi was one of the most distinguished Arabic poets who flourished in India. His political genius is best illustrated by his famous eulogy on the Prophet

Muhammad known as 'Lamiyyat al-Hind' (the ode of India rhyming in '1') which he composed in imitation of the universally celebrated ode Lamiyyat al-Ajam (the ode rhyming in '1' of the non-Arabs) composed in the year 1111 A.D. by Al-Husain bin 'Ali al-Tughra'i (1063–1120 A.D.) of Persian origin and a native of Isfahan.

His panegyric on the Prophet is followed by his glorification of the latter's companions, who sacrificed their lives fighting in the path of Allah. He has also paid high tributes to the four Righteous Caliphs. He has invoked the Prophet's intercession for him. He has also admitted that it was beyond his power to adequately eulogize the Prophet even with the best of his eloquence.[61]

Malkushora Sheikh Faizi

He was a very good poet and writer, who had translated the Quran that is called *Savet-ul-illham.* This he had done without using any *nukta* (point). He had written poetry of all sorts. He was the poet of Akbar's period and also the Noble of the court. He took inspiration from his father for writing. He was born at Agra and died at Lahore in 1004 Hijri at the age of 45 years. He was the son of Sheikh Mubarak Nagori. He was buried at Agra in the tomb of Abul Fazal, who was his elder brother. His famous poetry is related to *bhakti* of God and intoxication in the idea of God.

Maulana Navi Khabushani

He was also a poet in Akbar's time. His name was Mohammad Riza, born in Khabusan, in Khurasan (Iran). He came to India with his father at very young age. He went back to Iran but again came to India. He came in contact with Prince Daniyal. Navi was a very good marksmen. He has written in favor of the practice of Sati. He died at Burhanpur in 1018 Hijri.

Urfi Siraji

He was also a poet in Akbar's period and was very near and dear to Akbar. He had written his poetry in praise of Md. Ali and Prophet Mohammad. He died in 909 Hijri at Lahore.

Mirza Sarfe-Jahan, Khwaza Husain Thesnai', Mirza Ghazi were also in the court of Akbar.

Talib Amuli

He was the poet of Jahangir's period, who had written in praise of Jahangir. Hakim Faghfore Lahi Zani, Maulana Mohammad Sufi, Mazindrani, Hakim Rukn-ud-Din Kasani, and Naziri Mirpeni were also famous poets of Jahangir's period.

Anand Ram Mukhlis (1696–7 to 1758 A.D.)

He was an eminent poet, who wrote a large number of ghazals, rubaiyat and fragments in verses.

The following are the works of Mukhlis:

1. *Diwan-i-Mukhlis*
2. *The Safar Nama*
3. *The Letters of Mukhlis*
4. *Badaye-i-Waqae or Tazkira Waqaya-i-Anand Ram Mukhlis*
5. *Mirt-ul-Istilah*
6. *Hangama-i-Ishq*
7. *Karnama-i-Ishq*
8. *Nuskha-i-Chamanistan*

Bedil and Arzu who were famous poets of the time had inspired Mukhlis with the real taste of poetry. He wrote in a uniformly serious style. He seemed to be a very calm and composed writer. Mukhlis tried to blend with success, the native and imported elements.

Persian in those days was the court language. People of the court were thought to be versatile either in politics or the language. He had mastery over the language.

His Persian verses possessed sweetness and were common among the people. He was sentimental and humorous, but did not copy his contemporaries very much; wherever he copied them, he honestly acknowledged it.

He had considerable influence among the poets of the age. He was educated to be successful courtier in the Mughal court. He had a fine nature, sweet and wholesome, devoid of bitterness and cynicism.

Nadir Shah's invasion not only impacted the poetry of Mukhlis but it also scattered the whole world of poetry.

His style was quite unique; he described a vast subject in a few words. He was the son of Raja Hirde Ram Khatri who belonged to Sodharah, a place near Lahore. His father, uncle and grandfather were courtiers (*Vakils*) in the king's courts. Mukhlis also followed in his forefather's footsteps. He was fond of gardening and kite-flying. He used to go to coffee-houses regularly and exchanged his views with his friends. He was very broad minded in religious affairs and used to visit the Dargah of Qutub-ud-Din Bakhtiar Kaki and Nizam-ud-Din. Mukhlis never tasted wine. His house was a grand building with a garden in Parijahat Pura, Vakil Pura in Shahjahanabad. He loved his two sons Rai Kirpa Ram and Rai Fateh Singh and gave various references about them. He loved the city and depicted it in his writings. He also wrote about trees, fruits, Sati, social life, music, trade and administration of his period.

He was a very renowned Hindu poet of Persian. Mukhlis respected other poets of his time and he was also respected by others. They never felt jealous of him. Mukhlis was considered a great, honest man.[62]

Other Hindu (Persian) Poets of Delhi

The following poets of Delhi were known for their poetical excellence in Persian.

Chunni Lal 'Ahsan', Kishan Chand 'Akhlash' during the period King Ahmad Shah, Amanat Rai 'Amanat' (disciple of Mirza Bedil), Rai Sanat Singh 'Bedar' (a courtier of Safdar Jung), Rai Surab Singh 'Diwana', Roshan Lal Roshan', Rai Manka Rai 'Shak', Bal Mukand 'Shoud' (from Bihar, during the reign of Mohammad Shah), Jai Kishan 'Ishrat' (who wrote a story of Ram Sita in Persian), Sangam Lal 'Izzat' (he has compared the life and works of Khwaja Muhi-ud-Din Chishti in Persian), Kishan Chand 'Qarib' (during the reign of Mohammad Shah), Rai Sahi Mal 'Mana' and Rai Punjab Rai 'Wali'.[63]

European Urdu and Persian Poets of Delhi

Alexander Headerly 'Azad' was born in 1829. His father, James Headerly, was a British and his mother a Muslim lady. He was a very good scholar of Urdu and Persian and was adopted by Mirza Ghalib as his son. Nawab Zamul Abidein Arif was his *Ustad. Matba-i-Ahmadi* was his literary work from Agra in 1863 A.D. His father worked at Fort William with the Nawab of Jhajhar (Nawab Faiz Mohammad Khan in 1833 A.D.).

Alexander Skinner was the son of James Skinner. In 1841, James Skinner died at Hansi. After the death of his father, Alexander lived at Kashmiri Gate, Delhi. During his stay at Delhi, he came in contact with Mirza Ghalib and in his company he refined his poetical skills in Urdu and Persian under the pen name 'Sikandar'. In 1869, he became member of the Delhi Society. His wife, Alice, died in 1881 and was buried in St. James Church at Kashmiri Gate.

Major A.R. Filler was an administrator in education at Punjab in 1860-61. He was the patron of a publishing house, 'Anjuman-i-Uloom', at Lahore. He recommended the booklet of Ghalib on Persian Grammar in Urdu language for study at madarsas.

The other British literary people who have shown interest for the promotion of Urdu and Persian languages were: Sir George Frederick Edminstone, Lord Ellenborough, Francis Howkins, William Fraser, Charles Metcalf and John Jacob (1812–57/58) who came to Balli Maran on 14 October 1844 as a guest of Ghalib. Ghalib had written six letters to him in Persian. He was a disciple of Ghalib.

The following noted scholars who wrote Urdu poetry were: Dr Howard, Dr Hoey, Dr Fisher, General Joseph Bensley *Fana* (*Diwan-i-Fana* was published in 1876, Meerut), Gardner 'Fana' and George Pucch 'Shoere'.

Hindu Urdu Poets of Delhis

The following were the noted Hindu Urdu poets of Delhi: Shiv Narain Aram (1833–98), Munshi Makkhan Aram Dehlvi who died in 1858 at Delhi, Munshi Hargopal 'Tufta' and Master Pyarelal 'Ashob' (1838–1914).

Shahjahanabad: The New Walled City and its Environs

Before Shahjahanabad was built on the western bank of Yamuna by Shah Jahan, several cities with different names had been founded on the various sites of Indraprasth. Since the beginning of first city the stones in large numbers have been used are the same as those used in Indraprasth or later cities.

During the time of Sher Shah, Delhi remained only an administrative centre and provincial Headquarter. The Lodi's had shifted their capital to Agra, till Shah Jahan, the Mughals kept Agra as their capital. Only Humayun restored the citadel of Indrapat and named it 'Dinpanah' (asylum of the faith). Sher Shah destroyed the Delhi of Ala-ud-Din and used its stones to build its own town. Firoz Shah built his own town while using the stones of Tughlaqabad and Mehrauli.

Shah Jahan built his city using the red stones from Dholpur, and other stones from Firoz Shah Kotla and Bhojla hill. The Muslim culture and civilization had reached its climax of development during this period.

Kos Minar near Apollo Hospital, Mathura Road.

Some of the cities (Lahore, Multan, Jaunpur, Agra, Ajmer and Delhi) were not only the seats of governments and administration, the centre of trade, industry, commerce, academic, literary and spiritual activities, but with the passage of time, they also became the centre where a new Indo-Muslim culture based on a peculiar synthesis of Indo-Muslim values, beliefs, and cultural traits was fashioned.

The city of Shahjahanabad was built between 1639 and 1648 A.D. This city remained the home of the Mughal Emperor until 1858 A.D. But it ceased to be an imperial capital after 1739 A.D., the year of Nadir Shah's invasion, which not only massacred its inhabitants, but also looted them and the fort, burned and ransacked this city. This city (now onwards will be addressed as Delhi) has been a witness to several turmoil and upheavals of local and foreign invasions as well as internal feuds since its early days. These had affected the political, social, religious and economic life of this city. Chander Bhan Brahman, who was a noble at the court of Shah Jahan, was present when this city was built and inaugurated. He narrates 'its towers are the resting place of the Sun. Its avenues are so full of pleasure that its lanes are like the roads of paradise. Its climate is beautiful and pleasant.'[64]

The city was surrounded by gardens from three sides and on eastern side the Yamuna river was flowing touching the walls of Red Fort. Ali Mardan

Digambar Jain Temple, Chandni Chowk.

Khan, who was the Minister of Shah Jahan, brought a canal from western side of Delhi. The canal not only irrigated the gardens around it, but also supplied water to Red Fort and a moat around it. This canal entered into the city from Khari-Baoli side crossed the whole Chandni Chowk area and entered in the Red Fort. On both side of this canal there were big trees. This was restored in 1829 A.D. Many changes in the geography of this canal were made after 1857 A.D. and it was closed in 1910 A.D. Stephen P. Blake, called this city as the capital of the patrimonial-bureaucratic Empire; he had taken this concept from Max-Weber, who believe, 'Patrimonial State is the Patriarchal family and the central element is the imperial household. The Patrimonial ruler tried to assimilate state to household: he attempted to administer, control and finance the entire realm as if it were part of his own private domain.'[65]

But this concept of sovereignty was against the concept of sovereignty in Islam. The Islamic conception of economic life has no distinct theory. Sovereignty in Islam cannot be confined to political supremacy alone. It must be, all embracing; the very basis of Islamic sovereignty will be those principles or fundamentals which were revealed to the prophet of Islam. In Islam, Allah is the Sovereign. No individual, group, society, nation or international authority can lay claim to sovereignty. The Islamic state must be based on the basic principles laid down in the Quran. The state and the government must act on these principles. None can transgress the limits set up by Allah.[66]

It was totally un-Islamic that state exchequer spent on personal use even for the marriage of the members of the royal family. Aurangzeb had out of many, one such complaint against Shah Jahan that he had emptied the royal treasury in building the huge structures during his reign. The Europeans of this period may not like the city and its buildings, they may have compared it with the structures of Paris, London or Amsterdam, but they have forgotten the very fact that the buildings built at Lahore, Agra and Delhi were built to suit its climate, 'Thus Delhi also may possess beauties adapted to a warm climate.'[67]

The shifting of the capital from Agra to Delhi was one such reason: that the city was exposed during summer and rendered it unfit for the residence of a monarch. Its roads and streets got narrow and congested for royal processions. Bernier describes, that 'Delhi' was a city which could be circled in three hours on horseback. This did not include the suburbs, only the walled city, and the walls were broken at many places. In fact, Lord Lake got these rebuilt when the British took over Delhi in 1803, originally it was made of mud and not of mortar. The suburbs were only three or four and not exceeding 1½ 'league' and these suburbs are on the side of Lahore and surrounded by gardens and open spaces. Outside the fort there was a garden, filled at all times with flowers and green shrubs. 'Next to the garden of the fortress, and on the opposite side of which terminate the two most considerable streets of the city.'[68]

Percival Spear writes,

> Shahjahan built three great streets in Shahjahanabad. ... These three great streets were the Chandni Chowk, a road from Delhi Gate of the Red Fort to the Jama Masjid, and a road from the Delhi Gate of the Red Fort to the Delhi Gate of the city. Part of this road is now the Faiz Bazar. The road to the Jama Masjid and its bazar was destroyed after the Mutiny when all the houses on the present ground were also demolished (Zakaullah's grandfather had one such house in this place, which he had described to C.F. Andrews in his interview to C.F. Andrews, Zakaullah of Delhi, London, 1919). This road was used by the Emperors when they went on state to the Jama Masjid. The Chandni Chowk was the chief road for processions. Here Shah Jahan and Aurangzeb passed in pomp; here Dara Shikoh was led as prisoner through the sorrowful Delhi crowds; here Nadir Shah and Ahmad Shah Abdali rode in triumph, here at Kotwali Guru Tegh Bahadur along with his associates was executed; here in a house of Begum Samru, Bahadur Shah II was kept as prisoner and here came Madhav Rao Sindhia, the Maratha, and Ghulam Qadir who took away the eyes of Shah Alam II. The last state procession was in 1912 A.D. when Lord Hardinge entered Delhi, for the first time. The Chandni Chowk is one of the most historic streets in the world.[69]

The Mughal rulers kept the Chandni Chowk street for their own use, for state processions so that no untoward incident could occur between various communities in Delhi; but the British started allowing it for the use of all, however with permission. The city was built in a planned way, keeping in view of the difficulties at Lahore and Agra. The street originated from a distance of 50 yards of the main gates of the fort. At the end of the streets, there were magnificent mosques, with sarais and *hamams* attached to them. The Jama Masjid was the Friday mosque for the Emperor and his household and the Princes and great Amirs attended the mosque on holidays and festivals. It was in addition, the public forum for Muslims of the city and, to a certain degree, for Muslims of the empire at large. It was the place where changes in ruler and dynasty were announced and the place where people congregated to register displeasure with religious, political or social policies.[70]

This masjid was completed in 1658 and Shah Jahan was confined at Agra the same year. Till the completion of Jama Masjid, Shah Jahan used to perform his prayers at Shah Jahani Masjid (near Pataudi House).

The Eastern Gate of this mosque was connected with Khas Bazar where cloth and pigeons were sold. On the western side stood a madrasah and a hospital, where sick people were treated at the Emperor's expense. The area was the rallying point for the inhabitants of the city. Faqirs and mendicants roamed in large number. Eight other big mosques were also built by Begums and great Amirs.

From 1639 to 1739 A.D., ninety one mosques were built by noble men and women, Amirs, mansabdars, merchants and caste/craft groups, and were located in mansions and walled neighborhoods throughout the city.[71]

To build a mosque was a virtuous act. It is believed that whoever built a place of worship of God, God built a house for him in Paradise.

Early in his reign, Shah Jahan had ordered the building of mosques in every city that contained Muslims. The command was followed in Shahjahanabad 'In every lane, bazar, square, and street they have erected mosques'. In the early 1740's, Joseph Tieffenthalar, a German Jesuit, observed:

> Delhi contains a great number of Mosques built at great expense; there are two constructed of red stone transported here from Fatepouer, two others whose domes are gilded with gold. The number of small ones is unknowable.[72]
>
> The archeological survey of the city (List of monuments I) conducted in the early part of this century, listed 410 structures in the walled city and 378 outside the Palace-fortress, 202 (53 percent) were Mosques. Two hundred of these were built between 1639 and 1857 and one hundred between 1639 and 1739.[73]

Bazars

For royal members, nobles and commoners, bazars (shops) were planned on the main streets of Shahjahanabad on both sides of the streets. One from Lahori Gate of the fort to Fatehpuri Mosque was built in 1650 A.D. by Jahan Ara Begum, this street was 40 yards wide and 1520 yards long and held 1560

Ghantewala, one of the oldest sweet shops, Chandni Chowk.

shops and porticos. The canal (brought to Delhi by Ali Mardan Khan) flowed through its middle; on both sides of it there were big trees that provided shade. Originally this street had no name, but, sections of it were named such as starting from Lahori Gate, the Chowk, then Kotwali Chabutra, then Urdu Bazar, Asharfi or Jauhri (Jewellers) Bazar. In the north of this area, Jahan Ara Begum built a *caravansarai* (inn) and a garden. Both of them were very beautiful. In front of Fatehpuri Mosque was a platform and below that a pool. A sarai for scholars and travellers stood nearby; near it Khari Baoli and a vegetable and fruit market was there. Every day a caravan used to come from Afghanistan and other places laden with fruits.

All kinds of goods from India and abroad were displayed in these shops, above it were the residences of shopkeepers.

Coffee Houses

Coffee drinking is not just a modern activity; there are records that coffee drinking was very popular during the Mughal period. There were coffee houses in Chandni Chowk. These places were the rendezvous where literary people and poets met each other and the poets recited their new poetic compositions. Topics concerning war often discussed. Anand Ram Mukhalis used to go to these coffee houses very often.[74] The other famous bazar was Chowk-i-Sa'dullah Khan; this was named after the Wazir of Shah Jahan, (now it is leading to Darya Gunj or Subhash Park area). In this bazar, there were many shops of the Punjabis, the natives of Lahore. On both sides of this street there were spacious and decorated shops in a distance of an arrowshot. Among other famous bazars—the Bazar of Khanum, Khas Bazar, Faiz Bazar, Urdu Bazar, Bazar-i-Jami masjid, Bazar-i-Sadar, Bazar-i-Lahori Darwaza, Khari Baoli. Ghuzri ka Bazar, Bazar-i-Lal Shah, Bazar-i-Sita Ram, Qumar-ud-Din Chowk ka Bazar, Bazar-i-Chah Khari, Bazar-i-Charkhawalan, Bazar-i-nau, Bazar-i-Chabyan,, Bazar-i-Zer-i-Jami masjid, Bazar-i-Kashmiriyan, Dariba Bazar, Bazar-i-Chakla, Bazar-i-Fatehpuri, Bazar-i-Sadat Khan, Bazar-i-Chauri ('Chauri' is a Marathi word which means a Police Post). During the predominance of the Marathas at Delhi, there was a police station in this bazar. This bazar was also very wide so it was also known as Chaura Bazar, now it has come down to Chauri Bazar, on the upper stories of this bazar, the prostitutes used to live.[75] Other famous bazars were Bazar-i-Jauhri and Bazar-i-Amir Khan.[76] Some bazars were destroyed after 1857 A.D. by the British.

Shah Jahan shifted his capital to keep wide streets, which was not possible at Agra. However, later on the main streets of the city could not be maintained in their original form, and there were encroachments on the roads, hence they did not remain as wide as they were when Twining visited Delhi in 1794 A.D. He observed,

> Passing through several streets of which one alone was remarkable. It was very wide and formerly a canal, formed of red stone, received the waters of the Yamuna, several miles above Delhi, and conveyed them through the city to the palace. Now there was no water in the canal, and small houses of mean appearance having been built on each side of it, neither the original width nor beauty of the streets had been preserved.[77]

In fact, all the major cities from the ancient time had been built either on the banks of some river or near the source of water. Shahjahanabad was also built on the western bank of river Yamuna. Yamuna was fulfilling the need of water of the city; a large number of wells were there in the city. The city was surrounded by gardens on three sides, to meet the requirement of water for these gardens and the city, a noble of Shah Jahan, named Ali Mardan Khan brought a canal from Sirhind to Delhi which ended in Red Fort. This canal passed through Chandni Chowk and was called Nahar-i-Bahisht. The other view is that Sultan Firoz Shah Tughluq had brought a canal from the Pargana of Khizrabad to Safidaun. During the reign of Akbar, Shihab-ud-Din Khan, the Governor of Delhi, repaired that canal, but the succeeding generations paid no attention to it and it fell into disuse. The ponds were there in large number and the water table of Delhi was not as low as it is today. The rainy seasons were for nearly four months. There was no crisis of water as it is today despite the fact that animals were there in the city in large numbers who consume lots of water. There were wells in almost every mansion and the street, the Panch-Kuyan Road of that time, denotes that there were five wells on that road. There is no record of fight over drinking water as is seen today.

In the neighbourhood of Delhi, in the direction of Faridabad, a noble of Shah Jahan built a dam, a bridge and a sarai which became a small town later. Bakhtawar Nagar area also had a huge water reservoir.

In 1715 A.D., Qutb-ul-Mulk Sayyid Abdullah Khan had provided water to the residents of Patpar Ganj by cutting a branch canal from the main river.

The Hauz (Pond) Qazi, Hauz Shamsi, Hauz Khas were there to provide water. Every Sarai had a well and a pond near it. There were *Baolis* inside and outside the city such as Khari Baoli, Agrasen ki Baoli, Rajo ki Baoli (Mehrauli).

Gardens and Suburbs

The walled city of Shahjahanabad was only the hub of an urban complex that extended several miles into the countryside on all directions. Nearly half of the population resided in the suburbs, and the ring of gardens, tombs, bazars and *Mohalla*s contained a good deal of economic, cultural and social activities of the city. The Mughal rulers, Nawabs and the Begums of the royal family were keenly interested in laying out gardens; even the big Zamindars had their garden, and it was the economic culture of that period. It was not only a place

Tripolia, Rana Pratap Bagh.

of amusement and status but also providing the fresh breath to the city as well as fruits and vegetables. The gardens were also adding to the beauty of the city. The gardens were there inside the city and in the Red Fort (Hayat Bakhsh), a large garden adjoining the ditch of the fort, filled with all kinds of flowers and green shrubs.

Shah Jahan had a country house in a large and beautiful garden called Shalimar Bagh, some three-four miles away from the walled city. In this garden Nadir Shah stayed for a day; here Aurangzeb performed his coronation ceremony. But in course of time, this garden got ruined and deserted; only the name is left. Jahan Ara Begum, the eldest daughter of Shahjahan, also built a big and beautiful garden along with a beautiful Sarai, the place now is Town Hall, opposite the Old Delhi Railway Station; earlier it was called Queen's Garden by the British; now it is no more there. The Bagh-i-Anguri was situated adjacent to the Qila-i-Arak. There was a big garden of oranges, outside the Kashmiri Gate, which had to be cleared by the British in 1857 to bombard Kashmiri Gate, as it was a hurdle for the attack. Tees Hazari was a garden; now the District Courts are there. Roshan Ara Begum, the younger daughter of Shah Jahan, also built a garden and a sarai, now it is in ruin, located at Roshan Ara Road. She is buried in that garden. Paen Bagh of Kamgar Khan is situated near the Takiya of Majnu Shah. There was a garden on the plain in front of the

First gate of Bagh-i-Nazir built by Mahaldar Khan in 1728 A.D. (later on taken by David Ochesterlony), Rana Pratap Bagh.

Second gate of Bagh-i-Nazir built by Mahaldar Khan in 1728 A.D., Rana Pratap Bagh.

Jharokha (Red Fort) in which Nargis flowers were planted, Bagh-i-Jawed Khan, Bagh-i-Shaista Khan Bagh-i-Gulabi, Andha Mughal, and Bagh-i-Golapa. Chahar-Bagh, Bagh-i-Khirabad, Bagh-i-Jugal Kishore, Bagh-i-Jharokha, Qudsia Bagh, Bagh-i-Jafar Khan, Bagh-i-Sahibabad, Bagh-i-Talkatora, Karoli Ka Bagh, Bagh-i-Zia-ud-Daula Asadullah, Jor Bah, Lodi Garden, Sunehri Bagh, the Khan-i-Saman, situated near the Sarai Rohilla, Mochi or Moti Bagh, Baghichi-i-Nili Chattari, situated between Nurgarh (Salim Garh Fort) and Nigambodh, and the gardens of Dhirpur.

Bagh-i-Farhat Afza, situated in the town of Loni, Bagh-i-Musharraf, Bagh-i-Sarhindi, Bagh-i-Mahaldar Khan were situated in the Old Subzi Mandi (laid in 1728 A.D.), Bagh-i-Nazir (laid in 1748 A.D.) by Nazir Roz Afzun, an eunuch of Mohammad Shah. Baghs were attached to the havelis of Burhan-ul-Mulk Sa'adat Khan and Mujaddid-ud-Daula Abdul Ahad Khan. Bakhtawar Khan had also laid out some gardens at Bakhtawar Nagar.

During the last quarter of the eighteenh century, all these gardens were in a state of decay.[78]

The names had also changed with the change of its owners. Now it is very difficult to find out the exact location of these gardens. The city has expanded so much and houses have come up all over the place, where once the trees were there.

Shahjahanabad was not limited to the area enclosed by the walls. The influence of the city extended several miles into the countryside on the north, south and west along the opposite bank of the river on the east. The ring of gardens, tombs, bazars and mohallas contained a good deal of the economic, social, and religions activity of the city. The exact area of the suburbs cannot be measured as Bernier writes, 'I cannot undertake to define exactly the circumference, because these suburbs are interspersed with extensive gardens and open spaces.'[79]

In the north and south of the city, the suburbs were extended from 3 to 7 Kos.[80]

It was extended to Arab ki Sarai in the South; in the west to the tomb of Qutab al-Qutab.

The total area in 1739 A.D. was probably about 3300 acres: 1500 acres for the walled city and about 1800 acres for the nearby suburbs of Mughalpura, Subzi Mandi, Paharganj, Jai Sing Pura and the rest.

The suburbs contained as many as fifty-two bazars and thirty-six mandirs; the tombs of holy men and saints, and the gardens and garden-tombs of important men and women.[81]

Paharganj was the largest and most important of the suburban mohallas. It was the main grain market, where food grains from across the river were stored before being distributed to shopkeepers and peddlers for sale within the city, linking Paharganj to the Akbarabadi gate was another wholesale bazar called Shah Ganj. Patpar Ganj and Shahadara were another wholesale grain markets, which were destroyed in the mid-eighteenth century.

Jai Singh Pura was also a well-known mohalla near Paharganj named after Raja Jai Singh of Jaipur. In the Kothi or Mansion of Raja Jai Singh now there is Bangla Sahib Gurudwara. Near to it was Rakab Ganj. It was the Mohallah of Banjaras (grain dealers), who were in the household or stirrup (*rikab*) of the Emperor. Gurudwara Rakab Gunj was erected there. The remains of the body of Guru Tegh Bahadur are still preserved there. Beyond Kabul Gate of the city lay Mughalpura; the canal split this suburb. There were watering gardens and houses on its way into the city. The Mongols from Central Asia resided in this place since the days of the Khilji Sultans. North of Mughalpura is the Subzi Mandi, which was earlier in the Khari Baoli area. Mori and Kashmiri Gates were connected by a row of bazars and mohallas that were destroyed in the mid-eighteenth Century. Other Mohallas were Malka Ganj, Sayyidwara, Tarka Ganj, Abdullah Nagar, Wakilpura and Najaf Ganj.

Around the city, the tombs of saints, rulers and important men and women, were the sites for celebrations of *urs* (death and birth anniversary) and place far rest and relaxation. Other such places were: Humayun's tomb, the Tomb of Sheikh Nizam al-Din Aulia, Qadam Sharif, Tomb of Ghazi-al-Din Khan, Sayyid Husain Rasul Numa, buried at Gulabi Bagh; Tomb of Baktiyar Kaki at Mehrauli, Nasir-al-Din Mohammad (Chiragh-i-Delhi).

The nobles and rich people laid out gardens around the city. While the city was being built, Shah Jahan laid out a garden called Khizrabad on the banks of the river Yamuna about five miles south of the Akbarabadi Gate of the city. Here, in 1658 A.D., Aurangzeb imprisoned his brother Dara Shikoh.[82]

Outside the Kabul gate of the city, Jahan Ara Begum constructed a garden filled with neem trees and called it Tis Hazari Bagh (now the District Courts). Malika-i-Zamani, wife of Mohammad Shah, was buried there.

It was difficult to estimate the population of the city in 1650 A.D., however Bernier estimated it around 3,75,000–4,00,000 persons; Jean de Thevenot, a French who travelled in western India during 1666 A.D. stated that Shahjahanabad had a population of about 4,00,000 persons.[83]

During Nadir Shah's invasion, the city experienced great fluctuations in size, population and activities.

In 1679 A.D., Aurangzeb left the city for the Deccan and so the population of the city declined.

Bahadur Shah returned to North India (Lahore) in 1707 A.D. and the city began to revive. But since he spent the five years of his reign in touring, never really living in the palace-fortress, the full rebirth of the city had to await Bahadur Shah's successor in 1712 A.D. With the return of the men, the animals and equipment of the great camp, the city quickly regained its former size and population probably gained about 4,00,000 persons until the invasion of Nadir Shah in 1739 A.D.

Mansions of Shahjahanabad

With the building of Shahjahanabad, the Amir, Umrah and the princesses built their mansions in the city and this process continued. As and when the capital was shifted by the rulers either to Agra and Lahore these people built their mansions in that city. When Nadir-Shah left Shahjahanabad he took a map of the city and he was so impressed by its plan and buildings, that he constructed a city one-quarter the size of Delhi in Khurasan in 1741 A.D. There are some mansions whose structure is not left today in the same fashion as it was in its origin.

The Mansion of Safdar Jang

Dara Shikoh, son of Shahjahan, built a magnificent mansion on the banks of Yamuna in four years (1639–43 A.D.) at a cost of four hundred thousand rupees. In the late seventeenth or early eighteenth centuries, the original mansion was divided. Safdar Jang, Wazir of Ahmad Shah occupied the structure nearest the fort. He was the nephew and son-in-law of Sa'adat Khan, Nawab of Oudh and succeeded to the Nawabi on his uncle's death in 1739 A.D.

In 1662 A.D., Prince Muazzam, son and eventual successor of Aurangzeb lived there. The mansion was damaged during the invasion of Nadir Shah. Safdar Jang occupied it from 1744 to 1752 A.D.

Najib-ud-Daulah lived here from 1755 to 57 A.D. and 1761 to 70 A.D. In 1785 A.D., Asaf-al-Daulah got this property. On the British takeover in 1803 A.D., the mansion was turned into quarters for garrison officer and later it was converted into a munitions storehouse.[84]

The Mansion of Dara Shikoh

It was also used by Dara Shikoh as his library as he was a great literary person. In 1639 A.D., Ali Mardan Khan also lived here. In 1803 A.D., the mansion became the British Residency. In a part of it, Delhi College was housed for some years.

The Mansion of Ali Mardan Khan

He was a Persian and came to India during the time of Shahjahan in 1637 A.D. He was given the task of bringing the canal to Red Fort, which he did skillfully. He built his own mansion in the new capital. Prince Azam Shah, third son of Aurangzeb, lived here during most of his father's time. In 1713 A.D. during the time of Farrukh Siyar, Sayyid Abd al Allah Khan, the elder of the two famous Sayyids of Barha took over this Mansion.

The Mansion of Lutfullah Khan

He was an Amir of the early eighteenth century. This Mansion was also taken by the elder Sayyid brother in 1715 A.D.

The Mansion of Majid al Daulah

He was an Amir under Mohammad Shah and Ahmad Shah. He lived in this mansion in the early eighteenth century. His son, Abdul Ahad Majid-al-Daulah, who took a prominent role in the political intrigues of 1780 A.D., lived in this mansion.

The Mansion of Shaista Khan

He was the Wazir of Shahjahan who constructed this mansion opposite the Lahori Gate of the Palace-fortress. Asad Khan Asaf al-Daulah and his son Zulfiqar Khan Amir al-Umrah lived in this Mansion during the reign of Aurangzeb. Zulfiqar Khan was killed in 1713 A.D. and Sayyid Hussein Ali Khan took this house. Farrukhsiyar gave this house to Mir Jumla and later to Samsam al-Daulah. In 1757 A.D., when Ahmad Shah looted Delhi, this house was dug up by the Afghans in search of buried treasure.

The Mansion of Ghasi Ram

He was the astrologer of Shah Jahan. This house was built during the early days of the city.

The Mansion of Habshi Khan

Sadi Miftah Habshi Khan, an Amir under Shahjahan and Aurangzeb, constructed this mansion near the Fatehpuri Mosque. Sidi Faulad Khan, Kotwal under Mohammad Shah repaired this house and lived there.

The Mansion of Sa'adat Khan

This mansion was one of the largest in the city built near the Kabuli Gate. It had six separate gateways. Sa'adat Khan Burhan al-Mulk, was the first Nawab of Oudh; he resided during the early time of Mohammad Shah's reign. He died on the eve of Nadir Shah's invasion and his house was looted and ransacked by the Persians.

The Mansion of Haidar Quli Khan

Haidar Quli, an Amir under Mohammad Shah, was appointed commander of the artillery by Sayyid Hussein Ali of Barha. This house is now occupied by various people near Fatehpuri.

The Mansion of Sher Afghan Khan

This mansion was named after Sher Afghan Khan. The poet Gulshan was the member of Sher Afghan's house.

The Mansion of Sipahar Khan

Sipahar Khan was the son of Aurangzeb's foster brother, achieved a rank of three thousand *zat*. His palace was on the periphery of the city near the wardrobe gate.

The Mansion of Adina Beg Khan

He was the noble of Mohammad Khan. His mansion was on the road from the Lahori Gate to the Turkman Gate.

The Mansion of Qamar al Din Khan

He was the Wazir of Mohammad Shah from 1724 to 1728 A.D., he lived in one of the largest and finest mansions of the city. He was a very indifferent administrator and the Mughal Empire drifted during his tenure. In 1761 A.D. Najib-ul-Daulah resided here. In 1788 A.D. one of the lieutenants of Ghulam Qadir, occupied the place. The British converted it into the custom house.

The Mansion of Muzaffar Khan

This mansion was at Turkman Gate. He was the noble of Shahjahan.

The Mansion of Mir Khan

Mir Khan's father was the Governor of Lahore, under Aurangzeb for twenty years. He did not hold a high position but was a confidant of Mohammad Shah, and invited scholars, artists, poets and musicians to the court.

The Mansion of Afghan Khan

This mansion was near the Jama Masjid. Azam Khan was the son of Amir Khan during the reign of Mohammad Shah.

Matiya Mahal

The builder of this mansion is unknown, but a number of important Amirs lived here. It is said to have been the home of Shahjahan during the construction of the Red Fort. It was also the residence of Azizabadi Begum; later Bahadur Shah II conferred it on one of the grandsons.

The Mansion of Bakhtawar Khan and Other Mansions

The mansion of Bakhtawar Khan (outside the city wall). The mansion of Ahmad Ali Khan, the Mansion of Khan Duran (near Jama Masjid), the mansion of Sarbuland Khan, the mansion of ustad Hamid (near Jami Masjid, the mansion of Shahji, the mansion of Sa'adullah Khan/Ghazi al-Din Khan, haveli of Nar Singh Das, haveli of Harun-un-Nisa Kaka, these two havelis were plundered by Jat invaders.

There were so many havelis or mansions of Amirs and merchants built from time to time and occupied by various persons. Some were hereditary, some were taken by others than its builders.

The havelis of nobles which were constructed in front or near the Red-Fort, are no more there. In the same way, there were houses at the place that is now old Delhi Railway Station. These were demolished by the British. No trace of these havelis can be found now.[85]

The palaces and mansions of the noblemen were the central institutions of Shahjahanabad. The mohalla was the major form of residential organization. Neighbours were 'people of the mohallah'—persons who occupied an adjacent house or who attended the mosque of the mohalla—and one of the first duties of a city magistrate was to see that the urban area was divided into mohallas; the mohallas were constructed on the basis of caste/craft and elitism. The chiefs of the mohallas were to decide the local issues. Mohallas were surrounded by high walls and contained houses, shops and stalls where food, clothing and other supplies were sold, wells and tanks for water and rest houses for travellers. People gathered in mosques and temples to listen to political announcements, celebrate marriages and exchange gossip. The inhabitants were grouped in self-contained self-governing wards, where the men were usually united by the sameness of profession or the patronage of one common protector such as a nobleman or a saint, around whose mansion or shrine they clustered.

Anarchy followed the decline of the Mughal power, each ward or lane had to fortify itself by building defensive gates at its two ends which were closed at the evening or at the first alarm of an invasion or riot. This system was called Kucha Bandi and it lasted down to the time of the mutiny of 1857 A.D. The city of Delhi was divided into mohallas, kuchas and katras, signifying the racial and professional, groups lived therein that is, Ahdipura (a kind of Indian military group) situated adjacent to Shah Ganj, Khari Baoli, Chowk-i-Sa'adullah Khan, and Chandni Chowk. In every mohalla there was a Mir-i-Mohalla, it was the duty of the Kotwal to administer the city. For his help, horsemen and soldiers were provided; the Qazi had to decide on religions matters.

Agra was much superior in mansions, houses, and trade and industry than Delhi. Delhi was the second important provincial city in the Mughal Empire for trade and industry during 1629–43 A.D. 'This city is much resorted to by merchants on account of the varied kinds of merchandise found there, especially indigo, cotton cloths, mostly dyed in various colors, and stuffs which they call Chitas.'[86]

The artists and craftsmen who had the patronage of the king and the nobles had good fortune; the rest of them were considered low and had to give their goods and services to the nobles at low rates or they were beaten.

Hooka-bottoms were manufactured in large scale as smoking of tobacco became very popular during the Mughal period.

Bernier writes that there were many Karkhanas or workshops meant for the artisans inside the Delhi Red-Fort.[87]

The capital town of Delhi was not safe from the menace of the robbers. The dacoits and bandits were very active on the highways. Most of the people kept arms not only for personal safety but also for fashion as a consequence of which Iron industry might have been established to meet the local consumption of arms.

The industries for manufacturing coats for men, bows and arrows, shawls were established in Delhi.

The people of Turkey, Zanzibar, Syria, England, Denmark, Yemen, Saudi Arabia, Iraq, Khurasan, Kabul, Zabulistan, Cathey, Khotan, China, Machin, (Great China) Kashghar, Qalmquistan, Tibet, Kashmir and other provinces of India had already chosen to settle in Delhi. They learnt the language of the city and kept themselves engaged in various commercial activities of their interest.[88]

By 1748–54 A.D., at the time of Emperor Ahmad Shah 'the dignity of the Mughal royalty has fallen to such a low ebb that even the bankers and money-lenders refused to advance any money on loan.'[89]

Delhi could not recover from the setback it had suffered at the hands of Nadir Shah, its cultural and commercial activities could not be revived.[90] The king and his dependents lived in miserable condition.

Shahjahanabad became an important centre of educational and spiritual activities. During the period of Shah Jahan and Aurangzeb, the spiritual and educational activities increased and continued till the reign of Mohammad Shah. Apart from the earlier khanqahs; there were twenty two Sufis during the reign of Mohammad Shah. Among the famous khanqahs of the period were that of Shah Kalimullah, Shah Fakhruddin Dehlvi, Mirza Mazhar Jan-i-Janan, Khwaja Mir Dard, Sa'dullah Gulshan, and Mirza Abdul Qadir Bedil. People from far and near thronged at those khanqahs to quench their spiritual thirst. Besides the above mentioned Sufis, others such as, Shah Bhik, Shah-Abdul Rasul, Shah Sharif, Shah Basit, Shah Abdul Mannan, Shah Faqirullah Ambalvi, Shah Sondhi Ambalvi, Shah Bayazid, Shah Fuzail, Shah Ghulam Mohammad Jhatlavi, Shah Abdus Samad, Shah Kamal, Shah Budh, Shah Mubarak, Shah Ramz, Shah Abdullah, Shah Karimullah, Shah Nasir, Shah Abdul Latif, Shah Hussein Waiz, Sayyid Mohammad Khan, Saeed Khan, Shah Kazim, Mir Mohammad Shafiz.

In the eighteenth century, Qadam Sharif became the popular place for pilgrimage in Delhi. In thirteenth and fourteenth century the tomb of Bakhtiyar Kaki at Mehrauli and Nizam-ud-Din Aulia at Nizam-ud-Din, become very popular. Khari Gujrat and Rajasthan merchants controlled trade in Shahjahanabad along with other traders. Like mosques and khanqahs, Hindus were also allowed to build their religious places, but this was done after 1648 A.D.; so between 1648 and 1857 A.D., ninety-six temples were erected in Shahjahanabad, twelve of which had inscriptions and could be dated. Of the twelve, ten were constructed during the British period (1803–57 A.D.), two during the period of destruction and decline in the eighteenth century (1739–1803 A.D.) and none at all during the period of Shahjahanabad's glory (1639–1739 A.D.).[91]

Early in his reign, Aurangzeb had ordered against the construction of new temples and the repairs of the old ones.[92] Image worship came to be regarded as an evil practice and a crime necessary to be suppressed[93] Aurangzeb also ordered in 1665 the discontinuation of the festivals of Holi and Diwali.[94] The pilgrimages of the Hindus were also stopped.[95] The burning of the dead on the bank of Yamuna had been prohibited.[96] Only the Rajputs and the Marathas were allowed to mount (Turki) horses. The ordinary Hindus were not allowed to mount such horses.

After the invasion of Nadir Shah, the decline of Shahjahanabad started. The decline was also due to luxurious life of the Emperors and nobles, engrossed in sensual pleasures, wine-drinking, dance and music, division of court on factional lines, nobles at court pulling down one another and without any qualm of conscience seeking help from the enemies of the Empire in a bid to settle scores with their rivals and total indifference to the interests of the state. The imperial treasury was drained and the nobles were shorn off their wealth. The soldiers were not paid salaries, and they became rowdy and created commotion due to pain of hunger. The poets, the soldiers, the courtiers, the jesters, the mimics, storytellers, cooks and prostitutes, migrated to newly risen provincial towns in general and Lucknow in particular.

The glory and prosperity of Shahjahanabad, a city developed in twenty years (foundation 1638 A.D.) as an important centre of Indo-Muslim culture, literary and spiritual activities, could not survive more than a hundred year. (Nadir Shah invaded in 1739 A.D.).

From 1748 to 1769 A.D. Ahmad Shah Abdali invaded India about nine times. The inhabitants of Shahjahanabad were subjected to all kinds of inhumane treatments.

Sack of Delhi by Nadir Shah

Mohammad Shah was the ruler of Delhi when Nadir Shah invaded it in

1739 A.D. Asif Jah Khandoran was the *Bakshi* (Paymaster General); he was given so much of respect by the king that whatever he demanded was accepted, but the same person was denied all the things during the time of Aurangzeb. Nizam-ul-Mulk was also one of the Amirs of Aurangzeb. The King, Mohammad Shah, remained always in the company of loose women and buffoons; he had no time for state affairs. The Marathas under Baji Rao I increased their power and positions; the Sayyid brothers who were all powerful at the court before the appointment of Mohammad Shah as king, had taken away all the buried treasures, jewellery, armory and all the imperial establishment from Delhi and Agra. The Sayyid brothers and Nizam-ul-Mulk were in open rebellion. By 1732 A.D., the Marathas partly occupied Gujarat, Bundelkhand and temporarily overrun Mewar. They spread themselves from Gwalior to Ajmer. In 1737 A.D. Baji Rao I reached Delhi, near the Dargah of Nizam-ud-Din Aulia; after looting the people he withdrew from there.

Nizam-ul-Mulk, who had left Delhi was again called back; he reached Delhi on 17 April 1737. It is believed that there was correspondence between Nizam, Sa'adat Khan and Nadir Shah to invade India.[97] In Europe, Nadir Shah is known by the Name of Quli Khan; he was born at Calot in the province of Khurasan. His father was the chief of a clan of Afsar (a tribe of Turkman). His father died when Nadir Shah was a child; his uncle did not give him his share when he came of age; he went to the city of Mashad, here he behaved so well that he was given the command of a troop of 1000 horses. He remained in this position till the age of 32 years. The Safavi king had been driven out by an Afghan soldier, whose father had freed Kandhar. He conquered heart and Khurasan and in 1722 A.D. occupied Isfahan the Safavi capital. Nadir Quli, acting in the name of Safavi king, defeated the Afghans and in 1729 A.D. expelled them from Iran.

In 1736 A.D. he ascended the throne as Nadir Shah. He wanted to punish the Afghans, who still held Kandhar. He sent envoys to Mohammad Shah requesting him to close the frontiers of the Mughal province of Kabul to the fugitives from Kandhar. Nothing was done, he sent another envoy with the request to do the needful within 40 days but many Afghans escaped from Kandhar to Kabul and no reply was received.

After a year, he captured Kandhar, Ghazni and Kabul in June 1738 A.D. He also captured Peshawar and Lahore. He wrote a letter from Lahore to Mohammad Shah, complaining about his discourtesy not replying his letter and desired to come to Delhi to punish the responsible officials. Mohammad Shah, along with his large army, reached Karnal, but the Indian army was out maneuvered; no major clash took place. Burhan-ul-Mulk, the Subedar of Awadh, was captured, the premier noble, first Bakshi of Mohammad Shah, was fatally wounded, Nizam ul-Mulk was not involved in action. Burhan-ul-

Mulk was originally from Nishapur, was taken to Persian camp. He persuaded Nadir Shah to agree to take 20 million rupees as an indemnity. Leave Mohammad Shah on the throne and make Burhan-ul-Mulk as Amir-ul-Umara in place of Khan-e-Duran. But Mohammad Shah did not agree to make Burhan-ul-Mulk as Amir-ul-Umara and made Nizam-ul-Mulk instead. Burhan-ul-Mulk now advised Nadir Shah to not to content with 20 million and to move to Delhi.

The news of the outcome of the battle of Karnal reached Delhi, the Kotwal of the city, Haji Faulad Khan, took all steps to prevent any panic and lawlessness. He closed all the gates of the city. Nadir Shah decided to go to Delhi. He sent Tahmasp Khan and Sa'adat Khan in the advance party and himself marched towards Delhi along with Mohammad Shah with the orders of the Governor, Lutfullah Khan the gates of the city were opened, the keys of the fortress and the treasuries and store-houses were given to Tahmasp Khan.

Travelling via Panipat, Sonipat and Narela the two monarchs reached Shalimar Gardens on 18 March. Nadir Shah remained in Shalimar Garden till 20 March. Nadir Shah was on horseback, lined with troops and headed by 100 elephants, he reached the Red Fort on 20 March, and there he was given salute of guns. He was received with great pomp and given costly presents. Mohammad Shah offered to Nadir his entire royal treasures and jewels. This was what his forefathers could accumulate from the loot in 348 years. After reception and entertainment by the Emperor, Nadir Shah stayed in Diwan-i-Khas, the Emperor stayed in Asad Burj, some Qizilbash troops were kept in the fort and the rest were quartered around the fort and in the city. Next morning (21 March) it was Persian Nou Roz and the Id-ul-Juha (Feast of Sacrifice). The Khutba was read in Nadir Shah's name in all the mosques of Delhi. Coins were also struck in Delhi in the name of Nadir Shah. The same day Sa'adat Khan died. (It is believed that he took poison as Nadir Shah spoken roughly to him at the public Durbar (Delhi Chronicle); some say that he was injured in the foot and because of gangrene he died.)

In the afternoon of 21 March, a rumour was spread in the city that Nadir Shah was arrested; a rumour also spread that Nadir Shah was killed by some women guards of the Emperor. These rumours spread in the whole city like fire and people started gathering in open places; the Qizilbash troops who were in the city were also attacked by the people. In the Paharganj granaries some soldiers of Nadir Shah were killed. When reports of Nadir Shah reached the soldiers, they could not resist much. Some Indian Nobles such as Sayyid Niyaz Khan, a son-in-law of Qumar-ud-Din Khan and Shah Nawaz Khan collected 500 men and captured Salim Garh fort. By some estimate, 3000 to 7000 Persians were killed.

In the first instance, Nadir Shah refused to believe such rumours. He ordered one of his Yasauls to go and ascertain the truth. He was killed as he came out of the Red Fort; a second Yasaul also suffered the same fate. Now Nadir Shah sent 1,000 Jazayirchis to quell the rioters, but due to darkness and small numbers they could not do much. To this, Nadir Shah ordered his troops to remain under arms all night to defend themselves, if attacked. He could not sleep the whole night.

Next morning at sun rise Nadir Shah mounted his horse and with a strong escort, reached the Roshan-ud-Daulah Mosque (this mosque is in the middle of the Chandni Chowk); when he was approaching this mosque someone fired at him, Nadir Shah escaped but, one of his officers died. He mounted the roof of the mosque. He ordered his soldiers to kill everyone. The killing started at nine in the morning and continued till three o'clock in the afternoon, when the Emperor sent the Nizam-ul-Mulk and Qumar-ud-Din Khan to the Shah, to implore him to be merciful. Nadir gave the order to stop the massacre; it was obeyed instantly. Nadir Shah ordered to restore to their families the prisoners whom they had taken. How many were innocent and guiltless, who were killed will never be accurately known. The houses were burnt. Animals were killed. The estimated total that were killed range between 8,000 to 400,000 persons. (Abdul-Karim, according to the manuscript written by Sir J. Sarkar 8000 and Maratha's office letters 400,000)

Nadir Shah punished (put to death) Sayyid Niyaz Khan and Shah Nawaz Khan, who captured the Salim Garh fort and royal elephants. Nadir Shah also took vigorous punitive measures against the people of Sarai Rohilla and Mangol Pur. Haji Faulad Khan was confirmed as the Kotwal of Delhi with the beat of the Drums. Streets remained littered with corpses for some days. In the interest of public health, Nadir ordered the Kotwal to collect the bodies and burn them. Thousands of dead bodies were thrown into Yamuna and thousands were piled, Hindu and Mohammedans alike and timber was taken from wreaked houses, they were burnt.

> After killing human beings, Nadir Shah exacted his tribute of money and jewels. The possessions of Khan Dauran and Muzaffar Khan were seized. Even soldiers were sent to Awadh to confiscate the possessions of Sa'adat Khan. No one was allowed to go out of the city and the granaries were sealed. This time, the sack of Delhi was much more severe than the sack of Delhi by Timur in 1398 A.D.; this signifies Nadir Shah's massacre and high handedness'.

Baji Rao I, who had not responded to help the Emperor of Delhi, was also alarmed after the sack of Delhi. Nadir Shah ordered it to be announced that, for the next three years, no tax would be taken from any province of Persia. All the soldiers were paid their dues and all were given 60 to 100 rupees extra as per their status. The people of Delhi were still mourning their dead but Nadir Shah had got married his son, Nasrullah, with the great-granddaughter of

Aurangzeb, a daughter of Yazdan-Baksh. Aiffat-un-Nissa, after the death of Nadir Shah, was taken by Ahmad Shah Abdali in to his harem. As per Mughal etiquette, Nasrullah was required to give the account of seven generations, to this Nadir Shah said, 'Tell them that he is the son of Nadir Shah, the son of the sword, the grandson of the sword, and so on, till they have a descent of seventy instead of seven generations'[98]

Nadir Shah had ordered illuminations, display of fireworks and lavish entertainment. Some soldiers of Nadir Shah danced and sang in Turki on the night of the marriage. Next day they were killed as Nadir Shah regarded it as anti Quranic and against the tradition. Their bodies remained in the open, as a warning to others. Emissaries of Kotwal and a Persian Nasaqchis went from house to house to make the inventories of all that the owner of the house possessed for individual contribution. Now Delhi was assessed for two crores. Nadir Shah ordered some Nobles to collect the money; some families were entirely ruined, a number of persons were driven to desperation and some committed suicide. In some cases, torture was employed to enforce payment.

The value of the money, jewels and other objects which Nadir Shah obtained from the Emperor, his nobles and people must have been at least 70 crores of rupees. Some exaggerate it to a total of 111 crores, including the loot done by the soldiers. Anand Ram remarked, 'The accumulated wealth of 348 years changed owners in a moment.'[99] Anand Ram himself had to pay Rupees 5 lakh. The Peacock Throne, the most famous and valuable of Nadir's spoils was Kohinoor diamond.

On 12 May, Nadir Shah held a Durbar, he invited the Emperor and other nobles; with his own hand he placed the crown of Hindustan on the head of Mohammad Shah, and handed him a belt and a sword set with jewels; and gave splendid coats to nobles. He advised the king and warned the nobles.

In gratitude for his reinstatement as Emperor, Mohammad Shah offered all the territories of the Empire situated to the west of the Indus such as Tibet, Kashmir, provinces of Thatta including the forts. In fact some part of this offer was already with Nadir Shah; he accepted it.

Mohammad Shah's name was substituted for the name of Nadir Shah in Khutba and on coins. On 16 May, Nadir Shah left Delhi and took along with him many artisans, physicians, and others. An immense baggage train consisting of mules, camels, several hundred elephants and horses were included in the spoils. He halted at Shalimar Bagh and next day marched ahead. On the way his spoils were looted; he also looted the nobles, the rulers and people on the way. One fourth of his booty was drowned in the Chenab and Jhelam rivers.

The defeat of Indian army at the hands of Nadir Shah, the plunder and massacre of the people of Delhi, destroyed the prestige of the Mughal government and ruined it financially; this emboldened the Sikhs, the Marathas and the Jats.

Nadir Shah was a great admirer of Timur; he used to carry Timur's autobiography with him on his campaigns, and had not the heart to ruin Timur's lineal descendent in India.

Nadir Shah and Mohammad Shah remained on good terms till the death of Nadir Shah. In his last days, Nadir Shah's character underwent a rapid decline. He became a fierce tyrant, reveling in wanton bloodshed and cruelty, giving vent to frequent outbursts of fury and insane suspiciousness. He lost confidence in his officers and people. Rebellion broke out in many parts of his empire. The ceaseless warfare had emptied his treasury, to fill the coffers he had to be crueler. In this way, he lost many of his valuable officers. He killed his best soldiers, Qizilbashes, on 9 July 1747 at the northeastern corner of Khurasan; thirteen Qizilbash entered Nadir Shah's tent and killed him. The death of Nadir Shah left the field open for Ahmad Shah Abdali.

Invasions of Ahmad Shah Abdali

After the death of Aurangzeb, the Mughal Emperor and the empire grew weaker and weaker; and by the middle of the eighteenth century, the authority of the Emperor became nominal and the empire shrunk. The provinces became very strong and in the centre the nobles were getting stronger but not united. Everyone was looking after his own interest and self aggrandizement; the atmosphere of the court was spoiled by factionalism and internecine struggles; the Emperor was incapable of any reforms. The Marathas took full advantage of this situation. Many times Marathas raided the northern part of India.

Nizam-ul-Mulk died in the Deccan in 1748 A.D. and Najib-ud-Daulah, was with the Emperor but was waiting for Ahmad Shah Abdali to invade India, so that he could support him. After the assassination of Nadir Shah, Abdali, who was the famous General of Nadir Shah, established his authority over Afghanistan and started invading the sub-continent. He first attacked in 1744 A.D. but was repulsed by Ahmad Shah, the heir apparent to the Mughal Empire. After two years, Abdali again attacked and plundered some parts of Punjab. In 1751 A.D., he again attacked and took hold of Punjab and Kashmir but, in 1756 A.D., the Mughal Wazir, 'Imad-ul-Mulk', took back Punjab from the hold of Abdali. This was the challenge to Abdali. He forced a march on Delhi. The Emperor was so weak that it was agreed to cede the territory of Kashmir, Sind and Sarhind. Najib-ud-Daulah helped Abdali who defeated Marathas near Delhi. Imad-ul-Mulk was re-instated as Wazir and Najib-ud-Daulah as Wakil; Punjab was left to the charge of his own son Timur Shah.

Timur Shah was unable to control Punjab after the departure of his father. The brutal flogging was inflicted on Baba Badbhag Singh of Kartarpur. He was the Sikh leader having a considerable following. Enraged Sikhs came out in open rebellion. He also annoyed Adina Beg who fled to the hills. The people of Delhi had suffered immensely from the civil war with the withdrawal of Abdali. Now Delhi was the city of bureaucrats and most of them were living in great distress as they had ceased to receive any receipts from their jagirs which had been usurped by Rohilla Pathans, Marathas, Jats or other outlaws. The city was rife with incidents of robbery and house-breaking, and many sons of the Umrahs and lesser Mansabdars had taken to brigandage. The Kotwal himself was suspected to be in league and accused of sharing the fruits of their depredations.[100]

By July 1757, Raghunath Rao had entered the Delhi Region from Rajasthan and on 11 August 1757, the Marathas launched their attack on Delhi. Desultory fighting went on for a month and Maratha shelling did some damage to the palace (Red Fort) and two bastions near the Delhi Gate were destroyed. Eventually, Najib-ud-Daulah, submitted to the Marathas. On 3 September 1757, terms of truce were finalized. A few days later, he marched out of Delhi, with his property and followers to Saharanpur from there he used to write to Ahmad Shah Durani (Abdali) to come back and expel the unbelievers from Delhi.

Now Ahmad Khan Bangesh was appointed the Mir-Bakhshi in place of Najib. Najib's appointees were replaced by those of the Marathas. Antaji Mankeshwar was appointed the Fauzdar of Delhi Sarkar. Najib's brief dictatorship was over.

In February 1758, the Marathas, along with Sikhs and Adina Beg conquered Punjab. They looted Sarhind, the Afghan officials were captured, and the people of Sarhind were looted so thoroughly that its inhabitants were left with barely the cloths on their body. The Marathas marched ahead. On 19 April, Lahore was captured, and then Multan till the Indus River, the Marathas and Sikhs had dominated for few months.

In Delhi, Ali Gauhar, the heir apparent along with Vithal Shivdev plundered the suburbs of Delhi, and ultimately he established himself in Ali Mardan Khan's House and Vithal Shivdev camped in Qudsia Bagh. But Ali Gauhar was driven out by the Wazir; he went to Hissar, then to Muzaffar Nagar, then to Lucknow, for Shuja-ud-Daulah, on 2 January 1759.

A few weeks later, the Marathas, led by Dattaji Scindia and Jankoji, arrived in Delhi and Punjab to collect the arrears of tribute. Adina Beg, the Faujdar of Sarhind and Jalandhar, had died. All the forces of the Marathas came to Punjab. They appointed their Subedars in Lahore and Sarhind.

Ahmad Shah Durani could not remain a silent spectator, he sent an army, which met reverses at the hands of Sabaji; Dattaji came to Delhi and plundered some villages, Najib went to Sukratal, and the Marathas also followed him there.

After the repulse of the Afghans, Jahan Khan, Abdali himself had taken the field and his army swept everything that lay in its path. Many in the Marathas' forces were killed.

Imad come to Delhi and, he had the emperor murdered on 29 November 1759 and next day his old rival Intizam was also strangled to death. At the field of Taraori, Afghan forces defeated and killed many Marathas. On 9 January 1760, Dattaji was killed and his head was sent to Abdali. Jankoji Scindia and later Malhar Rao Holkar fled to Rajasthan; they reached Bharatpur and met Surajmal. The eternal friendship was sworn over *bel* leaves and Ganga water. But it was all empty form. The Marathas were hated in the North because of their regular plunder. People knew from the past experience that Abdali's incursions were of short duration; after this, they would again face the wrath of the Marathas. So, most of the northern rulers would prefer to sit on the fence and watch. Ahmad Shah Abdali was a prudent politician and successful warrior. He made Afghanistan as an independent power. A large number of Afghan nobles were attached to him, due to constant employment and much gain by carrying on military operations in India. He had marched twice to

The mutineers damaged this cross which was later on repaired and placed on St. James Church, Kashmiri Gate. (Old_cross_from_top_of_St_James_Church,_Delhi__January_1891.JPG)

The graveyard of the British between Red Fort and Daryaganj, the army was stationed here from 1857 to 2009.

Delhi and eight times to different parts within India. The Punjab was his tributary. He wanted to crush the Marathas and in 1761 A.D. he fought with them and crushed the Maratha power. He also wanted to punish Jawahar Singh, the ruler of Bharatpur.

Apart from the famous third battle of Panipat (1761 A.D.) he invaded India in December 1766 and 1769 A.D. as well. In all his invasions he got uncounted booty in the form of cash, jewellery, diamond, animals, men, women, children and territory.

Similarly the Marathas, the Jats, the Sikhs and the Rohillas plundered the inhabitants of the city and towns and villages around Delhi.

In 1803 A.D., British established their administration in Delhi. The British army occupied the land north and south of the Red-Fort. All the havelis from Red Fort to Jama Masjid were razed to ground. One battalion laid out a bazar, setup a hospital, and built accommodation for guns and stables near Kashmiri Gate. Dara Shikoh's mansion became the headquarters of the Resident and other places were used for official activity. Two battalions were quartered in the Daryaganj area east of Faiz Bazar. Qamar al-Din Khan's mansion near Ajmeri Gate became the custom house.

In 1817 A.D., Jama masjid was renovated. In 1828 A.D. British shifted their cantonment to North of Kashmiri Gate (now Delhi University area). During 1830-57 A.D. British laid out a cemetery, built a church near Kashmiri Gate, established a college in the old residency, constructed a club, a bank, post office, printing press, and photographic studio. In 1852 A.D., Calcutta Gate was opened in the south eastern wall of the city. With the shift of the cantonment, Europeans began to settle in the civil station (Civil Lines area).

Villages of Delhi

Like the city of Delhi its villages which had been established at different periods and its people had also played a great role in the socio-cultural, political and economic life of Delhi and Hindustan at large.

During the reign of Akbar, the records of the land were kept in the record office of Todarmal and these were called 'Bahi Kalan'.

During British period (in 1842 A.D.), Delhi settlement of land was done along with its population. In 1864 A.D., again the settlement of land was undertaken. Delhi was a District and Bawana was its Tehsil. Some villages of Najafgarh were attached to Punjab, which later attached to Tehsil Mehrauli and Narela. In 1880 A.D. the land settlement was again undertaken in Delhi. In 1857 A.D., all these villages that took part in the revolt, their land was confiscated by the British. In 1880 A.D. all the villages related with Mehrauli Tehsil were attached to Ballabgarh Tehsil, which came under the jurisdiction of Punjab Government

In the beginning of British Delhi, only two villages, that is, Baskoli and Andhavli, were attached to Delhi city. Some land was taken from the villages and enclosure Jahanuma was created and was continued till 1905–6 A.D. Later on, this area was merged in the city, but still the area is called Deewar Jahanuma. In 1908–9 A.D., the settlement of land for Delhi and east of Yamuna was undertaken. All these villages attached with Tehsil Ballabgarh were merged with Tehsil Mehrauli; the villages related to Sonipat (Punjab) were merged with Delhi. In 1842, 1864, 1880 and 1908–9 the settlement undertaken is called 'Misal Hakiyat'.

In 1915–6 A.D. some villages withdrawn from Meerut and Bulandshahar were merged into Delhi. The remaining villages were covered by the Punjab Act.

All those villages which were east of Yamuna are now villages under the D.D.A. The settlement of these villages was undertaken in 1926–7 A.D. From 1842 to 1964 A.D., the settlement of land was undertaken; the number of villages in Delhi comes to 448.

Patwari's Jurisdiction and Names of Villages[101] of Mehrauli Tehsil

S. No.	*Patwari's Area*	*Village*
1.	Mehrauli	Mehrauli
2.		Masud Pur
3.		Laddho Sarai (*Be Chirag* Village, not habited)
4.	Mahipal Pur	Mahipal Pur
5.		Rang Puri (Its earlier name is Malik Pur Kohi alias Rang Puri)
6.		Rajokari
7.	Khan Pur	Khan Pur
8.		Tigri
9.		Madangir
10.		Devli
11.	Bijwasan	Bijwasan
12.		Bharthal
13.		Kapashera
14.		Sahlapur
15.	Tughlaqabad	Tughlaqabad
16.		Tehkhand
17.	Badarpur	Badarpur
18.		Aali
19.		Molarband
20.		Tajpur
21.		Meetha Pur
22.		Pul Pehlad Jaitpur
23.	Madanpur Khadar	Madanpur Khadar
24.		Saidabad Saeedabad
25.		Jasola
26.		Kotal Mahigaran
27.		Okhla
28.		Joga Vai

29.		Khizrabad
30.	Mohammad Pur Munirka	Mohammad Pur Munirka
31.		Katwaria Sarai
32.		Jiya Sarai
33.		Vasant Nagar Manakpur alias Basant Nagar
34.		Muradabad Pahari (*Be Chirag* Pahari)
35.	Munirka	Ber Sarai
36.		Kasum Pur
37.	Chirag Dilli	Chirag Dilli
38.		Shahpur Jat
39.		Khirki
40.		masjid Moth
41.		Yusuf Sarai
42.	Chhattar Pur	Chhattar Pur
43.		Satwari
44.		Rajpur Khurd
45.	Bhati	Bhati
46.		Shahur Pur (is *Be Chirag*)
47.		Asola
48.	Lado Sarai	Lado Sarai
49.	Said-ul-Ajaiv	Said-ul-Ajaiv
50.		Naiv Sarai
51.		Hauz Rani
52.		Maidan Garhi
53.	Sulatan Pur	Sulatan Pur
54.		Aaya Nagar
55.		Ghitorni
56.		Gadai Pur
57.	Fateh Pur Beri	Fateh Pur Beri
58.		Dera Mandi
59.		Chaandan Hula
60.		Jona Pur
61.	Naangal Devatta	Naangal Devatta
62.		Bagrola
63.		Sambhalka
64.		Toganpur
65.		Shahbad Mohammad Pur
66.		Sahupur
67.	Mubarik Pur Kotla	Mubarik Pur Kotla
68.		Garhi Jharia Maria
69.		Baha Pur
70.		Yakut Pur
71.		Khurd

72.	Kilokari	Kilokari
73.		Sahupur Khadar
74.		Bahlolpur Khadar
75.		Sarai Kale Khan
76.		Chakchilla
77.		Nangli Razapur
78.	Kharhera	Kharhera
79.		Tota Sarai
80.		Kalu Sarai
81.		Begam Pur
82.		Sarai Shahji
83.		Hauz Khas
84.		Humayun Pur
85.		Adhchini

Patwari's Jurisdiction and Villages of Palam Circle

86.	Palam	Palam
87.		Bindapur
88.		Luhar Hairi
89.		Asalatpur Khadar
90.		Mirzapur
91.	Hastsal	Hastsal
92.		Razapur Khurd
93.		Ranhola
94.		Shafia Bad
95.		Neelothi
96.		Tilangpur Kotla
97.	Naseerpur	Naseerpur
98.		Dabri
99.		Burhala
100.		Kaishopur
101.		Posangi Pur
102.		Nangli Jalab
103.	Shadipur	Shadipur
104.		Chaukhandi
105.		Tatarpur
106.		Jwala Heri
107.		Khyala
108.	Jhatikara	Jhatikara
109.		Ragho Pur
110.		Nanak Heri
111.	Badusara	Badusara
112.	Shikarpur	Shikarpur
113.		Daulatpur
114.		Hasan Pur
115.		Asalatpur Sabad

116.		Jain Pur
117.	Kakraula	Kakraula
118.	Matyala	
119.		Navada Majra Hastsaal
120.	Revla Khanpur	Revla Khanpur
121.		Rajpur Khurd
122.		Goyla Khurd
123.		Aimavaat
124.		Kutbapur
125.	Rani Khera	Rani Khera
126.	Mubarak Pur Dabas	Mubarak Pur Dabas
127.		Madanpur Dabas
128.		Rasul Pur
129.	Poothkalan	Poothkalan
130.		Kirari Suleman Nagar
131.		Begampur
132.	Mundaka	Mundaka
133.	Kamruddin Nagar	Kamruddin Nagar
134.	Mangolpur Kalan	Mangolpur Kalan
135.		Mangolpur Khurd
136.		Garhi Piran
137.		Rithala
138.	Chhawla	Chhawla
139.		Kangan Heri
140.		Dhool Siras
141.		Ambarhaai
142.		Baaproli
143.		Pochan Pur
144.	Nangloi Jaat	Nangloi Jaat
145.		Nangloi Sayyad
146.		Sultanpur Majra
147.	Tihar	Tihar
148.		Narayana
149.		Sagar Pur
150.		Nangal Rai
151.	Jadeed Chhawni	Jadeed Chhawni
152.	Pandwaala Kalan	Pandwaala Kalan
153.		Pandwaala Khurd
154.		Kaal ki Rond
155.		Kharkhari Jatmal

Patwari's Jurisdiction and Villages of Delhi Circle

156.	Burari	Burari
157.		Kamalpur
158.		Salimpur Majra Burari
159.		Badarpur

160.	Sadhohra Khurd	Sadhohra Khurd
161.	Wazirpur	Wazirpur
162.		Chaukri Mubarik Pur
163.		Nimri
164.	Sadhohra Kalan	Sadhohra Kalan
165.		Rajpur Chhavni
166.		Milakpur Chhavni
167.		Wazirabad
168.		Timarpur
169.	Shakoorpur	Shakoorpur
170.		Naharpur
171.		Pitam Pura
172.		Salimpur Majra Shadipur
173.		Yakoot Pur
174.	Chandrawati Urf Shahdara	Chandrawati Urf Shahdara
175.	Mandoli	Mandoli
176.		Karkardooma
177.	Azad Pur	Azad Pur
178.		Bhalswa Jahangir Pur
179.		Bhadola
180.		Pipal Thala
181.		Mahipur
182.		Haidarpur
183.	Ghidoli	Ghidoli
184.		Kondli
185.		Dallu Pura
186.		Khichari Pur
187.		Kotla
188.		Ghonda Nimka Bangar
189.		Ghonda Nimka Khadar
190.	Chilla Saroda Bangar	Chilla Saroda Khadar
191.	Rajapur Sharki	Rajapur Sharki
192.		Shamaspur Jaagir
193.	Khureji Khaas	Khureji Khaas
194.		Shakarpur Khaas
195.		Shakarpur Baramad
196.		Mandawali
197.		Faajalpur
198.		Haseen Pur
199.		Ghazi Pur
200.	Babar Pur	Babar Pur
201.		Ziauddin
202.		Gokul Pur
203.		Khanpur Tahaani
204.		Jeevan Pur urf Johri Pur
205.		Maujpur
206.		Sakandar Pur

207.		Jaafarabaad
208.		Saboli
209.	Karawal Nagar	Karawal Nagar
210.		Saahdatpur Goojraan
211.		Saahdatpur Musalmanan
212.		Bihar Pur
213.		Badarpur
214.		Sabhapur
215.		Bakiyabaad
216.		Sabhapur Shahdara
217.		Pur Shahdara
218.		Pur Dilli
219.	Seelampur	Seelampur
220.		Ghondli Meer Pur Shark
221.		Ghonda Goojran Khadar
222.		Garhee Mandi
223.		Mustafabaad
224.		Ghonda Chauhan Khadar
225.		Ghonda Chauhan Bangar
226.		Khajuri Khaas
227.		Oldanpur
228.	Baadli	Baadli
229.		Samaypur
230.		Libaspur
231.	Dhaka	Dhaka
232.		Dheerpur
233.		Jagatpur
234.		Badodara Majra Burari
235.		Mukandpur
236.		Sanjarpur
237.		Jagatpur Elaaka Shahdara
238.	Basai Dara Pur	Basai Dara Pur
239.		Toda Pur
240.		Azadpur
241.		Shadipur
242.	Civil Station	Civil Station

Patwari's Jurisdiction and Villages of Najafgarh Circle

243.	Najafgarh	Najafgarh
244.		Deendaar Pur
245.		Roshan Pura
246.		Haiwat Pur
247.		Masudabaad
248.	Jaunti	Jaunti
249.		Nizampur Rasheed Pur
250.		Garhi Randhala
251.		Chatesar

252.	Mandela Kalan	Mandela Kalan
253.		Mandela Khurd
254.		Shamaspur Khalsa
255.	Bakar Wala	Bakar Wala
256.		Baap Rola
257.		Jafarpur urf Hiran Koodna
258.		Neelwaal
259.	Dichaaun Kalan	Dichaaun Kalan
260.		Nangli Sakrawati
261.	Ghooman Hera	Ghooman Hera
262.		Dariya Pur Khurd
263.	Rawta	Rawta
264.		Devrala
265.	Karala	Karaala
266.		Mohammadpur Ghazi
267.	Teekri Kalan	Teekri Kalan
268.		Ghevra
269.		Saavda
270.	Milakpur zer Najafgarh	Milakpur zer Najafgarh
271.		Jhuljhuli
272.		Sanragpur
273.	Isapur	Isapur
274.		Qazi Pur
275.		Baakargarh
276.	Kanjhawla	Kanjhawla
277.		Laadpur
278.	Surhaira	Surhaira
279.		Khair
280.		Khera Dawar
281.	Mitraaun	Mitraaun
282.		Kharkhari Naahar
283.		Khaira
284.	Dhansa	Dhansa
285.		Ghalibpur
286.	Jhaardheda Kalan	Jhrhonda Kalan
287.		Surkhapur
288.		Ujaba
289.		Sherpurdahri
290.		Jafarpur Kalan

Patwari's Jurisdiction and Villages of Narela Circle

291.	Palla	Palla
292.		Jhangola
293.		Kalakpur
294.		Akbarpur Majra
295.		Sungarpur
296.		Tigipur

297.		Fatehpur Jat
298.		Sungarpur elaka Shahdara
299.	Auchandi	Auchandi
300.		Harevli
301.		Bhorgarh
302.		Kureni
303.		Rajapur Kalan
304.		Tikri Khurd
305.	Singhu	Singhu
306.		Singhola
307.		Baakoli
308.		Khampur
309.	Jatkhorh	Jatkhorh
310.		Katewara
311.		Mungash Pur
312.	Salapur Majra	Salapur Majra
313.		Chaandpur
314.		Budanpur
315.	Qutubgarh	Qutubgarh
316.		Panjab Khorh
317.	Nangal Thakran	Nangal Thakran
318.		Baajidpur Thakran
319.	Barwala	Barwala
320.		Pahladpur Bangar
321.		Pansali
322.	Bakhtawar Pur	Bakhtawar Pur
323.		Taayarpur Kalan
324.		Hamid Pur
325.	Pooth Khurd	Pooth Khurd
326.		Sultanpur Dabas
327.	Hiranki	Hiranki
328.		Mohammadpur Ramjanpur
329.		Abrahim Pur
330.		Mukhmel Pur
331.		Kaadipur
332.		Garhi Khasraw
333.		Jeend Pur
334.		Tehrih Daulatpur
335.	Daryapur Kalan	Daryapur Kalan
336.		Ghogha
337.	Bawana	Bawana
338.	Bankner	Bankner
339.		Laampur
340.	Narela	Narela
341.		Maamoor Pur
342.	Alipur	Alipur
343.		Boorhpur Bijapur

344.		Nangli Poona
345.		Siras Pur
346.	Sanauth	Sanauth
347.		Holambi Kalan
348.		Holambi Khurd
349.		Shah Pur Garhi
350.	Khera Khurd	Khera Khurd
351.		Aradat Nagar urf Naya Baans
352.	Khera Kalan	Khera Kalan
353.		Shahbaad Daulatpur

Be Chirag Villages (which are not inhabited)

(According to Bandobast of 1908–9 A.D. there was no habitation in these villages)

1. Sanjarpur (is a village by the name Ber Sarai. The land has been acquired. Nowadays there are IIT quarters and Jawaharlal Nehru University nearby.)
2. Kamaal Pur
3. Garhi Khasraw
4. Rajapur Kalan
5. Pansaali Bangar
6. Sherpur Dairy
7. Jainpur
8. Qutubpur
9. Haibatpur
10. Masudabaad (Najafgarh Circle)
11. Rajapur Khurd
12. Safipur
13. Chaukhandi (Near Tilak Nagar)
14. Loharheri
15. Tongapur
16. Mirjapur
17. Sahupur
18. Saalaahpur (Veeran)
19. Yaaqut Pur
20. Sarai Shah Ji (Mehrauli Circle)
21. Kotla Mahi Giran
22. Saeedabad
23. Saoopur
24. Gattu Sarai
25. Bahlolpur Khadar
26. Kasum Pur
27. Muradabaad Pahari

List of Urbanized Villages

The list of villages which were under Land Reform Act, 1954 but later on put under Commissioner, Delhi Municipal Corporation, were urbanized by Section 507 of Delhi Municipal Corporation Act, 1957 (66 of 1957):

Number and Date of Gazette Notification
No. RNZ/526, dated 28-5-1963

	Name of Village	*Circle*
1.	Khureji Khaas	Delhi
2.	Sadhora Kalan	Delhi
3.	Sadhora Khurd	Delhi
4.	Chaukri Mubarakabaad	Delhi
5.	Neemri	Delhi
6.	Dhaka	Delhi
7.	Saalaahpur Majra Maadipur	Delhi
8.	Azadpur	Delhi
9.	Shakoorpur	Delhi
10.	Maadipur	Palam
11.	Khyala	Palam
12.	Keshopur	Palam
13.	Basai Darapur	Delhi
14.	Najafgarh	Najafgarh
15.	Masoodabaad	Mehrauli
16.	Haibatpur	Najafgarh
17.	Ladho Sarai	Mehrauli
18.	Mehrauli	Mehrauli
19.	Khirki	Mehrauli

Note: The villages at S. No. 1 and 2 (Khureji Khaas and Sadhora Kalan) have been transferred to DDA on 20.8.1974.

Number and Date of Gazette Notification
No. F 2(49)65 LSG dated 3.6.1966 and F 9 (2)/65-Law-Corporation dated 28.5.1966

	Name of Village	*Circle*
1.	Budhela	Palam
2.	Jasola	Mehrauli
3.	Madanpur Khadar	Mehrauli
4.	Tehkhand	Mehrauli
5.	Hauz Rani	Mehrauli
6.	Ber Sarai	Mehrauli
7.	Katwadiya Sarai	Mehrauli
8.	Madan Geer	Mehrauli
9.	Badarpur	Mehrauli
10.	Khanpur	Mehrauli
11.	Tughlaqabad	Mehrauli
12.	Dheer Pur	Delhi
13.	Bhadola	Delhi
14.	Peepal Thala	Delhi
15.	Wazeer Pur	Delhi
16.	Ghonda	Delhi
17.	Maujpur	Delhi
18.	Karkardooma	Delhi

19.	Seelam Pur	Delhi
20.	Kondali	Delhi
21.	Mandaawali	Delhi
22.	Ghazi Pur	Delhi
23.	Khichri Pur	Delhi
24.	Hasan Pur	Delhi
25.	Shakar Pur Khaas	Delhi
26.	Saboli	Delhi

Number and Date of Gazette Notification
No. CTO/82/47 dated 6.5.1982

	Name of Village	*Circle*
1.	Garhi Peeran	Palam
2.	Nangloi Sayyad	Palam
3.	Maqsoodpur	Najafgarh
4.	Sarai Kale Khan	Mehrauli
5.	Nangli Rajapur	Mehrauli
6.	Jiya Sarai	Mehrauli
7.	Mahipal Pur	Mehrauli
8.	Laado Sarai	Mehrauli
9.	Naaharpur	Mehrauli
10.	Baadli	Mehrauli
11.	Reethala	Palam
12.	Wazirabaad	Delhi
13.	Samayapur	Delhi
14.	Mangolpur Kalan	Palam
15.	Usmaanpur	Delhi
16.	Mandoli Kachchi	Delhi
17.	Ghonrah Neem Ka	Delhi
18.	Kotla	Delhi
19.	Haidarpur	Delhi
20.	Sahipur	Delhi
21.	Mangolpur Khurd	Palam
22.	Jawala Heri	Palam
23.	Peetampura	Delhi

List of Urban Villages

Names of 106 villages which are in urban area under Master Plan, 1981 and have been declared urban by Notification under Section 507 (9) of the Municipal Corporation Delhi Act:

Name of Villages

1. Asaalat Pur
2. Aazaadpur
3. Basant Gaon
4. Basaidarapur

5. Begampur (Mehrauli)
6. Ber Sarai
7. Bhadola
8. Budhela
9. Dheerpur
10. Garhi Jharia Maria
11. Garhi Peeran
12. Ghazipur
13. Ghonda
14. Haidarpur
15. Hari Nagar Aashram (Note: Hari Nagar Aashram is not a revenue estate and this colony is inhabited on the land of village Kilokhari.)
16. Hasanpur
17. Hauz Khaas
18. Humayunpur
19. Jheel Mil Tihaarpur
20. Jogaabai
21. Jawala Heri
22. Kaachhipur (Kaachhipur is not a revenue estate and this colony is inhabited on the land of Mandoli village.)
23. Kaalu Sarai
24. Karkardooma
25. Katwaariya Sarai
26. Khayala
27. Khirki
28. Khijrabaad
29. Khureji Khaas
30. Kilokari
31. Kishan Garh (Kishan Garh is not a revenue estate. The colony is inhabited in Mehrauli rakaba.)
32. Kotla Mubaarakpur
33. Laado Sarai
34. Maadipur
35. Maqsoodpur
36. Mangolpur Khurd
37. Mandaawali Fajalpur
38. Masih Garh (Masih Garh is not a revenue estate. This colony is inhabited on the land of Bahapur.)
39. masjid Moth
40. Maujpur
41. Mehrauli
42. Munirka (It is in the revenue estate of Mohammadpur village.)
43. Nangal Rai
44. Nangali Jalib
45. Nangaloi Saeed
46. Narayana
47. Okhla

48. Peepal Thala
49. Peetampura
50. Pausangipur
51. Rampura (Shakoorpur) Rampura is not a revenue estate. This colony is inhabited on the land of Shakoorpur.
52. Sahipur
53. Sarai Julaina (Now Sarai Julaina is not a revenue estate. It is revenue estate of Bahapur village.)
54. Shahpur Jat
55. Shakoorpur Khaas
56. Shakarpur
57. Shaalimaar (Haidarpur) Shaalimaar Bagh is not a revenue estate. This colony is inhabited on the land of Saheepur village.
58. Taimoor Nagar (Taimoor Nagar is not a revenue estate. This colony, now known as Friends Colony, is inhabited on the Land of Kilokari.)
59. Sheikh Sarai
60. Taataarpur
61. Tehkhand
62. Wazeerpur
63. Adhchini
64. Akbarpur Bagh Mochi
65. Badarpur
66. Baadli
67. Bahlolpur
68. Chaukhandi
69. Chiragh Dilli
70. Dhaka
71. Ghonda Neemka
72. Ghondli
73. Hauz Rani
74. Jasola
75. Jiya Sarai
76. Katewara
77. Keshopur
78. Khaampur Rai
79. Khaan Pur (Hissaa)
80. Kharera
81. Kotla
82. Madangeer
83. Madanpur Khadar
84. Malikpur Chhawni
85. Mandoli Kachchi
86. Mangolpur Kalan
87. Mahipaal Pur
88. Mohammad Pur
89. Naaharpur
90. Nangli Rajapur

91. Rajpur Chhawni
92. Reethala
93. Saboli
94. Sadhora Kalan
95. Samayapur
96. Sarai Kale Khan
97. Sarai Shah Ji
98. Shaadipur
99. Seelampur
100. Tihaar
101. Tughlaqabaad
102. Shahdara
103. Usmaanpur
104. Wazirabaad
105. Yusuf Sarai
106. Jamroodpur

Religious Strife, Social Tensions and Political Conflicts in Delhi (1803–57)

From the dawn of history, foreign tribes, some as peaceful immigrants and others as valiant invaders, have come through the northwestern mountain passes of the Indian peninsula. Many of them were able to reach the very heart of the land while others settled in groups in the bordering regions and worked

Gaurishankar Temple, Chandni Chowk.

as intermediaries in between different cultures, which approached India in successive waves. During a foreign domination, these tribes took active part in enriching the Indian civilization. Overtime, they mingled into each other, and their history of their true origin has disappeared into the darkness of oblivion. However, from the very beginning, the Islamic movement in India had been different. Muslims did not deliberately mingle with the earlier people. This movement had two salient features: political power and *Tasawwuf*. The first devastating conquest of India gave a blow under which it reeled and which it has never quite forgotten nor forgiven. This stand persisted, interwoven into the whole subsequent history of the community. And indeed, the Pakistan movement may be seen as in a sense an affirmation that Islam cannot exist in the subcontinent without political power.

Some Muslim rulers desecrated or demolished temples, deliberately economically exploited the Hindu moneyed class and put jizya on the non-Muslims. On the other hand, there were Muslims like Dara Shikoh and some Sufi saints who always preached universal love.

The evolution of Islam in Delhi in particular can be seen in three phases in relation with Hindus. The first begins with the violent arrival of the armies of Mohammad of Ghazna and Mohammad of Ghori and their successors. It was a period of vehement iconoclasm and exclusivism. The second, the Sufi presentation of Islam, which gathered strength, won much of India's heart and indeed, in later centuries, formally and chiefly converted many millions from the lowest castes of Hindus. The Sufism also influenced the spread of Hindu Bhakti movements (eleventh to sixteenth century). The relations between two communities not only improved vastly but even reached a stage where syncretism seemed a possibility. Akbar and Dara Shikoh tried for it, but some Muslims viewed the process as threatening the utter absorption of Islam within Hinduism and its eventual death. So they started the movement of the Revival of Islamic tenets. A reaction set in; this was the third phase.

The ruling classes, who were mostly believers in the orthodox Sunni sect of Islam, were not only intolerant towards Hindus and Sikhs but were also intolerant towards heterodox Muslim sects such as the Shias and the Caramathians (Qaramita). Firoz Shah Tughluq describes his persecution of the Shias in the following words:

> ... the seat of Shias, also called Rawafiz, had endeavoured to make proselytes. They wrote treatises and books and gave instruction and lectures upon the tenets of their sect. And traduced and reviled the first chief of our religion. I seized them all and I convinced them of their error and perversities. On the most zealous I inflicted punishment, and the rest I visited with censure and threats of public punishment. Their Book I burnt in public, and so by the grace of God, the influence of this sect was entirely suppressed.[102]

In 1803, British took over the administration of Delhi after defeating the Marathas. In fact, the King had asked the British to help defend Delhi against the growing Maratha power and re-establish the old Mughal order. The King was a defender of the faith, apart from being a political sovereign. In fact, during the negotiations with the Badshah, immediately before the battle (1803), the British offered nothing but a vassal's protection of their Lord. The Badshah after it reduced to a pensioner of the East India Company, in fact the same position he was having during the Maratha period.[103]

Population-wise, the Hindus and the Muslims were almost equal in Delhi. The Historians in modern India treated resistance movements as a rural phenomenon,[104] and urban riots are generally portrayed as manifestations of older pre-colonial social tension, though the colonial record is dotted with instances of well-organized urban resistance against British rule.

The British planned their expansion slowly and steadily. In 1801, the Nawab of Awadh was made to cede the districts of the Ganga-Yamuna Doab to the East India Company to fund the maintenance of British subsidiary troops at his court. In 1805, the British finally took over rest of the Ganga-Yamuna Doab. They established military cantonments throughout the conquered provinces such as Meerut, Delhi, Mathura, Agra, Etawah and Kanpur; despite this North India continued to see unrest till 1857.

Many of the towns were also affected by disturbances during the first half of the nineteenth century such as Banaras hit by riots in 1809 and a hartal in 1810–11, Bareilly in 1837, Aligarh in 1853, Delhi in 1807, 1824 and 1856; Faizahad-Ayodhya, clashes between Hindus and Muslims took place in 1856, Lucknow in 1843, 1853 and 1856. Mubarakpur in Eastern Awadh, economic riots took place in 1813, 1834 and 1842.[105]

The period in Delhi between 1803 to 1857 was crucial in which the urban poor, traders and craftsman, an emerging 'middle class', the urban elite, the Badshah and the British vigorously competed for influence and control. So it led to clashes.[106]

After the advent of the British in Delhi, Municipal politics emerged—what was to be known as the 'Delhi system' of administration. Its principal architect was Charles Metcalfe who served as an Assistant to the Delhi Resident from 1811 to 1819 and as Resident from 1824 to 1829. The British regarded Red Fort as the centre of political intrigue and subversive intelligence, so they were very careful. During the riots of 1807, the Resident transferred about one thousand soldiers from hinterland cantonments and permanently stationed them at Delhi, thus raising British military strength from a battalion to a regiment. This force was further augmented during the food riots in 1837. The British never stationed European troops within the walls of Delhi except the *sipahi* regiments. The British did not want to provoke unnecessarily the

Badshah and the inhabitants of Delhi with the presence of the foreign and white troops in the city. The British did not feel safe within the walls of the city. They resided mostly in the vicinity of Kashmiri Gate in the North and in Daryaganj in the southeast.

The walls of Delhi had crumbled due to the assaults of the British and the Marathas; till 1820, the repair work could not be taken over due to shortage of funds and that it was a difficult task. In 1820, the work started. Many occupants were taken out from the area of the wall. Many Muslim tombs and houses were demolished to allow for the extension of the glacis. The British overseers exercised 'great caution and forbearance' so as 'not to excite the jealous feelings or the religions prejudices of the natives.'[107]

Of course, the British doubly profited from the eviction of the wall dwellers, but the eviction of these poor people aggravated their economic circumstances, and this may well have translated into a sense of grievance against the British and they were potential rioters.

The British were aware of Delhi's symbolic character as the Badshah's residence. At the same time they became more and more obsessed by the idea of a Muslim conspiracy against British rule in India centred in Delhi as the nodal point of Badshah's sovereignty and legitimacy. The British wanted to occupy the Red-Fort before 1857, and they tried for it and asked the Bahadur Shah II to vacate it and go to Mehrauli or Shahdara (for him some houses were built there) some security measures were taken by the British such as early closure of city gates; the famous Mirza Ikram Sarai outside the Lahore Gate was demolished in 1824. Only this sarai was giving facilities to travelers and old Id-compound which had been abandoned by the Muslims and was now occupied by Hindu grain and cattle merchants. It helped the British to extract custom duties.[108]

The revenue demand was solely determined by the needs of the Government and not by its potential economic impact or the financial capacity of the inhabitants.

Thomas Fartesque, the Civil Commissioner of Delhi, listed 562 items which were taxed at five percent, and 51 items for ten percent duty. It was really a great hardship on the poor and needy classes' labour for their daily bread.[109]

In 1729, a Hindu jeweller, Shubkharan's court dress caught fire on his way to the Red Fort. This led to a riot between members of the new Arab, Abyssinian, Afghan and Turkish court elite against the old Turani and Irani military elite which were still backed by the Badshah. It was a small issue which was exploited by rival court factions to settle political scores.

With the British occupation of Delhi, the issue of authority and sovereignty started. Soon, the matter of a Muslim ruler and the Muslim population of his residence being forced to live under the authority of a non-Muslim power, excited the attention of the city's Muslim theologians, such as Shah Abdal Aziz, who issued a fatwa in 1809. The British used all methods like appeasement and crushing the political opponent. In 1806, they used military force to pursue the Mughal party. When in 1835 William Fraser was assassinated and Ahmad Bakh Khan, Nawab of Firozpur Jhirka, was held responsible for it, he, along with Karim Khan, was publicly hanged on 3 October 1835.

In 1807, when Har Sukh Rai, a Jain merchant along with others wanted to organize a Rathyatra to build a temple, he was opposed by a Muslim mob, which looted his and others houses at Jama Masjid; Rafi-al-Din, the brother of Shah Abdal Aziz, was found to be the main instigator; Resident Seton wanted to punish him. Some riots broke out in the city. Rafi-al-Din was exiled for four months but the British paid all his family debts and he was later allowed to come to the city.

The Jains of Delhi were wealthy merchants, they were only three percent of the population but they gained prominence particularly for advancing credit to the peasants and Zamindars in the city's rural vicinity. The Jains had spent more than twenty-five lakh rupees on religions edifices and public facilities in Delhi during 1790 and 1820.[110]

The issue of Dar-ul-Islam and Dar-ul-Harb gained momentum in the 1820s. After Badshah, Shah Alam, himself a Sunni, had returned to Delhi in 1785 and the Shias' influence grew further. Therefore, the riots of 1807 also point towards an increasing rivalry between the Shia and Sunni sects and polarization of political influence between the two orders.

The problem of cow slaughter proved to be the touchstone of British attempts to defer to local customs and, at the same time, to establish equal rights for all religious communities. When Scindia occupied Delhi, his lieutenants allowed resident butchers to kill cows in deference to earlier Mughal tradition and contrary to the inclination of the Maratha rulers at large to impose a general ban on cow slaughter. When the British took over the government, the Badshah confirmed this arrangement, yet refrained himself from the sacrifice of cows; however, the sacrifice of cows on Id was performed at private houses in the city. There were few public altercations over the sacrifice of cows, but there was always an undertone of tension. In 1819, the Delhi Magistrate Thomas Metcalfe (younger brother of Charles Metcalfe) permitted the slaughter of cows within houses but, in 1821, he revised this decision and put a general prohibition on cow slaughter in the city. However, by the threatening petition of some Muslims, the order was withdrawn next day. The issue of cow slaughter also had come up in 1835. In 1835, cow slaughter was allowed in the city at certain places; the Hindu shopkeepers went on three days hartal and in the last the order was rescinded. In 1816 and 1834, clashes occurred between Hindus and Jains on the grounds their dissimilarities in ideology and religious practices.

In 1827, for the first time in centuries, a public Dashehra festival took place in Delhi near the police station at Kashmiri Gate mainly hosted by the influential Bengali Babu, Ram Gopal, Babu of Resident Colebrook. Some Muslims protested against the celebrations but Colebrook provided military escort. This episode indicates the growing prominence of Bengalis in the political landscape of Delhi in the first half of the 19th century.

Shia-Sunni riots broke out, too, after Magistrate Lindsay altered the traditional proclamation about Taziyah in favour of the Shia in 1837.

After a series of insufficient rains since the beginning of the 1830's, the monsoon almost failed completely in the region between Allahabad and Delhi in 1837. Soon the availability of basic food items deteriorated rapidly in the countryside. When the rains again failed in 1838, destitute people left the North Indian plains en masse-perhaps eight million in all.[111]

Serious food riots broke out in Delhi in 1837. Due to the policy of Laissez-Faire of the British Administration prices of grain raised up to 12 sears for one rupee instead of 25 sears for one rupee. Numerous food riots occurred due to the deterioration of agrarian conditions in North India which made the region increasingly vulnerable to ecological disasters and the greed of grain dealers.

The uproar afflicted Delhi through the first half of the nineteenth century for a variety of reasons. The simultaneous presence of two, authorities—the British and the Badshah in the city was a major reason for much of the discontent among the upper echelons of the population. The British wanted to oust the Badshah from the Red Fort and for that matter they tried in various ways but could not succeed. In 1856 they announced that they would not recognize the rights of the heir to the Delhi Throne, Mirza Jiwan Bakht, after the death of the Badshah.

A few months before the rebellion, a rumour spread in Delhi and a notice appeared on the walls of Jama Masjid that Shah of Persia would assist the Badshah and Muslims should unite and wait for outside help. After 1857, the British became very strong and Badshah was exiled to Rangoon and the main rivalry of the British ended.

Sarais

From earlier times, the city of Delhi was not only an imperial city, it was also a commercial town. People from all over the world used to come here. Earlier they came either on animal back or assistance or on foot. They used to bring their merchandise. They required a safe place to keep this merchandise and also require safety and a safe place for rest. Caravansarais were some such places for this purpose. Sher Shah had built sarais at a distance of 2 *kos*, where

2 horses were kept in each sarai to transmit the message to the next. There was good provision for food, medicine and security.

This was a place where animals can be kept, information can be passed; food of a particular type can be taken. It was also a resting place. Information can be gathered about, who had come from where. Because with the increase of cities and other dwellings and means of transport such as railways, these Sarais had become obsolete for its purposes. They had served useful and important purpose in the medieval period. The usefulness of Sarais in and around the city of Delhi also became insignificant after the shifting of capital from Delhi to Calcutta, the change of the seat of power. One must note that after the 1857 'Mutiny', the British deliberately destroyed sarais or converted them into buildings for other uses such as hospitals, schools or government quarters. This was a conscious attempt to obliterate Mughal structures used by the mutineers. Though the name 'sarai' exists all over Delhi, the buildings and their original purpose, are lost to history.

Some of the famous Sarais were as follows:

More Sarai

Before 1857, there was a Kagzi Mohalla (village) at this place. This is situated in front of old Delhi Railway Station, on the road leading to Sis Ganj Gurudwara (in front of Haradyal Library). In 1861–2, Hamilton, the Commissioner of Delhi built it in Rs. 10,517 and it was called Hamilton Sarai, later Mr. More, the engineer of Delhi, got erected a peacock on the dome of this sarai so it was called More Sarai. In 1901, the municipal committee sold it to East India Railway for Rs. 1, 65,000. Now the Railway Employees are residing in it. This was a very good and big building at that time only a masjid is left at this place.

Jahan Ara Begum Sarai

This was built by Begum Jahan Ara, the daughter of Shah Jahan along with a beautiful garden. This sarai was demolished in 1858 by the British and Delhi Institute was started at this place. One gate opened on South, towards Chandni Chowk and other towards North to the Garden. In the courtyard of the Sarai there were two wells and one masjid. This Sarai was two story building. Mostly Uzbek traders and other traders of various countries used to stay there.

Bernier described Begum Sarai (built by Jahan Ara Begum, the daughter of Shah Jahan),

> This place is the rendezvous of the rich Persian, Uzbek, and other foreign merchants, who in general may be accommodated with empty chambers, in which they remain with perfect security, the gate being closed at night. If in Paris we had a score of similar structure, distributed in different parts of the city, strangers

Ahmad Pai Masjid, Fatehpuri, near St. Stephen's Church.

on their first arrival would be less embarrassed than at present to find a safe and reasonable lodging. They might remain in them a few days until they had seen their acquaintance, and looked out at leisure for more convenient apartments. Such places would become warehouses for all kinds of merchandise, and the general resort of foreign merchants.[112]

Shiv Sahay ki Sarai and Ahmad Pai Sarai

This sarai was for Hindus, built near the sarai of Ahmad Pai. Its main door was near the Begum Sarai towards its garden. This was a double story building. The main gate was 28 feet long and 11 feet high, a masjid was also attached with this sarai. It was called Ahmad Pai Masjid; a well was also erected and dedicated to Sheikh Ahmad Pai, who was a Punjabi.

Phoons ki Sarai

Once upon a time it was a very wide sarai. It was probably built of straw huts and so it is called Phoons ki Sarai. Now potters live there. An old small masjid along with a well is still remains there. Nanu Singh Katra was there at the time of this Sarai; this person was a Jat by caste. This katra was inhabited by potters and grass cutters. It was not a hygienic locality.

Badli ki Sarai at village Pipal Thala near new Subzi Mandi. Earlier the G.T. Road was passing through the two gates of this Sarai. In 1857 a fierce battle was fought between the British forces and the mutineers and the Sarai was destroyed by the canon shells.

Badli ki Sarai

This Sarai was built by some Mughal ruler. It was situated a mile to north of Azadpur village. Earlier, a small road used to pass through the two gates of this Sarai. On the East of this Sarai a small garden with a big pond used to be there. Now between the Sarai and the earlier pond a new road is built. The mutineers laid a heavy gun on 8 June 1857, and British had to lose so many soldiers. It was destroyed during the 1857 assault and now only remains are there.

Farid Khan ki Karvan Sarai

Farid Khan was the Subedar of Shah Jahan. He was the Subedar of Gujarat. He also built a small town of Faridabad near Tilpat. He also built this Sarai. Later the British converted this Sarai into a Jail, near it a hospital (Irwin Hospital) was also built by the British. It was situated on the place, where now is Maulana Azad Medical College. Mirza Ghalib (a poet) was interned twice in this Jail (once for two months and the second time for four months).

Mirza Ikram ki Sarai

This sarai was situated near Sarhindi Begum Masjid near Khari Baoli. This was a very busy Sarai and in the evening many people used to display their goods, so a big bazar came up there.

Arab ki Sarai

This sarai was erected by Haji Begum, wife of Humayun and mother of Akbar, her name was Hamida Bano Begum. This Sarai was built in 1560 A.D. She brought 300 Arabs from Macca-Madina and put in this Sarai. Out of these 100 were Sayyids, 100 were Sheikhs and 100 were those who used to serve the two mentioned earlier. Later they were scattered to other parts of the Empire due to their livelihood, nothing is left except the doors of this Sarai.

Sarai Bangash

This sarai was situated near Fatehpuri masjid. Now it is under the control of Lala Narain Dass and his descendents who made so many shops in it.

Koria Pul Sarai Top Khana

Earlier it was a Top Khana during Mughal period; it was situated near Koria Pul, then a Sarai was made in that place.

Achan-Machan ki Sarai

This structure, which is now near Delhi High Court and also near the Madarsa of Mahim Anaga, the step-mother of Akbar, was built in 1642–3 A.D. by the step-brother of Akbar, Zeen Khan for his daughter; this is the version of Sir, Syyad Ahmad Khan but Mr. Vogel had said that it was not mentioned that this structure was not in any body's name and it was a Sarai. This Sarai was built by Achan-Macham two brothers, as per the version of Bashir Ahmad Dehlvi.

Ajim Ganj or Sarai Mughalia

This is in front of the present Oberai Hotel. Only the Eastern Gate is left, which is occupied by various people who were uprooted from Old Fort in 1858. It was 430 sq. feet structure. A masjid was also there in its compound. It had four gates. It had 100 rooms; one room was 23 sq. feet in its compass.

Sarai Sahi

It is behind Khas Mahal. This structure is well built and spacious.

Badshah Pasand Sarai

It was in Mehrauli area. It was well built in earlier times, it was away from the Basti. It had many rooms and *hujras*.

Lado Sarai

This is also near Mehrauli. It was called Chandal Pur. There were many *bastis* earlier, but no signs of Sarai. Now village Lado Sarai is there. The famous Sufi Saint Mir Baqi is buried there along with his Pir.

Yusuf Sarai

Now it is a village, earlier it was a sarai. It is in South Delhi near Green Park.

Kalu Sarai

It is near Malviya Nagar, near Begum Puri Masjid.

Jia Sarai

Now there is a village at this place near Mehrauli.

Sarai Rohilla

It is near old Rohtak Road, a *basti* is flourishing at this place, and some part of it is taken by Railway.

Sarai Roshan Ara

It is now in a residential area, a school is run in it. It is in front of Roshan Ara Garden, near Ghanta Ghar (old Sabzi Mandi).

Mughal Sarai near Kishan Ganj, and others such as Katwaria Sarai, Ber Sarai, Sarai Kale Khan are now urban villages in South Delhi. There were many more Sarais, whose existence is not traceable.

Mohallas

The city of Shahjahanabad was a populous city and its radius was nearly seven *kos*. Its population was settled in Mohallas, according to a particular region, caste, profession and role et cetera. Bernier described this city:

> I have accomplished the circuit (of the city) with ease in the space of three hours, and notwithstanding I rode on horseback, I do not think my progress exceeded a league per hour. In this computation I do not however include the suburbs, which are considerable, comprising a long chain of buildings on the side of Lahore, the extensive remains of the old city, and three or four smaller suburbs. By these additions the extent of the city is so much increased that a straight line may be traced in it of more than a league and a half; and though I cannot undertake to define exactly the circumference, because these suburbs are interspersed with extensive gardens and open spaces, yet you must see that it is very great.[113]

It was one of the duties of the Kotwal to prepare the list of the inhabitants of the city or town with the help of the clerks. He should ensure in the list of economic status of the house holder, his profession. He should also appoint the headman (Mir-i-Mohalla) for any omission and commission of the inhabitants of that Mohallah (Street).

Nadir Shah got the survey of the inhabitants of Delhi in 1739 for their economic status and with the help of the Kotwal tax was lavied on each inhabitant, it was immaterial whether they were in position to the pay or not.

The inhabitants were grouped in self-contained, self-governing wards; the inhabitants were united by the similarity of profession or the patronage of one common protector such as nobleman or a saint, around whose mansion or shrine they clustered. During the repeated invasion and the decline of Mughal power, each ward or lane had to fortify itself by building defensive gates at its two ends, which was closed by the evening or at the time of invasion or riot. This system was called Kucha Bandi and lasted till 1857.

The city was divided into Mohallas, Kuchas and Katras that was, Ahdipura (a kind of Indian Military Corps) was situated adjacent to Shah Ganj, Khari Baoli, Chauki-Sadullah Khan and Chandni Chowk, Suhagpura, a Mohalla of royal widows, after the demise of the king or other prince, the ladies used to live in this Mohalla, the Mohalla-i-Wakilpura, was an important ward where several of the nobles had built their residential houses. Anand Ram Mukhlis resided here. A canal passed through this ward, but with passage of time this ward suffered a complete ruin, and people have forgotten its very name.

Kucha-i-Rai Man, Rai Man was Mansabdar during the reign of Emperor Ahamad Shah; Kucha-i-Chelan, Mohalla-i-Khakhriyan (situated on the bank of the river Yamuna) Mirza Bedil lived there. He was poet philosopher born in 1644 A.D., at Azimabad (Patna) in the reign of Shah Jahan. He died in 1720/1721 A.D. in Delhi and his tomb is situated in Bagh-i-Bedil near the National Sports Club, opposite old fort (Purana Qila); Mohalla-i-Mughalpura was a very important Mohalla, originally the Mongols used to live there during the time of Ala-ud-Din Khilji. This is near Roshan Ara Bagh. This Mohalla was burnt on account of some treachery and suspicion of a plot against the Sultan. There are also two small villages— Mongol Pur Kalan and Mangol Pur Khurd, earlier they were only one village, it was also the village of Mongols, who looted one party of Nadir Shah, while they were coming to Delhi via this village. Nadir Shah ordered to burn this village and kill all the inhabitants; Now it is near Rohini in North-West Delhi and inhabited by Jats and other communities, Mohalla-i-Kashmiriyan was inhabited by the natives of Kashmir and their descendants, who had taken up abode in the city; it is near Sita Ram Bazar, the last Kotwal of Delhi in 1857 was Ganga Dhar, the father of Moti Lal Nehru; Kamla Nehru, wife of Pt. Jawahar Lal Nehru was also the resident of Bazar-Sita Ram. Mohalla-i-Sa'adat-i-Barha was inhabited by Barha Sayyids, who were very influential during later Mughals.

The Sayyid Brothers made and unmade Emperors at will. Farrukh Siyar hated them; Mohalla-i-Afghans, the Afghans lived there. Some of the Mohallas are known by a prominent Haveli in that area, such as the Haveli-i-Sayyid

Firoz; Haveli-i-Ismail Khan, a noble of Safdarjung; Haveli-i-Malika-i-Zamani, daughter of Farrukh Siyar and the wife of Mohammad Shah; Haveli-i-Shabbir Jang, Haveli-i-Haider Quli. The Chowk-i-Sa'dullah Khan; the Chowk-i-Sa'adat Khan (Burhan-ul-Mulk); and Phatak Habash Khan, the Mohalla-i-Chitli Qabr, the Mohalla-i-Haveli wa Bazar-i-Nawab Amir Khan; Tiraha-i-Bairam Khan; Mohalla-i-Faulad Khan (The Kotwal of Delhi during the reign Mohammad Shah); Mohalla-i-Kanchanis; the butchers lived in the Qassab Pura; Farangpura, the Europeans lived there, they were employed in the department of artillery, in the capacity of Surgeons, Physicians and joiners of bones. This Mohalla was ruined during the time of Nadir Shah. Their Church was also burnt; the Mohalla-i-Ajmeri Darwaza, was an important ward because the Wazir, Itmad-ud-Daula Qumar-ud-Din Khan lived there.

There were nearly 146 Mohallas, Katras, and Bazars, every Mohalla was confined within an enclosure having main gates on two ends. Many of the old Mohallas are still remembered by their old names. Beyond the city wall, there were inhabited quarters. In the vicinity of Old Fort there was Khankhariya Mohalla; near Kadam Sharif, Bakhtawar Nagar a colony founded by Bakhtawar Khan in 1671–2. A mosque and a reservoir were there. Bahadur Khan purchased 900 Bighas of land from the Government and some private owners and founded a colony, near Paharganj, outside the Ajmeri Gate area; Dilipura, was also founded by Dilir Khan near Jai Singh Pura, the ice makers used to live in Dilipura. Jai Singh Pura was from present Bangla Sahib Gurudwara (This was the Haveli of Raja Jai Singh) to Paharganj; Mohalla-i-Nau was founded by Emperor Mohammad Shah. It is not in existence. When in 1753 A.D. Suraj Mal invaded the city, the people of Delhi took shelter in this Mohalla, but it was also burnt and looted; the Kasalpura and Mohalla-i-Nagal were also founded by princes and great officials have built elegant mansions and laid out extensive charming gardens, and in subsequent period after the invasion of Nadir Shah in 1739 A.D., the population of Delhi increased for some times.

The settlement west of the city wall in early nineteenth century had a large non-agricultural population. Subzi Mandi, consisting of houses, high walls, gardens et cetera.[114] was located in Mughalpura. The South of this was Dargah Nabi Karim (around the Shrine of Qadam Sharif); Teliwara and Shidipura (granted to Meher Ali Shidi in 1773), these were all in the revenue estate of Jahan-Numa village, and the revenue of village Jahan-Numa was going to Jama Masjid for its upkeep. In the later period say in the middle of the nineteenth century Pahari Dhiraj, Bara Hindu Rao also came up as residences.

Bara Hindu Rao, was a place where Hindu Rao, a hereditary title of Jai Singh Rao Ghatge. The brother of Baiza Bai, the favourite wife of Daulat Rao Scindia, kept his animals, force and a small house. Hindu Rao, incurred the displeasure of his nephew Maharaja Jankoji Scindia, of Gwalior, for his many alleged intrigues against the young ruler and was obliged to leave Gwalior and go into voluntary exile under the protection of the British Government. His good services and friendly attitude towards the British induced R. Cavendish, the resident at Gwalior, to procure for him the promise of monthly pension of 10,000 Chandorie Rupees from Jankoji Scindia. The British Authorities at Fort William considered it very liberal. At last Hindu Rao marched towards Delhi on 11 August 1834. Daulat Rao Scindia died in 1827, his widow, Baiza Bai, adopted a son 'Jankoji'. She expected to rule in her own right but the British backed Jankoji and Baiza Bai was compelled to retire when her young son died in 1835, she had to leave Gwalior state and joined his brother at Delhi.

Emperor, Firoz Shah Tughluq has built a hunting lodge in about 1360 A.D., which is now called Hindu Rao Hospital. Sir Edward Colebrooke, the resident of Delhi, further built some structures here. Near this place is Asok Pillar on which his edicts are engraved, one such Asok pillar is placed on the structure of Firoz Shah Kotla. One edict of Asok is marked on a rock in East of Kailash near the ISCKON temple.

To make the days of his exile as comfortable as possible under the circumstances, Hindu Rao bought this place from John Fraser, the brother of William Fraser, who was in occupation of this place for Rs. 20,000 and a title deed was drawn up in the proper Department of the Civil Judge's office, authenticated by official seal and signature. The estate comprised, besides, 323 bigha of land, a spacious bungalow with a compound of 169½ bighas. 'In some of the portions more or less wells were situated and on some were buildings. Mr. Fraser, having made these purchases, united the lands, built a dwelling house in the midst of them, to which they served as a compound and they appear to have been (if not actually are yet) enclosed by a wall of masonry.'[115]

As soon as the property was bought, Hindu Rao was involved in a law suit as a defendant. In 1839 the title of land was granted to Hindu Rao; the letter of Secretary to the Governor-General N.W.P. (F. Curie) to H.M. Elliot, Secretary, Sadar Board of Revenue, dated 5 December 1839, No. 1613, writes that, the first parcel was purchased on the 25 May 1824 from Tuz Khan and others for Rs. 1,000. The second parcel including 'a well, a Baolee, a Pucka Tank and a Bungalow on 26 April 1823 from Khwajah Meer Khan of Delhi for Rs. 500. The third parcel was purchased in August 1823 from Mohammad Sala of Delhi for Rs. 900. The fourth from Sheikh Hatim Aleeh and Sheikh Gul Mohammad of Delhi for Rs. 675 in January 1823 and the fifth parcel was purchased in November, 1823 from a woman named Uchan Koonwar for Rs. 375.[116] William Fraser, Governor-General's Agent and Commissioner at Delhi, also lived in this house, he was assassinated in 1835. Fraser purchased the proprietary right of the land from the Zamindars of the village of Chundrawal; but he never purchased from the Government share of the land and consequently always paid his portion of the assessed revenue of the estate. In 1842 the matter come to a close. Hindu Rao's house was acquired by the Government from the heirs of Hindu Rao after the Sepoy Mutiny and turned it into a hospital which it has remained ever since. Bara Hindu Rao had become a residential colony. In 1857 British took shelter in the House of Hindu Rao. On the victory British erected a memorial there which is called 'Jeet Garh' Memorial. Flag Staff Tower was also built on the other side by the British on the Ridge.

Shahjahanabad and the Red Fort

Geographically, climatically, strategically (from the Military point of view) and environmentally, the Indo-Gangetic plains are more suited for an Imperial city. That is why the triangle along the river Yamuna was selected by the rulers from time-immemorial for their capital cities. Shahjahanabad (Delhi) is no exception in this category. In fact

> for nearly a thousand years the rulers of North Indian States established their capitals in the Delhi area. The Delhi triangle, a sixty-square mile area bounded by the Aravalli Hills on the West and South and the Yamuna River on the East occupied a strategic position in upper India. It commanded the 115 mile wide corridor that, on the one hand, separated the Deccan tableland and the Thar Desert from Himalayas and, on the other, separated the Punjab and the lands of the North-West from the rich unbroken flood plain of the Ganges. Touching the Yamuna at its Northern-West point of year-round navigation, the Delhi triangle encompassed the major break in transportation between the two great river systems of the sub-continent, the Ganges and the Indus.[117]

Shah Jahan ascended the throne on 24 January 1628. After reigning for eleven years from Agra, his seat of Government, he decided to shift his capital from Agra to Delhi just before his expedition to Deccan in 1635 A.D., he summoned Makramat Khan, the Chief-Supervisor of buildings and ordered to build a new city of his taste in Delhi. There are various reasons for shifting the capital from Agra to Delhi. From the Deccan expedition, Shah Jahan got lots of money and other articles in booty, he wanted to use it. He was known for constructing good buildings, and called the Architect King. After the death of Mumtaz Mahal in June 1631 A.D. at Burhanpur in Madhya Pradesh, Agra became distasteful to the king. Agra also became hot and the king wanted to escape from the excessive heat, the fort of Agra was not very big to accomodate the needs of the Empire, even the streets of the city were narrow for the elephants and troops. Agra was an old capital and became very congested over the years; it was not built by Shah Jahan. The Mongol invasions had also ended, due to which earlier the capital was shifted from Delhi to Agra. Even when Shah Jahan visited Delhi he stayed in Salim Garh fort and liked the environs of Delhi and wanted to live here. The search for the new capital started. Ultimately a place suitable for the fort and city was chosen near the Yamuna, adjacent to Salim Garh Fort.

This was done after long and intense consultations with astrologers, Maulvis, Ministers, Nobles and others. Shah Jahan laid the foundation of the fort on Friday night, 12 May 1639. (Sir Syed Ahmad Khan, Asar-us-Sanadid) Some writers say it was on the night of Friday, the 9th of Muharram, 1049 A.H. (1639 A.D.).[118] The popular understanding is that one head of a male was required in the foundation before starting its construction. The Zamindar of village Narholla, near present Nangloi village was given this order to bring the person, but in the night the villagers fled out of fear and the watchman of this village reported this matter to the king. He also offered his head for the purpose, on the condition that the land of the vacated village be given to his son Madari Khan. It was agreed and the head of the Shamsher Khan, the watchman of village Narholla was buried in the foundation of the fort.[119] The Red Fort was built under the supervision of Makramat Khan, other associated with building were Ghairat Khan, the then Governor of Delhi, Izzat Khan, who later became the Governor of Sind, Ali Wardi Khan, later became Governor, Hamid, a master builder (in his name a Kucha is there near Jama Masjid), and Ahmad.

For building this fort and later the city, the stones and materials of ancient Delhi and Tughlaqabad were used. Shah Jahan expended large sums in the construction of this city and in the foundations he ordered several decapitated criminals to be placed as a sign of Sacrifice.[120] This was a common practice while building a fort even hundreds of heads of Mongols were buried on the gates of Siri by Khilji. It took nine years, three months and some days to complete it with the cost of 100 lacs of rupees. Karamat Khan asked the Emperor, who was then in Kabul, to come to see it, on 24th Rabi 11 of A.H. 1058 (1648 A.D.) Shah Jahan entered the Fort through the gate facing the river Yamuna. This first entry of the king to the fort was marked with great fanfare. He held his first court in the Diwan-i-Aam. Gems, gold, silver were used at the appropriate places. Silk was used enormously. In keeping with the grandeur of the occasion, Shah Jahan distributed lavish gifts to commemorate the day that saw the birth of the Red Fort. He also built the wall around the city, initially it was made of mud, but rain played havoc with it, so it was later made of stone, bricks and lime. In 1634 and 1635 he visited Delhi. He got his first grandson from Dara Shikoh to sit on Peacock Throne which was made in seven years. Shah Jahan who got built his splendid monuments was not destined to enjoy it for long. His last days were dotted with intrigues and mishaps, sorrow and tragedy. He was imprisoned at Agra by Aurangzeb and died a broken man in January 1666.

> In 1657 he was seized with a paralytic stoke at Delhi and was only relieved by copious bleeding. The people were much concerned and all business was suspended until the bulletins announced his convalescence. He was then moved to Agra by boat, under the superintendence of Dara Shikoh; but the news of his death had reached the provinces and each son moved his powerful army towards Agra ... Aurangzeb imprisoned his father ... and proceeded to Delhi, where he ascended the throne at the Shalimar Gardens in the year 1658.[121]

Shah Jahan had to eat only one grain (Chana) till his death as ordered by Aurangzeb.

Yamuna was flowing at that time along the wall of the fort on the east side, it used to recede after rainy seasons, then the vacant place was used for military drills, elephant fights and for other entertainments. The Yamuna changed its course towards farther East after the construction of the railway bridge by the British in 1864. The river not only provided the security from eastern side but also was the source of entertainment, business, transportation and communication. But the unfortunate part is that most of the invasions of Delhi were undertaken from the river side. The principal residence of the Emperor and his ladies are on the river side. On the city side of the fort there is a deep moat, once kept filled with water, since 1875 no water had been allowed to stand in the moat. On the city side lofty battlements walls were carried round and houses were built along with it. The fort had four gates; Delhi Gate and Lahori Gate were two main Gates, Calcutta and Agra gates were also used for that direction. The fort was connected with a bridge to the fort of Salimgarh, which is older than Red Fort. This fort was built by Salim Shah Sur during his brief reign from 1545–54 A.D. Humayun again conquered Delhi from here and used it as a place for recreation and retreat for which he built a pavilion whose dome sits on four arches.

> By 1619, a new palace (Daulat Khana) had been constructed by order of Jahangir. In 1621-22 Jahangir also built a bridge between the South-Western part of Salimgarh and the raised ground on the opposite bank of Salimgarh of the Yamuna which was later to be occupied by Shah Jahan's Red Fort. A baoli situated in this very area (enclosed by the walls of the Red Fort) to the South of the bridge dates from the same period. The Daulat Khana at Salimgarh served as residence for the Mughal court whenever it passed through Delhi until Shah Jahan's new fortress palace was constructed across from it.[122]

Jahangir called this fort Nurgarh.

In the construction of Red Fort, a huge contingent of trained stone-masons, skilled in both plain and decorative work, builders and carpenters were brought from all parts of the kingdom even some forigners were also employed. The large army of various animals was used to carry the materials from near and far off places. Red Stone and Marble was used for the construction, the main building was Naqqar Khana, beyond this no noble could go on horse or elephant, they had to go on foot, from this place the arrival of the Emperor was announced by beating of the drums and other musical instruments, the Diwan-e-Aam, was the Hall of public audience, the Emperor sat on his raised throne, which was a peacock throne, said to be taken by Nadir Shah; under which the Nobles had to sit according the their positions. The Emperor held his court and also inspected the animals, birds, goods and soldiers et cetera brought for the Emperor.

On its other side, there were gateways which led to the storerooms where various state appurtenances were kept and to the Imperial Kitchens. To the left of the Hall on East side, there was another gate, which led to Rangilla Chambers; the Diwan-i-Khas was close to the river wall. The privilege of entering this court was only accorded to those when emperor wants to consult, or to Ambassadors or persons invited by the king for interview. Near it, was Pearl Mosque, and Hayat Baksh Garden, Hammam, Moti Mahal, Mehtab Garden, Khas Mahal, Rang Mahal, Khurd Jahan. The Red Fort, as it was constructed by red stone to its walls, originally known as Qila-i-Mubarak or Qila-i-Molla. In 1659–60, Aurangzeb, the son of Shah Jahan built Moti Masjid inside it. In 1809 Akbar II added a balcony projecting from the central side of the Mussaman Burj, Bahadur Shah Zafar added, Moti Mahal, the Hira Mahal and the Zafar Mahal in this fort.

After 1857 the British occupied this fort and demolished many structures inside the fort, they also demolished many structures around the Red Fort (1860) to make clear the way to shoot anyone from the fort if needed. They demolished many Havelis (including Akbarabadi Begum Masjid) up to Jama Masjid and other Havelis on the site of present Old Delhi Railway Station.

They added new structures in the Fort for the use of Army, many times it was vandalized during Mughal period and thereafter, so the original garden and glory of this fort cannot be seen or described. The military occupied it till 1993. The buildings, within the Red Fort, as they stand today, are but a shadow of what they were in the time of Shahjahan and Aurangzeb, after being deprived of their gold plating and other precious decorations by the Marathas, the Afghans and the British. A large number of the original buildings have been razed to the ground.

Bahadur Shah Zafar and his Trial

He was the last Mughal Emperor of Delhi. The British called him King and not Emperor. From 1857 onwards *Dehli* is spelt as Delhi, *Dehli* is more native

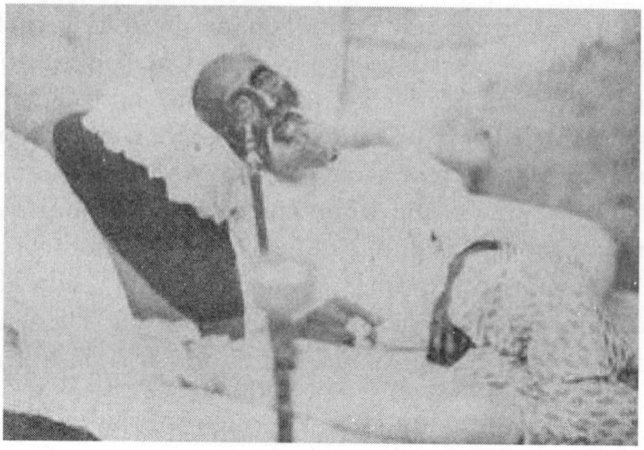

Bahadur Shah Zafar in his last days.

and it has its meaning—'threshhold'—culturally rich and significant in all quarters of the subcontinent. Bahadur Shah II was the son of Akbar Shah and his Rajput wife Lal Bai. Akbar Shah's mother was also a Hindu by birth. Akbar Shah died in 1837 and Bahadur Shah II (Zafar) succeeded him at the age of 62 years. He was of a mystic frame of mind. He had a natural outlook and kind to the Hindus, which he inherited from his father. He reposed great faith in Hindus and banked on Hindu-Muslim unity. He also visited Hindu Temples, got hallowed mark on his forehead. He observed the Hindu festivals of Rakhi Bandan, Basant, Holi and Diwali and granted 'Bakhshish' to the Hindu servants. He honoured many Hindus during his reign some of them are: Babu Suraj Narain, Muktar of Banaras, Pandit Nand Kishore, Raja Bhola Nath, Kunwar Salag Ram, Debi Singh, Gainda Mal, Lala Shiv Lal, Jagjivan Das, Lala Mukand Lal, his Private Secretary. Zakaullah, who had seen Bahadur Shah, and close to the British also said about the Emperor, 'if you, Muslims are to me like one eye, verily the Hindus are dear to me like another eye. C.F. Andrews who had written on Zakaullah says 'Bahadur Shah was highly respected by the inhabitants of the royal city-Delhi ... he was dearly loved by Hindus and Muslims alike for his good manners.'[123] The grandfather of Zakaullah, Hafiz Mohammad Khalil was the teacher of Bahadur Shah apart from Hafiz Ibrahim and Sayyid Jalal-ud-Din Haider.

Zakeer Dehlvi who was closely connected with the royal palace since his boyhood, who later became the courtier of Bahadur Shah; had seen him in different capacities describes that Bahadur Shah was yet in his teens when he became an athlete, an archer, a good shot, a master rider and a specialist in horses apart from this he was a good architect. He built buildings inside the Fort, Palace of Zinat Mahal, his wife, at Lal Kuan in 1846 A.D., a Palace of Taj Mahal for his another wife inside the Katra Khushal Rai, one of the Gateways

Zeenat Mahal.

at Qutb Shrine in 1847 A.D. and Hawa Mahal at Qutub. He was the lover of Birds. He was a good poet and respected the literary people. When Shah Alam died in 1806 A.D., Bahdur Shah was 32 years old. By this time his character was formed. He possessed all the good qualities of his ancestors 'without sharing their vices'. He never tasted wine and abstained from all drugs including opium, later he only indulged in hookah and paan. His favorite past-time was cock-fighting and partridge-contest. He spent most of his time in reading, writing and comparing verses in 'Roshan Ara Garden'.

Charles Metcalfe who saw him about 1828 was impressed by his conduct and accomplishments. However, other Europeans (Emily Eden and Orlich) did not appreciate his plain apparel. He wrote five Diwans of mixed Urdu, Panjabi and Persian poetry, one was published from the Royal Press, under the supervision of Hakim Ahsanullah in 1845 A.D., Another in 1850 A.D.; Sheikh Sadi's Gulistan, the forth from Nawal Kishore Press, Lucknow, his fifth Dewan is missing.[124]

The verses give the picture of his mind, beliefs, temperament, habits and outlook towards life. His Ghazals did much more to damage the British in 1857 than all the combined guns of the mutineers.[125] He wanted to free himself and all the Indians from British thraldom. He was philanthropic, generous and charitable. He used to give fixed amount to disabled on the 1st of every month, when he had no money he used to take loans from the Mahajans to pay the salaries to his servants, awarding gifts to intending travellers, deserving poets and needy persons and to his courtiers. Sir, Syed had not written well for the Emperor, so about Zakaullah, but later he felt sorry for it. Ghalib faced many difficulties, but never wrote badly for Bahadur Shah. Bahadur Shah joined Chishti order at an early age. Hakim Ahsanullah was allowed to officiate as Wazir because Mehbub Ali Khan had fallen ill during the Mutiny. Bahadur Shah did not like Ahsanullah as Wazir, but he was associated with the fort since the time of his father. Bahadur Shah did not heed his advice not to have association, with the mutineers. From 12 May 1857 he considered his interests identical with the mutineers. When mutineers wanted to kill Ahsanullah, the king threw himself on his body and saved him. Later Hakim Ahsanullah, Mirza Ilahi Bakhsh and Munshi Rajab Ali proved adverse to the interests of Bahadur Shah.

He issued many orders between May–September 1857. However Bahadur Shah did not wield the sword during the war and killed no one though he visited the battlefield and frequently inspected the batteries.[126] After the battle of Patparganj in 1803 when Marathas, who were the protectors of the king, got a crushing defeat from the British, General Lake captured the city. The city and fort having been evacuated by the Marathas, the Emperor Shah Alam, a blind king sent a message to General Lake, appealing for protection by the British Authorities, till the date of the successful assault of 1857 by the British, the kings of Delhi have become pensioned subjects of the British Government. The king had no power whatever beyond the precincts of his own palace; he had only the power of conferring titles and dresses of honor upon his own inmates but was prohibited from exercising that power upon any others. He and the heir-apparent alone were exempted from the jurisdiction of the company's local courts but were under the orders of the Supreme Government. After the victory of Patparganj, Shah Alam congratulated Lord Lake. It is said by Europeans that Shah Alam welcomed the British as liberator who had rescued him from the ignominious thralldom of the Marathas. It is a fact that the emperor had been in secret communication with Lord Lake before the battle of Delhi; but it was the traditional pattern of imperial diplomacy.

The British were not new to him. He had spent Nine years under the protection of the English crown at Allahabad, but at that time there was no dearth of revenue. In fact from his heart he wanted French as his protectors, but French had no army of their own. General Peron was only the Agent of the Marathas.

The King Shah Alam had no idea that something revolutionary had happened with this battle; it was not only the change of guards. Since this battle onwards the behavior of the British changed towards the king and the people. Now they became the sovereign power in India. The King, who was the symbol of power of Indian people, the Princes, the Rajas, Nawabs, would pay their respects by offering compliments and Nazars to their overlord; the Emperor of India lost this symbol. The failure of the British to appreciate the power exerted on the Indian imagination by this emperor was a large measure responsible for muting apart from other factor.

Bahadur Shah was anxious to help his countrymen against the English 'tyrants'. East India Company's officers were committing violence and fraud, they had exceeded all bounds in their attempts to satisfy their unbridled ambition and their thirst for Gold and Power. This was the common belief of the Indians.

The outbreak of 1857 had been foreseen in England and France much earlier to it. It is evident from a letter dated 30 May 1850 written by Sir Charles Napier, conqueror of Sind to a higher officer of the company. He writes:

"No, No, I will not concede to you that we are strong, just or punctilious (strictly following the rules) or that we take from the people only that which law empowers us to take or that we pay them (their dues) all the months. We do not pay ourselves, nor do we pay others. Here is a fact: The coolies who were called to carry the baggage of the Governor setting out on a journey and meet at Simla. They are each paid two annas per day and are treated with great cruelty. But I understand that by the negligence of the officers and perhaps also through defalcation, 8,000 to 10,000 of these coolies who had been employed for carrying and transporting the luggage of a certain Englishman going out of India have not obtained those miserable wages of their for three years. In Calcutta you live in an enchanted circle. You know the Indian Government only in theory, just as if you were the Governor-General. The atrocities which are committed here baffle description. You cannot know that much from your book-shelves of Calcutta but I, who have travelled over all parts of the country sometimes on foot and sometimes on horseback, have been seeing the conditions of the Indians for years.

...I had left Sind contented but now it has been made unhappy and discontented. To remove the political disaffection that has set in, the Government has employed military force. Therefore I do not associate myself with the praises that you bestow on the Indian Government; my opinion is just the reverse... We force the Indian to work at the plough and we force him to walk thousands of miles carrying the luggage of the English soldiery. The Indian peasant loses his harvest, his land remains uncultivated and his family perishes; his oxen, over worked by the soldiers, fall on the way and he does not receive a farthing as compensation for this. His broken plough is left on the way and he is dragged to shoulder another plough whose master has fled away in desperateness. And after six or eight months the peasant is sent back ruined to his house where he used formerly to live happily and peacefully before our arrival there. There he may find his wife and children alive; but if the wife is beautiful, he will (have the misfortune to) hear that the European magistrate has taken her for himself.

I am told that these magistrates have no scruples about taking the Indian women. The only thing one might say in their favor is that they do not openly practice severity and violence vis-à-vis the women as the Indians do."[127]

Sir Thomas Munro held similar opinion in 1822:

> The army will not wait for the long process of the spread of Education and the growth of freedom. It well hurry to do things which it will consider practical for subverting the Government and recovering its national independence, the achievement of which the press will teach them before long to consider their duty. They will experience great difficulty in finding leaders ... A military revolt which will come about through some temporary or partial courses can be suppressed but a movement which arises from a change in the character of troops and from systematic opposition becomes irresistible. We shall never be able to recover our present ascendancy; all confidence in the Indians will be destroyed. After one series of civil and sanguinary wars, rather amidst mutinies and massacres coming off alternatively we would be compelled to leave no support from the people. The traders and shopkeepers whose interests we have promoted may desire our success; they cannot help doing otherwise. It will be only to deceive ourselves if we believe that gratefulness to, and love for, our Government will raise a considerable number of Indians to rally to our side, should a war break out with the army.[128]

After Vellore mutiny of 1806, the British Government adopted the policy of divide and rule. In 1821 a British Officer, wrote in the Asiatic Journal 'Divide et empera' should be the note of our Indian Administration, whether political, civil or military. In 1843, Lord Elenborough openly adopted the policy of favouring the Hindus, he said, "I cannot close my eyes to the belief that this race (Musalman) is fundamentally hostile to us and therefore our true policy is to consider the Hindus."[129]

He brought the gates of the temple of Somnath from Ghazna supposed to be taken by Mahmud of Ghazani, to elate the feelings of Hindus and keep alive the feeling of bitterness among Hindus and Muslmans. He got arranged a procession from Firozpur to Somnath. Sometimes the Government favoured the Hindus and so on. After 1857 they deliberately followed the policy of divide and rule.

On the morning of 11 May 1857 after killing their British Officers, the mutinous troops from Meerut arrived in Delhi, Bahadur Shah confronted a very difficult situation. In fact he knew that the troops from Meerut had left the incomplete task and he could foresee the reactions and results. The Indian historian writes, '... when after a great deal of delay and wavering Bahadur Shah at last accepted the title of Emperor of Hindustan, he assumed the responsibility of the position which had been forced upon him.'[130]

As a matter of fact as soon as the preliminary obstacles had been removed, Bahadur Shah declared war on the British and made no secret of his hatred for them.[131]

Bahadur Shah sent a letter on the 12th May 1857 to the Indian Princes and soliciting their help, he made it quite clear that he was waging the country's war (letters were dispatched to Raja of Patiala, Nawabs of Jhajjar, Ballabgarh, Bahadurgarh and Alwar) on 4th September 1857 to Bikaner and Alwar. The king was in want of troops and was desirous of annihilating the British.

On 11 May he took the reins of administration into his own hands and appointed Hamid-ud-Dawla Mirza Mughal eldest and most experienced son as Commander-in-Chief of the Army and other sons and grandsons as Colonel of each Regiment. He arranged for the supply of the food for the army, hospital for the wounded; report from the Kotwal, collection of revenue and loans; salary-sheet of the Sepoys.[132]

On 25 August 1857 Bahadur Shah issued a firman for the welfare of Zamindars, sepoys and artisans. But in the third week of May 1857 he wrote a letter to Mirza Mughal, the commander of the Armed forces about, the behaviours, highhandedness, lethargy, non-compliance of the orders of the king, their rude behaviour towards the royal servants, their looting, killing the shopkeepers, demanding more money and positions and their connections with the British. The British on the other used their spies and spread all sorts of wrong news. In this letter Bahadur Shah had threatened to go to the Dargah of Khwaja and then to Mecca if the sepoys did not mend themselves. This letter is an indication of Bahadur Shah's sincerity of purpose at this ripe age.

He was requested by Mirza Ilahi Bakhsh to start negotiations with the British, but Bahadur Shah considered it a crime to negotiate with the British. On the night of 19 September 1857 he sent out the Queen, other ladies and children in the dark of night to the house of Mirza Ilahi Bakhsh. He was alone, in the fort. On 20 September 1857 in the early morning he went to the shrine of Hazrat Nizam-ud-Din Aulia. He sat down by the side of the sacred Tomb and burst into tears. He looked to Shah Ghulam Hasan, the custodian of the Shrine, he talked to him, gave him a box which contained the three hairs from the sacred beard of Prophet Mohammed, which had passed on as a sacred trust from father to son in the house of Timur since the fourteenth century, now the relics are with the shrine of Hazrat Nizam-ud-Din Aulia. For two days Bahadur Shah did not get the food. He was given something to eat by the caretaker of the durgah; after that he went to Humayun's tomb; there he was he was captured by Hudson at the direction of Ahsanullah; two of his sons and one grandson were also captured and shot dead near Khuni Darwaja. Bahadur Shah was taken as prisoner to Delhi and lodged as a prisoner in the house formerly the residence of the Begum Samru. He was guarded by fifty soldiers under the command of a lieutenant. He was guarded by European sentries, with fixed bayonets stood on both sides of Bahadur Shah. The orders given to them were that on any attempt to rescue the King, the Officers were immediately to shoot the king with their own hand.

On the other side in the morning of the 21st the British captured the Red Fort and General Wilson established his Head-Quarters in the Dewan-i-Khas. The search for other members of the Bahadur Shah's family was on. It is the second time in a century (First in 1803) that Delhi and its forts were captured by the British.

Trial of Bahadur Shah

Bahadur Shah was tried in the Red Fort before the Military Commission, assembled on 27 January 1858, upon a charge of rebellion, treason and murder. The following was the composition of the Court, President: Lieut. Colonel Davis, Horse Artillery;

Members:

1. Major Palmer, H.M. 60th Rifles.
2. Major Redmond, H.M. 61st Foot.
3. Major Sawyer, H.M. 6th Carbineers.
4. Captain Rathney, 4th Sikh Infantry Interpreter: Mr. James Murphy, Prosecutor for Government, Major F.J. Harriott, Deputy Judge Advocate General.

After a lengthy trial he was found guilty on every charge. Being saved from a severer penalty by a guarantee of his life which he had received from Major Hudson at the time of his surrender, he was sentenced to perpetual banishment. By Government orders he was removed to Rangoon, where he died, a prisoner of the British Government, on 7 October 1862. Following is the list of the Mughal Princes, who were executed by orders of Delhi Special Commissioner for rebellion:

(1) Mirza Nadir Bakht son of Mirza Iqtedar Bakht,
(2) Mirza Moula Bakhsh son of Mirza Rahim Bakht,
(3) Mirza Kureen Bakhsh son of Muhboo Mirza,
(4) Mirza Abu Abbas son of Mirza Muzaffar,
(5) Mehmood Shikoh son of Mirza Abbas Shikoh,
(6) Mirza Husain Bakhsh son of Mirza Qadar Bakhsh,
(7) Mirza Ahmad Bakhsh son of Mirza Qadar Bakhsh.

(8) Mirza Abidoodin Abbas son of Mirza Zahooruddin,
(9) Mirza Musheeruddin son of Mirza Qadar Bakhsh,
(10) Mirza Moinuddin son of Mirza Ala Bakhsh,
(11) Mirza Qadar Bakhsh son of Mirza Makhoo,
(12) Mirza Nooruddin son of Mirza Abboo,
(13) Mirza Qutbuddin son of Mirza Qadar Bakhsh,
(14) Muizzuddin son of Mirza Medhu,
(15) Mirza Inayat Husain son of Mirza Iqtidar Bakht,
(16) Mirza Mohammad Bakhsh son of Mirza Ezad Bakhsh,
(17) Ghulam Mohammadi son of Mirza Karim Bakhsh,
(18) Mirza Ghulam Bakhruddin son of Mirza Agha Jan,
(19) Mirza Ghulam Abbas son of Mirza Agha Jan,
(20) Mirza Kabiruddin son of Mirza Qutbuddin,
(21) Mirza Bahadur son of Mirza Baland,
(22) Mirza Wala Shikoh son of Mirza Balan Dey,
(23) Mirza Nannhey son of Mirza Karimuddin,
(24) Mirza Mubarak son of Mirza Munjhley,
(25) Mirza Balan Day son of Mirza Mukarram,
(26) Mirza Kaley son of Mirza Agha Jan.[133]

Following is the list of Mughal Princes who died shortly after their arrest or subsequently to the pronouncement of sentence of imprisonment for life:

(1) Mirza Kamran
(2) Mirza Babur Shihab
(3) Mirza Ilahi Bakhsh
(4) Mirza Bahadur
(5) Mirza Husain Bakhsh
(6) Mirza Karim Bakhsh
(7) Mirza Ghulam Inammuddin
(8) Mirza Mohammad
(9) Mirza Husain Bakhsh
(10) Mirza Kadir Bakhsh
(11) Allah Bakhsh
(12) Mirza Ghulam Naeemuddin
(13) Mirza Ahmad Jan
(14) Mirza Inhan Sultan
(15) Mirza Rihazuddin, (He died during trial)

The following Princes were sent to jail for life, first they were confined in Agra, then in Kanpur and then in Calcutta and Alipur Jail; but they were ultimately sent to Moulmein and Karanchi:

(1) Nazim Shah, son of Mohammad Akbar Shah (Brother of Bahadur Shah)
(2) Mirza Khuda Bakhsh
(3) Mirza Farrukh Shah
(4) Mirza Imam Bakhsh
(5) Turab Shah
(6) Zakiruddin
(7) Husbhuddin, directed to be sent to Karachi:
(8) Mirza Babur
(9) Mirza Nizamuddin
(10) Mirza Khuda Bakhsh
(11) Mirza Chhotey,
(12) Mirza Ahmad Shikoh
(13) Mirza Asghar[134]

Nominal roll of the State Prisoners Proceeded to Calcutta

(1) Abu Zafar Bahadur Shah, Shah Ghazee, ex-king of Delhi.
(2) Mirza Jawan Bakht, son of the above by ex-queen Zint Mahal.
(3) Mirza Shah Abbas, son of the above by a Harem woman.
(4) Zinat Mahal, ex-queen of Delhi,
(5) Nawab Shah Zamani Begum, wife of Mirza Jawan Bakht.
(6) Ruqaiya Sultan Begum, sister of Nawab Shah, Zamani Begum has one female baby.
(7) Mumtaz Dulhan Begum, mother of Shah Zamani Begum and Ruqaiya Sultan Begum.
(8) Nawab Taj Mahal Begum, a wife of Ex-king of Delhi.
(9) Sultan
(10) Rakeena
(11) Ishrat — Harem of the ex-king
(12) Taharat
(13) Mubarakunisa, mother of Mirza Shah Abbas
(14) Mirza Keiser,
(15) Abdur Ruhiman,
(16) Ahmad Beg,
(17) Inzzur
(18) Khwaja Bakhsh, Eunuch (male attendants).

Female attendants

(19) Sandal
(20) Niazoo
(21) Husani
(22) Kimeian

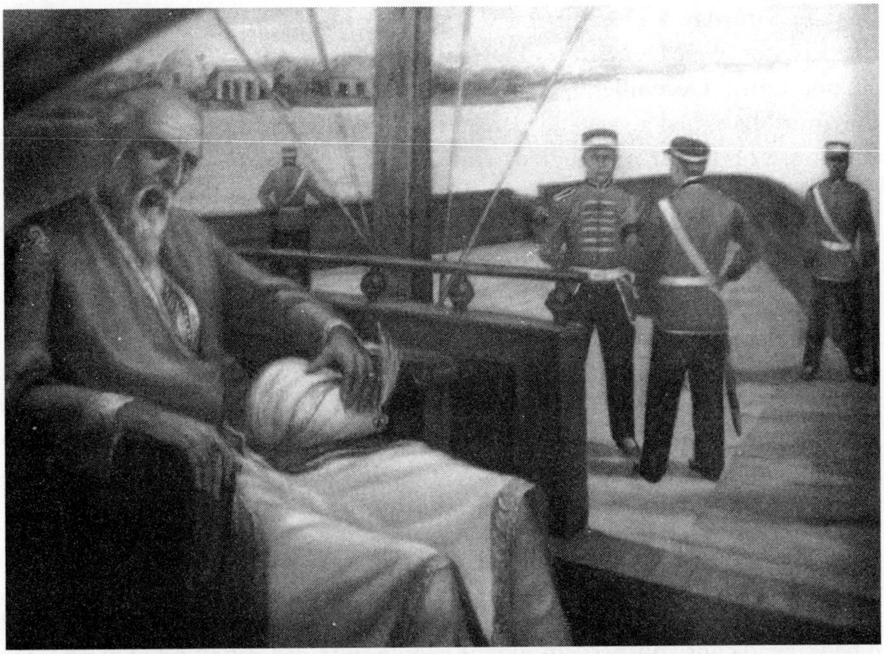

A sketch of Bahadur Shah Zafar in a boat at Delhi before deporting to Rangoon.

(23) Wafldar
(24) Rahat
(25) Jumayat
(26) Mubarak
(27) Sakina Khanum
(28) Hurmat Bhai
(29) Lutfan.

On 7 October 1858, the above mentioned left by land route, under the escort of 9th Lancers, to Allahabad, and reached Allahabad on 13 November 1858. The 14 members of the party whose names are given below expressed a desire to go back to Delhi, so they were detained in the fort of Allahabad: 1.Mirza Kaiser, 2. Jaffar, 3. Khwaja Bakhsh, (Eunuch) 4.Taj Mahal, wife of Bahadur Shah, 5. Sakina Khanum, 6. Mumtaz Dulhan, mother-in-law of Jawan Bakht, 7. Ruqaiya Sultan Begum, sister-in-law of Jawan Bakht, 8. Raheena, 9. Taharat, 10. Kimeian, 11. Wafedar, 12. Rahat, 13. Junayat, 14. Mubarak.

From Allahabad the prisoners were taken to Mirzapur where they embarked on board the' Soorma Flat' a steamer and were accompanied by eleven followers who having received the option determined to go with the prisoners to their destination (Rangoon).

On Saturday 4 December 1858 it arrived at Diamond Harbor; from it the prisoners were boarded on H.M.'s ship Megara. It arrived at Sandheads at 12 noon on 5 December 1858 and reached Rangoon on 9 December 1858. Bahadur Shah died a very sad person on 7 October 1862 and with his death the house of Timur or Mughals ended. He was buried in Rangoon like an ordinary person. On the other hand, Delhi remained sometimes under the military Authority and whole population was expelled from the city. The order of expulsion was afterwards modified, Hindus being generally admitted but Mohammedans still rigorously excluded. People were allowed to enter the city by issuing the permit.

In July 1858 civil courts were reopened and the city gradually resumed its wanted appearance. Calcutta was made the capital of India. The cantonments were constituted in 1859. Red Fort was taken over by military. The administration was transferred from East India Company to the Crown. There onwards the development of the city started.

Indian National Army Trials

The Mutiny (1857–8) may not have succeeded to achieve its goal, but certainly it had spread consciousness among the people and a different kind of movement began to take shape, different political, social and cultural organization began to form. Indian National Congress was one such organization which was formed in 1885, by 1905 it has given birth to extremists and militant groups. In the beginning the British were sympathetic towards Congress, but by 1905 they become indifferent and followed the policy of divide and rule. In 1906 Muslim league was formed. The European literature and English education definitely encouraged the Indian leaders for self rule; the Jalianwala Bagh (1919) incident had also contributed to intensify this movement.

Netaji Subhash Chandra Bose become the president of Indian National Congress, despite the opposition of Mahatma Gandhi, this proved that the opinion of the masses was not for peaceful means to achieve the political freedom. But Bose soon got disenchanted with the leadership of the Congress and resigned, he formed the Forward Block, but soon arrested for his inflammatory speeches. In 1941 he escaped to Afghanistan, from there to Russia and then to Germany and finally to Japan.

Some Indians who were outside India, were also feeling to liberate their motherland by armed struggled, they did try many times for it, one such person was Mohan Singh in Malaya. He formed an idea to form an anti-British force to liberate India, as well as to check Japanese misconduct towards Indians in South-East-Asia. By then Japanese had allowed only the civilian Indians to form Anti-British organizations. On 17 February 1942, Lieut. Colonel Hunt, as representative of the British surrendered the Indian Officers of the British Army to the Japanese. The Japanese handed over these men to Mohan Singh, who acted as GOC and conceived Indian National Army (INA) Subhash Chandra Bose, arrived in July 1943 and received the support of Germans and Japanese and took over the command of INA or 'Azad Hind Fauj'. On 21 October 1943 he proclaimed the provisional Government of Free India, and declared war on Britain and United States, and its allies. Subhash Chandra Bose gave two slogans, 'Tum Mujhe Khoon do Main Tumhain Azadi Dunga (give me blood and I will give you the freedom)'; the second slogan was 'Dilli Chalo (March to Delhi)'. The INA was successful in capturing some outlying territory in India, but it could not make much head way as the Axis powers collapsed. Subhash Bose was also declared dead in a plane crash. There is still some debate on this issue. The INA was forced to surrender. The British imprisoned the INA Officers, transported them to India and lodged them at the Red Fort. About 17000 men of the INA believed to have been held as prisoners of war. Ironically, the very men who ought to have marched to Delhi as victors, hosted the National Flag on the ramparts of the Red Fort and held a victory parade there, were now declared prisoners, inside the Red-Fort, they awaited a trial for waging war against the British.[135]

On 20 August 1945, Jawaharlal Nehru in his first statement to press said, "It would be a very grave mistake, leading to far-reaching consequences, if they were treated just as ordinary rebels. The punishment given to them would in effect be a punishment to all of India and all Indians and a deep wound would be created in millions of hearts...'

This set the tone for the whole country and the INA became a burning topic. The public demanded the release of the INA prisoners. Mahatma Gandhi met the INA officers at the Red Fort. The surrendered men were put to trial in court Martial Conducted in Red Fort in Delhi. The Court Martial began on 5 November and ended on 31 December, 1945.

The three main persons were charged, Capt. Shah Nawaz Khan, Capt. P.K. Sehgal and Lt. G.S. Dhillon. The Court Martial comprised seven members headed by Maj. General A.D. Baxland; Col. F.C.A. Kerin, was the Judge Advocate, Advocate General of India Sir Naushirwan P. Engineer represented the prosecution and Bhulabhai Desai headed the defense team including Jawaharlal Nehru.

The main charge of prosecution was that the accused had waged war against the King and forced the POW's to join INA. Individually they were charged with murder or abetment to murder. The accused pleaded not guilty.

The defense argued that men had voluntarily joined INA without any coercion, INA was the organized army, and its main objective was to free India from the British. It was a wing of a regular Government, when British had given over the soldiers to the Japanese, the relations of soldiers with the Crown was severed. The Government of INA had its own structure along with institution like Bank and issue of Postal Stamps et cetera. The INA could not be tried under the domestic law, for it the case of American and British to free French to liberate France and 1918 of Polish National Army's examples were cited.

On 3 January 1946, the court martial found the three accused officers guilty of waging war against the king and sentenced them to transportation for life, cashiering and the forfeiture of arrears of pay and allowances. The Commander-in-Chief, General Auchinlek, well aware of the explosive political situation commuted the sentences of all three to that of cashiering and forfeiture of pay and allowances. Some more trials took place; however, as these trials were heading towards a politically explosive situation and mass protests, the Government gradually preferred to withdraw them.

The British categorized all the INA personnel into three categories, Black, Grey and White. White was allowed to rejoin the army, Grey was to be retired with their dues and pensions, while Blacks were to be dismissed and their dues confiscated.

The country went delirious with joy and the heroes of the Red Fort trial were overwhelmed by the uproarious welcome they received wherever they went. History was once more created in the fort and the Red Fort remained silent witness to these happenings.

The Trial of Nathu Ram Godse

Nathu Ram Godse was born in a devotional Maharastrian Brahmin family in 1911. He instinctively revered Hindu religion, Hindu history and Hindu culture. He was proved to be Hindu but he was against caste system. He worked against caste system and joined many anti-caste movements. He believed that all Hindus are –equal in status. He was influenced by the writings and speeches of Dadabhai Naoroji, Vivekananda, Gokhale, and Tilak and read the history of England, America, France and Russia. He studied the tenets of socialism and marxism. He also studied the writings of Veersavarkar and Gandhiji, the two ideologies molding the thoughts of Indian people at that time. After reading all this he believed that it was his duty to serve Hinduism and Hindus, while doing that he would be serving the Nation, because thirty cores of Hindus overwhelmingly constitute the well-being of all India. He believed that Hindu ideology would win the National independence.

Godse did not personally disliked Gandhiji, he respected Gandhiji's slogans of truth and non-violence as nothing was new in that, he believed that they are implicit in every constitutional public movement. But these ideals according to his beliefs cannot be scrupulously adhered by the bulk of mankind. In fact, honour, duty and love of one's own kith and kin and country might often compel the person to disregard- non-violence and to use force. He never believed that an armed resistance to an aggression is unjust. It is a religious and moral duty to resist and, if possible, to over power such an enemy by use of force. He had case to site Ram in Ramayana, Krishn in Mahabharat, Shivaji, Rana Pratap and Guru Gobind Singhji: 'Gandhiji has merely exposed his self-conceit. He was, paradoxical as it may appear, a violent pacifist who brought untold calamities on the country in the name of truth and non-violence, while Rana Pratap, Shivaji and Guru will remain enshrined in the hearts of their countrymen for ever for the freedom they brought to them.'[136]

"The accumulating provocation of thirty-two years, culminating in his last pro-Muslim fast, at last goaded me to the conclusion that the existence of Gandhi should he brought to an end immediately".[137]

Godse believed that Gandhiji had done very good in South Africa, but returning to India he developed a subjective mentality under which he alone was to be the final judge of what was right and wrong.

"He alone was the judge of everyone and everything; he was the master brain guiding the civil disobedience movement; no other could know the technique of that movement. He alone knew when to begin and when to withdraw it. The movement might succeed or fail, it might bring untold disaster and political reverses but that could make no difference to the Mahatma's infallibility. 'A satyagrahi can never fail' was his formula for declaring his own infallibility and nobody except himself knew what a satyagrahi is."[138]

Godse also did not like Gandhi's pro-Muslim policy on the question of the National language of India, earlier Gandhiji advocated for Hindi and afterward for Hindustani, which is not a language; it is only a dialect which has no grammar and no vocabulary. From August 1946 onwards the private armies of the Muslim League began to massacre the Hindus, with some retaliation by the Hindus. The interim Government formed in September 1946, the Muslim League members became disloyal to it, Lord Wavell, had to resign. Gandhiji and Nehru had to accept what Jinnah wanted. The official date for handing over power was fixed for 30 June 1948 but Mountbatten after ruthless surgery gave a gift of vivisected India ten months in advance.

Mosques which were occupied by refugees in Delhi, Gandhiji got it vacated by what was happening in Pakistan with the Hindus did not bother, Gandhiji, this infuriated Godse.

Godse knew it that killing of Gandhiji will ruin him and his relatives, but the Nation would be saved from the inroads of Pakistan. "People may even call me and dub me as devoid of any sense or foolish, but the Nation would be free to follow the course founded on the reason which I consider to be necessary for sound nation-building".[139]

Gandhiji was staying at Birla House in Delhi. He used to address the gathering and perform his prayer and in the evening of 30 January 1948 while going to this meeting place Gandhiji was shot by Godse. Godse was arrested immediately after Gandhi's assassination. Nandlal Mehta, an eye witness to the murder and an associate of Gandhiji filed an F.I.R. at the Tughluq Road Police Station. Godse and his fellow conspirators were tried in the Red Fort. The trial began on 27 May 1948 and lasted till 10 February 1949 and Godse was given a death sentence. The High Court at Simla upheld the sentence. On 5 May 1949 Godse made a statement to the court, exploring his motivations for the murder.

First Battle of Panipat 1526 A.D.

Ghazni was small kingdom in Afghanistan which was founded in the tenth century by a Turkish nobleman. One of his successors Mahmud Ghazani wanted to make Ghazni into a big and power kingdom, for that he required money and army. He heard that India was extremely rich and politically divided. So he planned on raiding India. The first raid began in 1000 A.D. In short period of twenty five years Northern India was terrified, anyone who tried to stop him was destroyed. Later he annexed the Punjab and made it a part of his kingdom.

Between 1010 A.D. and 1025 A.D. Mahmud attacked only temple towns in Northern India. He had heard that there was much gold and jewellery kept in the big temples of India. So he destroyed the temples and took away the gold and jewellery. One such temple was at Somnath in western India. He had another advantage in destroying these temples, he could claim, that he had obtained religious merit by destroying images. In 1030 A.D. he died.

In the twelfth century another Afghan ruler, Mohammad Ghori, was interested to invade India and to add-Northern India into his kingdom. Punjab was already a part of the Ghazni kingdom; it gave advantage to him. In the second battle of Tarain in 1192 he defeated Prithvi Raj Chauhan III, ruler of Delhi and Ajmer. It is believed that Mohammad Ghori was invited by Jai Chand, the ruler of Kannauj, the rival of Prithvi Raj III, to come to India and attack Delhi. This was the beginning of the Turkish rule at Delhi. In 1206 he was murdered.

The medieval period saw a change in the administration and economic structure of the country and this affected social life too. In the earlier period the king used to collect taxes directly through his officers, who were paid from the royal treasury. But now the officers were granted the revenue from land and the amount of revenue was normally equal to the salary which he had received. The persons who received such land grants or right to collect revenue were known as feudatories. The feudatories were responsible for the maintenance of law and order in their territory and were also required to maintain soldiers for the king. The system of feudatories made the position of the king weak. When a feudatory considered himself powerful enough, he often declared his independence and established his own rule. They spent (the king and feudatory) much of the revenue on themselves.

The Lodi Dynasty was the last dynasty of the Sultans who ruled Delhi before the Mughals conquered India. The Sultanate had become small and weak, since many of its provinces had become independent kingdoms. The noble wanted to get rid of Lodi Kings. Babur considered the Punjab as a right belonging to him, as it was a part of Timur's Empire and he was the descendent of Timur. He was invited by Daulat Khan Lodi the Governor of Punjab and by Alam Khan, a noble of Sultan Ibrahim Lodi. In 1523 A.D. Babur undertook five expeditions on India, some of it were preparatory. He attacked India but retired to Afghanistan due to Uzbek's pressure. But soon in November 1526 A.D., he again attached India, Daulat Khan had come out with 40,000 soldiers, his force melted away at the approach of Babur's army.

Ibrahim Lodi marched from Delhi along with the right bank of Yamuna, with 10000, troops, including many war elephants. A subsidiary force moved from Hissar under Hamid Khan. This force comes in the contact of Humayun, at this time 18 years old and Humayun defeated the forces of Hamid Khan. Babur arrived at Panipat where he occupied a strong position, protecting his right along the town, and his left by ditch and branches of trees. The centre was protected by rows of carts, seven hundred in number, tied together with twisted bull-hides gaps were kept at convenient distances for the army to sally forth to attack the enemy. Babur had a few pieces of camels and some musketeers as well (gun powder was used by him for the first time), whom he stationed behind the wagons. For eight days Ibrahim hesitated to attack this strong position. Babur then sent a small force to mark a night attack which roused Ibrahim Lodi. Approaching Babur's strong position Ibrahim had to shorten his line by slanting it, which resulted in confusion. At this time Babur sent his 'Tulghana' or flanking parties of light cavalry armed with bows and arrows which took the Afghans on the flanks and in the rear, thus increasing the pressure on the front of Lodi's Army. The Lodi's Army thus became a dense mass of men without room to move or manoeuvre. The Mughal fell upon them and the battle turned into a slaughter. The Lodi's soldiers were killed in large numbers and the road up to Delhi was strewn with the dead as Babur's army pursued them.

Humayun was sent to occupy Agra where his courteous treatment of the family of the raja of Gwalior who had fallen into his hands earned him not only their gratitude but also presents including the famous Kah-i-Noor. In 1527 A.D. Babur defeated Rana Sanga; the defeat of Medini Rai of Chanderi completed the collapse of the Rajputs. In 1529 in the battle of Buxar a treaty was made between Afghans and Babur. On December 1530 A.D. Babar died at

Agra; with a short break of Sur dynasty, the Mughals ruled Delhi and its Empire till 1857. So the first battle of Panipat had a long and far reaching effect on the socio-economic and cultural life of Delhi.

Second battle of Panipat 1556 A.D.

After the death of Islam Shah, son of Sher Shah Suri, Adil Shah seized the throne but taking advantage of state of anarchy, the real power passed into the hands of Himu, a Bania by caste of Rewari. Akbar was only thirteen in 1556 A.D. when his father died and he was proclaimed king at Kalanaur by Bairam Khan, who acted as his guardian till Akbar started doing administrative work himself. As a child Akbar was more interested in pigeon-flying and hunting. Humayun did not have time to strengthen Mughal power in North India, this job was later undertaken by Akbar. The first conflict came with Himu, who was the General of one of the Afghan Princes. So another battle was fought in 1556 A.D. at Panipat. Himu had a strong army, initially the Mughal army was divided on the issue of battle, but Bairam Khan prevailed on others. Within 30 years the Mughal army had become ready to fight the throne of Delhi at Panipat. Himu had 100000 soldiers while Mughals had only 20,000 soldiers, even there was disparity in resources and equipment. There were many problems on the side of Mughal army; in fact few kings in the History of India had left so many problems for his successor as was left by Humayun. On the other hand Himu was sure for an easy victory. He sat on the back seat of an elephant and leading an attack on the heart of the Mughal army when suddenly an arrow pierced his left eye. He fell down senseless, his elephant ran away and his men fled for their lives. His entire army became panicky and then dispersed, while Himu was captured and later beheaded. After capturing Delhi, Mughals resumed their operations against Sikandar Shah Sur. He was soon forced to offer submission and accepted a Jagir. Meanwhile Mughal army captured Jaunpur and Gwalior. Later Akbar extended his Empire.

Third Battle of Panipat 1761 A.D.

Balaji Vishwanath was the first Peshwa. The Peshwa was technically a minister of the king (Chhatrapati) of the Maratha kingdom. Baji Rao was the son of Balaji Vishwanath, who followed the policy of conquest, if he had lived little longer he would have consolidated his conquests. His son, Balaji Baji Rao (1740–61) continued the policy of his father. During this period the power of the Marathas were at its zenith. The year of his death saw it terribly decline.

Shahu, who had ascended the throne of Chhatrapati in 1707, died in 1749. He was in detention of the Mughal court. From 1720 he was hardly the centre of politics in Maharashtra. The Shivaji's family was fighting the succession issue and the family was highly devided. So the Peshwas became the real power and over the years the office of the Peshwa, became hereditary. After the death of Sahu, no one bothered about his capital at Satara and the power shifted to Poona the home of the Peshwa's.

During the power of the Peshwa, Nizam was defeated at Udgir in 1760, and many forts such as Asirgarh, Burhanpur, Ahmadnagar and Daultabad were taken by Marathas, states of Rajasthan were compelled to pay the chauth; the Gangetic Doab and Punjab were taken over. Punjab was in the possession of Ahmad Shah Abdali; in 1756-57 he raided Delhi and committed the same atrocities as was done by Nadir Shah.

The Peshwas occupation of the Punjab therefore brought the Peshwas into conflict with Ahamad Shah Abdali. The expansionist policy of Marathas created many enemies around the country. The Rajasthan Rajput rulers were not happy with Marathas, the Jat ruler of Bharatpur did not want to indulge in war with Afghans, the Sikhs were also not prepared for the war, the Nawab of Awadh and the Nizam of Hyderabad were not with the Mrarthas. The Najib-ud-Daulah and his other companions went over the Abdali, the Muslims of Delhi were not happy with the Marathas; in the victory of Marathas they feared the anarchy and plunder.

The Peshwa dispatched Sadasiv Rao Bhao to oppose Abdali who had already captured Punjab. Bhao marching on the borders of East-Rajputana reached Delhi and captured it. In November 1760 the Maratha's and Abdali's forces stood facing each other in the battlefield of Panipat. Abdali's army was sixty thousand strong. Shuja-ud-Daulah and Najib-ud-Daulah were also with him. Najib-ud-Daulah rendered extremely valuable service in this battle. He helped the Afghans with money as well as by sending a contingent of fifteen thousand soldiers. The other Rohilla chiefs, Hafiz Rahmat Khan, Dundey Khan and Sadullah Khan also came to help the Abdali. The difficulties of Marathas was multiplying with the passage of time without provisions of fresh supply. Bhao begged for peace, but Najib-ud-Daulah opposed it.

On the Morning of 14 January 1761 fighting began. The initiative was taken by the Marathas, whose left wing was under Ibrahim Khan Gardi, launched a fierce attack. Bhao himself pushed back the centre of the Afghan Army, which was led by Shahwali Khan. When the battle was at its peak, Ahmad Shah attacked the centre and the left wing of the Marathas with a fresh army of thirteen thousand soldiers. This unexpected blow broke the spirit of the Marathas' army. When Marathas army showing the sign of weakness, they were fired by musketeers. At 2, o'clock the Peshwa's son Vishwas Rao, died of a bullet shot. Bhao was also killed. By 3 p.m., Marathas began to lose ground. The Afghan rushed at them from all sides by sunset huge piles of dead appeared on the scene. Holkar himself immediately left the field and fled promptly followed by the Gaikwad.

"The early escape of Holkar, on a day so fatal to his Nation, has given rise to some reproaches; but his advocates ascribe his safety to his superior knowledge as a leader, which made him, when he saw the action lost, keep his party together, and retreat with an order that none of the others preserved".[140]

The fact is that Holkar advised Bhao to delay the action for one or two days, but the commander did not agree to it. So the Holkar did not fight with his commitments.

The ferocious victors beset the camp all night. On the morning, they divided amongst themselves as slaves, the women and children and slaughtered the male prisoners in cold blood.

The Jat Prince treated the fugitives with much kindness Vishwas Rao's body was found, and the barbarous chieftains assembled around the Afghan sovereign at first insisted that the corpse of the king of the unbelievers should be stuffed and carried back to Kabul, but by Shuja-ud-Daulah's intercession, it was eventually burned. A headless trunk was displayed as that of the Bhao. But it remained uncertain whether the body was actually his.

With the third battle of Panipat, the native period of Indian History may be coming to an end. Henceforth the merchant Princes from the west became more powerful and ultimately they captured the fort of Delhi. It is estimated that more than 30 thousand Maratha soldiers lost their lives. The Marathas had never suffered such a disastrous defeat. There was hardly a family in Maharashtra which had not lost one or the other of its members. For the Peshwa the shock was so great that he died within few months of this disaster. The defeat of Marathas broke their back bone. The influence of Najib-ud-Daulah had increased. The Jats looted Delhi. The Sikhs attached Delhi. By 1770 the Marathas again invaded the Doab and established their supremacy in the region, until the British defeated them in 1803.

The Problem of Succession

Red Fort was not an enclosure of stones and bricks. It was quite different from other forts. In fact it was the centre of political power and authority. The major events enacted in it ultimately related to succession of the power.

The problem of succession had been very intricate in the history of India since the time immemorial. But it became more intricate during the time of Mughal Dynasty. The questions-whether the eldest son alone is entitled to rule or every son of the deceased ruler has some share in the kingdom, whether the nomination of a dying Emperor is enough to ensure the succession of the nominee or is there any necessity of selection or approval by the nobles, whether the kingship can be challenged during the life time of the ruler by any of his sons, or has the grandson any right to be preferred in comparison to his father.

It is difficult to answer any one of these questions without taking into account all the forces of thought that had been operating at that time.

The Hindu period, the Slaves, Khilji's, Tughluq, Sayyids and Lodi's had something to give on any, all or some of the questions of succession. The Muslim theory of kingship owes a good deal to the institution of the Caliphate.

Babur was descended from a Mongol mother and a Timurid father. He had imbibed both the cultures. Apart from these two, he had the Islamic culture as his back ground. Mohammedans had been ruling in India long before Babur's advent.

In Timurs conception of kingship the partner had no place. He did not divide his kingdom among all his sons, who were four in number. Probably he believed in the right of primogeniture. But Timurs will remain only a pious wish. Immediately after his death the succession was contested between his sons and grandsons. The Principle of Primogeniture was not recognized as a right.

Humayun's troubles were in a large measure due to unfixed and uncertain laws of succession. Babur's mother was the daughter of a Mongol Khan. The laws of succession among the Mongols were quite different from those of the Turks. Among the Mongols a man was not succeeded by his son so long as he had brothers living. When the brothers were exhausted, the inheritance is reverted to the family of the eldest brother. Babur enters into India with two principles of succession. He wanted to make Humayun supreme but at the sametime desired to give something to Kamran by way of right. This attitude of Babur is partly responsible for many of the misfortunes of Humayun. Humayun's entire reign is a sad commentary on the principle of the divisibility of the Empire. Jahangir (younger brother of Babur) had troubled him and all his predecessors had quarreled amongst themselves. The Principle of Primogeniture was not fully recognized.

Humayun was bound to forgive and forgive helplessly, and his brothers were let loose to do whatever they liked. The Pathan Kings of Delhi had left a very bad tradition so far as the problem of succession was concerned.

Firoz Shah Tughluq was elected to kingship in spite of the claims put forward by Mohammad Tughluq's sister's son and his own. The former was declared incompetent and the letter rejected on account of his being a minor. The Sayyids have nothing very positive to contribute. The Lodis again turn over a new leaf. Islam Khan dies after appointing his nephew Bahlol as his heir-apparent. His son Qutub Khan was alive but he was superseded. He was elected after great bitterness and hart-burning. Bahlol went a step further. Azam Humayun, son of his eldest son was alive, yet he appointed as his heir Sikandar who was supposed to have been born of a goldsmith woman. So even in Muslim rulers of India, any favorable bias for the Principle of Primogeniture is not found.

Humayun, Akbar, Jahangir, Shah Jahan and Aurangzeb had to struggle for the succession. In Jahangir's accession involves the quarrel of a son with his father. Jahangir's reign opens a new chapter in the problem of succession. The laws of succession were so uncertain that Salim (later on Jahangir) had become hopeless. The claim of first born was not at all recognized. This alone was not the deciding factor. This king's declaration – rather nomination – was the chief thing along with the approval of the nobles. Since Muslim theory of kingship desires its inspiration from caliphate. When Mohammad died he nominated no one as his successor. The first four caliphs who succeeded him were elected in the spirit of Islam and in the most democratic manner. Muawaiyah, the founder of the Umayyad dynasty was the first man to introduce the principles of heredity and nomination and had him accepted as such by the people. It was with reluctance they gave their consent.[141]

In 676 A.D. Yazid was accepted by reluctance by the people. The principle of nomination was followed by the Abbasids also. In case of first 24 caliphs of the Abbasid's dynasty that for a period of more than two centuries (759 – 974 A.D.) only six of them were succeeded by a son. After the Abbasid's it became more common for a son to succeed his father, but throughout the whole period political theory maintained that the office was elective. By the sheer force of time and events the office which was originally elective in theory became almost hereditary and nominative in practice. Among the Mongols the system was a bit curious. It was nomination-cum-election.

From Iltutmish (Slave Dynasty) down to the Sayyids one can see a set of ideas ruling the government. The Afghans under the Lodi had their own peculiar notions about the government. The earlier was the 'absolute monarchy' and in the latter case the power of the king was limited by the tribe to which the king belonged.

Before the Babur's advent into India the following principles of succession were more or less recognized:

(a) The ruler before his death was expected to nominate a successor, usually his nomination was respected,
(b) The successor was formally raised to the throne by the common consent of the nobles and the chiefs.
(c) A son who was near to the dying king had surer and greater chances of succeeding to the throne.
(d) The omras, grandees and chief of the realm began to make themselves felt more in matters of succession. This was due to the influence of Afghan thought.
(e) According to the Afghans even two rulers could rule at the same time.

It was due to their allegiance to tribal headship. Fortunately this practice could not be followed.

Khurram (later on titled as Shah Jahan was born on Thursday, 15 January 1592 at Lahore, he was brought up by Akbar's childless wife, Ruqaiah Begum. At an early age he showed an interest in arms rather than the pursuit of knowledge. During the life time of Jahangir he had organized successful victories in Mewar, Deccan and Kangra campaigns. Up to 1622 he worked in close collaboration of Nur Jahan, but after that he fell out of favour and sent to Deccan. Nur Jahan wanted Shahryar, his son-in-law to succeed the throne after Jahangir, but Asaf Khan the father-in-law of Shah Jahan wanted, Shah Jahan for the kingship.

In the war of succession, Dawar Bakhsh, (son of Khusrau, who was already blinded by his father Jahangir and killed by Shah Jahan) Prince Danial, Shahryar, Gurshasp, Tahmurs and Hoshang were killed at the instance of Shah Jahan. Similar tragic incident enacted by the son of Shah Jahan, Aurangzeb, while ascending the throne of Delhi. He imprisoned Shah Jahan at Agra fort and killed all living brothers and nephews. Mohammad Salih Kambu, the author of Amal-e-Salih, justifies this action. The execution of the Princes in the following callous and unceremonial manner. "It is entirely lawful for the great sovereigns to rid this mortal world of the existence of their brothers and other relations, whose total annihilation is conducive to the common good......and leaders, spiritual and temporal, justify the total eradication of rival claimants to the fortune throne on grounds of expediency and the common welfare."

After imprisoning his father (Shah Jahan) Aurangzeb ascended the throne at Delhi on 21 July 1658 A.D. By May 1662 he killed all his brothers and nephews. He was a fearless soldier and a skillful general and in his dealings with men he was cool and cautious. After his second and formal coronation on 5 June 1659 he issued orders which were calculated to please the orthodox.

During the first half of his reign, Aurangzeb had been busy in the North and left the administration and military operations of the Deccan in the hands of his viceroys but not able to overcome over the Marathas, especially Shivaji. He decided to handle the situation of the South himself. So he left, the Red Fort of Delhi in late 1681, but Aurangzeb could not do much by 1695 A.D. The position of the Mughals was very miserable. In July 1697, the Mughal army suffered a great misery due to the heavy flood of the Bhima River.

On 11 March 1689, the elder son of Shivaji was killed. Raja Ram Shivaji's another son was enthroned on 8 February; because of the capture of Shambhaji, he also died on 2 March 1700. On 19 October 1689, the surviving grandson of Shivaji, Sahu, a boy of seven years of age and other widows of royal family of Shivaji were taken prisoners.

> All seemed to have been gained by Aurangzeb now, but in reality all was lost. It was the beginning of his end. The saddest and most hopeless chapter of his life now opened. The Mughal Empire had become too large to be ruled by one man or from one centre. ... His enemies rose on all sides; he could defeat but not crush them forever. Lawlessness reigned in many parts of northern and central India. The administration grew slack and corrupt. The endless war in the Deccan exhausted his treasury. The Deccan ulcer ruined Aurangzeb.

Centrifugal forces were let loose by the emperor's long absence from the capital and the lack of strong administration at the centre. Besides the risings in the Jat territories, Rajasthan, Bundelkhand and Malwa, rebellions broke out in Gondwana, Bihar and Bengal, resulting in utter lawlessness and anarchy which ultimately sapped the foundations of the Mughal Empire.

Like waves in the ocean the Mughal Empire reached the highest point only to break down, Aurangzeb's grave defects in his character are mainly responsible for the sudden collapse of the mighty empire which then included nearly the whole of India and Afghanistan. During this period Maratha Nationalism flourished with all its vitality as a triumphant force.

In the midst of these disorders and sufferings from bereavements due to the death of two daughters, one daughter-in-law, one sister and two nephews and deep anxieties for the gloomy future of the Empire, specially because of an apprehended civil war among his sons, Aurangzeb breathed his last in his 90th year at Ahmadnagar in the morning of 3 March, 1707 (Friday). During the time of Aurangzeb the Red Fort remained empty without king for nearly 26 years.

Aurangzeb was a fanatic religious person; perhaps he did so because of his compulsions of political reasons. He got built a Mosque in the Red Fort of Delhi; he lived a simple life used to eat a vegetarian food. He used to sew the caps himself and out of that proceed he maintained himself. He was very critical of Shah Jahan who had emptied the exchequer in constructing the buildings. But to show himself a scrupulous observer of the Faith, he did many ridiculous things; such as he ordered that no Mohammedan should wear a beard longer than four finger-breadth and appointed officials for checking it, who used to move in the city to measure the beard of persons. The common people suffered badly in this venture. He also ordered that Muslims should clip their moustaches to uncover the lips. It was done because when pronouncing the name of Allah, there might be no impediment to the sound ascending straight to heaven.

Delhi was a big centre of culture and music was the part of that culture. Both Hindus and Muslims were found of hearing the sound of singing and instrument. Aurangzeb ordered to ban it. On one Friday when Aurangzeb was going to Jama Masjid, the musicians came out with highly ornamented biers, as per the custom of the country, and started crying. While king saw this, he enquired and came to know that it was due to the order to ban the music, these musicians were doing it. So he ordered that they should pray for the soul of music, and see that she was thoroughly well buried. The fact is that Aurangzeb was a good singer himself and used to sing till he was a prince. He had good knowledge of music, but because of his over zealousness for religious practices, he did so. Due to it many good musicians and singers left Delhi during this period (1653–1760).

Twelve holy men of Delhi prophesied to Dara Shikoh that he would be future king and they will pray to God for it. After he had arranged matters in the Empire, Aurangzeb called these holy men and gave them three days time to perform miracles, so that he becomes their disciple. After three days they were again called in the presence of the king, they failed to perform any miracle, the king sent some of them to jail and some were ordered to banish and leave the city.

Sarmad, an artist, a saint always went naked in Delhi. He was very much liked by Dara Shikoh, Aurangzeb considered Dara as a 'Kafir'. Sarmad was beheaded by the order of Aurangzeb because he did not read the full Kalima. His grave is still there near the eastern gates of Jama Masjid at Delhi.[142]

Aurangzeb had five sons and five daughters.

Sons:

1. Eldest son Mohammad Sultan was born near Mathura on 30 December, 1639 and died on 14 December 1676.
2. The second son Mohammad Muazzam, born in Burhanpur on 14 December 1643 from Nawab Bai, daughter of Rajah Raju of Rajauri in Kashmir, she was also the Mother of Mohammad Sultan the eldest son.
3. The third was Mohammad Azam born on 9 July 1653 from Dilras Banu, daughter of Shah Nawaz Khan Safawi.
4. The forth was Akbar born on 21 September 1657 after rebellion joined Rajputs in 1681, he fled first to the Maratha court of Sambhaji and thence to Persia, he died at Mashhad on 31 March 1706.
5. The fifth son was Mohammad Kam Bakhsh born on 7 March 1677 from Bai Udipuri, who died at Gwalior in June 1707.

Daughters:

1. Zeb-un-Nisa Begum born on 26 February 1637 died unmarried at Delhi on 1702 as state prisoner.
2. Zinat-un-Nisa Begum born on 16 October 1643 from Dilras Begum and died on 18 May 1721, at Delhi.
3. Badr-un-Nisa Begum was born on 28 November 1647 from Nawab Bai, died on 20 April 1670.

4. Zubdat-un-Nisa Begum, born on 13 September 1651 died on 17 February 1707. She had been married to her cousin Siphr Shikoh, son of Dara Shikoh. Begum Jahan Ara arranged this marriage in Delhi. She also brought up Zubdat-un-Nisa.
5. Mihr-un-Nisa Begum born on 29 September 1661 from Aurangabadi Mahal. She was married to Ezad Baksh, son of Prince Murad Bakhsh. She died on 1 April 1706.

The first son Sultan Mohammad was imprisoned and he died in prison. Aurangzeb's second son Mohammad Muazzam now became heir apparent from 1664 to 1687 he remained with his father in southern campaign, but Aurangzeb became suspicious of him and on 4 March 1687 he was arrested and remained in prison for seven years. In 1695 he was released and made Governor of Agra, then to Lahore, then to Kabul. He was addressed as Shah Alam. On 25 November 1706 he pitched his camp at Jamrud, twelve miles west of Peshawar, there he heard the news of the death of his father. Azam Shah, the another son of Aurangzeb became ambitions for the throne of Delhi as his other brother was imprisoned and he had a quarrel with his younger brother, Kam Bakhsh. Aurangzeb knew it well that his end is approaching and it will hasten if Azam Shah and Kam Baksh remain hostile to each other. So Aurangzeb decided to separate them, Kam Baksh was sent to Bija Pur as Governor and Azam Shah to Malwa as Governor.

A will was prepared by Aurangzeb, for the distribution of the Empire among his three sons and also the place of his burial. This will is said to be found under the pillow after his death by Hamid-ud-Din Khan, head of the household. After the burial and mourning having elapsed, Azam Shah on 14 March 1707 ascended the throne with the usual ceremony. Kam Bakhsh did try to come to Aurangabad but he was deserted by his own persons; he went to Bijapur and somehow managed to enter the fort.

In Jamrud on 22 March 1707, twenty days after the death of Aurangzeb, Mohammad Muazzam heard the news of the death of his father. There is distance of 1,400 miles between Jamrud and Ahmadnagar. It was a race between the competitors for the throne. Whoever could first reach Agra or Delhi and obtain the wealth stored at one or both cities, would be almost certain to overpower his rival.

The distances to be traversed were from Ahmadnagar to Agra about 700 miles, from Jamrud to Agra about 715 miles. Mohammad Muazzam (Bahadur Shah) also started from his destination. In fact he was earlier pretending that after the death of his father he will go to Iran and not contest for the throne. At Lahore he declared himself as the king and entitled himself as Bahadur Shah. He collected lots of money, arms and other provisions of war on the way and reached Delhi on 1st June, 1707. He took lots of money from the treasury, paid the visits to the Dargah of Saint Bakhtiyar Kaki and Hazrat Nizam-ud-Din Aulia. This was the last visit of Bahadur Shah to Delhi. He reached near Agra on the 12 June, 1707. Azam Shah reached Gwalior on this day. Bahadur Shah sent a latter by hand through a holy man, Mir Abd-ud-Karim, 'the patch wearer', to Azam Shah for division of the Empire, but it was not accepted by Azam Shah, who was prepared for war. Bahadur Shah wanted to fight on 20 June 1707 as was advised by his astrologers. So he was delaying the direct war but on the other side Azam Shah was making haste. The area of Dholpur becomes very dangerous without water to fight, many soldiers and animals perished from Azam Shah's side due to heat and without water.

The battle commenced on 20 June 1707 at Jajau near Dholpur. In this battle Azam Shah was killed as he had not sufficient artillery. His head was cutoff and presented to Bahadur Shah who did not reward the person who did it. Bahadur Shah sent his trusted persons to bring the bodies of the sons of Azam Shah and Azam Shah. He wept for the dead and promised to be kind to the other sons of Azam Shah. The other sons and grandsons and ladies of Azam Shah were received well. The main reason of defeat of Azam Shah are his over haste and excessive rashness, failing to reach Agra before his rival, little or no money in comparison of his rival, he left much of war equipment behind, his army was composed of fresh and untrained troops, half-heartedness of his nobles, and the leaders decided the outcome of the war.

The policy of Bahadur Shah was throughout his reign one of conciliation. He pardoned other persons who sided with Azam Shah before the war and during the war. After Azam Shah, the king had to deal with Rajputs, with war and diplomacy; but soon he had to deal with Kam Bakhsh, who had till than not accepted Bahadur Shah as the king on 12 January 1709 Bahadur Shah came to Hyderabad and a battle ensured in which Kam Bakhsh and his sons were captured, later Kam Bakhsh died of his wounds; in spite of the efforts of the royal surgeons. Again there was rebellion in the Rajputana and Sikhs were at arms in Punjab, the king had to make treaty with Rajputs and he soon went to Punjab. Under Banda Bahadur Sikhs were occupying many parts of Punjab. Reaching Lahore he ordered the inclusion of the word "Wasi" after the name of Hazrat Ali in the Khutba to be delivered in every mosque in Public Prayer, this was resented by Sunni Ulema. The order was not followed in Delhi. The order was withdrawn, but again an attempt was made, he debated with Ulemas, the second order he gave to kill all dogs of the city and in the camp. Bahadur Shah died on 28 February, 1712 of a sore in his stomach. But Dutch Ambassador said, '[t]hat he was stabbed.'[143]

Gurudwara Nanak Piyau.

The Rise of the Sikhs

The West and North-West part of India was regularly invaded by Muslims till the Mughals established their rule in India. Guru Nanak, the first Sikh Guru, was born to Hindu father and mother had the influence of Islam. In 1489 at the age of 30 years after a great deal of meditation, he had a revelation or as the Janam Sakhi narrate, was led to the presence of God; and commissioned to propagate his massage to mankind. This led the foundations of his mission. In 1504 A.D. he said, "There is no Hindu; and there is no Musalman." "Na Koi Hindu, Na Musalman." His religious movement wanted to bring Hinduism and Islam closer; the popular saying was:

Nanak Shah Fakir,
Hindu ka Guru, Musalman ka Pir

He had conversation with Sheikh Farid of Pak-Pathan, a famous Pir. In fact 112 verses were taken from him into the 'Adi Granth.' He used to say "There are only one Lord, and only one tradition."

He asserted a universal humanism. Everyone was the child of one God. He undertook the tour of the sub-continent and beyond. He went to places for worship of all denominations-Indians and Semitic. He went to Tibet, Middle East and Central Asia. He also went to Kamrup, Orissa and Sri Lanka. He did come to Delhi and stayed for three days at two places- now the Gurudwara at 'Nanak Pyau' and 'Majnu Ka Tila' are there.

Gurudwara Majnun ka Tila.

The Brahmins and hill chiefs did not like the Guru Nanak's movement. Guru Nanak preached in the language of the people; Punjabi, which had its own script Gurmukhi. He instituted the concept of Sangat (congregation) and Panget (common kitchen) Guru Nanak's greatest contribution for consolidation of his mission was appointment of his successor in Bhai Lehna (born in March 1504) as Guru Angad and asked him to settle in Khadur. He did not go for hereditary Guruship. Humayun had met Guru Angad at Khadur Sahib, while enroute to Lahore after the defeat in the battle of Kanoj from Sher Shah Suri.

Guru Angad appointed Guru Amar Das as his successor. During this period the difference between Hindu and Sikh (Shishe) became more pronounced and the Sikhs (Shishe) began gradually, to drift away from the orthodox Hindu society and formed a class by themselves.

Guru Ram Das was the next Guru and this time witnessed a far reaching development. In 1577 Guru Ram Das obtained a grant of the site together with 500 bighas of land, from the Emperor Akbar on payment of Rs. 700 Akbari to the Zamindars of Tung who were the owners of the land. He also got dug a tank and laid the foundation of the city of Amritsar.

Guru Ram Das appointed Guru Arjun Dev as his successor who was a great scholar, who completed Adi Granth.

Guru Arjun got the foundation of the Harimandir Sahib (Golden Temple) laid down by Mian Mir, a prominent Muslim saint of Lahore. He also founded the town of Taran Taran in 1590; and Kartarpur (Jullundhar) and Hargobind Pur in the name of his son Hargobind on 14 June 1595. Many Jats from Majha became the Sikhs (Shishe) during this period. By the organization of Masand system, he ensured the solidarity of the Sikh community. The Masands, not only collected the offerings of the Sikhs from the important centers but also propagated the religion of Guru Nanak.

The growth and achievements of Sikhism under Guru Arjun Dev aroused envy and malice in the orthodox section of Muslims. Sheikh Faizi Sirhindi Mujjadid-i-Alif Sani was exceptionally hostile to the rising popularity of Sikhism. To him even a slight concession to the Hindus was an act of hostility. Emperor Jahangir was his staunch follower.

During this period Prince Khusru also visited Guru Arjun Dev. This gave an opportunity to the rival of Guru Arjun to instigate Jahangir to take action against the Guru. He ordered the execution of the Guru, without enquiry and trial; Guru Arjun Dev was killed after five days torture. The Guru with his martyrdom cemented the Sikh community to resist and sacrifice for righteousness and just demand. One of Guru Arjun's last instructions to his son, Guru Har Gobind, was to sit fully armed on his throne and maintain army to the best of his ability. The concept of 'Miri' and 'Piri'. This worldly and other worldly started from now onwards, the new Guru kept two swords then he sat on the throne, one is called 'Miri' and another is called 'Piri. This was the turning point in the Sikh History. The growing military strength and the royal pomp of the Guru and his worldly spirit and tastes made a conflict between him and the Government of Delhi. The conflict broke out after Shah Jahan's accession.

In 1628, the Mughal Army was defeated by the Sikhs, but ultimately over taken. Guru Har Gobind fled to the hills. On his death in 1645, the Guru was succeeded by Guru Har Rai, who tried to help Dara Shikoh in the war of succession. On his death in 1661, Aurangzeb was asked to intervene in the dispute between his sons, but before he could give his verdict, the dispute was resolved by the death of one of the two claimants.

The ninth Guru, Tegh Bahadur, who came to the gaddi in 1664; served in the Mughal Army on the Assam frontier for some years; but later returned to Eastern Punjab and settled at Anandpur. As per Cunningham Guru Tegh Bahadur called himself as Sachcha Badshah, he levied Tax on the people, plundered between Hansi and Satluj, gave asylum to fugitives.[144] He wanted to protect the Brahmins of Kashmir.

Guru Tegh Bahadur was ultimately captured and brought to the court at Delhi. He was kept as prisoner in Kotwali along with Bhai Mati Das and Jati

Gurudwara Bangla Sahib.

Das. There he predicted that a new race with blue eye will come to Delhi and destroy the Muslim rule. This so happened in 1803. The British came to Delhi and in 1858 they destroyed the Mughal rule in Delhi and ultimately in India. Guru Tegh Bahadur was beheaded at the place where is now situated Gurudwara Sis Ganj, Chandni Chowk. His head was taken by a disciple to Kiratpur Sahib and his trunk of the body was carried by Lakhi Shah, Banjara to Rakab Ganj village where now stands a Gurudwara Rakab Ganj.

Even before Guru Tegh Bahadur, Guru Harkishan also came to Delhi and stayed with Raja Jai Singh at his Bungalow. He visited the patients of Small Pox near Nizam-ud-Din and got infected with Small Pox and died on 30 March 1664 a Gurudwara is also built and called Damdama Sahib, at Jai Singh's Bungalow Gurudwara Bunglow Sahib was also built.

Guru Tegh Bahadur, in order to keep the flames of Sikhism lighted up, established closer links with the Sangats of distant places and also undertook personal tours to these places. Aurangzeb was already suspicious of the Sikh Movements in the Punjab. During these days a deputation of Brahmins from Kashmir came to Guru Tegh Bahadur to seek protection from the tyranny of the Mughal Government. This required sacrifice, and Guru Tegh Bahadur got prepared for it.

Even Guru Tegh Bahadur came to Delhi on 8 November 1665 he met first time Emperor Aurangzeb who ordered for his execution, but for Raja

Gurudwara Sis Ganj.

Ram Singh son of Raja Jai Singh, he was imprisoned and later released, he then went to Patna.[145]

Guru Tegh Bahadur was arrested by Nur Mohammad Khan Mirza, Kotwal of Ropar, for helping the Kashmiri Pandits. He was brought to Delhi in November along with, Bhai Mati Das, Sati Das and Dayal Das. Along with these three companions he was martyred on 11 November 1675.

The seventeenth century was a period of turmoil, struggle and serious conflicts for the Sikhs. They had to fight not only for their own survival but for the protection of the down-trodden and to challenge the evil forces to protect dharma after the martyrdom of Guru Arjun Dev. The coming Guru's changed from peaceful devotees into saint-soldiers. The Sikh became militant and they realized the need of the army. So Guru Gobind Singh founded the Khalsa in 1699.

During this period Indian society was divided into Muslims and Hindus; the upper classes of Muslims, Ulema, Ahl-i-Tegh and Ahl-i-Kalam, were comprised the government. Parda system, slavery, drinking, caste system and child marriage were prevalent both in Hindus as well as in Muslims. Sati system, untouchability and superstitions were prevalent in Hindus. Jizya was imposed on Hindus; the Muslim rulers required the sanctions of Caliph or the ruler of Egypt. The Hindus or non-believers in Islam were hated and persecuted. Guru

Gurudwara Bala Sahib.

Gurudwara Nanak Pura, Moti Bagh.

Gurudwara Damdama Sahib.

Gurudwara Mata Sundari.

Arms of Gusru Gobind Singh, Gurudwara Mata Sundri.

Gobind Singh was the Saint-Soldier, he had to fight much against his wishes as the exigency of the time so demanded. He had to fight a number of battles against the hill chiefs and the Mughal forces such as battle of Bhangani, battle of Nadaun, Khanzada's expedition, battle of Guler, and Shahzada Muazzam's expedition. In 1699 he created the Khalsa; the literal meaning of the word is pure. It was nominally used for Government land. It also connotes piety. It has been used in the Adi Granth in this context. Saint Kabir writes:

Kaho Kabir Jan Bhaye Khalsa
Prem Bhagat Jeh Jani[146]

The world Khalsa had been derived from the Arabic word 'Khalis'. The Guru Gobind Singh used this word for his Sangat. The real mission of the creation of Khalsa can be understood by the description of Senapat, a contemporary chronicler of Guru Gobind Singh. He writes:

Guru Gobind Singh Gur Karanhar Kartar
Jagat Udharan Aayo Janhu Sab Sansar
Jagat Singharbe ko Dorjan Ka Marhe ko
Sankat Nivarbe ko Khalsa Banayo He[147]

Also he writes:

Khalas Saroop, Anoop Roop
Geh Tegh Leen Ate Judhe Keen.[148]

To fulfill his mission described above, it became essential for Guru Gobind Singh to create Khalsa. He created Khalsa to bring internal reform in the Sikh Sangat. The Khalsa was born out of the ashes of Guru Tegh Bahadur.

General Gordon writes, "The dragon's teeth thus sown at Delhi in the blood of the martyred Guru Tegh Bahadur soon brought to harvest an abundant crop."[149]

Some Guru's Sikhs were there in Delhi, the Masands used to come to them. Bhai Lakhi Das, also called Lakhi Shah Banjara, and his three sons Nigahia, Hema, Harshi and Naik Dhomma son of Bhai Nannu had shown a great courage in taking the body of the Guru Tegh Bahadur to Rakab Ganj village and cremated it with all basic rites.

Earlier, the bodies of Guru Har Kishan and Baba Gurditta's were cremated (near Humayun's Tomb). Now there is Guru Dwara at this place. In Delhi Guru Teg Bahadur's martyrdom led to the two incidents, a person flung a stick at Aurangzeb in June-July, 1676 when he was mounting a horse in the compound of Dewan-i-Aam, on Friday October, 1676 a disciple of Guru Tegh Bahadur flung two bricks at Aurangzeb, one of which reached the choir where he was seated.[150]

All such incidents led to 'dharmayudh', waging war against the forces of evil, tyranny and oppression of all sorts using religion as a social catalyst.

Minas and other dissident Sodhis were also persecuted. Dhirmal was detained in the fort of Ranthombore who died in 1677 and in 1678 his 30 year old son was burnt alive in Chandni Chowk.

In 1687 Guru Gobind attended the Bhog ceremony of Ram Rai and helped his widow Punjab Kaur. Aurangzeb, who had been operating in the South since 1682, was ruthlessly pursuing his policy of suppression of infidels which included not only various dominions of Hindus including Marathas and Rajputs, but Shia Muslims too.

By the order of Aurangzeb, to expel the Sikhs from Punjab, Dilawar Khan, the Governor of Lahore in 1695, Husain Khan in 1695, Jujhar Singh in 1696, and Prince Muazzam (later Bahadur Shah I) made attack on the Sikhs in the Punjab.

In 1697-8 Guru Gobind Singh took serious note of the misdoings of the Masands, who became corrupt and ordered for their abolition.

On 29 March 1699 he founded, the Khalsa, and Five Beloved ones were administered by him to the fold of Khalsa, they were, Mohkam Chand, a washerman from Dwarka, Sahib Chand a barber from Bidar; Dharam Das, a

Jat from Hastinapur, and Himmat Chand a cook from Jagannath Puri (His elders were in contact with earlier Guru's) in turn he was Baptised by them. He gave them the common appellation of 'Singh' for male and 'Kaur' for women. He also said to greet each other by saying, 'Waheguru ji ka Khalsa, Waheguru ji ki Fateh' (The Khalsa belongs to God; victory be to Him). He pronounced certain ideas, and Five Ks are essential for any Khalsa, i.e. Kes (hair); Kangha (Comb); Kara (bracelet); Kachha (underwear) and Kirpan (Dagger). After the establishment of Khalsa, the hill chiefs and the Governor of Sirhind were alarmed, they approached Delhi authorities and in turn Aurangzeb who was in Deccan, ordered to help the hill chiefs with all remaining forces in Delhi, Sarhind and Lahore. Senapat the contemporary historian had given the account of these battles, fought by Guru Gobind Singh with hill chiefs and Mughal Army i.e. Battle of Anand Pur in August-September 1700 A.D. Battle of Basoli 1700 A.D.; First Battle of Chankaur-1702 A.D.; Battle of Anand Pur 1704–5 A.D.; Battle at Parivar Bachhora Sahib on the bank of river Sirsa, 1705 A.D.; the Battle of Chamkaur, 1705 A.D.; and the Battle of Khidrana (Muktsar) May, 1706 A.D.

During the battle of Chamkaur and Muktsar, Guru Gobind Singh wrote a historic letter to Emperor Aurangzeb from 'Dina'. This letter is called Zafarnama in history. The Guru sent this letter to Emperor Aurangzeb through his trusted Sikhs, Bhai Daya Singh and Bhai Dharam Singh, they took a long journey of about 1600 km. from Dina to Ahmadnagar, where Aurangzeb was staying, they with great difficulty took some months to deliver this letter to Aurangzeb. The Zafarnama commenced with the adoration of God. The Bakhshis and Diwans of the Emperors were biased and were not true to the oaths taken on the holy Quran, as it was the condition that if Guru leaves Anand Pur he will not be attacked. He writes that had I sworn on Quran, even secretly, I would have abided by that but you did not.[151] Let me know how could I believe your oath[152] God shows the right Path to those who believe in the oath of Quran[153] I believe you are a liar, throwing away your religion and faith to the winds[154] A man who is firm believer of religion stands by his promise.[155] When all means fail, it is lawful to hold a sword in one's hand as a last resort.[156] In his letter the Guru made mention of the battle of Chamkaur.[157] He described the loss of the Mughal army and his personal loss.[158]

The Guru says that the Emperor should not shed innocent blood for the final vengeance is in the hands of God before whom even he would have to stand and give an account of his atrocities.[159] "Do not wantonly spill the blood of any one for your own blood as surely will be spilt by death."[160] The Guru also writes that it mattered least if his four sons had been killed; the venomous snake (the Khalsa) was still alive.[161] In the last days of his life Aurangzeb became physically weak and emotional; this is reflected in the letters which he had written to his sons Azam and Kambaksh from the death bed.[162]

Ultimately the Guru decided to meet the Emperor, personally at Ahmadnagar, so he started for South along with his disciples. Passing through Marwar, the Guru met Daya Singh and from him he got the information of the Emperor's Camp. There the Guru received the news that on 20 February 1707 Aurangzeb died. He decided to return to Punjab via Delhi; this was middle of March 1707.

In the battle at Parivar Bachhora Sahib in 1705 A.D., the family of Guru Gobind Singh was divided in two groups, Mata Sundri and Mata Sahib Kaur accompanied by Mani Singh went towards Ambala to Delhi. In Delhi, they found shelter with Jawahar Singh, at Gali Dil Wali Singh at Teliwara. After this Mata Sundri lived outside the walls of the city and organized the Sikh Sangat, now there is Gurudwara Mata Sundri. The other party was of Guru's mother and his two sons, Zorawar Singh and Fateh Singh were taken by Gangu, an old domestic servant of the family to his village Saheri, on the Ropar, Marinda Road. The Jani Khan and Mani Khan local Ranghars of the town Marinda captured them and gave them to Wazir Khan, the Governor of Sarhind. They did not accept Islam so they were bricked alive in Sarhind; the Nawab of Malerkotla did try to save the children but failed. Mata Gujri died of grief caused by the sad demise of her grandsons.[163]

Mata Sundri, after knowing the death of her sons in the battle, adopted a child and named him Ajit Singh, after the name of her own son, when Guru Gobind Singh visited Mata Sundri in mid March 1707, he did not relish the idea of this adoption. When Bahadur Shah was going to Agra from Lahore, Guru Gobind Singh met him, he was given a mansab of 5, 000 Sawars.

His soldiers under Kuldipak Singh with 200 to 300 horses fought at Jajau, when Bahadur Shah's army won the battle.

When Bahadur Shah was going to South to punish his younger brother Kambaksh, Guru Gobind Singh accompanied him. At the bank of Godavari he met a Mendicant, Madho Das Bairagi, whom he had already met at Haridwar. He was known for his occult powers. Madho Das was informed by Guru Gobind Singh for what had happened to him and his family and Baptized Madho Das, who was given Guru's weapons to take revenge against the Nawab of Sarhind. Banda Singh Bahadur accompanied by about 25 Sikhs, Nishan Sahib, five arrows of Guru and a seal from the Guru left for Punjab.

The same day Guru Gobind Singh was stabbed by two Pathans. There are variations in this story. Some historian writes that Guru had taken horses from the father of these Pathans but could not pay back the price. So these Pathans took revenge. The other writes that the Nawab of Sarhind got this action done, as he feared revenge from Guru Gobind Singh. The Guru was treated by a British Surgeon Dr. Cole, but after few days the wound leaked and Guru Gobind died on 7–8 October, 1708. His mortal remains were consigned to flames by Bhai Daya Singh by the following dawn. The Bhog ceremony was performed on 17 October 1708. On 5 October 1708 knowing his end near, Guru Gobind Singh passed on the spiritual Guruship to the Adi Granth. (Bhat Vehi Talunda Pargana Jind and Bhat Vahi Bhadson, Pargana Thanesar)

Banda Bahadur

Banda Bahadur has created a significant place in the history of the Punjab of the eighteenth century. Guru Gobind Singh met him second time at Nander in 1708 just before his demise. After this interaction, Banda Bahadur marched towards the Punjab and waged a series of fights against the Mughal rulers. It was not a religious war, nor it was against Islam nor was it vindictive war. In fact it was a war against the tyranny and injustice of the rulers of that time. He tried to chastise the evil-doers for their sins and excesses perpetrated on innocent people, including the sons of Guru Gobind Singh. Banda Bahadur was called Lachhman Dev, son of Ram Dev of Rajauri, Jammu, born on 16 October, 1670. His father was an ordinary agriculturist and could not provide education to his son. But Banda Bahadur with practice became a good hunter and marksman. At the age of fifteen he killed a pregnant female deer, this incident changed his future life; he decided not to hunt and thereafter he became a Bairagi. He became the disciple of Janaki Prasad. He came in contact of Bairagi, Ram Das and then to Aughar Nath, along with them he come to Nasik and learned the good knowledge of Jantar Mantar (occult science). His Guru died in 1691, Madho Das came to Nander, East of Godaveri and established his dera. Here he met Guru Gobind Singh. After Guru's instructions along with 25 Sikhs and weapons, Banda came to Delhi (Bawana village). It took nearly a year to reach Delhi. He met the Jamindar of Kharkhoda (a small town, thirty five Miles West of Delhi) from here he was accompanied by 500 farmers to Sonipat, and attached it, the Nawab of Sonipat fled to Delhi. He attacked Kaithal and there he got the treasury and some horses; he pillaged Samana, Sadhaura, Ropar, and Sarhind.

On 24 May 1710 Wazir Khan, the Nawab of Sarhind was killed and the Sikh Army entered Sarhind, plundered and killing continued for three days and the city was burnt. After capturing Sarhind and killing Wazir Khan and Sacha Nand, who instigated Wazir Khan to murder the sons of Guru Gobind Singh and cremated the bodies of Bibi Anup Kaur, who committed suicide, as she was carried away by Sher Mohammad Khan.

Banda Bahadur now established his own government. The entire administration was taken by the Sikhs. Baj Singh was appointed the Governor

Gurudwara Banda Singh Bahadur, Mehrauli. (b. 16.10.1670 and d. 12.01.1716).

of Sarhind with Baba Ali Singh as his Naib. Fateh Singh, who had been earlier detained Governor of Samana, was confirmed in the same appointment. Binod Singh and Ram Singh (brother of Ali Singh) were jointly appointed Governor of Thanesar. Hindu officials were appointed in other subordinate posts in the place of Muslim officials. The Khalsa flag was hoisted on the fort of Sarhind.[164]

From Sarhind, Banda sent out parties to occupy the country to the South, the East and the West. One party was sent across the Satluj, to take Sultanpur and other places, in the Doaba of Baith Jallandar. Sikhs took Saharanpur and Jalalabad. The Sikh Army reached near Lahore walls.

The first news of the Sikh outbreak was brought to Bahadur Shah on 30 May 1710 when he as approaching Ajmer on his return March from Dakhin (South India). On 10 September 1710 the Emperor was at the town of Pataudi, he ordered that no one is allowed to visit Delhi nor any members of the family from Delhi can meet any one in the camp. He also ordered that no Hindu can keep the beard in the camp. He also ordered the forces from all areas to come to a point and attack the Sikhs.

By 11 August 1711 the Emperor and his sons reached outside the city of Lahore. Before this on 28 February 1711 Munim Khan the chief Advisor of the Emperor died. On 27 February 1712 Bahadur Shah died. The Emperor had hardly breathed his last, before his sons were raged against each other in contest for Empire. Maulvi Muradullah, Mahfuz Khan and Abdul Qadir prepared the body for burial and laid it in a bier. It lay unburied until the succession. It was dispatched to Delhi on 11 April 1712 in the charge of Bibi Mihr Parwar, the Emperor's widow. It arrived on 15 May 1712 and was buried in the court yard of Qutub-ud-Din Kaki at Mehrauli.

For two years Sikhs were hiding and now and then making some attack on Mughal Army. By April 1714, Banda Bahadur held a Darbar at Amritsar and he appeared in a royal dress as a Guru. While in fact Guru Gobind Singh forbade every one not to act as Guru and Adi Granth be treated as the Guru for future. He paid a visit to the Golden Temple at Amritsar. He gave out that he had been empowered by the Guru to claim succession to the Guruship. The Sikhs did not like it.

Emperor Farrukh Siyar got tired of the reports he received about Banda. He created a rift in the Sikhs, the Sikhs were divided into Tat Khalsa and Bandai Khalsa, the Bandai Khalsa was not taking meat as Banda was not taking meat.

The Emperor also got a letter written by Mata Sundri from Delhi, to Banda to desist from all attacks as the task has been fulfilled but Banda did not accepted it. So Mata Sundri wrote a circular letter to the Sikhs asking them to dissociate themselves from Banda. He was charged with the disregard of the Guru's commandments.

In the battle of Gurdas Nangal where Sikhs were divided, Banda and his followers were captured. They were tied with fatters and tied to elephants. At Lahore they were kept in the fort for some days.

Along with 1000 Sikhs, Banda Bahadur was sent to Delhi via Sarhind. At Sarhind they were paraded on the streets and abused by the people. On the 27 February 1716 Banda and his comrades were conducted to Delhi in a procession. At the end of the procession was a dead cat to indicate that every living creature in the fortress of Gurdas Nangal down to a cat had been destroyed.

In Delhi they were paraded in the Streets. When the procession arrived at the fort, Banda and some of his leading comrades like Baj Singh, Fateh Sigh were handed over to Ibrahim-ud-Din Khan, Mir Atish, on the orders of the Emperor and others were handed over to Kotwal for execution.

Every day 100 Sikhs were executed opposite the chabutra Kotwali or Police Station from 5 March 1716. If the Sikhs accepted Islam, they were pardoned but none did so. The British, who saw this execution, reported to their higher officer that 100 Sikhs were executed every day and the prisoners were patient and courageous.[165]

The execution of the prisoners went for seven days. Banda Bahadur and his other companions were kept in Red Fort for three months just to know about their treasure. Not getting the clue of their treasure, it was decided to execute them.

On 19 June 1716 in a procession all were paraded to Mehrauli, near the Dargah of Bakhtiar Kaki, the son of Banda was put in his lap, Banda was asked to cut this boy, Banda refused, so the boy was cut into pieces his intestines were put over the neck of Banda, his flesh was put into the mouth of Banda. After this Banda was asked by the Emperor how he would like his death to which Banda replied "just the way in which his majesty would like to meet his own death".

His left eye was taken out by a Butcher's Knife, then his right eye; then his left arm, then his right arm was cut, his left leg was cut and then his body was cut into pieces, but Banda Bahadur did not utter a single word. The wife of Banda (the Rajkumari of Chamba) accepted Islam. But this view was resented by Mata Joginder Kaur. After the execution of Banda a general proclamation was issued that whosoever finds a Sikh, he should be hunted down like beasts and anyone who kills a Sikh could claim a reward from the Governor of Lahore.[166]

Guru Gobind Singh before his demise declared that then on words Adi Granth be treated as Guru as he had no surviving natural issue. But Mata Sundri who was living in Delhi adopted one boy named Ajit Singh. He received an imperial Mansab and was raised to the seat of the head of the sect. In Farrukh Siyar's reign, when he grew up to manhood, evil advisers persuaded him to set up entirely on his own account. Mata Sundri was turned out; she established her own separate spiritual headship. On the 18 January 1725 Ajit Singh was killed in Shahjahanabad (Delhi) for rebellion, as he was charged for killing a Benava Faqir, or Khirkah posh (very well respected Darvesh in the court) Ajit Singh did not appear before the Emperor when he was asked to do so. Jahi Singh, son of Ajit Singh was very young at that time, he was taken to Mathura by his followers and his dissendants are still living there. Mata Sundri died forty years after the death of Guru Gobind Singh and Sahib Devi succeeded her, who also died after a year.

After the demise of Farrukh Siyar, Sikhs got some relief. But they needed a wise leadership to ingrain the concept of the Granth and the Panth into the Sikh psyche; it was provided by Bhai Mani Singh. In his missionary tour he explained the Shabad contained in Adi Granth, without any distinctions, including the hymns of Bahktas which the Guru to be shown an equal degree of respect and reverence and Adi Granth was not worshiped as an idol, but its word, the hymns were revered.

Since the first recession of Adi Granth had been installed at Harimandar Sahib, it helped to assert the position of Amritsar as the politico religious headquarters of Sikhism. Bhai Mani Singh also contributed for the emergence of the medium of Ardas, the Prayer, as a continuous evolutionary process, recounting the deeds of Sikh heroes and martyrs to serve as a beacon light to the community in those hard pressed days of the eighteenth century. Zakaria Khan, the Governor of Lahore initially co-opted the Sikhs in to the system, he offered Jagir to Kapur Singh, who in turn organized the Sikhs into Bhudda Dal (over 40 years of age) and Tarun Dal (under 40 years). The Imperial Authorities at Delhi were concerned for this consolidation of Sikhs and Sikhs were persecuted. Golden Temple was taken into government possession and Diwali could not be celebrated there. Bhai Mani Singh along with others were cut into pieces in June 1734 at Nakhas, horse market, outside Delhi Gate (Lahore); where Gurudwara Shahid Gunj stands now during this period under the leadership of Kapur Singh. The Sikhs trampled the chiefs of Jhaffar, Dadri, Dujana, Bahadur Garh, Faridabad, Mehrauli, and Gurgaon up to the outskirts of Delhi.

In 1739 Nadir Shah shattered the areas of Punjab and Delhi, the Sikhs took advantage of this situation and looted the baggages of Nadir Shah. Nadir Shah advised Zakaria Khan to exterminate the Sikhs or in future they will become the rulers. So Zakaria Khan now onwards followed the policy of exterminating the Sikhs. He pursued the policy of genocide of the Sikhs. A graded scale of rewards was offered to the people for cutting the Sikhs hair – one blanket; for information of a Sikh – Ten Rupees; for a Sikhs scalp – fifty rupees; plunder of Sikh home was made lawful; giving shelter to Sikh's or withholding information of their movement was made a capital offence.[167]

Massa Ranger committed the heinous crime of converting Harimandar into a dancing hall where he smoked and wined. In 1740 Mehtab Singh, a devoted Sikh chopped off his head, but later Mehtab Singh was arrested and tortured and crushed to death in 1744. Zakaria Khan died on 1 July 1745.

The dispute between the sons of Zakaria Khan over the succession to Governorship of Lahore gave time to the Sikhs to organize. On 14 October 1745 Sikhs assembled at Amritsar under the command of Kapur Singh; Jassa Singh Ahluwalia, Hari Singh Bhangi, Jai Singh Kanahya, Naudh Singh of

Sukrachak played a great role in organizing the Sikhs. The Sikhs looted Lahore, in turn on Amavas, 10 March 1746 general massacre of Sikhs were committed. It is called chhota ghallughara (small holocaust, in which 7, 000 Sikhs were killed and 3, 000 were prisoned, the big holocaust happened in 1762).

The first invasion of Ahmad Shah Abdali in January, 1748 was welcomed by the Sikhs, they wanted that Mughals and Afghans should fight and weaken themselves. From 1748 to 1765 Ahmad Shah Abdali invaded India seven times; and between 1766 to 1769, three times. The Sikhs formed 11 misls under the leadership of Jassa Singh Ahluwalia as Kapur Singh became old and sought retirement.

Phoolkia was the twelfth Misl under Ala Singh of Patiala but it was not the part of Dal Khalsa as it sometimes worked against the interests of the community. In 1762, near village Kup, Ahmad Shah Abdali killed 30, 000 Sikhs, so it was called great holocaust. The Sikhs earned wrath of Abdali who on three occasions, 1757, 1761, and 1762 pulled down Harimandar and defiled the sacred tank by carcasses of cows.

In 1765 Sikhs captured Lahore and established their administration. The people wanted the Sikh administration as they were fed up with Ahmad Shah's invasions. Three generations of the Sikhs perished before the Sikhs emerged sovereigns of the Punjab.

During Banda Singh Bahadur, 25,000 Sikhs lost their lives; Abdul Samad Khan killed 20,000, Zakaria Khan(1713–26) and (1726–45) killed an equal number, Yahya Khan (1746–7) destroyed about 10,000, Mir Mannu (1748–53) more than 30,000, Adina Beg (1758) 5,000, Abdali's Deputy, Najib-ud-Daulah 20,000, petty officials and public must have killed 4,000. This makes a total of about 200,000 Sikhs.[168]

For two decades, Northern India was conducive for Sikhs. The Afghans had exhausted and retreated from Punjab. The Mughals had collapsed. The Marathas were a spent force. The English were still for away; Rohillas, Jats, Rajputs and the Nawab of Oudh were week, disunited and declining.

From 1763–88, seventeen incursions were made by the Sikhs in Gangetic valley. They also captured Red Fort and for six months Nishan Sahib was put on Red Fort. Jassa Singh Ahluwalia built eight historic Gurudwaras in Delhi where the Guru's had either stayed or cremated or martyred. In 1784 Shah Alam appointed Mahadhji Scindia as Wizir-ul-Mutlak. So the Sikhs could not invade Delhi.

The Sikhs did stop Shah Zaman to come to Delhi. For four decades, the Kingdom under Ranjit Singh symbolized the crowning of the Sikh efforts to seize power. The loss of political power in 1849 to the British had its concomitant impact on the Sikh Faith and ecclesiastical polity.

In 1857–8 Maharja Patiala sent his army to help the British against the rebellion or the people who fought the war against the British, this army was highly dominated by the Sikhs.

But, the Sikh made sacrifices for the fight for freedom during the freedom struggle 73 of 121 persons executed were Sikhs and 2147 of 2664 sentenced to life imprisonment in the Andaman's were the Sikhs. In the Jalianwala Bagh massacre which brought to head the demand for freedom, out of 1302 men, women and children gunned down by General Dyer, 700 were Sikhs. Bhagat Singh who played a noted role in the freedom struggle was a Sikh.

In the partition of India many Sikhs suffered at the hands of Muslims, they were converted to Islam especially in Rawalpindi. Many came to Delhi and settled here.

In the past, happenings in Punjab have influenced the social, religious and political life of Delhi. Even after partition of India, the incidents in Punjab were directly affecting the socio-cultural-religious and political life of Delhi. Delhi bore the burnt of assassination of the then Prime Minister Mrs. Indira Gandhi resulting in unprecedented anti Sikh riots in 1984 and its fallout.

Jats and Their Early Activities

The origin of the Jats is a disputed subject. Some scholars believe them to be the descendants of "Getai" of the Greeks, the Yue-Chi of the Chinese. They settled in Northern Afghanistan before the Christian era.

Some scholars hold that Aryans and Scythians are identical entities, the Jats are of Aryan/Scythian ancestry, the original home of the Aryan/Scythians/ Jats was in the Sapta Sindhu, which included the Indus or Sindhu with its principal tributaries on the west and the Saraswati on the east. The Yamuna and the Ganga have certainly been mentioned once or twice, but they have not at all been included in computation of the seven rivers that gave the country its name. The Ganga and Yamuna were, in those days (Rigvedic period), comparatively insignificant rivers with very short courses to run into the Aryavarta Sea. The land inhabited by the Aryans appears to have extended as far to the North-West as Gandhara, (modern Kandhar and Kabul) and as far to the North as Bacteria and Eastern Turkistan across the Himalayas up to the Oxus Valley. In the South was Rajputana Sea and in the East was the Gangetic Sea, both of which disappeared after 7500 B.C., due to upheavals caused by volcanic and seismic eruptions. Within these bounds was situated the ancient Sapta Sindhu. This sacred land witnessed the composition of the most ancient hymns, extant of the Aryan race and the early growth and development of their most wonderful civilization.[169]

They did not come from outside. At the time of the invasion of Sind by the Arabs, they were to be found in Baluchistan and along the course of the Indus. Amir Timur found them around Bhatinda. While some of them adopted

Islam, others adopted Hinduism and later Sikhism. By the time of Alamgir, Aurangzeb, they had spread as far east as Agra, Mathura and Bharatpur.

The first rebellion of Jats under Gokla was aggression in origin; it was due to the mal-administration and high-handedness of Mughal officers. In 1669 A.D. there was local rising of the Jat peasants in Mathura district. It was suppressed but the *faujdar* of the district, 'Abd-un-Nabi', who was slain in the action. The rebel leader, Gokla of Tilpat was subsequently captured by the new Faujdar, Hasan Ali Khan.

In 1685, the Jats began to give trouble again. They commanded the great royal road from Delhi to Agra and Dholpur connecting it with the road through Malwa to the Deccan. After Gokla, the leadership of Jats passed on to Raja Ram and Ram Chehra, the Zamindars of Sinsani and Sagar. They had trained the hardy peasants as soldiers, formed them into regiments and mounted and equipped them as freebooters. By 1690–1 under the directions of Fauzdar Raja Bishan Singh Kachhwah the Jats of Sinsani and Sagar were captured. But Jat leader Churaman again organized the Jats as freebooters. By the time of Mohammad Shah they had become a terror for the countryside and plundered the royal baggage with impunity several times. He was present with his armed bands at the battle of Jajau where he plundered the camp of 'Azam Shah' and acquired rich booty.

On 5 October 1713, Churaman was asked to submit to the king, he was given the wardenship of one of the main road running from Barapulla up to the bank of Chambal. But his high handed dealing with the fief-holders and other officers of the government provoked the Emperor to retaliate. Raja Jai Singh was summoned from Malwa to crush Churaman Jat, he did so but with the help of Abdullah Khan, a Sayyid brother, he got the Mansab of 5,000 Jat and agreed to pay the tribute of Rs. 50,00,000 on 19 April 1718.

By 1752, Balram Jat, son of a petty revenue collector, had considerably strengthened his position in Faridabad by emulating other Jat chiefs in defying the imperial authority. Safdar Jang had personally conducted campaign against him and the Jat leader submitted and was given the lease of Palwal and Faridabad which he controlled from his newly built mud-fort of Ballabgarh. From there they also plundered the crown lands in Sikandrabad. Ahmad Shah (1748–54) became angry with Safdar Jang, due to the death of Jawed Khan. In the middle of March 1753 Safdar Jang relinquished the office and left the city, but remained around the city. During the first week of May Salabat Khan and Suraj Mal Jat joined Safdar Jung. On 9 May 1753 Jats plundered the old city of Delhi. On 29 September the Jats and Safdar Jung were defeated.

Aqibat Mahmud Khan Kashmiri, conquered the district South of Delhi from the Jats, but the peasants did not pay the revenue. Bala Jat was treacherously murdered on 29 November 1753. The fort of Ballabgarh was captured. The Jats were expelled from Kol (Aligarh) and Jalesar also.

The battle of Panipat in 1761 created new problems for Najib-ud-Daulah, he was relieved from the Marathas, but Shah Alam II was still a fugitive. Surajmal Jat wanted Imad to restore to power but could not succeed. Najib was all powerful at the capital. He had to struggle with the Jats.

Surajmal captured Farrukh Nagar in 1763; Najib tried his utmost to maintain amicable relations with Jat Raja, but the latter flushed with recent success and proud of his wealth and army refused any compromise. Suraj Mal was defeated in the battle of Hindan on 25 December 1763 and was killed near Delhi (now Suraj Mal Vihar in East Delhi). Jawahar Singh continued the fight, Najib advised him for peace, but Jawahar Singh attacked Delhi in early 1764. The city of Delhi was bombarded and the countryside plundered. Failing to capture the city, Jawahar Singh had to conclude peace and marched away on 16 February 1764, having spent 160 lakhs in this fruitless venture.

Najib now started establishing his authority over the districts around Delhi. The petty Zamindar had become refractory and withheld the payment of revenue. He attacked Bawana village, Hissar and Rohtak, with firmness and punitive measures he restored law and order there.

Shah Alam II (1760–1806)

Prince Ali Gauhar, the eldest son of Emperor Alamgir II was thirty years of age when his father was assassinated. After the accession of his father he received the title of Ali Gauhar on 16 August 1754 and Shah Alam on 24 April 1759. He was intelligent, self-controlled, well-educated, studious, inquisitive and free from sloth and vice. In February, 1757 he was made Chancellor by Abdali, but without resources and army, he was not given any maintenance. But soon was replaced by Imad. The Prince tried to collect the revenue from Jhajjar, Hansi and other places but could not do much as his soldiers rebelled. He was called to Delhi, and he stayed outside the fort in Ali Mardan's House with 2,000 soldiers for his safety, ultimately he was attacked by Imad's soldiers but Marathas saved him. He went to Najib Khan, who sent him to Shuja-ud-Daulah in Lucknow, from there he went to Allahabad, the Prince was declared as a rebel. He captured Patna from there he went to Rewa. He again entered South Bihar and while encamped at Khotaub he heard the news of the death of his father. He proclaimed himself Emperor under the title of Shah Alam on 24th December, 1759. He appointed Shuja-ud-Daulah as Mir Bakshi and Moin-ud-Daulah as his agent to the court of Shah Abdali. His son Jawan Bakht, was put on the throne at Delhi in 1760.

In 1759, 1760 and 1761 Shah Alam could not gain over the superior forces of Ram Narain in Bihar. He made a treaty with English in 1760. The

English settled an allowance of Rs. 1800 a day on the Shah, in return for confirming their political arrangement in Bengal and Bihar.

In the battle of Buxar on 23 October, 1764 British defeated Shah Alam, Nawab Qasim of Bengal and Shuja of Oudh. Battle of Buxar and the treaty of Allahabad set the seal of British gains after the battle of Plassey. The Emperor became the prisoner of the British and Shuja their vassal. In 1766 Clive entered into a formal agreement at Chhapra with the Shah, Shuja, the Jat Raja, and the Rohilla Chiefs "for mutual defense against any Maratha aggression."

In 1756 a large army of Marathas was sent to assert Maratha supremacy in Doab and with the half of Jats and local officials of Delhi Government they attacked Delhi and in 1757 forced Najib-ud-Daulah to surrender. Imad was established in Delhi. In Lahore Maratha's established Adina Beg, who died on 13 October, 1758 and the whole of the Punjab fell into anarchy. In 1759 new enforcement of Maratha came to North, but Ahmad Shah recovered Punjab and marched towards Delhi. On 19 January, 1760, Datta, the General of Maratha forces, fell on the battle field near Burari (Delhi) and Malhar fled to Agra. New force under the Bhao come to North, he contacted Shuja-ud-Daulah, but Shuja did not agree to help the Marathas, Najib was in favor of war, because he wanted to take back his position and take revenge against Marathas. In the battle of Panipat on 14 January, 1761 Maratha forces were defeated badly. The power of the Marathas was crippled without destroying it and within 10 years they were again threatening the Muslim powers whom fear of a common enemy had united but who fell apart soon after the immediate purpose was achieved.

The battle of Panipat in 1761 changed the political scene. Ahmad Shah Abdali invited him to Delhi. He left for Patna in May, 1761. During 1762–3 he was occupied in Bundelkhand. He returned to Allahabad as dissension between Shuja, Ahmad Khan Bangash, Rehmat Khan, Dundey Khan and Najib made it impossible for Shah Alam to go to Delhi.

Imad-ul-Mulk was appointed Wazir and Najib as Bakhshi by Ahmad Shah Abdali, leaving the Mughals to fend for themselves.

The coins were struck in the name of Shah Alam but for all practical purposes Ahmad Shah was the ruler.

Najib-ud-Daulah as Dictator of Delhi (1761–70)

Imad was made Wazir by Ahmad Shah Abdali, because he realized with extraordinary insight and political shrewdness, that neither Shuja-ud-Daulah nor Najib would be acceptable to the Princes of India—the former because of his being a Shia and his luke warmness in the last conflict, and the latter because all the important personages were jealous of him and would not render him cooperation. Further, Najib could not be a pliant tool in his hands. Abdali wanted to get his tribute punctually year after year. Imad was at Mathura living on the bounty of Raja Suraj Mal of Bharatpur, he did not join his Wizarat. In 1762 Ahmad Shah again arrived in India and stayed till 12 December, Najib-ud-Daulah visited him twice and as Imad had failed to take over the office of Wizarat, and so Ahmad Shah appointed Shuja-ud-Daulah as Wazir. He was made Wazir at this time against his will after some times he retired to his Subah. At this time Shah Alam II was a fugitive and lived in Bihar, Oudh and Allahabad and had no will and strength to come to Delhi and assume his throne. Suraj Mal and the Sikhs were emerging very strong. Marathas were the strong enemy of Najib and vice-versa. From 1761 till his death 1770 Najib was all powerful at Delhi.

He was an illiterate soldier, sprung from the lowest rank. He had no patron, he came to India from Afghanistan, of an Umer Khel tribe, as a grown up man. He had first rate military and administrative capacity, diplomatic skill and tact in dealing with others and above all in his instinctive perception of the realities of the politics of his day and concentration on the essentials he had no equal in that age except Ahmad Shah Abdali.[172]

He captured main Daob country such as Meerut, Sikandrabad, Dasna, Baghpat and seven Mahals of Marathas. He paid every month a small sum for the maintenance of Zeenat Mahal, the mother of the Emperor Shah Alam II and Mirza Jawan Bakht.

In 1764 Ahmad Shah again came to India and stayed at Amritsar, he devastated Hari Mandir Sahib. Najib helped Ahmad Shah in defeating the Sikhs especially Ala Singh (the founder of the House of Patiala who died in 1765).

Shuja-ud-Daulah called Shah Alam from Patna put on the Khilat of Wazir and started towards Delhi in the way he faced the army of Ahmad Khan Bangash, Najib who came from the side of Ahmad Shah Abdali advised Shuja not to make any haste. He reached Delhi and came to the camp of Shuja and advised him not to take that venture, after knowing the reality Shuja and Emperor Shah Alam II returned. Najib came to Delhi. He founded a city of Najibabad its building, gardens and mansions. There was a Meo named Sanulba, who used to commit highway robbery with ten horsemen, near the fort of Dig used to loot caravans and used to reach the stations of Hodal and Barsana repeatedly after two days. They used to give the material to the Nawab of Farrukhnagar and stationed in a fort named Tauru. Jawahar Singh wanted to punish them, with the assent of Suraj Mal; Jawahar Singh raided many times these Meo's and ultimately captured them along with their children and women and sent them to Dig. He also captured some of the territory of Najib. Najib wrote many times to Surajmal and sent his messengers not to repeat it. But Suraj Mal defended his son. Ultimately Surajmal wanted to attack Najib, with a strong army he come to river Hindan. Najib also came to Delhi from Najibabad and reached in front of Hindan. He tried to advise Suraj Mal not to go for war, but ultimately it was not heeded and in the war Suraj Mal was killed, his head and hand were cut and sent to Najib. The Sikhs had plundered the country of Barah and took lots of valuables from there.

In twenty days time Jawahar Singh son of Suraj Mal got an agreement for help from Sikhs and Marathas. Jawahar Singh came to Delhi and reached old fort and his army moved to Firoz Shah Kotla, Malhar Rao who had an understanding with Najib did not move further to old fort.

The Sikhs also came to North of Delhi; they put their conditions on Jawahar Singh. The Jats crossed Yamuna to East side and looted the grain merchants of Shahdra. From East side of Yamuna they bombarded the city some shots also fell on Red Fort. The Nagas also joined Jawahar Singh. For fifteen days fighting went on like this.

Imad and Malhar Rao were luke warm towards Jawahar, they had secret pact with Najib-ud-Daulah. News spread that Ahmad Shah has crossed Atok and coming to Delhi. This compelled Jawahar to go for peace and on 19 February 1765, peace treaty was made. On the other hand Ahmad Shah was making haste to come to Delhi, he sent a message of his arrival soon, but by that time a peace treaty was made. Khutba was not read in the name of Shah Alam as was suggested by Imad. Ahmad Shah Abdali had reached 30 miles away to Delhi near Bawana; there he came to know that peace treaty had already been signed and all the forces of Jawahar, Imad, Malhar and others had gone away from Delhi, he marched back and went to Kabul and Qandhar. In 1770, Etawah and Shikohabad were surrendered to the Marathas, when they again appeared in the North. In 1771 Rohilas suffered an irreparable loss by the death of Najib-ud-Daulah and Dundey Khan.

The Maratha Movement

The Maratha came from the dominant peasant clans living in the western territory of India where Marathi language was spoken. During the 16th century the Sultans of Bijapur and Ahmadnagar had recruited them to serve as light cavalry to balance the political ambitions of the Mughal soldiers in the army. The Brahmans were divided into Deshastas and Chitpavans also got benefits from Muslim overlords. They had their high positions because of their standing in administrative service to Muslim regimes and their participation in the Bhakti cults of Maharashtra.

The Deccan territories were administered by local persons, that is, Deshmukh was the head of 20 to 100 villages, each of the village had a powerful headman (Patil), assisted by the keeper of records (Kulkarni). Headmen were inevitably drawn from the Maratha peasant castes and village accountants were from Brahmans. Heads of Deshmukh was Sardeshmukhi and Chief of account was, Dash Kulkarni. The role of external authorities such as Deccan Sultans or later occasionally the Mughals was minimal. Shivaji as a king sought greater control over the autonomous countryside.

Aurangzeb initially wanted to punish Shambhaji the son of Shivaji, who offered shelter to the rebel Prince Akbar. Subsequently the Emperor found other reasons to try to rid the Deccan of Marathas predations. Shambhaji faced execution, his son Shahu - who ruled from 1708 to 1749 left to Maratha fighting bands which regularly raided and pillaged Mughal tracts along the northern frontier. Soon they were reaching towards Delhi.

During the warfare period many talented Deshmukh families got opportunities to expand Maratha power, the Chitpavan Brahmans who were holding the position of Peshwas under king Shahu became very influential and powerful.

Originating modestly as keeper of records, under the Peshwas Balaji Vishwanath, the office was transformed into that of Prime Minister of the kingdom and hereditary later on. His son Baji Rao held the post from 1720 to 1740 and his son Balaji Baji Rao from 1740 to 1761. During most of Shahu's reign, there was a steady increase in the territory under Maratha sway, from which tribute was extracted, after his death in 1749 and until 1761. Baji Rao extend the boundary of Maratha Empire in the South in the area of Nizam of Hyderabad, Gujarat, Malwa, and even Delhi was not ruled out, this not only accrued the glory for the king but wealth as well.

Baji Rao was astute in his choice of commanders for the undertakings, passing over the established elite of the Deshmukhs; commands were given to new men of the Gaikwad. Holkar and Shinde families, who had been loyal to Shahu and to his father and now to himself. Enhanced armies were formed, and when they were not deployed on the Peshwa's conquests they served his interests by leaving hired out to lesser Lords in some remote conflict.

In 1728 Nizam was trapped and forced to recognize Peshwa as king and overlord of Deccan. In 1737 Delhi was raided. In 1739 a treaty was agreed at Bhopal in which the area from Narmada to Chambal was ceded to Maratha. The Mughals were weak so the Marathas were gaining. From 1747 to 1751 plundering expeditions were launched by Maratha chieftain Raghoji Bhonsle. Instead of territorial expansion the policy of receiving Chauth was followed.

The treaty of April 12, 1752 had granted the Marathas the provinces of Agra and Ajmer. The ambitious Maratha chiefs attempted to establish their sway in these provinces even after the above mentioned treaty reduced to a scrap of paper. Soon after Khande Rao Holkar plundering the Jat villages near Palwal, he started his war against Suraj Mal in January 1754 but was killed by chance with the bullet. Same time after the march of Khande Rao, Jayappa Scindia also invaded Marwar. He was killed at Nagaur in 1755.

The Mughal-Maratha treaty of April, 1752 brought the Marathas to North India and gave rise to many new problems and complications in Indian politics, Rajput-Maratha conflict in Rajasthan, the Jat-Maratha conflict in central India, and Afghan-Maratha conflict in the Punjab. The ever increasing ambitions of the Marathas and their plundering raids in central India and Rajputana were mainly responsible for Sadashiv Rao Bhao's tragic failure in the game of diplomacy and beating the allies on the eve of the third battle of Panipat. The Rajput resentment against the Maratha actions in Rajputana were too fresh for them to go to the aid of Bhao, the Jats kept aloof because of their homes had been ravaged by them. Thus the treaty which was the main source of bringing Maratha influence to the North became eventually responsible for their defeat at the hands of a foreign invader in 1761.[173]

The Marathas not only raided territory, imposed Chauth but they also administered their territory directly under their control. They accurately accessed proceeds from the land and kept its proper record. The British later followed the same policy.

The battle of Panipat in 1761 with Ahmad Shah Abdali brought the end of the strong, centralized Maratha power. The Marathas were now divided among several commanders. The new kingdom were at Baroda in Gujarat under the Gaikwad family, at Indore in Malwa and in the central Deccan tracts north of the Narmada under the Holkars, South of Delhi at Gwalior was with Scindia family; at Nagpur in western Maharashtra the Bhonsles endured; and in Pune region, descendants of the Peshwas retained a territorial sway made fragile by competing smaller houses in the heartland of the former State.

The Marathas appeared in North India again in 1770. Najib by that time became old, weak and not secure and assisted by foreign power. He now seriously wanted Shah Alam to come to Delhi who was the prisoner of the British at Allahabad with the help of the Marathas he wanted to do so. As early as 26 May 1761 the English had promised to escort him to Delhi. This promise was repeated again and again but not fulfilled. Ahmad Shah Abdali and Najib had also asked the Emperor to come to Delhi in October 1765. By 1768 Najib was broken in health and spirits

Najib had been a dictator for ten years at Delhi. The fear of Afghan invasion was over; the Sikhs were busy in Punjab. Najib died on 9 February 1771, the Marathas, with whom Shah Alam had been in negotiation for his restoration at Delhi, bombarded Delhi and captured it. Zabita Khan for fear of Marathas had left Delhi and retired to his Jagir. Shah Alam left Allahabad on 13 April 1771 and entered Delhi on 6 January 1772 on the eve of Id-ul-Fitr under the escort of Marathas.

Shah Alam Emperor at Delhi

On the first day of Shah Alam in Delhi, Id was celebrated. People of Delhi, who had suffered poverty and humiliation under the fear of Jats, Marathas, Afghan raids, believed this restoration of Shah Alam as opening a new era of peace, prosperity, and freedom from fear. But Shah Alam did not have the material means, the will, the determination or political acumen to restore the fallen fortunes of his dynasty. He was dependent on others and surrounded from all sides by strong forces who would like to take over Delhi. During the last 20 years some of the ablest nobles had either died a natural death or got killed. Some had created their own principalities some got involved in their personal rivalries and petty feuds. Ghazi-ud-Din Imad-ul-Mulk had been tried and failed and was in exile. Shuja-ud-Daulah was busy in his own affairs. Munier-ud-Daulah, Saif-ud-Din Mohammad Khan and Husain-ud-Daulah were neither soldiers nor administrators.

The two leaders who dominated the stage during the years 1772 to 1782 were Najaf Khan and Abdul Ahmad Khan.

Mirza Najaf Khan

He came to India along with his sister from Iran. He was born in a respectable family. He served at many places, such as Allahabad, Bengal and Bundelkhand. When Shah Alam left for Delhi through Kora, Najaf Khan was appointed by Shah Alam.

Najaf Khan was a capable military officer with a considerable political insight, vision and realism so rare amongst his contemporaries. He died in 1782 and mourned by all.

On the death of Najib-ud-Daulah his son, Zabita Khan, was invested with the office of Mir-Bakhshi and the title of Amir-ul-Umara. He was asked to pay the customary succession fee and settle the accounts of the crown lands and Privy Purse estates held by his father. Zabita Khan accepted the office but insolently refused to comply with other demands.

Najaf Khan with Maratha troops brought Zabita Khan to submission in January 1772. He was brought before the king but fled again to his Jagir, but was again captured, his Jagir was looted and his family was captured, he was asked to pay 40 lacks of rupees to Marathas, which Shuja-ud-Daulah stood security but this money was never paid. The rivalry between Najaf Khan and Marathas increased because the division of the levy from Zabita Khan could not be divided with satisfaction.

Now to counter the growing popularity of Najaf Khan Marathas supported Zabita Khan. Shah Alam knew the plans of Marathas that they will attack Delhi, so he asked Medec to come to Delhi from Jat service on 17 November, 1772 he met Shah Alam and entered in the service of Shah Alam on

17 December, 1772. Marathas fought a battle at Purana Qila and entered Delhi and plundered it. Emperor had no alternative but open peace parleys and Zabita Khan was made the Mir Bakhshi, Medec was relieved, Jats were given back their Jagir. Now Marathas invaded Rohilkhand and the territory of Shuja, but British supported Shuja, the Marathas were defeated. Zabita Khan also left the Marathas camp. Najaf Khan returned to Delhi on 20 May 1773 and appointed second Bakhshi in June, 1773. On his advice Abdul Ahad Khan a Kashmiri Muslim, a smooth polish, perfect suavity of temper and false bewitching tongue and soon grew into the best loved personal friend and private companion of Shah Alam, was appointed Deputy Wazir on 22 May 1773.

Najaf Khan with a force of 20,000 men defeated the Jats and cleared South-East of Delhi of them. Medec joined Najaf Khan. Najaf Khan second time defeated Jats in 1775 and captured Kama and Dig. Abdul Ahad Khan poisoned the mind of Emperor and he was called to the court.

Zabita Khan defeated imperial army with the support of Sikhs on 11 March 1776. Ghulam Qadir Khan, the son of Zabita Khan fled from Delhi and joined his father. The emperor asked Zabita Khan to pay the revenue arrear or yield the crown lands held by him. He declined to do so the imperial army under Najaf Khan defeated Zabita Khan in September, 1777. Zabita Khan fled to Punjab along with Sikhs, his forts, property, was taken. Ghulam Qadir was taken prisoner along with his family. Zabita Khan was made destitute and he converted into a Sikh and named Dharam Singh. In 1778, Najaf Khan with his political insight and far sighted statesmanship restored the property and family of Zabita Khan to him; married the daughter of Zabita Khan and secured the pardon of the Emperor, who gave him a robe of honor and a letter of patent for the district of Saharanpur on 30 January 1779.

When Najaf Khan was away in Alwar the Sikhs entered Delhi. They demolished a mosque near Rikabganj and built a Gurudwara; in the memory of Guru Teg Bahadur, as the trunk of the body of Guru Tegh Bahadur was cremated there by Lakhi Shah Banjara's family.

On 19 November 1779 Abdul Ahad Khan was removed from his position, this brought the relief to the people of Delhi, who were much harassed by Ahad Khan. Najaf Khan gave to pleasure and the instrument of his degeneration was a woman, who was introduced in to his wine parties by her husband, Latafat Ali Khan. Najaf Khan died on 6 April 1782. During the last year of his life the administration had passed into the hands of Latafat Ali Khan; the poor peasants suffered, army was in arrears, the Emperor and the Princes did not receive their allowances. Even the Emperor and the ladies of the harem had to go without food and the latter even thought of drawning themselves in the Yamuna.

Mirza Najaf Khan was the last great Muslim Minister, but the administration was in the hands of Kashmiri Brahmin Diwans, and Muslim officers of average ability. During his time the Shias again came into prominence. He wanted to oust Shah Abdul Aziz from Delhi.

Afrasiyab Khan

After the death of Najaf a political void was created. Emperor got too much engrossed in pleasure. On the recommendation of Najaf, Afrasiyab Khan, who was his slave and Hindu convert was appointed his successor. He was hot tempered. So it was a bad choice. Najaf Quli Khan, Mirza Mohammad Shafi, Mohammad Beg Hamadani, these persons dominated the court and camp from 1782 to 84. They were more absorbed in promoting their own selfish interests and by their intrigues after intrigues further lowered the prestige of the Emperor. This set the stage for the tragic events which led to the blinding of the Emperor and restoration of Marathas influence in northern India through Mahadhji Scindia.

Mirza Safi was engaged against Sikhs. He was also an ambitions person. The elder sister of Najaf wanted him to be Mir Bakhshi. She had also promised to give one daughter of Najaf to him in marriage. On 11 August 1782 in a street fight between the soldiers of Safi, and Ahad Khan Safi won. He was appointed Mir Bakhshi, but the outcry of the people against him compelled him to flee from Delhi. In June 1783 he met Scindia and invited him to Delhi to restore the confused imperial administration.

Afrasyab arranged a meeting of Hamadani with Safi on 23 September 1783 in this meeting Safi was treacherously murdered.

Afrasiyab, who was the Mir Bakhshi also, could not manage with Hamadani the Emperor and Abdul Ahad Khan. He was also murdered on 2 November 1784. The rapid and unexpected changes compelled Shah Alam to seek the help of Mahadhji Scindia, and despite the opposition of Narayan Das and Himmat Bahadur Gosain, Shah Alam, appointed Mahadhji Scindia as his deputy and Bakhshi-i-Mumalik also as his agent and Wakil at the Mughal court to perform the functions of these officers.

But to gain resources for the maintenance of Emperor and army he had to capture, Dig and Agra in January–March, 1785. Aligarh on 20 November 1785. But at Jaipur he was defeated at Lalsot in 1787. Meanwhile Ghulam Qadir was appointed Mir Bakhshi and regent by the Emperor on 24 August 1787 in his place. Scindia perforce had to retire south of the Chambal and reorganize his resources as there was no support from the Peshwa for the present. Rane Khan supported him in June 1788 and cleared the country west of the Yamuna of Scindia's enemies.

Ghulam Qadir

He was the son of Zabita Khan, had succeeded his father on 21 January 1785. His first move to drive out the Marathas from upper Doah succeeded. He wanted to attack Shahdara, the Emperor called Ghulam Qadir in his presence on 26 August 1787 and appointed him Bakhshi-i-Mumalik, Naib and granted him a Khillat. He went to Aligarh. When he wanted to come back to Delhi he was prevented. At Shahdara he was supported by material and men by Mansur Ali and Ram Rattan on 1 July 1788. He captured Delhi and occupied it from 18 July to 2 October 1788. He inflicted unspeakable suffering and dishonor on the royal family and ruined the prestige of the Empire beyond recovery. It was first to get money. Servants were beaten till they died; Shah Alam was deposed (20 July) and blinded (10 August); tender children and helpless women were done to death by denying them food or drinks. The Princesses were raped. Even the palace was denuded of its pearls and other articles even Jama Masjid was not spared. The rich and wealthy persons of the city were robbed of their wealth. In this action he was helped by dowager Empress Malika-i-Zamani, who had offered 12 lakh to Ghulam Qadir to place her grandson Bidr Bakht on the throne. Bidar Bakht, the son of Ahmad Shah was placed on the throne and other princes were made prisoners. Malika-i-Zamani and Sahiba Mahal, who had been instrumental in bringing Ghulam Qadir to Delhi, were exposed to the sun and the public gaze. Mansur Ali was severely beaten and his house was ransacked. The spoils estimated from Delhi were 25 crores. Gold coating, one cupola of the Jama Masjid was removed.

Scindia when heard all this sent Rane Khan to Delhi on 14 September 1788. On 2 October 1788, Delhi was captured. Ghulam Qadir went to Aligarh fort he was pursued, he went to Meerut, there he was also pursued. He was captured at Bamrauli near Meerut on 19 December, 1788.

Ghulam Qadir and Mansur Ali were executed. His headless trunk was hung upside down from a tree; a black dog with white rings round its eyes set below it and lapped up the blood dripping from the neck. It happened for two days; after that the trunk and the dogs were not seen. The head was sent to Shah Alam. The two enemies of Scindia, Ismail Beg died on 20 June 1790 and Najaf Khan on 23 August 1791. Now the Emperor remained a vessel of Scindia. Mahadhji left for Poona in 1792, leaving his agent at Shah Alam's court. Anand Rao Narsi Yerulkkar was the agent of Mahadhji Scindia at Shah Alam's court from 1780 to 1786.

Shahji acted as Scindia's Subedar of Delhi from August 1789 to June 1796. He was replaced by Shah Haji, a personal friend of Prince Ahmad, but was re-appointed in May, 1798. In October 1799 Prince Akbar seized Shahji, had him beaten and confined to the palace. He was later released and continued as Subedar till 1803; when he was replaced by Pearson.

Scindia had fixed the Emperor's allowance at 300 rupees a day and later at 1,50,000 annually. This amount was not sufficient for the Princes and many took asylum in Awadh, in Deccan and Afghanistan. Shah Alam, though he was blinded but had 500 women in his seraglio. He had married a dancing girl of Delhi, Azizan by name. She would often get angry and the old dotard would humiliate himself to placate her. He was addicted to sensuality and love for pleasure. Shah Alam contained to live in penury as a non-entity as Sindhia had his hands full elsewhere and could do little to relieve the distress of the royal family.

The Anglo-Maratha (1803–05) war resulted in the complete discomfiture of the Marathas.

Mahadhji Scindia of Gwalior

The Empire of the Mughals, which Babur established after the first battle of Panipat in the beginning of the sixteenth century, had been dissolved in the eighteenth century. The scepter of sovereignty had slipped from the feeble grasp of the successors of Aurangzeb, for they had become mere puppets in the hands of their powerful subordinates. The whirlwind incursions of Nadir Shah and Ahmed Shah Abdali during the years 1739 and 1761 had sapped whatever yet remained of the great Mughal dominion. In northern India the Jats and Rohilla challenged the powers of Mughal emperors; and practically the whole of Deccan had become independent of the irksome yoke of Delhi. The growing British power, which was destined to establish a great empire in India, had not yet entered upon its glorious career. In this situation, on the ashes of the towering Mughal Empire in India, some self growing states, most of them ephemeral, but other containing the germs of a future worthier existence came into being. One such state was of the Gwalior, which played an important part in the politics of the eighteenth and the nineteenth century.

J. Sutherland, who was the resident at the Scindia's court, wrote to Mr. W.H. Macnagten, Secretary, on 12 August 1838 from Gwalior residency.

"The ancestors of Scindia family, used to live in the South India, one branch of which held the hereditary post of Patel in the village of Kooserkera in the District of Satara. The head of the family received a patent of rank from the Emperor Aurangzeb, while a daughter of this family was married to Raja Sahu, grandson of Shivaji. The first appearance of this family in central India was early in the eighteenth century in the person of Ranoji Scindia, a scion of an impoverished branch of the family; who began his career as the slipper-bearer of the Peshwa Balaji Baji Rao; and rose, owing to his military abilities, to be commander of his bodyguard. From this position his rise to the first rank of the Maratha chief was rapid. Ranoji Scindia fixed his headquarters at

Ujjain, which rose to be the first capital of Scindia's dominion. Ranoji Scindia died at Shinghalpur (Shujalpur) about the year 1750."[174]

Ranoji Scindia left three legitimate sons, Jayapa, Dattaji, and Jatila, and two illegitimate sons, Tukaji and Mahadhji; all of whom, except Tukaji, survived their father, Jayapa's life was cut short; he died at the hands of an assassin at Nagaur in 1759, Dattaji and Jatila were killed during fourth invasion of Ahmad Shah Abdali (1759–61).

Only Mahadhji survived, who narrowly escaped with his life from the terrible slaughter in 1761 A.D. at the battle of Panipat. It was a crisis in the history of the family of Scindia's. He not only received back his father's territories but established one of the most powerful and lasting Hindu monarchies in India and played a paramount role in the drama of Anglo-Scindia relations in India. It was true that Mahadhji Scindia could not oppose successfully Generals Goddard and Camac in the first Maratha war. He was the greatest of his age and country could produce at the time, but the army and soldiers were worthless in comparison to the British. He got the Gwalior, with some difficulty from the Peshwa as his father's fief in the year 1769. In the struggle of Peshwaship he sided with Nana Fadnavis. Narain Rao, the fifth Peshwa was murdered in 1772. In 1775 when Raghunath Rao the uncle of late Peshwa, claimed the post of Peshwa under the aid of East India Company, Mahadhji Scindia supported the claim of Madhu Narayan Rao.

In 1779 British wanted a treaty with Scindia but Scindia declined. After the first Maratha war in 1779 East India Company again came with the initiative of a treaty with Scindia on 13 October 1781 a treaty of Salbai was concluded which was further ratified on 17 May 1782; which was further ratified on 20 February 1783. With this treaty Mahadhji Scindia became very powerful; he could re-establish Shah Alam to his kingship in 1785. This treaty not only gave a political stability to Gwalior but also commercial boost. Mahadhji Scindia now employed Benoit de Boigne to train Gwalior's army. Scindia wanted to wipe out the disgrace of the third battle of Panipat. But he could not do it. On 12 February 1794 he got a violent fever, and died. He passed away at a time when success, seemed almost within his grasp. Ultimately one by one the rulers of India seized by the strong tentacles of the great octopus, the East India Company's expansionist policy, the disunity and the utter lack of any political sense in the Indian ruling classes of the eighteenth century led them to their pre-destined doom of subjugation.

REFERENCES

1. Hamoodur Rehman, 'The Islamic Concept of State', Hamdard Islamicus, vol. II, No.1, 1979, pp. 51-52.

2. Hamoodur Rahman, 'The Islamic Concept of State', Hamdard-Islamicus, vol. II, No.1, 1979, pp. 51-64.
3. W. Montgomery Watt, *Islamic Philosophy and Theology,* Edinburgh, The Universal Press, 1962, p. 24.
4. D.B. MacDonald, *Development of Muslim Theology, Jurisprudence and Constitutional Theory*, Reprint, The Premier Book House, Lahore 1960, 1964, p. 103.
5. Elphinstone, Monstuart, *The History of India*, 6th Ed., London, 1874, p. 476.
6. Murray T. Titus, *Islam in India and Pakistan; A Religious History of Islam in India and Pakistan*, Munshiram Manoharlal, New Delhi, 2005, p. 92.
7. Najm-ul-Ghani Khan, *Madhahib-ul-Islam*, Nawal Kishore Press, Lucknow, 1924, p. 441.
8. A. Halim, 'Justice of Sikandar Lodi', Journal of Pakistan Historical Society, II, October, 1954, pp. 272-279.
9. Chach-Namah, E.D., I, p. 206
10. Elliot, Sir H. M. and Dawson, J. *The History of India as Told by its Own Historians*, vol. I, p. 462.
11. Arnold, *The Caliphate*, Oxford University Press, p. 86
12. Arnold, p. 116.
13. Ziya-ud-Din Barni, *Tarikh i-Firuz Shahi*, tr. by Elliot and Dowson, vol. III, pp. 249-250.
14. Arnold, op cit., pp. 159-62.
15. Murray T. Titus, op. cit., p. 61.
16. L.F. Rush Brook Williams, *India in 1920*, Calcutta, 1921, pp. 51-3.
17. Williams, op. cit., p. 34.
18. Elphinstone, Monstuart, *The History of India*, 6th Ed., London, 1874, pp. 533 and 672.
19. Khafi Khan, *Muntakhab-ul-Lubab*, tr. by Elliot and Dowson, vol. VII, pp. 420 and 427.
20. Narayani Gupta, *Delhi between Two Empires, 1803-1931*, Oxford University Press, Delhi, 1986, p. 10.
21. D.C.O.F. I/1878.
22. P. Jackson, 'The Mongols and the Delhi Sultanate in the Reign of Mohammad Tughluq (1325-1351)', *Central Asian Journal*, vol. XIX, 1975, pp. 118-160.
23. J. Talboys Wheelar, *The Religious and Cultural History of India*, Sanjay Prakashan, New Delhi, 1988, pp. 333-4.
24. Quran, Chapter 72, Ayet 18.
25. Hamida Khatoon Naqvi, 'Urban Growth in Hindustan circa 1000-1550: An Exploratory Study', *Studies in Islam*, Vol. 16, 1976, p. 150.
26. Al-Tawbah, Al-Anjal (8) 41, 69.
27. Ziya-ud-Din Barni, *Tarikh-i-Firozshahi*, S. A. A. Rizvi, translated, Aligarh Muslim University 1955, p. 70.
28. Agha Mahdi Hussain, *The Rise and Fall of Mohammad Bin Tughluq*, London, 1938 and R.C. Majumdar (Ed), 'The History and Culture of Indian People', vol. VI, The Delhi Sultanate, Bombay, 1960, p. 106.

29. Amir Khurd, *Siyar-ul-Aulia* (Lives of the Saints).
30. Barni, *Tarikh-i-Firoz Shahi*, p. 332.
31. Dara Shikoh, *Safinat-ul-Aulia.*
32. Barni, *Tarikh-i-Firoz Shahi*, p. 343.
33. Dara Sukoh, *Safin-ul-Aulia*, Sabri Book Depot, Deoband, pp. 27–8.
34. Tamhidat; Diwan of Mas'ud Bakk; Mirat-al-Arifin, (The Mirror of the Gnostics)), (Abd-al-Haqq-Tales of the Great Ones).
35. Mohammad Gul Ahmadpuri, *Takmila-i-Siyar al-Awlia*, also Carl W. Ernst, 'From Hagiography to Martyrology: Conflicting Testimonies to a Sufi Martyr of the Delhi Sultanate', History of Religion, May 1985, vol.24, No. 4, pp. 30827.
36. Shu'ayb Firdawsi, *Manaqib al-Asfia*, Calcutta, Nur al-Afaq, 1313/1895.
37. Iqtidar Husain Siddiqui and Qazi Mohammad Ahmad, 'An Arab Account of India in the Fourteenth Century', Studies in Islam, October 1970, p. 219.
38. Chandra Bhan Brahman, *Guldasta-i-Chahar Chaman*, p. 13, and Sujan Rai Bhandari, *Khulasatut Tawarikh*, p. 31.
39. Malfuzat-i-Shah Abdul Aziz, p. 34.
40. Simon Digby, 'Abdul Quddus Gangohi: The Personality and Attitudes of a Medieval Indian Sufi', Medieval India, A Miscellany Aligarh, 1975, vol. 3, pp. 36-39; also see, Iqtidar Hussain Siddiqui, 'Sufis and Sufism in the Territory of Kalpi, 15th and 16th Century', Pakistan Journal of History and Culture, vol. V, January-June, 1984, pp. 63-69.
41. Tuzuk-i-Jahangiri, 1 232-233.
42. Tuzuk-i-Jahangiri, 1.56.
43. Waldemar Hausen, *The Peacock Throne*, Motilal Banarsidass, Delhi, 1972, p. 451.
44. Ippolito Desideri, *Tibet-A Chronicle of Exploration*, Ed. by MacGregor, London, 1970, pp. 62-63.
45. Dr. Vasundhra Filliozat, 'Juliana: An Influential Portuguese Lady at the Moghul Court', Quarterly Journal of the Mythic Society, pp. 195-203.
46. Aziz Ahmad, 'Epic and Counter-Epic in Medieval India', Journal of the American Oriental Society, vol. 83, 1963, p. 470.
47. "Ashiqa', tr. from Elliot, III, p. 546.
48. Amir Khusrau, *Nuh Sipihr*, Ed. by Wahid Mirza, Calcutta, 1950.
49. Isami, *Futuh al-Salatin*, Ed. by A. S. Usha, Madras, 1943, pp. 17 and 114.
50. Ibid., pp. 230-6.
51. Ahmad, p. 472
52. Babur, *Tuzuk* (Leyden and Eraskine), II, p. 241.
53. K.M. Ashraf, '*Life and Conditions of the People of Hindustan (1200-1550)*', JRASB, Calcutta, 1935, p. 142.
54. Har Bilas Sarda, 'The Prithviraj Vijay', in JRAS, 1913, I, pp. 260-1.
55. G.A. Grierson, *The Modern Vernacular Literature of Hindustan*, Calcutta, 1889, p. 6.
56. Grierson, pp. 1-2.
57. Maheshwar Prasad, Purush Pariksha of Vidyapati, 20 et sq.
58. G.A. Grierson, 'The Popular Literature of Northern India', BSOS, 1/3, 1920, pp. 97-100.

59. Wide the Third Sipahr in *Nuh Sipahr*, Ed. By M. Wahid Mirza, Lucknow University, Bombay, 1950, p. 147-202.
60. Abdul Ali, 'Qadi Abd al-Muqtadir of Delhi: A Distinguished Eulogist of the Prophet Muhammad', Islamic Culture, October 2001, p. 39.
61. ibid., pp. 45-46.
62. George Mcleod James, *Anand Ram 'Mukhlis', His Life and Works, (1695-1758)*, pub. by Henrietta Yasmin James, n.d.
63. Bhagwan Das, (Hindi), *Safina-i-Hindi*, Patna, 1958.
64. Chander Bhan Brahman, *Chahar Chaman*, pp. 141-142.
65. Stephen P. Blake, *Shahjahanabad: The Sovereign City in Mughal India, 1639-1739,* Cambridge University Press, 1991, p. XII.
66. Yusuf Abbas Hashmi, 'Sovereignty in Islam in Theory and Practice', The Proceedings of the Pakistan History Conference, 2nd Session, Pakistan Historical Society, 1952, pp. 87-96.
67. Francois Bernier, *Travels in the Mogul Empire,* A.D. *1656-1668*, S. Chand & Co., 1968, p. 240.
68. Bernier, op. cit., p. 243.
69. Percival Spear, *Delhi, its Monuments and History*, 3rd Ed., Oxford University Press, 1994, pp. 9-10.
70. Stephen P. Blake, p. 54.
71. Stephen P. Blake, p. 55.
72. Quoted in Stephen P. Blake, pp. 51–2.
73. Stephen P. Blake, p. 53.
74. *Muraqqa-i-Delhi*, p. 39, Qahwa Khani-Guldasta-i-Chandra Bhan Brahman, Waqa-i-Anand Ram Mukhlis, p. 177 a.
75. *Waqi'at-i-Darul Hukumat-i-Delhi*, vol. II, pp. 184–5.
76. *Waqi'at-i-Darul Hukumat-i-Delhi*, vol. II, p. 123; *Asar-us-Sanadid*, vol. I, pp. 214 and 366; Muraqqa-i-Delhi, pp. 84-7.
77. Bernier, *Travels in the Mugul Empire*, p. 239–88.
78. Twinning, *Travels in India*, p. 240; Bernier, p.283; and, *Asar-us-Sanadid*, pp. 287-8.
79. Bernier, Travels, p. 242.
80. R. C. Temple, *The Travels of Richard Bell*; and John Campbell, 'East Indies, Persia and Palestine'; The Indian Antiquary, 35 (1906), p. 173; and, Hakim Maharat Khan, "*Bahjat at-Alam*" fol. 35.
81. T. Fortescue, 'Report on the Revenue System of the Delhi Territory, 1820, in records of the Delhi Residency and Agency 1807-87', Lahore: Punjab Government Press, 1911, p. 169.
82. Manucci, *Storia do Mogor*, 1, p. 377.
83. Sen (Ed.), *India Travels of Thevenot and Careri*, p. 61.
84. Stephen P. Blake, p. 75-76.
85. Stiphen P. Blake, p. 75-81; and, Shah Nawaz Khan, *Ma'asir al-Umara*, pp. 463-6 and 476.
86. Manrique Froy Sebastien II, p. 180.
87. Bernier, *Travels in India*, pp. 258-59.

88. Munshi Chandra Bhan Brahman and Sujan Rai Bhandari, p. 6b.
89. Shakir Khan, *Tarikh-i-Shakir Khani,* p. 49 b.
90. Percival Spear, *Twilight of the Mughals-Studies in Later Mughal Delhi,* Cambridge University Press, 1951, p. 64; Mirza Mazhar, *Jan-i-Jaman-Makatib-i-Mazhar;* and, Ghulam Hamadani Mushafi, *Mushafi Aur Unka Kalam,* p. 64.
91. Stephen P. Blake, p. 111.
92. Sri Ram Sharma, *Religious Policy of the Mughal Emperors,* Second Ed., p. 131.
93. Orme's Fragments, Notes, 85.
94. News Letters, 20th November 1665; 1st April 1692; Manucci, II, p. 154; Mirat, I, pp. 154-55.
95. *Muntakhab-ul-Lubab,* Text, II, p. 212.
96. *Akhbarat-i-Darbar-i-Mu'alla,* 16th April 1694.
97. James Fraser, *The History of Nadir Shah,* London, MDCCXLII, pp. 69-70.
98. Sir John Malcolm, *History of Persia,* Vol. II, pp. 46-47.
99. *Ashub,* Vol. II, p. 369.
100. J.N. Sarkar, *Fall of the Mughal Empire,* p. 106.
101. Prakash Gupta, *Delhi Tera Itihas Nirala,* (Hindi), Prem Prakashan Mandir, Delhi.
102. Elliot and Dowson, *History of India as Told by its Own Historians,* vol. III, pp. 377-8.
103. Frederick W. Buckler, 'The Political Theory of the Indian Mutiny' in Michael N. Pearson, Legitimacy and Symbols. The South Asian Writings of F.W. Buckler, Ann Arbor: Centre for South and Southeast Asian Studies, University of Michigan, 1985, pp. 43-74 and 55-61.
104. *Subaltern Studies,* I-IX, Delhi, Oxford University Press, 1982.
105. Gyanendra Pandey, *The Construction of Communalism in Colonial North India,* Oxford University Press, Delhi, 1990, p. 134.
106. Shama Mitra Chenoy, *Shahjahanabad - A City of Delhi, 1638-1857,* Munshiram Manoharlal, New Delhi, 1998, pp. 144-5.
107. Major Archor, *Tours in Upper India and in Parts of the Himalaya Mountains,* 2 vols., London, 1833, vol. I, pp. 104-5 as quoted in Kaul, *Historic Delhi,* pp. 204-1.
108. Jitendra G. Borpujari, 'The Impact of the Transit Duty System in British India', Indian Economic and Social History Review, vol. 10, 1973, pp. 218-43.
109. 'Turbulent Delhi: Religious Strife, Social Tension and Political Conflicts, 1803-1857', in South Asia: Journal of South Asian Studies, vol. 28, 2005, pp. 5-34.
110. Bayloy, Rulers, *Townsmen and Bazars,* pp. 30-31, 123-5 and 141-2.
111. Mann, *British Rub on Indian Soil,* pp. 175-7.
112. Francois Bernier, *Travels in the Mogol Empire,* S. Chand & Co., Delhi, 1960, p. 281.
113. Bernier, *Travels in the Mogol Empire,* p. 242.
114. F. Roberts, *Letters written during the Indian Mutiny,* London, 1924.
115. 'T. T. Metcalfe, Agent, Governor-General, N.W.P. to T. H. Maddock, Officiating Secretary', Pol. Department N.W.P., dated 12th November 1839, No. 1258.
116. 'Metcalfe, Commissioner of Delhi Division to Elliot, Secretary', Sadar Board of Revenue, Allahabad, dated 31st January 1840, No. 24.

117. Stephen P. Black, *Shahjahanabad: The Sovereign City in Mughal India, 1639-1739*, p. 5.
118. Mohammad Tahir-Inayat Khan, *Shahjahan Nama*, in Elliot and Dowsan, p. 85-86), on the 25th Dhul Hijja of the 12th year, 1048 A.H. (19th April 1639) Shams-ud-Daula 'and Abdul Havy, *Maathir-ul-Umara*, tr. by H. Beveridge, 2 vols., Reprinted, Janaki Prakashan, Patna 1979, vol. 2, pt. 1, pp. 226-8.
119. Prakash Gupta, *Delhi Tera Itihas Nirala*, (Hindi), Prem Prakashan Mandir, Delhi, pp. 217-218.
120. Niccoloi Manucci, *Storia do Mogor* or *Mogul India*, tr. by William Irvin, 4 vols., London, John Murray, 1907, vol. I, pp. 183-5.
121. G.S. Hearn, *The Seven Cities of Delhi*, Ed. and revised by Nalini Thakur, Aryan Books International, Delhi, 1906, p. 128.
122. *The Delhi of the Mughals prior to Shahjahanabad as reflected in the patterns of imperial visits* by Ebba-Koch quoted from Ahsan Jan Qaiser and Som Prakash Verma (Eds.) Felicitation volume in honour of Prof. Nurul Hasan, Publication Scheme, Jaipur, 1993, pp. 11-12.
123. C.F. Andrews, *Zakaullah of Delhi*, Heffer, p. 13.
124. Mehdi Husain, *Bahadur Shah II and the War of 1857 in Delhi with its Unforgettable Scenes*, M.N. Publication, New Delhi, 1987, pp. 42-45.
125. Spear. P, *Twilight of the Mughals*, 1951.
126. Mehdi Husain, pp. 66-67.
127. Quoted in Mehdi Husain, *Bahadur Shah II and the War of 1857*, pp. 3-4.
128. op. cit. pp. 4-5.
129. Caveeshar, S.S., *India's Fight for Freedom*, p. 427. Quoted by Mehdi Husain, op. cit. pp. 14-15.
130. R.C. Majumdar, *The Sepoy and the Revolt of 1857*, p. 118.
131. Mehdi Husain has seen the Mutiny papers Box 94, No 1; Box 73 No. 146-201; Box 2 No. 29,31.28, 29 of July 5 to August 12, 1857.
132. S.N. Sen, *Eighteen Fifty Seven*, pp. 109.
133. Mehdi Hasan, pp. 405-06.
134. Mehdi Hasan, p. 412.
135. N.L. Batra, *Delhi's Red Fort by the Yamuna*, Niyogi Books, p. 25, and p. 207.
136. Godse's speech Quoted in Rudrangshu Mukhrjee (Ed.), *Great Speeches of Modern India*, Random House India, 2007, p. 201.
137. (op. cit. p. 201).
138. op. cit. p. 201.
139. op. cit. pp. 203-04.
140. Sir John Malcolm, *Central India*, vol. I, p. 153.
141. Arnold, Caliphate, p. 22.
142. Niccoloi Manucci, *Storia do Mogor*, pp. 14-15 and 223.
143. *Dutch Embassy to the Court of Bahadur Shah*, Journal of Punjab Historical Society, vol. I, Pt. I, p. 21.
144. Cunningham, Joseph Davy, *A History of the Sikhs from the Origin of the Nation to the Battles of the Sutlej*, London, 1849 and S. Chand & Co., Delhi, 1966.
145. Sangat Singh, *The Sikhs in History*, Uncommon Books, New Delhi, 1966, p. 61

146. Guru Arjun (Ed.), *Adi Granth*, p. 654; ref. Kahan Singh, *Gurshabad Ratnakar Mahan Kosh*, Patiala, 1930, pp. 1117-18.
147. Senapat, *Sri Gur Sobha*, (Ed.) Ganda Singh, Patiala, 1967, p. 20.
148. ibid. p. 31.
149. Gordon, *The Sikhs*, London, 1905, p. 36.
150. *Maasir-i-Alamgiri*, p. 94; and also Gopal Singh, *A History of the Sikh People 1469-1978*, World Sikh University Press, New Delhi, 1979, p. 282.
151. Zafarnama, p. 18.
152. Zafarnama, p. 18.
153. Zafarnama, p. 4.
154. Zafarnama, p. 4.
155. Zafarnama, p. 47.
156. Zafarnama, p. 23.
157. Zafarnama, p. 19, 41 and 46.
158. Zafarnama, p. 39-40, 44.
159. Zafarnama, p. 62, 67.
160. Zafarnama, p. 66.
161. Zafarnama, p. 91.
162. D.K. Verma, *Guru Gobind Singh*, Harman Publishing House, New Delhi, 1985, p. 125-127.
163. C.H. Payne, *A Short History of the Sikhs*, London, n.d., p. 40.
164. G.S. Deol, *Banda Bahadur*, New Academic Publication Co., Jallandar, 1972, p. 51.
165. In Wheeler J.T., *Early Records of British India*, Calcutta, 1878, p. 180.
166. Payne, C.H., *A Short History of Sikhs*, London, n.d., p. 45.
167. Khushwant Singh, *A History of the Sikhs*, Princeton, 1963, p. 127.
168. Hari Ram Gupta, *History of the Sikhs*, vol. II, p. 255-56.
169. A.C. Das, *Rig-Veda Culture*, Calcutta, 1920, referred in Hukam Singh Pawar, *The Jats, their Origin, Antiquity and Migration*; Mamtha Publication, Rohtak, 1993, p. 214.
170. Jadunath Sarkar, 'Delhi During the Anarchy 1749-1788, as told in contemporary Records', Indian History Records Commission, vol. III, 1921, p. 4-5.
171. Abdur Rashid, 'History of the Muslims of Indo-Pakistan Sub-continent, 1707-1806', Research Society of Pakistan, University of Punjab, Lahore, 1978, p. 99.
172. Jadunath Sarkar, 'Najib-ud-Daulah as the Dictator of Delhi, 1761-1770', Islamic Culture, October, 1933, p. 613.
173. Dharma Bhanu, 'The Mughul-Maratha Treaty of April, 1752', The Proceedings of the Pakistan History Conference, 2nd Session, 1952, p. 360.
174. Quoted in A.F.M. Abdul Ali, 'Mahadhji Sindhia of Gwalior', Indian Historical Records Commission, Proceeding, vol. XII, 1929, p. 109.

4

Delhi Before and After the British Conquest

The British Raj began from 1858 to 1947 A.D. However, in 1803, the Marathas, who were protectors of Shah Alam II, were defeated in the war at Patparganj (Patpaarganj). Since then, the system of Residency started in Delhi. All these residents were under the overall control of the Governor General and later on under the Viceroys.

The following are the high British officials who ruled India:

Governors of Bengal

(a)	Lord Clive	1758–60 and 1765–7
(b)	Warren Hastings	1772–4

Governors General

(a)	Warren Hastings	1774–85	(Sir John Macpherson 1785–6)
(b)	Marquess Cornwallis	1786–93	
(c)	Sir John Shore, Lord Teignmouth	1793–8	(Sir Alured Clarke 1798)
(d)	Earl of Mornington, Marquess Wellesley	1798–1805	
(e)	Marquess Cornwallis, (Second time)	1805	(Sir George Barlow1805–07)
(f)	Earl of Minto	1807–13	
(g)	Earl of Moira, Marquess of Hastings	1814–23	(John Adam 1823)
(h)	Earl of Amherst	1823–8	(W. B. Bayley 1828)
(i)	Lord William Bentinck	1828–35	(Sir Charles Metcalfe 1835)
(j)	Earl of Auckland	1835–42	
(k)	Earl of Ellenborough	1842–4	
(l)	Viscount Hardinge	1844–8	
(m)	Marquess of Dalhousie	1848–56	
(n)	Earl of Canning	1856–8	

Governors General and Viceroys

(a) Earl of Canning 1858–62

(b)	Earl of Elgin	1862–3 (Sir Robert Napier of Magdala 1863) (Sir William Denison 1863)	
(c)	Lord Lawrence	1863–9	
(d)	Earl of Mayo	1869–72 (Sir John Strachey 1872) (Lord Napier of Merchistoun 1872)	
(e)	Earl of Northbrook	1872–6	
(f)	Earl of Lytton	1876–80	
(g)	Marquess of Ripon	1880–4	
(h)	Marquess of Dufferin	1884–8	
(i)	Marquess of Lansdowne	1888–94	
(j)	Earl of Elgin	1894–9	
(k)	Marquess Curzon	1899–1905 (Lord Ampthill 1904)	
(l)	Earl of Minto	1905–10	
(m)	Lord Hardinge of Penshurst	1910–16	(14) **Delhi** – The capital of India, which was shifted from 'Dilli' to Calcutta in 1858 A.D., reshifted to Delhi from Calcutta in December 1911 A.D. and the Civil Lines were made the location for the new city.
(n)	Vicount Chelmsford	1916–21	
(o)	Marquess of Reading	1921–6 (Earl of Lytton 1925–6)	
(p)	Lord Irwin, Earl of Halifax	1926–31 (Viscount Goschen 1929)	(15) **New Delhi**–Now onwards Dilli was termed as Delhi by the British. They ultimately decided to build and name New Delhi and Shahjahanabad was called as Old Delhi. New Delhi was inaugurated in 1931 A.D.
(q)	Marquess of Willingdon	1931–6 *(Hon. Sir George Stanley 1934–6)	
(r)	Marquess of Linlithgow	1936–43	
(s)	Earl Wavell	1943–7	
(t)	Earl Mountbatten	1947 (April to August 1947)	

* During the occasional interim periods between Viceroys or when they were on leave, the Government was administered by the Senior Governor of a Presidency or a senior member of Executive Council.

At the end of the thirteenth century, Marco-Polo visited southern India, he wrote, 'You must not suppose that the diamonds of the first water come to our countries of Christendom. Actually they are exported to the kings and noblemen of these various regions and realm (Coromandel Coast that extends down the eastern shore of the Indian Peninsula) for it is they who have the wealth to buy the costliest stones'.[1]

At this time, southern India was still Hindu. In the second part of the thireenth century, Normans set foot in England and, after two centuries, Normans and Anglo-Saxons merged to form one nation and one culture but, in India at the same time, Muslim invaders thrust through the North-West passes into the Indian plains and beyond. Over the next five centuries in successive waves, the followers of the Prophet penetrated almost to Cape Comorian, the southern tip of the Indian Peninsula. In India, Muslims and Hindus never lost their separate identities, exhibiting so much more division in religion than in race. This fundamental divisiveness between its peoples, still bloodily apparent so many centuries later, virtually affected the social structure of India and needs to be taken into account when considering the impact subsequently made by the Europeans.

In 1526 A.D., Babar overthrew the ruling Afghan dynasty and entered into fragmented India, which was ruled by independent kingdoms, most of the Muslim kings reigning over subjects who clung to their ancient Hindu beliefs. Only in Rajasthan to the west and south of Delhi and the south of the Deccan Hindu Princes still ruled over independent realms. Before Babur died, he had conquered the kingdom of Delhi, the Hindu Princes of Rajputana paid him tribute and all Hindustan proper, up to the borders of Bengal in the east, acknowledged his authority. Only four great kingdoms beyond Narmada river remained unsubdued—the Muslim kingdoms of Ahmadnagar and Bijapur, in the west Golconda in the East, and the Hindu realm on Vijyanagar in the South.

At this time, the social structure of India was different to that of sixteenth century Europe. Most of the inhabitants lived in self-sufficient villages. Even before Babur established a Mughal Empire in India, tall masted European ships had cast anchor off the west coast of the Deccan. In 1498, Vasco da Gama circumnavigated Africa and, sailing across the Indian Ocean came to the sea port of Calicut. The ruler of this province who was a Hindu and was known as the Zamorin, welcomed him just, but the Arab traders who had already established themselves earlier in this province platted and later this friendship turned into open hostility. He went to Portugal and revealed the rich harvest waiting to be garnered in the East. Soon, fresh Portuguese fleets were sailing for the West coast of India.

After blows with Zamorin, the Portuguese were welcomed by the Raja of Cochin, who wanted to get rid of Zamorin. Cochin was better than Calicut, a profitable trade between Portugal and India began to spring up.

In 1507 A.D., the Portuguese sailed to India with twenty two vessels, carrying 1,500 men under the command of Don Francisco Almeida. They sought conqest as much as trade. The Portuguese entered into an alliance with the Raja of Cochin and waged a vigorous war against the Zamorin. The merchants of Venice helped the Sultan of Egypt to crush the Portuguese as they were their rival in trade.

The Portuguese under Almeida defeated the Egyptian fleet, but Almeida's personal triumph was short lived; owing to an intrigue in Portugal—he was abruptly superseded by Don Alphonso da Albuquerque, a man of outstanding ability. Under his command the Portuguese achieved complete supremacy at sea, a supremacy they consolidated by keeping a permanent naval presence in the Indian Ocean. He seized Aden, Ormuz, Malacca in Malaya, and captured Goa, and made it the capital of the Portuguese in India. Comparing the limited manpower of the Portuguese with the vast number of Indians, he tried to breed a race of Portuguese Indians to support the new empire he intended to create, and encouraged his men to take Indian wives, a policy they adopted with no little alacrity.[2]

The Failure of Shah Alam II, First Expedition to Delhi, 1765–6

After the battle of Panipat, (1761) Ahmad Shah Abdali nominated Ali Gauhar (a fugitive Prince), the son of murdered Alamgir II, as the Emperor of Delhi, who later titled him as Shah Alam II. The third battle of Panipat did not achieve its objective of re-establishing a centralized Islamic authority; it simply expelled the Marathas temporarily from upper India. Shuja-ud-Daulah was appointed Wazir and Najib-ud-Daulah as Amir-al-Umrah; became regents of Delhi. Ghazi-ud-Din disappeared from political life but lingered in obscurity till 1800. From 1761 to 1771, the capital (Delhi) was without a king. After Shah Alam's unsuccessful effort against the British at Buxar (1764), he settled down as their pensioner at Allahabad and did not return to Delhi till 6 January 1772. The Maratha's were instrumental in rescuing Shah Alam II in Delhi, but no Maratha chief really dominated the Mughal court until 1789, when Mahadhji Shinde took control. Shah Alam II resided at Allahabad for nearly six years and was given a pension of Rs. 26 lakh and the districts of Kara and Allahabad. He always looked upon to regain his ancestral throne and capital with which was associated, the sovereignty of the whole of the subcontinent of India.

Despite a fixed income and British protection, he was, at Allahabad, practically nothing more than a dignified royal pensioner, living in an atmosphere of suspicion, with no real power of even choosing his own ministers, to say nothing of the liberty of following a home or foreign policy—independent of the English. Shuja-ud-Daulah was forced upon him as his Chief Minister, against his pronounced wish, by Clive in 1766 and he was compelled to remove his own son from *wizarat*. In 1768, the Wazir was given full powers, despite the opposition of Shah Alam II. Kerelst, the successor of Clive, also supported this policy. Clive had promised Shah Alam II to give him protection and assistance to procure his throne, but was prolonging it. In fact, the British policy aimed at using every persuasion and argument to prolong indefinitely the imperial stay at Allahabad, as it was of great political advantage to the company.

In 1765, Shah Alam II desired to leave Allahabad for Delhi; he also received a letter from Najib-ud-Daulah that the Sikhs were intending to occupy the capital and the honor and safety of the imperial ladies was at stake and that his presence was required. Shah Alam II also conducted correspondence and negotiations with the Marathas. The help of the Marathas was not liked by the British as it was not in their interests and it also might threaten the security of Shuja-ud-Daulah.

Shah Alam took pains to assure the Governor that his march was intended only as far as Kara Jahanabad from where he would return after he had conquered the Agra fort from the Jats with Maratha assistance, and that he had no desire whatever of instigating the Marathas to invade Shuja-ud-Daulah's country. There is no doubt that the Emperor wanted to capture the Agra fort[3] but that was only a part of his scheme which aimed at the recovery of the Delhi throne.[4]

Along with 5,000 troops of the British, he arrived in the neighborhood of Kora, near Fatehpur, on the Yamuna. He started negotiation with Malhar Rao; in fact Shah Alam II wanted the united help of the Marathas, Shuja-ud-Daulah and the British to get his throne. Shuja-ud-Daulah and the Marathas agreed to this proposal but the British declined. The Emperor called Smith, the British representative, who negotiated with a select committee at Calcutta, which refused and instead proposed that the English escort him to Delhi "after the rains"—a promise never intended to be fulfilled—and the helpless Shah Alam II had no alterative but to return to Allahabad early in April 1766. He sent an envoy to the King in England.

In 1767, the Sikhs invaded the Doab and came as far as Nanouth. The Sikhs were defeated by Najib-ud-Daulah, but he had the disadvantage of old age, and henceforth raids from Punjab became so frequent that no count could be possibly kept of their numbers. In 1770 the Marathas again appeared in North India and Najib-ud-Daulah, knowing it fully well that he could not fight alone with the Marathas and that it was not possible to get help from outside, he allied with the Marathas, hoping to secure the return of Shah-Alam to his capital through them. He died on 31 October 1770.

Now, to return to Delhi became urgent for political and dynastic reasons for the Emperor. The English, the Jats, the Rohilas and Shuja-ud-Din were indifferent or unhappy about the emperor's natural desire to return to the Imperial capital.

On 9 February 1771, the Marathas, with whom Shah-Alam had been in negotiations for his restoration at Delhi, bombarded it and captured it. Zabita Khan, Najib's son, for fear of the Marathas, had left Delhi and returned to his Jagir. The Marathas made over Delhi to the Emperor's heir and quit the capital on 2 August 1771. Shah Alam left Allahabad on 13 April 1771 and entered Delhi on 6 January 1772, on the eve of Id-ul-Fitr.

Ahmed Shah Abdali also died on 13 April, 1772. He was succeeded without the usual war of succession by his son Timur Shah.

Shahu held a coronation in January 1708 and he selected Balaji for the office of the Premier as the ablest individual among his followers, devoted to his cause and capable of safeguarding the national interests. Shahu's release from Mughal captivity started a civil war, so conveniently planned by the dying Emperor. The long and successful War of Iindependence had infused a new war-like spirit among the rousing Maratha bands, who would surely have ruined their own country by taking opposite sides in the civil war if no new work had been supplied for their rising ambitions outside. Unlike Shahu, Shivaji considered himself a loyal vassal and supporter of the Mogul Empire, against which he would refuse to rise in open arms. Balaji, grasping these conflicting demands of the situation, with the shrewd foresight of a politician, created a useful diversion by engaging to employ Maratha arms in the Mogul court, thus covertly contriving to put an end to the disastrous civil war. He had already managed to silence the scheming Tarabai by getting her imprisoned through the instrumentality of her step-son, Sambhaji. Peshwa Vishwanath, from 1680 to 1710 cemented the friendship with the Rajput states of North India. His son Baji Rao also pursued this policy ably. In 1749, on 15 December, Shahu died; he made Balaji his real successor. Balaji, while cementing the state power, also created some blunders such as deliberately destroying the Angria's naval power with the help of the British and leaving the handling of North Indian officers, for eight years, in the hands of his incapable and inexperienced brother, Raghoba, which ultimately resulted in the disaster of Panipat. Baji Rao II's misrule and his presentation of the Chhatrapati cost him high his position and the British writers of those days found it convenient to denounce all the Peshwas as traitors to their masters, so as to defend their own assumption of power and justify their position as saviors of the situation.

Shortly after his assumption of kingship, Narayan Rao the fifth Peshwa, was murdered in 1772 during the scramble for the Peshwaship which followed. Mahadhji Scindia seized the occasion to extend his power and played an important part in the civil onslaught. In the year 1775, when Raghunath Rao, the uncle of the late Peshwa (better known as Raghoba), claimed for himself the post of Peshwa under the aid of the East India Company, Nana Fadnavis, the Minister of the then infant Peshwa, Madhu Narain Rao, invoked the help of the French. In the struggle, Mahadhji Scindia was the Chief supporter of the party of Nana Fadnavis.

The East India Company wanted to enter into an agreement with Mahadhji Scindia but failed as the terms of the agreement (at Wargaon 1779) was not favorable to Scindia.

The failure of the convention of Wargaon led to the First Maratha war in

1779 and soon the East India Company come in touch with the court of Mahadhji Scindia. In this war, the series of reverses, which Mahadhji Scindia sustained at the hands of Generals J. Comal and T. Goddard during 1779 to 1780, led him to appreciate the strength and discipline of this new power which had now entered into the arena of India politics. The capture of the fort of Gwalior by Major William Popham destroyed the morale of Scindia's troops as the fort was considered impregnable so far. A treaty of neutrality was signed by Scindia and status quo was restored.

On 17 May 1782 at Salbai, Mahadhji Scindia represented the Minister (Nana Fadnavis) and David Anderson, the East India Company (or Warren Hastings). This treaty not only brought about amicable political relations between the East India Company and the Scindia Darbar, but also initiated a healthy commercial relationship as well. Another treaty to clear the doubts of the earlier treaty was concluded and it was called the Treaty of Gwalior, on 26 April 1783.

During the closing years of Mahadhji Scindia's rule, his glory was at its zenith. He would be the virtual head of the Maharatha people and the ruler of the greatest part of India. He would be the Captain-General of the united forces of the Indian princes against the foreign intruders who threatened to absorb all India in their ever-growing Empire. He would bring under one standard the scattered horsemen and French Contingent of Tipu Sultan, the powerful artillery of the Nizam, the whole force of the Rajputs, and every spear which his influence could have collected from the Maratha confederacy and, at the head of these combined forces, fight the great battle of Hindu independence and would thus wipe out the disgrace of the third battle of Panipat. But such things were not destined to be. At Wanauli he was suddenly attacked with violent fever and died on 12 February, 1794.

At Delhi, anarchy started from the invasions of Nadir Shah in 1739 and intensified with the invasions of Ahmad Shah Abdali. The last Emperor, who deserved this title was Mohammad Shah who died in 1748. From 1749 to 1788, the anarchy prevailed in Delhi and its environs. In 1788, the Sindhias established their authority which lasted till 1803.

From 1749 to 1788, there was someone or the other calling himself Badshah, but he was never his own master, and still less the master of the provinces of the Empire. The city of Delhi was not under the control of this Badshah, but under the control of his keeper; or divided between rivals fighting for the position of his keeper. It was a direct negation of government, because a government implies an orderly state and habitual obedience paid by the people to the orders of a sovereign. The British did not come suddenly to Delhi as rulers; they became rulers of Delhi and India due to our own weakness and the rivalry of rulers and the prevailing conditions and the long suffering of the masses. There was no national outlook and strength to maintain internal law and order. Let us see in chronological order how the events happened and how a smooth way was cleared for the British.

From 1749 to 1788, is the saddest period in our history.

> It was a period marked by frequent bloody fights between rival nobles claiming the supreme control over the state, street brawls by solders mutinying for arrears of pay or between soldiers of different races who had quarreled in the Bazar. The Emperor was timid and imbecile, defeating the efforts his best friends by listening to base flattered and corrupt ministers for his pleasures, and vanity trying to recover his power by means of low and cowardly intrigue, such as creating a new Wazir for an old one or setting up his Commander-in-Chief (Bakhshi) against his Chancellor (Wazir) in the control of the imperial court and the nominal army of the Empire. The heir of the mighty Timur had fallen very low indeed, when he could not think of achieving his own emancipation by manly exertion or a manlier death. Delhi during these forty years is a sickening and monotonous tale of sack by Afghans and Marathas, Sikhs and Jats, even Gujjars and Pindaris; frequent panic among the citizens whenever only such attack was expected, the flight of the rich, the closing of the shops, the looting of the unprotected houses by the ruffians of the city population who took advantage of the public alarm and confusion; the utter spoliation of the peasantry and ruin of the surrounding villages by organized hands of brigands or soldiers out foraging, and consequent famine prices in the capital, the incurable intrigue, inefficiency and moral decay of the Imperial courts, culminating in the crowning agony of Ghulam Qudir's capture of the palace, outrage on the Emperor's family and blinding of Shah Alam II. The peasantries were so exasperated by their sufferings and the failure of the state to protect their life and property that they naturally regarded all strangers and even the forces of the crown as their enemy.[5]

A manuscript, which Jadunath Sarkar had got from Patna, narrates the following:

"On 14 March 1753 at night there was a tumult in the fort, on 17 March there was a tumult in the day time.

On 6 May 1753, the Jats and other people plunder the inhabitants of the old city in the neighborhood of Lal Darwaza at the instigation of Safdar Jang. On 12 June the role of Wazir was conferred on Intizam-ud-Daulah, who replaced Safdar Jang; for one prahar and a half a tumult raged, and the Jats and other classes looted the old city. Fight between Safdar Jung and the Bakhshi-ul-Mulk; Faridabad looted.

On 4 June 1754, a rumour spread that the Emperor was being deposed by the Wazir. A tumult broke out; the men of old Delhi fled from their houses and their property was looted.

Afghan troops burn Faridabad, cut off the heads of six or seven hundred poor people and bring them to Ahmad Shah Abdali, representing them to be the heads of Marathas killed in battle. The Abdali pays a reward of Rs. 8 per head.

In 1757, the Emperor walks from the harem to the mosque on foot for want of any conveyance or horse. The Rohillas loot Jaswantpura and some other wards.

In 1759, the Marathas loot Nizam-ud-Din Auliya Dargah and its houses and seize the men of the city for ransom.

The armies maintained by the imperial government and the nobles included many different races such as Jats, North Indian Muslims, Purbians or Awadh Hindus, Rajputs, Badakhshis his (men of Central Asia) Rohillas, Mughals (by which the Persians were designated) and Telingas (or European drilled Sepoys), and this diversity of rows did not contribute to the peace of the city.

On 20 September 1753, some soldiers got inside the fort and created a row for arrears of pay. They closed the treasury's office and the gates of the Begum's residence, and the Emperor himself had to come to the Diwane-Aam to pacify them.

On 13 February 1754, the soldiers who were sitting in the Qudsia's Masque for arrears of pay, created a tumult, prevented people from going to the fort and snatched away the turbans of the way farers and visitors to the Mosque, thus closing the public roads. The Wazir promised to pay them on Saturday next.

In April, 1754, the Badkhshis rose in violence, demanding their pay lighting the fuses of their matchlocks, they advanced to arrest the Emperor, the Wazir encountered them, the fort-guns also played on them. At last the Wazir triumphed, but the Khas Bazar and Khari Baoli were burnt. In June, 1754 the artillery men had meeting for arrears and closed the fort gates. The Wazir expels them.

In another event, the gunmen of the Wazir fought for arrears of pay. The shops near the Lahore Gate were looted and burnt; again soldiers stopped the burial of the Mir Bakhshi (Paymaster General) Khan-i-Dauran, demanding payment of their arrears. In 1776, Majid-ud-Daulah, the Emperor's favorite paltan of Bhawani Singh and Gangaram were on the road near Delhi Gate and were kept confined in the Mosque of Raushan-ud-Daulah. He was released next day at night, on giving security for the payment of their outstanding salaries.

In 1787, Telingas mutiny for arrears of pay. Tumult rages for two days in Deshmukh's camp. Three hours before sunset, the noise of muskets and artillery firing begins to be heard, one hundred men are slain and wounded on the two sides taken together.

In 1765, a Sikh raid was expected; it was proclaimed that none should leave the city of Delhi to make a pilgrimage to Kalika Devi temple.

In 1770, the Marathas burnt the villages near Sikandrabad from which the inhabitants had fled in panic. At midnight the Gujars burnt Sargani and Shahdara.

In 1773, the Sikh looted Shahdara till midnight and carry off 50 bags. They leave four hours before down. Thereafter in the very night the Gujars looted it.

In 1782, Sikhs from Kol (Aligarh) encamped at Burari, set fire to Malkaganj and Sabzi Mandi, and slayed the men of Mughalpura (now part of Arya Pura). The men of the city flee into the fort in terror.

Another year, no lamp lighted in any house up to Faridabad. The Jats looted the caravans of fugitives. Near Faridabad 2,000 corpses lie exposed, and the Persian followers of the Abdali dig up the floors of the houses in that city.

Another year, a proclamation was made that Ahmad Shah Abdali would enter the city, no one should sit on the roof of any house to behold the procession, that none should appear in arms in any street, and that the shops should remain closed. The Abdali's followers standing on the sand bank loot the people who went out to forage, attacked the houses in many of the lanes, broke the doors open and looted the property. The shops and bazars remained closed on account of their oppression. For one month the citizens of Delhi lay in a protracted morbid agony at the rumours of the coming of the Abdali, who was fighting the Marathas at Kunj Pura. The Afghans leave Delhi, and the joy of a second life appears in the city."[5]

The agony of Delhi during these forty years of anarchy is not without its lessons, each living its own life in selfish isolation, taking no thought of the interests of the country as a whole, robbing and devastating its neighbors in this common fatherland of us all as remorselessly as foreigners from beyond the frontier. Our leaders and chieftains were without foresight or the larger patriotism, but seeking only the aggrandizement of their families or clans. The central government was paralyzed. There was no federal army or treasury for India as a whole capable of repelling foreign invasions and maintaining internal order. Personal selfishness and parochial patriotism divided India. The result was the weakness of the country as a whole, the agony of forty years, and finally foreign conquest—which last came as a relief to the long-suffering masses.[6]

The economic condition of the Emperor was not good. This can be gauged from the letter of Shah Alam written to King George III of England, in which, besides containing a reiteration of the Emperor's grievances regarding the non-payment of the Bengal tribute, there is a request for the payment of the dues of the part amounting to one crore and sixty-eighth lakh of rupees. There is a note of confidence, and an implied threat at the end of the letter; it also depicts the political and economic conditions of the country.[7]

In December 1787, Shah Alam relieved Mirza Jawan Bakht (Jahandar Shah) from important duties after discovering that he was plotting to seize the throne and appointed him as the Subedar of unconquered Agra Province.

Jahandar Shah left Agra in disgust and proceeded towards the British territory. Lord Cornwallis promised to give him asylum in Raj Mahal in Bihar, but the building of Raj Mahal was declared to be unsafe for the Prince, and he was asked to reside in Banaras. On 31 May 1788, he proceeded to Chunargarh early in the morning to pay a visit to the tomb of one of his wives and returned the same evening. Next day, he died; according to Abu Talib he died of cholera. He had pronounced that, in case of his death, if the Emperor should send for the members of his family, they must not he sent to Delhi and the allowance that was paid to him should be continued to his wife, His successors were not invited in the matters of allowances and the property. The two sons left Banaras and resided in Lucknow. The pension and property dispute continued for long. Meanwhile, the eldest wife of Jahandar Shah, Qutluq Sultan Begum, died in 1818.[8]

The royal family had become very destitute.

In 1778, Sikh Chiefs, camping near the Shalimar Bagh demolished a mosque at Rakab Ganj and built a Gurudwara on the sport as the remains of Guru Tegh Bahadur were found in a pot at this palace. Lakhi Shah Banjara had brought the remains from Kotwali. The Seventh and Eighth Gurus stayed at Raja Jai Singh's House, so Gurudwara Bangla Sahib was built at that place.

During this period the treasury was empty, the troops were not receiving their pay and the terrible 'Chalisa' famine aggravated matters so much that no revenue was forthcoming. The regent was unable to pay even the Emperor's monthly expenses.

There is considerable evidence to suggest that Delhi, at this time was also unusually pestilential. There were illness and premature death, even in the imperial family. Probably the water was infected; the old irrigation system of the Persian genius, Ali Mardan Khan, had fallen into disrepair and was chocked at many places.

Mirza Najaf Khan, the Wazir, was a noble person, but in the company of Lutafat, who was a eunuch and had 'married' a dancing woman, Najaf Khan plunged into debauchery, business was abandoned to his Kashmiri Diwans. Afrasiyab controlled Najaf's domestic finance. The Emperor's Privy Purse, the allowances of the Princes, the Princesses, the Begums, and the salatins, fell into arrears. On one occasion, the princesses protested that they would join hands and jump into the Yamuna to end their lives of humiliation. The shopkeepers of Delhi stopped their credit, and Shah Alam, ' Emperor of the World', moaned that the humiliation was insufferable. With characteristic hyperbole, he declared to Maulvi Ataullah that he had no second coat left in his wardrobe.[9]

Latafat and Afrasiyab helped themselves to the coffers of the degraded Mughal state. The Jaipur state and the house of Mirza Raja Jai Singh and its condition were no better than the Mughal House.

Shuja-ud-Daulah had died and was succeeded by Asaf-ud-Daulah in 1775. Asaf was even more spoilt than his father and his administration was capricious. The treasury was further emptied for the expedition against Jaipur and the Sikhs; ultimately, as usual the Mughals conceded the Maratha claims in the Deccan, the empire succumbed to the Sikhs. The English had already swallowed Bengal with its dependencies of Bihar and Orissa. The Nawab of Awadh was their puppet.

The death of Peshwa Madhav Rao in 1772 had been the signal for civil war; Raghunath Rao staked a claim for Peshwaship.

English had already seized the entire Andhra coastline and they were in the process of swallowing up Mysore; Salsatte and Bassein had been ceded to them at the outset. Goddard swept through Malwa; the fort of Gwalior, considered impregnable, was taken by surprise and a treaty was signed by Mahadhji Sindhia with the British. After the departure from Allahabad, Shah Alam was not paid the Bengal tribute, for which he had written to Clive at Calcutta many times and to George III in England but, at the last, the English pretended that, since Shah Alam had left against their advice, they were justified in withholding the tribute.

On 2 May, 1781, the Emperor designated Prince Akbar Shah as his heir with great pomp and ceremony. Only four months later, Farkhunda Bakht, a much loved Shahzada died. He had been a scholar. The same night, his infant daughter passed away.

On 11 June 1781, a fearful dust storm of unusual violence was followed by an earthquake; a meteor fell near Jhajjar. By then, it was also clear that the regent was on his deathbed. He lingered for some months until 6 April 1782 when he breathed his last. After the death of Najib, the struggle for the office of regent started: on one side were Afrasiyab, Najaf Quli, Lutafat and Abdul Ahad and, on the other, Mirza Shafi, Begum Khadija (sister of Najib) and the soldiers of the absent Hamdani. Initially, the religious subsectional angle of Shia and Sunni also played a role.

Mirza Shafi was killed on 23 September 1783 by Hamdani and his associates and the Emperor was again without a Keeper. Afrasiyab's complicity was suspected in the murder of Shafi. However, he was called to Delhi to take charge of the position of Keeper. On 14 April 1784 occurred the curious flight of Mirza Jawan Bakht. Nothing illustrates so well the vacuity of life in the Qila-i-Maulla as this incident. Twenty five years earlier, his father, the young Shah-Alam, had also fled Delhi, but the circumstances on that occasion were entirely different. During the long years of his father's exile he had deputized for him in the Qila-i-Maulla (Red Fort). The real master was Najib and he, merely a puppet. He expected a change in life after Shah Alam's return to Delhi, but life seemed to have got set in a standard format. And it seemed that these substituted Wazirs had great difficulty in governing what remained of the Empire of Delhi. Indeed, words like Empire, Badshah or Emperor sounded embarrassingly pretentious for the shrunken realm of Badshah Shah Alam.

The Prince wanted to get the support of the British but could not succeed. He eventually did return in 1787 but not before Ghulam Qadir had blinded his father. He was thus again entrusted with the role of being his father's deputy but, failing to receive the necessary support, he left, and died at Banaras on 1 June 1788. It was his younger brother who was ultimately destined to sit on their father's throne.

The four successors to the heritage of Mirza Najaf, Afrasiyab Khan and Mirza Shafi were dead while Hamadani's power had been destroyed (by the Marathas). Najaf Quli alone survived, but he was dissipating himself in drink and debauchery. Now the road was wide open for Scindia as he was the master of most of North India.

It had long been the desire of Mahadhji Scindia to take the Emperor under his protection. In 1772, he escorted Shah Alam to Delhi from Allahabad. But the death of Peshwa Madhav Rao forced him to withdraw from Delhi; he got entangled at Poona and Gwalior. He also had to pay a large amount to his troops. So he wanted some such opportunity from where he could acquire money as well as prestige. Shah Alam after various trials, thought of Mahadhji Scindia. He appealed to Scindia to come to his help. In 1785 Scindia become the regent, but found many financial, administrative and military hurdles. Scindia, after becoming the regent, could not get the amount required from Aligarh and Jaipur; rather his forces were repulsed at Lalsot near Jaipur. Some of his soldiers, on account of the non-payment of their dues, joined the Rajput forces. His old distrust of 'Hindustanis' was confirmed.[10] The battle of Lalsot/Tunga near Jaipur could not give any good results to Scindia, rather, the rumour of the debacle reached the imperial court. The Emperor was planning to replace him. Ghulam Qadir, son of Zabita Khan, had nursed and abided a grudge against the imperial house. Ambaji Ingle was called by Mahadhji Scindia for his help. In Delhi at this time Ladoji Deshmukh Sithole and Shah Nizam-ud-Din were there from Scindia's side, they were not the soldiers. Ghulam Qadir took advantage of this time; he had some supporters in the Royal harem like Mansur Ali Khan, harem Nazir, a eunuch and some royal aspirants for the throne. Imad-ul-Mulk had placed Alamgir II on the throne after murdering

Ahmad Shah in 1762. Secondly, Shah Alam had some private assets with him from Allahabad, which he never spent on salatins; even when they were crying like beasts.

Thirdly, the Begums Malika-i-Zamani and Sahiba Mahal, Mohammad Shah's windows, who lived in ample comfort in mansions outside the fort, were ready to pay Rs. 12 lakh to Ghulam Qadir if their grandson Bidar Bakht was restored to the throne.

The triumph of the two dowagers, Malika-i-Zamani and Sahiba Mahal was short lived. Ghulam Qadir now demanded the price for the enthronement of their grandson. The old ladies protested that he had already realized much more from the plunder of the palace. The old ladies were subjected to insults.

On 10 August 1788, Shah Alam was dragged out from his cell; Rohilla threw him down and gouged out his eyes and walked away with a parting kick at the bleeding old man. For two days, no one was allowed to approach Shah Alam.

Ghulam Qadir not only looted the fort and its inhabitants but also took away one of the cupolas of Jama Masjid. He sent out his looted treasure and baggage to Ghausgarh, but much of it was plundered on the way by Sikhs, Marathas and Gujars.

On 18 December, while taking shelter in Bamrauli near Shamli (in Meerut District) he was caught by Maratha forces. His eyes were also taken out and sent to Shah Alam. His head was cut later. It is not known where he was buried. During his period, the salaries of the traditional *fauj* of Indian generals were, even in the best of times, heavily in arrears.

About this time armies of most Indian Princes and Generals could be divided into two distinct divisions, the European trained and officered *paltan* and *campoo* and the native fauj.

At the end of the eighteenth century, India was an exhausted country, incapable of producing men of mettle. Haidar Ali, Tipu Sultan and Ranjit Singh were exceptions to some extent.

Scindia was bankrupt; so were his masters. The Peshwa, Nana Fadnavis had full control over the infant Peshwa. Holkar and Scindhia were having great enmity among themselves. Everything was rotten; the ruling class, the Princes and the Umrahs, and their petty accountants, Serishtadars and Karkoons, all had been corrupted to the hilt. The soldiers were not getting their pay regularly; they were deserting and joining the bandits in order to survive.

In 1763, Suraj Mal, a Jat ruler was killed. In 1770, Najib-ud-Daulah died; In 1774 Ahmad Shah Durrani died. In 1782 Najaf Khan died. It was he, who conferred the Jagir of Sardhana on Walter Reinhardt "the Sombre his wife Begum Samru managed it later and took active part in the affairs of

Delhi. In 1785 Zabita Khan died and Ghulam Qadir succeeded his estate. In 1788 Shah Alam was blinded and in 1789 he again was restored to the throne of Delhi. Mahadhji Scindia died in 1794, Daulat Rao Scindia succeeded him, De Boigne, and the Maratha General was replaced by Pearson in 1795.

By now, the East India Company, a private firm was permitted to do trade; now submitted to state control, and was the representative of the British nation. "Between their territories and those nominally under the sway of the Mughal king there was nothing but an imaginary and weak frontier, insufficient to hold back those who had the power, and who could not be expected for ever to refrain from using it."[11]

On 31 December 1802, the Peshwa made a treaty of Bassein with the East Indian Company and placed his fortunes in the hands of East Indian Company; and the chiefs of Daulat Rao Scindia, the Raja of Berar, Jaswant Rao Holkar and others were still independent. The territory around Delhi was held in Jagir by M. Pearson. Napoleon had invaded Egypt and it was feared that he might also invade India, the British were apprehensive of it. Shah Alam was practically in French hands, and his name might be implicated in causing a rising against the English.

On 11 September 1803, refusing to declare his intentions Lord Wellesley gave orders to advance against him. In the middle of the monsoon, after a

British Memorial of 1803 in Golf Course, NOIDA.

rapid advance from Kanpur and Fateh Garh, the capture of the fortress of Aligarh, General Lake appeared before Delhi, near the village of Patparganj. In this battle, the Maratha troops, under the command of M. Louis Bourquein, were defeated by General Lake and as a result of the action, the city of Delhi and, the Mughal Emperor, Shah Alam, passed under the British supremacy.

The battle was fought in the tract between the rivers *Hindan* and Yamuna to the south-east of Delhi, the exact site on which the engagement took place was near the village of Sadarpur or Chhalera.

There is a monument and inscription at that place; the original one was replaced in 1899. The inscription now runs:

> Sacred to the memory of the under mentioned gallant officers.
>
> Major Middleton 3rd Regiment Native Cavalry, Capt. McGregor, Persian Interpreter. Lieut. Hill, 2nd Battalion 12 Native Infantry. Lieut. Preston, 2nd Battalion 15th Native Infantry, Cornet Sanguine 27th Dragoons "Quarter Master Richardson 27th Dragoons.[12]

The British force consisted of H.M. 27th Dragoons and 76th Foot, two regiments of Native Cavalry and seven of Native Infantry or four thousand and nine hundred men in all. It was relatively small, but the troops were excellent; the capable general and the result of a long march and action from 3.00 am to 7.00 pm completed the rout of the Marathas. Sixty-eight guns were captured and the British loss was 461 killed and wounded. M. Bourquain plundered the city and made off, but surrendered subsequently. On 14 September 1803, the head of the British force entered Delhi. Two days later, General Lake had an interview with the old blind king in the Diwan-i-Khas, receiving from him the insignia of second noble of the new imaginary Mughal Empire; the first was Daulat Rao Scindia.

As a special distinction, the Governor-General presented an honorary colour to each regiment which had been engaged in the battle; Rs. 4,000 left by M. Drugeon were distributed among the troops as prize money.

Lt. Colonel Ochterlony, commanding the 2nd/12th B.N.1, which had fought at Plassey and Dy Adjutant General of the company's troops, was appointment Resident at Delhi.

In 1805, it was settled that Shah Alam should received a monthly allowance from East India Company of 60 thousand rupees, and to other relatives Rs. 30 thousand rupees per mensem and rupees 10 thousand on the occasion of certain festivals annually. No death sentence was to be passed on the citizens of the city without the sanction of the King. Sentences of mutilation were to be commuted at the rate of five years imprisonment for each limb. He was exempted from the jurisdiction of local courts.

In 1805, Marquis Cornwallis, sent out for the second time as Governor –

General in place of Lord Wellesley and with orders to 'stop the war' as Lord Lake was pursuing against Holkar but Lord lake did not agree with it. Lord Cornwallis died soon; he was replaced by Sir George Barlow. On 7 January 1806 at Amritsar a treaty was signed between Holkar and Lord Lake. In 1806 Shah Alam died and was buried in the royal enclosure, near the Shrine of Bakhtiyar Kaki at Mehrauli.

He was succeeded by his son Akbar Shah II. He had fewer powers than his father had enjoyed. In 1808 his son Mirza Jahangir fired a pistol at the British resident, Mr. Archibald Seton, and was removed to Allahabad. Akbar Shah had favoured him for succession instead of Abul Muzaffar (afterwards Bahadur Shah II), on whose sanity doubts were cast; investigation, however, proved that he was sane. In 1809, the allowances of his and his family were increased to one lakh rupees. He erected a balcony on the Mosaman Burj. In 1811, Charles Metcalfe put certain restrictions but coins were still continued to be struck in his name until the reign of William IV.

Generally it is presumed that the period from 1803–57 in the History of Delhi is the period without disturbance. The Mughal King and Princes were docile persons. However, even during this period, we come across events where bold spirits dared to challenge the might of British Empire. Mirza Jahangir, the third son of Akbar Shah was born in 1790 from Nawab Mumtaz Mahal. He was a very brave and daring youth, a fine marksman and a veteran rider. He had out witted many contemporary British officers in these exploits. These exploits of chivalry greatly displeased the British authorities. Repeated attempts made by the King to procure the sanction of the British Government to his nomination as *Wali Ahad* (Heir Apparent) proved quite futile.

Different versions have been made by various writers such as Bishop Hurber, Major Sleeman and Maulvi Zafar Hassan that Mirza was of a violent nature and wanted to kill his eldest brother who had annoyed the King. However, the fact is different for the banishment of the Prince to Allahabad. Mirza Jahangir used to keep daring troopers in the Red Fort which was not liked by the Resident, Mr. Seton. He asked the King to desist from the practice, but Mirza did not comply. He used to call the Resident Mr. Seton 'Lo Lo' (a bug-a ben figure dressed up to frighten children) in the open darbar of the King. There is a traditional song very popular among the old families of Delhi, which can be translated like:

> Why did Mirza call Seton Lo Lo?
> Red curtain hardly escaped being hit;
> Regiments came, Platoons Came;
> Red Curtain hardly escaped being hit;
> Why did Mirza call Seton Lo Lo?

On 20 July 1809, someone from the party of Mirza Jahangir fired at Seton, the Resident. They were prevented from entering the fort. The Resident complained to the King. Earlier, Mirza was banished to Allahabad, but after an undertaking given in writing he was allowed to reside in the fort. However, this time the resident was so furious that he asked his troops to fire. The king ultimately agreed for Mirza's banishment to Allahabad where he remained till the last. He did try to restore the power and position of the King but could not.

On return to Delhi on earlier occasion, the Mother of Mirza Jahangir went to the Dargah of Qutub-ud-Din Bakhtiar Kaki and from then a festival of Phool-walon-ki Sair started. After a brief interval during the partition of India it started again and every year Dargah of Bakhtiyar Kaki from it starts and ends at the temple of Yoga Maya.[13]

The British Residency at Delhi was set up in 1803. The most important duty of the Resident at that time was the management of British relations with the Mughal Emperor. John Hope has defined what resident used to be. He says,

> ...a resident is a man who has gained one of the richest prizes in the lottery of a public servant's career in India. He occupies in or near the capital of the native princes a splendid Mansion, which was erected and furnished at the expense of the supreme government receives a salary varying in amount, according to the

Mubarak Begum Mosque (Chawri Bazar) built by one of the wives of David Ochesterlony, the Resident of Delhi.

importance of the state from £5,000 to £10,000 a year and as the representative of the Governor-General, himself takes precedence at all ceremonials of everyone in the state, except the Maharaja (ruler). The most distinguished civilians and officers were selected for the office.[14]

After the defeat of the Marathas, Delhi was captured by the British in 1803. Col. (later Sir) David Ochesterlony held the post as First Resident at Delhi from 1803 to 1806. He was barely a year in office when Delhi was besieged by Jaswant Rao Holkar, who was repulsed after a gallant defense lasting nine days.

Delhi Residency and Agency 1803–57

1803–06	Col (later Sir) David Ochterlony
1806–10	Mr A. Seton
1810–18	Mr C.T. Metcalfe
1818–21	Sir David Ochterlony
Nov 1821–April 1822	Mr H. Middleton (Acting Charge)
May 1822–3	Mr A. Rose
1823	Mr William Fraser (For Few Months)
1823–5	Mr C. Elliot.
1825–7	Mr C.T. Metcalfe (As Resident Commissioner with control over Rajputana and to conduct foreign Relations with Kabul and Lahore
1827	Sir E. Colebrooke
1827	Mr William Fraser (For few weeks)
1827–30	Mr F. Hawkins
1830–2	Mr N.B. Martin. Agent at Delhi (Residency abolish and Rajputana Made a separate charge)
1832–5	Mr. William Fraser. (was murdered)
1835–3	Mr T.T. Metcalfe (Agent to the Governor, Agra. Later as Agent to the Lt Governor, N.W. Provinces)
1853-57	Mr. Siman Fraser (Agent to the Lt Governor N.W. Provinces and Commissioner, Delhi, Killed during the Mutiny on11 Mar 1857.

The following District Officers who have successively held charge of the District since annexation:

1.	Mr W. Clifford	14 September 1857	30 September 1857
2.	Sir Theophilus Metcalf	1 October 1857	22 November 1857
3.	Mr P.H. Egerton	23 November 1857	20 March 1860
4.	Mr W.C. Plowden	21 March 1860	30 April 1860
5.	Mr F.H. Cooper	1 May 1860	26 October 1860
6.	Lt F.C. Bewsher	27 October 1861	14 November 1861
7.	Major Stuart Graham	15 November 1861	16 February 1862
8.	Mr F.H. Cooper	17 February 1862	11 May 1863
9.	Mr T.H. Thornton	12 May 1863	2 October 1863

10.	Mr F.H. Cooper	3 October 1863	13 December 1863
11.	Mr T.H. Thornton	14 December 1863	27 May 1864
12.	Mr D. Fitzpatrick	3 October 1864	9 October 1864
13.	Captain C.A. MacMohan	10 October 1864	2 September 1865
14.	Lt A. Harcourt	2 September 1865	2 October 1865
15.	Captain C.A. MacMohan	3 October 1865	1 September 1866
16.	Mr T.W. Smyth	2 September 1866	1 October 1866
17.	Captain C.A. MacMohan	2 October 1866	22 February 1867
18.	Mr D. Fitzpatrick	22 February 1867	4 November 1868
19.	Major C.A. MacMohan	5 November 1868	5 September 1870
20.	Mr A.W. Stogdon	6 September 1870	20 October 1870
21.	Major C.A. MacMohan	21 October 1870	1 June 1871
22.	Mr G. Knox	2 June 1871	29 February 1872
23.	Mr A.H. Benton	1 March 1872	26 March 1872
24.	Major R.T.M. Lang	27 March 1872	27 May 1872
25.	Mr G. Knox	28 May 1872	10 December 1872
26.	Major C.A. MacMohan	11 December 1872	22 February 1873
27.	Mr W.M. Young	23 February 1873	11 March 1873
28.	Lt. Colonel R. Young	12 March 1873	15 June 1873
29.	Major Jas Tighe	16 June 1873	15 January 1874
30.	Mr J. Frizelle	16 January 1874	13 November 1874
31.	Mr T.W. Smyth	14 November 1874	5 May 1875
32.	Mr G.L. Smyth	6 May 1875	13 May 1875
33.	Mr T.W. Smyth	14 May 1875	19 August 1875
34.	Mr J. Frizelle	20 August 1875	30 September 1875
35.	Mr T.W. Smyth	1 October 1875	31 August 1876
36.	Captain C.H.T. Marshall	1 September 1876	30 September 1876
37.	Mr T.W. Smyth	1 October 1876	14 August 1877
38.	Mr A.W. Stogdon	15 August 1877	14 October 1877
39.	Mr T.W. Smyth	15 October 1877	15 April 1878
40.	Mr D.G. Barkley	16 April 1878	22 April 1878
41.	Mr George Smyth	23 April 1878	13 August 1878
42.	Lt Col F.M. Birch	14 August 1878	11 November 1878
43.	Mr G. Smyth	12 November 1878	1 September 1879
44.	Mr J.R. Maconnachie	2 September 1879	29 September 1879
45.	Mr G.Smyth	30 September 1879	14 November 1880
46.	Mr T.W. Smyth	15 November 1880	31 January 1882
47.	Mr G. Smyth	1 February 1882	23 March 1882
48.	Major A.S. Roberts	24 March 1882	18 April 1882
49.	Mr J.R. Drummond	19 April 1882	20 April 1882
50.	Mr T.W. Smyth	21 April 1882	17 July 1882
51.	Mr A.W. Stogdon	18 July 1882	6 October 1882
52.	Mr T. Troward	7 October 1882	17 December 1882
53.	Mr T.W. Smyth	18 December 1882	6 April 1883
54.	Mr G. Smyth	7 April 1883	9 October 1883
55.	Major W. J. Parker	10 October 1883	17 October 1883
56.	Mr J.W. Gardiner	18 October 1883	9 November 1883

57.	Mr G. Smyth	10 November 1883	15 July 1885
58.	Mr R. Clarke	26 July 1885	19 October 1885
59.	Mr G. Smyth	20 October 1885	21 August 1886
60.	Mr A. Meredith	22 August 1886	16 September 1886
61.	Mr G. Smyth	17 September 1886	5 December 1886
62.	Mr Denzil Ibbetson	6 December 1886	5 April 1887
63.	Mr E. O'Brien	6 April 1887	10 August 1887
64.	Mr W.R.H. Merk	11 August 1887	27 October 1887
65.	Mr R. Clarke	28 October 1887	14 July 1890
66.	Mr J.R. Drummond	15 July 1890	16 October 1890
67.	Mr R. Clarke	17 October 1890	16 September 1891
68.	Mr W. Chevis	17 September 1891	9 November 1891
69.	Mr R. Clarke	10 November 1891	6 August 1892
70.	Mr P.D. Agnew	7 August 1892	6 September 1892
71.	Mr R. Clarke	7 September 1892	11 March 1893
72.	Mr Alex. Anderson	12 March 1893	18 May 1893
73.	Mr R. Sykes	19 May 1893	10 July 1893
74.	Mr Alex. Anderson	11 July 1893	21 December 1893
75.	Lt Col C.F. Massy	22 December 1893	18 July 1894
76.	Mr J. G. Silcock	19 July 1894	9 November 1894
77.	Captain H.S.P. Davis	10 November 1894	2 August 1897
78.	Mr C.L. Dundas	3 August 1897	2 November 1897
79.	Captain H.S.P. Davis, (Major from 1st May 1898)	3 November 1897	19 July 1898
80.	Mr A. Langlay	20 July 1898	4 September 1898
81.	Major H.S.P. Davis	5 September 1898	26 March 1899
82.	Captain M.W. Douglas	27 March 1899	6 June 1900
83.	Mr T.P. Ellis	7 June 1900	6 July 1900
84.	Captain M.W. Douglas	7 July 1900	14 May 1901
85.	Captain R.M. Lowis	15 May 1901	14 June 1901
86.	Captain M.W. Douglas, (Major from 6th February 1902)	15 June 1901	25 March 1903
87.	Major F.E. Bradshaw	26 March 1903	23 November 1903
88.	Major C.G. Parsons	24 November 1903	7 July 1904
89.	Mr O. Lumsden	8 July 1904	20 October 1904
90.	Major C.G. Parsons	21 October 1904	20 October 1905
91.	Mr R. Humphreys	21 October 1905	5 June 1908
92.	Mr E. Burdon	6 June 1908	28 June 1908
93.	Mr R. Humphreys	29 June 1908	28 March 1909
94.	Mr C.A. Barron	29 March 1909	1 January 1912
95.	Major H.C. Beadon	2 January 1912	4 June 1912
96.	Mr S.M. Jacob	5 June 1912	1 October 1912
97.	Major H.C. Beadon	1 October 1912	Capital was shifted from Calcutta to Delhi.

Christians and Their Churches in Delhi

It is not easy to write a complicated and varied story within the limits of a few pages, without reducing it to a mere catalogue of events and missing sight of the wide variety of character and spiritual experiences of bishops, chaplains, missionaries and Indian Christians who, in fact, planted the Church of Christ on Indian soil, especially in Delhi.

The earliest Church in India is the Syrian Church, a branch of the Nestorian community, in Malabar. This community came to India in the fifth century A.D. The evangelization in India, now the old Malabar Church, have some 200,000 souls attached to it.

From Portugal in the fourteenth century, the Roman Catholic Church entered into the field of evangelization of India. It operated through Dominican and Franciscan orders. Christianity in India prospered with colonization, Vasco da Gama discovered the sea route to India in 1498 and on 25 November 1510, another Portuguese leader, Alfanso de Albuquerque, conquered Goa with this various priestly orders (Franciscans, Jesuits, the Dominicans and Augustinians) who arrived in India. The Mass conversions were possible in the remote villages of Goa, Madras and Kerala. (Priest Francis Xavier reached India in 1542 and the process of conversion started). The successors of Xavier's Jesuit order could not establish themselves in Northern India of course, they preached less rigid Christianity and in vernacular languages. They were more successful in tribal areas, such as Dadra, Nagar Haveli, Bastar, Ranchi and Andaman Islands; they concentrated more on education than on conversion. Tipu Sultan was against their activities in Mysore and they suffered due to his attitude, about 1784 he forcibly converted the people to Islam and deported a large number of Christians.

The Catholic Missions in northern India were not as successful as those of the south, but were established due to the tolerant attitude of Akbar and his successors. Myriam Begum, a Portuguese by birth, was one of the wives of Akbar. Efforts were made to translate the Christian religious literature into Persian to make the gospel understandable to the people. The Quran was also translated into Portuguese. During the famine in the valley of Kashmir in 1597, when the Jesuits accompanied Akbar, many mothers put their children on the road to die; these children were recovered and Baptized by the Christian priests.

During the rule of Jahangir, Sir Thomas Roe visited the Mughal Court but nothing was done to patronize the Jesuits. Shah Jahan was not a lover of Christianity. He distrusted the foreigners; he found in them a threat to the stability of his Empire. When Shah Jahan, as a prince, rebelled against his father, the Portuguese refused to help him. They also incurred the wrath of the Emperor when two slave girls were taken away by the Portuguese. In 1632,

Sagar Island was attacked and Christian captives were forcibly converted to Islam. During Aurangzeb's rule, the reimposition of jizya (tax) in 1679 made it impossible for non-Muslims to survive in his empire and Tukaram and others also influenced Hinduism. The second half of the seventeenth century was also not favorable for Christianity, due to political instability and the Mughal-Maratha conflict.

The Augustinians came in 1599 and Carmelites came to Goa in 1616 but found obstacles in establishing themselves.

When the East India Company acquired Bombay from the British crown in 1668, the Carmelites started their religious activities. English merchants built the first Church in 1675 in Madras, which was a village at that time.

In the seventeenth century, the European powers encroached on the Indian scene and established enclaves with an intention to stay. The Dutch expelled the Portuguese from the coast of Malabar and established their enclave. The French established themselves in the eighteenth century at Pondicherry. Seram Pur and Calcutta played an important part in spreading Christianity in India.

Protestant Missions to India came in the eighteenth century under the royal patronage of King Fredrick IV of Denmark. The arrival of the English coincided with the Dutch. The British East India Company came to India in 1600, but not until 1681 could the first English Church begin and, in 1708, the services of chaplains and school masters be put to regular footings. The Society for the Propagation of Christian Knowledge (S.P.C.K.) was established by Dr Thomas Bray in 1698 at Madras in 1720 at Guddalore, Calcutta, Trichinapally, Tinnevally and Tanjore. Baptist Mission Society (BMS) reached Calcutta in 1793. The London Missionary Society established in 1795 and sent its first Missionary, Nathaniel Forsyth, to India in 1798.

After 1813, the Mission Societies did not follow the pattern of colonization countries which did not have any colonial stakes in India and had also their missionary representatives in India, such as, the American Quakers, Unitarians, Presbyterians, Free Will Baptists, Methodists, the German and American Lutherans and the Canadian Baptists. These organizations worked through voluntary societies, with great earnestness, self-sacrifice and often with abundant blessings.[15]

Glancing through contemporary literature relating to the city of Delhi, it appears that the city was divided into Mohallas, Kuchas and Katras, signifying the racial and professional groups who lived therein. From Manrique's account, it seems that Delhi was an important centre for trade and industry from 1629–43. The accounts of Munshi Chandra Bhan Brahman[16] and Sujan Rai Bhandari[17] reports that the people of Turkey, Khurasan, Kabul, Zabulistan, Cathay, China, Zanzibar, Syria, England, Denmark, Yemen, Saudi-Arabia,

Iraq, Khotan ... and those of the provinces of India had already chosen to settle in Delhi.

The Europeans were employed in the department of artillery in the capacity of surgeons, physicians and joiners of bones. Their chiefs enjoyed the title of Farangi Khan and Francis Khan. There was a *mohalla* of *farangi*. This Mohalla was well-populated. It had a chapel in it. It was ruined during the invasion of Nadir Shah.[18]

In 1803, the British, under General Lake, defeated the Marathas at Aligarh and Patparganj. They defeated Bourquien, a French General of Marathas, and established British ascendancy in North India. Shah Alam had asked Lord Lake for protection and a formal treaty was concluded in 1805. The terms of the Marathas and the British were not different. Both gave the Emperor a pension, took over revenue administration, established an agent at court and retained a monopoly over the use of force. The relationship between the British and the Mughal ruler remained strained until 1858, when Bahadur Shah II was deposed and exiled.

The arrival of Lord Lake in 1803 immediately caused land values to double and it increased steadily. Before this it was not so, it may be to escape the taxation. North and South of Red Fort were occupied by British Army. Near Kashmiri Gate, a bazar was built, a hospital, accommodation for guns, stables were laid out, and two battalions were quartered in Daryaganj. Qamar-al-Din

Remains of the walls of the Mission Hall, Daryaganj.

Central Baptist Church, Chandni Chowk.

Grave of Master Ramchander, Nicholson Cemetry.

Khan's Mansion near Ajmeri Gate became the Custom House. A chapel was established in the Military area near the wall of Red Fort. Religious zeal was often noticed, but did not destroy the harmony. In the 1850's exited debates were held in Jama Masjid between Maulvis and Dr Pfander of the Church Missionary Society. The Resident did not prohibit all such debates and lecturers, as Wahabi, leader Shah Mohammad Ismail and Shah Abdul Aziz were also doing so. Shah Abdul Aziz, the son of Walliallah said that 'in this city (Delhi) the Imam-al-Muslimin wields no authority while the decrees of the Christian leaders are obeyed without fear'.[19]

Master Ram Chander (1821-1880)

Delhi Club in front of Red Fort.

The Baptist Missionary Society (from 1818) and the Society for the Propagation of the Gospel (from 1852) alienated the conservative people of Delhi with their activities, especially converting Master Ram Chander and Doctor Chaman Lal.

Master Ram Chander edited two Urdu newspapers published from Delhi the Fawaid-ul-Nazarin and the Kiran-us- Sadain. In July 1847, he published a translation of Macaulay's Minutes on education and commented sadly 'Dekhiye Hindustan ke Din Kab Phirenge' (Let us see when the great days of India will return).

Bishop Herber reached Agra on 11 January, 1825. There he met Abdul Mashie. Heber spoke of Abdul Mashie's earnest desire for Anglican orders, which he hoped in 1824–5. Bishop Hurber spent the winter in Delhi. He had an audience with the pathetic Akbar Shah, the nominal Emperor, who was impressed by him as a most sincere Christian, quite free from all conceit or enthusiasm.

In 1828, on the fifteen hundred acre site (now University of Delhi and its adjoining area) the British shifted their cantonment, constructed branches, offices, storerooms and Parade Grounds. The North wall of the city, the ridge, and river became a triangle and houses of agents, merchants and low ranking officers started coming up. Metcalf built his own house in 1854 on the bank of Yamuna uprooting the villagers of Chandrawal; who took revenge in 1857, while looting and burning this house.

During 1830–57, the British laid out a cemetery at Rajpura (now Reids Line), built a church, James Skinner (November, 1836), at Kashmiri Gate, established a college in the old residency, a club, a bank, a post office, printing press and photographic studio.

After the Mutiny, the British army took over Jama Masjid, Zinat-ul-Masjid and Ghata Masjid. Before 1850, no non-Roman Catholic Mission existed in Delhi, apart from a rather weak Baptist Mission and the occasional visit paid by Anand Mashie. In that year, however, a group of English Christian officials began to collect money for a mission, and, in 1851, their efforts received vigorous reinforcement on the arrival as Chaplain of Midgley John Jennings. In 1852, two Hindus were baptized. Ram Chander from Panipat, born in 1821, educated at the Government College in Delhi, a teacher of Mathematics was baptized by Jennings on 11 July 1852 in St. James' Church along with Chaman Lal, a Sub-Assistant Surgeon.

Rajpur Cemetry, Patel Chest Institute, Delhi.

Injured Nicholson before death.

A crowd of nearly 200 Hindus surrounded the Church on that day and nearly 200 watched the ceremony inside the Church.

St. Stephen's Church, Fatehpuri.

In 1854, two S.P.G. Missionaries, J.S. Jackson and A.R. Hubbard, both from Coirs College, Cambridge, arrived in Delhi along with their wives. Some 20 Indian Christians who were re-admitted to their old-society were allowed to dine along with Hindu friends but on a separate table. The Indian Christians were assembled in St. James' Church every Sunday by Mr. Steward, who was a teacher in Delhi College. Jackson soon started service in Urdu.

Baptist Mission Church, Mukim Pura, Malka Ganj.

Brotherhood, Rajniwas Marg.

A school was started and a college was projected. In 1856, the Mission was joined by Danial Carrie Sandy, a catechist from Bishop's College; he was just 22 years old. He was made the in- charge of the Mission School, which by then had 170 students. Jackson already left India at the end of the 1852 and L. Koch from Bishop's College replaced him. The Delhi Mission was prospering.

But in the Mutiny of 1857, apart from other distractions and murders of men and women, the mutineers turned in fanatical fury on the Missionaries and their converts. Jennings died weapons in hand; his daughter was killed at the breakfast table, with her friend, Miss Clifford. Hubbard remained in the Mission House on the morning of 11 May, 1857. A friend took him to his house where all were massacred and the house was burnt.

Sandy was also murdered. Chaman Lal, Koch and the steward of the Government College were killed. Only Ram Chander managed to escape. The Delhi Mission was completely wiped out.

By the end of 1857, the British rule was effectively re-established in North India. On 20 September, Delhi was taken over by the British. The country entered upon a new era in its history. By the act of 1857, the East India Company was abolished and the Authority of the Government of India was transferred to the Crown. Till now, the Directors of the East India Company were suspicious about Missionaries and their work, but, the Queen in her declaration considered all communities equal and indicated that she herself was a Christian. The religious policy of the Government remained the same, but the provision of a state establishment of chaplains for its English Christians servants in India was created, and freedom for Christian Missions on a voluntary basis. It created liberty for Government servants to subscribe to and promote Missions as private persons; and it also involved the protection of the civil rights of converts. The educational dispatch of 1854 of Macaulay, which outlined a national system of education, helped in the spread of English as a common language of an elite, English literature, Philosophy and General History provided opportunity for developing their Christian content.

The coming of the railways and the other public works such as irrigation canals and bridges involved the coming to India of a new type of Englishman. The Railways and Printing provided employment for Anglo-Indians and Indian Christians. There came up railway colonies of Anglo-Indians and Indian Christians. In 1866, East Indian Railway entered into an agreement with S.P.G. by which the Society was to supplement a grant by the share holders of the Railway of £ 7000 to provide an endowment for clergy to be established along the line from Calcutta to Delhi; and for every clergyman so stationed, the Government promised an additional £ 180 a year. So there came about the Railway Chaplain and the Railway Parish with its Church, parsonage, school and railway institute. In 1860, Robert Reynolds Winter arrived in Delhi along with his wife and remained in Delhi till his death in 1891. The foundation stone of a Church for the Indian congregation was laid by Bishop Cotton in 1865. The Church was consecrated on 17 October 1867 by Bishop Milman in the name of St. Stephens and a memorial to those of the Delhi Mission who laid down their lives in the Mutiny. Some communities with their Headquarters in England, like the Missionary Brotherhoods, started their work in Delhi.

Cambridge Mission House.

One such Brotherhood was the Cambridge–Brotherhood of Delhi. The earliest community which converted to Christianity in Delhi was from a section of Dalits.

In the middle of December, 1877, Bickersteth and Murray arrived at Delhi. Murray fell ill and went on furlough. Bickersteth single-handedly managed the Brotherhood for some time; he faced many problems from their new converts, who were admitted by Winter through baptism. These new converts were living with their relations and marring in their old society according to their own customs; they were also celebrating their festivals. In 1884 and then in 1887 these new converts held their Panchayats (Assembly) and finally only 60 out of six hundred remained attached to the Brotherhood, despite the attraction of houses given to them in New Basti, which was created in Daryaganj. At this time, French was appointed Bishop of the new diocese of Lahore, in which Delhi was included.

Government College (now Zakir Husain College and earlier Delhi College) was closed and a need for a Christian College was realized. Bishop French supported this idea and, by 1882, St. Stephen's College was established. It was affiliated to the New University of Punjab; this was the only college outside Lahore. Due to ill health, Bickersteth returned to England in August, 1882. Mrs Winter died in 1884, but Mr. Winter lived on until 1891. Of the original six, Carlyon, Allnutt and Lefroy remained. Lefroy, though the youngest, headed

Bickersteth Hall.

the mission, until 1899, when he was made the Bishop of Lahore. In Delhi, when Lefroy was preaching Christianity, a blind Maulvi, who knew the Quran by heart and had been to Mecca his name was Maulvi Ahmad, later became Maulvi Ahmad Masih. He opposed Lefroy for some time, but ultimately converted to Christianity. During the time of Lefroy, St. Stephen's Hospital for women was started in 1885. When Lefroy became Bishop of Lahore, Samuel Scot Allnut become head of the Brotherhood of the Mission. He remained the head of Brotherhood from 1891 to 1917 when he suddenly died.

In 1890, St. Stephen's College acquired a new building, designed by Sir, Swinton Jacob. This was at Kashmiri Gate, which by then became the centre of attraction of British. In 1904 at Maitland House, a residential system was established. In 1886 Sushil Kumar Rudra, joined the college. His father worked for C.M.S. in Bengal and Missionary at Burdwan, who died due to malignant malaria in 1889. In 1902, S.K. Rudra was appointed as Vice-Principal of the college and warden of the Hostel. In 1906, when the Principal Hibbert-Ware went on furlough, Rudra became acting Principal and was confirmed as Principal in 1907. He was the first Indian to be appointed Principal of any mission college in India; he continued until 1923, till his resignation due to ill health.

With the rise of nationalism, Missionaries found themselves awkwardly placed between two worlds: one evidently declining towards its end and the other striving to be born. The attitude of Missionaries was different in villages and cities. They knew the conditions of the people of India and were sympathetic towards it, but condemned violence and terrorism. In fact, most missionaries felt that the Indian Nationalist Movement was a matter for Indians. But some like C.F. Andrews had sympathies with Indian ideals.

Charles Freer Andrews was born in 1871; his father was a Minister of the Catholic Apostolic Church. Before going to Pembroke College Cambridge, in 1890, he underwent a mystical experience which gave him a living certainty of faith in Christ. This he never lost in spite of intellectual doubts at times, and some great changes of outlook. He did brilliantly at Cambridge. In 1904, he joined the Cambridge Brotherhood. His friend, Basil West Cott, had already come to India and died in Delhi in 1900. It became certain that Andrews had to go to India for work. In 1907, he came to India, joined St. Stephen's College, made friendship with S.K. Rudra and Sunder Singh, met Rabindra Nath Tagore in London in 1912, and Gandhiji in South Africa in 1914. For some time he taught at Shanti Niketan. From 1925 onwards, he grew more towards Christianity. From 1928, for ten years, be returned to the West. He met Gandhiji in 1931 at the Second Round Table Conference in England.

In 1936, he resumed his ministry as an Anglican Priest by celebrating the Holy Commission at St. James Church Delhi. He was never a physically strong man; he had many a time breakdown in his health. He died in Calcutta on 5 April 1940 and was buried in the cemetery in the Lower Circular Road.

The Second World War affected India more directly then the first war had done. Mission institutions soon began to suffer; new men from England neither came nor sent money and all British laymen of military age were conscripted at once; the attack of Japan in Burma and Kohima created many problems for Missions.

In 1947, new dioceses was formed in Delhi, the idea for the same was mooted as far back as 1912. The first Bishop of Delhi was Aurobindo Nath Mukherjee, a Bengali, who worked in Delhi and was the Principal of Delhi United Christians School. In New Delhi with the help of Lord Irwin, the Viceroy of India, the Church of Redemption was built near the Central Secretariat, for the service of Government Servants. In February 1927, Irwin laid the foundation of this church and consecrated it in February, 1931.

The Partition of India also made a dent on the Churches in Calcutta and Lahore and a part which has gone to Pakistan. Since the coming of the Europeans and the British especially for the first time in Delhi, the following Churches and cemeteries have been serving the Christian community in the city.

1. Delhi Mission House and Church - Christian Mohalla (now extinct)
2. Trinity Church – Turkaman Gate

Trinity Church, Turkman Gate.

Armenian Cemetry, Kishan Ganj.

3. Armenia Church – Kishan Ganj – Chapel
4. Baptist Church – Chandni Chowk (Begum Samroo)
5. Church Julaina – Sarai Julaina (a village)
6. Skinner's Church – Kashmiri Gate
7. Fatehpuri Church (1867)
8. Chapel at Old Fort
9. Chapel at Cantonment in Daryaganj near Red Fort wall
10. Church – Rajpur Cemetery
11. Church – Dhaka
12. Baptist Church - Mukim Pura
13. Church – Phoons Ki Sarai
14. Church – St. Thomas at Panch Kuiyan Road
15. St. Antony Church – Gol Dak Khana
16. Church – Central Secretariat (Kendriya Sachivalaya)
17. Church at Mehrauli
18. Church at Jantar Mantar
19. Modern Church at Jungpura
20. Church at R.K. Puram
21. Church at West Punjabi Bagh
22. Church at Karol Bagh

St. John's Church (Mehrauli) was founded by Bishop S. S. Allnutt in 1927. This Church is a mixture of Hindu, Islamic and Christian architecture.

23. Church at Mayur Vihar
24. Cemetary at Auranzeb Road
25. War Cemetery at Cantonment
26. Nicholson Cemetery
27. Cemetery at Andha Mughal

St. Mary's Church, Mor Sarai.

28. Cemetery at Lothian Bridge
29. Cemetery at Coronation Grounds
30. Cemetry at Paharganj
31. St. Mary's Church

Armenians

Captain Manual Deremao was an important military officer of the Delhi territory and had surrendered the fort of Hansi to the British in 1803. Lieutenant Domingo Manual Deremao was another military officer who had also served in the Maratha army, but had joined the British when Lord Wellesly asked all the European officers to leave the service of the Marathas on the eve of Anglo-Maratha war in 1803. Their family cemetery is at Kishan Gunj, Delhi, known as Deremao Cemetery; which is now on the verge of elimination as many houses have been erected over the graves in this cemetery.

James Skinner, a Eurasian, also left the Marathas just before the Anglo-Maratha war of 1803.

Cremation and Burial Rites at Delhi

The Hindus of Delhi traditionally cremate their dead. They used to cremate their ancestors at the designated cremation grounds and used to immerse the remaining bones in the river Ganga either at Garh Mukteshwar (Gan Mukteshwar) or at Haridwar. So, there was no one fixed place for the cremation and other rites of the Hindus. But when Shahjahanabad was built, Nigambodh Ghat became the cremation ground for the Hindu inhabitants of the city. However, Aurangzeb made an order that no one should cremate the dead at Nigambodh Ghat. The Lalas of the city defied this order many times and ultimately it was agreed to cremate the body at the Nigambodh Ghat. It was also due to the fact that Aurangzeb remained out of Delhi for 25 years and never returned to Delhi.

The Muslims from the Turkish period, used to bury their dead initially in and around Qutub Minar area. As and when the new city was developed, this activity was also shifted. It was the desire of the Muslims to be buried near his Peer or some spiritual person. That is why there are many graves in and around the Dargahs, mausoleums or graves of spiritual leaders. The following are some of the important burial grounds of Delhi:

Mehrauli (Bakhtiyar Kaki); Nizamuddin (Hazrat Nizamuddin Aulia); Chiragh Delhi; Mehdiyan; Khwaja Baqi Billah, Qutub Road (there are many graveyards in the Qutub Road area near Nabi Karim); near Filmistan there are two big graveyards; one large graveyard was at Panchkunya Road; one is at Sarai Kale Khan; there is one big graveyard in the walled city; and an other big graveyard is at Bahadur Shah Zafar Marg, near Link House, Qabristan at Mohalla Qabristan, Old Delhi.

The Christians also bury their dead like the Muslims. But they make pucca graves and also put a slab on the grave providing name and dates of birth and death of the dead. There are some old graveyards of the Christians such as the Armenian graveyard at Andha Mughal, Kishan Ganj, the other at

Lothian Bridge, and also the Nicholson cemetery. Some graves are in the St. James Church. The Paharganj area also has some graveyards. One graveyard is near Golf Links. One old cemetery is near the University of Delhi at Rajpur (near Patel Chest Institute) and the other at Rajpur Road.

It is isomic that both Muslims and Christians leave in the preservation the body of their ancestors in the grave and protect it and honour it. Not only has the government dismantled many graveyards and erected buildings over there, individuals have also done the same and, in many graveyards, buildings and other encroachments are quite evident.

The Status of the Mughal Emperors and Their Relations with the Residents

After the departure of Warren-Hastings, Lord Wellesley assumed charge of Governor-Generalship of India in 1798. The British Government in India was consciously pursuing the policy of non-intervention which considerably weakened many Indian powers due to their mutual aggrandizement and recriminations Marathas and Mysore consolidated and strengthened their resources and power. During his tenure of office, the British expanded their territorial authority. In North India, the British experienced conflict with the Marathas. By 1803, the Maratha power was crippled and the Emperor came under the protection of the Resident (the residency at Delhi came into existence on 24 September, 1803).

The maintenance of law and order in the Red Fort was, among others, a tough and complicated problem for the Resident. Just after the death of Shah Alam II on 19 November, 1806, the Resident got the information that Mirza Izzut Baksh, the second son of Shah Alam II would contest the title to the throne against his elder brother, Mirza Akbar Shah. The Resident, David Ochesterlony took precautionary measures and next day, Akbar Shah succeeded the throne. During the reign of Akbar Shah II, the royal palace was a hot-bed of villainy, conspiracy and debauchery.[20]

Mirza Jahangir, the third son of the Emperor was always fomenting trouble in the palace by infringing the code of sanctity and laws. He adopted an inimical attitude towards Abu Zafar, the eldest son of the Emperor (latter the last Emperor of Mughal Dynasty).

Next month on 17 December 1806 the Emperor wrote a letter to Mr. Seton, the Resident, expressing his desire to bestow honors upon the Prince, Mirza Jahangir, for appointment as the heir-apparent. The Resident advised the Emperor 'to take the advice of the Governor-General, who is paramount authority; and it was not in the interest of the Mughal House. It is also not essential as the Emperor is very healthy still'. The royal palace now became the arena of active intrigues in which Mumtaz Mahal, Qudsia Begum, the Emperor's mother and Daulat-ul-Nisa Begum were the major participants.

They were for Mirza Jahangir. A plan was also executed and Abu Zafar, the elder son was accused by the Emperor of seducing of one of his wives at the time of Shah Alam II. The Resident enquired with this matter in detail and found no substance in it. A letter was also obtained from Abu Zafar expressing denial for having the throne; but Seton again got it verified and found that the letter was signed under duress.

Mirza Jahangir was ousted to Allahabad again because of his violent activities. Even Seton, the Resident, was adopted by Begum Mumtaz Mahal as his son; which was neither liked by Seton, nor by the Governor-General.

Akbar Shah II sent two missions to Calcutta (to the Governor General): the Mission of Shah Haji and that of Raja Pran Kishan and another to England, the Mission of Ram Mohan Roy. However, this was also decidedly opposed by the British Residents for various reasons. The Emperor intended to be enthroned in the city of Agra, from which plan he was dissuaded with great difficulty by the Resident. To make distant excursions from Delhi was considered a part of his strategy to assert his sovereignty. The Government felt that the attempts of the Emperor to obtain a degree of ascendancy and latitude of independent action could lead to consequences of the most serious embarrassment and even danger to the interests of the British Government in India.

The proposal to appoint Mirza Jahangir was not approved by the British Government at Calcutta; it was conveyed by the Resident to the Emperor and Prince Abu Zafar was elevated to the exalted position of the heir-apparent on 16 January 1810. The appointment of Abu-Zafar as the heir-apparent increased his prestige and influence. It created a strong impression among the palace circles that the authority of the Resident was indomitable. The influence of Mumtaz Mahal virtually became nullified and the Emperor henceforth gave head to the advice of the Resident more readily than before.[21]

Akbar Shah II later became very unhappy with Resident Seton, and he had written a complaint against the Resident to East India Company's authorities to replace Seton with a more helpful and least interfering Resident. But the successive Residents did not toe His Majesty's line of action on many issues. Mr C.T. Metcalfe, the Resident did not approve the policy of importing slaves from abroad; he advised the Governor-General not to approve of this business, as it was inhumane. At last, Lord Moira stopped this trade for good on the recommendation of A. Ross, the Resident.

In the first half of the nineteenth century, the Resident decisively wanted His Majesty's attempts to augment the royal stipend and restore imperial privileges with the help of any other country power. In 1811, C.T. Metcalfe, the Resident got hold of some papers from Lucknow which gave the impression that Qudsia-Begum was involved in a clandestine transaction with Bahu Begum, the Queen of Oudh. But the Emperor and his mother (Qudsia Begum was the mother of Akbar Shah II) pleaded that the alleged letters were written without their knowledge.

In 1811, another clandestine Mission known as the Prankissen Mission also ended in a dismal failure owing to the exertions of the Resident.[22]

In 1811, the Emperor consented to further restrictions at the instances of Charles Metcalfe, coins however still continued to be struck in his name until the reign of William IV (the year 1818).

After the abolition of the Delhi Mint which was near the Akbarabadi Begum's Mosque, the Resident urged the Governor-General to grant compensatory allowances to the employees of the Mint.

In 1820, a considerable amount of treasure had been unearthed on the bank of the river Yamuna. The Governor-General took the decision to deposit it in royal treasury. The Resident carefully avoided doing anything which would cause pecuniary loss to His Majesty. In 1822, Nuckee Ali Khan, the manger of the household of Mirza Jahangir was paid Rs. 69,000 as his salary from the treasury of the Delhi palace household. In 1828, the Resident, E. Colebrooke, proposed and the Governor-General permitted that Emperor be allowed to purchase any piece of land, the cost would be borne by the company's treasury. In 1823, British authorities helped the Emperor to realize the royal revenue from the Zamindars. In 1824, the Resident advised the Governor-General to sanction money for creating several houses for the benefit of His Majesty at Shahdara, Delhi. On human considerations, the British Residents were trying to improve the economic condition of the Emperor, so that he may not ask to increase his royal stipend.

In 1811, Holkar threw off his yoke of allegiance to the house of Timur and struck coins in his own name. The Emperor complained to the Governor-General who reprimanded Holkar for it. In the same way, the Resident sided with the King, when in 1814, the King and Abu Zafar had some tussle over the receipt of the expenditure by Abu-Zafar. No one was allowed to disobey or disrespect the King. Even the Resident was liable to be removed from the Residency office if he incurred the King's displeasure and failed to satisfy His Majesty's mind. Thus in 1811, Minto effected Seton's dismissal in deference to His Majesty's wishes.[23]

In 1830, Francis Hawkings, the Resident was also dismissed for not respecting His Majesty's sentiments. In 1825, when a slave girl who was not treated well by her keeper and wanted to escape from the fort, was rescued by the British officer, the King took the serious view of it. He advised the Resident, C. Metcalfe, not to interfere in the domestic affairs of the royal family; but at the same time, he ordered all in the fort to treat the servants compassionately.

On the request of the King in 1833, William Fraser, the Agent, ordered that payment be made for the royal stipend on the first of every month, even if it was a Sunday.

The King was fully authorized to appoint any officer of his choice; even if he was not liked by the Resident. In 1828, one Daulat Ram who had not cleared the debts to the king was kept under the King's protective custody. He informed T.T. Metcalfe the Magistrate and Judge of Delhi, who sent a peon to release the Daulat Ram. The King complained to the Resident, who in turn reprimanded T.T. Metcalfe and advised him not to interfere in the domestic matters of the King. But when Kabul King shown the desire to send his army to overthrow the company's rule, the King did not respond to it; in the same way when Shahzada Yunus, Timur Shah's grandson expressed a desire to visit Delhi, the Delhi King did not show any inclination to it. It was all done to maintain good political relations with the British.

Many times, noteworthy gifts were received and exchanged between the King, the Residents and the Governors-General. Since 1813, the presentation of *nazars* to the Emperor by the Indian Princes and Chiefs considerably reduced. The Governor-General also stopped it. In fact, the Resident continued an annual nazar to the King the Indian Princes stopped it of their own and not by any order of the British.

In 1836, it was decided to discontinue nazars at the expense of the Government except those presented by the Resident to the Emperor, the Queen and the heir-apparent on customary occasions.

It was Lord Ellenborough who dealt a final blow. He disliked half measures and was highly indignant to learn that the Resident still continued to offer nazars to the Emperor. He considered this token of feudal submission inconsistent with the relative position of the Emperor and the British Government. He had neither sympathy nor regard for the feelings of the Emperor.

The Court of Directors took a humane view of the situation. They were not inclined to introduce any change during the life time of Bahadur Shah and ordered to continue the practice. Hardinge who succeeded Ellenborough did not implement the orders of the Home authorities. Lord Dalhousie had succeeded Hardinge; he was more vehemently opposed to the Emperor's regal prerogatives than his predecessors and was waiting for Bahadur Shah's death to effect some sweeping innovations. He turned down all earlier requests of the King regarding the nazars and cleared this issue for ever.

The Court of Directors agreed to this change. With the discontinuance of nazars the policy initiated by Lord Moira was almost complete. The King was reduced to a cypher in the political life of the country. What was left to him were only the kingly title and the royal palace at Delhi. During the 1820s and 1830s many changes in the personal, status and jurisdiction of the Residency could be seen. Ochterlony, Metcalfe and Seton's period was considered as the 'Golden Age' of Residency. Edward Colebrooke was dismissed on the charge of corruption and nepotism on the complaint of Charles Trevelyan, an assistant in the Residency, who was the brother-in-law of Macaulay. In 1832 William Bentinck separated the Rajputana states from the Delhi Residency. A separate Residency was erected for Rajputana and Delhi Residency was relegated to the position of an Agency and the Civil Commissioner of Delhi was entrusted with political duties. He was designated "the Civil Commissioner and Agent to the Governor-General at Delhi." William Fraser was the first Agent, who was murdered on 22 March 1835. Thomas Theophilus Metcalfe, the younger brother of Charles Metcalfe, then took over charge and held this office till his death in 1853.

The Charter Act of 1833 divided the Presidency of Bengal into the Presidency of Fort William in Bengal and the Presidency of Agra. Delhi Agent was sub-ordinate to the Governor of Agra. In 1836 the Presidency of Agra was converted into the Northwestern provinces under the Lieutenant-Governor with all the political duties formerly attached to the Governor of Agra. The Agent at Delhi came under him. From 1834 onwards, the Agent at Delhi was relegated to a comparatively insignificant position, he had only to manage the relations with the Mughal Emperor. Bahadur Shah II, who ascended the throne in 1837, was allowed by the British Government all privileges enjoyed by his predecessors. But most of the British officers were not in favour to give any lenient and considerate treatment to the Mughal Emperor. On the conclusion of the Afghan war in 1843, Lord Ellenborough, decided to make sweeping changes in the privileges enjoyed by the Mughal Emperor. Nazar by any British official in the presence of Agents was prohibited.

The Emperor employed Thompson to represent the Emperors view to the Queen in England; but he was not allowed to meet her, the Board of Directors and the members of the Board of Control decided against the Mughal Emperor. At this time, Bahadur Shah II was 75 years old, devoid of energy, perhaps even of any ambition and was mainly given to literary pursuits. The Government was not prepared to extend the same consideration to his successor. The palace had both political and military importance to the British Government. They wanted to get it vacated by the Mughal ruler and his family. The powder magazine of the Government was not at a suitable place, they wanted to bring it to Red Fort. The British Government by 1848 had by slow degrees deprived the Emperor of the various prerogatives of sovereignty and assumed them largely to itself. Now, apart from the royal title, the palace was the only remnant of imperial dignity left to the Emperor. Its occupation by the British Government would then symbolize the final transfer of sovereignty from the Mughals to the British. The British wanted that the Mughal ruler be shifted to his residence at Qutub and other family members to live elsewhere.

Prince Dara Bakht, the heir-apparent, was fifty-seven years old; in appearance and constitution scarcely less feeble them his father, the next claimant was Fakhr-ud-Din. On 11 January, 1849, Prince Dara-Bakht died. Consequently, the Governor-General proposed an end to the royal privileges of the house of Timur on the demise of Bahadur Shah II. There was also a controversy for the nomination of heir apparent, in the royal house. The Emperor, under the influence of his wife Zeenat Mahal recommended her son Mirza Jawan Bakht. He objected to Fakhr-ud-Din on grounds of illegitimacy and mutilation. On January 23, 1852 he made an agreement with the British to evacuate the palace, but, urged the revision after the agreement. On 10 July, 1856 Fakhr-ud-Din unexpectedly died, for Zinat Mahal it was a golden opportunity for Jawan Bakht to get him appointed for heir-apparent. A document was produced, signed by Mirza Koeash the eldest surviving son containing a request in favour of Jawan Bakht as the heir-apparent. Mirza Koeash, however, presented a separate memorial in which he advocated his claims to be recognized as the heir-apparent.

Simon Fraser took over from Thomas Metcalfe who died in Calcutta. Lord Canning had replaced Dalhousie. The death of Mirza Fakhr-ud-Din also provided an opportunity to the British Government to reconsider the future of the Mughal Dynasty. The Mughal Emperor had outlived his usefulness to the British.

The supremacy of the British in India had by now been established beyond doubt and, therefore, to the mind of Lord Canning, the preservation of a titular king paramount of Hindustan appeared a serious anomaly.[24]

The decision of the future of Mughal dynasty started at the time of Wellesley, Canning merely tried to fix the last nail on the Mughal coffin. The revolt of 1857 provided a convenient opportunity to the British to end the royal privileges of the Mughal dynasty without conditions and guarantees.[25]

Lord Ellenborough discontinued the practice of offering presents at the two Ids, the Nauroz, and the King's birthday, and his authority was restricted to the precincts of the palace. In 1848, the Marquis of Dalhousie visited Delhi, but did not visit the King.

On 10 July 1856 Fakhr-ud-Din the heir apparent died of poison. Before his death he had to retire to the residence at Qutub.

English officials started ridiculing the royalty. William Fraser, on returning from a durbar at the palace, handed over the robes with which he had been honored to the first beggar he met outside the Delhi Gate.[26]

By now, in all the annexed territories, the higher offices of state were reserved for the younger sons of English squires and clergymen. The army of the company remained dependent on its mercenary sepoys recruited from

Court Building, Kashmiri Gate.

Lock up, Kashmiri Gate Courts.

Torture Cell, now Urdu Academy Library, Kashmiri Gate.

among the 'martial' communities of India. The troops of the army were paid in time, but it was a direct discrimination that no Indian was given the higher position in the army.

The Emperor tried to imitate his mighty ancestors in holding durbars, conferring titles and Khilats, enjoying the performance of dancing girls but otherwise he had to seek assistance of the British Agent posted at Delhi, concerning a theft in the palace for importing commodities in the fort and to move out of his residence to visit important places in the city and its suburbs.

Emperor was free from communal prejudices. The Emperor celebrated Hindu- festivals and on Id cow was not sacrificed. The Holy water of the Ganges was used for sacred purposes.

Begam Samru had sent a letter along with nine maunds of Khas (a sort of cool grass) and four maunds for the heir apparent; and hundred large fans sent to be distributed in the palace.[27] The British Empire was different from the preceding systems. It was a colonial complex, the colonies existed for the benefit of British merchants. The doors for Indians were opened in the British Empire but for lower ranks. The British created a new class of Khan Bahadur and Rao Sahib in place of the old peerage; they were only honorary titles for those who were supporting the British system politically. The revenue system of the British was more rigid than in old native states. A new justice system was introduced.

With the shortening of the voyage to India, the arrival of the 'Memsahib' started in India. There was wide difference in the social status of Indian soldiers and a soldier in England—the position of Indian soldiers was more honorable.

It was evident from the war in Punjab, the Gorkha war in Nepal and the Crimean war that the English were not invincible.

The suppression of abominable practices like sati and female infanticide gave rise to suspicions in the Indian mind for interference with the faith.

The annexationist zeal (through policy of lapse) of Lord Dalhousie had created fear in the mind of Indian rulers.

With the annexation of the Punjab after the Sikh war, the British frontier had reached the utter most limits of traditional border of India.

The claims of the adoptive prince at Satara in 1848 were rejected and the state was annexed. Towards the end of 1853 the Bhonsle state of Berar suffered similar fate. Jhansi was also annexed. Sambhalpur in Orissa, Jaitpur in Bundelkhand and Tanjore in South India extinguished without a murmur. The extinction of the title of the Nawab of Arcot is a footnote in history.

The last Peshwa who was living on pension died on 28 January 1851 at the age of 77, his adopted sons were not granted the position of Peshwaship. Awadh was also annexed after much of exploitation. The establishment of few decades was seething with the spirit of revolt. Dispossessed princes were plotting revenge; those that still retained their thrones were apprehensive and fearful. The native army, on which the company's rule depended, could see no future for a man of honor in the company's service.

They grumbled that the *sipahis* of the Nizam and the Maratha chiefs were better off than the company's Subedars and Jamadars. They rode horses or ponies purchased from their savings, the English officers frowned on them as upstarts.[28]

The Englishman of the age of Victoria looked down on the ignorant native and treated him with withering contempt. Orientalism was out of fashion. The royal family was described as 'that great evil of rotting royalty which had so long polluted the atmosphere of Delhi.'[29]

The Mutiny of 1857

There were widespread rumours that the cartridges of the new Enfield rifle were enclosed in paper greased with the fat of cows and pigs – offensive equally to Hindus and Muslims; the rumor was that the polluted sepoys should be left with no option but to embrace the Christian faith.

There was the phenomenon of *chapaties* being passed from village to village as a forerunner of some news or mysterious orders to come. Wandering faqirs and sadhus of both faiths spread the belief that the English rule was fated to last a hundred years, from the centenary of Plessey (1775).

Memorial of the Rebel Soldiers, Meerut.

विक्टोरिया पार्क जेल तोड़कर छुड़ाये गये सैनिक
10 मई – 1857

1. हवलदार मातादीन	2. शेख पीर अली (नायक)	3. अमीर कुदरत अली (नायक)
4. शेख हुसैनुद्दीन (नायक)	5. शेख नूर मोहम्मद (नायक)	6. शीतल सिंह
7. जहांगीर खान	8. मीर मौसिम अली	9. अली नूर खान
10. मीर हुसैन बख्श	11. मथुरा सिंह	12. नारायण सिंह
13. लाल सिंह	14. पृथ्वीदान सिंह	15. शेख हुसैन बख्श
16. साहिबदाद खान	17. बिशन सिंह	18. बलदेव सिंह
19. शेख नुन्दू	20. नवाब खान	21. शेख रमजान अली
22. अली मोहम्मद खान	23. मक्खन सिंह	24. दुर्गा सिंह (प्रथम)
25. नसरुल्ला खान	26. मेहराब खान	27. दुर्गा सिंह (द्वितीय)
28. नबी बख्श खान	29. जुरखान सिंह (प्रथम)	30. भुदनू खान
31. जुरखान सिंह (द्वितीय)	32. अब्दुल्ला खान	33. हसन खान (प्रथम)
34. जबरदस्त खान	35. मुर्तजा खान	36. मजजूर खान
37. अजीमुल्ला खान (प्रथम)	38. अजीमुल्ला खान (द्वितीय)	39. कल्लू खान
40. शेख साहुल्ला	41. सालार बख्श खान	42. शेख रजा अली
43. द्वारिका सिंह	44. कालका सिंह	45. रघुवीर सिंह
46. बलदेव सिंह	47. दर्शन सिंह	48. इमदाद हुसैन
49. पीर खान (प्रथम)	50. मोती सिंह	51. शेख फजुल इमाम
52. हीरा सिंह	53. सेवा सिंह	54. मुराद पीर खान
55. शेख आलम अली	56. काशी सिंह	57. अशरफ अली खान
58. कादरदाद खान	59. शेख रुस्तम	60. भगवान सिंह
61. मीर इमदाद अली	62. शिव बख्श सिंह	63. लछमण सिंह
64. शेख इमाम बख्श	65. उस्मान खान	66. [illegible] सिंह
67. मकबूल अली खान	68. शेख गफ्फार बख्श	69. शेख उम्मीद अली
70. [illegible]	71. राम सम्पत सिंह	72. पनाह अली खान
73. लछमण दुबे	74. रामसरन सिंह	75. शेख रमजान अली
76. शिव सिंह	77. शीतल सिंह	78. मोहन सिंह
79. [illegible] अली खान	80. शेख मोहम्मद खान	81. सुन्दर सिंह
82. [illegible] खान	83. गेन्दा सिंह	84. शेख [illegible] अली
85. [illegible]		

List of soldiers who were released after breaking Victoria Park Jail, Meerut, on 10 May 1857 and then they proceeded to Delhi along with the rebels.

The Rebel soldiers prayed at this temple before proceeding to Delhi from Meerut on 10th May 1857.

Between January and April 1857, Nana, the ruler of Bithur visited Kalpi, Delhi and Lucknow and met many rulers. Till the middle of the nineteenth century Britain ruled only about 40 percent of India; and it was only until a few years before the mutiny of 1857 that the territorial balance was definitely weighed against the states. The annexations of the great kingdoms of the Punjab, of Nagpur and of Oudh gave the predominance to British India and incidentally were largely the cause of the general uneasiness throughout Northern India of which the Mutiny was only a symptom.

The obnoxious cartridges were the apparent cause of the disaffection and in the month of February 1857 Mangal Pandey attacked an officer at Barrackpur and Behrampur (Calcutta), the 19th Native Infantry and the 34th were disbanded. Mangal Pandey was hanged in April 1857. Some trouble took place in Lucknow on 7 May 1857, but the big explosion took place in Meerut on 10 May 1857. This had immediate repercussions in Delhi.

The sepoys at Meerut mutinied, shot their officers, and started in a wild rush for Delhi. The immediate cause of the Mutiny had been the sentencing of eighty five troopers of the 3rd Regular Bengal Light Cavalry to considerable terms of imprisonment, owing to their refusal to handle cartridges which for years they had used without the slightest protest.

At Delhi, on the morning of the 11 May, there was no sign of the coming storm; the Magistrates attended court at six in the morning, as it was usual in the hot weather and business was as usual. A report was there that the toll-house at the far end of the bridge of boats was in flame, and the Calcutta Gate had been closed against the Mutineers. Information was sent to the Head Magistrate of the cantonments behind the Ridge, to request assistance from the Brigadier, who at once ordered down the 54th regiment of Bengal Native Infantry and two guns to deal with any riot that might arise. There were no European troops in Delhi at all as they were in Punjab as Delhi was considered unhealthy for them, and the authorities had easily deferred to a request of the King of Delhi that none should be stationed there.[30]

Soon all the principal civil authorities proceeded to the Calcutta Gate of the city, in order to interview the rebels accompanied by the Captain of the palace. The rebels entered in the fort from Rajghat Gate and reached Lahore Gate. They were massacred by the King's retainers, with them perished the Chaplain of Delhi, his daughter and a lady friend of hers, who were staying there on a visit.

The Mutineers entered into the city through Kashmiri Gate, they were charged by 38th light infantry but they killed all the European officers, till 4 p.m. none from the cantonment proceeded beyond the Kashmiri Gate to quell the riot. In the mean time the Europeans living in Daryaganj including children and women were made prisoners and taken to Red Fort and kept prisoners and after five days they were massacred.

The officer in charge of the arsenal near Kashmiri Gate, Lieutenant Willoughby including nine Europeans, as native soldiers fled from the arsenal, defended till last, the Mutineers tried to scale the wall of the arsenal through the ladders. In the end the arsenal was fired; the small arm magazine went up into the air, arraying with it a number of the attackers and shaking the whole city. It deprived the Mutineers of two million rounds. On the midnight of 11-12 May a 21 gun salute was fired to proclaim their return of the Moguls rule to Delhi. The King had quailed and temporized but he was bludgeoned into ascending the throne. On 12 May 1857, Emperor Bahadur Shah II paraded the streets of Delhi mounted on a richly caparisoned elephant appealing to the citizens and traders to resume their normal life and advising the unruly sepoys to exercise restraint. On the same day, the English who were in panic, had evacuated their families from the cantonment (at present Delhi University) and huddled them up for security in the Flag Staff Tower. The city of Delhi

Flag Staff, Ridge near University of Delhi.

was in confusion and chaos. Arson, murder looting and bloodshed were prevailing; sepoys and unlawful elements went out on the rampage.

Two signalers in the telegraph office, outside the city flashed a message to Ambala warning the British administration.

'The 3rd Cavalry, the 20th and 11th Native Infantry at Meerut revolted, the 54th Native Infantry and 38th Native Infantry joined them at Delhi.'

There were little military activities till 8 June when the English won their first victory at Badli ki Sarai and moved the Headquarters of their Delhi field force to the Ridge which was bare, rocky and hot, before this on 30 May British forces coming from Karnal marched to Ghazi-ud-Din Nagar (now Ghaziabad), it gave rebels two sharp lessons and repulsed their attacks with the loss.

During this period, Hindu Rao House (now the Hospital), the Flag staff tower and an old Pathan Mosque afforded shelter and accommodation to the British troops. Many attempts were made to dislodge the English from the Ridge and the biggest on 23 June 1857, the day which marked the hundredth anniversary of the battle of Plassey. It had been predicted that the English rule would disappear exactly a hundred years after Clive's victory. Meerut and Delhi sepoys fought violently but the English won. Superior weapons, better leadership and better organization helped them. There was a heavy toll on the English place due to heat, cholera and dysentery. The supply of food stuff was becoming irregular and insufficient.

On the other hand, the Emperor was not happy with the sepoys and the General. He was finding it difficult to conduct the affairs of the state with an empty treasury and an unruly mob of sepoys.

There was shortage of food and gun powder. There were palace intrigues, mutual suspicions and constant espionage conducted by the Agents of the English. There was no thought out plan, discipline and leadership were lacking and treachery was prevalent. Situation changed for the British when John Nicholson arrived on the Ridge on 7 August. Five days later the Mughal army was driven out from the Ludlow Castle and on 24 August the British gained an important victory at Najafgarh. On 11 September, the English commenced a final assault on Delhi. Four batteries opened up. Mori Gate and Kabul Gate were breached and captured. At Kabul Gate, Nicholson received a fatal wound and he died later. It was the third English column, which achieved spectacular success. It blasted the Kashmiri Gate. The column came up to the Church and the college, and then worked its way to the Jama Masjid. The English troops fanned out in various directions. On 20 September the Red Fort and the Salimgarh Fort were taken. A terrible retribution followed; Delhi got its blood bath. English troops plundered and ravaged, shot the people of Delhi. Emperor Bahadur Shah was taken prisoner from Humayun's tomb on 21 September.[31]

Mirza Ghalib

Mirza Ghalib was one of the greatest figures in Urdu and Persian literature, he had poetical talents of a high order, and he was attached to Bahadur Shah II for his poetical talents. Ghalib was in Delhi when the Mutiny broke out on 11 May 1857 and remained in Delhi till the fall of Delhi. He was living in Mohalla Balli Maran, in the House of Hakim Mohammad Hasan Khan; the Raja of Patiala had taken a promise from the British that the Mohalla would not be ransacked after the re-occupation of Delhi. The Raja's guard took charge of the Mohalla after the British victory. The brother and father of Hakim Ajamal Khan were the Hakim of Raja of Patiala. Mirza Ghalib had written many letters to his friend and described the events of the period of Mutiny. These letters were written to Munshi Har Gopal and published in 1869 as 'Urdu-i-Mulla' and 'Dastanbu'. Ghalib was arrested on 15 October, 1857 and he was brought before Colonel Brown; a friend of Ghalib was sitting with Colonel who recommended his case and he was released. Delhi was handed over to the Military authorities and remained under their control up to the 24 February 1858. The British forces shot dead many persons. Many were hanged in the Chandni Chowk. The British authorities admitted that 392 persons were hanged and quite a large number were shot dead.[32] Ghalib wrote to Mirza Hatim Ali,

> Thousands of my friends died. Whom should I remember and to whom should I complain! Perhaps none is left even to shed tears on my death.[33] Some times innocent persons are killed along with the sinners. This is what happened after the Mutiny. The English soldiers began to shoot whomsoever they met on the way. Among the men who remained in the city, there were some whose equal has never been born nor shall be born. Mian Mohammad Amin Panjakush, an excellent writer, Maulvi Imam Baksh along with his two sons Mir Niaz Ali and the persons of Kucha Chelan (It is said they were fourteen hundred in number) were arrested and taken to Raj Ghat Gate. They were shot dead and their dead bodies were thrown into the Yamuna. As for the women, they came out of their houses along with their children and killed themselves by jumping into the wells. All the wells of the Kucha Chelan were filled with dead bodies. My pen dose not write more.[34]

On the morning of 21 September a royal salute was fired to celebrate the victory. The fort was taken a day before. On this day Bahadur Shah II was captured from the Humayun's Tomb on the condition to save his life. On

Hindu Rao House, Azad Market, where mutineers placed their guns in 1857.

Lothian Cemetry near GPO.

22 September Mirza Mughal, Mirza Khizr Sultan and Mirza Abu Bakr were captured from Humayun's Tomb and were shot dead at Khuni Darwaza near Delhi Gate; their bodies were hanged at Kotwali Chowk for a day and nobody knows where they were put later on.

On the 27 of January 1858, Bahadur Shah II had been brought to trial in the Privy Council Chamber of Red Fort. He was charged with devising war against the British Government; with abetting rebellion and with numerous other seditious wrongs. After a patient trial in which Bahadur Shah II denied the charges and blamed the British for dishonesty and not following the agreement made by them. This trial extended for forty days and Bahadur Shah II was declared to be guilty of the main points of the charges and sentenced to be transported for life. He was sent to Pegu (now Burma, Myanmar) where he died in 1862, bringing the Mughal dynasty to an end. In 1877, Queen Victoria assumed the title of Empress of India on the advice of Prime Minister Benjamin Disraeli.

The number of the Europeans/British were small during and just after the victory, and they were apprehending the attack from within, as some mutineers were still at large, so they killed all those, who were seen, others fled the city with the families, especially women and children remained in open for two years, only then they were allowed to enter in Delhi, that too only by permission and thorough checking. Their houses were ransacked and damaged. Few rich persons purchased the Havelis of all those who could not come back; or were killed in the Mutiny. Fatehpuri Masjid, was given to Lala Chhunna Mal, and restored later. Jama Masjid was captured by the British soldiers and restored after six years; Sunehri Masjid and Ghata Masjid were used as bakeries by the British soldiers, the religious sanctity of these places was destroyed. The whole city looked like a jail. The population decreased tremendously. The Mutineers and their allies fought stubbornly, but were always at a disadvantage as they had no effective central command. On 14 September 1857, the British paid a heavy cost, they lost sixty-six officers and 1,104 men were killed and wounded; General Nicholson was also wounded and died after taking Delhi. In all, roughly 4,000 officers and soldiers of the British army lost their life in this action in Delhi. It is not estimated how many rebels lost their life.

The siege of Delhi had brought out the qualities which distinguish the British soldier; like his endurance of hardships, his eagerness for enterprise, were the Gurkhas of the Himalayas, the hardy Baluchis, the daring Sikhs, and the resolute Pathans. Among the most remarkable to occupy centre stage were the names of Baird-Smith; Nicholson, Barnard, Neville Chamberlain, Charles Reid, James Brind, Frederick Roberts, Hope Grant, John Jones; Edwin Johnson, Alac Taylor, Tait, Lockhart, Turnball, Seaton, Hudson, Dighton Probyn, Daly, Tombs, Renny, Jacob, John Coke, Speke, Greville, Watson, Medley, James

Lahore Gate of the Palace (Red Fort) as seen from inside in 1858. (http://www.columbia.edu/itc/mealac/pritchett/00routesdata/1600_1699/redfortdelhi/redfortphotos/redfortphotos.htmla photo by Robert and Harriet Tytler, 1858)

Hills, Quentin Bettye, Rosser, Aikman, Salkeld, Home. The Mutiny was not a mere movement that took shape just in a day. Various causes were there for its happening. The country was going through a tumultuous phase; the youth were disillusioned. Some prominent causes are as follows:

(1) Political Causes

From 1757 to 1857 East India Company had gained control over whole of India. The policy of expansion pursued by the British created discontentment among the Princes. By the Doctrine of Lapse, of Lord Dalhousie, a number of independent kingdoms were annexed to the British Empire. Sind in 1843 and Punjab in 1849 were the last.

(2) Social Causes

The English Administrators were gradually becoming arrogant and they were interfering in the basic way of living of the people, their traditional beliefs, values and norms. Their social reforms such as customs of Sati, female infanticide made many people unhappy. The Act XXI of 1850 which enabled the converts to inherit ancestral property led to believe the people that Government is bent upon to converts them to Christianity.

(3) Economic Causes

Most of the soldiers in the East India Company's army came from peasant families which were deeply affected by their impoverished status. Lots of partiality was done against Indians, like not giving them posts above the rank of Subedar and salary being less than their English counterparts. A general discontentment grew rapidly and strongly in Indian soldiers. British economic policy was adversely affecting the Indian Economy; its trade and industry especially Indian handicrafts; the British drained India of her wealth and all her natural resources.

(4) Religious Causes

The introduction of telegraph, railways and the spread of western education, causesed suspicion and fear in the people's minds. They were convinced that the English were conspiring to convert them to Christianity. The Religious Disability Act was an indication towards it.

(5) Military Causes

Most of the sepoys of the Bengal Army belonged to high casts of Oudh and the North-West province. They fought and won many battles for the Company but did not get a fair deal. Their loyalty was always undermined; their avenues of promotion were negligible. They had an aversion to overseas service, as travel across the seas meant loss of caste to them. They were pressed to go to Burma. They were getting less salary than their counterparts.

(6) Immediate Causes

The discontentment was rampant among the Indians, especially soldiers and some Princes; they were waiting only for an occasion to revolt. The introduction of greased cartridge in 1856 sparked fire. The Government decided to replace the old-fashioned musket, 'Brown Begs' by the 'Enfield rifle'. The loading process of the Enfield rifle involved bringing the cartridge to the month and biting of the top paper. There was a rumour among the sepoys that the greased cartridge contained the fat of the cow and pig; both were prohibited for Hindus and Muslims. Later, the British reflected to reduce the displeasure by allowing the sepoys to use their own grease made of Ghee. Lord Canning approved a proposal of Major-General Hearsay to this effect. However, the proposal was voted down by the Meerut based Adjutant-General of the Army Colonel C. Chester, who felt it would be equivalent to an admittance of guilt and therefore worsen the matter.

Causes of the Failure of the Mutiny

There were many causes responsible for the failure of revolt of 1857. The causes of the failure of the Mutiny were very much embedded in the revolt itself.

(1) The Indian forces were a complete mismatch to the British forces against whom they fought.

(2) The revolt was localized. There were many parts of India which were not affected by the revolt at all. South of the Narmada River remained undisturbed, Sind was quiet; Rajputana and Punjab were loyal.

(3) The rebels worked without any common plan, they were short of modern weapons and other materials of war, they were ill disciplined, and there was no centralized leadership and no experienced General. The rebels were joined together by a common feeling of hatred against foreigners and when British power was overthrown from an area, they did not know what sort of power to create in its place. They were often suspicious and jealous of one another and often got involved in suicidal quarrels. The peasantry having destroyed the revenue records and account books of the money lenders became passive and did not know what to do next.

(4) The British succeeded in crushing the leaders of the revolt one by one.

(5) The money lenders were the targets of the attacks by villagers. They were naturally hostile to the revolt. They supported the British. The educated Indians did not support the revolt. The rebels stood for the old order along with its superstitions.

(6) The personal character of the Bengal troops was also responsible for the failure of the Revolt. They were arrogant and were hated in every part of India to which they were sent. At many places, the rebels were crushed by the people themselves.

(7) Internationally, the rebels were isolated.

(8) As the British had control over the sea, they were in a position to pour into India both men and material with no difficulty, the rebels were short of finance and materials of war.

(9) The Mutiny at best was a religious riot of the Hindu and Muslim soldiers and not based on national outlook and alternative political and economic system.

(10) Double role of the ruling chiefs also strengthened the British.

(11) The King himself had no faith in the sepoys or in the success of the Mutiny.[35]

(12) Hindu-Muslim conflicts also weakened the success of the revolt.

Dr R.C. Majumdar, Dr Jadunath Sarkar, Dr S.N. Sen, Ganda Singh, Abul Kalam Azad and many historians declared it a sepoy mutiny and not a War of Independence.

The History of no other country in the world has been as tragic as that of India. Repeatedly the peoples of India have had to bend their neck to the yoke of foreign conquerors. Some historians believe that about 4000 years ago came the Aryans, who met the aborigines. (It is not a fact.) After the Aryans came Greeks, Scythians, Parthians, Kushans and the Huns. They were followed by the Arabs, the Turks, the Pathans and the Mughals. Wave upon wave the invaders came, conquered and subjugated the land, founded great empires and then passed away. Last of all came the English, who ruled over India till 15 August 1947; but the English language and culture is still ruling India.

The conquest of India by the English is different from the conquests of earlier invaders in many respects. The former invaders came without exception from the North-West, whereas the English started their conquest from Bengal in the East; the former came by a land route, whereas the latter came by a sea-route. The earlier invaders came as invaders; the English came as traders, without any notion of territorial conquests. The earlier invaders came with one full swoop; they fought a few brilliant battles, conquered the land and established a mighty empire in a couple of years. The English, on the contrary, from 1608, when they first landed on the soil of India to 1849 with the last conquered and annexed Indian province, took nearly 250 years to bring the country under their sway. When they started their work of conquest in 1757, it took them a full 100 years (1858). For one century and a half they lived as mere traders. No former conqueror even succeeded in bringing the whole of India under his power, but the English did so. For the first time, India that is geographically one country, brought into political unity under one Government. This was possible only by the British due to their command over the sea, improvement in land communications and modern science. The earlier invaders invaded India for their lust for conquest and territorial aggrandizement. The English were forced to conquer the country by the confusion and anarchy prevailing in India after the death of Aurangzeb.

Later they continued for their preservation. The earlier conquerors were absorbed in Hinduism; the Muslims refused to become so absorbed and maintained their separate religious identity. But politically later they became one with the Hindu inhabitants of India. The Hindu Rajas had many Muslim soldiers and Ministers and many Muslim rulers had many Hindu soldiers and Ministers. The British conquerors had not made India their home; India had become a 'dependency' of a distant country situated on the other side of the Globe. They ruled it from their own motherland and did not identify themselves with their subjects as the Muslim conquerors did. This affected the whole administration, finances, its economic policy and foreign policy.

The question arises, how is it that an old civilization and geographically large country having better resources overcome by a small nation of the British?

There are many factors responsible for this. The trading British learned the benefit of subjugation from French, Portuguese and Dutch.

On 12 December 1687 a letter was written by the Court of Directors to the Governor at Fort St. George (Madras), 'It is our object to establish such a policy of civil and military power and to create and secure such large revenue as may be the foundation of large well-grounded sure English dominion in India for all the time to come.' This policy was restated in 1698 and, on the renewal of its charter in 1702, the East India Company was authorized to raise troops for that purpose. The factors which operated in India in eighteenth and nineteenth century were also in favour of the English. Apart from it, religious doctrine also contributed to the weakness of the country. The early Aryans were a joyous people full of hope, faith and ardor. But from sixth century BC onwards they began to believe and cultivate a philosophy of pessimism, fatalism and renunciation. Karma, ahimsa had their devastating effect upon the average men.

The caste system of India had been a great source of our national weakness. By this system, three-fourths of the people were thrown out of commission and rendered unfit to bear arms. The soldiers were born and not made.

The division of the people into a multitude of hidebound castes has acted as an effective check to the growth of the sentiments of nationality and patriotism.

People were attached to their caste and not to the nation. India was not a nation. A nation cannot be conquered by another people as was done repeatedly. It was a geographical expression and not a political entity. In fact, India was also not conquered by the English with the help of British troops. India was conquered by the Indians and with Indian money for the British.

The absence of a central authority and government helped the British to conqueror India, after the fall of the Mughal Empire many new states emerged, the British took advantage of this situation and one by one, step by step they were taken over. In the eighteenth century the country was divided into many principalities. The British took advantage of this division. The English had no serious opposition, the local chiefs were not united, they had no patriotism they were having mutual jealously. On the other hand the British had a trained and disciplined force superior in arms to the native rulers. The troops of the East India Company were mainly recruited from among the Indians, the proportion of the British element in the army being about one to five. Discipline, skill, unity and resources were pitched against divisibility and absence of discipline, skill, resources and talents and the British therefore won.

Vincent Smith also gives one reason for the defeat of Indians on account of deterioration of character he writes

> In the eighteenth century during the anarchical period which intervened between the death of Aurangzeb and the establishment of British supremacy, the character of the Princes and other public men of India had sunk to an extremely low level. Thereby all the notable men of that age lived vicious lives, stained by gross sensuality, ruthless cruelty and insatiable greed.

The above mentioned were some of the reasons for the subjugation of India by the British. The sepoy Mutiny had effected the India in different ways, even the British living in England. The British army were in a year able to recapture, Delhi, Kanpur, Lucknow, Gwalior and Meerut; thousands of native army-men were slaughtered mercilessly without any valid reason. The British justified these killings; Bahadur Shah II was exiled in Rangoon, here he died a lonely man. Then East India Company's rule ended and India was formally annexed under the direct rule of the Queen by the Act of 1858. A new British Government department, the India Office, was created to deal with the governance of India; and its head, the Secretary of State for India, was entrusted with devising Indian Policy. The Governor-General of India gained a new title (Viceroy of India) and enforced the policies formulated by the India Office. The Viceroy put an end to land grabing, ordained religious tolerance and included Indians into civil service, although primarily as subordinates. The old East India Company's bureaucracy essentially remained the same, though there was a major alteration in attitudes.

In November 1858, Queen Victoria's proclamation stated that, 'We hold ourselves bound to the natives of our Indian territories by the same obligations of duty which bind us to our other subjects ... It is our further will that ... Our subjects of whatever race or creed, in our service, the duties of which they may be qualified by their education, ability and integrity, duly to discharge.'

British increased the ratio of British to Indian soldiers. Regiments, which had remained trustworthy, were kept back, and the number of Gurkha units, which had been fundamental in the Delhi campaign was increased. The sepoy artillery was abolished, leaving all artillery in British hands. The post-rebellion alterations formed the root of the military organization of British India until their rule in India.

The capital was shifted from Delhi to Calcutta and remaind there until 1911 when again it was shifted to Delhi.

Delhi after 1857

After the capture of Delhi by the British, the loot, massacre, hanging, digging of houses and arresting of people started. Lord Canning declared that all properties whose owners were not identified or had taken part in the Mutiny were the property of the Government.

The native inhabitants of the city were all turned out, and after some time, Hindus were allowed to return. It was thought that the palace, Jama Masjid and some part of the city were to be demolished but it was not executed. Only some Havelis around the palace were demolished, so that guns could be used if required from the palace.

On 13 October 1857, two more sons of the old King, Mirza Bakhtawar Shah and Mirza Mahndu, having been found guilty, were shot down at the Yamuna river bed by a party of riflemen. Then followed the trials of Nahar Singh, Raja of Ballabgarh and Nawab Abdul Rahman Khan, of Jhajjar. They were hanged.

On 11 January 1858 Delhi was handed over to the civil authorities and the civil courts were reopened in the following July. Most of the records had been destroyed. On 6 February 1858, Delhi territory was transferred from the jurisdiction of the North-West provinces to the Punjab, as by right of Conquest Hissar and Delhi Districts were formed.[36]

Ghalib was perturbed by the large scale demolition made by the British: 'Here, the city is being destroyed, big and famous markets; Khas Bazar, Urdu Bazar and Khanum Bazar, which in it self were equal to a town have been demolished and no body can make the marks of residences and shops.'[37]

In another letter Ghalib writes,

> Here, we have two roads: 'Thandi Sarak' (Yamuna Road) and Iron road (Railway line), both are apart. Moreover, a barrack for 'Goras' would be constructed in the

A well in Fatehpuri Masjid

This is a well, the water was brought from Lal Diggi and through Persian Wheel it was lifted and channeled to Jama Masjid for ablution. (The Lal Diggi was also called Ellenborough Tank which was destroyed after 1857.) Shri Abdul Muqeet Makki Niazi, Mohalla Paiwalan, seen in the photo has helped us to identify the well.

city and, in front of Quila, a ground would be cleared, where the 'Lal Diggi' is presently situated. The shops in south, the houses of bird-catchers, elephant stables (Hathi Khana), from the entry of Kucha Bulaqi Begum till the moat of Fort, no building would be spared except Lal Diggi* and some wells. ... Today, the

Memorial Tower at Ridge, near Hindu Rao Hospital.

> demolition of 'Chhatta' of Jan Nisar Khan has started. Why I would not be happy on Delhi's destruction? When the residents have not been left, what I would do with the city?[38]

(* Lal Diggi was a pond built of Red stones in front of Red Fort. It was filled with sweet water of Nahr-i-Bahisht which was running through Chandni Chowk to Red Fort. The water used to be channelized to the well behind the

Jama Masjid (as the water of this well was not sweet) from Lal Diggi and through a Persian Wheel it was lifted from the well to be sent to Jama masjid for 'Wuzu' (ablution); there were wells in front of Red Fort, a well at Begum Bagh which was filled by the British in 1858, in Chawri Bazar there was a Rehat (Persian Wheel) ka Mohalla which was demolished by the British in 1860.)

He further writes in another letter, "Qazi's well has become dry, the wells of Lal Diggi became brackish. Even we could have drunk brackish water, hot water is emanating. ... Now from Calcutta Gate to Kabuli Gate the buildings have been leveled for railway line. Punjabi Katra, Dhobi Wara, Ramji Ganj, Katra of Sa'adat Khan, the Hveli of General's wife, the hose of Ramji Das godownwala, Sahib Ram's orchard, his haveli have become untraceable now. In short, the city has become a desert. Now, when the wells have dried up and water has become a rare thing, this desert, would become the desert of Karbala"[39]

In 1870 the Mutiny Memorial on the Ridge was erected in the memory of the officers and men who had died during the reign. In 1865 Dr Cotton, Bishop of Calcutta, laid the foundation-stone of St. Stephen's Church, near the Queen's Garden (now Fateh Puri), as a memorial to the martyred Christians who fell at Delhi. The Church was opened on 10 May 1867 the tenth anniversary of the massacre. There had been a Delhi Mission for some years previously to 1857, started by voluntary contributions from those who attended St. James Church. One of the Missionary, the Rev A.R. Hubbard was killed in Mutiny; he was working for the society for the propagation of the gospel since 1854. The Mission was re-established and in 1877 the Cambridge University Mission was amalgamated with it. There was a Baptist Mission since 1813 and the Rev J. Mackey, took a notable part in the defense of the House in Daryaganj in 1858, he was taken prisoner and murdered. The Mission in Delhi took great efforts in the field of education and establishing hospitals.[40] The Indian Christians used to pray there but it was not called a 'Church'. The public called it a 'Girja' and a 'Dawakhana' (dispensary) was there in this structure. The mutineers assaulted and destroyed it on 11 May 1957.[41]

The population of Delhi in 1847 was a hundred and sixty-thousand and after 1857 it was just above twenty thousand but after 1875 it again rose to the population of the year 1847. In 1881 it was 1, 73, and 393; in 1891 it was 1, 92, and 579, in 1901 it was 2, 08, and 575; in 1911 it was 2, 32, and 837.[42]

In 1864, the Railway Bridge over Yamuna was still under construction but the Railway was opened, the first regular train entered into Delhi from 1 January, 1867. In the same year the Sind, Punjab and Delhi Railways entered by means of running powers granted from Ghaziabad junction. In 1873, the Rajputana state Railway connected Delhi with Bombay and in 1881, the Delhi-Ambala-Kalka Railway gave a shorter rout to North. In 1897, the Southern

Punjab Railway was opened while afforded a shorter route to Karachi. In 1900, the Ghaziabad-Muradabad Railway was opened. In 1905 Agra-Delhi chord Railway till Bombay was connected.

The Prince of Wales' Visit and Lord Lytton's Durbar of 1877

In 1876, the Prince of Wales visited Delhi and the regiments which had garrisoned the Main piquet in Hindu Rao's house took up their old positions on the Ridge.

When the Prince of Wales visited India it was felt that the title of the sovereign of India as mere Malika was not significant enough of the rule she had not only on the British Indian territory but also on the native states whose rulers owed her allegiance.

So it was announced in the speech from the throne in the Parliament sessions of 1876 that her Majesty deemed it necessary that the omission made at the time of her assumption of the direct government of the Indian Empire in making suitable addition to the style and titles of the sovereign should be supplied. The term Emperors of India with its Persian synonym Kaiser-i-Hind was decided upon.

> Sound benevolent and even-horded administration alone could not captivate the imagination and win hearts in a country where the exercise of power had always been associated with outward magnificence. This had been understood by Lytton, a Tory with Bohemian inclinations, who had decided to revive Mughal traditions in the grand manner for the formal declaration of Queen Victoria as Empress of India in January, 1877.
>
> At the heart of India's theatre of power was the Monarchy. The first royal tour of India had been made in 1875-76 by the Prince of Wales, and was a prelude to the announcement of his mother as Queen Empress. It was a vital in this and future royal progress that representatives of the house of Saxe-Coburg-Gotha conducted themselves in ways which would win the admiration of the Indian aristocracy... In 1890 the grand-son of Queen Victoria the Duke of Clarence, also visited Khyber Pass and shook hand with Ayub Khan, the exiled Afghan Prince who had led resistance against the British ten years before.[43]

In 1880, Queen Victoria was a cult figure: her image on coins was revised and in Kashmir many Hindu homes had her portrait. Soon after the Queen Empress's death early in 1901, Curzon claimed that every one wholeheartedly backed his plan for a Victoria Memorial Hall in Calcutta. This was to be like Taj Mahal, but there were no artists alive who could match its craftsmanship.[44]

The concept of Queen Empress as a distant goddess was owed something to her attempts to learn Hindustani as well as her intense interest in Indian affairs. In 1887, she took a Munshi, Abdul Karim, son of an Agra Prison Pharmacist; he was also an unofficial advisor on India; the Queen grew found of Abdul Karim, but of course it was not relished by Ministers and Viceroys; yet nothing could be done. In 1894, Hindu-Muslim clashes took place in Bombay. She remarked on the advice of Karim that Mohammedans should be protected, and their worship not disturbed. They are the real supporters of the British Government Brahmins were at the root of the trouble and Muslims needed to be protected from insults and disturbance in their peaceful and quiet worship which is so opposed to idolatry. Elegan, the Viceroy, was then asked to deliver his respects to Karim's father in Agra.[45]

It was a U-turn in the British policy towards the Muslims. In the Mutiny and after it, Muslims were not treated by the British on the same footing as the Hindus.

At Lytton's invitation, over 400 Indian Princes and their retinues converged on Delhi during the closing weeks of 1876 for a dazzling display of imperial theatre, devised to show them the majesty, permanence and sheer strength of the Raj. There were 15000 red coated British soldiers, the muscle of the empire, and its brains, the immaculately uniformed, plumed and bemedalled British officers. The Delhi Durbar emphasized the new unity of India as well as resurrecting the grandeur of the Mughals.[46]

The Durbar was held on the historical plain in Delhi near village Burari on 1 January, 1877. Altogether 68,000 were invited and did actually reside in Delhi and in its surrounding camps, during the fourteen days of the assemblage. It costs 60 lac rupees.[47]

Lady Betty Balfour in her history of Lord Lytton's Indian administration has set out in great deal the object and origin of the first proclamation Durbar held at Delhi in 1877:

(i) Queen Victoria was titled 'Kaiser-i-Hind'.

(ii) Services hitherto inadequately recognized were rewarded: pensions enjoined by ancient native families whose unquestioned legality had rendered them deserving of assistance were increased; salaries for life to native Princes; a large silken banner bearing on one side the royal Arms and on the other their own was given to the chiefs along the recognition of their gun salute; gold medals were given to selective persons; the pay and allowances to the commissioned and non commissioned officers and men of the native army in India were increased.

(iii) Three large pavilions had been specially erected for the occasion.

(iv) The Viceroy arrived at the place of assemblage a little after noon along with Lady Lytton.

(v) The proclamation formally declaring her majesty the Queen to be Empress of India was then read in English by the chief Harold and afterwards in Urdu by the Foreign Secretary.

(vi) Lord Lytton's made a Durbar Speech; in which he spoke of the purpose of the Durbar, the title of the Queen, the loyalty of the native rulers, chiefs, soldiers and people at large.

The message of the Queen Victoria, which the Viceroy received that day, was read by Viceroy.

The Effects of the Proclamation

The supremacy of the British Government had of course been long admitted as a practical fact by all the Native states of India, but in many cases their chiefs gave themselves, when opportunity offered and it seemed safe to do so.

The twenty-one guns salute ceased after the Delhi Assembly to be a sign of equality with the representative of the sovereign. Now the British Crown was the paramount superiority and it had effect also beyond the frontiers of the Indian Empire.

The Durbar was praised by British authorities and the Native Princes and chiefs. After the Mutiny, Delhi College was facing the financial crisis the Government was not ready to help; rather the Lieutenant-Governor announced that Delhi College classes would be amalgamated with those at Lahore. This was an unexpected blow. The Durbar was criticized all over India as being in bad taste because it was held at a time of severe famine. To the people of Delhi the decision about their college appeared to be another example of bad timing. Surindra Nath Banerjee publicly denounced the government which 'could not spend Rs. 12,000, a year for the maintenance of an ancient and time-honoured seat of learning, (when) the Delhi Assemblage cost Rs. 60 lac.'[48]

Delhi Durbar of 1903.

The Durbar of 1903

On 22 January 1901 on the death of Queen Victoria, Edward VII ascended the throne of United Kingdom of Great Britain and Ireland, Defender of the Faith, and Emperor of India. These circumstances, the proclamation and the announcement made to this effect, prompted Lord Curzon, the Viceroy, to hold the Durbar for Indian Princes, Chiefs, solders, officers and civil persons. At the end of 1902 Delhi was again enfate, when not only the ruling chiefs of Indian Empire were gathered together but also their Royal Highnesses, the Duke and Duchess of Connaught (who was sent by the King his brother, to represent him at Durbar) accompanied by many English notables. The Viceroy (Lord Curzon) made a state entry into Delhi on 29 December 1902. On 1 January 1903 all the ceremonies of previous (1877) Imperial Assemblage were repeated with the addition of an investiture and State Ball. The Durbar and its concomitant pageants were on a much large scale in numbers and brilliancy, as was only to be expected by the great development in Railways and resources which had occurred in the interval of a quarter of a century, sports, tournaments, and art exhibition and history, a review of native state retainers lent a color which was missed in 1877. The ceremonies closed on 10 January 1903 with the public departure of His Excellency the Viceroy and their Royal Highnesses the Duke and Duchess of Connaught.[49]

The Durbar was attended by 100 ruling chiefs, representatives from Australia and South Africa, Governors and envoys from Portuguese India the French settlements in India, Afghanistan, Siam, Japan et cetera.

The Viceroy made his speech then he read the Message of His Majesty, the King. In the message the important issue for the Indian people was the waving of the interest on loans. "Neverth, it has been a pleasure to us to propose that Government shall cease to exact any interest for a period of three years upon all loans that have been made or guaranteed by the Government of India to native states in connection with the last famine; and we hope that this benefaction may be acceptable to those to whom it is offered."[50]

The Durbar was meant to remind all the princes and people of the Asiatic Empire of the British crown that they had passed under the dominion of a new and single sovereign, to enable them to solemnize that great and momentous event, and to receive the Royal assurance and greetings.

The Coronation Durbar of 1911

The partition of Bengal in 1905 brought more political problems for the British than it actually solved. Even before the partition there was one opinion that the capital of the Empire be shifted to Delhi, but after the partition of Bengal the idea of shifting the capital accelerated. The right movement came when

King Edward VII died on 6 May 1910 and George V ascended the throne and he also became the Emperor of India, to be known to Indian Princes, the officials and the public at large, the king charged and commanded the Charles Baron Hardinge, the Viceroy and Governor-General of India to take all necessary measures to hold the coronation Durbar in Delhi on 12 December 1911.

The King Emperor George V and Queen Empress Marry arrived at Bombay on the 2 December. Their Majesties stayed at Bombay till the 4th, and visited the caves of Elephanta on the 5th and left for Delhi the same night. The King and Queen arrived in Delhi on the 7th morning by train; the Royal couple received formal homage from Lord Harding, the Governor-General, and the highest officials of the Raj. Over a hundred Princes were formally presented. The entire gathering of Imperial functionaries, together with their many attendants, then commenced upon the formal state entry in to Delhi.

George V flatly refused to mount the Royal Elephant urged upon him by Lord Hardinge; he rode a horse instead. Before him, down avenues lined with soldiers, pranced squadrons of Dragoons, Guards and Lancers, their polished gear and harness glistening in sunlight. Through the Red Fort and onto the great maidan between the Fort and the Jama masjid, the parade then moved straight down the most famous street (Chandni Chowk) of Delhi. Slowly the great five-mile long procession moved along until, at last, it reached the imperial encampment on the far side of the city; to its North and West. Here the King-

Coronation Memorial and assemblage point of the Royal Aristocrates, High Military Officers, Governors and Governors General and other dignitaries in 1877, 1903 and 1911.

Statue of King George V, the Coronation Ground

Emperor and Queen-Empress were escorted to their own pavilion. The state entry was over.[51]

Five days later on 12 December, 1911, the coronation Durbar was held. Preparations had been going on for over a year, ever since Lord Hardinge had first arrived in India. He had appointed Sir, John Hewett, and Lt. Governor of the United Provinces, to head the Durbar Committee. A special crown of India for the king was made, which was taken to England; and later placed in Tower of London. The site had been just as carefully prepared, with details arranged down to the smallest point. The Durbar itself began with the formal

This building was constructed as a platform for railways (Kingsway Railway station) to bring the dignitaries to the Coronation Ground for the Coronation ceremony in 1911. Later in 1935 it was converted into a Tuberclosis Hospital which was inaugurated by Mr. J. N. G. Johnson, Chief Commissioner of Delhi Province. Now it is Rajan Babu Tuberclosis Hospital governed by Delhi Corporation.

Post Office built by the British in 1911, Timarpur.

British Cantonment Dispensary on the back side of Daulat Ram College, University of Delhi, now under the control of Delhi Police.

entry of army veterans from past wars. These were led by more than a hundred survivors of the great Mutiny. It was followed by the Viceroy and Lady Hardinge, various guards, and Royal Guards. As a 101 Gun salute began to echo and as rolling drums and a fanfare of trumpets sounded, the entire throng came to its feet. The Royal Landau arrived at the double-tired dais. The King-Emperor and Queen-Empress, arrayed in their crowns and coronation robes of ermine-lined deep purple were greeted by the Viceroy and led to gilt chairs on the dais, other took their places.

Sir Henry McMahon, master of ceremonies approached and asked permission to open the proceedings. Again there was a roll of drums and a flourish of trumpets. The King rose to his feet and delivered a short address. He indicated joy and thankfulness at being able to come to Delhi, to announce in person his coronation which had been celebrated in Westminster Abbey on 22 June, 1910 to renew past pledges to maintain rights and privileges in India, and to express earnest concern for the welfare, peace and contentment of India's peoples. Recalling with gratitude his previous visit to India, he voiced bright hopes for the future and tendered his 'loving greetings' to all present. All of the great notables of India came forward, one by one to do homage. The Governor-General bowed, kissed the royal hand, the commander in-chief saluted. Members of Council bowed, Princes, each according to custom, bowed, bent low, placed swords on the ground, or tendered their submission by other gestures, Begum of Bhopal in *burqa* made obeisance, Governor, Judges of

High Courts, other civil and military persons did the same one by one.

Lord Hardinge stepped forward to read the list. The boons, commencing with the smallest mounted upward step by step; Money for the advancement of education, half a month's extra salary for all Government servants in India, medals for meritorious service, remissions of debts, release of prisoners from jail. The reading ended with innovation of 'God save the King-Emperor'!

Then suddenly, to the surprise of all, the King-Emperor took a document from Hardinge, the, Governor-General's hand and began to read in a loud voice:

> we are pleased to announce to our people that, on the advice of our Ministers, tendered after consultation with our Governor-General in Council, we decided upon the transfer of the seat of the Government of India from Calcutta to the Ancient capital of Delhi, and, simultaneously, and as a consequence of that transfer, the creation at as early date as possible of a new Governorship for the Presidency of Bengal, of one Lt Governorship in Council administering the areas of Bihar, Chota Nagpur, and Orissa, and of a chief-Commissionership of Assam, with such administrative changes and redistribution of boundaries as our Governor-General in Council with the approval of our Secretary, of state in Council, may in due course determine.[52]

After some wilder cheering, yet another playing of the National anthem and a final artillery salute, the royal party made a dignified departure from the amphitheatre and returned to the Royal Pavilion. The Coronation Durbar was officially over. The king went to Nepal and the Queen to Taj Mahal.

The decision to move the capital of India from Calcutta to Delhi was received differently by different people; it depended upon where they had originated and from whom. Outside Calcutta, it was enthusiasm or indifference. The people of Delhi were delighted. The people of united province, Punjab and Rajputana were pleased as their new proximity to the centre of power. Bombay, long resentful of Calcutta's supremacy was not sad to see the humbling of a rival. As for Madras and other cities, they remained largely unruffled.

The Bengalis of the two Bengals were enthusiastic over the revision of their province. Congress Moderates under the leadership of Surendra Nath Banerjee felt vindicated. Most Calcutta gentry seemed to have been anything but enthusiastic. 'They have wiped our eyes and knocked out one eye in doing so'.[53]

Some blamed terrorists for bringing such loss to Calcutta. Muslim League was not happy with this decision as some Muslims were getting jobs, and after this they will be devoid of it.

The Durbar announcement was read in Parliament on the same day that in 12 December 1911. It was a surprise to the opposition leaders but a fait accompli, as the King had already taken a stand and announced it.

The preparation of this declaration was going on for a year but it was kept a top secret. On 15 December 1911, their Imperial Majesties laid the first stone of the new capital of India. The place was selected in the Government of India camp, which had been decided to be the centre of the Imperial Delhi that is to be. Later it was shifted to Raisina Hills. It can be seen now while going from Raj Path to Rashtrapati Bhawan. It lies between North Block and South Block.

Delhi during 1911-31

A high priority was accorded by the British to make Delhi a safe place for the soldiers from 1860. But now the capital has been declared to be shifted to Delhi from Calcutta, again more priority was given to make Delhi and its neighborhood more attention for its development. The Delhi Municipal Committee was not ready to take up all the development work, due to lack of funds. It was also not ready to levy taxes on common people as it was done in the recent past.

> What ever extra taxation was laved fell on the lower classes, as had happened earlier. In 1914 the wheel tax was enhanced, and the protest by the thelawalas of Idgah was ignored. In 1916 the buffalo tax was raised to a steep Rs. 5 per month, to induce the gwalas to move out beyond Yamuna. There were protests from impoverished gwalas in Subzi Mandi and from the militant leather merchants of Sadar Bazar..... The electoral rules of the Municipality were revised upwards in 1914. The voter now needed to be the occupier or owner of premises within his ward rated at a house-tax of at least Rs. 1-8 as per annum. Candidates for election had to be owners or occupiers of premises valued at Rs. 13-2 as per annum for house tax, or who had paid Rs. 35 per annum in income-tax for the past three years.[54]

On 23 December 1912 Lord Hardinge, the Viceroy, made a state entry into the capital city of Delhi. As he was leaving Government House, Calcutta, the flag staff was struck by lightning and the flag turn to ribbons. Fifty elephants took part in the procession from central station (Old Delhi Railway Station) through the Chandni Chowk to the palace. One elephant did not complete the journey. As the Viceroy with Lady Hardinge beside him passed the Punjab National Bank building, some one threw a bomb; which burst just behind the *howdah* killing the Chobdar holding the state umbrella. Fortunately the Viceroy was only wounded, Lady Harding escaped unhurt. Lord Hardinge subsequently recovered from his wounds.

The procession proceeded with a slight delay, and the city was handed over by Sir Louis Done: Lt Governor of the Punjab, in the Dewan-i-Aam. He referred the actions of the Punjab and Sikh chiefs in the Mutiny, after which Delhi became a province of the Punjab for fifty-five years. Sir Guy Fleetwood

Ludlow Castle where Delhi Club was shifted from the site in front of Red Fort.

Wilson read the Viceroy's reply, Delhi then became a separate province under a Chief Commissioner, on a parallel to the District of Columbia, surrounding Washington in the U.S. the Chief Commissioner's role in the Government of Delhi city was to be considerable, because the province was an Imperial Enclave and also because his residence was in Delhi, whereas earlier the Lieutenant-Governor had been more remote, in Lahore. The Cantonment Act, as desired by Craddock, was not implemented but effective self-government was considerably reduced. Delhi Municipality's territory and authority were truncated, and it came to be sandwiched between two 'Imperial' areas. It was shorn of the civil lines, which, with the addition of five-hundred acres to the north, was formed into a Notified Area Committee. From 1912 to 1922 (that is, until New Delhi was partly built) this area was maintained as a temporary capital. A Viceregal Lodge was built North of the Ridge (later it was occupied by Delhi University) the Secretary's office at Alipur Road, (now 5, Sham Nath Marg), the Commander-in-Chief's office was at Alipur Road (now Indraprastha College since 1932) and Assembly (now Old Secretariat). The Government was not eager to spent expenditure on temporary Delhi which is evident from the records.[55]

World War I Slow Down Town-planning Schemes

The Western extension area originated with a scheme to use Karol Bagh (a earlier Bagh Karoli) for settling the families of workers employed in the construction of the New Capital and families of tanners from Pahargunj. This would be adjacent to two settlements inhabited by those displaced from the capital. The area between the western extension and the city was to be improved with a wide road linking the Civil Lines and the Imperial city, through the Sadar Bazar and Jhandewalan. The Burn Basin Road was to accommodate the spillover from crowded Khari Baoli and the Jhandewalan Road. Improvement scheme would prove good sites for shops. The city wall from Kabul Gate to Ajmeri Gate was demolished and the ditch filled. Beadon, who was the Dy Commissioner of Delhi, wanted the Western extension to be controlled by the Imperial Government The earlier extension of Western suburbs had occurred largely spontaneously, but the extension from 1912 to 1919 was due to an artificial stimulus which went against the more natural tendency to extend south and parallel to Sadar Bazar. New roads became necessary, and the two biggest ones planned were new Jhandewalan Road (east-west) and the Idgah Road (north-west) Sadar Bazar was initially established for the needs of those soldiers who were quartered in the Idgah and on Pahari Dhiraj. Many of the shopkeepers, who had been displaced by the clearance around the fort, were given cheap plots of land in the new Sadar Bazar; the old Sadar Bazar was at Khyber Pass. It was for the facilities of the soldiers of the Rajpur Cantonment. At new Sadar Bazar Punjabi Muslims, who were traders dominated the area and after 1877 through Fateh Puri Masjid they also influenced the politics of the city.

In 1830, Charles Trevelyan, the brother-in-law of Macaulay, spent his own money to establish a small suburb outside Lahore Gate. After the capture of Delhi in 1858, there was a debate that the city and fort be demolished, but Trevelyan wrote to Lawrence that the city be repaired and it should be improved. Ultimately, excepting some part around the fort, the city was spared.

In 1915 a new slaughter house at Kadam Sharif near the Idgah was built, which sparked protest by the Hindus who patronized the Jhandewalan Temple nearby; and become implacably hostile to Beadon. The Muslims of Phari Dhiraj and Sadar Bazar (The Punjabi Muslim) purchased, the Shidipura cemetery (Kabristan) in 1904, it was restored in 1915 to these Muslims.

By the 1890's the Civil Lines population was a mix of Europeans who were working in Railways and Mills. The racial polarization became clear. The club (in front of Red Fort) was shifted from the city to Ludlow Castle in 1898; it may be due to 'Plague Scare'. Some new Hotels were built in Civil Lines i.e. Laurie's Hotel, Maiden's Hotel (which started with a single story in 1900 but did well enough to justify a second story within seven years), and in 1920s Hotel Suisse, at the place of Curzon House (new Swiss Apartments are built there, it is near Nicholson cemetery) and Cecil Hotel. In 1908 the army moved to a new cantonment on the Ridge, and the offices of the Deputy Commissioner and of the Commissioner shifted from Kashmiri Gate to the Civil Lines. By 1903, the Indian owners of the plots such as Lala Ram Chand, Lala Sri Ram, Lala Basheshar Nath Goela, Sheikh Hafizullah and Sheikh Abdul Ghani also shifted their activities to this place. In 1912 this area was constituted in to the Notified Area, and building activities increased, and the inhibited area extended

Chandni Chowk, 1860.

beyond the Ridge. The temporary capital occupied buildings sprawling from the Ridge down to Metcalfe House. During first World War the Land Lords push up rents further, this increase in rent tapered off by the mid-1920s, when official started to move to houses in the new capital in Raisina. Many buildings in Civil Lines played different roles at different times, that is, Curzon built an official house in 1903 for Durbar. In 1920's it housed offices of Delhi University, after it was Hotel Suisse, and now 'Swiss Apartments'. The cantonment at Rajpur remained there from 1828-57. Then it was shifted to the city. Sadar Bazar area also increased in population especially due to Railways and expansion of trade. Pahargunj after 1871 became very important, till now it was the residence of tanners.

They were shifted to Karol Bagh area, and Railway Quarters were built and in the early years of twentieth century, New Delhi Railway Station also came into being.

In the early 1880s, there was no industrial establishment in Delhi to which the Factory Act was applicable. Some small *karkhanas* were there.

In 1885 ten such industries were there in Delhi that is one at Bara Hindu Rao, where cotton machines were used by Mr. Wilson, and employed two hundred men, other an ice factory in Kauria Pul employing twelve persons, By 1888, the cotton spinning and ginning and the flour industries were beginning to be mechanized. The Delhi Cloth Mills and the Delhi Cotton Mills established in 1889. The Indian shareholders were local Banias and Khatris, the Chief contributors being Lala Ram Kishan Das. By the end of nineteenth century there were ten cotton factories and in 1900 there were more than 2,500 workers in the twenty Mills in Delhi.[56]

In 1890's additional railway lines were constructed in Delhi and the number

Railway Bridge over Jamuna.

of industries increased; in 1902 electricity also added the incentives. The Northwestern Railway initially benefited Delhi merchants and industrialists by opening up the Karachi route. By the beginning of twentieth century Delhi became the major railway junction in North India.

In 1905, the Punjab Chamber of Commerce established its head-quarters in Delhi and its branches in Amritsar and Lahore. After the capital was moved to Delhi, many joint-stock banks, British and nationalist Indian, established branches. But still the bulk of banking business at Delhi was carried on in the indigenous fashion. The Kayasth Mercantile Bank started in 1880's which break down the monopoly of the Khatris and Banias. This was a symptom of the caste-conflict which in the presidency towns took the form of competition for white-caller jobs. In 1898 a native commercial Bank was established for the purpose of lending money, buying and selling hundis, and undertaking insurance, an attempt to combine Indian and European banking methods.[57]

By 1912, Delhi became politically and economically the centre of North-India and Railway played a great role in this. There was no village of Delhi which was 12 miles away from Railways. The Railways and factories changed the pattern of Urban Delhi. The road from Sabzi Mandi through Sadar Bazar to Panchkuyan became important. It attracted many people to settle for residence and business purposes. In Karol Bagh, Tibbia College and other educational institution came in to being in 1920's. A road was built between the Civil Lines and the new city lay through Faiz Bazar, in Daryaganj. Since this was Nazul property or an 'extension,' the Municipality had to bear the huge cost of 'improving' Daryaganj. The cantonment was situated in Daryaganj, It was shifted from this place in 1916 it was thought that a large number of plots be sold. In 1920, it was sold to people at higher premium and for schools at lower premium. In 1913, the Sunehri Masjid (south of the Red Fort), which falls in the vicinity of the cantonment area, the prayers were stopped there. The pipal park (People Park), which was the venue of the gathering, was now given to an Imperial Institution for a low sum. Now some shops, parking area and State Bank of India came over it.

In 1925 a resolution was moved in Municipality which was turned down by the Chief-Commissioner and vetoed down by Deputy Commissioner. In 1928, Johnson, the Chief-Commissioner dismissed Improvement Trusts as an expensive error. Delhi acquired an Improvement Trust only in 1937. By 1921, the imperial Government reduced the power of the Municipality 'local-self-government' became a 'transferred' department. In the 1940s and 1950s, Karol Bagh was used for the refugees who came to Delhi due to strain of partition. The transfer of the capital from Calcutta to Delhi and later the World War I sparked off a sudden rise in the cost of living in Delhi. To popularize the Karol Bagh a bus-service was introduced from Bara Hindu Rao to Ajmeri Gate via Karol Bagh. After the transfer of the capital, many inhabitants who had hitherto been only lethargically interested in national politics came into contact with politicians of an all-India reputation. Slogans and ideologies that formed part of national politics started to be used for local grievances. After the attack on Hardinge in 1912, the beautiful trees along Chandni Chowk were cut down, and the canal bricked over.

Amir Chand was condemned to death, which sparked great indignation, But it was not so in the case of Rash Behari Bose. From 1912, many Bengalis came to Delhi with the shifting of the capital from Calcutta to Delhi. Dr H. C. Sen and later Rash Behari Bose entertained all Bengalis visiting Delhi. In Delhi, Ajmal Khan, Girdhari Lal, Wazir Singh, Amba Prasad, the Ali Brothers, Ansari, Abdullah Churiwala, Obeidullah Sindhi, Saif-ur-Rehman, Umrao Mirza, Abdul Ghani, Shardhanand, Pyareylal, Abdul Rehman, Mrs Besant, M.K. Gandhi, Abdul Aziz, Shiv Narain, S.N. Bose, Lala Ram Kishan Das, Lala Sri Ram, Raj Narain, Sultan Singh, Shankar Lal, Mr Gidwani, Principal of Hindu College, Principal, Allnut of St. Stephen College, K.A. Desai, Beadon, Barron, and Hailey played the prominent role in the politics of Delhi from 1912 to 1931 in relation to Hindu-Muslim politics, in the improvement of the old city, in relation to representation in Municipality in relation to Jallianwalan Bagh agitation, in relation to Khilafat Movement, in relation to Home Rule League and various satyagrah and other movements started from time to time.

The water, sewer and electricity were provided to the old city. By 1931, the transfer of the capital from Civil Lines to New Delhi became clear. After Delhi became the seat of the central Government, political activity was constant and on occasion, when connected with local problems affected the local inhabitants. This political activity was carried on in the 'old city'. Which remained the political heart of the urban Area, though sandwiched between the arid stretched of New Delhi and the apolitical bureaucratic Island of the Civil Lines.

The seeds of British rule were planted in 1714 when British succeeded in establishing in Delhi an Embassy of the East India Company. The English influence in Delhi since then became pronounced. It was more due to the weak Mughal administration, throughout the late seventeenth and eighteenth centuries, that European style buildings started coming up, which intercepted the façade of Mughal and Indian architecture. Besides quite a few townhouses, bungalows, churches and cemeteries were built in the European style. Even the narrow streets of the walled city were visible with the imported architecture.[58]

After defeating the Marathas (1803), who were the protectors of Mughal ruler, the British became the rulers of India.

In 1824, Town Duties Committee was established. In 1828, British troops shifted from old city to Ridge Cantonment, Rajpur Cantonment and Khyber Pass. In 1833 in the first census of Delhi 1,19,800 persons were living in Delhi. In 1843 Delhi's population was 1.31 lakh people. In the same year water sources were surveyed. It was found that water in 555 wells out of total 607 wells was brackish and drinking water from the river was considered necessary. The census of 1853 recorded a population of 1.51 lakh. In 1915, 193 sq. miles were included in Delhi's territory from the districts of Meerut and Bulandshahar across the river Yamuna.

After the Mutiny of 1857, one-third of the city was razed to the ground. Almost the entire population of the walled city was ejected. Muslims tried to settle down in the suburbs of Motia Khan, Idgah, Qadam Sharif, Nizam-ud-Din, Mehrauli, Shahdara, and Paharganj and many migrated to Lucknow, Hyderabad and Jaipur. The infantry was centralized in Daryaganj and Kashmiri Gate. Lahore and Delhi Gate of the Red Fort were renamed as Victoria and Alexandra Gate and a town hall was built in Chandni Chowk. In 1863, Delhi Railway Station was constructed on the debris of the houses demolished by the British after Mutiny.

In 1863, the Delhi Municipal Committee was given control and jurisdiction over the walls and adjacent area were transferred to Civil Authority. In 1867, Delhi was given the status of a First Class Municipality. In 1874, Delhi Municipal Committee was given control of Nazul (government) Lands up to three mile radius of the city walls that enlarged its functions and jurisdictions. In 1881, the 'Building Bylaws' were passed by the Municipal

Committee. The Delhi Durbar of 1877, signified the importance attached to Delhi and boosted the development and expansion of Civil Lines and the area towards the north of the walled city. In 1892, a waterworks was opened, which introduced in Delhi prepped water piped in the buildings. In 1895, sewer constinction in the Chandni Chowk area was undertaken. In 1901, electric lighting was provided to the walled city. In 1902, tram transport in the walled city was another achievement of technological progress. In 1902, house tax was introduced. In 1908, the cantonment was shifted from Daryaganj to Northern Ridge.

When King George V proclaimed the shifting of the capital from Calcutta to Delhi on 12 December 1911, he desired that the planning and designing be done with the greatest deliberations and care.

A temporary capital was constructed towards the north of the Civil Lines and became functional from December, 1912. The Town Planning Commission, Comprising of G.S.C. Swanton, Edwin Lutyens and J.A. Bordie, after a long deliberations and search, recommended the location of the new capital in the area around Raisina Hill.

The new city was planned to accommodate a population of 65,000 people; it was planned adjacent to Shahjahanabad yet separated from it by an open space buffer and Railway embankment. Minto and Lady Harding Bridges

Christian Colony, Daryaganj.

made it accessible to the old City. New Delhi was laid in a geometric pattern over a triangular base formed by Connaught Place, Government Complex and the India Gate. The centre piece of the plan was the central vista. The residential areas were laid with lower and middle income employees to the north of the fashionable shopping centre of Connaught Place; New Delhi Railway Station was laid. This insulated the new capital from the old city. The villages within the limits of Imperial Delhi were: Shadipur, Todapur, Dashghara, Malchha, Alipur Pillanji, Arakpur, Bagh Mochi, Mohammad Pur, Munirka, Mujahidpur, masjid Moth, Gathusarai, Kushak, Kayasthpura, Shalimar, Ghondli, Jatwara Kalan, Firoz Pur Khadar, Firoz Pur Bangar, Mubarak Pur Reti, Nagla Machi, Samaspur Jagir, Pehladpur Rig, Mubarak Pur, Kotla Khurd, Rai Pur Khurd, Jamrsud Pur, Garhi Jhandia Mandia, Kilokhri, Nizampur, Behlolpur Bangar.[59]

C. F. Andrews.

The whole city, covering about 3,200 acres, was nestled between two ecological features of the site, which were river Yamuna on the East and the Aravali Ridge on the West.

> The main feature of New Delhi's street pattern is a broad processional avenue, which was known as the king's way and now called Rajpath, linked India Gate with the Viceroy's residence. Various roads cross this main avenue at right angles, but the general street pattern is diagonal to the main axis. The system of Diagonal Avenue in Delhi provides directness of movement for vehicular traffic which has much to command it. Lutyens had far sighted perspective and planned the roads with liberal widths. Delhi has multiplied ten times than what it was planned for, most of the roads have been able to bear the burden of multiplying Traffic.[60]

About Rs. 115 millions were spent on building a new city; which was completed in 1931. The New Delhi was not built simply to provide housing and office space for bureaucrats. From the outset it was charged with symbolic meaning, and the two architects, Edwin Lutyens and Herbert Baker, who laid out the city, put up its principal structures with a carefully thought out set of objectives in view. Lutyens, as the chief designer and architect, has won much deserved fame for his work in Delhi. Baker by contrast has been often disparaged. Yet the buildings Baker designed are central to any understanding of architecture of Imperial Delhi. By extension they may tell us something about the character and purpose of the British Empire itself.

Herbert Baker was the architect of Parliament building; Robert Tur Russell was the architect of Connaught Place. E.L. Lutyens was the Architect of Vice-regal Estate and also layout the details of capital complex at Raisina.

The British built New Delhi as if they will be rulers for eternity. But events took such a shape and so speedily that by 1947 the British had to leave India. However, before they left, they divided the country. The partition brought its own problems. With the partition and independence of India, Delhi witnessed one of the largest immigration in the human history. Delhi was not prepared for this exodus of population; Ministry of Relief was created by the central government. New townships in the urban fringe of Delhi were planned during 1948-52, by the Delhi Improvement Trust and the Central Public Works Department for the Ministry of Relief (later Ministry of Rehabilitation) these schemes housed the refugee population. Thirty-six rehabilitation townships were developed, on all sides of Delhi that is, Sheikh Sarai, Kalkaji, Tihar, Nizam-ud-Din, Lajpat Nagar, Jung Pura, Old and New Rajinder Nagar, Patel Nagar, Malviya Nagar, Moti Nagar, Ramesh Nagar, Kingsway Camp, Gandhi Nagar, for Government employees, who were multiplying with the fast growing central government, five townships, namely Vinay Nagar, Sarojini Nagar, Kaka Nagar, Lodi Road and Moti Bagh were developed. To meet the needs of the rich and the business class, Sunder Nagar, Jor Bagh and Golf Link were developed. In December, 1957, Delhi Development Authority was created which has built many colonies since then. The slum clearance and improvement work was transferred to the Municipal Corporation. Over the years, due to lack of political will and apathy of the politician and bureaucrats, they created many authorities to function in Delhi at one and the same time, such as Land Development Office, C.P.W.D., D.E.S.U. (now private companies), D.D.A., D.W.S. and S.D.U. and D.T.C. and no one is answerable to the other or any one Agency. The lack of proper interaction among them creates further problems for people.

Delhi is drifting slowly towards its own death. It is choking. Its environment pollution level is highest among the cities of the world. The Yamuna is dying; it floods during the rainy season. Transport service is a total failure despite a metro system recently introduced. The town-planning is awful; the civic services are criminally neglected. The population, especially the migrants are increasing everyday in thousands and the amenities like, electricity, roads, health, education, water, sanitation and land are not impowering in the same proportion, the problem of law and order is increasing day by day. Fear of terrorism is increasing, police atrocities and indifference is on the rise. Apathetic administration can be gauged from the complete lack of interest in solving the problems of the people, ensuring viral fever, safe water and health care, quality of construction, illegal encroachment on government land. The increase in the number of beggars price rise, education and power crises are such issues that any Government and its leaders should rise above petty politics and solve these problems or certainly these will eat the vitals of Delhi.

Freedom Movement in Delhi and Hindu-Muslim Relations

India was the first in Afro-Asian countries that got independence from the British Imperialism; this example was later emulated by other Afro-Asian countries. It was a long fought movement, in which many people sacrificed their life, liberty and property. So many events took place. Many leaders emerged; various issues became the focal points of the movement. There were many trading companies, like the Dutch, French and Portuguese but they could not survive, it was only the British East India Company founded in 1600, with the grant of limited trading privileges from the Mughal rulers, with the decline of Mughal power in eighteenth century and a series of battles with the Marathas, the French and local rulers, in 1757, 1764, 1803, 1818 and 1849—the British East India Company established a firm foundation of its rule.

By the middle of the nineteenth century, the whole of the Indian Sub-continent had passed under the British control either directly or through the various subsidiary treaties, as in the case of Princely States ruled by the Indian rulers.

The British conquest of India was, in essence different from the earlier conquests of India by the Muslims; the dominance the latter had exercised was mainly military and political, leaving the social structure of Hinduism more or less intact. The British rule resulted in many socio-economic revolutions, culminating in the development of the infrastructure of modern state such as a uniform system of law, education, transportation and communication, and a highly centralized and professionalized bureaucracy; the emergence of political institutions and associations such as legislatures, local councils and interest groups and political parties; and the birth of new social groups, professions and occupations, especially the English-educated new middle class.[61]

The Indian National Movement can be divided into three main phases—(1) Politics of Social Reforms and Colonial liberalism, the Nationalism of social reformers and the moderates of the Indian National Congress. (2) The politics of terrorism, Hindu revivalism, and Swaraj. (3) The Gandhian synthesis (1920-47).

The reprisals after the revolt are also one of the reasons of freedom movement. The discontent and helplessness was simmering in the masses.

They were killed and looted ruthlessly, even the scale of Nadir Shah's atrocities on Delhi people had been crossed. British terror was everywhere. Even the villages in the neighborhood of Delhi were plundered; people were hanged, even innocent old people were not spared; religious places like the Jama Masjid, Fatehpuri Masjid, Kala Masjid and a masjid at Sadar Bazar were not spared; temples were looted and even the idols were broken, just to take the booty buried under it.[62]

The Gurudwaras were not touched, as the Sikh army of Patiala, Jind and Nabha were helping the British and the Government believed that the rebellion of 1857 was overwhelmingly a Muslim movement 'and with them alone was there any trace of National feeling' which the 'Hindus as a body acted very differently'. It was quite natural that the Government followed a policy of repression towards Muslims.[63]

Wahabi Movement

This movement was named after Mohammad-bin-Abdul Wahab (1703-87) of Arabia; while the Wahabis contented that they were Ahl-i-Hadis working for restoration of Islam to its pristine purity. The loss of socio-religious decay of the Muslim community and its loss of political power in the eighteenth century gave rise to Wahabi activities in India especially in Delhi. In Delhi, Shah-Walliullah (1702-63), who was the contemporary of Mohammad-bin-Abdul Wahab, was the leader of the Wahabi movement; later his son, Shah Abdul Aziz, led it. The two main features of this movement was to ameliorate the Islamic social structure and to fight against the infidel rulers. At first it started from the North-West Frontier under the leadership of Sayyid-Ahmad of Rae Bareli (1786-1831), their activities spanned from 1820 to 1870. Patna was its headquarter. Through the traders the money collected from Patna and Delhi was sent to North-West Frontier, in the hope that someday the Russian Government shall attack India and it will be possible to restore the Muslim rule in India. One such literature was sent to the Delhi-Municipal Committee, and also found from the houses of the activists. Maulvi Nazir Hussain, Maulvi Salim-ud-Din, Maulvi Hamid-ud-Din and Amir Bakhsh were prominent persons in Delhi.[64]

From 1869 a discernible shift in the British policy towards Muslims was noticed. In 1869-70 Syed Ahmed Khan of Delhi visited England; he was welcomed, recognized and presented to Queen. He was decorated. In 1859; he had also propagated the policy of 'Divide and rule' through his treatise – 'causes of Indian Revolt'; in 1860-61 he published a work on 'Loyal Muslims of India.' Some royal descendants like Zamani Begum, the wife of Jawan Bakht, the son of Bahadur Shah II came to Delhi from Rangoon on medical grounds. People of Delhi thought that royalty was being restored. Firoz Shah, the descendent of Akbar Shah, did try to restore royalty but the British checked his activities.

In 1876, some 300 Wahabis of Punjab gave a petition and declared that they were not Wahabis. The British government accepted it. The scale turned in favour of Muslims who were devoid of English education for a century. The Mutiny of 1857 was, to some extent a turning point in the progress of India and in its relationship with the colonial power. The British realized that the accomplishment made by Clive in the battle of Plassey, needed a continuous process, which further needed tact and diplomacy, with a capacity for giving occasional concessions to Indian demands. The effects of British rule up to the Mutiny were not completely negative, but they were imbued with white arrogance and utter disregard for Indian emotions. They unwittingly festered Indian Nationalism which, combined with the communal sentiments, but could lead sooner or later to the creation of an independent Pakistan and India.

The spread of the Western education gave rise to modern political awakening. The English education, based on Lord Macaulay's historic minutes, believed in the inherent superiority of Western culture and civilization. The revival of the old Delhi College in 1858, when a collegiate-school was established, was an event of great significance. To meet the onrush of students in 1862, branches of the collegiate-school were opened in different part of Delhi.[65]

The school was affiliated to Calcutta University in 1862. The spread of Western education was mainly confined to Hindu classes such as Khatris, Kayasthas and Suds. The courses taught were modern history, modern politics, modern economics and the english language and literature. It is reported that by 1860 'the feeling of freedom is daily gaining strength in the hearts of thousands. Universities and schools are doing their work well, and those who are educated are beginning to see that Education is the foundation of wealth and honour'.[66]

The writings of Thomas Pain, Locke, Burke, Macaulay, Mill, Bentham, Rousseau, Voltaire and the pioneers, of the French Revolution, inspired the ideas of liberalism, Individual liberty and national freedom, equality, national unity and fraternity. They also came to know of the leaders of Italian unity, the war of American Independence, the Irish struggle for freedom and free political institutions of the West. This made the people of India, especially the youth of Delhi, the discontented lot.

The Western political ideas found their expression in the growth of the Indian Press. By 1876 there were 15 newspapers in Delhi. These papers ventilated the grievances of the Public. The newspapers highlighted the incidents of insecurity (robbery), famine (1865), poverty. In 1866, the Delhi literary society was formed for social and intellectual intercourse. It was pleaded that civil service examinations be held in India and Indians be placed in higher positions.

Apart from social indignities inflicted upon Indians, the justice administered in British courts was also tainted, if one party was Indian. This factor also produced the discontentment and reaction in the minds of Indians. The represented cases are: (i) Brahmani Bull case, 1868, (ii) Indian Mason Murder case 1870, (iii) Punkha Coolie Murder case 1877, (iv) Kishan Chand Murder case 1886, (v) Corporal Rigney case 1890, (vi) Davis Trial Case 1908. In these cases a murder was committed by an Englishmen, but he was let off, with a fine of Rs. 15 to 25 only. But in the same nature of cases, Indians were punished for murder. Another factor which contributed to the growth of political awakening was the effort of Christian missionaries to the spread the message of gospel.

The Missionary work in Delhi was started by Ram Chander soon after the suppression of the revolt of 1857. He was born at Panipat in 1822, a teacher of Mathematics in the Delhi College, who was converted to Christianity in 1853. In the post-1857 he was appointed Headmaster of a Government High School in Delhi. Thomas Skelton came to India in October in 1858. He learned Urdu from Sarfaraz Ali, a student of Ram Chander; Sarfaraz Ali and Tara Chand were baptized. Chaman Lal was also baptized along with Ram Chandra and was killed in 1857. Hira Lal, Qasim Ali and Sara, the widow of Chaman Lal assisted the Delhi Mission in spreading the Christianity in Delhi. Edward Bickersteth, the son of Henry Edward Bickersteth, a Bishop in England and a literary person was the first Head of the Cambridge Brotherhood, who converted many people from a section of Dalit community of Delhi to Christianity. A hall in his name 'Bickersteth Hall', was erected later on in walled city to baptize the people. In 1882, St. Stephen College was established. It was affiliated to the New University of the Punjab. Mr Winter, Lefroy, Allnut, Mrs. Winter before her death looked after the medical and zenana work in Delhi. She, along with a team of doctors and Nurses, also took medical case of women in villages around Delhi. In 1891, Dr Jennie Muller, a qualified medical Doctor took charge of St. Stephen's Hospital. No caste was recognized in this hospital, and all who were in need of healing, whether high born or low, were treated without distinction. The Mission also started St. Elizabeth's School for Handicraft, to help women to support themselves. Many were converted to Christianity in such places. In 1913, a Board of Missions was formed for examining nurses. St. Mary's Home was also established for blind and crippled women.

The Rev H.C. Carlyon, one of the original six of the Cambridge Brotherhood, used the method of establishing itinerary Camp in the villages for spreading the Christianity.

In 1913, Mission's teachers were stationed at Mehrauli and a small Christian congregation was built at Fatehpur. A Priest was also stationed in Rohtak and village Kharkhoda near Delhi in Sonipat district. In Sohna, a village in Gurgaon, families of a section of Dalits[67] were baptized in large number and so was the case in Delhi.

After the revival of the Delhi Mission, the Missionaries started preaching in bazars and streets, mainly in Chandni Chowk. When Muslim and Hindu religious leaders started doing the same, the administration protected the Missionaries. By 1877, the Missionary activities had longer among Muslims in the city. In 1890, the Missionaries were facing considerable obstacles to their strat preaching. A blind maulvi followed Mr Lefroy, Head of the Cambridge Brotherhood, like a ghost and made his life miserable. He had to ask for police protection 'against Muslim rowdy population', which was granted.[68]

At various occasions, discussions amongst the Missionary and the local Hindu-Muslim leaders took place at Fatehpuri masjid on the issue of conversion. Lala Chohak Chand, Lala Himmat Rai, Lala Jai Dayal and Sahai Mal among the Hindus and Ahmad Hassan, Din-Mohammad, Hakim Ahmadullah, Mohammad Yakub, Maulvi Ahmad-ud-Din and Maulvi Mohammad Yasin among the Muslims were vocal critic of conversion.[69]

In July 1873, there were frequent reports of people bitten by mad dogs. It may be due to unusual heat. The civil surgeon brought this to the notice of Deputy Commissioner, who in turn, issued an order to catch the dogs. In the process, some pet dogs were also caught by the Kanjars, who were assigned this job. One such dog belonging to a shopkeeper from Nai Sarak, was also taken captlured on 12 July 1873. Next day, the bazars of the whole dity were closed, a *hartal* (strike) was observed by Hindu and Muslim shopkeepers.

The observance of hartal by the people of Delhi, marking their protest against the local authorities, was obviously due to a spirit of self-assertion that was sweeping through the Indian community.

In the 1870s, India was definitely in a state of political fermentation, before the formation of Indian National Congress in 1885, the sporadic outburst of political and religious excitement was also more national and critical of British domination.

The British Crown took over the administration from the East India Company in 1858 but the new title was not assumed. This gave embarrassment to successive Indian administrations. So the Royal Titles Act was adopted by British Parliament on 27 April 1876, and Queen Victoria was declared the 'Empress of India. In 1875-6 Prince of Wales visited India. In 1877, a Durbar was held in Delhi. Queen Victoria was declared as the 'Qaiser-i-Hind', which was criticized as it did not specify any gender.[70]

The people of Delhi also complained of much harshness and oppression on the part of the police on the day the Viceroy entered the city.[71]

(a) People were discontentd and they expected and desired that they would be given equal responsibility in administration;

(b) No opportunity was given to Indians to sit for the ICS Examination; they also wanted that Examination to be held in India.

(c) Nothing was done to improve agriculture, which was deteriorating day-by-day. The government revenues, after defraying ordinary expenses of the state, mostly went into the pockets of Europeans and the remainder was sent to England. Indian commerce, industry and art revived. 'Europe has drained India of all her wealth.'[72]

(d) The Indian chiefs were awarded honorific appellations, without any material benefit. The gain of the Durbar was that the development of railways and other means of communication brought different parts of India into contact with one another and endeavored to obliterate their divergence. It also brought the conception of National unity.

In Poona and Bengal, the activities of national unity and social and political work were started by the elite.[73]

The vernacular press expressed the people's expression in their papers especially the Durbar of 1877 and Afghan war; so the Vernacular Act IX of 1878 was passed; for the better control of Publications in the oriental languages; which was highly disliked and criticized by the people and it was withdrawn after four years.

The growth of a National consciousness also emerged due to a number of Socio-religious reformation movements, they were the expressions of rising national consciousness. In 1876, in Delhi, a branch of the Banaras Theosophical Society was established with a view to removing mutual differences as well as to create love for the country.

At this time Swami Dayanand came to Delhi. He preached that the Vedas are the revelation of God. This was not accepted by the people who attended his meetings. He again came to Delhi on 3 October 1878 and established a branch of Arya Samaj in Delhi. In the first edition of Satyarth Prakash, published in 1875, Swami Dayanand held that it was lawful to kill a sterile cow and eat its flesh. He also advocated that flesh should be used in performing *hawan* morning and evening and otherwise sanctioned the killing of animals.[74]

He also criticized the Muslims, Christians and Sikhs, the caste system and idolatry. Later Swami Dayanand turned against cow slaughter.

A Jain Sabha was formed in Dharam Pura, Dariba to protect the Jain religion from Arya Samaj. In 1889, the Kayasth Self Advancement Society was set up in Kucha Chilpuri, Dariba. In 1892, Vaish Young Men Association in Mohalla Imli was established. Ram Sabha was established in Sita Ram Bazar in 1884. In 1896 in Mandir Chipiwara, Dariba, another organization came up, the Nawal Ram Sabha. Gopal Ram Sabha in 1891 near General Civil Hospital in Kucha Chelan. In 1895 a Sanatan Dharam Sabha at Haridwar and Delhi was established to counter the Arya Sabha.

In 1899 Hindu College was established at Delhi to give Education to Children on Sanatanist lines.[75]

In August 1900, the revivalist meeting of Sanatanist, under the Presidentship of the Maharaja of Darbhanga, was held in Delhi which was attended by 60, 000 persons. The Arya Samajists were alarmed due to this and they held a big meeting under the leadership of Lala Munshi Ram, later known as Swami Shradhanand. Sir Syed Ahmed Khan of Delhi started encoveraging adopt Muslims to a modern outlook. In 1863 he established a scientific society at Ghazipur, he was assisted by Munshi Amu Jan from Delhi. After some time, Sir Syed Ahmed settled at Aligarh and the society's headquarter was shifted to Aligarh. He established the Anglo-Mohammedan College, which later flourished into Aligarh Muslim University.

Maulvi Zakaullah.

Grave of Zakaullah at Dargah of Hazrat Abdul Salam, opposite Marina Hotel, Connaught Place.

Haveli of Nazir Ahmad, Gali Patishan, Khari Baoli.

Maulvi Nazir Ahmad.

In Delhi Sir Syed Ahmed was assisted by Maulvi Altaf Hussain Hali, the famous Urdu poet and a teacher in the Anglo-Arabic School at Delhi, Maulvi Zakullah (1832-1910), Maulvi Nazir Ahmed, a famous novelist and renowned for his erudite scholarship.

After the Mutiny of 1857, there was a sharp cultural, political and economic deterioration in the life of Muslims; it was partly caused by the suspicious attitude of the British toward Muslim ambitions and partly by the inability of the Muslims to adapt to the changed situation. The Hindus' grasped the opportunity of English language and western pattern of education. The Muslim gentry, proud of its traditional culture and resenting the intrusion of a foreign culture fell behind. As a consequence, Hindus entrenched themselves in government service from which the Muslims were excluded. The Hindus succeeded in taking advantage of the opportunities offered by the English commercial and industrial expansion, thus succeeded in creating a western minded Hindu middle class which the Muslim Society lacked. The situation changed somewhat around 1870. The English began to realize that they had made a mistake in putting all the blame for the Mutiny on the Muslims. They also conceived that the Muslim community could be an effective weapon against the rising demands of the Hindus; a small Muslim upper class was, at that time, under the leadership of Sir Syed Ahmed Khan; completely loyal to the crown.

Syed Ahmed's loyalty to the British was of old standing. During the Mutiny he supported the British, for which he was decorated by the Government.

The horror of the Mutiny, his guilt in 1857 and the second Mutiny in which the whole community would be annihilated, made Syed Ahmed to draw a plan to bring the Englishman and Muslaman near to each other. In 1869, he visited England, was presented to Queen Victoria, praised western culture, was given the title of Sir, in 1875, and with the help of the British established Mohammedan Anglo-Oriental College, which later developed into the Aligarh Muslim University. It soon became the cradle of Muslim political thought in India. He wrote in favour of English and worked on 'a radically new interpretation of Quran and Islam in the light of nineteenth century rationalism.'[76]

Syed Ahmed admired western achievement; he founded a movement in favour of contemporary western culture.

Prof Symonds summarizes the activities of Syed Ahmed Khan as follows:

> In theology he had reconciled Islam with western learning. In Education he had given the Muslims their own college where they could pursue western studies without becoming worse Muslims. In government service and commerce he had made openings for the new educated Muslim middle class. In politics he had stated that the Muslims were a Nation who could not and must not be submerged

in a system of government by majority vote. The Pakistanis rightly claim him as one of the fathers of their country.[77]

The policy of the Syed is contained in these three words: Education, Loyalty and opposition to the Hindus.[78]

The University movement, according to Syed,

> is the starting point of more extensive movement. The Question is nothing less than the political and religious awakening of the Indian Musalman. All thoughts of aggression, for the present, and for the future, against the English domination, have been discarded from it from the outset. On the contrary the Muslims offer themselves as allies, as Mamelukes, of the existing regime. To be the best Muslims means at the same time the most loyal subject.[79]

He also said that,

> When the English established their dominion in India, the latter was a poor widow waiting for a husband ...and we helped in the extension of the British rule, in furtherance of our well-being. We and the English nation, are joined together like the two blades of a pair of scissors...it is our ardent desire that British rule should continue not for a long time, but till eternity in the interests of our country. Therefore, there is no reason to suppose why there should not be sympathy between ourselves and the English.[80]

Syed had also said earlier that "the Hindus and the Musalmans are like the two eyes of a beautiful Maiden."[81]

Syed Ahmed Khan advocated for western achievement. He founded a movement in favour of cotemporary western culture.

Another Muslim leader, Amir Ali, advised Islam in its simplicity, purity and dynamism. He started a movement in favour of the Islamic culture of the past.[82]

Amir Ali was more aggressive and positive than Syed Ahmed: while Syed tried to prove the advantages of western learning to Indian Muslims, the former triumphantly proved the historical achievements of Islam.

The Hindus were crying for 'Back to Vedas' and the Muslim outburst was for 'back to the early Khilafat'; it was the call of revivalism which egged them to conceive of the good old days.[83]

The Pan-Islamic feelings found its expression in 1856 during the Anglo-Persian war and in 1877-8, during the Russo-Turkish war. In Delhi, Hasrat Ali, the editor of Hasrat-Ali-Akhbar, was the leader, who collected funds for Turks. Turkey was regarded as a symbol of Islamic power. A number of religious schools were established in Delhi such as the Arabic Madarsa in Kucha Rehman founded by Maulvi Abdul Rabb, it was re-established in 1867 by Maulvi Abdullah.

In 1847, the Madarsa Hussain Bakhsh was established which ceased to function in 1857. It was reopened in 1875. Madrasstul Quran in Chitli Darwaza was established in 1879. After the restoration of the Fatehpuri masjid, the committee under the guidance of Maulvi Mohammad Shah established the Fatehpuri-Maktab. In 1880 Maulvi Nazir Ahmed established his school at Phatak Habash Khan, assisted by his son, Maulvi Sharif Hussain. In 1871, Maulvi Ulfat Hussain, a teacher in the Normal School, established the Anjuman-i-Imamia (Religious Society) in Delhi with the object to reform the customs and ceremonies of the Muslims, particularly of the Shia Sect.[84]

In 1888, Anjuman-i-Muaiad-ul-Islam was established in Delhi in Kamra Bangash with an object to support and look after the education of destitute children. It was later assisted by Madarsa Rahimia Islamia Arabia in Bara Hindu Rao, Sadar Bazar in 1892, and Madarsa Aminia established by Maulvi Amin-ud-Din in masjid Panipatian, Kashmiri Gate. In the beginning of 1880s, the Indian Press, such as papers from Delhi that is, 'Khair Khwah-i-Alaam' (a weekly) and 'Delhi Punch', criticized the administration of English. In 2 February 1883 the 'Ilbert Bill was introduced in the legislative council, which debarred Indian judges to try Europeans; this Bill was criticized by Indians. The Europeans formed a defense association and held a protest meeting at Delhi and urged that it would be degrading for European women to appear before Indian Magistrates.[85]

This bill was a humiliation for educated Indians. The controversy taught them an object lesson about the enormous possibilities of a well organized political agitation. The period saw a mushroom growth of political associations in almost all parts of the country. One such association was the Bombay Presidency Association (31 January 1885) to which A.O. Hume was associated. He had arrived in Bombay in December 1884 to bid farewell to Lord Ripon with whom he had worked for Indian political reform. He wanted to direct the rising discontent as aspirations of educated Indians into constitutional channels and meet them by political reform. He visited Madras and, Calcutta in that connection. He also visited Simla and on his way from Simla to Calcutta, he met Lord Duffrin in early May 1885. Lord Dufferin agreed with Hume for an organization, through which the administration would know the mind of the educated Indians, but, at the same time, he warned that the administration should remain detached from such associations. The Indian National Congress had a modest beginning of 72 delegates who met in Bombay from 28 to 30 December 1885 under the Presidentship of A.O. Hume. The Conference decided to form itself into the Indian National Congress, drew up its aims and objects and decided to meet every twelve months to continue its work.

The Congress grew its popularity amongst educated and semi-educated Indians. It was not a mass organization and certainly not revolutionary one. The early Congress had misconception of British Imperialism. They admired the blessings of British rule. They were hardly ready to suffer personal sacrifice. However the work of the early Congress cannot be minimized. It did a great deal of spade work in furthering the cause of political education and National awakening and a feeling of common suffering under the foreign rule had developed.

By this time Syed Ahmed Khan had made clear his ideas, he believed that the Anglo-Muslim alliance would ameliorate the condition of Muslims, while the nationalist alliance would again lead them to disaster. He advocated that Muslims should remain loyal to British Government and stay out of all disloyal organizations.[86]

In 1886, the Congress session was held at Calcutta. Amir Ali, Secretary, Calcutta Mohammedan Association declined the invitation and also requested his fellow co-religionists not to attend Congress session. Nawab Abdul Latif, the Secretary of Mohammedan Literary Society also declined to have any truck with Congress.

On 28 December 1887 at Lucknow and on 16 March 1888 at Meerut, Syed Ahmed Khan made two pronouncements, which formulate his ideology. He said "Now suppose that all the English were to leave India, then who would be the rulers of India? Is it possible that under the circumstances two nations, the Mohammedan and the Hindu could sit in the same throne and remain equal in power? Most certainly not ... the rigour of religious institutions has kept neighbours apart."[87]

In 1888, Syed Ahmed and Raja Shiv Prasad of Benaras, who was the member of the Viceroy's Executive Council, established the Indian Patriotic Association as an ultra-loyalist organization to counterpoise the aims and objects of the Indian National Congress. The educated Muslims in North India had the effect of Syed Ahmed Khan ideas; so much so even Badruddin Tyabji, who presided the Congress Session in 1887, felt that the Congress should suspend its organization for five years.[88]

Lord Dufferin dubbed the Congress as a seditious organization.[89]

The Muslim distrust for the Congress was born out of mutual jealousy and religious conflict between the Hindus and the Muslims.

Communal Conflict in Delhi

The Indian Nationalism also carries with it the emergence of a religious conflict between the two major communities, the Hindus and Muslims. It expressed itself in two phases, anti-British and inter-communal. The stress and strain of communal tension was not unknown, but by and large, the contact between the Hindus and Muslims was one of co-existence with mutual tolerance rather than domination of one culture by the other, though in the process the Muslims occupied a position of slight vantage. In 1852, when Muharram and Dussehra fell on the same day, the authorities, following the old Mughal practice, decided in favour of the Muslims with the result that Dussehra celebrations in Delhi were postponed for 13 days. As late as 1875, the Hindu festival at certain places was put off for eight days.[90]

The Muslim communal movement in India, which sprang up after the Indian Mutiny of 1857-9, culminated in the establishment of Pakistan. An upshot of the British 'Divide and rule' policy, the religious communal problem gained increasing prominence in the country's social affairs at the end of the nineteenth century. It is not the orthodox Ulemas, but the European educated class, who helped to spread European culture; it also promoted the first Muslim organization. The early ideologists of religious communal—exclusiveness also advocated modernization of Islam and its adjustment to the changed social environment.

'The National Muslim Association' and the 'Mohammedan Literary Society' were founded in Bengal; the cradle of Indian nationalism. Abdul Lalif, associated with the western-educated Bengal landlords, was conferred the title of Nawab by the British government in 1880 and the Nawab Bahadur in 1887.

The Muslim section of Indian intellectuals was un-acquainted with European education and English literature and was throught to be inimical to their spread in India. This is not so, but it is true that Muslim society did not take the British educational system close to their hearts. Many young people of the Muslim landlord families and the younger generation of divines were enrolled in Delhi College. Many members and leaders of the 1857-9 uprising came from this college. By the middle of nineteenth century there existed in north-west India, especially in Delhi a group of western-educated Muslim Intellectuals but it was insignificant as the grey-bearded Mullahs and the Ulemas, keepers of the orthodox faith, still ruled the minds of the landlords, the Merchants, the petty traders and artisans, semi-literate themselves, the Mullahs were also the sole 'bearers of culture' in the villages. The 'National Muslim Association' opposed Muslim to Hindu Intellectuals and called for the exclusion of Muslims from the all-Indian national-organizations.

The early Muslim Educational Societies had a marked influence on the socio-political development of Muslim intellectuals outside Bengal and, in particular, on the development of the outlook of Syed Ahmad Khan (1817-98), known as the architect of the Muslim communal movement.[91]

He was highly influenced by the ideas of Shah Walliullah for his ideas on the revival of the original purity of the Holy Quran and later a pupil of Mohammad Ismail, the most prominent continuator of Shah Waliullah. But in the course of time, Syed Ahmad Khan's ideals changed. He described the enthusiasms of his youth as a 'sweet dream'. In 1847, he entered the British Civil Service.

He began studying the History of India. His historical conception reveals the duality of his socio-political views, which led up to the subsequent ideological substantiation of the Muslim communal movement. His utterances about the crisis and decay of the feudal Mughal Empire were best formulated by him in his Asar-us-Sanadid (Antiquities of Delhi). He differed in conclusions of Shah Walliullah; he believed Britain's conquest of India was a fait accompli, he believed that since India's old political system had become invalidated, British rule was inevitable and beneficial.

He considered the struggle of 1857-9 to be merely an attempt at restoring the old feudal order, and, deeply convinced in its futility, took the side of the British. He was also displeased with Britain's policy on the eve of the uprising and believed that the British authorities had insulted Indian 'National Pride' and given the Indians ample cause for discontent.[92]

He believed that Muslims should strive to combat poverty and ignorance; he also urged the admission of Indians to the legislative Assembly. His political ideas of the 1850s and 1860s reflected the ideas of the smaller landlords and intellectual class of North India. He believed that the Muslim landowners were ruined by Hindu Money-lenders and despised by the British authorities after the 1857-9 rising. This is evident from his book 'Asbab-i-Bagavat-i-Hind', in which he appealed to the British authorities to change their treatment of the Muslims, alternated with anti-Hindu utterances, subsequently employed by him and his followers to propound Muslim communal exclusiveness. By 1860, he became a popular educator in North India. In 1877 with the help of British he founded the Muslim College at Aligarh; which developed into the biggest ideological and political centre of the Muslim propertied classes in India and Educated many generations of Muslim intellectuals. The college was headed by English principals, Indian princes and landlords who were its trustees. It spread separatist sentiments, a spirit of loyalty to the British, and sought to keep the Muslims away from joining the Indian National Congress. But, concurrently, it did much to rouse the Muslim intellectuals politically, and further the emergence of a Muslim political party in India.

The Muslim intellectuals read Syed Ahmad Khan's journal, *Tehzib-ul-Akhlaq* (Social Reformer) where he urged the development of Urdu, European culture, and deplored the ignorance of the people. The course of theology was based on the notion that the tenets of Islam were proved by their conformance to the laws of nature, the name of Syed Ahmad Khan's philosophical school was 'Nachari', ('Natural', close to nature) and till the establishment by Congress in 1885, he was the champion of Hindu-Muslim unity but after it he became the founder of a separatist movement with a communal religious foundation. The Muslim communal movement came into being at about the same time as the All-Indian National-Liberation Movement. Through the open encouragement of the British Authorities, Muslim educationalism assumed an anti-congress and later also an anti-Hindu orientation. The reasons for that were multiple. The association of Muslim Educational Societies being the feudal leadership than their Hindu-counterpart, the British encouragement for the Muslim Education, the British gave prominence to minorities and divided Hindu-Muslim communities. The Congress disappointed the British Colonialists. They expected it to operate as a purely Hindu organization. It proclaimed an All India Party and later also timidly criticized the British Authorities and made some democratic demands. Soon after its formation, the Hindu movement against cow-slaughter arose in North India. This provoked the first Hindu-Muslim riots. The movement arose as one of the trends for the purity of the faith and in defense of religious customs and rites, but later due to British policy, it acquired an anti-Muslim tenor.

On 28 December 1887 Syed Ahmed Khan made a speech at Lucknow; he appealed to people of means, the middle classes and the nobility to be loyal to the British and to rely on the latter's support and assistance in their work for social progress. It was the first time anyone had stated so emphatically that he did not think the Muslims of India would gain anything from the country's liberation from British rule.[93]

This Lucknow speech was discussed in every intellectual Muslim house. The educational societies of the Muslims denounced the congress, and opposed it.

To combat 'the political ideals and activities of the congress' Syed Ahmed Khan in 1888 organized the first All-Indian Anti-Congress Organization of Muslims—the United Friends of India Society. In 1893, Anglo-Oriental Defense Association of upper India, with a similar object, was organized. Theodore Beck, the English Principal of the Aligarh College, declared 'that Muslims and Englishmen should unite in opposing them (the congress and the movement against cow-slaughter) and that the establishment of democratic political institutions should be opposed as they are not suitable to this country.'[94]

In 1890, a petition drawn up by Beck bearing 50,000 signatures (chiefly those of Anglo-Indian officials and Muslim landlords) was submitted to British Parliament, stating that Democratic Institutions were unsuited to India, because there were different communities inhabiting it.[95]

Beck's ideas became the pivot of British propaganda in India and exercised a strong influence on the socio-political views of Syed Ahmed Khan. Syed's another reason for congress and Hindu opposition was the competition of Bengal and Bombay people for private enterprise and civil service. He preferred political parties based on religious bases and not a country wide organization. From separatism in the field of education he also passed to separatism in the political field. He turned from an advocate of Hindu-Muslim unity into an advocate of Hindu-Muslim discard; contending that the various castes and religious communities of India had no common national interests.

People gave an ear, he was very popular among the Muslims, and his opinion was respected. As a result, while All-India National Organizations took strength, the religious communal movement also won a hold upon the minds.

Along with Modern Educational organizations there existed in North-West India the 'half-monastic and half-Knightly' medieval Muslim secret societies, they cherished the traditions of the liberation struggle of 1857-9; like the Wahabi Societies of 1840's, and Dar-ul-Ulum in Deoband; founded by Mohammad Qasim in 1867. He studied at Delhi College and took part in the uprising of 1857-9 and remained staunchly anti-British till the end. The Deoband centre gravitated towards the congress and was closely associated with the radical wing of the Indian Nationalists on the eve of the First World War.

In the fourth session of the congress, Badruddin Tyabji was its president he was for Hindu-Muslim consolidation and propagated that Muslim and Hindu should work for National interests with shoulder to shoulder.

The correspondence between Tyabji and Syed Ahmed Khan illustrates the general situation in which the Muslim Communal movement came into being.[96]

The Muslim League

The Muslim section of Indians gained increased economic and political weight in the first three decades of the twentieth century. This coincided with the awakening to political affairs of the middle sections of Muslims, causing a split within the older upper-crust Muslim educational societies and a new attitude on their part with regard to the All-Indian National-Liberation Movement. The early controversies among the moderate, pro-British Muslims, which dated back to Syed Ahmed Khan's life time, often assumed a religious complexion.

In the Punjab, traders, money-lenders and landlords formed a new Muslim Sect-the Ahmadiya or Quadiani Movement (1889). Ahmad Quadiani, founder of the sect, was proclaimed the new Muslim prophet, and his followers set out to adopt Islam to the news socio-economic and political setting.

While preaching Islam among Christians and Hindus, they supported the British rule. The other Muslim group, the Anjuman-i-Himayat-i-Islam (1890s) attacked Ahmadiya movement for departing from orthodox Islam and supporting the British colonial rule.

In Bombay and Calcutta, some Muslim intellectuals opposed the Anti-Congress stand of the Aligarh centre. In 1894, a new Muslim Educational Society, the Nadwat-ul-Ulema was founded in Lucknow.

The Society was founded by Nomani Shibli, a former teacher at the Aligarh College. In the early period this society was not opposed to Syed Ahmad Khan. But after 1905-08, it took a stand with Congress and Theodore Beck, the Principal of the Aligarh School opposed it.

The Muslim intelligentsia in North India could no longer stand aloof from the national movement and political life. The progressive element was eager to co-operate with the congress, the others who were affected by the British 'divide and rule" policy and the separatist notions advocated the establishment of an independent Muslim political party. The founding of such a party dates to 1905-8; a period of high tide in India's movement for National liberation. It was during this period that the peoples of India made their first steps towards conscious mass political struggle for National freedom and democratic rights. When Bal Gangadhar Tilak, Aurobindo Ghosh and others entered political field at the turn of the twentieth century, the National liberation movement showed more than just moderate constitutional opposition to the colonial authorities, the colonial authorities went to great pains to put Muslims against Hindus in the country's political life. They partitioned Bengal in 1905. With that ultimate purpose in view, supported the establishment of Muslim communal party (Indian-Muslim League) in 1906, and introduced separate electorate in 1909. The split caused by the British 'divide and rule' policy and the religious background of many of the anti-imperialist actions of the time tended to weaken the Indian National-Liberation Movement.

The partition was opposed by Congress, also opposed by most of the Hindu landlords; it was also opposed by Muslim traders, moneylenders and landlords, but Lord Curzon toured Bengal and told that the partition of Bengal would benefit the Muslims. The partition of Bengal, wrote the *Statesmen* was calculated 'to foster in Eastern Bengal the growth of Mohammedan power, which it is hoped will have the effect of keeping in check the rapidly growing strength of the Hindu community'.[97]

Muslims brought from the united provinces replaced many of the Hindu police officials and civil servants.[98]

The Nawab of Decca, Salimullah, assumed an anti-Hindu attitude after the Bengal partition Bill was published. The Aligarh Institute Gazette welcomed the move.[99]

The Muslim upper crust countered the slogans of Swaraj and Swadeshi with Swajaati (own-community), urging purely Muslim commerce, purely Muslim Industry, Muslim Schools and Muslim Business associations.[100]

The Congress Session in Benaras in 1905 was attended by only 17 Muslim delegates, whereas previous sessions saw as many as 700. Hindu-Muslim-riots broke out in Bengal.[101]

Abul Kalam Azad (1888-1958), a youth of 21 years, participated and advocated for Hindu-Muslim unity; also Shibli and the Nadwat-ul-Ulema cooperated for Hindu-Muslim unity. In 1906 a deputation under the leadership of Archbold, Aligarh College, met the Secretary to the Viceroy at Simla for separate electorate.

The Muslim deputation, was chiefly composed of Aligarh group; Aga Khan III (1877-1957) who led the deputation along with other 69 Muslim leaders, met the Viceroy Lord Minto on 1 October 1906. It had the sympathy of Badruddin Tayabji, who had presided the congress session.

In a private conversation with Mohsin-ul-Mulk, Lord Minto stressed that Muslim political activities should be aimed at achieving community representation, which he guaranteed in the projected reforms, so as to combat the growing political and economic influence of the Hindu community. The Viceroy pointed out that the British authorities pinned strong hopes on the good sense and loyalty of the Aligarh group.[102]

The Indian Council Act of 1909 instituted separate electorates for Hindus and Muslims. This act of the British also encouraged the establishment of communal political parties - The Muslim League and the Hindu Mahasabha.

Aga Khan visited Aligarh in 1906, he believed that the hope lay along the lines of independent organization (Muslim League) and action and that 'we must secure independent political recognition from the British Government as a Nation within the Nation.'[103]

Archbold, the Principal of Aligarh College was the 'secret' Counsellor of the Muslim politicians. The second conference of the Muslim League adopted a resolution welcoming the partition of Bengal and condemning the Swaraj and Swadeshi movements.[104]

Aligarh was named the permanent seat of the Muslim League but in the Delhi session of December-1909-January-1910 it was moved to Lucknow. The British were so frightened by the movement of Anti-partition of Bengal that, in December, 1911 it was decided that the capital of India be shifted to Delhi from Calcutta and the British were compelled to repeal the partition of Bengal; a person like Nawab Salimullah, the author of the original plan for the establishment of the league, lamented the reunification of Bengal as the end of his political career.

Muslim Radicals on the Eve of the First World War

The propaganda of the British "beneficence" by the Muslim League leadership fell on increasingly barren Soil. The British authorities had failed to isolate the Muslims of East Bengal (now Bangladesh) from the mounting revolutionary movement. In 1911, they were compelled to repeal the partition of Bengal. The middle strata of Muslims were greatly influenced by the rising revolutionary tide of 1905-1908.

Shortly before the First World War the Muslim League began to gravitate left wards. Newspapers and Magazines mostly in Urdu were founded, differing from the older Urdu periodicals, and they had greater circulation, and had anti-imperialist attitude. Nomani Shibli; from Lucknow, through 'Muslim Gazette' informed the Muslim Masses. He urged the Muslim League to alter its attitude towards congress. He termed the pro-British standpoint of the Aligarh College as 'a slavish mentality'.[105]

He was also not free from religious prejudice; he clothed his liberation ideas in the religious fabric of Pan-Islamic propaganda. He coined his motto, 'Islam in Danger'. Later, Muslim reactionary groups gave this slogan an entirely different construction, proclaiming Hindu domination, the chief danger to Islam.

During this period the Egyptian educators and the Young Turk movement exercised a strong influence on the emergence of Pan-Islamic views among India's Muslim Intellectuals. In 1908, Maulana Abul Kalam Azad tours the Eastern countries and was affected by this view.

Al Hilal (the crescent), a periodical founded by Azad in June, 1912 soon become a popular organ of the new trend.

Al Hilal did not directly oppose the separate electorate system, or the Muslim communal party. It focused its criticism upon the separatist attitude of the Aligarh group, Azad wrote, 'Aligarh movement has paralyzed the Muslims.'[106]

Al Hilal was for Hindu-Muslim unity against foreign oppression. It was candidly anti-imperialist, but like most of the patriotic newspapers of the time it clothed its liberal ideas in religious forms. The pro-Congress newspapers were 'Bengalee' and 'Tribune'.

The radical intellectuals in the league argued for the cooperation with other political parties, especially Congress in December, 1912 at Lucknow session of the council. But in December 1913, at its seventh session at Agra, this was achieved. The Turkish Sultan was considered 'the commander of the faithful, Turkey, at the time, claimed leadership of Islam and its domestic and foreign policy attracted the attention of Muslims in all countries of the Near and Middle East. Mass meetings swept the country in 1911-3, condemned the situation in the Balkans and prayed for a Turkish Victory. The students of Aligarh College also joined it and raised funds for the aid of Turkey. This alarmed the British Authorities. Deoband Dar-ul-Ulum became the centre of extremist underground Muslim politics. The conspiracy was headed by Mahmud Hasan who was in 1920 conferred the title of Sheikh-ul-Hind; an uprising of 1857-9 was to be repeated. The Afghan Muslim leaders were also involved in it. A provisional Indian government was formed in Kabul. The movement could not be successful as the leaders were arrested, but it gave a start to the Khilafat Movement, which involved large masses of people during the revolutionary upswing of 1918-22.

Mohammad Ali Jinnah and the Lucknow Pact

For the Muslim League, the period before the First World War was of great importance, during this period Mohammad Ali Jinnah (1876-1948) joined the Muslim League. Until 1906 he took no part in the country's political affairs and devoted himself entirely to his legal practice. In 1906 he first attended the National Congress Session as Secretary to Dadabhai Noroji, under the Indian Council's Act of 1909 he was elected member of the Bombay Legislative Council from the Bombay Muslim Electorate (representing essentially Muslim merchants and mill owners). His Business connections and his marriage to the daughter of Dinshaw Petit, one of the city fathers, linked Jinnah with the Parsi community, which was very prominent in Bombay's business world. He was strongly influenced by British liberals of the Morley type and close to Gokhale, but was opposed to Bal Gangadhar Tilak's radical programme. His espousal of the Muslim League began after the revolutionary tide of 1906-8 had been suppressed.

As a far-sighted leader of his class, he was awake to the need for united action by the different political parties in the constitutional struggle against the British. He worked for the Hindu-Muslim unity and agreement between Muslim League and the Congress.

Jinnah attended his first session of the league in 1912. In 1914 he went to England and led the delegation for the proposal to inducting Indian members elected by the central and the provincial legislative assemblies in to the London Council of the Secretary of state for India. The Congress, the Muslim League and other political parties declared their support of Britain in the War.

In December, 1915 he convened the Congress and Bombay league session in Bombay, which was attended by prominent congress leaders like, Annie Besant, Sarojini Naidu, and Mahatma Gandhi, who had then came from South Africa.

In 1916, the league and the congress concluded an agreement signed by Jinnah on behalf of league and by all Congress leaders. It was endorsed by the two parties at their respective sessions held simultaneously in Lucknow; it came to be known as Lucknow Pact. It was to establish self-government. Bodies by direct elections, preferably on the territorial principle; they made the reservations, however, that it would be wise to keep the separate representation system for at least 10 years. (For Muslim representation in various provincial legislatures: 50% seat in Punjab; 40% in Bengal; 33½ in Bombay; 30% in Central Provinces; 5% in C.P. and 15% in Madras).[107]

The Lucknow pact had its strong and weak points. Its acceptance of the principle of separate electorates was unquestionably negative. The British government could, on the strength of it, regard the Lucknow pact as an agreement between the Hindu and Muslim religious communities, rather than between two political parties. Many landlord groups described the Lucknow pact as recognition of the exclusive rights held by the league to represent the

'Muslim Nation'. Mohammad Durrani, a prominent Advocate of Pakistan, wrote, 'By that pact, the congress acknowledged the fact that the Hindus and the Muslims were two separate nations, and while the congress itself was the representative of the Hindus, the Muslim League represented the Muslim community.'[108]

On the other side the pact drew broader sections of Muslims into the All-Indian National-Liberation Movement.

The Muslim League and the Khilafat Movement

Due to the October Socialist Revolution (1917) in Russia, the Afghan war of Independence and the Economic contradictions between Indian Business Class and the British Imperialists the rank and file of the Muslim League rose up to the National-Liberation Movement.

When the Montague-Chelmsford Report appeared in 1919, some of the Moderates split away from the Congress, but the left wing of the League welcomed the non-cooperation launched by the Congress in 1919. Some of the Muslim radicals continued to favour religious forms of struggle.

The Khilafat Movement of 1918-22 appealed to the masses, and in that lays its basic difference from the earlier Indian Muslim activities. A Khilafat Committee held in November 1919 in Delhi. By 1920, the Khilafat Movement had spread far and wide. In January, 1920 a Khilafat Manifesto was issued. It called on India's Muslims and the Muslim states to safeguard the prestige of the Turkish Sultan and appealed to the congress for support.

The National Congress welcomed the Khilafat Movement from the outset. The All-India Khilafat Conference and the league session held in 1919 at Amritsar, which coincided with the session of the congress, were attended by Moti Lal Nehru, Mahatma Gandhi, Annie Besant and many other prominent congress members. In Delhi, speaking at Khilafat Conference, Gandhi suggested a campaign of Non-cooperation.[109]

In May 1920, the Khilafat Committee approved the idea, in June, 1920, a Hindu-Muslim unity conference was convened, civil disobedience was launched and the Khilafat Movement proclaimed a part of it. In 1920, all Ulemas of Calcutta welcomed the rapprochement of league with Congress.

At the League session in Calcutta, Jinnah attacked the Khilafat Movement and Gandhi's programme. He stated plainly in a letter to Gandhi that he would not support his programme because it set the masses in motion, which would lead to complete disorganization and chaos.

Gandhi's way, Jinnah said at the session of Calcutta, was the wrong way. 'Mine is the right way' he declared, 'The constitutional way is the right way'.[110]

In 1921, Jinnah resigned from the Congress. It was at this point that once 'ambassador of Hindu-Muslim unity began to change into an ideologist of

Muslim separatism. The Aligarh group, too from the very outset assumed a hostile attitude towards the Khilafat Movement. In 1919 and 1920, 17 October was marked the Khilafat day. From 1912 to 1921, the Muslim League played a prominent role in influencing the people.

British Constitutional Devices and the Muslim League (1922-37)

By 1921, the Muslim League returned to the path of religious sectarianism, which led up to its demand of an independent Pakistan. The Muslim League leadership stood aloof from the various national-liberation movement of 1929-33 and adopted a hostile attitude to it.

In 1921, the Muslim League refused to back the campaign of civil disobedience, and this was the first violation of its agreement for united action with the congress.

The moral blow to League-Congress cooperation was delivered by the reactionary course of the British Authorities and the Hindu-Muslim riots of 1923-27, which they provoked.

The Muslim educators appealed for religious separatism. The British went out of their way to set Muslim against Hindu. The few religious riots in the cities towards the close of the 19th century and before and during the First World War were local and sporadic. It was different in 1923-27. Incitement of Hindu-Muslim clashes became part of reaction's general offensive. The venom of Hindu-Muslim discord spread to the countryside. Riots caused reactionary demonstrations by religious fanatics throughout the country and new reprisals against workers, peasants, artisans and progressive Intellectuals.

Between 1923 and 1927, more than 5,000 people suffered harm in the religious riots in different parts of India, and 450 losing their lives.[111]

At the close of 1921 and early 1922, some Muslim leaders started Tabligh movement, in which they preached the conversion of the people of other religion to Islam, in the same way Hindu Mahasabha launched a campaign for converting Muslims to Hinduism (the Shudhi Movement) Rajendra Prasad wrote, 'that year the seed of distrust was sown, and it took root gradually in the course of time a wide gulf came to separate the two communities. The British saw their chance and stepped in.... By skillful manoeuvres they kept the fires of communal distrust burning.'[112]

The division among the radical Indian Intellectuals hampered the fight against religious separatism and the reactionary maneuvers of the British imperialists, and this in turn, brought M.A. Jinnah to prominence. Until 1935, he was not appealed to the Muslim working people. He speaks of the 'Mob' with mingled contempt and mistrust. Jinnah's constitutional movement for dominion status was more popular than Aligarh group. He wanted home rule within the British Empire. He was for special privileges for Muslim.

In 1925 a conference of Hindu-Muslim unity was convened; an appeal was made not persecuting Muslims by Hindus and Hindus by Muslims.

Gandhi and Ajmal Khan were entrusted the responsibilities to investigate the causes of riots.

But no far-reaching change occurred in the relations between the Muslim League and the Congress; grave differences arose within the Muslim League over its cooperation with the congress after the British Government appointed the Simon-Commission to revise the Government of India Act. The Indians Public resented the fact that no Indians were included in the Commission. A mass campaign of protest was launched. Various political groups had to make clear their stand point concerning the future constitutional make up of India.

In March 1927 a document, known as the Delhi-Manifesto, was drawn up by M.A. Jinnah and Maulana Mohammad Ali, and backed by the entire leading Muslim group. The Muslim League was prepared to disown the separate representation system on the terms set out in the Manifesto and maintained this position until 1937.

Movement for Pakistan

After the close of the first non-cooperation movement the league and congress were never on the same side again. They worked like two titanic forces against a common enemy, but they were themselves unable to come to terms. The breakdown of the early 20's unity between league and congress were manifold. In general, they naturally can be derived from the deeply ingrained cultural differences that made prolonged partnership between the two-communities impossible. In particular, the fall of the Turkish Caliphate brought the Indian Khilafat movement to an end, while simultaneously the breakdown of the non-cooperation movement awakened the deep-seated antagonism of some Hindu segments of the population against the Indian Muslim. Congress continued its struggle for freedom un-interruptedly. The league, however, fell into a stupper from which it did not wake up until the disastrous elections of 1937. All in all, the Muslim League won 108 of the total of 482 Muslim seats in the provincial Legislative Assemblies; that is, less than 3 per cent of all the seats. Out of the 7, 319, 445 Muslim electors, only 321,772 voted for the league nominees.[113]

The tragic results of these elections had an electrifying effect on Muslim leadership. Urged by Mohammad Iqbal, a vigorous propaganda campaign was conducted in the country to shake off the apathy of the Muslim population. The torch of Indian Muslim Nationalism was finally beginning to burn brightly under the auspices of the league led by M.A. Jinnah. No half measures were to be taken. The league was fighting on all sides: against congress, against the English and against the lethargy of its own followers. The culmination of this upheaval was the Lahore Resolution of 26 March 1940, demanding the establishment of an independent Muslim state in India.

The Lahore Resolution of 26 March 1940

The idea of creating a Muslim state independent from the rest of India was first advanced at the Round Table conference. The British seized on the plan, framed by Choudhury Rahmat Ali, a Cambridge University student, and financed his Press Campaign.[114]

Although, the Muslim delegation to the Round Table Conference rejected Rahamat Ali's plan, the British Parliamentary Committee brought it up once more in 1933. After this, the problem of partitioning India kept recurring in Parliament dealings and the plans of the conservative party.[115]

A theory of 'Two-Nations'—the Hindu and Muslim was brought to light as an ideological basis for India's division.

Syed Ahmed Khan never contemplated a political division of India along religious lines. As far Mohammad Iqbal was concerned, he proposed an autonomous Muslim state within a Federation of India. But these two leaders are said to be the ideologist of Pakistan.

In 1940, at Lahore session, the league formally endorsed the creation of an independent Muslim state as its main objective.[116]

The resolution ostensibly came as a reply to the futile and protracted efforts of the Simon Commission 1927-9, the Round Table Conference 1930-2, and the Government of India Act 1935, to form a workable scheme of federation in the country.

Ambedkar summarizes the Muslim demands expressed at Lahore as follows:

(1) What the Muslims are asking for is the creation of Administrative areas which are ethnically more homogeneous.

(2) The Muslim want these homogeneous administrative areas which are predominately Muslim to be constituted into separate States:

  (a) Because the Muslims by themselves constitute a separate nation and desire to have a national home and,

  (b) Because experience shows that the Hindus want to use their majority to treat the Muslims as though they were second-class citizens in an alien State.[117]

If we analyse all the above arguments given in favour of the creation of Pakistan, we come to the conclusion that all are redundant and the conditions of Pakistan are of a failed State.

The Muslims received Lahore declaration with enthusiasm; Hindu leaders considered it as a chimerical play or as a treacherous act to break the integral unity of India and refused to take it seriously. But their opposition could not stop that flow of nervous energy, creative enthusiasm, nationalist feeling and religious devotion that was led into positive channels by the Lahore Resolution; that opened a new vista of action, achievement, and glory to a people downtrodden and trampled upon, which could be satisfied only with the achievement of an independent sovereign Islamic State of Pakistan.[118]

'Modern nationalism has displaced religion as the chief factor in human group relationships. Throughout human history, however there has been a constant interplay between religious denominationalism and those basic elements of state and territory, ethnic descent and language which have always constituted the major ingredients of National feelings.'[119]

Because of this interplay between Nationalism and religion the latter has a strong appeal to Nationalist elements and continues to be a powerful force even in those countries where Church and state are separated. The Religion can became Nationalized, assuming the aspect of cultural nationalism which again often turns into political nationalism.

Religious consciousness and the power of religion was intense, until the British occupation the country had lived for hundreds of years under governmental systems where religious law was the law of the state; with the advent of the British rule there was substantial 'secularization' on the subcontinent. Still religion continued to be the directing principle in everyday life of the masses. Before long, religious differences was an effective political weapon in India and was used by the interested parties to their greatest advantage under the collective term 'communalism'. Communalism in a popular sense could be considered an acute self—consciousness of the different religious groups in India. It also entails 'the sense of insecurity which any community feels and the accompanying action it takes to protect itself and further its own interests'.[120]

The appeal of Nationalism—popularly known on the subcontinent as communalism—was strong enough to unite the various economic, political and cultural factions of the Muslim community or nation. Facing the danger of losing their identity in the face of an overwhelming Hindu majority, the different interest groups among the Muslims allowed any inner conflicts to give way to mutual cooperation. The common cause was paramount in the eyes of the Muslim populace. It is thus, possible to equate communalism in pre-partition India with Nationalism, religion and culture, being the uniting factors of the group subject to a common emotional appeal.

Hindu-Muslim Existence

There are evidences in history that communal loyalty was not always as overwhelming as it appeared to be in the twentieth century; neither was communal antagonism. The reign of Akbar was one such example; Lucknow Pact of 1916 is another, but it last not so long.

There are two views of writers on communalism on Pakistan and pre-partition India: one view is that communalism is an artificial cleavage; the other is that it is embodied in the history of the subcontinent.

One writer writes, 'The Hindu-Muslim problem is an artificial English irritant.'[121]

"Muslims are not a reporate people. They are Indians who happen to attend a Muslim Mosque instead of a Hindu temple."[122]

W.C. Smith writes, "It is usual now to recognize that the communal antagonisms of India's middle class are due to British imperial policy of 'Divide and rule'.[123]

Brailsford writes, 'It was the Marley-Minto Reforms that inaugurated modern Indian Political Communalism.' By introducing Principle of communal representation through separate electorates, having adopted this measure that retarded the development of India's social consciousness for purely selfish-end in the long run detrimental reasons.[124]

Some writers like Rawlinson write that 'There is of course no foundation for the accusation that the British government pursued a policy of divide and rule... The authors of the Montage-Chelmsford Reforms, like Morley, were deeply reluctant to accept communal electorates.'[125]

Some believed that while the British did their best to take advantage of prevailing communal sentiments, communal friction existed from the moment when Hinduism and Islam first met. In spite of centuries of association, Hindus and Muslims represent two distinct cultures; their religious conceptions stand as a great barrier against a complete merging together. There is no inter-dining and inter-marriage and these two factors has been a bar to social assimilation. Their admired legendary heroes and historical personalities are different; in fact, those revered by one group are either hated or ridiculed by the other..."[126]

The author goes on enumerating the striking differences in food, dress, personal appearance, and names between the two communities. No unanimous opinion of the nature of communalism and its development will ever be reached. The fact, however, is that as a political weapon it was frightfully effective, leading to the partition of India on a communal basis. The underlying factor of communalist feeling is religion and culture, although they developed side by side for a thousand year, difference on more points than they have in common. The religious differences between Hindu-Muslim communalism happen to coincide with the economic differences to such an extent that it is sometimes difficult to distinguish between the two.

Hindus ruled India in the beginning, and then the Muslims ruled it, the British ruled after Muslims. Changes came about with British penetration. The Hindus did not lose much with the coming of the British; to them it was a routine change in masters to which they adopted themselves as quickly as conditions permitted. The Muslims resented British interference in their affairs that culminated in the destruction of the Mughal Empire, their loss of liberty and self-determination. The resentment was shown in their reluctance to assimilate western culture.

In the beginning, the British suspected the Muslims and were more favourable towards the Hindus. The 1857 Mutiny further victimized the already backward Muslim upper and middle classes.

By the end of nineteenth century, the British realized that Muslims could be utilized in hampering resurgent Hindu Nationalism. The British leaned towards Muslims and helped them economically. The economic differences were directed into communal channels. The half of the twentieth century in India can plainly be called communal history.

Independent Muslim State

With the progress in the twentieth century, a curious dichotomy developed in the Muslim Nationalistic aspirations on the Indian sub-continent. On one side they demanded more freedom from the British rule; and on the other side as more freedom was given by the British, the closer came the day of final liberation from the colonial power, the more obstructionist did the league become, the greater were its demands and the more frequent were the bloody communal riots.

'The more sharply the contours of Indian Nationalism stood out in the congress party, the more widespread grew the anxiety among the Muslim best, failing timely precautions; Islam should be submerged in a Hindu sea. As the prospect of Indian self-government drew nearer, anxieties and hesitations naturally grew still more acute.'[127]

While desiring to throw off the foreign yoke—the Muslims were not willing to exchange it for the yoke of a seemingly antagonistic, indigenous Hindu majority. They were scorching in haste for a solution to their weighty problem.

Until the election of 1937, the Muslim League at least half-heartedly cooperated with Congress in the fight against the British. It was more for separate electorate and grater weightage in representation.

But the situation changed radically in 1937 as the league made a poor show in the provincial elections. An All India Committee was formed, presided over by the Raja of Pirpur to establish the grievances of the Muslim against Congress domination and oppression. It was to arouse widespread sympathy among the Muslims and turn against the congress.

The report stated that 'Muslim children had been made to worship the portrait of Gandhi, that they were forced to sing the anti-Muslim *Bande Mataram*, that Muslims were intimidated from eating beef etc.'[128]

Within a short time Muslim League became the only popular rallying point for the Muslims of India. Rigorous discipline was enforced in the league. Double allegiance was forbidden. Nobody could be a member of the Congress who joined the League. At the outbreak of World War II, Congress ministers resigned in protest as they had not been consulted before India was drawn into war; by a declaration of the Governor-General, the league celebrated a 'Deliverance Day'. The resignation of the Congress strengthened the influence of the League—substantially.

The English cabinet, seeking to gain full cooperation from the people of India, sent out Sir Stafford-Cripps in 1942, with the promise of Dominion Status, but complete freedom was requested in turn, not after the war, but immediately, Elections were held in 1946, which decisively proved that the league commanded the support of the overwhelming majority of the Indian Muslims. The Indian Independence Act was passed in July, 1947. Partition and Independence came into effect on 15 August 1947.

Congress Party and Delhi

On 10 September 1888, Ali Mohammad Bhimji paid a visit to Delhi, a large public meeting was presided by Sheikh Hafizullah, Municipal Commissioner, Ali Mohammad Bhimji, explained the aims and objects of the Indian National Congress.[129]

This meeting was also addressed by Lala Murli Dhar, Pleader, who was a founder member of the Indian National Congress, and president of the Arya Samaj at Ambala. Due to utterances of Syed Ahmed Khan, the people of Delhi were bi-polarized. It was the Central National Mohammedan Association of Punjab that decided to counter the spread of influence of Congress ideology. After a sometimes strong reaction of ultra loyalist elements among the Muslims at Delhi took place and under pressure, Sheikh Hafizullah recounted and admitted his mistake.

The Muslims conducted a number of meetings as against one for congress. In one such meeting in late September 1888, Maulvi Abdul Haq spoke against the Indian National Congress and said that Muslim cause would suffer by its identity with the congress movement, which was calculated to create disaffection towards the government. Another meeting was held on 5 October 1888 in Town Hall, it was presided over by Shahzada Suleman Shah. Maulvi Nazir Ahmad, a retired Deputy Collector, delivered a long speech and drove home the idea that Muharram, Dussehra, Holi and Id riots fully proved the truth of assertion that "Hindus and Muslims cannot be one Nation."[130]

On 15 October 1888 another crowded meeting was held in which congress was condemned and resolutions were passed in support of the Indian Patriotic Association. These elements also received great encouragement when Lord

Duffrin condemned the Indian National Congress as a seditions organization. But despite it a sizable number of Muslims supported the congress.

On 2 December 1888, a meeting of the Congress was organized at the house of Babu Kedar Nath, a pleader at Delhi, Khan Bahadur Hadi Hussain Khan and Maulana Abu Mansur took part in it.

On 19 December 1888, in another meeting, delegates were elected for the forth coming (4th) Congress session at Allahabad, twenty delegates from Delhi (14 Hindus and 6 Muslims) participated in the Congress proceedings. Umrao Mirza Hairat, spoke on elective elements in legislative councils. In 1889, when Charles Bradlaugh introduced in British Parliament a Bill, seeking introduction of representative institutions; Beck, the Principal of Aligarh College, opposing the Bill, tried to make Muslims conscious of their separation, he obtained 20,000 signatures, took a batch of Aligarh boys to Delhi, stood near Jama Masjid on a Friday and collected 3,036 signatures of Muslims by representing the memorial to be against Hindu efforts for stopping cow killing.[131]

To counteract the propaganda of the Aligarh School of thought, a fatwa by leading Maulvis of Delhi was issued pronouncing that there was nothing un-Islamic in joining the congress. In 1890, for the aims and objectives of the Congress, in its session; Maulvi Rukn-ud-Din Jadoo from Delhi spoke in favour of congress and political consciousness.

In the Congress session, Maulvi Umrao Mirza Hairat, spoke in favour of congress aims and objects, and being a Muslim, he had no problem to join the objects of the congress, but at the same time he said, 'we have the pride of being the subject of the British Government, God willing we shall not be the subjects of any power.'[132]

In 1889 congress session held on 24 November 1889 20 delegates from Delhi (13 Hindus and 7 Muslims) attended the session and Rs. 500 was collected for congress fund.

The public of Delhi during this period was divided, the interest in congress dwindled in Delhi. It was the outside Delhi leadership which was stimulating the influence of the congress in Delhi.

In 1891 Pandit Ajudhia Nath came to Delhi and a public meeting was organized which was attended by Dr Hem Chandra, Babu Kedar Nath, Babu Pyarelal, Pleader, and Hafiz Aziz-ud-Din, Pleader. Congress was condemned in a meeting of the Muslim on 16 September 1891.

In 1890, only four (one Hindu and three Muslims) delegates attended the Congress session at Calcutta. In 1892 at Allahabad only six (five Hindus and one Muslim) delegates attended the congress session. In 1893, at Lahore session of the Congress, 28 delegates attended the session from Delhi, there after the interest in congress movement lacked. No delegates from Delhi attended the annual sessions of the congress held at Madras (1894), 1898 and 1903 at Poona in 1895, at Amravati in 1897, at Ahmedabad in 1902 and at Bombay in 1904. The general tone prevalent during this period, was one of the loyalty to the British Crown. On the death of Queen Victoria, a public meeting was held on 18 February 1901 and it was decided to raise fund to build memorial to the Queen. By February 1902, collections rose to Rs. 1.5 lakh. James Skinner presented Rs. 10,000 for a bronze statue of the Majesty. The fund was utilized in founding 'The Public Library' now known as Harding (Hardayal) Municipal Library in 1902 and Victoria Zenana Memorial Hospital, the inauguration ceremony of the hospital was performed by Sir Charles-Rivaz, Lt.-Governor of Punjab, on 19 February 1904. Two days after the death of Queen Victoria, on 24 January 1901, King Edward VII was proclaimed Emperor of India. On 2 January 1903, a durbar was held at Delhi, the king was expected earlier to come in person, but the British Cabinet deterred the king. So the Brother of the king, the Duke of Connaught and the Duchess represented the king. Nothing very significant was announced, as was expected, for the masses; rather they were saddled with the cost of the Durbar. Lord Curzon's Administration produced a wave of discontent in the Mind of Indians. Curzon antagonized Indian public opinion by various Acts of omission and commission, such as Calcutta Corporation Act, Indian Universities Act, official secrets Act and other pieces of legislation, besides his utterances against the Indians in the Calcutta University convocation address in February, 1905, 'truthfulness of the west and the craftiness of the east', as well as denying that there was anything as 'any Indian Nation'. Japan's Victory over Russia had an electrifying effect on the morale of Indians; it proved that east can defeat the west; so Indians can also achieve their independence.

The Partition of Bengal followed the bombshell. It was promulgated on 19 July 1905. Its aims were not administrative but political and he succeeded into dividing the two communities—Hindus and Muslims. It was an attack on Bengali nationalism. Swadeshi and boycott resolution were adopted by Indians. In the congress session, the programme of passive resistance and National reconstruction came into surface. This has its repercussions in Delhi too. Protest meetings were convened in the city. Both Hindus and Muslims declared the boycott of foreign goods. In 1905 at Benaras Congress Session, Delhi sent six delegates.

By their efforts and actions, the British not only further divided the Hindus and Muslims, (Partition of Bengal, establishment of Muslim League communal electorate), they also divided the Congress in to two groups (moderates and extremists). British patronized discussions were going on with Gopal Krishna Gokhale, Lord Minto did so since 1905 and Lord Morley continued it when Gokhale visited England in 1906. This ultimately led to split in the Congress.

In recognition of the rising discontent, the Congress in 1906 at Calcutta adopted resolutions on self-government: Swadeshi, Boycott and National Education.

By 1907, foundations of revolutionary nationalism were laid in several provinces. The extremists advocated the passive resistance to the Government; whereas the moderates laid emphasis on constitutional methods for achieving their goal. In the Surat session, the moderates dropped the boycott resolution due to coquetting with the British. Over the issue of the election of President, the Congress broke up on 28 December 1907; with violent actions and scenes at the session. Lokmanya Tilak still prepared for compromise if the last year's resolutions were adhered to, but there was no response,

> Shorn of its left wing, the Indian National Congress went into wilderness and till the Great War, it played no part worth the name in furthering the cause of Indian Nationalism. The National workers from Delhi completely refused to align themselves with the moderate congress and significantly not a single delegate from Delhi attended any of the Congress sessions held from 1908–1915. The period in between was marked by the rise of extremist movement and revolutionary Nationalism.[133]

Rise of the Extremist Movement

All those nationalist, who wanted to achieve Indian's independence by any means and not necessarily constitutional or peaceful, were turmed as extremist. For these leaders, there was no coherent political party with a common programme, but there were certain ideas from which the revolutionaries drew inspiration of violent acts. The Partition of Bengal had given rise to agitation not only in Bengal but in other provinces of India, in Punjab Sardar Ajit Singh, in Delhi Syed Haider Raza of Delhi, Master Amir Chand, Prof Raghbar Dayal they were assisted by Sultan Singh, Madan Mohan, Pyarelal, Syed Haider Raza was teaching on leave vacancy at St. Stephen College, from where his services were terminated, he edited 'Aftab' a newspaper, actively participated in Hindu-Muslim unity, Swadeshi and Swaraj movement. At Lala Lajpat Rai's arrest, he organized many public meetings in Delhi in 1907. After the release of Lalaji, who was invited to Delhi, Raza organized a meeting with the student's of St. Stephen's College.

Sawan Singh, Mahant-cum-Granthi of Gurudwara Rakab Ganj, Delhi, helped in raising the funds.

Syed Haider Raza had a strong influence over the student community, he used to take the parties of school boys to the Eastern Bank of the Yamuna, in the united provinces and inculcate in them a spirit of renaissance.

He also organized meetings of Mr Keir Hardie, the founder of the British Labour Party, while in Delhi.

Tramway Transport System started in Delhi by the British in 1903.
(http://www.flickr.com/photos/mayankaustensoofi/3736234192/)

The meetings were held for opposing the seditious-meetings Act of 1907.

On 24 January 1908, a protest meeting against increase of house tax was organized, which became very popular.

Tilak's conviction greatly infuriated the Nationalist at Delhi. Embers at Tilak's conviction had hardly died down another object of attack found out, this time it was the Delhi Electric Tramways, opened on 3 June, 1903. A public meeting was held on 14 August 1903, in the house of R.S. Girdhari Lal, pleader, when Master Amir Chand violently criticized Delhi Tramways and its promoters 'The Company' he denounced, 'was foreign, its capital was foreign and the material used in the construction of the tramway was foreign. The tramways made a daily profit of Rs. 400 to 500 and India was impoverished daily by that amount.'[134]

To boycott the tramways, Syed Haider Raza, announced the holding of another meeting on August 19, 1908 in Queens Garden. But British issued a notice not to hold this meeting, the public gathered at Queens Garden, but moved to eastern bank of the Yamuna, which formed part of Meerut district in the united provinces. Syed Haider Raza addressed the meetings and criticized the government and urged a boycott of the foreign enterprise.

Haider Raza used to write articles in his paper 'Aftab' against the British rule; he was fined Rs. 200 for it; which was very heavy for him.

For Khudi Ram Bose a meeting was organized to raise funds (50 thousand rupees were collected by the Bengali community) but Khudi Ram Bose was hanged, and it was decided to pay this amount to Bose's family.

In the beginning of 1909, Haider Raza, accompanied by Asif Ali and Rauf Ali, left for England on the invitation of Shyamji Krishan Verma. He also worked with V.D. Savarkar, Madan Lal Dhingra, V.S.S. Aiyer and S.M. Master.

After Raza left Delhi, Master Amir Chand took over the revolutionary activities, he was working in St. Stephen's School, from where he resigned. He was a disciple of Swami Ram Tirath. His nationalism based on Hindu religion, it took to the extremist and revolutionary lines. The revolutionary and nationalist movement got a setback when in 1909 All India Muslim League opened a branch in Delhi and propagated for separate electorate. The Hindu-Mahasabha was also formed, a language controversy erupted between Muslim and Arya Samajist, which diverted the popular enthusiasm and damped it into unprofitable channels. The ill-feelings accentuated by a great output of booklets and pamphlets in the city by individual Arya Samajists and Muslims denouncing each other's religion in abusive language. Some new converts from Islam to Arya Samaj, irritated the Muslims. Their preaching also irritated the Sanatani Hindu; this ill-will remained for a considerable period in Delhi, without open clash, due to the precautionary measures by the authorities, the temper on both sides died down over the period.

By December 1910, Master Amir Chand along with others revived the cause of revolutionary nationalism; and established a society on the Bengal Pattern, the object of which was kept a profound secret. The object of the society was production and distribution of inflammatory literature. The society was to distribute revolutionary literature received from abroad. Tara Chand and Sunder Lal were from Allahabad and Jatindra Mohan Chatterjee from Saharanpur, Dwarka Nath Bose was also from Saharanpur. They were in touch with, Har Dayal in England.

On 23 December 1912 when Lord Hardinge entered Chandni Chowk in a procession, in front of Punjab National Bank at Katra Dhulia, opposite Moti Bazar, a bomb was thrown at 11.45 a.m.; at Lord Harding which exploded in the 'howdah' occupied by him. The explosion of the Bomb was so loud and crushing that it was heard six miles away, the hearing of Lord Harding was paralyzed by the Bomb before the sound could be heard. His helmet was on the road. The attendant seated just behind the Viceroy was killed instantaneously while the other attendant on the left of the 'howdah' was maimed in hands and body; four persons in the crowd were wounded, one boy on the right side in the crowd was killed. Lord Harding was wounded and caused some deafness, Lady Harding escaped unhurt but received severe shock which at least hastened her premature death.[135]

The Viceroy ordered the procession to reform and proceeds but shortly afterwards he lost his consciousness and had to be conveyed by car to the Viceroy Lodge. The Durbar ceremony was held as scheduled; senior member of the council, Sir Guy Fleetwood Wilson, delivered the Viceroy's replies to the addresses of non-official members of the council and the Lt. Governor of Punjab; the return route was changed as the original route considered unsafe.[136]

The news of the Bomb outrage evoked a wave of General denunciation of the incident throughout all classes in India. At Delhi the General consensus of opinion among the residents was one of grief and sorrow and this found its expression in a thickly attended public meeting in Queens gardens in 24 December 1912, when Madan Mohan Malviya, Pandit Harnarain Shastri and Hari Ram Multani expressed regret and abhorrence at the incident, similar feelings were expressed by Hindus, Arya Samajists, Muslims, Sikhs and Jains, as well as Delhi Municipal Committee. All shops were closed as a mark of sympathy.[137]

Besides the feelings of sympathy, various chiefs of Indian States and other prominent persons, to show their spirit of attachments to the Government, announced the award of a reward to anyone disclosing information leading to the arrest and conviction of the accused. Prayers were held in the city Hindu temples for the speedy recovery of Lord Hardinge.

The investigation of the Hardinge bomb incident was entrusted to Mr D. Petri, Additional Superintendent of Police, Delhi. Rewards were offered for any useful information relating to the incident. The Funds collected for receiving the information was ultimately spent on the construction of Lady Hardinge Medical College (The foundation of Lady Hardinge Medical College for women was laid on 17 March 1914 and the college opened on 17 February 1916).

The money collected for Lord Hardinge, was spent to build a library (Hardinge Library). Which is now called Hardayal Library.

On 25 December 1912 Hardayal convened a meeting in Berkley, California, and spoke to the people there about the Hardinge Bomb incident and said that it was the work of his men.[138]

The interception of letters written by Hardayal to his relatives and friends from 3 July 1913 to 11 December 1913, was singularly inept in yielding any information as to the identity of persons connected with the Bomb incident. Other eye witnesses such as constable Ram Singh's wife, Lallu a boy, records of the House where the persons who threw the Bomb stayed (near Dass's House), the records of the Imperial Forest Research Institute, Dehra Dun, where Rash Bihari was a clerk, (his leave records) the revolutionary literature hailed the incident of throwing of Bomb considering it a Brave act said 'Man' has not died in India...'. 'This Bomb of December, 1912 opens up a new epoch in the history of the revolutionary movement in India...' May Durbars and bombs go together till there are no more Durbars on the face of earth? Yugantar Ashram was circulating the literature in favour of the incident of bomb throwing. The Hardinge bomb incident showed in unmistakable terms that the revolutionary activity followed in the work of the transfer of capital from Calcutta to Delhi and infused in the adjoining provinces of the Punjab and the united provinces the bomb and cult of assassination.

Rash Bihari and Basanta Kumar were identified for the Hardinge bomb incident.

The secret society which were doing the throwing of bombs at Delhi, consisted of Master Amir Chand, Hanwant Sahai, Avadh Behari and Ram Lal alias Chhote Lal, who had links with Jaipur, the Lahore group consisted of Dina Nath, Bal Mukand, Bal Raj with Avadh Behari as a link connecting with Delhi, others were Raghobar Sharma and Khushi Ram in Lahore, Manoo Lal in Delhi and Charan Dass in Gurdaspur, trials were conducted against many revolutionaries from Delhi and Lahore; only Master Amir Chand, Awadh Behari and Bal Mukand were hanged on 8 May 1915, in Delhi district Jail while Basanta Kumar Biswas was hanged the same day in Ambala district Jail.

This incident gave a big blow to revolutionary movement in Delhi.[139]

Gurudwara Reform Movement

Soon after the announcement of the transfer of the capital from Calcutta to Delhi in December, 1911, the Committee was appointed to search the suitable site for the Buildings of new capital. It took time for the committee to select the site, one day Lord Harding himself rode on horseback and galloped over the plains of the hill by the side of Gurudwara Rikab Ganj. He at once declared 'This is the site of the Government House.'[140]

Gurudwara Rikab Ganj is a historic place. It was a village of Lakhi Shah Banjara who used to supply the provisions to the Red Fort during the period of later Mughals. He brought the trunk of the body of Guru Tegh Bahadur, the 9th Guru of the Sikhs, to this village after the execution at Chandni Chowk Kotwali (where the Sis Ganj Gurudwara is situated). Lakhi Shah, along with his relations, with all due regards cremated the body of the Guru and he buried the remains in a vessel at the place where Gurudwara Rikab Gunj exists. Later, Sardar Baghel Singh along with other chiefs of Sikh misals came to Delhi and built the Gurudwara at this place along with other historic Gurudwaras. The remains of Guru Tegh Bahadur are still preserved in this Gurudwara. This site was declared by Lord Hardinge for government buildings did put an end to the controversy on the question of the selection of the site for government building, but it definitely brought an estrangement between the Sikhs and the government and it led to the beginning of the Gurudwara reform movement.

For the Viceregal Lodge (now Rastrapati Bhawan), central secretariat and other buildings, proceedings for acquiring land whatever privately owned were taken up. Lists of buildings, tombs and graveyards had already been prepared; villages were shifted from this site. Categories of (i) buildings of historical or

Gurudwara Rakab Ganj.

antiquarian value not to be destroyed, (ii) the category of building not to be destroyed, unless it becomes imperative, and (iii) the category that was not of any historical value. The Gurudwara was in the first list at S. No. 10, Raisina Village, Khasra No. 396-398 'Gurudwara Tegh Bahadur' owned by Gurbax Singh and few others. The remarks column reads, 'Much respected by Sikhs. Ashes of Guru Tegh Bahadur, the father of Guru Gobind Singh.'[141]

To make the road straight, some portions of the land of the Gurudwara were acquired, even the proposal to pull down the wall 'to beautify the inner Dalan as a part.' The Government thought that the walls enclosing the historic shrine were too ugly to be allowed near the vicinity of the Viceregal Lodge. This all happened in the middle of 1913.[142]

After the Kuka suppression in 1872 Singh Sabha movement emerged, which did pioneering work to rekindle the Sikh faith.

The acquisition of a portion of the Gurudwara land spread a wave of resentment in the Sikh Community. The Government went ahead with its plans, and pulled down a portion of the Wall. Attempt was also made to pull down the wall at another point in the beginning of November, 1913, but hue and cry raised by Sham Kaur, mother of the Mahant, put a stop to this and the matter was referred again to New Delhi Committee. This act of sacrilege singularly unleashed dynamic forces in Sikhism.[143]

For the first time in the History of Sikhism in Delhi the Sikhs of Delhi took out a procession on the eve of the birth anniversary of Guru Gobind Singh in December 1913, which became a regular feature thereafter. A Diwan was held in Gurudwara Sis Ganj Delhi, when the Sacrilege Committee against Gurudwara Rikab Ganj was condemned in most unequivocal terms and the Chief Khalsa Diwan, Amritsar was requested to take up the matter with the authorities.

Layalpur Singh Sabha, Khurdpur village, Jullundur, Master Tara Singh, chief Khalsa Diwan, Harchand Singh, played a prominent role in raising the issue. The whole Punjab was agitated except few who were the stooges of the British Administration. 'Sikh Review', a paper had already been started at Delhi in April 1914, under the patronage of Bhai Arjun Singh, a close friend of the Maharaj of Nabha; he was a pioneer in opening a second front at Ludhiana. Meeting at different cantonments were held. Sikhs in Vancouver, America, also expressed resentment. The constitution of the 'Khalsa Gurudwara Committee, Delhi' was framed. The Punjab Government decided on a policy of repression to suppress the agitation of Gurudwara Rikab Gunj affair. The agitators pushed the discontent underground and channelized it into revolutionary lines. The Kamagata Maru incident and Budge riot in the last days of September 1914 created sensation in Punjab and released a fresh wave of indignation.

In the following months there was a great onrush of emigrants to Punjab under the aegis of Gadar Party of America, with the declared object to fight of Indian independence.

The emigrants came by the following ships:

Jardine and others arrived at Calcutta on 29 September 1914; Nam Sang arrived at Calcutta on 13 October 1914; and Kores en route Tosha Maru arrived at Calcutta on 29 October 1914; Randhir Singh an activist for Gurudwara affairs came into contact with Rash Behari Bose. The emigrants came in contact with the extremists of Ludhiana School of thought. Some cantonment at Lahore was seduced.

Some revolutionary were captured and tried in the second Lahore conspiracy case. The judgment was announced on 30 March 1916, when six were sentenced to death, 45 to transportation for life and fifteen were acquitted.[144]

The agitation over the wall of Gurudwara Rikab Ganj infused a new spirit in the Sikh community and emphasized upon it the necessity of controlling the religious shrines by the community itself rather than leave them at the mercy of a few Mahants.

The Government entangled in the 'Punjab and Khilafat Groups' saw discretion to be the part of velour and decided to readjust the proposed roads so as to abut Gurudwara Rikab Gunj leaving it in the form of a rectangle with extra land to the Gurudwara. An agreement to this effect was signed on 1 March 1920.

With the inauguration of Non-cooperation movement from 1 August 1920, the Gurudwara reform movement worked in close collaboration with it.

Pan-Islamism was on the rise when Ali Brothers came to Delhi in 1911, the rich Punjabi Muslim Merchants were the earliest supporters of the Ali Brother. The ground for the Pan-Islamism of Mohammed Ali was already prepared by 'Faqir', Nusrat Ali, Mohammad Din and Obeidullah. Arya-Sanatan rivalry, a conflict between generations as well as between provincial groups, was less linked with political issues than was Muslim factionalism. The loyalist and the nationalist Hindus were not as clearly distinguished from each other as were the loyalist and the Nationalist Muslims. The Municipality was dominated before and after 1884 by the mercantile and banking groups, the burden of taxation fell chiefly on the professional and lower paid sections. The rich were, however generous in their philanthropy, because of which the Municipality was able to execute many public works and carry out effective famine-relief. (Drinking water was supplied in 1903 so the electricity) donations and not taxes, had been the traditional method of contributing on public services, and this continued till the late nineteenth early twentieth centuries.

Muslims did become a minority as a result of death and exile in 1858 and they had reason to be bitter because many of them had been impoverished, all of them were under suspicious and their Mosques were confiscated and desecrated. However as a community they were invigorated by the immigrant Punjabi Muslim merchants, who stridently took up Pan-Islamic issues and whose wealth fed the Mosques and Madarsas.

The Era of Mahatma Gandhi

On the scale of political creativity and representatively the leaders of the congress never touched the high level mark. None of them could give new political ideas to build a highly efficient political system. In fact, till M.K. Gandhi came on the scene, the congress leaders had not even thought of a completely independent India. They were struggling for more and more representation in the Legislative Assembly for themselves. Either their Instinct to serve the people was missing or weak. If they had wanted to represent the people, they would have de-classed themselves. Their living style, their language, their areas of activities hardly showed any sign of their instinct to identify themselves with the interests of the masses. They did talk of the miseries of Indian people in the AICC sessions. But no action flowed. In fact, their political creativity was so low that they could neither think of systematically involving the masses in the struggle nor of making them capable of running a political system by raising their political consciousness. They wanted power and were not public oriented.

However, there was a gradual rise in political creativity and representativity of the Indian National Congress. The radical group in the congress did operate among the masses and tried to mobilize them. With the arrival of M.K. Gandhi on the scene, the congress leadership entered a phase of fairly high political creativity and representativity. Gandhi because of his wide and long experience in mass mobilization on the non-violent path did not take much time to involve the masses in the freedom struggle. Moreover, he trained the congress leaders in the technique of mass mobilization. He could generate a sense of mission in them to work among the rural people.

Led by Gandhiji, the Congress leadership was apparently flowing in one current, but inside there were two currents, not quite compatible with each other. One comprised of sincere congressmen who were guided by a missionary Zeal; the other of opportunist elements. They had joined the Congress only to take advantage of the situation. Gradually, they began to dominate the Congress while marked the turning point in the quality of Congress leadership. The Congress was no longer guided by men committed to the welfare of the public. This became clear long ago during the short period of 1937-9, when the congress got an opportunity to form the government in the provinces. Gandhiji had already resigned from the primary membership of the congress party.

The evolution of the Congress elite can be divided in to four periods till the death of Gandhiji, each of which produced a slightly different type of leader drawn from a different complex of social strata:

(i) From 1885 to 1900 non-creative and non-representative;
(ii) From 1900 to 1920 (the period of radicals) non-creative but partly representative;

(iii) From 1920 to 1946 (Gandhian Era) creative and representative;

(iv) The past-independence period, (till J.L. Nehru) Predominantly under the leadership of Jawahar Lal Nehru, Non-creative but partly-representative.[145]

Under Gandhi's leadership the congress became a powerful mass organization with a widespread network all over the country. The main organizational objective of the congress now was to bring as many in the fold of the organization as possible and make then politically conscious. Gandhiji evolved programs so that all congressmen could contribute to the best of their capacity in cutting the roots of the British rule and ameliorating the socio-economic conditions of Indian people. Through these programs Gandhiji imparted massive political education to the people living in remote villages and good democratic political training to a large number of the congressmen. Gandhiji made them struggle for their self-respect. And this was not possible without making them fearless and self-sacrificing; ready to defend their dignity and self-respect even at the cost of property and life. Under his leadership the Congress became the true national organization and it stood for the collective strength of the Nation. Through the use of Satyagraha Gandhiji was able to broaden the base of the Congress by recruiting new elements in the movement. This gave the Congress the impetus to develop organizational methods of reconciling conflict among such diverse elements.

Gandhiji made the Congress into a representative institution with an almost authoritarian high command, combining a democratic spread of its field of action with a firmly controlled central focus of decision-making. Despite Gandhi's use of a tremendous amount of creative energy to transform the character of the congress, the latter could not became a powerful beacon. In fact, during his life time this organization developed weaknesses, and the vested interests had come to dominate it. It had lost its missionary zeal to a large extent. It had also lost the sense of purity of means and ends. All these led Gandhiji to resign from the primary membership of the congress. When he resigned he told one of his co-workers '...My retirement can only lead to purging the congress of cant and hypocrisy. Today violence and non-violence, truth and untruth, Khadi and non-Khadi seem to be the same to congressmen...'[146]

In 1948, when Gandhiji was on fast for restoring communal harmony, he read out one of the letters written to him from one of his co-workers from Andhra Pradesh.

> The one great problem, apart from many other political and Economic issues of very complicated nature is the moral degradation into which the men in the congress circles have fallen... the taste of political power had turned their heads, several of MLA's and the MLC's are following the policy of making hay while the sun shines ... Swaraj was the only all absorbing passion which had goaded men

and women to follow your leadership; but now that the goal has been reached, all moral restrictions have lost their powers on most of the fighters in the great struggle, who are joining hands even with those who were sworn opponents of the national movement and who now, for their personal ends, enlist themselves as congress members. The situation is growing intolerable every day with the result the congress, as well as the congress Government, have come into disrepute.'[147]

Gandhiji, after Independence, foresaw that unless the congress maintained its momentum and dynamism, purged itself of the lust for power for power's Sake, and returned to its old standards of austerity, integrity, and service, it would lose its hold on the masses and ...wither away.

On 9 January 1915 Gandhiji and Kasturba landed at Apollo Bunder, Bombay. In the interview he said he would follow Gokhale's advice and pass some time in India observing and studying.

On the following dates, Gandhiji came to Delhi:

- On 12 April 1915, arrived in Delhi with Kasturba and others.
- On 26 November 1917, had interview with Chelmsford and Montague at Delhi
- On 27 November 1917, had interview with Tilak and Montague.
- On 25 March 1918 Met Private Secretary to Viceroy regarding release of Ali Brother.
- From 25 April 1918 till May 1, 1918 Gandhiji remained in Delhi, met Viceroy, spoke at war conference supporting resolution of recruitment.
- On 6 March 1919, he had interview with Viceroy.
- On 7 March 1919 attended protest meeting at Delhi, Mahadev Desai read out speech, met Sir, James Duboulay, Home Secretary.
- On 9 April 1919 – on way to Delhi at Kosi served with orders restricting entry into Punjab and Delhi. Message to countrymen not to resent arrest or commit violence. Ram Navmi Day celebration. Peaceful procession at Amritsar.
- On 1 November 1919 he attended a public meeting at Pataudi House, the meeting could not be held due disturbances.
- On 2 November 1919 Delhi martyrs meeting was resumed, Gandhiji addressed gathering.
- On 23 November 1919 spoke at Khilafat Conference at Delhi, attended exclusively by Muslims. M.A. Jinnah regretted inability to attend.
- On 24 November 1919 Gandhiji presided over joint Hindu-Muslims session of Khilafat Congress; spoke in Hindi, Resolution declared India's unwillingness to participate in peace celebrations until Khilafat question was settled.

Gandhiji Returns to India from South Africa in 1915 (Gandhi%20and%20Kasturba_imgres.htm)

- On 16 January 1920 reached Delhi.
- On 18 January 1920 met Maulana Abul Kalam Azad.
- On 19 January 1920 had interview with Viceroy, as member of Khilafat Deputation.
- On 31 August 1920 took pledge to wear Khadi for life, at Ahmedabad.
- On 13 February 1921, at Delhi, spoke at opening ceremony of Tibbia College, Karol Bagh.

- On 4 November 1921 in Delhi, spoke on civil-disobedience resolution at the AICC meeting.
- On 5 November 1921 spoke on resolution regarding renouncing of Government Service including service in Army.
- On 26 February 1922 at Delhi, Gandhiji gave interview to Press on AICC, meetings and its resolutions
- On 14 September 1924, reached Delhi, in connection of Hindu-Muslim riots.
- On 15 September 1924 in Delhi inaugurated, the Hindustan Times.
- On 17 September 1924 commenced 21 day fast at Mohammad Ali's house.
- On October, 1924, in Delhi at 12 noon, broke his fast after making statement on Hindu-Muslim unity, Mohammad Ali presented Gandhiji with a cow purchased from a butcher for being sent to Pinjrapole.
- On November, 1924 Gandhiji left Delhi, but during this period he met many people, along with Rabindra Nath Tagore he appealed to international opium conference, Geneva, to adopt measures to suppression of opium traffic except for medical purposes, he sought Viceroy's permission to visit Kohat, in a message asked Transvaal Indian to continue struggle for honourable existence.
- On 2 November 1924, he interviewed by Associated Press of India.
- On November, 1924 visited Modern School and Ramjas College, addressed the students, and attended the funeral of Bi-Amma, mother of Ali Brothers.
- On 18 November 1924 left Delhi for Bombay.
- On 23 January 1925 at Delhi he presided a meeting of all party conference committee for Swaraj and Hindu-Muslim unity; Moti Lal was the Secretary of this meeting.
- On 3 February 1925 he left for Rawalpindi.
- On 8 February 1925 reached Delhi, Met leaders.
- On 27 February 1925 he reached Delhi.
- On March 1, 1925 presided over the meeting of All Party Conference Committee on Hindu-Muslim unity.
- On 8 March 1926 in a letter to Abul Kalam Azad described the pathetic condition of disunity within the congress.
- On 1 November 1927 in Delhi attended meeting of Khadi Pracharak Mandal.
- On 2 November 1927, He met the Viceroy, Lord Irwin, visited Jamia Millia Islamia and spoke to students.

- On 4 January 1929, Halted at Delhi; met Dr. Zakir Husain; reached Ahmadabad at night of 5th.
- On 19 February 1929, attended with Viceroy, Vithal Bhai Patel's Party.
- On 27 March 1929 reached Delhi, Attended meeting of congress working committee, left for Ahmadabad.
- On 5 July 1929 he reached Delhi from Kashipur and left on 6 July 1929 reached Sabarmati Ashram.
- On 1 November 1929 arrived in Delhi; leaders met at Vithalbhai Patel's House to prepare drafts of joint statement; Gandhiji emphasized that Viceroy's offer could not be accepted without fulfillment of conditions.
- On 2 November 1929 Conference of Prominent leaders at Delhi unanimously issued statement in reply to Viceroy's offer of Round Table Conference, Gandhiji spoke at the Town Hall; received addresses from congress committee, Mazdur Sabha and a purse from citizens.
- On 28 December 1929 Attempt was made to blow up Viceroy's special train near New Delhi. Gandhiji reached Delhi; met Viceroy.
- On 2 January 1930, reached Delhi, working committee fixed 26 January as Independence Day.
- On 15 February 1930 Addressed Public meeting. Rafi Ahmad Kidwai, ex-member of legislative Assembly and substitute member CEC, handed over Gandhi's letter to Viceroy in Delhi 'Motilal Day' observed, Motilal died in Lucknow on 6 February 1930.
- On 17 February 1931 Gandhiji detained at Ghaziabad; after morning walk at Shahdara, drove to Dr. Ansari's house, spoke to people gathered in the park; received Lal Bahadur Sastri, Sapru and Jayakar, before meeting Viceroy; RTC terms and scope of congress participation discussed. Gandhiji held prayer meeting at Dr. Ansari's house in the evening.
- On 18 February 1931 – talked to Viceroy.
- On 19 February 1931- Summoned by Viceroy; held consultation with Jawahar Lal Nehru, Vallabbhai Patel, Abul Kalam Azad and other CWC members; communiqué issued.
- On 20 February 1931 – Gandhiji Addressed Public meeting.
- On 22 February 1931 – Addressed council of All-India Muslim League.
- On 25 February 1931 – Gandhiji spoke at Hindu College, Delhi.
- On 26 February 1931 – Spoke at Sisganj Gurudwara.
- On 27 February 1931 summoned by Viceroy; no final agreement, CWC met after Gandhi-Irwin Talks.
- On 1 March 1931- CWC altered draft formula of Gandhi-Irwin

agreement without affecting the principle of its terms for truce. Gandhiji met Viceroy at 9.00 a.m. talk continued till 12.15 a.m. on return to residence at 1.00 a.m. informed CWC members about his discussion with viceroy; at 2.00 p.m. began his silence day.

- On 4 March 1931 at Viceroy House Lord Irwin and Gandhiji signed the provisional settlement which was officially announced at 5.00 p.m.
- On 9 March 1931 Reached Ahmadabad at 9.30 p.m.
- On 19 March 1931-Reached Delhi, Met Viceroy regarding commutation of death sentences of Bhagat Singh, Sukhdev and Rajguru. Met H.W. Emerson, Home Secretary.
- On 21 March 1931 attended a conference convened by Viceroy along with Salvia for framing the new constitution, ruling princes attended it.
- On 23 March1931 in a letter to Lord Irwin he appealed for reconsideration of question of commutation of death sentences of Bhagat Singh and others. Issued statement of Bhagat Singh on execution, left Delhi for Karachi.
- On 6 April 1931 – in Delhi, issued press statement on communal problem. Interview with H.W. Emerson.
- On 7 April 1931-At Council Hall, he spoke to federation of Indian Chambers of Commerce and Industry.
- On 10 December 1933-Arrived in Delhi in morning; addressed labourer's meeting. Visited Harijan quarters, Khadi Bhandar and Jamia Millia Islamia. Had discussion with Harijans.
- On 11 December 1933 – At Delhi, Silence Day.
- On 12 December 1933 – Conferred with congress leaders.
- On 13 December 1933 – Had discussion with Sanatanists. In morning visited Alipur and spoke at public meeting. Addressed student's meeting and unveiled portrait of Motilal Nehru met Japanese delegation, in a statement reply to Iqbal's charge.
- On 14 December 1933 – Discussion with Abul Kalam Azad, Jawahar Lal Nehru, J.B. Kriplani, Jamnalal Bajaj and Syed Mahmud. Addressed Harijan's and women's meetings. Left for Bezwada at 4.00 p.m.
- On 18 July 1934-At New Delhi Station en route to Calcutta, interview to Associated Press of India.
- On 29 December 1934-reached Delhi in the morning. Gave interview to Associated Press.
- On 30 December 1934-spoke at Harijan Industries Exhibition, Delhi.
- On 1 January 1935 Gave interview to the Hindustan Times.
- On 2 January 1935, had discussion about new constitution of Harijan

Sewak Sangh. Laid foundation stone of Harijan Colony, Delhi. Opened Harijan conference at Narela.

- On 3 January objection to joint Parliamentary Committee report
- On 4 January, he met a deputation of a section of Dalits, who had been ill-treated by Zamindars of their village;
- On 5th he attended a meeting of Central Board of All-India Harijan Sevak Sangh.
- On 8 January, he met the deputation of Ahmadabad Mill owners.
- On 9th he gave interview to Halide Edib Hanum.
- On 10th interview regarding rural development.
- On 12 January visited Cattle breeding farm, Delhi, till 28 January 1935 he met various leaders and people and visited village around Delhi like Sultanpur, Bawana, Hamayunpur, Munirka and spoke at MLA's meeting at Delhi.
- On 28 January 1935 he left for Wardha.
- On 8 March 1936 arrived in Delhi. Stayed in Harijan Cottage. He remained at Delhi till March 30, 1936, during this period he met various congress leaders like Nehru, Jamnalal Bajaj, Harijan workers sent draft for Rs. 60,000 to Rabindra Nath Tagore.
- On 27 October 1936 arrived in Delhi, met Mrs. Ansari, and ailing mother of Brij Kishore Chandiwala.
- On 15 March 1937 Gandhiji arrived in Delhi, attended AICC meeting (on March 16) which passed resolution on office-acceptance.
- From 19-20 March 1937 In Delhi, convention of newly elected congress members of legislatures and other AICC members was held to take oath of national independence and allegiance to Indian people.
- On 22 March 1937-Gandhiji gave interview to leaders of Jamiat-ul-Ulema-i-Hind, visited Industrial Training School.
- On 22 March left for Segaon.
- On 4 August 1937-Reached Delhi. Had interview with Viceroy regarding question of lifting ban on Abdul Ghaffar Khan's entry into Frontier Province.
- On 14 April 1938, arrived in Delhi.
- On 15 April 1938, had interview with Viceroy, left Delhi for Wardha.
- On 20 September 1938 arrived in Delhi, Called on ailing Begum Ansari.
- From 21 September to 4 October 1938-he attended congress working committee meetings, gave interview to F.S. Young, Inspector-General of Police to Jaipur State; left Delhi for N.W.F.P.
- On 10 November 1938, arrived in Delhi, called on Begum Ansari, left for Segaon,.

- On 15 March 1939 in Delhi had two-house meeting with Viceroy. In Delhi Jail, he persuaded prisoners to give up hunger strike.
- On 16 March 1939, Gandhiji had another meeting with Viceroy.
- On 18 March 1939-spoke at opening ceremony of Lakshmi Narayan Temple and Buddha Vihar at Mandir Marg, Delhi.
- On 20-23 March 1939 statement on Travancore Satyagrahis and Jaipur Satyagrahis.
- On 6 April 1939-Had meeting with Viceroy.
- On 27 July 1939-At Ghaziabad Station in the morning, Gandhiji Got down and proceeded to Delhi in motorcar. At 10.30 a.m. at Harijan colony presided over first convocation of Harijan Industrial Home and gave away certificates to students. In the afternoon, interview to Ghanshyam Singh Gupta, speaker, central provinces legislative Assembly. He also met other leaders and left Wardha by G.T. Express.
- On 2 October 1939-he had discussion with Rajendra Prasad and Jawahar Lal Nehru before their meeting with Viceroy.
- On 3 October 1939, Through the Manchester Guardian he appealed the British people for sincerity in "Professions about Democracy."
- On 5 October 1939 he had an interview with Viceroy.
- On 1 November 1939 he along with Rajendra Prasad and M.A. Jinnah had conference with Viceroy. He also expressed sympathy with Chinese children, for the hardships caused by Japanese aggression.
- On 2 November 1939 spoke at opening ceremony of Prayer Hall in Harijan Niwas.
- On 4 November 1939 Interview with Viceroy.
- On 4 February 1940 – Reached Delhi, Met Sir Sikandar Hayat Khan.
- On 5 February 1940 – at 11.00 a.m. had interview with Viceroy.
- On February, 1940 – Gave statement to Press about, differences between congress demand and Vice regal offer left Delhi for Wardha.
- On 28 June 1940-arrived in Delhi. Had discussion with Asaf Ali, left for Simla.
- On 29 June 1940 – Met the Viceroy.
- One 30 June 1940 – New Delhi, attended Public Prayer at Harijan Colony.
- From 2 July to 7 July 1940 – he attended congress working committee, and declared complete independence for India, left for Wardha.
- On 26 September 1940 arrived in Delhi in the morning and left for Simla in the Evening.
- On 27 September 1940, he met Viceroy also on September 30.
- On 1 October 1940, in Delhi, had a long talk with Bhulabhai Desai

and J.B. Kriplani; attended a function at Harijan Colony to celebrate his 72nd birthday, left for Wardha.

- On 27 March 1942, attended congress working committee meeting. Telegraphed condolence to Prabhavati Devi Bose on reported death of Subhas Chandra Bose.
- On 30 March 1942 – sent telegram to Prabhavati Devi Bose expressing relief at contradiction of the news. British war Cabinet's proposal released to Press. Remained in Delhi till April 5, 1942.
- On 21-22 June 1945, attended C.W.C. meetings.
- On 23 June Halted at Delhi on way to Simla.
- On 24 June 1945, met Viceroy in afternoon.
- On 17 July 1945-Gandhiji arrived in Delhi, visited Satyavati and Saukat Ansari, left for Wardha.
- On 1 April 1946 – In Delhi, he met cabinet Ministers in the evening; spoke at prayer meeting.
- On 3 April 1946, in letter to Lord Pathick-Lawrence, pleaded for abolition of Salt Tax and release of prisoners.
- On 4-5 April 1946, he met INA. Men and paid tribute to INA men and Subhas Chandra Bose.
- From on words till 28 May 1946 he remained in Delhi met number of people, attended congress working committee meetings, met many times the Viceroy; Addressed INA officials.
- On 8 June 1946 came to Delhi from Mussoorie, till 29 June 1946 he remained in Delhi, met Cabinet Mission; on 26 June Viceroy and Cabinet Mission announced that a temporary caretaker government of officials would be set up, during this period he attended CWC meetings met Viceroy and other leaders.
- On 16 August 1946, Four days rioting started in Calcutta as the consequence of Direct Action Call by Muslim League.
- On 26 August 1946 he arrived in Delhi.
- On 27 August 1946 with Jawahar Lal Nehru he met Viceroy.
- On 2 September 1946, interim Government took office, Congress Ministers before taking oath called on Gandhiji.
- On 26 September 1946, he met Viceroy.
- On 10 October 1946 – communal violence broke out in Noakhali and Tippara.
- On 15 October 1946 – Muslim League announced its decision to join interim Government
- On 28 October 1946 he left by train for Calcutta.
- On 12 November 1946, Madan Mohan Malviya died.
- On 31 March 1947, reached Delhi in the morning met Nehru,

C. Rajgopalachari, Sucheta Kriplani, G.D. Birla and Vallabbhai Patel. Met number of people in Delhi, also visited ailing Sarojini Naidu left Delhi at Night.

- On 1 May 1947 reached Delhi remained in Delhi till 7 May 1947.
- On 9 May 1947 reached Calcutta.
- On 25-26 May 1947 in Delhi remained in Delhi till 20 July 1947, left Delhi,
- On 15 August 1947 he was in Calcutta, observed Independence Day by fasting, working on spinning wheel and prayer.
- On 9 September 1947 reached Delhi, put up at Birla House, till 30 January, 1948 he remained in Delhi, met various political leaders and delegation of people, and visited many places in Delhi such as Dargah of Bakhtiyar Kaki at Mehrauli. Met Viceroy.
- On 30 January 1948, revised draft constitution of congress. Had talks with Pyarelal, Sudhir Ghose, Maulanas and Sindhi deputation. Had discussion with Vallabbhai Patel, took his evening meal at 4.30 p.m. while discussion continued, Maniben Patel interrupted discussion to remind Gandhiji that it was time for prayer. Gandhiji started for prayer meeting supported by Manu Gandhi and Abha Gandhi on either side. As he was approaching the prayer place, three shots were fired at him at close range. Gandhiji Sank to the ground breathing his last at 5.17 p.m.[148]

Apart from Gandhiji, many known and unknown people and leaders from Congress and other political parties, groups, organizations took part in the struggle for National Independence; it is not possible and in some cases feasible to name them, but they had definitely contributed immensely in achieving the political freedom. Gandhiji did play very noted role. He politically organized the divided masses of India under his leadership, through non-violent means, based on truth and fair means. He travelled immensely; met various people. He was opposed by many and also opposed others, but never treated them as enemy. Many leaders who worked along with him died during his lifetime; this also gave him rude shocks. The death of Kasturba Gandhi shattered him; she was a true companion in his political life. He got political freedom from the mighty empire through non-violent means, which was not only a strategy but the creed of his life.

The East India Association with the overseas league held a condolence meeting on 3 February, 1948 at Overseas House. In his condolence Lord Scarbrough said,

> For thirty years Mr. Gandhi was the dominating figure in the Indian Sub-continent. No important move, no large policy, could be undertaken by men of wisdom without taking into account what Mr. Gandhi might think of it and

what he might decide to do about it. It was something quite remarkable that one man, whose only armory was his character and his personality, should attain such power and influence. Inevitably, the British rulers in India came into collision with so powerful a figure, but he understood that, and I believe never resented it, so far above the little feelings of ordinary men was he able to lift his spirit.

In addition to his great position in public affairs, his personal influence on the lives of individuals must have been immeasurable. Many changed their whole lives because of him; some followed him as disciples follow a master; men of wealth honoured him for a life of sacrifice which they could not emulate; men in high positions at times took their personal difficulties to him for solution. No one talked to him without experiencing the charm of his personality. Not all, perhaps very few, understood him, but he penetrated the thoughts of many men and ruled the hearts of multitudes.

He will be remembered in the world as a great teacher, particularly of simple folk, and as a great leader who devoted his life to his fellow-countrymen. His influence on the recent history of India will in time be properly assessed; it cannot fail to be found to be a great influence, perhaps a decisive one. In this country, he will have no enemies, but he will have recognition as a very remarkable man, who was often our opponent, but one whom we honoured. It is indeed a great tragedy that in these most critical early days in the existence of the two new free Dominions, when his great influence was so much needed and was being used on the side of restraint and moderation, he has been struck down...[149]

The Partition of India—India, Pakistan and the Indian States

The sentiments of Indian Nationalism started from 1885 in systematic manner within the congress, this organization was representative and national but not the organization of masses as it became later on with the leadership and control of Gandhiji; the Muslims considered it as Hindu organization. In 1906, the All-India Muslim League was formed with favourable relations towards British rule; but by 1913, the League changed its stance and shifted its focus and began to view Indian self-government as its goal. It continued to favour Hindu-Muslim unity towards that end; but in 1940, the league began to call for a separate Muslim state from the projected independent India. It has penetrated into middle class and lower class, which it was not related to so far. The League had the impression that a united Independent India would be dominated by Hindus. The British authorities welcomed the idea of Pakistan and campaigned at the Round Table Conference for the partition of India, because they were bent on splitting the National forces of the country. Whenever the prospect of agreement arose between the League and Congress, no matter on what terms, the British authorities always said it was unacceptable.

Rajagopalachari suggested that the final decision on whether or not the establishment of Pakistan was desirable, should be postponed until authority would pass to an Indian Government and a referendum could be held in areas with a Muslim majority. The proposal was favourably received not only by Muslim League rank-and-file, but also by some of its leaders. But the British authorities opposed the project.

Viceroy Linlithgow declared at the Calcutta chamber of commerce on 17 December 1942 that the British solicitude for the unity of India had increased in proportion to the prospect of a Hindu-Muslim settlement on the basis of partitions.[150]

The utterances were hypocritical through and through, and even the leaders of the Pakistan movement realized it.

Jinnah wrote, 'The British are not honest in their solicitude for the Muslims and whatever regard they show for the Muslims is in the interest of their traditional policy of "divide and rule".'[151]

The attitude of the British authorities contributed greatly to the failure of the league-congress negotiations of 1942.

The Cripps Mission fell through

The 1945-6 elections reflected the alignment of the class forces in provinces with a Muslim majority. The Indian National Congress had lost its hold on the middle strata of Muslims. The small owners and the middle strata of Muslim intellectuals in north-west India and Bengal mainly followed the League.

In the Second World War, League supported the British. After the war, the British forces became so weak economically that it became impossible to rule India, but the British Government was determined to keep the country economically and politically dependent on Britain, and therefore dragged out the transfer of power, fostered the most reactionary schemes of partition and abandoned the country in a condition which made normal relations between the two newly-created states practically impossible.

Under the Pethick Lawrence Plan (1946), India was granted dominion status after the Constituent Assembly drew up the new constitution. The constitution envisaged the country's partition into three zones; provinces with a predominantly Hindu population forming one zone, the Eastern provinces (Bengal and Assam) forming another, and the Western provinces (the Punjab, Sind and North-West Frontier Province) the third. The zones and the various provinces in them were granted autonomy in administration of all matters, same matters of defense, external relations, and communications, which were to be a Central Government responsibility. In the provisional Indian Government envisaged in the British proposals, 40 per cent of seats were to go to Hindus nominated by the Indian National Congress, 40 per cent to Muslims nominated by the league and 20 per cent to the Sikhs, 'untouchables', Parsis and Christians.

In April 1946, Congress accepted the constitutional proposal, also the Muslim League. The elections to the Constituent Assembly were held in June 1946 of the 389 deputies elected, 192 belonged to the Congress and 70 to the Muslim League.

In reply to a congress statement that the Constituent Assembly should be a completely sovereign body, the British Government was bent on restricting its authority. The Pethick Lawrence mission declared that its terms of reference would not extend to the minorities problem and the question of India's relations with Britain. Jawahar Lal Nehru attacked this notion on 10 July 1946,

> We shall have no treaty, if they seek to impose anything upon us, and we shall tear up any treaty they try to impose... In regard to the minorities it is our problem, and we shall no doubt succeed in solving it. We accept no outside interference in it – certainly not the British Government interference in it – and therefore, these two limiting factors to the sovereignty of the Constituent Assembly are not accepted by us.[152]

In the press conference, Nehru replied to the question that the congress had agreed to participate in the Constituent Assembly but did not consider itself committed to the scheme as a whole. This statement was used as a pretext by the British and the Muslim League; to spread the charge that the congress did not intend to recognize provincial autonomy. The full interview was not published. On 29 July 1946, the League Council revised its previous decisions, rejected Pethick Lawrence proposals and announced 'direct actions' to achieve Pakistan, charging Jinnah to draw up a programme. The programme envisaged a boycott of the Constituent Assembly and set 6 August as 'Direct Action Day.'

The leaders of the Pakistan movement hoped to achieve two ends; one to force the British Government, into immediately declaring its agreement to an independent Muslim state, two at the same time, by organizing anti-Hindu campaign and charging the Congress with partiality to Hindu interests, they wanted to press the congress into consenting to a division of the country into two states. This campaign caused bloody Hindu-Muslim riots. 'The events after it made it almost impossible to expect a peaceful solution by agreement between the Congress and the Muslim League. This was one of the greatest tragedies of Indian History.'[153]

The Provisional Government of India was formed in August 1946 under Jawahar Lal Nehru, the Muslim League initially boycotted it, but on 15 October 1946 agreed to join it. Liaquat Ali Khan, Ismail Ibrahim Chundrigar, Sardar Abdur Rab Nishtar, Ghasanfar Ali Khan and Jogendra Nath Mandal were introduced into the Government at Jinnah's proposal. Very important and influential members of the League were left out. Though, it joined the Government; the Muslim League persisted in its boycott of the Constituent Assembly. This was motivated by procedural differences with the Congress.

The National-Liberation struggle of the people of India, which had by 1947 spread from British India to the Indian States, loomed as a serious threat to Britain. Any further maintenance of India's colonial status held seeds of fresh revolutionary outbursts. So P.M. Clement Attlee officially declared in the House of Commons on 20 February 1947, that Britain would begin transferring power to the Indians not later than June 1948. If no constitution is acceptable, then authority would be transferred to the existing provincial government Lord Mountbatten was appointed the new Viceroy.

The Pakistan movement entered a new stage. Hindu-Muslim killings started. In Punjab, the Muslim proclaimed that Sikh landlords and Hindu-money lenders were their sub-enemies.[154]

The attitude of the British government and the situation in the provinces with a Muslim majority compelled the Indian National Congress to consent to the Pakistan scheme. Gandhiji was very opposed to the idea of partition and urged Mountbatten to offer Jinnah leadership of a united India instead of the creation of a separate Muslim State. However, Nehru would not agree to that suggestion.

The statement containing the final decision of the British Government regarding 'the method of transfer of power,' known as the Indian Independence Act, was published on 3 June 1947. Under this Act, India was divided into two parts—the Hindu State of Hindustan (India) and the Islamic State of Pakistan, both with dominion status. Whether North-West Frontier Province and Assam's Sylhet district would join India or Pakistan was to be decided by a referendum; in the case of Sind, this was to be decided by voting in the Sind legislative assembly whether the Punjab and Bengal would join one of the dominions integrally or be divided, was also to be decided by vote in the legislative assemblies of the two provinces. The voting was to be separate—by deputies of districts with Muslim and with Hindu majority. If one of the two groups of deputies favoured partition, the provinces would be divided.

The princely states were allowed to decide for themselves whether they wished to join either one of the dominions, or preserve their former relationship with Britain. The status of the Pakistan tribal border areas was to be determined by negotiation between tribal representatives and the government of the dominion to which North-West Frontier Province would go after India and Pakistan were established. The sovereign rights of India and Pakistan were thus curtailed by dominion status, but since the Indian Independence Act envisaged the termination of India's Colonial Status, on the one hand and the establishment of Pakistan on the other, it was endorsed with reservations by both the Indian National Congress and the Muslim League. In July British Parliament passed the Indian Independence Act, Pakistan celebrated it on 14 August and India on 15 August 1947. As a result, at least 10 million Hindus,

Muslims and Sikhs fled their homes to seek sanctuary on whichever side of the line was favorable to them. The ensuing communal massacre left at least one million dead.

The wholesale massacres, demolished town blocks, and gutted villages in Lahore, Rawalpindi, Amritsar and other Punjab cities. There were riots and killing in Delhi, united provinces and Bihar, in states of Rajputana and Hyderabad. Compelled to abandon India, the British colonists did everything they could to complicate the work of establishing the developing normal relations between the newly constituted states—Pakistan and the united India.

Jinnah presided as the Governor-General of Pakistan, which was geographically divided into East Pakistan and West Pakistan and separated by Indian Territory (including half of Punjab and half of Bengal). The issue of Kashmir remained in dispute. Mysore was the first state to accede to the Dominion of India followed by others.

The people of India and Pakistan (now) lived on these political geography for centuries with common history and various commonality, the people of both the countries and its leadership after the experiences should think and act sincerely that either India and Pakistan must draw closer together or they drift further and further apart, with disastrous reactions on both in every sphere: political, economic, military and social.

REFERENCES

1. James P. Lawford, *Britain's Army in India*, George Allen and Unwin, London, 1978, p. 11.
2. ibid. p. 15.
3. S.P.D. XXIX, 99.
4. C.P.E.I. 2754, 2759, 2760.
5. Jadunath Starker, 'Delhi during Anarchy 1749-1788, as told in contemporary records', Indian Historical Records Commission Proceedings, vol. III, 1921, pp. 6-8.
6. Jadunath Sarkar, 'Delhi During the Anarchy 1749-1788, as told in contemporary records', Indian Historical Records Commission proceedings, vol. III, 1921, pp. 6-9.
7. Sayyid Hasan Askari, 'A newly-discussed letter of Shah Alam to George III', Proceedings of the Indian Historical Records Commission, vol. 20, 1943, pp. 47-9.
8. K.P. Srivastava, 'Jahandar Shah and His Successors in Banaras', Journal of Indian History, 1973, pp. 495-500.
9. Sarkar, Sir Jadunath, *Fall of the Mughal Empire*, M.C. Sarkar, Calcutta, 1932, vol. II, p. 121.
10. G.S. Cheema, *The Forgotten Mughals—A History of the Later Emperors of the House of Babur*, 1707, Manohar, 2002, p. 402.

11. Colonel Sir Gordon Hearn, *The Seven Cities of Delhi*, 2nd Ed., Thacker Spink Co., Calcutta, 1928, p. 200.
12. Sir Edward Maclagan, The Site of the Battle of Delhi, 1803, Punjab Historical Society, 1914, pp. 127-141.
13. Krishan Lal Sachdeva, 'Mirza Jehangeer's Revolt', Indian Historical Records Commission Proceedings, vol. XXXI, 1955, pp. 97-101.
14. John Hope, *The House of Sindhia*, p. 38.
15. S. Neill, *A History of Christianity in India, the Beginnings to* A.D. *1707.*
16. *Guldasta-i-Chandra Bhan Brahman*, p. 6B.
17. *Khulasatut Tawarikh*, p. 30.
18. Bernier, *Travels in India*, pp. 217, 274 and 300-1; *Tarikh-i-Shahadat-i-Farrukhsiyar-wa Julus-i-Mohammad Shah II*, p. 286 b and 288 a.
19. M. Mujeeb, *Indian Muslims*, London, 1966, p. 390.
20. T.W. Kaye, *The Life and Correspondence of Charles, Lord Metcalfe*, vol. I, London, 1858, p. 344.
21. K.N. Panikkar, *British Diplomacy in North India: A Study of the Delhi Residency 1803-1857*, Associated Publication House, New Delhi, 1968, p. 41.
22. Gouri Sankar Mukherjee, 'Nature of Political Relationship between the Residents and Akbar Shah II', Journal of Indian History, 1982, p. 58.
23. Minto papers, VIII, King to the Resident, 29th July, 1811.
24. K.N. Pannikar, Ibid. p. 178.
25. ibid. p. 179.
26. Fane, Sir H., *Five Years in India*, 2 vols., rpt. Punjabi Languages Dept., Patiala, 1970, pp. 137-8.
27. Hari Ram Gupta, 'Delhi Diary of 1825', Indian Historical Records Commission, vol. 25, Pt 2, 1948, pp. 162-8.
28. Kaye and Malleson, *History of the Indian Mutiny*, 6 vols., W.H. Allen, London, 1888-89, vol. I, p. 161.
29. ibid. II, p. 7.
30. Colonel, Sir Gorden Hearn, *The Seven Cities of Delhi*, Thacker, Spink & Co., Calcutta, 1928, p. 217.
31. V. Longer, *When Delhi was lost and won by the English*, in H.S. Bhatia (Ed.), *Political Legal and Military History of India*, Deep & Deep Publication, Delhi, 1986, pp. 112-114.
32. Delhi Gazetteer, 1883-84, p. 30.
33. H. S. Bhatia, ibid. p. 120.
34. Hazrat Zahir Dehlvi, *Dastan-i-Ghadar*, p. 127.
35. Ganda Singh, *The Indian Mutiny of 1857*, in H.S. Bhatia, ibid, pp. 182-83.
36. Gorden Risley Hearn, *The Seven Cities of Delhi*, Aryan Books International, New Delhi, 2005, p. 162.
37. Ghalib's Urdu letters to Abdul Ghafoor 'Suroor', September 1860.
38. Ghalib's Urdu letter to Yusuf Mirza, 26th July 1859.
39. Ghalib's Urdu letter to Meer Mehdi 'Majrooh', 1860.
40. Hearn. ibid, p. 163.

41. Zakaullah- 'Delhi ki masjid aur Muabid ki Sarguzisht' in Fikrenau, Delhi College Magazine, 2010-2011, p. 165.
42. G.A. Natesan & Co., *Delhi, The Capital of India*, Madras, 1918, pp. 171-2.
43. Lawrence James, *Raj-The making and unmaking of British India,* Little Brown & Co., 1997, pp. 316-18.
44. ibid. p. 118-119.
45. ibid. p. 319.
46. op. cit. Lawrence James, p. 316.
47. Narayani Gupta, *Delhi Between Two Empires 1803-1931, Society Government and Urban Growth,* Oxford University Press, Delhi, 1986, op. cit. p. 109.
48. Narayni Gupta, op. cit. pp. 108-109.
49. Delhi Gazetteers, 1912, pp. 36-7.
50. G.A. Nateson & Co., op. cit. p. XX.
51. R.E. Frykenberg, 'The Coronation Durbar of 1911, Some implications', in R.E. Frykenberg(Ed), *Delhi Through the Ages; Essays in Urban History, Culture and Society*; Oxford University Press, Delhi, 1986, pp. 376-7.
52. R.E. Frykenberg, op. cit. pp. 379-80.
53. ibid. p. 381.
54. Narayani Gupta, op. cit. pp. 187-8.
55. N.A.I., Home (Delhi), 38-41 A/July 1912.
56. Census of India 1891, vol. XIX, pt. II, table 93; Ibid, 1901, vol. XIV, pt II, table XV.
57. P.H.P. (Registration) 33A/June, 1899.
58. A.K. Jain, *The Cities of Delhi*, Management Publishing Co., New Delhi, 1994, p. 81.
59. Ved Parkash Gupta, *Dilli; Tera Itihas Nirala (Hindi)*, Prem Prakashan Mandir, Delhi 1997, p. 96.
60. A. K. Jain, ibid. p. 97.
61. M.P. Singh, *The Indian National Movement: A Psycho-Cultural Approach*, in Varinder Grover, *Political System in India*, Deep & Deep Publications, 1989, p. 12.
62. Griffiths, Sir Percival, *British Impact on India*, London 1952, pp. 245-246.
63. Annual Report of the Deputy Commissioner, Delhi, for the year 1858, P.R.O.: Delhi Division, Bundles for 1871.
64. Sangat Singh, *Freedom Movement in Delhi-1858-1919,* Associated Publishing House, New Delhi, 1972, p. 25.
65. Sangat Singh, *Freedom Movement in Delhi,* 1858-1919, Associated Publishing House, New Delhi, 1972, p. 35.
66. Sangat Singh, ibid. p. 35.
67. Delhi Gazetteer 1912, pp. 84-5.
68. Montgomery, *The Life and Letters of George Alfred Lefroy,* London, 1920, pp. 67-70.
69. Sabri, *Farangion Ka Jaal*, Delhi, 1949, p. 154.
70. The Urdu Akhbar, December 30, 1876, pp. 1-2.

71. 'The Rajputana Social Science Congress Gazette, (Jaipur)', January 12, 1877, p. 29.
72. The Tajul Akhbar (Rampur), February, 1877, pp. 45-8 and 109-10.
73. Mazumndar, *Indian National Evolution*, Madras, 1917, p. 33.
74. Sangat Singh, op. cit. p. 64, also, *The Satyarth Prakash*, 1875 Edition, p. 45, 71, 302, and 399.
75. Delhi District Gazetteer, 1912, p. 212.
76. W.C. Smith, *Modern Islam in India*, Lahore, Minerva, 1943, p. 10.
77. R. Symonds, *The Making of Pakistan*, London, Faber, 1949, p. 32.
78. E. Pircoie, 'The Muslim Opposition', The Modern Review, vol. I, 1907, pp. 584.
79. E. Pirion, op. cit., p. 587.
80. op. cit. p. 587.
81. op. cit., p. 587.
82. W.C. Smith, *Modern Islam in India*, Lahore: Minerva, 1943, Chapter, I & II.
83. Sangat Singh, op. cit., p. 67.
84. Sangat Singh, op. cit., p. 68.
85. Sangat Singh, op. cit., p. 70.
86. Mehta and Patwardhan, *Communal Triangle in India*, Allahabad, 1942, p. 24-7.
87. Sachin Sen, *Birth of Pakistan*, Calcutta, 1955, p. 42.
88. Letter dated, October 27, 1888 from Badr-ud-Din Tyabji to A.O. Hume. Quoted in Sangat Singh, op. cit., p. 74.
89. Sangat Singh, op. cit., p. 74.
90. Sangat Singh, op. cit., p. 83.
91. Y.V. Gankovesky and L.R. Gordon-Palonskoya, *A History of Pakistan,* "Nauka" Publication House, Moscow, 1964, p. 12.
92. Syed Ahmad Khan, *Asbab-i-Bagavat-i-Hind*, Aligarh, 1903, p. 65.
93. S. Sen, *The Birth of Pakistan*, Calcutta, 1955, p. 42.
94. R. Prasad, *India Divided*, Bombay, 1947, p. 105.
95. Ibid, p. 104.
96. Y.V. Gankovsky and L.R. Gorden, op. cit., p. 23.
97. R. Prasad, *India Divided*, p. 111.
98. The Indian Review, June, 1906, p. 411.
99. Lal Bahadur, *The Muslim League, its History, Activities and Achievements*, Agra, 1954, p. 30.
100. M. Minto, *India Morley and Minto, 1905-1910*, London, 1936, pp. 30-40.
101. A.B. Rajput, *Muslim League Yesterday and Today*, Lahore, 1948, p. 17.
102. 'The Aligarh Institute Gazette', April 22, 1908, Lal Bahadur, *The Muslim League*, op. cit. pp. 39-40.
103. *The Memoirs of Aga Khan*, p. 33.
104. R. Prasad, *India Divided*, p. 115.
105. A.H. Albiruni, *Makers of Pakistan and Modern Muslim-India*, Lahore, 1950, p. 125.
106. A.H. Albiruni, op. cit., p. 135.

107. The Indian Review, January, 1947, p. 9.
108. R. Prasad, *India Divided*, op. cit., p. 18.
109. Lal Bahadur, op. cit. p. 140.
110. H. Bolitho, *Jinnah, Creator of Pakistan*, London, 1954, p. 84.
111. Indian Statutory Commission, vol. I, London, 1923, p. 27.
112. R. Prasad, *Autobiography*, p. 142.
113. S. Ansari, *Pakistan, the Problem of India*, Lahore, 1945, p. 9.
114. S. Ansari, *Pakistan*, op. cit. p. 7.
115. S. Ansari, op. cit., pp. 4-6.
116. B.R. Ambedkar, *Pakistan*, Bombay: Thacker, 1946, p. 3.
117. B.R. Ambedkar, op. cit. p. 2.
118. Journal of the Pakistan Historical Society, 1956, p. 163.
119. S. Baron, *Modern Nationalism and Religion*, New York: Harper 1947, p. 7.
120. W.N. Brown, *The United States and India and Pakistan*, Cambridge University Press, 1955, p. 113.
121. F. Gunter, *Revolution in India*, New York: Island Press, 1948, p. 12.
122. ibid. p. 21.
123. Smith, *Modern Islam in India*, p. 208.
124. H. N. Brailsford, *Subject Indian*, New York; J. Dey 1943, p. 125.
125. H.G. Rawlinson, *British Achievement in India*, London: W. Hodge, 1938, p. 188.
126. Nafis Ahmad, *The Basis of Pakistan*, Calcutta: Thacker, 1947, p. 27.
127. Fernau, *Muslims on the March*, New York: Knopf, 1954, pp. 199-200.
128. Journal of the Pakistan Historical Society, 1956, p. 171.
129. The Koh-i-Noor (Lahore), September 15, 1888, p. 222, ref. Sangat Singh, *Freedom Movement in Delhi*, Associated Publishing House, New Delhi, 1972, p. 97.
130. ibid. p. 98.
131. Tufail Ahmad, *Musalman Ka Roshan Mustaqbil*, Badayun, 1938, p. 293.
132. ibid. p. 100.
133. Sangat Singh, op. cit., p. 108.
134. Quoted in Sangat Singh, op. cit., p. 130.
135. *Chirol, India, Old and New*, London, 1921. p. 130.
136. *O' Dower, India as I knew it,* London, 1925, p. 170.
137. Sangat Singh, op. cit., p. 179.
138. Sangat Singh, op. cit., p. 182.
139. Sangat Singh, op. cit., pp. 182-183.
140. Quoted in Sangat Singh, op. cit., p. 198.
141. Sangat Singh, op. cit., p. 199.
142. The Khalsa Advocate, July 26, 1913.
143. Sangat Singh, p. 200.
144. Sangat Singh, op. cit. p. 213.
145. Ram Avtar Sharma and Anil Karan, 'Congress-Leadership on the Touchstone of Creativity and Representativity'; Democratic World, vol., XIV, 1985, p. 9-12, No. 3 and No. 4, p. 12-14.
146. Sharma and Karan, op. cit. p. 12.

147. Sharma and Karan, op. cit., p. 12.
148. The dates have been taken from the book: Anil Dutta Mishra, Saroj Kumar Jha, and Sohan Raj Tatar, *A Chronological Biography of Mahatma Gandhi*, Abhijeet Publication, Delhi, 2010.
149. The Asiatic Review Vol. XLIV, 1948, p. 139-140.
150. S. Ansari, *The Problem of India*, Lahore, Pakistan, 1945, p. 65.
151. ibid. p. 66.
152. Speeches and Documents on the Indian Constitution, 1921-1947, vol. II, pp. 612-613.
153. M.A.K. Azad, *India Wins Freedom*, p. 159.
154. People's Age, March 23 and 30, 1947.

5

Amusement and Entertainment

In ancient Indian literature, one finds the absence of discontentment and rebellion. This was due to the influence of the philosophy of karma and rebirth. This attitude towards life rendered all the human conditions (good or bad) as being full of joy and happiness.

The ancient seer, Acharya Barat, has said that dance, song and drama are not only for amusement, but are creators of happiness. If one were to perform them in a procedurally correct manner, all the barriers and hurdles caused by one's bondage to ones desires and karmas evaporate and the accumulated sins of many lifetimes get washed away.

> Mangalyam lalitshchaiv brahmno vadanodabhavam,
> Supunyam ch pavitram ch shubham paapvinashanam.[1]

He also said that gods do not get so happy with flower and garlands as they do with dance and drama.[2]

During the Mahabharat period, amusements could be classified into four categories: 1) personal, 2) familial, 3) social, and 4) religious. Festivals like Holi, Dashahra, Diwali, Shivratri, were celebrated by the people with great delight, pomp and show. People were fond of music, dance and drama. They staged plays and shows, rasa dances were performed, musical instruments were played like the vina, drum, flute. Stringed instruments and trumpets were also common. Hunting was a populer means of entertainment among the princely class and nobility. Arjun killed various birds, animals and Naga people to build Indraprasth. People enjoyed the swing (Jhoola); young boys, girls and women took great delight in the swing. Bards sometimes provided enjoyments. They recited praises, extolling one's predecessors. Chandra Bardai was one such Bard of Prithvi Raj Chauhan. People played indoor games like chess and passas (gambling). Pandavas lost their kingdom and wife (Dropdi) in this game.

During Hindu period, kings, princes, nobles and upper classes of society had high standard of living. Untouchability and slavery were unhealthy features sof the Hindu society. People had great faith in religious superstitions and pilgrimage. The ages old sentiment of veneration of the cow has continued till date.

The third phase of the Turko-Afghan invasions and conquests (like the Greeks, Sakas and the Hunas) from ninth century till seventeenth century. This brought the Hindus and Muslims in India in a relationship of a very different nature, that of the ruled and the ruler.

Mongol pressure had driven away many refugees from the heartlands of Islam to India, to seek a safe home in Hindustan. Delhi being the political capital of India, many foreign people took refuge in it and along with them they brought various new features of social life. During the reign of Sultan Iltutmish the capital city of Delhi was a cosmopolitan Muslim city having a separate Mohalla assigned to the emigrants from Islamic countries.[3]

From the period of Sultan Mahmud of Ghazani down to the Sayyid and Lodi Sultans, a very large number of emigrants came to Delhi from different Islamic countries, like Arabs, Turks, Khurasanis, Afghans, Persians, Mongols, Egyptians and Abyssinians They in the course of time formed the class of Muslims of Hindustan. The Hindu converts to Islam were called Nau-Muslims.

The converted Muslim population was small in the beginning, began to increase gradually with the expansion of the authority of the Delhi Sultanate. These were mostly Hindus of low casts who had embraced Islam due to various reasons. They had submitted themselves to their fate, though no less murmuring and frowning at being inferior in status.

The lowest strata of the Muslim society comprised the artisans, workmen, domestic servants and peasants and cultivators, usually of Indian origin.

Sultana Raziya and Rukn-ud-Din were fond of music. Prince Bughra Khan, son of Sultan Balban was exceedingly fond of music and he set up an association of musicians, dancers and actors. He was a patron of Amir Khusrau, one of the great musicians of his time. During the reign of Sultan Kaiqubad and Jalal-ud-Din Khilji musical concerts were organized. Many male and female musicians were brought from Persia. Turmati Khatun, a skilled musician was the in charge of female musicians during the time of Ala-ud-Din Khilji.

Superiority complex of the foreign Muslims was maintained; Shia-Sunni relations were bitter and sharp and pervaded all the ranks of the Muslim society alike. The Muslim who came to India did not like to go to Indian villages. Life in the village was dominated by the Hindus was intolerable to them. They had entertained a strong aversion for country life.

Slavery was the established practice. Their number was very large. Slaves were sold and bought like commodities in the markets. Delhi was a good market for slaves.[4]

Chinese slave girls were also seen in Delhi. The price of a young girl for domestic work did not exceed eight Tankas at Delhi. Young girls worthy of being concubine and fit for domestic work were purchased for fifteen Tankas. Probably the price of slave girls in Delhi being the capital was higher as compared to other cities of India. Handsome slave boys were priced higher.[5]

The kings, princes, nobles and notables had their own occasions of entertainment and rejoicing. Birth and marriages of royal and nobles (sons and daughters) were celebrated with great pomp and splendour. Music and dances were organized in the palace; drums were beaten, gifts and sweets were distributed and people indulged in merry-making activities.

Hunting and hawking were popular outdoor games among the Sultans and nobles. Chaugan (Polo) was played on horse back with a stick or club and a ball. Sultan Qutub-ud-Din Aibak and Sikandar Lodi were very fond of this game. Aibak died while playing Chaugan. Hunting was another favourite outdoor sport of the Sultans and nobles. Iltutmish, Balban, Ala-ud-Din Khilji, Mohammad Tughluq and Firoz Shah took special interest in hunting excursions. There were special officers appointed for hunting. They were Mir Shikar and Shikar Bak.

Birds were hunted and killed with the help of falcons. Falcon and falcon keepers were maintained. Hare and deer were hunted with the help of red coloured ravenous animals called Seyah gosh and hunting leopards. Tigers were hunted with swords and arrows.

The forests of Dipalpur, Sursuti and Badaon were famous for wild asses, deers and wild cows (Neelgay).

Outdoor game like Guru was played by many boys. The main interest of the game was throwing of the ball by a player at his opponent and catching the ball by him. Sultan Bahlol Lodi also played this game in his childhood.[6]

Kite flying was also an outdoor entertainment. It was a favourite pastime for boys.[7]

People enjoyed wrestling and there were wrestling competitions on the occasion of Id.[8]

Id-ul-Zuha has been an important festival of the Muslims, which is the twelfth month of the Islamic Calendar. "It is a festival held in commemoration of Prophet Abraham offering his second son Ismail, who miraculously escaped the atonement through a 'dumba' (a kind of sheep with a thick tail)."[9]

Animals were killed on this day of Id-ul-Zuha. Girls played with dolls. Pigeons were reared and baited upon their flight and people indulged in Kabutarbazi. Chess was a favourite indoor game of the Sultans and nobles. It was also a favourite game of the Afghans.[10]

There were gardens and Hauz (public tanks) where pleasure-seekers used to go for amusements and relaxation. Also, there were male and female dancers, conjures, acrobats, rope dancers and jugglers, who provided considerable entertainment to the people. The Muslim jurists and theologians repeatedly mentioned that dancing and singing have been prohibited, yet Muslims in medieval India practiced and enjoyed dancing and singing. They were fond of both vocal and instrumental music. There are many references to music in Amir Khusrau's Masnavis, especially in Qiran-us-Saadain and Nuh Sipihr. Musical instruments like Chang, Rabab, Nai (flute), Duff, Shahnai, Udd, Tabl (drum), Dhol-i-Hindi (drum) are mentioned in these Masnavis. The Arabs, the Turks and the Persians had their own musical systems which they followed in India.

In the Sultanate period moral tone of the Muslim society was low. A large section of the Muslims practiced prostitution, harlotry, gambling, wine-drinking and other unnatural activities. There were professional eunuchs who adorned themselves charmingly like women and performed derogatory things. Beardless boys were in great demand in society.[11]

Sensuality, drunkenness, prostitution and night revelry were very liberally practiced. Soldiers, officials and nobles participated in the night revelry and enjoyed profusely.[12]

At times even learned scholars and theologians being over sexed misbehaved with women; Maulana Shams-e-Said, who was so much over-sexed that he even neglected his obligatory prayers and ran after slave women; a Muezzin used to enter the mosque in drunkenness and polluted the atmosphere of the sacred mosque.[13]

A large number of persons were addicted to wine and women. Sultan Mubarak Shah adorned himself with the garments and trinkets of women and appeared in assemblies. He danced and drank.[14]

Sultan Kaiqubad indulged in drinking, dancing and singing. During his reign, 'Parasites and pimps flocked in the city (Delhi) under the shade of every wall, persons of both sexes were seen mingling freely and from every house top beautiful women exhibited their beauty.'[15]

Amir Khusrau had invented new rags with the Indian tunes such as Yaman, Ushaq, Muafiq, Ghanam, Mujir and Farghane. He developed a judicious combination of Persian melodies with Indian music. He also invented Khayal, and also evolved light songs, popularly known a *Qawwalis*. He invented a new musical instrument called Sitar. His impact on Indian music is indelible.

During the time of Ala-ud-Din Khilji, who brought Gopal Nayak from South, a musical contest was arranged between Amir Khusrau and Gopal Nayak; in which Khusrau's rapturous melodies surpassed those of Gopal Nayak.

Other well known musicians were, Muhammad Shah Changi and Nusrat Khatun Mehro Afroz. During the Tughluq period music received a set back. Sultan Ghiyas-ud-Din Tughluq banned music in his kingdom. His son and successor, Sultan Muhammad Tughluq was a lover of music, but because of his preoccupations with other things he could not give mush time for the development of music. The general condition of music declined considerably.

Ibn Batuta observed about it, "The music was limited like water in a pond, which has no way to flow like water in a pond, which has no way to flow out, nor water comes from out. The water grows stagnant and such is the condition of music."[16]

Firoz Tughluq was little interested in music. Sikandar Lodi was fond of music and patronized musicians to some extent.

Many saints of the Bhakti movement and Sufis contributed considerably to the development of devotional music. Sufi saints especially those of the Chishti order patronized music. Singing was considered by them as a support to the soul.

The first Mughal ruler, Babur took Agra from Lodi rulers, Humayun lived shortly in Delhi and Akbar made Fatehpur Sikri and Agra his capital, Jahangir loved Lahore and Agra, of course all these rulers frequently visited Delhi, Shah Jahan founded, Shahjahanabad in 1639 A.D. All the Mughal rulers were fond of hunting. Along the course of the Yamuna, on both the sides of it, there was a large quantity of uncultivated land, covered either with corpse wood or with grasses six feet high. This land was guarded with the utmost vigilance, excepting patridges, quails, hares, which the natives catch with nets, no person was permitted, who he may be to disturb the game, which was consequently in abundance.[17]

Palam (Delhi) was one of the established hunting grounds (Shikargah Muqarrer, Saidgah Muqarrer) of the Mughal emperors since the days of Akbar. The hunt at Palam has been referred extensively in Jahangir Nama. Inayat Khan's Shahjahan Nama also refers Palam as hunting place.

Hastsal Minar at village Hastsal, near Uttam Nagar, is still there. It was constructed by Shah Jahan as hunting tower.

> According to the Mughal theory of kingship – patterned on ancient Persian models – the hunt of the ruler symbolized in a general sense his power to overcome the forces of evil, often meant in a political sense. In a more specific argument, the hunt was defended as a means to know about the condition of the subjects and to administer justice on the spot without any intermediaries. In other words, hunting made it possible to win over the subjects by peaceful means.[18]

Animal-fights like elephants, dumba, oxen and buffaloes also bird-fights like cock and teetar, flying of pigeons were organized. The site behind the Red Fort along the river Yamuna was very common for such activities. Kite flying was very popular. Families used to go for picnics in the gardens of Mehrauli and to North areas.

Jama Masjid (mosque) was the centre of the city's religious, intellectual and political life. In fact the mosque created the city.

> ... it was more central to the social and leisurely concerns of the city's inhabitants. Adjacent to it was the prostitutes' bazars – the Chawri Bazar. By the steps of its Jama masjid) these gates were Chauks (Squares) where a lot of recreation went on, particularly in the evenings. Books and armaments were sold side by side; magicians and jugglers entertained; eatables like kababs, chicken and sweet drinks could be bought; a story teller (dastan-go) recited anecdotes and tales from the classics; and birds (especially pigeons), animals, cloth, and other knick-knocks were sold. The recreational spirit surrounding the Jama masjid, however, found unrestrained expression at the Chauk Sa'ad-Allah Khan which therefore became the centre of popular culture in the city. Seated on colourful carpets, wearing expensive clothes and conical caps, they peddled cures for everything under the Sun; and such magical cures for sexual dysfunctions that men were only too willing to part with much. There were naqqals (mimics) and flatterers, busy entertaining. Beautiful lads danced at intervals. The place was full of catamites and beardless lads. ... the Chowk was a melee of people. The hub of the city, on the other hand, was the palace-fortress. The main bazars were adjacent to it; it was more central to the material concerns of the inhabitants of the city. The main streets radiated from it.[19]

The most important aspects of popular culture in Shahjahanabad in its early period were the celebrations at the tombs of Sufi Saints. In thirteenth and fourteenth centuries the Urs at the tombs of Bakhtiyar Kaki and Nizam-ud-Din were the most popular and in early eighteenth century, the most popular festival of any kind was held at the Qadam Sharif (Sacred-Footprints) built by Firoz Shah Tughluq, (1351-88 A.D.) for his favourite son, Fath Khan, who died unexpectedly before him. Firoz Shah's spirited guide, Makhdum Jahanian Jahan Gasht brought from Mecca a stone bearing the Prophet's footprints and it was placed on Fath Khan's tomb (now near Sadar Bazar). At the tomb of Hazrat Nasir-al-Din Chirag-i-Delhi, both Hindus and Muslims gathered, on Sunday, especially during the month of Diwali. Qutb Sahib Tomb; Tomb of Hazrat Shah Hasan Rasul Numah, tomb of Shah Turkman and the tomb in Ahadipurah were visited by large number of people.[20]

There were also celebrations at the tombs of several other less popular Saints; Hazrat Shah Hasan Rasul Numah, Mirza Bedil (1685-1720 A.D.), the famous poet of the city. The Urs at Humayun's tomb was brilliantly lighted and drew great crowds; there was no intervention by the mutashib (censor) for drunkenness, male and female prostitutes.

On the 10th of Muharram, it was the special time for the Shi'as of the city, commemoration of the death of Hussain, son of Ali, at the tomb of Shah Aziz Ullah, many marssiyas were sung.

Majnun Nanak Shah was very emaciated and poor and practiced strict austerities, on the bank of river Yamuna. He gave audience to both Hindus as well as the Muslims. He gave food, fruits and sweets to the poor people. During the rainy season there were drunken bouts in the area around his abode.

The residents of Shahjahanabad had a deep love for poetry. Many people gathered at their homes and other places to listen to their recitations; Mirza Bedil, Mirza Mazhar Jan-i-Jahan (1702-81 A.D.). Mani Khan, one of the favourites of the Emperor, was an expert at reciting *ghazals*; Muhammad Ali Hazin; Siraj al-Din Ali Khan Arzu, Mir Mohammad Afzal Sabit; Mir Shamsuddin Khan Majnun; Mir Abdul Razzaq Warasta and Mirza Abu al-Hasan Agah were famous, and they recited their poetry to people.

The flowering of Urdu literature took place in the early decade of the eighteenth century. The Urdu poetry of course had flourished in the sixteenth and seventeenth century, it had an aristocratic origin. The earliest Urdu poets were people from the aristocratic Muslim families attached to the courts. A poetry recital is called a *Mushaira*, where thousands of people listen to famous poets reciting their latest work. The original aristocratic Mushairas have given way to modern ones.

During the period of later Mughals Mir, Hali and Mirza Ghalib were famous poets of Delhi. They were associated with royalty. Mirza Ghalib was very popular but he used to drink and gamble. He was punished twice for drinking and gambling, for the first time in August 1841 and fined Rs. 100 or four months jail, it seems that Ghalib somehow paid this amount and escaped jail. But he repeated the same offence second time on 25 May 1847, he appealed, the judgement came on 2 July 1847, He was prisoned for six month and fined Rs. 200. This time he went to jail. He suffered badly in jail. After some time, Dr. Ross, Civil Surgeon of the jail, visited the jail and enquired from Ghalib to which he responded:

> Jis Din se ke Hum Ghamzạda Zanjir Be Pa Hain
> Kapron Mein Juein Bakhye ke Tankon se Siva Hain[21]

(Since the day I have been afflicted by the chains, the number of lice are more than the stitches on the cloths.)

After listenning this *Sh'er* and seeing the condition of Ghalib, the Civil Surgeon recommended for the reduction of the prison term for three months and Ghalib came out of the prison after completing three months. He remained dejected and shattered after that. In his letters he had indicated his inclination to go out of Hindustan, even to Mecca and also desired to commit suicide.

Islamic culture had banned drinking of wine and prohibited the use of music and love affairs. During the time of Aurangzeb, music and poetry had declined. Even Nadir Shah did not like it. At the marriage of his son to the grand daughter of Aurangzeb, some soldiers danced and played some music in the night. Next morning they were called by Nadir Shah and they were killed.

There were coffee houses in the Chandni Chowk where literary persons used to gather every day and discussed literary topics. Anand Ram Mukhlis used to go to such gathering very often. He was also a very popular poet and disciple of Mirza Bedil.

After the revolt of 1857-59 tremendous changes took place. In the second half of the nineteenth century the impact of British rule and of Victorian values was so great that the whole character of Urdu literature was changed by it.

The old order had gone for ever and its survivors must either come to terms with the new order or perish. Sharp differences of opinion remained regarding the revolt of 1857-58, the regeneration of Islam and the recovery of an elite position in the subcontinent. Some men of immense energy and determination took stock of the situation after the defeat and evolved the policy for the future.[22]

The middle of the nineteenth century may be called the period of Urdu renaissance. During this period Urdu periodicals exercised a profound influence on society, arts and literature. Urdu prose and poetry was revolutionized by Syed Ahmed Khan, Azad, Dhakaullah, Pyarelal, Madan Gopal and Altaf Husain Hali.

The progress of this renaissance was largely due to the work of the cultural societies which flourished in northern India in the later half of the nineteenth century. These societies gave the people hope, faith and courage and within a decade and a half they grew to be a force in the country and gained power and developed a sense of responsibility. One such society was 'The Delhi Society'. Maulana Hali has referred it in his Hayat-i-Jawid. Ram Babu Saxena, in his 'History of Urdu Literature' introduces the Society in these words, 'Another Literary Society was formed in Delhi in 1864 of which Rai Bahadur Pyarelal Ashob was the able Secretary. Under its auspices many lectures were delivered and the lamp of Urdu though dim was kept alive.'[23]

> On the morning of 28th July 1865, Col. Hamilton, Commissioner of Delhi, Held at his kothi a preliminary meeting which was attended by prominent Indian and European gentlemen, nobles and officers. Explaining the object of the meeting, the Commissioner said that Delhi, the seat of Mughal culture, should not lag behind her sister cities which had stolen a march over her in the field of knowledge and culture and so a society similar to that of the Punjab or Lucknow societies should be started to keep the torch of knowledge bright. ... The aims and objects of the Society should be to promote, develop and stimulate interest in literature, history, numismatics, archaeology and bell letters by means of reading of papers and discussions. It was further decided that there should be a literary and a reading room and that arrangements should be made to acquire a building to house the

library. It was also resolved that the minutes of the meetings and the papers contributed or read in the Society should be published in a Journal of the Society.[24]

In its first General Meeting hesld on 1 August 1865, the following office bearers were declared elected;

1) Col. Hamilton, Commissioner of Delhi, Patron;
2) Capt. MacMohan, Deputy Commissioner of Delhi and Mirza Ilahi Baksh, Presidents (He was related to Bahadur Shah Zafar, the last Mughal King);
3) Lala Sahib Singh Sahib, Vice President;
4) W. Coldstream, Judge, Small Cause Court, Honorary Secretary;
5) Pyarelal, Secretary.

Other prominent members were: Wilayat Husain Khan and Jeevanlal.

It started from the two rooms of Delhi Museum. Donations and gifts were also received by the Managing Committee which was duly acknowledged in the Society's Journal. Whenever a State dignitary visited Delhi, it became a convention of the Delhi Society to present him with an address of welcome.

When in October 1866, Lt. Governor, Sir Donald McLeod visited Delhi and held public Durbars an address was presented to him. He was made the Grand Patron of the Society. Col. Hamilton was the Patron from its very foundation till 1867 when he resigned. On another occasion when Duke of Edinburgh visited India, the Society presented him an address. On 24 January 1873, Lt. Governor Sir William Muir attended the meeting of the Society. On another occasion the Society presented an address to the Prince of Wales in 1875. Lord Lytton, the Governor General and Viceroy was presented an address on 26 April 1876. The Society paid respect to high dignitaries of its province. It had its opinion on important issues and government and other agencies sought its opinion on such matters.

On educational matters it always reflected its opinion. The Society published many books. In 1866 the Society expressed its views to establish a university either in Delhi or Agra. It also gave its views for reforms in Calcutta University and medium of instruction.

It had the patronage of the British. The other prominent members and office bearers of the Society were; Lala Rami Mal, Rai Chhuna Mal, Rai Mahesh Dass, Mr MacNeil, Col. Nick, Mr Fitz Patricks, Mr Boilon, Judge of Delhi, Mr Smith, Padre Whatley, Mr Carr Stephen, Padre Winter (1876), Mr Chandulal, Maulvi Dhakaullah, Mr Lala Chaman Dass, Lala Madan Gopal and Prof Ram Chander.

It was not only a literary and cultural society but also created an opinion on the burning issues and many prominent and literary persons (British as well as Indians) were attached with this Society.

The other society like 'The Archaeological Society of Delhi', 'The Delhi Vernacular Translation Society'; many magazines, newspapers in English, Urdu and Persian, the Delhi Sketch Book, calligraphy, paintings, poetry, European music (at St. James Church) and Libraries satisfied the cultural and literary needs of the people of Delhi. Apart from the poets, musicians and singers who were clients of the great men, there were a number of independent artists who played an important role in the cultural life of the city.

Niamat Khan, a 'Been' player, singer of *Khayal* and was the head of the singers of the city. He was very wealthy person. He sang and played at all the major Urs, and every month on the 11th the Amirs of the city gathered at his mansion.

Qasim Ali, the disciple of Niamat Khan was honoured by the Amirs because of his beauty. Panna Bai, another disciple of Niamat Khan had voice like nightingale. Taj Khan, qawwal, was very famous, on the seventh of every month there was a gathering at his house attended by the Faqirs and Sheikhs. His sons Jani and Ghulam were also popular. Ghulam Mohammad, the Sarangi player, Jimsen and Tansen were the equal of their famous ancestor Tansen Akbarshahi, Ghasi Ram played *Pakhavaj*, Husain Khan was the Dhulak player, Muin al-Din had a unique talent for *Qawwali* and was not at all interested in wealth. Burhani, a *Qawwal*, the power of his voice made the hair on the bodies of his listeners stand up and brought them in ecstasy. Dervish invented a combined instrument that produced the sounds of the *Dhulak*, the *Pakhawaj* and the Tambur.[25]

Jattah Qawwal, Rahim Khan, Daulat Khan, Kiyan Khan and Haddu were unequalled in the art of *khayal*. Nur Bai, a popular singer was approved by the lords of music and she played popular tunes for a group of high-ranking women of the court. Chamani was one of the famous singers. She was honoured in every mansion and given money by the Emperors and Amirs.

In the early eighteenth century in Shahjahanabad there were many talented dancers like: the mistress of Abu-al-Hasan Khan. A crowd gathered every day to watch eunuch Miyan Haiga dance in the square of the Urdu Bazar in front of the palace-fortress. Sultana, another eunuch dancer was twelve year old. His dancing and singing captivated the city and he was in great demand; Dargahi, Saras Rup, Ad Begum, Asa Pura (a Hindu dancing girl), Chak Mak and Mani, Kaki Kanba, Zinat and Bahaq were beautiful dancers. Ramzani, Rahmani Bai and Rupan Bai danced as freely as the breeze of spring. Panna and Tannu captured souls with their beauty and amorous glances. Taqi, the head of the actors of the imperial household, Shah Daniyal Surkhi, Khwasi, Ansusha and Bari were the great actors and mimics of the time.

There were many suberbs and villages around Delhi. Some of them were very old. The people resided in these villages had their entertainment with sports and other activities.

Wrestling was one such popular sport. Wrestling is the most ancient sports in the human civilization. It started in some form when man tried to save himself from wild animals or to defend oneself from other human beings or to establish supremacy over others. Later ist developed into a game. In India one can find the references of wrestling in Ramayan relating to Hanuman, Angad, Bali, Sugriv, Jamvant and Vibhishan. In the same way one can see the reference of wrestling in the *Mahabharat* as well; Bhim, Balram, Krishan, Duryodhan, Jarasandh and Ashvathama were the great wrestlers. Kans was the great patron of wrestling in Mathura before the Mahabharat period.

Wrestling was not only popular in the villages but it was also popular in the city as well. Some famous *Akharas* are still there in Delhi; Chiranji ka Akhara, Chandgi Ram ka Akhara, Sadiq Akhara (infront of Red Fort, Lajpat Rai Market), Madho Das ki Bagichi, Munni ka Akhara (Panchkuyan Road), Brahmchari ka Akhara, Shekhu wale ka Akhara, Bhure wale ka Akhara, Gandi Shah ka Akhara, Mira Shah ka Akhara, Badri Akhara (Ghanta Ghar), Sonkar Akhara, Birla Mill Akhara/Guru Hanuman ka Akhara, Jhandewalan Akhara, Bal Akhara (Teliwara). There are some other Akharas on the bank of Yamuna.

Bhagwan Singh was one such wrestler who fought with lion in Kolhapur and killed the lion. He was born in 1882 or 1885 at village Naraina (Delhi). He served in police and army and fought many wrestling bouts with noted wrestlers such as Gama. His *Akhara* is still in Loha Mandi (Pusa, Delhi).

Fares (melas) were organized in various parts of Delhi where wrestling was the main attraction. Apart from wrestling *Kabaddi* and Tug of War was also commonly prevalent in Delhi. The rural folk used to organize the 'Swang' or 'Nautanki'. Ram Lila, Diwali, Holi, Teej and Dashehra were not only religious festivals but other activities were also organized during this period for the amusement and entertainment of the people.

The British first took over Delhi after defeating the Marathas who were the protectors of the Emperor. They found the city exhausted. Charles Metcalf wrote, 'Robbing in the city of Dihlee was organized in a systematic manner. ... The city was shared in districts among the villages of the environs, and the plunder of particular districts was the property of particular villages.'[26]

In the late eighteenth century under the rule of the Marathas land in Shahjahanabad was sold for a trifle or even given away to escape taxation and extortion.[27]

The arrival of the British caused the value of the land to double. There were large and great mansions but most of them were in an advanced state of despair. The British Army occupied the land north and south of the palace-fortress. One Battalion laid out a Bazar, set up a hospital and built accommodations for guns and stables near Kashmiri Gate. Dara Shikoh's Mansion became the headquarters of the Resident and other palaces to the north were renovated and turned to official use. Two Battalions were quartered in Daryaganj area east of Faiz Bazar. A Magazine was built, a bazar was constructed and stables for camels, bullocks and horses were established.[28] Qamar al-Din Khan's mansion near Ajmeri Gate became the Custom House.

The wall of the city was repaired in 1803, and in 1817 the minaret of the Jami Masjid was renovated. By 1820's middle class houses were constructed between the Jami Masjid and the palace-fortress. The sarai of Jahan Ara Begum was converted into a shopping area. Many shops came up near the Mosque of Raushan al-Daula. In Daryaganj timber merchants resided alongside British soldiers; in 1821 Paradise canal had been reopened; but it soon became clogged again. During the 1820's, the expansion of the city was confined almost exclusively to the area of the city walls. Bishop Hurber, who spent the winter months of 1824-25 in the city, wrote of houses that were large and high, fine looking mosques with minarets and domes, streets that were wide and handsome, and rich bazars. Outside the walls, however, from the Akbarabadi Gate to Humayun's tomb, the eye was assaulted by the ruins of mansions, Mosques, gardens, and tombs.[29]

Qutub Minar was also repaired during this period. In 1828 began a change, the British shifted their cantonment to the ridge and fifteen hundred acre site (the part of which is now Delhi University) was used for constructing barracks, offices, store rooms and parade grounds. The triangle: ridge, the river and the North wall of the city began to fill with houses, gardens of merchants and officials. Thomas Metcalf, the Resident built a house on the bank of Yamuna uprooting the residents of village Chandrawal. It became the seat of many activities, but during Mutiny (1857) it was burnt and looted by the villagers of Chandrawal as revenge. Metcalf also built an outhouse for recreation at Mehrauli. David Ochesterlony, the first Resident also occupied Shalimar Bagh and its structure for recreation. Fraser also purchased the house (now Hindu Rao Hospital).

> During the period 1830-57 the British laid out a cemetery, built a Church near Kashmiri Gate, established a college in the old residency, constructed a club, and founded a bank, Post Office, printing press and a photographic studio. In 1852 they opened the Calcutta Gate in the south-eastern wall of the city. At the same time the city Magistrate ordesred the bazars to clean, the platforms in front of the shops restored, and the drains repaired and built. As a result, Chandni Chowk and Faiz Bazar began to look as they had in the palmy days of the mid seventeenth century. With the shift of the cantonment to the ridge and the resettlement of a section of the European enclave in the triangle (Civil Lines), Muslims and Hindus began to move outside the walls and the repopulation of the suburbs to the south and west began.

By the late 1820s, the British arms had succeeded in establishing a seemingly unassailable dominance over the Indian polity that altered the nature of collaborative relationships not only with Indian commercial and banking groups, but with Indian society at large. The Mutiny of 1857 and its result not only sealed the fate of Bahadur Shah II and the Mughal dynasty but also greatly affected thousands of families in Delhi. The British recaptured the city, the army confiscated the houses and goods of many Muslims, expelled them from the city, and allowed some with entry passes, major Mosques were used for military purposes, a number of buildings were razed to the ground. Bahadur Shah II was imprisoned and sent to Rangoon, where he died. The army occupied the palace-fortress. From 1857 to 1861 Shahjahanabad was an occupied city; its inhabitants were impoverished and demoralized. But with the mid of 1860, the city began to recover. It was slowly rebuilt and repopulated and it increased in size and activities in the rest of the century. During the period from 1739-1857 the economy changed, It further changed with the introduction of rail and mills and *karkhanas*. This period witnessed the demise of the patron-client system centered on the palace-fortress and the mansions of princes and great amirs.

Under the British a new system of society founded on different principles and staffed by different men began to emerge. The socio-cultural system which was dependent on the Emperor and the old nobility, turned towards Hindu-Muslim merchants, bankers, lawyers, teachers and administrators. New cultural and educational institutions emerged. Drinking was one of the modes of entertainment. In the days of Shah Jahan people drank with full liberty. He left everyone live at his own will. It was also common to drink spirits when Aurangzeb ascended the throne. He once said that only two persons, himself and the Chief Qazi, Abd-ul-Wahab did not drink but, Niccolo Manucci said, with respect of Abd-ul-Wahab he was in error, for "I myself sent him every day a bottle of spirit, which he drank in secret."[30]

Aurangzeb wished to repress this disorder, and therefore ordered that all Christians, except physicians and surgeons should leave the city and remove to near the park of artillery, which was beyond the suburbs at one League's distance from the city. There they had leave to prepare and drink spirits on condition that they did not sell it. Strict orders were there for Kotwal that if he finds any Hindu or Muslim for selling spirit, cut his one leg and one hand. But little by little these orders were relaxed. Christians had leave to prepare spirits for their own consumption, but were prohibited from selling it.

People invented another beverage, called 'Bhang'. Aurangzeb also wanted to suppress this disorder. He therefore appointed an official under the title of Matusin (Muhtasib). But seeing that the Ministers themselves also drank and loved to get drink, the rigour of prohibition was lightened by degrees.

With the establishment of Residency, the focus shifted from the Red Fort to the British Residency. As the first half of the nineteenth century progressed and the power and arrogance of the British grew, so the Resident came to act less and less like Ambassador to the Great Mughal, and more and more like the Mughal's paymaster and overlord."[31]

David Ochterlony was fond of hookahs and nauch girls and Indian costumes. He lived the life of a Mughal gentleman. Every evening all of his thirteen Indian wives used to go in procession around Delhi behind their husband, each one on the back of her own elephant. One of his wives Mubarak-un-Nisa built a mosque which is now near Hauz Qazi Police Station. Earlier people did not perform namaz in this masjid as they considered it 'Haram'. Later on it was repaired and now namaz is performed regularly. David Ochesterlony died on 15th July 1825 at Meerut as a dissatisfied man. William Fraser, another British official had taken on the customs and dress of the Indians from the very beginning of his residence in the subcontinent. He raised and trained a force of irregular cavalry. He had one wife named 'Amiban' a Jat women of Rania, whose delicate beauty was beyond compare. ...[32]

From 1803 to 1857 there was a good growth of the middle class, consisting of doctors, teachers, traders, government servants and employees of banks and press. A small but a very influential Eurasian and European community also developed during this period. Nobles like Hindu Rao, Deremao, Col. James Skinner and Begum Samru depended more on the pleasure of the British Resident and Commissioner than on the Mughal Emperor. With the establishment of the British rule, European wines became more popular. Soda water factories were established in Delhi. Hindu Rao and Col. James Skinner gave feasts to Europeans and they were in turn invited to the parties. Indian cooks learnt the art of preparing European dishes. Indians began to imitate European dress as well. (Prince Babar and Mirza Salim remained in the dress of English Generals)

With the growth of the Christian community, Christmas began to be celebrated with great enthusiasm. The birthday of the King and Queen of England was also celebrated after the establishment of British rule.

Begum Mumtaz Mahal introduced the fair of 'Phool Walon ki Sair' at Mehrauli when her son Mirza Jahangir was permitted to come back from Allahabad where he had been exiled by the British authorities.

Cricket, horse-race and billiards were favourite games of the new European community. (Roshanara Cricket Club was established for this purpose.) British conquest changed the social habits of many communities.

Christianity had existed in Delhi since the foundation of Shahjahanabad by Shah Jahan in 1639. Two churches were burnt by the soldiers of Nadir Shah in 1739. Systematic efforts were made to propagate the gospel started by the Baptist Mission in 1814. The Church Missionary Society sent Anand

Masiah to Delhi in 1820. The vigorous efforts of Rev. M.J. Jennings led to the establishment of Delhi Mission.

The establishment of the British rule also brought about many changes in the educational sphere. In Delhi a number of Darbars were held since it ceases to be the capital of Mughal Empire. However, on 12 December 1911, The King declared, 'We are pleased to announce the transfer of the seat of the Government of India from Calcutta to the ancient capital of Delhi. ...' Since then, the Civil Lines area became a concentration of British offices and residences. New clubs and recreation areas were developed. In 1931, New Delhi was inaugurated; it had been planned with wide roads, gardens and water channels, single story buildings, trees around them, bazars like Connaught Place, Rajpath, Parliament House, Rashtrapati Bhawan, the Supreme Court and clubs like the Gymkhana and the Chelmsford and other hotels, et cetera.

Changes have come to Delhi since the ancient period; and they will continue in future.

REFERENCES

1. *Natyasastra* 37.73
2. Ibid.
3. *Isami: Futuh-us-Salatin*, Ed. By A.S. Usha, Madras, 1943, pp. 114-15; and Tabaqat-i-Akbari, Text, 1, p. 216
4. Barni, *Tarikh-i-Firozshahi,* p. 314, and *Siyar-ul-Auliya*, p. 393
5. *Tabqat-i-Nasiri*, p. 183; Barni, *Tarikh-i-Ferozshahi,* p. 183
6. Yadgar, *Tabqat-i-Nasiri*, p. 138
7. Annals of the Bhandarkar Oriental Research Institute, XXXVII, 1956, p. 113
8. Afif, *Tarikh-i-Firozshahi*, p. 367
9. A Rashid, *Society and Culture in Medieval India*, p. 123
10. Shaikh Md. Kabir, *Tarikh-i-Afghani*, f 138a
11. Barni, *Tarikh-i-Firozshahi*, p. 384
12. S. H. Askari, 'Historical Value of Basatin-ul-Uns', Journal of Bihar Research Society, XIVIII, 1962, pp. 20 and 124
13. Amir Khusrau, *Ijaz-i-Khusravi*, IV, p. 175-76, and 206
14. *Tabaqat-i-Akbari*, pp. 179-80
15. Barni, *Tarikh-i-Firozshahi*, p. 116
16. Quoted in B.N. Lunia, *Life and Culture in Medieval India*, Kamal Prakashan, Indore, 1978, p. 624
17. Francois Bernier, *Travels in the Mogol Empire* A.D. *1656-1668*, S. Chand & Co., 1968, p. 375
18. Ebba Koch, *The Delhi of the Mughals Prior to Shahjahanabad as Reflected in the Patterns of Imperial Visits*, In Felicitation Volume in Honour of Prof. S. Nurul Hasan, Publication Scheme, Jaipur, 1993, p. 15
19. Urvashi Dalal, 'Shahjahanabad: An Expression of the Mughal State's Legitimacy',

Islamic Culture, vol. LXXIV No. 3, 2000, pp. 12-13; also Dargah Quli Khan, *Muraqqa-i-Delhi*, tr. and Ed. English, Chander Shekhar and Shama Mitra Chenoy, Delhi, 1989.

20. *Risalah-i-Salar Jang*, Fols. 97-9
21. Nisar Ahmad Farooki, *Talash-i-Ghalib* (Urdu), Lahore, 1989, pp. 83-96, and *Diwan-i-Ghalib*, Ed. Dr. Md. Hasan Maneri, (Persian) 1997, Tehran, p. 20
22. Ralph Russell, *The Pursuit of Urdu Literature, A Select History*, Oxford University Press, 1992, pp. 77-79
23. Ram Babu Saxena, *A History of Urdu Literature*, p. 289
24. K. Sajan Lal, 'The Delhi Society, Islamic Culture', July, 1952, pp. 55-56
25. *Risalah-i-Salar Jang*, fol. 117a
26. Quoted in Stephen P. Blake, *Shahjahanabad: The Sovereign City in Mughal India* 1639-1739, Cambridge University Press, N. Y., 1991, p. 170
27. ibid. p. 170
28. ibid.
29. C.F. Andrews, *Zaka Ullah of Delhi*, Cambridge, W. H. Heffer and Sons Ltd, 1929, pp. 3-4
30. Storio do Mogor
31. William Dalrymple, *The Early Days of the British* in Khushwant Singh (Ed.), *City Improbable, An Anthology of Writings on Delhi*, Viking, 2001, p. 44
32. ibid. p. 50

Further Readings

Articles:

Alam, Muzaffar. *Sikh Uprising under Banda Bahadur, 1708–1715,* Panjab Past and Present, vol. 16(1), April 1982, pp. 95–107

Anthony, D'Costa. *Invasion of Nadir Shah as Seen Through the Bombay Records,* Indica, vol. 4(1), Mar 1967, pp. 43–53

Arnold, David. *Industrial Violence in Colonial India,* Comparitive Studies in Society and History, vol. 22, 1980, pp. 234–255

Arulanandham, J. T. *Harijan Christians Versus High Cast Christians,* Organiser, vol. 18(29), 1st Mar 1965, p. 12

Asghar, Mohammad. *Mughaliyah Hindustan key Kutabkhane (Libraries of Mughal India),* Pakistan Library Bulletin, 15(3–4), 1984, pp. 1–22

Aziz, A. *Origin and Growth of Delhi,* Geographer, vol. 14, 1967, pp. 101–118

Aziz, Abdul. *Thrones, Chairs and Seats used by the Indian Moghals,* Journal of Indian History, vol. 17, 1933, pp. 181–228

Bal, S.S. *Circumstances Leading to the Martyrdom of Guru Teg Bahadur,* Sikh Review, vol. 16(166), May 1967, pp. 22–7

Bali, Yogendra. *Ninth City of Delhi is True Mirror of Mixed Cultures,* Times of India, (Supplement), 12 Feb 1970, 10 May 1970 and 30 Jun 1970

Banerjee, Anil Chandra. *The Influence of Islamic Traditions on the Sultanate of Delhi,* Journal of Indian History, vol. 16, 1937–8, pp. 151–68

Banerjee, R.C. *State Patronage to the Hindu and Muslim Religions during the East India Company's Rule,* Bengal Past and Present, vol. 56(1–2), Jan–Jun 1939

Bannerjee, G. Nath. *The Peregrinations of the Ancient Hindus,* Hindustan Review, vol. 27, 1913, pp. 261–269

Banerji, S.K. *Muslim Contributions to Medieval India,* Indian Review, Jul. 1945, 46(7), pp. 382–6

Banerji, Adris. *Fifteen Cities of Delhi,* Link, 6(1), 15 Aug 1963, pp. 51–2

Banerji, Adris. *Delhi under the Early Muslim Rulers (c. AD 1193–c. 1388),* Journal of Asiatic Society of Bangladesh, (Bengal), vol. 6(1), 1964, pp. 5–14

Banks, Marcus J. *Defining Division: An Historical Overview of Jain Social Organization,* Modern Asian Studies, vol. 20(3), 1986, pp. 447–460

Baquir, Mohd. *Lahore Islamic Culture,* vol. 18, 1944, pp. 19–35

Batra, N.D. *Famous Churches of India,* Indian and Foreign Review, vol. 22(4), Dec. 1984, pp. 20–21 and 27

Bhatia, S.S. *Historical Geography of Delhi, Indian Geographer,* vol. 1, Aug. 1956, pp. 17–43

Bhatnagar, I.C. *Mystic Monasticism during the Mughal Period,* Islamic Culture, XV, pp. 79–90

Bhuyan, S.K. *Annals of the Delhi Badshahat,* Islamic Culture, vol. 7, 1933, pp. 22–49 and 249–276

Bhuyan, S.K. *Annals of the Delhi Badshahat,* Islamic Culture, vol. 8, 1934, pp. 66–91, 263–272 and 425–438

Blake, Stephen P. *The Urban Economy in Pre–Modern Muslim India: Shahjahanabad, 1639–1739,* Modern Asian Studies, vol. 21(3), 1987, pp. 447–471

Blunt, James T. *A Description of the Cuttub Minar,* Asiatic Researches, London, 1861

Bond, Ruskin. *Lady of Sardhana,* Imprint, vol. 18(2), May 1978, pp. 61–65

Bordey, Jeffrey and Others. *Cast Factors and the Church in India,* Sevarthan, vol. 7, 1982, pp. 123–35

Browser, S. *Delhi Before I was Born: As Gleaned from Newspaper Files,* Hindustan Times, Sep. 24, 1967

Buch, M.N. *Delhi 2001, Land Policy Implications,* India International Centre Quarterly, vol. 8, 1981, pp. 159–68

Bullock, Humphry. *The Architecture of the Delhi Sultanate,* Islamic Quarterly, vol. 1, 1954, pp. 144–51

Campbell, Robert. *Crisis in Christianity,* Prabuddha Bharata, vol. 74(3), Mar 1969, pp. 122–6

Campbell, C.J. *Notes on the History and Topography of Ancient City of Delhi,* Journal of the Asiatic Society, No. IV, 1866, pp. 199–217

Chatterji, Nandlal. *Communal Reppprochement in Medieval Indian Literature,* Prabuddha Bharata, vol. 47, 1942, pp. 149–52

Chatterji, Nandlal. *The Conception of History in Ancient India Prabuddha,* Bharata, vol. 58, 1953, pp. 13–16

Chatterji, Nandlal. *The Architectural Glories of Delhi,* Alpha Pub. Concern, Calcutta, 1969

Chaudhari, Jatindra Vimal and Jagannatha, Pandit Raja, *Court Poet of Shah Jahan,* Prabuddha Bharata, vol. 47, 1942, pp. 436–40 and 475–80

Chaudhury, Jasbir. *Chee Chee and half–cast: The Anglo Indians in Fact and Fiction,* New Quest, vol. 39, May–June 1983, pp. 147–53

Cheshire, Leonard. *How Christ Was Crucified,* Illustrated Weekly of India, 89(15), 14 Apr. 1968, pp. 8–16

Chopra, P.N. *Dress, Toilet and Ornaments During the Mughal Period,* Proceedings of the Indian History Congress, 1952, p. 33

Choudhury, N.N. *Ancient History of the City of Delhi in the Epics and the Puranas,* Purana, vol. 6(1), Jan. 1964, pp. 174–80

Chughtai, M. Abdulla. *The So called Gardens and Tombs of Zeb–un–Nisa at Lahore,* Islamic Culture, vol. 9, 1935, pp. 610–20

Cole, Juan R.I. *Of Crowds and Empires: Afro–Asian Riots and European Expansion, 1857–1882,* Comparitive Studies in Society and History, 31(1), 1989, pp. 106–33

Cullen, G. *IXth Delhi,* Architectural Review, London, Feb. 1960, pp. 110–117

Datta, Kalikankar. *India in the Eighteenth Century,* Journal of Indian History, Golden Jubilee Volume, 1973, pp. 687–702

Derbyshire, I.D. *Economic Change and the Railways in North India, 1860–1914,* Modern Asian Studies, vol. 21(3), 1987, pp. 521–45

Dharamvira. *Delhi,* Dec. 23 1912, Organiser, vol. 22(1), 15 Aug. 1910, pp. 9–10

Digby, Simon. *Sufi Shaikh as a Source of Authority in Medieval India,* Purusartha, vol. 9, 1986, pp. 57–78

Dinno, Bokdawala. *Aurangzeb and the Non–Muslims,* Sikh Review, vol. 16(174), Jan. 1968, pp. 45–6

D'Souza, P.P. *Saint Thomas in India,* Indian Horizons, vol. 23 (2–3), 1974, pp. 21–24

Edgley, N.G.A. *Saints of Delhi and Their Shrines,* Prabuddha Bharata, Golden Jubilee Volume, 1945

Erdosy, G. Early Historic Cities of Northern India, South Asian Studies, vol. 3, 1987

Fawcett, R.H. *Railways in India from a Military Point of View,* Calcutta Review, vol. 66, 1878, pp. 616–36

Fischel, Walter J. *Jews and Judaism at the Court of Moghal Emperors in Mdieval India,* Islamic Culture, vol. 25, 1951, pp. 105–32

Francklin, W. *An Account of the Present State of Delhi,* Asiatic Researches, London, 1801

Fraser, T.G. *Transfer of Power in Divided Societies: Partition in India, Ireland and Palestine,* Indo–British Review, vol. 14(2), 1988, pp. 61–9

Fritag, Sandria B. *Sacred Symbol as Mobilizing Ideology: The North Indian Search for a "Hindu" Community,* Comparitive Studies in Society and History, vol. 22, 1980, pp. 597–625

Fusfeld, Warsen. *Communal Conflict in Delhi, 1803–1930,* Indian Economic and Social History Review, vol. 19(2), 1982, pp. 181–200

Gasling, David L. *Hindu and Christian Ashrams in India,* Aryan Path, vol. 46(2), Feb. 1975, pp. 76–80

Ghatak, Taraprasanna. *Origin and Growth of Communal Tension in India,* Journal of Indian History, vol. 36, 1958, pp. 199–214

Gokhale, B.G. *Tobacco in 17th Century India,* Agricultural History, vol. 48(4), 1974, pp. 484–92

Gray, Hugh. *Synthesis of Indian and British Institutions,* India International Centre Quarterly, vol. 2, No. 1, 1975, pp. 48–56

Green, Burger and Allan J. *Partition: The Legacy of the Raj,* Indo–British Review, vol. 14(2), 1988, pp. 57–60

Gupta, M.R. *Delhi Diary of 1825,* Proceedings of the Indian Historical Records Commission, Silver Jubilee Session, vol. 25(2), Dec. 1948

Gupta, Sir Krishna ji. *The Position of Hindus in India,* Hindustan Review, vol. 27, 1913, Feb.–Mar., pp. 113–126 and Apr. 1913, pp. 183–193

Gupta, O.P. *Nawab and Their Servants,* Times of India (Annual), 1968, pp. 29–38 (also see other articles in this issue)

Habib, Mohd. *Shaikh Nasiruddin Mahmud Chirag–i–Delhi as a Great Historical Personality,* Islamic Culture, vol. 20, 1946, pp. 129–153

Habib, Mohd. *Chishti Mystics Records of the Sultanate Period,* Medieval India Quarterly, vol. 1, No. 2, Oct. 1950, pp. 1–42

Habibullah, A.B.M. *Sultanah Raziah,* Indian Historical Quarterly, XVI, pt. 4, 1940, pp. 750–772

Hashmi, B.A. *Sarmad: His Life in Quatrains,* Islamic Culture, vol. 7, 1933, pp. 663–672 and vol. 8, 1934, pp. 92–104

Hashmi, Syed. *Tughulaq Namah,* Islamic Culture, vol. 8, 1934, pp. 301–312 and 413–424

Hashmi, Syed. *The Real Alamgir, Islamic Culture,* vol. 11, 1928, pp. 183–203 and 622–633

Hasrat, Vikramajit. *Dara Sikoh, Mulla Shah and Other Saints,* Vishva Bharti Quarterly, VI, pp. 331–345

Hopkins, E.W. *Position of the Ruling Caste in Ancient India,* Journal of the American Oriental Society, vol. 13, 1889, pp. 57–72

Hurst, B.C. *The Myth of Historical Evidence,* History and Theory, vol. XX, 1981, pp. 278–290

Husain, Yusuf. *Nizam–ul–Mulk Asaf Jah I,* Islamic Culture, vol. 8, 1934, pp. 341–360, 550–559 and vol. 9, 1935, pp. 22–38, 224–267 and vol. 10, 1936, pp. 299–323

Husain, Mahdi. *Contest for Legal Sovereignty between the Last Three Mughal Emperors and the East India Company,* Journal of Asiatic Society of Bangladesh, vol. 17(3), 1972, pp. 35–63

Husain, Sheikh Fida. *The Origin of Tazia–Keeping in India,* Hindustan Review, vol. 31, 1915, pp. 530–537

Ilse, Liechtenstedter. *From Particularism to Unity: Race, Nationality and Minorities in Early Islamic Empire,* Islamic Culture, vol. 23, 1949, pp. 251–280

Islam, Riazul. *The Age of Feroz Shah, Medieval India Quarterly,* vol. 1, July 1950, pp. 25–41

Jafri, S.N.A. *Islamic Mysticism: Its Effect on Urdu Poetry,* Aryan Path, vol. XII, pp. 511–513

Jhabvala, R.P. *Open City: Letter from Delhi Encounter,* vol. 22, May 1964, pp. 40–44

Keene, H.G. *Anglo Indian Mufasal Life in the Last Generation,* Calcutta Review, vol. 66, 1878, pp. 712–728

Khan, Yusuf Husain. *Why was Nasir Jung Summoned to Delhi?* Islamic Culture, vol. 17, No. 1, 1943, pp. 57–64

Khan, Baloch Nabi B. *The Burial Place of Sultan Muhammad bin Tughlaq,* Islamic Culture, vol. 21, 1947, pp. 70–74

Khuluse, S.A. *An Account of Nadir Shah in an Eighteenth Century Arabic Ms.,* Islamic Culture, vol. 25, 1951, pp. 146–154

Kozlowski, Gregory C. *Muslim Women and the Control of Property in North India,* Indian Economic and Social History Review, vol. 24(2), 1987, pp. 163–181

Krishanan, Y. *European Travellers in Mughal India: An Appreciation,* Islamic Culture, vol. 21, 1947, pp. 215–230

Kunte, B.G. *Mughal–Maratha Conflict, 1680–1707, A Few Original Documents,* Journal of University of Bombay, vol. 33(1–4), July 1964–Jan. 1965, pp. 1–20

Lafont, Jean Marie. *Bennon Pan Dei Allord and the Family of General Allord,* Panjab Past and Present, vol. 15(1), April 1981, pp. 28–63

Lal, A. *Delhi, A Capital City,* Focus, vol. 19, Sep. 1968, pp. 7–11

Lal, K. Sajun. *Professor Ram Chander as Urdu Journalist,* Islamic Culture, vol. 23, 1949, pp. 22–36

Lal, K. Sajun. *The Delhi Urdu Akhbar and Its Importance,* Islamic Culture, vol. 24, 1950, pp. 16–44

Lal, Krishan. *The Sack of Delhi as Witnessed by Galib,* Bengal Past and Present, vol. 74, Jan.–Dec. 1955

Lal, K.S. *Food and Drinks in Medieval India,* Indian Historical Quarterly, XXVIII, pt. 2, 1952, pp. 192–196

Loharry, N.C. *Delhi Rotarian,* Evanston: USA, vol. 92, Mar. 1958, pp. 10–13

Macmilan Margaret. *Anglo–Indians and the Civilizing Missoon, 1880–1914,* Contribution to South Asian Studies, vol. 2, 1982, pp. 72–109

Mahmud, Syed. *Political Police of the Mughals,* Modern Review 21(2) Feb. 1917, pp. 164–168

Malik, Zahiruddin. *Khan–i–Duran, The Mir Bakshi of Muhammad Shah,* Medieval India: A Micellany, 1969, pp. 134–232

Malik, Zahiruddin. *Some Aspect of Mughal Culture During the First Half of the 18th Century,* Studies in Islam, vol. 2, 1965, pp. 17–44

Malik, Ziauddin. *Financial Problems of the Mughal Government During Farukhsiyar's Reign,* Indian Economic and Social History Review, vol. 4(3), Sep. 1967, pp. 265–75

Malik, S.D. *Mutiny and the Muslim World: A British View Point,* Islamic Studies, vol. 5(3), Sep 1966, pp. 283–304

Marcia, Hermansen. *Shah Wali–Ullah of Delhi's Hujjat Allah Al–Baligha: Tension* Between the Universal and the Particular in an Eighteenth *Century Islamic Theory of Religious Revelation,* Studia Islamica (France), vol. 63, 1986, pp. 143–157

Margul, Tadeusz. *Present Day Worship of the Cow in India,* Numen, vol. XV, 1968, pp. 63–80

Masumi, M.S. Hasanal. *An Appreciation of Shah Waliyullah Al–Muhaddith –Dihlawi,* Islamic Culture, vol. 21, 1947, pp. 340–352

Mathur, Y.B. *Religious Disturbances in India,* Studies in Islam, vol. 8, 1971, pp. 81–131

Mathur, B.S. *Malik–ul–Umara Fakhruddin– The Kotwal of Delhi,* Islamic Culture, Vol. 39, 1965, pp. 205–208

Menezes, S.L. *The Military History of the "Habash" in India from 1200,* Journal of the United Service Institution of India, 114 (475), 1984, pp. 78–84

Menezes, S.L. *Tales of Former Government Houses,* Journal of the United Service Institution of India, 114(478), 1984, pp. 335–339

Menezes, S.L. *"White Mutinies" in India Before and After 1857,* Journal of the United Service Institution of India, 116(486), 1986, pp. 354–359

Mitra, Saratchandra. *Medieval and Modern India through French Spectacles,* Hindustan Review, vol. 32, 1915, p. 115–124 and Sept. 1915, pp. 125–132

Mleeko, Joel D. *The Guru in Hindu Tradition,* Numen, Vol. XXIX, 1982, pp. 33–61

Mohammed K.K. *Hammams (Baths) in Medieval India,* Islamic Culture, LXII, No. 4, Oct. 1988

Muhammad Rustam Ali Diwan *Muslim Contribution to Libraries during the Medieval Times,* Islam and Modern Age, vol. 9(2), May 1978, pp. 19–34

Mukerji, Dhan Gopal. *Hindu–Moslem Tension,* Prabuddha Bharata, vol. 29, 1924, pp. 562–563

Mustafa, Khursheed. *Travel in Mughal India,* Medieval India Quarterly, vol. 3, 1958, pp. 270–284

Naqvi, S.A. Zafar. *Libraries in Muslim India, Islamic Culture,* vol. 19, 1945, pp. 329–347 and vol. 20, 1946, pp. 3–20

Naidu, P. S. *A Psychological Approach to Communal Unity in India,* Prabuddha Bharata, vol. 47, 1942, pp. 328–332

Naidu, W. S. *Building of the Indian Nation,* Hindustan Review, vol. 27, April 1913, pp. 229–31

Nath, R. *Panchmukhi Mosques of the Afghan Period,* Islamic Culture, vol. 50(1), 1976, pp. 33–39

Nath, R. *Important Christian Tombs at Agra,* Indica, vol. 4(1), March 1967, pp. 19–34

Nigam, S.B.P. *Nobility Under the Sultans of Delhi,* 1206–1398 AD, Quarterly Review of Historical Studies, (Calcutta) vol. 4(3), 1964–65, pp. 119–23

Nizami K.A. *Delhi Sultanate and the Mughal Empire: Genesis and Salient Features,* Islamic Culture, vol. 55, 1981, pp. 169–190

Nizami K.A. *Shah Wali–Ullah Dehlavi and Indian Politics in the 18th Century,* Islamic Culture, vol. 25, 1951, pp. 133–145

Nizami K.A. *Shattari Saints and their Attitude Towards the State,* Medieval India Quarterly, vol. 1, No. 2, Oct. 1950, pp. 65–70

Pandey, Dhanpati. *Nadir Shah's Exaction of Ransom from Delhi,* Shodhak, vol. 7, 1978, pp. 129–133

Panikkar, K.N. *Appointment of Abuzafar (Later Bahadur Shah II) as the Heir Apparent,* Journal of Indian History, vol. 42(2), 1966 Apr., pp. 585–90

Panikkar, K.N. *Delhi Residancy (1803–1856): A Political Study,* Quarterly Review of Historical Studies, vol. 3(4), 1963–64, pp. 208–10

Parel, A. *Political Symbolism of the Cow in India,* Journal of Commonwealth Political Studies, vol. 7(3), Nov. 1969, pp. 179–203

Pilania, G.S. *Surajmal of Bharatpur and His Contemporaries,* Journal of Rajasthan Institute of Historical Research, vol. 3(3), 1967, Jul.–Sep., pp. 33–48

Pant, N.G. *The Saga of Indian Arms,* Journal of Indian History, Golden Jubilee Volume, 1973, pp. 245–269

Qureshi, I.H. *A Year in Pre–Mutiny Delhi, Islamic Culture,* vol. 17, No. 3, 1943, pp. 282–297

Qutbi, M. Mahmood Ali. *Early Sufis and Earning of Livelihood,* Studies in Islam, vol. 18, 1981, pp. 101–9

Raizul Islam. *A Review of the Reign of Feroz Shah (1351–88),* Islamic Culture, vol. 22, 1949, pp. 281–297

Ram Sawrup. *Hinduism vis–à–vis Christianity and Islam,* Manthan, vol. 5(1), May 1983, pp. 5–12

Rand, C. *Letter from New Delhi,* New Yorker, vol. 32, Mar. 1956, pp. 88

Rawlinson, H.G. *Sir Saiyid Ahmad Khan,* Islamic Culture, vol.4, 1930, pp.389–386

Ray, Sunil Kumar, *Astride the Jamuna,* Indian Railway, vol. 13(4), July 1968, pp. 322–23

Reddi, V.S. *Medicine at the Mughal Court,* Journal of Indian History, vol. 17, 1933, pp. 165–174 and vol. 19, 1940, pp. 56–63

Reeves, P.D. *Soldiers and Policemen under the Raj,* South Asian Review, vol. 5(4), 1972, pp. 338–340

Rogers, John D. *The Historical Study of Crime in South Asia,* Criminal Justice History, vol. 7, 1986, pp. 145–154

Roy, Nirod Bhushan. *Raziyya,* Indian Historical Quarterly, VIII, pt. 3, 1932, pp. 449–461

Roy Chaudhury, P. C. *Military Cantonements in India,* Indo–British Review, vol. 10(1), June 1983, pp. 34–36

Sabikhi, R. *Delhi's Changing Skyline,* Indian and Foreign Review, vol. 6, Sep. 1, 1969, pp. 13–16

Sadhu, J.N. *Is Jesus Christ Buried in Kashmir?* Illustrated Weekly of India, vol. 93(14), 2 Apr 1972, pp. 34–35

Sain, Kunwar. *Dilli ki lat or Kutab Minar,* Hindustan Review, vol. 30, 1914, p. 541–558, vol. 31, 1915, pp. 46–67

Saksena, R.P. *Jesus Christ's Life in India,* Modern Review, 140(4) Oct. 1976, pp. 221–224

Sammadar, Jogendranath. *Rulers and the Ruled in Ancient India,* Hindustan Review, vol. 25, 1912, pp. 42–49

Sangar, S.P. *Religious Crime During the Reigns of Shah Jahan and Aurangzeb,* Bharatiya Vidya, Bombay, Nov.–Dec. 1945, pp. 252–258

Sangar, S.P. *Food and Food Habits in Mughal India,* Quarterly Review of Historical Studies, vol. 9(4), 1996–70, pp. 187–99

Sanial, S.C. *The 'Itimad–ud–Daulah Institution at Delhi,* Islamic Culture, vol. 4, 1930, pp. 310–328

Saniyal, S.C. *The News Papers of the Later Mogul Period,* Islamic Culture, vol. 11, 1928, pp. 122–140 and 453–463

Sareen, T.R. *The Simla Deputation, 1906,* Quarterly Review of Historical Studies, vol. 11(2), 1971–72, pp. 67–70

Sarkar, Jadunath. *Ahmad Shah Abdali in India 1748,* Islamic Culture, vol. 4, 1932, pp. 206–232

Sarkar, Jadunath. *An Original Account of Ahmad Shah Durrani's Campaigns in India and the Battle of Panipat,* Islamic Culture, vol. 7, 1933, pp. 431–456

Sarkar, Jadunath. *Najib–ud–Daulah as the Dictator of Delhi, 1761–1770,* Islamic Culture, vol. 7, 1933, pp. 613–639

Sarkar, Jadunath. *Life of Najib–ud–Daulah,* Islamic Culture, vol. 8, 1934, pp. 237–257

Sarkar, Jadunath. *Najib–ud–Daulah, Ruhela Chief,* Islamic Culture, vol. 10, 1936, pp. 648–658

Sarkar, Jadunath. *Breaking up of the Mughal Empire: Jats and Gujars,* Modern Review 34(4) Oct. 1923, pp. 450–455

Sarkar, Jadunath. *Companion of an Empress,* Modern Review 1(6) Jun. 1907, pp. 521–523

Sarkar, Jadunath. *Passing of Shah Jahan,* Modern Review 18(4) Oct. 1915, pp. 361–368

Sarkar, Jadunath (Tr.) *Account of Comte de Modave,* Islamic Culture, vol. 11, 1937, pp. 382–392

Sarkar, Jagdish Narayan. *Men and Beasts in Medieval Indian Warfare,* Journal of Indian History, Golden Jubilee Volume, 1973, pp. 463–494

Sen, S.N. *Lord Auckland on Delhi,* Bengal Past and Present, LXI, pp. 1–12

Sen, S.N. *A Note on the Purana Qila of Delhi,* Journal of Indian History, XX, pt. I, pp. 35–37

Seth, Mridula. *Cast System in the Capital,* Social Welfare, vol. 27(9), Dec. 1980, pp. 12–19

Sharma, Shriram. *Administration of Justice in Aurangzeb's Time,* Indian Historical Quarterly, XIX, pt. 2, 1945, pp. 101–104

Sharma, Arvind. *Alburini on Paralleis Between Hinduism and Christianity,* Bulletin of Institute of Islamic Studies, vol. 1(1–2), Jan.–Jun. 1978, pp. 24–29

Sharma, Dasharatha. *Prthviraja III, The Last Hindu Emperor of Delhi,* Indian Culture, No. II, 1944–45, pp. 47–73

Siddiqui, I.H. *An Arab Account of India in the 14th Century,* Studies in, Islam, vol. 7, 1970, pp. 205–227

Siddiqui, Iqtidar Husain. *Espionage System of the Sultans of Delhi,* Studies in Islam, vol. 1(2), Apr. 1964, pp. 92–100

Siddiqui, Iqtidar Husain. *Advent of the Afghans to Power,* Studies in Islam, vol. 1(4), Oct. 1964

Siddiqui, Noman Ahmad. *The Classification of the Villges Under the Mughals,* Indian Economic and Social History Review, vol. 1(3), Jan.–Mar. 1964, pp. 73–83

Simmons, Collin. *De–industralization, Industralization and the Indian Economy, 1850–1947,* Modern Asian Studies, vol. 19(3), July 1985, pp. 593–622

Singh, Amar Kumar. *Communalism in India: A Socio–Phychological Analysis,* India International Centre Quarterly, vol. 7, 1980, pp. 157–163

Singh, Songel. *Gurdwara Rikab Ganj: Origin and History,* Studies in Sikhism and Comparative Religion, vol. 4(1), Apr 1985, pp. 93–102

Singh, Patwant. *Delhi Past, Present and Future,* Design, vol. 14(3), Mar. 1970, pp. 23–28

Singh, Khushwant. *Massacre by Nadir Shah on 11th March 1739 in Delhi,* Times of India, Apr. 9, 1967

Sinha, S.K. *Military in Indian History,* Journal of the United Service, Institution of India, 115(479), 1985, pp. 1–21

Smith, W.C. *The Mughal Empire and the Middle Class: A Hupothesis,* Islamic Culture, vol. 18, 1944, pp. 349–363

Smith, W.C. *Lower Class Uprising in the Mughal Empire,* Islamic Culture, vol. 20, 1946, pp. 21–40

Spear, T.G.P. *The Mughal Family and the Court in the 19th Century Delhi,* Journal of Indian History, vol. 20, 1941, pp. 38–60

Spear, T.G.P. *The British Administration of the Delhi Territory, 1803–57,* 19 (2), Aug. 1940, pp. 235–48

Spear, T.G.P. *The British Administration of the Delhi Territory, 1803–57,* 'Journal of Indian History', 19 (3), Dec. 1940, pp. 320–35

Srivastava, K.P. *Jahandar Shah and His successors in Banaras,* Journal of Indian History, Golden Jubilee Volume, 1973, pp. 495–500

Srivastava, Harishankar. *Indian Famine of 1876–79, Journal of Indian History,* vol. 44(3), Dec. 1966, pp. 853–886

Srivastava, A.L. *Some Problems of the Medieval Indian History,* Quarterly Review of Historical Studies, vol. 3(4), 1963–64, pp. 168–71

Srivastava, A.L. *India's Resistance to Medieval Invaders: A Rejoinder,* Journal of Indian History, vol. 45(1), Apr. 1967, pp. 181–186

Stokes, Eric. *The First Century of British Colonial Rule in India: Social Revolution or Social Stagnation?* Past and Present, vol. 58, 1973, pp. 136–160

Talgeri, K.M. *Jantar Mantar Observatory,* Eastern World, Aug. 1953, pp. 29–30

Thomas, P. *Christian Saints of India,* Illustrated Weekly of India, 94(51), 23 Dec. 1973, pp. 6–13

Tikkiwal, H.C. *Sawai Jai Singh Kachhwaha and Emperor Jahandar Shah (1712–13 AD),* Journal of Rajasthan Institute of Historical Research, vol. 3(4), 1966, Oct.–Dec., pp. 25–28

Trimizi, S.A.I. *Record management in British India,* Indian Archives, vol. 29(2), Jul–Dec. 1980, pp. 1–6

Trivedi, D.S. *Vishnudhvaja of Delhi,* Organiser, (Souvenir No), 1973, pp. 49–51

Upadhaya, R.D. *Delhi as It Was 100 Years Ago,* Modern Review, vol. 117(3), Mar. 1965, pp. 199–200

Verma, C.L. *Delhi Water Supply and Sanitation,* India International Centre Quarterly, vol. 9, 1982, pp. 308–321

Verma, Birendra. *Shah Alum's Negotiations with Ahmad Shah Abdali,* Journal of Historical Research, vol. 9(2), 1967, Jan. 26, pp. 9–14

Wali, Maulvi Abdul. *Why Thursday is Called Jum–i–Rat in India?* Journal of the Anthropological Society of Bombay, vol. IX, No. 1, 1910, pp. 377–379

Wase, S.G. *A Neglected Aspect of Indian Politics,* Hindustan Review, vol. 32, 1915, pp. 95–103

Watson, F. *An Expanding Capital City,* Listener, May 1955, pp. 873–74

White, David L. *Parsis in the Commercial World of Western India, 1700–1750,* Indian Economic and Social History Review, vol. 24(2), 1987, pp. 183–203

Yang, Ananda. *Sacred Symbol and Sacred Space in Rural India: Community Mobilization in the "Anti–Cow Killing" Riot of 1893,* Comparitive Studies in Society and History, vol. 22, 1980, pp. 576–596

Yasin, Mohammad. *Jahingir and Nur Jahan,* Indian Historical Quarterly, XIV, pt. 4, 1938, pp. 817–821

Yusuf, K M. *The Judiciary in India under the Sultans of Delhi and the Mughal Emperors,* Indo–Iranica, vol. 18, Dec.

Yusuf, Ali A. *Social and Economic Life in Medieval India,* Islamic Culture, vol. 4, 1931, pp. 199–222

Books:

Alam, Muzaffar. *The Crisis of Empire in Mughal North India,* Oxford University Press, Delhi, 1986

Alexander, Llewellyn. *The Siege of Delhi,* Macdonald and Jane's, London, 1977

Ali, M. Athar. *Mughal Nobility under Aurangzeb,* Asia Publishing House, 1966

Ali, Ahmad. *Twilight in Delhi,* Oxford University Press, 1966

Azzizuddin, *History of Jama Masjid*

Barr, Pat. *The Memsahibs: The Women of the Victorian India,* Sacker And Warburg, London, 1976

Bashir–ud–Din. *History of Delhi,* 3 Vols. (Urdu)

Bayley, D.H. *The Police and the Political Development in India,* Princeton, 1969

Bayly, C.A. *Rulers, Townsmen and Bazaar,* Cambridge University Press, 1983

Beg, Mirza Sangeen. *Sairul Manazil (Urdu)*

Bhatia, L.M. *A Miscellany on the Raj,* Reliance Publishing House

Bhattacharya, V. *Delhi Through the Ages,* Delhi Metropolitan Book Co., 1977

Cecil, M. Martin. *Allnut of Delhi: A Memoir,* New York, The Macmilan Co., 1922

Chai – Shou Yu. *Early Buddhism and Christianity,* Motilal Banarsi Das, Delhi, 1981

Chakrabarty, Suhash. *The Raj: Syndrom*

Chaturvedi, Bharti (Ed.) *Finding Delhi, Loss and Renewal in the Megacity,* Penguin, Viking, Bombay, 2010

Clive, William. *Dandoo on Delhi Ridge,* Macmilan, London, 1971

Cumming, John (Ed.) *Political India, 1832–1932: A Co–operative Survey of a Century,* OUP, 1932

Dayal, Maheshwar. *Rediscovering Delhi, A Story of Shahjahanabad,* S. Chand and Co., Delhi, 1975

Dayal, Mala (Ed.) *Celebrating Delhi,* Ravi Dayal Pub., Viking, 2010

Diver, M. *The English Woman in India,* London, 1909

Dubey, Bala. *Galiyan Jahan Itihas Quaid Hai,* Parag Prakashan, Delhi, 1985

Dunbar, George. *A History of India from the Earliest Times to the Present Day,* Ivor Nicholson and Watson, London, 1936

Evelyn, Battye. *Costumes and Characters of the British Raj,* Rolly Books International, New Delhi, 1982

Fanshawe, H.C. *Delhi Past and Present,* Murray

Festing, Gabrielle. *When Kings Rode to Delhi,* Edinburgh, Blackwood, 1913

Francklin, W. *The History of the Reign of Shah Aulum,* Cooper, 1798

Galloway, Major General. *Notes on the Seige of Delhi,* (1804)

Gay, J. Drew– *The Prince of Wales in India: Or from Pal Mal to the Punjab,* Torento: Belford Brothers, 1877

Geffrey, Parrinder. *Jesus in the Quran,* Seldom Press, London, 1976
Gradidge, Roderick. *Edwin Lutyens, Architect Laureate,* George Allan Unwin
Griffiths, Charles John. *A Narrative of the Seige of Delhi,* John Murry, 1910
Gupta, A. *Police in British India, 1861–1947,* Delhi, 1979
Gupta, P.C. *The Last Peshwa and the English Comissioners (1818–1851),* S C Sarkar & Sons, Calcutta, 1944
Hugh, Col. *Pearse Life and Military Services of Viscount Lake*
Gupta, P.C. *Baji Rao II and the East India Company, 1796–1818,* Oxford, 1939
Hambly, Gavin. Cities of Mughal India: Delhi, Agra and Fatehpur Sikri, Eleck Books, 1968
Hamdani, Muhammad Kamal Husain. *Matab–e–Masih (Hakim Sharif Khan, 1790),* Aligarh, 1976
Haq, Sayed Moinul. *The Great Revolution of 1857,* Pakistan Historical Society, Karachi, 1968
Hasan, S. Nurul. *The Morphology of a Medieval Indian City: A Case Study of Shahjahanbad in the 18th and Early 19th Century*
Hoey, W. *Memorials of Delhi and Fyzabad*
Holzman, J.M. *The Nabobs in England: A Study of the Anglo–Indian, 1760–1785,* 1926
Horan, Barbara Gean. *The Use and Abuse of Power and Legitimacy in India's Constitutional History from 1935–1977,* New York University, 1983
Hudson, *Officers of the Bengal Army*
Irwin, H.C. *The Garden of India*
Jafri, Rais Ahmad. *Hazrat Mahal,* Lahore, Sheikh Ghulam Ali, 1969
John, Kaye. *Life and Correspondence of Lord Metcalf*
Joseph, Thekhedath. *History of Christianity in India,* (Two Volumes), 1982
Kaul, H.K. *Historic Delhi: An Anthology*, Delhi: Oxford University Press, 1985
Kaul, H.K. *Travellers India*
Kaye, John William. *Lives of Indian Officers,* London, 1867
Kaye, G.R. *A Guide to the Old Observatories at Delhi, Jaipur, Ujjain and Banaras,* Calcutta, 1920
Kaye, M.M. *The Golden Calm– An English lady's Life in Moghul Delhi,* Exceter, England: Web and Bower, 1980
Keene, H.G. *Madhav Rao Sindhia*
Keene, H.G. *Delhi 1899*
Keene, H.G. *Handbook for Visitors to Delhi,* 1899 Rev. 1906
Kerr, S. Parnell. *From Chasing Cross to Delhi,* T. Fisher Unvin, 1906
Kincaid, D. *British Social Life in India, 1608–1937,* George Routledge and Sons, London (Re. 1973)
Kington, William. *The Private Life of an Eastern King,* Humphrey Milford, Oxford University Press, 1921
Kudal, Vishnu Datt. Dhuliya Walon ka Itihas, 1696 se 1951 Tak (Hindi),
Lane–Poole, Stanley. *Medieval India under Muhammadan Rule,* Fisher Unvin, London, 1903
Lapel, Griffin and CharlesMassy. *Chiefs and Families of Note in the Punjab,* Lahore: Civil and Military Gazette Press, 1910

Laser, James. *Red Fort: An Account of the Siege of Delhi in 1857,* Warner Lansic, London, 1956
Leasor, James. *Red Fort,* London, 1856
Madho Parshad, Rai Sahib, *History of Delhi–Municipality 1863–1921,* Allahabad, 1921
Malik, S.C., *Indian Civilization: The Formative Period,* Indian Institute of Advanced Studies, Simla, Moti Lal Banarsi Das, Delhi, 1968 and 1987
Malik, Z.U. *Reign of Muhammad Shah (1719–1739),* Bombay, 1977
Mark, Bence Jones. *Palaces of the Raj: Magnificence and Misery of the Lord Sahibs,* George Allen and Unwin, 1973
Marry, Maj. Charles Francis. *Chiefs and Families of Note in the Delhi, Jalandhar, Peshawar and Derajat Division of Punjab,* Printed at the Pioneer Press, Allahabad, 1890
Martin. *Indian Empire*
Mason, Philip. *Skinner of Skinner House*
Mehra. *A Dictionary of Modern Indian History, 1707–1947,* Oxford
Metcalfe, C. T. (Ed.) *Two Native Narratives of the Mutiny in Delhi,* Constable, London, 1898
Metcalf, T.R. *The Aftermath of Revolt: India 1857–1870,* Princeton, NJ, Princeton University Press, 1964
Metcalfe, Thomas. *Reminiscences of Imperial Delhi*
Metcalfe, Thomas. *Delhi Book*
Mishra, Ram Gopal. *Indian Resistance to Early Muslim Invaders up to 1206 AD,* Arun Books, Meerut, 1983
Mishra, Rekha. *Women in Mughal India, 1526–1748,* Munshi Ram, 1967
Mookherji, Sudhansu Vimal. *India Since 1857,* Kitab Ghar, Gwaliar, 1968
Moose, Frederick V. *Christians in India,* Publication Division, Delhi, 1964
Nangia, S. *Delhi Metropolitan Region: A Study in Settlement–Geography,* Delhi, 1976
Nasir, Naseer Firaq. *Lal Qila ki Ek Jhalak (Urdu)*
Nasir, Naseer Firaq. *Dehli ka Ujra Hua Lal Qila (Urdu)*
Natesan, G.A. *All About Delhi: An Exhaustive Hand Book,* Madras, 1911
Nawab Jiwan yaar Jung Bahadur, (Tr.) *'My Life' – The Autobiography of Nawab Server–al–Mulk Bahadur,* Arthur H. Stockwell, London
Ojha, P.N. *Aspects of Medieval Indian Society and Culture,* B.R. Pub. Corporations, Delhi, 1978
Oldenburg, Philip. *Big City Government in India Councillar, Administrator and Citizen in Delhi,* Manohar Publications, Delhi, 1978
Page, J.A. *Guide to the Kutb Delhi,* Delhi Monograph Publication, 1938
Palmer, J.A.B. *The Mutiny outbreak at Meerut in 1857,* New York, Cambridge University Press, 1966
Pearson, Hesketh. *The Hero of Delhi: Life of John Nicholson,* London, Collins, 1939
Peck, Lucy. *Delhi, A Thousand Years of Building,* Roli Books, 2005
Pine, L.G. *Tales of British Aristocracy,* Burke Pub. Co., London, 1956
Potter, David C. *India's Political Administrators, 1919–1983,* New York: Oxford University Press, 1987
Potts, E.D. *Baptist Missionaries in India 1793–1837,* Cambridge, 1967
Qureshi, I.H. *The Administration of Sultanate of Delhi,* Lahore, 2nd Ed., 1944

Rao, V.K.R.V. and Desai, P. B. *Greater Delhi,* Bombay, 1965
Renton–Denning, J. *Delhi: The Imperial City,* Bombay: Printed at the Times of India Press, 1911
Richard, D.N. *Christian College in Developing India: A Sociological Inquiry,* OUP, 1971
Richards, John F. Ed. *Imperial Monetary System of Mughal India*
Rizvi, Sayed Athar Abbas. *Swatantra Delhi (Hindi), (11 May 1947– 20 September 1947),* Prakashan Bureau, Suchana Vibhag, Uttar Pradesh, 1957
Routledge, James. *English Rule and Native Opinion in India: From Notes Taken, 1870–74,* Trubner, 1878
Roy, Nirod Bhushan. *The Successor of Sher Shah,* Bengal, 1934
Russel, Ralf and Khurshid Islam. *Galib, 1797–1869, Vol. I,* London, 1969
Saksena, Banarsi Prasad. *History of Shah Jahan of Delhi,* Central Book Depot, Allahabad, 1962
Sanderson, G. *A Guide to the Buildings and Gardens,* Delhi Fort 1937
Sanderson, Gordon. *Delhi Fort,* 1914
Sangar, S.P. *Crime and Punishment in Mughal India,* Sterling, 1967
Satyaprakash, (Ed. and Compiled) *Christianity: A Select Bibliography,* Indian Documentation Service, Gurgaon, Haryana, 1986
Sharp, Henry. *Delhi: Its Story and Buildings,* OUP, 1921
Sharp, Sir Henery. *Delhi– Its Story and Buildings,* Oxford University Press, 1928
Singh, Roy (Ed.) *Chronicals of the British Indian Association,* 1851–1952
Singh, Ganda. *Ahmad Shah Durrani*
Singh, M.P. *Town, Market, Mint and Port in the Mughal Empire (1556–1707),* Adam Publisher and Distributor, 1985
Spear, Percival. *Delhi– A Historical Sketch,* Humphrey Milford, Oxford University Press, 1937
Spear, T.G.P. *The Nabobs, A Study of the Social Life of the English in 18th Century India,* 1932
Stanford, J.K. (Ed.) *Ladies in the Sun: The Memsahibs in India, 1790–1860,* The Galley Press, London, 1962
Stephen, Neil. *A History of Christianity in India: The Beginning to AD 1707,* Cambridge, CUP, 1984
Stephen, Carr. *Archaeology of Delhi, Ludhiana,* Supdt. Mission Press, 1876
Stocks, E. *History of the Church Missionary Society, 1899–1916, (Four volumes),* London
Thompson, Edward and Garratt, G. T. *Rise and Fulfilment of British Rule in India,* Macmillan, 1934
Trimizi, S.A.I. *Edicts from the Mughul Harem,* Idarah–i–Adabiyat–i–Delhi, 1979
Trotter, L.J. *The Life of John Nicholson,* London, John Murray, 1897
Varma, Lal Bahadur. *Anglo–Indians, Bhasa Prakashan,* New Delhi
Wahid, Mirza. *Life and Works of Amir Khusrau,* Punjab University, Oriental Pub. Series, Lahore, 1935
Waldemar, Hansen. *The Pecock Throne: The Drama of Mugul India,* Motilal Banarsi Das, Delhi, 1981
Westphal–Hellbusch and Westphal H. *Jat of Pakistan,* Duncher and Humbolt, Berlin, 1964

Wheeler, J. Tolboys. *The History of the Imperial Assemblage at Delhi: Held on the 1st January 1877,* R. K. Publishing House, Delhi, 1982

Wheeler, George. *India in 1875–76: The Visit of the Prince of Wales,* London, Champion and Hall, 1876

Whithorth, G.C. *Anglo–Indian Dictionary,* 1885

Yadav, C.S. *Land Use in Big Cities: A Study of Delhi,* Inter India Publications, 1979

Yang, Anand A. (Ed.). *Crime and Criminality in British India,* Tueson: University of Arizona, 1985

Yazdani. *Jahan Ara*

Young, K. *Delhi – 1857,* (Ed.) by Sir H.W. Norman, Chambers, 1902

Young, Keith. *Delhi 1857,* London, 1902

Zamir, Hasan S. *Galib ki Delhi (Urdu) The Other Side of the Medle*

Dissertations:

Bose, Pradip Kumar. *Bengali Voluntary Associations in Delhi,* (M. Phil Dissertation, SSS, JNU), 1973

Fusfeld, Warsen Edward. *The Shaping of Sufi Leadership in Delhi: The Naqshbandiya Mujaddidiyya, 1750–1920,* Ph. D. Dissertation of University of Pensylvania, 1981 (Teen Murti, Museum and Library), 1981

Goodfriend, Douglas E. *Delhi–Wala: Socio Cultural Aspects of Urban form and Policy in Delhi,* Ph. D. Dissertation of University of Chicago

Mathur, C.M. *Social Change in Delhi in the 20th Century,* (M. Phil Dissertation, SSS, JNU)

Manuscripts:

Lal, Sunder. *Majmua–i–Faiz,* Asafia, MS

Muzwar, Muhammad 'Aqil'. *Jalwa–i–Deedar,* Asafia MS, No. 130, 21

Reports:

Wood, Oswald. *Final Report on the Settlement of Land Revenue in the Delhi District Carried on 1872–77* by Oswald Wood and completed in 1878–80 by R. Maconachie, Lahore: Printed at the Victoria Press, 1882

Thesis:

Blue, Irvin Frederick. *Some Factors of the Hindu–Muslim Tension in India: A Study* of the Political, Economic, Social and religious Causes of the *Communal Difficulties,* University of South California, Thesis, 1941 (No. 533, Teen Murti Museum and Library)

Dhussa, Ramesh Chandra. *Urban Images of Delhi Through Literature: A Study in Humanistic Geography,* Kent State University, 1986

Ferrell, Donald Wayne. *Delhi, 1911–22: Society and Politics in the New Imperial Capital of India,* Australian National University, Thesis, 1969 (No. 184 Teen Murty Museum and Library), 1969

Sachdeva, Krishan Lal. *Socio-Economic and Cultural Studies in the History of Delhi, 1803-1857,* Agra University, Thesis, 1964.s

Index of Names

Index of Subject